Moreton Morrell Site

PATTERNS OF ENTREPRENEURSHIP MANAGEMENT

THIRD EDITION

Jack M. Kaplan
Columbia Business School

Anthony C. Warren
Penn State University

John Wiley & Sons, Inc.

VICE PRESIDENT & PUBLISHER	George Hoffman
EXECUTIVE EDITOR	Lise Johnson
ASSISTANT EDITOR	Carissa Marker Doshi
ASSISTANT MARKETING MANAGER	Diane Mars
DESIGN DIRECTOR	Harry Nolan
SENIOR DESIGNER	James O'Shea
SENIOR PRODUCTION EDITOR	Patricia McFadden
EXECUTIVE MEDIA EDITOR	Allison Morris
ASSOCIATE MEDIA EDITOR	Elena Santa Maria
PRODUCTION MANAGEMENT SERVICES	Aptara®, Inc.

This book was set in Times New Roman by Aptara®, Inc. and printed and bound by RR Donnelley. The cover was printed by RR Donnelley.

This book is printed on acid-free paper. ∞

To order books or for customer service, please call 1-800-CALL WILEY (225-5945).

ISBN-13   9780470169698

Printed in the United States of America

10 9 8 7 6 5 4 3 2

PREFACE

Working in a corporation, or even a smaller business, does not prepare you for the challenges, long hours, social sacrifices, and financial commitments involved in being an entrepreneur. If you know that your future goal is to become an entrepreneur, how can you truly understand the rewards and pitfalls of this choice? How do you acquire the information and skills needed to support you in realizing your goal? This book provides just that—the necessary information you need to get you started as a successful entrepreneur, even in today's ultracompetitive and hostile business environment.

We have had the privilege of teaching entrepreneurship courses for more than ten years—Kaplan at Columbia Business School in New York and Warren at Penn State. During this time, students, alumni, investors, small companies, and business colleagues have sought our advice regarding the topic of entrepreneurship. Both of us, being entrepreneurs ourselves, have also had the opportunity to gain extensive experience. Professor Kaplan served as president of Datamark Technologies, a technology marketing company engaged in loyalty and electronic gift card programs, and Professor Warren was a founder of several companies and was a venture capitalist for a number of years. We also stay active as entrepreneurs, Kaplan having recently founded "Robotics Systems and Technologies Inc." a hospital automation company, and Warren, "Airswim LLC", a networked telemedicine company. Thus, not only are we both in touch with the most recent academic research findings and best practices regarding entrepreneurship, but we have firsthand experience in starting and building companies and in advising other businesspeople on the concerns and trials facing entrepreneurs today. We hope to impart this experience, knowledge, and counsel directly to you through this book and its associated Web resources.

WHY THIS NEW EDITION

Patterns of Entrepreneurship Management, Third Edition, supports a greatly enhanced interactive learning experience that addresses the challenges, issues, and rewards faced by entrepreneurs in starting and growing a venture. It includes a major new theme on managing a start-up. The authors have spent many years both as entrepreneurs and teachers and passionately believe that entrepreneurial skills can be acquired only by actually confronting the problems that challenge every entrepreneur. This text and accompanying Web site, therefore, differ from others in that they challenge students with real situations and examples on which they can practice the broad range of skills required to start and build a company in today's complex world. Throughout this book you will find tips on how to become a successful entrepreneur, as well as issues to avoid. At the end of Chapter 2, you will have an opportunity to test your understanding by completing and answering a Personal Entrepreneurial Assessment on the Web site. In addition, the Web projects and cases that accompany this book focus on the successes and failures of entrepreneurs and offer valuable business plan examples and assessment tools. Other outstanding features that the book offers are as follows:

1. *Focus on Real Entrepreneurs.* Throughout the text, we relate the material to real entrepreneurs, helping you understand how entrepreneurs position their companies to meet the various marketing, financial, and technological challenges. For example, each chapter starts with a short profile of an entrepreneur that illustrates the key issues that will be covered. These engage students as they immediately see the relevance of the chapter and are intrigued by an actual case chosen for its learning impact.

2. *Management Track.* Most important, we have added an entirely new **learning track** embedded in the book. According to Timmons, (see note 11, for chapter 1), the failure rate of new companies is 24 percent within the first two years and 80–90 percent within the first ten years. Most companies fail not from focusing on a bad idea or having insufficient funds, but because inexperienced founders are confronting complex management decisions without knowledge of the tools to make them.

   The **"management track"** is based on a real company, Neoforma, which constitutes a **"master-case"** for the entire book. Wayne McVicker, one of the founders, reported, in diary form, the entire company history from concept to eventual sale, covering every conceivable management challenge that all entrepreneurs inevitably face. His book, *Starting Something,* became the basis of a new management course at Penn State. Students were so enthralled that we decided to enhance the materials. We took a film crew and interviewed many of the key characters—founders, investors, mentors, key hires, and even family members—who gave their personal views on many of the key management decisions that transpired. McVicker has agreed that we can embed elements of his book with the videos into this edition of *Patterns of Entrepreneurship Management* to provide a rich experience for students on the key management issues in entrepreneurship. We believe this is the first attempt to address important entrepreneurship management topics within a textbook. The materials have now been used at many universities within the United States and, indeed, around the world with great success, and we are pleased to incorporate them into this third edition to greatly enhance the learning experience.

   Because we view management skills as vitally important to entrepreneurs, we have added two entirely new chapters on this area. The first, entitled "What Is an Entrepreneur?" comes right at the beginning of the book, even before the more usual introduction to entrepreneurship and opportunity recognition. Only when a student has examined his own aspirations, lifestyle expectations, stress and risk tolerance, and management capacity does it make sense to seek an appropriate opportunity for study. Chapter 12, entitled "Managing the Team" covers the key "soft" human resources skills of building a corporate culture: hiring and firing and ethical decision making.

   Management topics are revisited in many of the remaining chapters with appropriate student exercises structured around the video materials on the book's Web site.

3. *Finance Track.* The second section of the book contains a complete set of materials covering entrepreneurial finance for non-finance majors. Every entrepreneur at some time needs to raise funds to grow the company. Many make fatal mistakes early on because they haven't clearly thought through the personal implications

imposed by the source of these funds. The issues of control, lifestyle, risk tolerance, and ambition all determine this choice. This book is the first to delineate funding sources between closely held private businesses and high-growth equity-funded companies, and these are dealt with in two chapters on financing. Understanding these two mutually exclusive routes for their companies can save a lot of heartache for entrepreneurs and their supporters. The third chapter in this module describes how to manage funds carefully once they have been raised.

4. *Roadmap Actions.* Each chapter begins with a list of "roadmap" actions that lay out the practical tasks you will accomplish in the chapter.

5. *Case Studies.* In addition to the "master-case," based on Neoforma, most chapters include a shorter case study that looks at a potential entrepreneurial opportunity. Answering the Case Study Questions allows you to think critically about the various aspects of launching a business. Several case studies touch on important aspects of business such as setting up the management team, financing for early and growth ventures, and expanding ideas into viable business opportunities. Longer cases appear on the Web site, which provides additional interactive cases.

6. *From Idea to Opportunity. Patterns of Entrepreneurship Management* is not merely a concept-oriented textbook. Through powerful examples, cases, and exercises, students explore important "soft" issues such as how to continuously innovate, design sustainable business models, and create a culture in their companies that will increase their chances of success as they launch a new enterprise.

7. *Innovation and Technology Venture Framework. Patterns of Entrepreneurship Management* stresses the importance of innovation and technology. Throughout the book are sections devoted to creating a framework for screening ideas, thinking about strategy and business models, determining the capital and resources required, attracting management talent, and preparing the plan to ensure that practices are accepted and implemented effectively.

ORGANIZATION OF THE BOOK

The book has been designed to support three different courses in entrepreneurship:

1. *Introduction to Entrepreneurship* teaches the student about the basics of the field, including the personal aspects of entrepreneurs, opportunity identification, and structuring. This course often includes teamwork in which students identify their own business opportunities and work them up into business plans and presentations to investors. For this course, some of the more detailed topics in management and finance can be omitted.

2. *Entrepreneurial Finance* is a subject that is rather different from corporate finance, which is taught in most business schools. Chapters 7 through 9 provide a complete set of materials for such a course, with supporting readings taken from elsewhere in the book.

3. *Entrepreneurial Management* is based on the master-case and the other management cases in the book. This is an experiential course and is best run in a seminar format.

The book is divided into four "roadmap" phases of entrepreneurship. Each chapter has been written to help students learn specific tasks needed to complete it with defined deliverables.

Part One, "Getting Started as an Entrepreneur," includes six chapters that establish the foundation for starting a venture, from understanding the personal attributes of an entrepreneur, developing ideas, and recognizing business opportunities to preparing a winning business plan and setting up the company. The master-case, Neoforma, is also introduced in the first chapter. Chapter 2 emphasizes the entrepreneurial process and the steps to becoming an entrepreneur. Chapter 3 explores the role of innovation and why it is important. Students learn techniques to become creative in developing new business ideas by building their own framework for analysis of situations. Chapter 4 discusses how to analyze markets and potential customers and how to conduct a competitive analysis and create a marketing plan for the venture. Chapter 5 shows how to start putting a complete plan together for a business, and in Chapter 6, the various forms that ventures may take are described alongside the processes of actually forming a company.

Part Two, "Money Sources—Finding and Managing the Process," constitutes a complete module on entrepreneurial finance. It describes the many ways start-up companies can access the resources they need, including funding at different stages of growth. Chapter 7 examines the methods entrepreneurs use to raise early-stage funding when their plan is to retain control of the company and make it a "lifestyle" business. These techniques, referred to as bootstrapping, are also important for entrepreneurs who later choose to grow a larger organization. Sources include friends, family, government grants, partners, and banks. Chapter 8 explains growth-funding sources from "angel" investors and venture capitalists whereby the entrepreneur sells shares in his or her company where ultimate wealth may be traded with loss of control. Finally Chapter 9 explains in detail how to manage the money once it has been raised, with ways of making it last a long while if possible. This chapter also teaches the fundamental financial management systems that should be installed early on in a company's development.

Part Three, "Implementation," focuses on three functions that must be actively managed as the company begins to grow. The first, covered in Chapter 10, is intellectual property explaining how to file patents, trademarks, and copyrights to build competitive protection. Chapter 11 describes how entrepreneurs continuously develop their business models for achieving rapid growth and maintaining high profits and barriers to competition. Chapter 12 covers the key skills in building and managing a team, including establishment of a strong culture; finding, hiring and even firing the right employees; and learning how to manage ambiguous conflicts of interest and ethical dilemmas. This chapter also describes key legal documents that a company will use.

Part Four, "Communicating and Exiting," examines the different alternatives for entrepreneurial businesses and exit strategies. Chapter 13 will equip students with the skills needed to communicate an opportunity to different audiences, including customers, investors, bankers, and employees. No entrepreneur can be successful without the ability to communicate passion and drive to those who can help her reach her goals. Chapter 14 describes the exit strategies entrepreneurs may wish to consider, including selling the business, going public, or being acquired.

SUPPLEMENTS

If instructors wish to incorporate all or part of the "management track" into coursework, then students can access the Neoforma case book on the book's Web site. This is a shortened version of the full text of *Starting Something* by Wayne McVicker. Students may want to read the full version if they seek an even richer insight into the life of an entrepreneur. In addition, for instructors, the Web site provides access to a test bank, PowerPoint presentations, sample cases and business plans, answers to end-of-chapter questions, and financial and legal templates you will need to set up a business. The Web site can be accessed at www.wiley.com/college/kaplan.

The Web site gives students access to a variety of resources:

- Additional case studies that allow students to review key entrepreneurial concepts.
- Audiovisual presentations by entrepreneurs, venture capitalists, successful students, and the Neoforma characters.
- Sample business plans. These plans are divided according to market and stage of development. Downloadable plans are available for students.
- Case summary reviews.
- Downloadable legal documents. Students can download sample legal agreements, including stock and shareholder agreements, consulting contracts, and employee option plans, among others.

ABOUT THE AUTHORS

Jack M. Kaplan is an adjunct professor of Entrepreneurial Studies at Columbia Business School and Penn State University, Smeal College of Business. He has taught the entrepreneurial courses for Launching New Ventures, The Business Plan, and The Entrepreneurial Manager. During his career, Mr. Kaplan started and managed three successful companies, concentrating on smart card technology, health-care information systems, and loyalty marketing programs. He was president of Datamark Technologies, Inc., an entrepreneurial business venture engaged in electronic gift card and loyalty marketing programs. Ceridian, a Fortune 500 company, acquired the company in November 2005.

Mr. Kaplan is the author of *Getting Started in Entrepreneurship,* published by John Wiley & Sons in January 2001. His previous book, *Smart Cards: The Global Information Passport,* and articles have appeared in *Technology News* and *Crain's of New York.*

His professional seminar experience includes conducting courses on new product strategies for Fortune 500 companies, including MIT Enterprise Forum, Aetna Insurance Company, Panasonic Global Sales Group, and Johnson & Johnson. He is judge for the Ernst & Young Entrepreneur of the Year® Award Program in New York and has appeared on A&E *Biography,* CNN, and CNBC. He is a graduate of the University of Colorado and received his MBA from the City University of New York.

Dr. Anthony C. Warren is the Farrell Professor of Entrepreneurship at the Smeal College of Business, Penn State University, named "the hottest school for entrepreneurship" by *Newsweek* magazine and the recipient of the NASDAQ Center for Entrepreneurial Excellence Award in 2005. He leads educational programs in entrepreneurship at the undergraduate, graduate, and executive levels. Under grants from the Kauffman Foundation, Dr. Warren created unique courses in entrepreneurship based on problem-based learning, which have been recognized by several national organizations as being at the forefront of teaching methods. These courses are being introduced into colleges and high schools across the country and overseas.

Prior to joining Penn State, Dr. Warren started and grew several companies and until recently was a venture partner in Adams Capital Management, a venture capital firm managing more than $720 million. He consults regularly with both small and large companies on subjects of innovation management. A regular speaker at national conferences, Dr. Warren is often quoted in the press regarding innovation and entrepreneurship. He has authored several patents and research papers on technical and business issues and has contributed to many books. He has a B.Sc. and Ph.D. from the University of Birmingham.

ACKNOWLEDGMENTS

It has been a privilege for us to work with many inspiring colleagues and entrepreneurs to collect material for this book. We relied on the contributions of many people in the preparation of this book to discuss trends and ideas in the exciting field of entrepreneurship.

Special thanks are due to Murray Low, executive director of Eugene M. Lang Center for Entrepreneurship at Columbia Business School; Michael Farrell and John and Bette Garber for their generous gifts and personal support for the entrepreneurship programs at Penn State; and the Kauffman Foundation for its continuing interest in and funding of pedagogy research in entrepreneurship. Special thanks to Deha Rozanes of Ernst & Young and Dr. Andrew Kaplan of the U.S. Department of Justice. We are indebted to the staff at John Wiley & Sons for their support, including Lise Johnson, executive editor; Jayme Heffler, senior acquisitions editor; and Carissa Marker Doshi, assistant editor.

We would also like to thank the following entrepreneurs for helping to add a real-world perspective to this project:

Jennifer Andrews	Jeff Kleck
Chuey Anima	Ed Marflak
Craig Bandes	Wayne McVicker
Matt Brezina	James Meiselman
Wally Buch	Ankit Patel
Denis Coleman	Donn Rappaport
Neal DeAngelo	Brian Roughan
Dan Eckert	Nikolay Shkolnik
William Frezza	Paul Silvis
Ted Graef	Anil Singhal
Linda Holroyd	Jack Russo
George Homan	Parviz Tayebati
Scott Johnson	Ethan Wendle
Dave Juszczyk	Anni Weston
Alvin Katz	Bob Zollars

And the following professors for insightful comments and guidance:

Tom Byers	Stanford University
Robert F. Chelle	University of Dayton
Alex DeNoble	San Diego State University
Sanford B. Ehrlich	San Diego State University
Raghu Garud	Penn State University

Nikolaus Franke	Vienna University of Economics and Business
Ralph Hanke	Bowling Green University
Liz Kisenwether	Penn State University
Rita McGrath	Columbia University
Robert Macy	Penn State University
Paul Magelli	University of Illinois
Jonathan Michie	University of Oxford
Robert Myers	Fairfield Resource International
Clifford Schorer	Columbia University
Michael Treat	Columbia University
Linda Treviño	Penn State University
Philippe Tuertscher	Vienna University of Economics and Business

We also acknowledge the support and appreciation of our spouses, Dr. Eileen Kaplan and Kirsten Jepp. Our personal thanks also go to the diligent research and support of many of our students. Particular mention is due to Anupam Jaiswal and Supreet Saini at Penn State and to Anna Mary Loope, administrative assistant at the Farrell Center, PSU, who managed to keep us all on track.

LIST OF CASES AND PROFILES

Profiles are entrepreneurs' stories; mini-cases are short, illustrative examples; and cases are full case studies for student analyses.

CHAPTER	TYPE	TITLE	ROADMAP TOPIC
1	Profile	Wayne McVicker	A Typical Entrepreneur
1	Case	Neoforma	Master-case for Entrepreneurial Management
2	Profile	Graef and Johnson	Getting Started with an "Off-the-Shelf" Idea
3	Profile	Minard and Gisholt	Identifying a Point of Pain
3	Mini-case	Greif Packaging	Listening to Customers, Services around Products
3	Mini-case	Blyth Candles	Incremental Innovation
3	Mini-case	Netflix	Points of Pain, Disruptive Innovation
3	Mini-case	Pizza on a Truck	Thinking Big, Analyzing Others' Weaknesses
4	Profile	Donn Rappaport	Marketing Visionary in Using Data
4	Case	SmartCard	Developing a Marketing Plan
5	Profile	Nikolay Shkolnik	Business Plan Turns a Dream into Reality
5	Case	SurfParks LLC	Business Planning
5	Case	Railway Innovation	Business Plan (on Web)
6	Profile	Wendle & Chverchko	When to Convert from an "S" to a "C" Corporation
6	Case	Health Care Co.	Setting up a Company
7	Profile	James Dyson	Bootstrapping, Perseverance, Corporate Innovation
7	Mini-case	Chasteen & Balch	Fighting for Their Rights

8	Profile	Matt Brezina	Staged Investments, Networking and Mentoring
8	Case	Coretek Inc.	Using Government Grants to Save Equity Dilution
9	Profile	Alvin Katz	Managing Cash in Tight Situations
10	Profile	Ian Kibblewhite	An Integrated Intellectual Property Strategy
10	Case	Ultrafast Inc. (1)	IP Strategy
10	Case	DataMark	Patent Analysis
11	Profile	Neal DeAngelo	Using Data Collection
11	Mini-case	Dell	Supply Chain Business Models
11	Mini-case	General Fasteners	Services and Customer Lock-in
11	Mini-case	ChemStation	Innovation, Data Management, and Franchising
11	Mini-case	Threadless	Customer Designed T-shirts, Social Networks
11	Mini-case	Syndicom	Vertical Market Social Networks
11	Mini-case	Go2Athlete.com	College Students' Social Network
11	Case	DBI	Business Model and Family Business Management
11	Case	Ultrafast Inc. (2)	Licensing
12	Profile	Paul Silvis	Building an Embracing Culture
13	Profile	Craig Bandes	Presentations to Excite Investors
13	Mini-case	Leaf-Busters	Teaser
13	Mini-case	Ankit Patel	Short and Long Pitches for RIT (on Web)
14	Profile	Alan Trefler	Private to Public Ownership

CONTENTS

Preface   iii
List of Cases and Profiles   x

PART ONE: GETTING STARTED AS AN ENTREPRENEUR   1

Chapter 1   What Is an Entrepreneur?   3
Introduction   3
Profile: Wayne McVicker—A Typical Entrepreneur   4
An Entrepreneurial Perspective   5
Commonly Shared Entrepreneurial Characteristics   5
Types of Entrepreneurs   6
The Need to Control   7
Entrepreneurship Roller Coaster   9
So Why Become an Entrepreneur?   9
Use the Master-Case to Develop Management Skills   10
Summary   11
Study Questions   11
Exercises   11
Interactive Learning on the Web   12
Appendix: The Master-Case, Neoforma, Inc.   12
Neoforma—A Summary of the Master-Case   13
Additional Resources   17

Chapter 2   The Entrepreneurial Process   21
Introduction   21
Profile: Ted Graef and Scott Johnson—Getting Started with an
    Off-the-Shelf Idea   22
The Spiderweb Model   22
Finding Early Mentors   23
Managing Stress   24
The Five-stage Entrepreneurial Process   25
The Growth of Entrepreneurial Companies   29
The Growth Period   29
Summary   30
Study Questions   30
Exercises   30
Interactive Learning on the Web   31
Additional Resources   31

Chapter 3   The Art of Innovation—Developing Ideas and
    Business Opportunities   35
Introduction   35
Profile: Becky Minard and Paal Gisholt—Finding a Point of Pain   36
Why Innovation Is Important   40
Definition and Types of Innovation   41
Frameworks for Learning Innovation Skills   43
Finding and Assessing Ideas   48
Converting an Idea into an Opportunity   49
Opportunity: Five Phases to Success   50
Summary   59
Study Questions   60
Exercises   60
Interactive Learning on the Web   60
Appendix: The Bayh-Dole Act   61
Additional Resources   61

Chapter 4   Analyzing the Market, Customers,
    and Competition   65
Introduction   65
Profile: Donn Rappaport—Marketing Visionary in Using Data   66
Formulating a Successful Marketing Plan   67
Preparing the Marketing Analysis and Plan   68
Defining the Market Segmentation   71
Conducting a Competitive Analysis   74
Preparing the Pricing and Sales Strategy   76
Penetrating the Market and Setting Up Sales Channels   78
Summary   80
Study Questions   82
Exercises   82
Interactive Learning on the Web   83
Case Study: Smart Card LLC Marketing Plan   84
Appendix: Marketing Research Techniques   86
Additional Resources   89

Chapter 5   Writing the Winning Business Plan   91
Introduction   91
Profile: Nikolay Shkolnik—Business Plan Turns a Dream
    into Reality   92
The Value of a Business Plan   93

Setting Goals and Objectives   94
Starting the Process to Write the Plan: Five Steps   95
Determining What Type of Business Plan Is Best   97
A Typical Business Plan Format and Content   99
Understanding Why Business Plans Fail   104
Summary   105
Study Questions   107
Exercises   107
Case Study: Surfparks LLC   108
Appendix: The Roadmap Guide for Writing a Business Plan   121
Interactive Learning on the Web   125
Additional Resources   125

Chapter 6   Setting Up the Company   127
Introduction   127
Profile: Ethan Wendle and Matt Chverchko—When to Convert from an
    S- to a C-corporation   128
Identifying What Form of Ownership Is Best   129
Forms of Doing Business   129
Sole Proprietorship   129
C-corporation   132
S-corporation   138
Partnership   140
Limited Liability Company   142
Business Start-up Checklist   143
Summary   147
Study Questions   148
Exercises   149
Interactive Learning on the Web   150

**PART TWO: MONEY SOURCES—FINDING AND
            MANAGING FUNDS   151**

**Chapter 7   Bootstrapping and Financing the Closely
            Held Company   153**
Introduction   153
Profile: James Dyson—Bootstrapping out of Necessity   155
Securing Early-stage Funding   157
Self-funding   157
Family and Friends   161
Using Factoring and Bank Loans as a Source of Cash   161
How to Use Commercial Banks   162
Using Government Sources of Funding   167
Summary   170
Study Questions   171
Exercises   172
Interactive Learning on the Web   172
Appendix: Start-up Entrepreneurs and Business Incubators   172
Additional Resources   176

Chapter 8   Equity Financing for High Growth   181
Introduction   181
Profile: Matt Brezina—Staged Investments   183
Equity Investment Fundamentals   183
Angel Investors   193
"Microequity"—Little Money with a Lot of Mentoring   194
Understanding the Venture Capital Process   195
Guide to Selecting a Venture Capitalist   198
Private Placements   199
Strategic Partnerships and Corporate Investments   200
Learning How to Value a Business   202
Summary   208
Study Questions   209
Exercises   209
Case Study: CoreTek, Inc.   210
Interactive Learning on the Web   211
Additional Resources   211
Appendix 1: Due Diligence Checklist   214
Appendix 2: Model Venture Capital Term Sheet—Series a Preferred
    Stock   219

Chapter 9   Managing the Money   231
Introduction   231
Profile: Alvin Katz—Managing Cash in Tight Situations   232
The Value of the Balance Sheet   233
Review and Analysis of the Balance Sheet   234
The Value of an Income Statement   241
How to Use Ratios for Profitability   242
The Value of the Statement of Cash Flows   243
Understanding Footnotes to Financial Statements   244
Preparing Financial Projections   245
Preparing a Cash Flow Forecast   249
Preparing a Breakeven Analysis   252
Analyzing an Investment Decision   254
Taxes and Filing   256
The Stresses of Managing Money   257
Summary   257
Study Questions   258
Exercises   258
Interactive Learning on the Web   259
Additional Resources   259

PART THREE: IMPLEMENTATION   261

**Chapter 10   Discovering Value in Intellectual Property: The
            Competitive Edge   263**
Introduction   264
Profile: Ian Kibblewhite—An Integrated IP Strategy   264

The Value of Trademarks   266
The Value of Copyrights   269
The Value of Patents   272
How to Protect Intellectual Property   278
Getting Started with the Patent Idea   280
What Is Prior Art?   280
Using Search Options   281
Progress from Idea to Patent to Enterprise   285
The Value of Trade Secrets   286
Reverse Engineering   287
Summary   287
Study Questions   288
Exercises   289
Interactive Learning on the Web   289
Internet IP Source Sites   290
Additional Resources   290

**Chapter 11   Business Models and the Power
                of Information   293**
Introduction   293
Profile: Neal DeAngelo—Using Data Collection   294
Definition of Business Models   297
Capturing Value in the Supply Chain   298
Using Databases to Create Value   299
Locking in Customers   300
Licensing and Franchising   301
Outsourcing Resources   307
Models Built around Social Networks   310
Corporate Partnering   311
Summary   312
Study Questions   312
Exercises   312
Interactive Learning on the Web   313
Additional Resources   314

Chapter 12   Managing the Team   317
Introduction   317
Profile: Paul Silvis—Building an Embracing
    Culture   318
Developing a Strong Corporate Culture   319
Finding and Hiring the Best People   321
Dealing with Firing an Employee   323
Dealing with a Resignation   325
Conflicts of Interest and Business Ethics   325
Legal Issues   327
Setting up Stock-Option Agreements   329
Summary   329
Study Questions   330
Exercises   330

Interactive Learning on the Web   331
Appendix: Legal Document Templates   331

PART FOUR: COMMUNICATING AND EXITING 343

Chapter 13   Communicating the Opportunity   345
Introduction   345
Profile: Craig Bandes—Matching Presentations to Investors   346
Locating Investors   347
Preparing a Teaser   349
The Elevator Pitch   353
After the Presentation   359
Summary   361
Study Questions   361
Exercises   362
Interactive Learning on the Web   362

Chapter 14   Scaling and Exiting the Venture   365
Introduction   366
Profile: Alan Trefler—Private to Public Ownership   366
Create an Exit Strategy   366
Selling an Equity Stake to a Partner   367
Implementing the Plan of Action   368
Selling the Business   369
Preparing a Selling Memorandum   370
Searching for Buyers   371
Evaluating Offers   372
Create the Letter of Intent   373
Performing Due Diligence   374
Closing the Deal   375
Merge with Another Business   375
Consider a Public Offering   376
Determining the Benefits of Going Public   376
Determining the Disadvantages of Going Public   378
Managing the IPO Event   379
Completing the Registration Process   379
Presenting a Road Show   381
The Expenses of Going Public   382
Delivering Value and Meeting Market Expectations   383
Summary   383
Study Questions   384
Exercises   384
Interactive Learning on the Web   385
Additional Resources   385

Addendum: Three Case Studies Covering the Whole Book   387
Notes   393
Glossary of Terms   403
Index   409

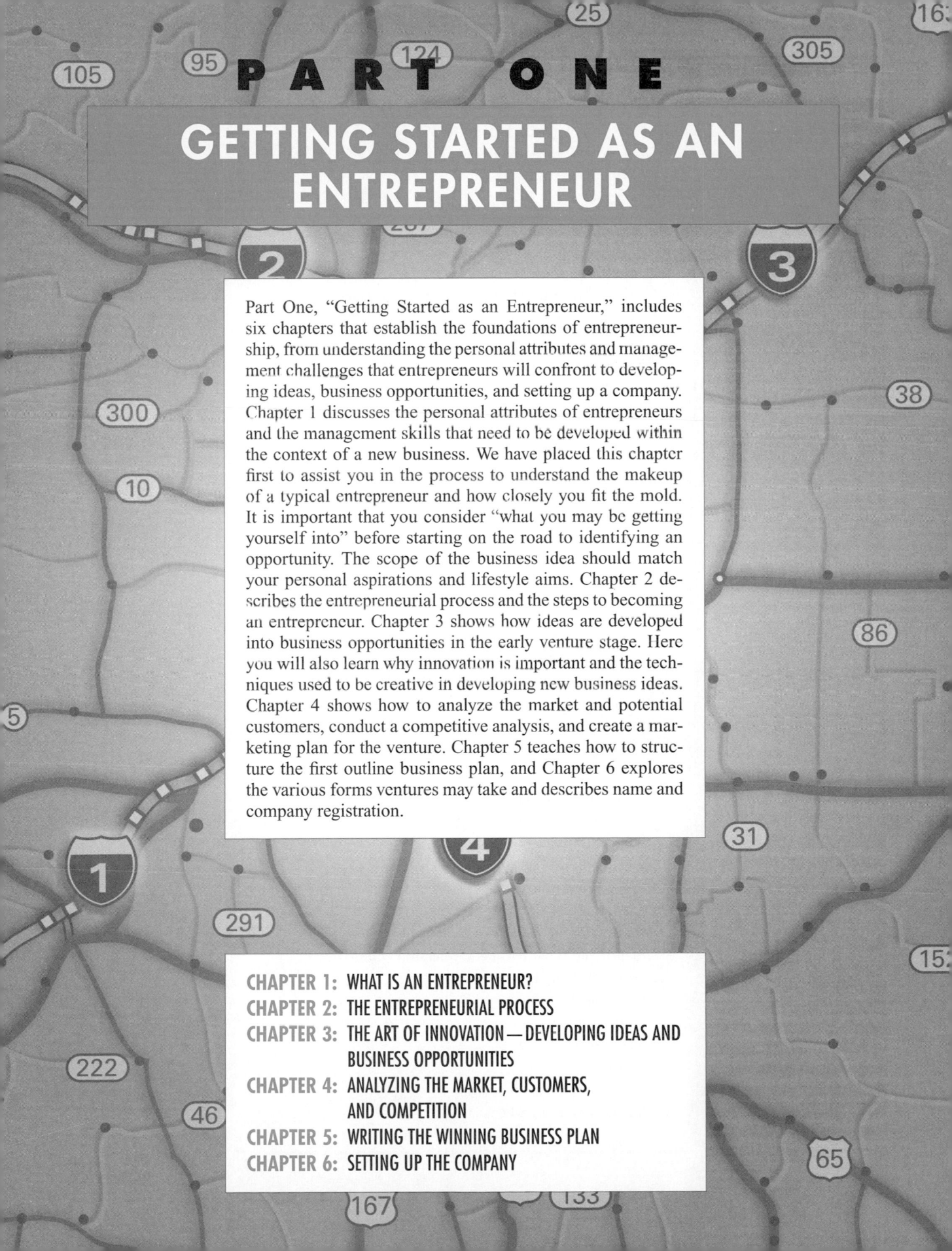

PART ONE

GETTING STARTED AS AN ENTREPRENEUR

Part One, "Getting Started as an Entrepreneur," includes six chapters that establish the foundations of entrepreneurship, from understanding the personal attributes and management challenges that entrepreneurs will confront to developing ideas, business opportunities, and setting up a company. Chapter 1 discusses the personal attributes of entrepreneurs and the management skills that need to be developed within the context of a new business. We have placed this chapter first to assist you in the process to understand the makeup of a typical entrepreneur and how closely you fit the mold. It is important that you consider "what you may be getting yourself into" before starting on the road to identifying an opportunity. The scope of the business idea should match your personal aspirations and lifestyle aims. Chapter 2 describes the entrepreneurial process and the steps to becoming an entrepreneur. Chapter 3 shows how ideas are developed into business opportunities in the early venture stage. Here you will also learn why innovation is important and the techniques used to be creative in developing new business ideas. Chapter 4 shows how to analyze the market and potential customers, conduct a competitive analysis, and create a marketing plan for the venture. Chapter 5 teaches how to structure the first outline business plan, and Chapter 6 explores the various forms ventures may take and describes name and company registration.

CHAPTER 1: WHAT IS AN ENTREPRENEUR?
CHAPTER 2: THE ENTREPRENEURIAL PROCESS
CHAPTER 3: THE ART OF INNOVATION — DEVELOPING IDEAS AND
BUSINESS OPPORTUNITIES
CHAPTER 4: ANALYZING THE MARKET, CUSTOMERS,
AND COMPETITION
CHAPTER 5: WRITING THE WINNING BUSINESS PLAN
CHAPTER 6: SETTING UP THE COMPANY

ROADMAP for

PATTERNS OF ENTREPRENEURSHIP
Getting Started as an Entrepreneur

- [x] **An Entrepreneurial Perspective**
- [x] **Commonly Shared Entrepreneurial Characteristics**
- [x] **Types of Entrepreneurs**
- [x] **The Need to Control**
- [x] **Entrepreneurship Roller Coaster**
- [x] **So Why Become an Entrepreneur?**
- [ ] The Spiderweb Model
- [ ] Finding Early Mentors
- [ ] Managing Stress
- [ ] The Five-stage Entrepreneurial Process
- [ ] The Growth of Entrepreneurial Companies
- [ ] The Growth Period
- [ ] Why Innovation Is Important
- [ ] Definition and Types of Innovation
- [ ] Frameworks for Learning Innovation Skills
- [ ] Finding and Assessing Ideas
- [ ] Converting an Idea into an Opportunity
- [ ] Opportunity: Five Phases to Success
- [ ] Formulating a Successful Marketing Plan
- [ ] Preparing the Marketing Analysis and Plan
- [ ] Defining the Market Segmentation
- [ ] Conducting a Competitive Analysis
- [ ] Preparing the Pricing and Sales Strategy
- [ ] Penetrating the Market and Setting up Sales Channels
- [ ] The Value of a Business Plan
- [ ] Setting Goals and Objectives
- [ ] Starting the Process to Write the Plan: Five Steps
- [ ] Determining What Type of Business Plan Is Best
- [ ] A Typical Business Plan Format and Content
- [ ] Understanding Why Business Plans Fail
- [ ] Identifying What Form of Ownership Is Best
- [ ] Forms of Doing Business
- [ ] Sole Proprietorship
- [ ] C-corporation
- [ ] S-corporation
- [ ] Partnership
- [ ] Limited Liability Company
- [ ] Business Start-up Checklist

CHAPTER 1

WHAT IS AN ENTREPRENEUR?

> "Good management is the art of making problems so interesting and their
> solutions so constructive that everyone wants to get to work and
> deal with them."
>
> PAUL HAWKEN

OBJECTIVES

- Place entrepreneurship in today's context.
- Understand what differentiates an entrepreneur.
- Classify different types of entrepreneurs.
- Explore what control means to you and the choices it affects.
- Learn the master-case story and context.
- Understand your strengths and limitations.

CHAPTER OUTLINE

Introduction

Profile: Wayne McVicker—A Typical
  Entrepreneur

An Entrepreneurial Perspective

Commonly Shared Entrepreneurial
  Characteristics

Types of Entrepreneurs

The Need to Control

Entrepreneurship Roller Coaster

So Why Become an Entrepreneur?

Use the Master-Case to Develop
  Management Skills

Summary

Study Questions

Exercises

Interactive Learning on the Web

Appendix: The Master-Case, Neoforma,
  Inc.

Neoforma—A Summary of the Master-Case

Additional Resources

INTRODUCTION

No sector of the economy is as vital, dynamic, and creative as entrepreneurship. For
the past thirty years, the impact of entrepreneurs and small-business owners in the
creation of new ventures has been felt in every sector of the United States and in
virtually all the world's mature economies. The startling growth of entrepreneurial
ventures forms the heart of our changing economic system as more employees work
for these owners than any other sector of the economy. In the United States today, the

3

number of employees in small and entrepreneurial ventures is growing faster than in any other sector of the labor force, and there is no sign of a reversal in this trend. The Global Entrepreneurship Monitor states that as much as one-third of the differences in economic growth among nations may be due to differences in entrepreneurial activity. A key factor affecting the U.S. economy is the annual creation of 600,000 to 800,000 new companies, which produces many new jobs.[1]

Entrepreneurship—the process of planning, organizing, operating, and assuming the risk of a business venture—is now a mainstream activity. Starting a business is never easy; it requires a special blend of courage, self-confidence, and skills, all of which determine the success or failure of an enterprise. However, a world of resources is now available to individuals who wish to launch ventures. The Internet provides access to up-to-date market and technology information and offers would-be entrepreneurs many useful support networks. In addition, business schools even *teach* the fundamentals of entrepreneurship, which were not even part of the curriculum until the 1990s.[2,3]

Throughout this text you'll read about entrepreneurs from many types of entrepreneurial businesses. Their stories will help you explore possible paths for building your own successful career. You'll also have the opportunity to assess your present career profile and strategy and contrast them with the approaches these entrepreneurs have developed. The career choices and paths you take are deeply embedded not only in relationships, but also in individual characteristics and valued outcomes. The course you follow will be based on a collected set of skills, knowledge, abilities, and experiences, as well as the recognition of unique opportunities.

PROFILE: WAYNE McVICKER[4]—A TYPICAL ENTREPRENEUR

Wayne McVicker, originally trained as an architect, first had the idea of starting a company while working for Varian Corporation in California. The idea to create a new and transparent way to market complex medical equipment did not get much support within Varian, so together with another employee, Jeff Kleck, he started Neoforma. (Interestingly, more than 60 percent of ideas for start-ups come when working for someone else!) They did this with full knowledge of their employer. At first McVicker worked out of his home, while still full time at Varian, but eventually he untied the knot. Using loans from family members, his home equity, and retirement and college funds, he started building the company. He was fortunate to meet Jack Russo, a local attorney who took Wayne and his partner under his wing. Jack gave them a little money and introduced them to some local successful entrepreneurs who eventually invested in Neoforma. The company grew rapidly, continually putting Wayne and Jeff under stress to find money, people, and advisors. They made a number of common mistakes, including wrong hires, chasing fruitless initiatives, not delegating tasks, and gradually losing control of their company as venture capitalists and new managers entered the picture. Despite these trials and tribulations, the passion that Wayne and Jeff had to make health care better carried the company through to a public sale of stock and an eventual purchase by a group of large health-care companies. After a short breather to get over the years of intense activity and stress, the founding partners started another company, Attainia, to do an even better job at opening up the health-care market. Using the lessons learned from Neoforma, they were better equipped to avoid most of the start-up traps. (See the Appendix to this chapter for more on Wayne and Neoforma.)

AN ENTREPRENEURIAL PERSPECTIVE

The word *entrepreneur* comes from the seventeenth-century French word *entreprendre,* which refers to individuals who "undertook" the risk of new enterprise. Early entrepreneurs were also "contractors" who bore the risks of profit or loss, and many were soldiers of fortune, adventurers, builders, and merchants.[5] Early references to the *entreprendeur* spoke of tax contractors—individuals who paid a fixed sum of money to a government for the license to collect taxes in their region. Tax entreprendeurs bore the risk of collecting individual taxes. If they collected more than the sum paid for their licenses, they made a profit; if not, they lost money.

Today the definition of *entrepreneurship* includes more than the mere creation of a business; it also includes the generation and implementation of an idea. Understanding this team concept is critical if you wish to be a successful entrepreneur. The idea of a sole individual being able to take on enormous risks, attempt innovations, leap without the appropriate background research, and succeed by working long hours and persevering at all costs is no longer relevant in today's global economy. Entrepreneurs also communicate effectively, not only to their teams, but also to external "stakeholders" such as investors, bankers, and corporate partners, which are necessary components of their growth path.

COMMONLY SHARED ENTREPRENEURIAL CHARACTERISTICS

"As professors of entrepreneurship, we are often asked if it is possible to 'teach' someone to be an entrepreneur. My response is that you can't teach someone to acquire the drive, the hunger, the passion, and the tenacity to pursue an entrepreneurial path. However, give me someone who has such 'fire in their belly' and we can help them to develop critical entrepreneurial skills which will guide them along their journey."

ALEX DENOBLE
Professor of Management and Director of Academic Entrepreneurship Program, San Diego State University Entrepreneurial Management Center

Entrepreneurs share a number of characteristics.[6] Often these seem to be paradoxical or even mutually exclusive, which highlights their first key attribute:

- They have the ability to deal with ambiguity. They are comfortable with making decisions based on apparently conflicting and incomplete information. They do not need to nail down every detail, yet they can apply analytical skills when appropriate and necessary. They are also comfortable in complex situations; indeed they can spot opportunities from what may seem to others a chaotic environment, often using an innate intuitiveness to extract patterns not obvious to competitors. Operating in fuzzy-edged gray areas is a natural habitat.
- They are self-starters, optimists, perseverant, energetic, and action oriented.[7] What to others may seem a fatal blow is an opportunity for entrepreneurs to learn, pick themselves up, and see a new opportunity. Threats are turned into great new ideas.
- They are persuasive leaders, people oriented, natural networkers, and communicators. Habitual entrepreneurs involve many people—both inside and outside the organization—in their pursuit of an opportunity. They create and sustain networks of relationships rather than going it alone, making the most of the intellectual and other resources people have to offer, all the while helping those people to achieve their goals as well.[3] They lead by example rather than dictating.
- They are often creative and highly imaginative.
- They passionately seek new opportunities and are always looking for the chance to profit from change and disruption in the way business is done.
- They tolerate risk, but great entrepreneurs temper risk with reality.
- They work with urgency but balance this with a focus on long-term goals too.
- They focus on execution—specifically, adaptive execution. People with an entrepreneurial mindset *execute;* that is, they move forward instead of analyzing new ideas to death.

- They are open to change and do not hang on to old plans when they are not working. But they pursue only the very best opportunities and avoid exhausting themselves and their organizations by chasing every option. Even though many habitual entrepreneurs are wealthy, the most successful remain ruthlessly disciplined about limiting the number of projects they pursue.

These skills clearly conflict with the old idea of an entrepreneur being a loner coming up with new out-of-context inventions in the basement without having the personal skills to create a valuable and exciting business from the creativity.

ROADMAP

IN ACTION

Entrepreneurs possess recognizable skills, many of which are embedded within us all. Understand these to uncover hidden traits, and develop them sufficiently to become a successful entrepreneur.

Many entrepreneurial skills do not apply only to starting a company but have broader applications to other career paths and, indeed, to the way one deals with many of the personal challenges in one's life. As the world becomes more complex and job security in large organizations is no longer the norm, the ability to create and successfully build your own opportunities is vital. Therefore, even if you do not decide to start your own company (at least not yet), the lessons learned throughout this book will help you in whatever you do.

TYPES OF ENTREPRENEURS

Until recently, people tended to think of the world of work in distinct categories. Most people worked either in someone else's business or in their own. The distinction between being an employee and being an entrepreneur was clear.

The rapid changes in the economy over the past two decades have blurred the lines between traditional employment and entrepreneurship. What counts now are portable skills and knowledge, meaningful work, on-the-job learning, and the ability to build effective networks and contacts, whether through teams or through the Internet. Many people now follow less predictable and even zigzagging career paths. The distinction between managing your own operations and working for others has become blurred. Owning your own business may be a lifetime pursuit or just one part of your career.[8] Some people, called *serial entrepreneurs,* start, grow, and sell several businesses over the course of their careers. In any case, to be successful, you must develop the appropriate skill sets, strategic plans, and management team to enhance your possibilities of survival. We return to this topic in Chapter 2.

There are several different approaches to identifying entrepreneurial types. Ray Smilor in his book *Daring Visionaries* recognizes three kinds of entrepreneurs: aspiring, lifestyle, and growth entrepreneurs.[7]

1. *Aspiring entrepreneurs* dream of starting a business; they hope for the chance to be their own bosses, but they have not yet made the leap from their current employment into the uncertainty of a startup.

2. *Lifestyle entrepreneurs* have developed an enterprise that fits their individual circumstances and style of life. Their basic intention is to earn an income for themselves and their families.[8]

3. *Growth entrepreneurs* have both the desire and the ability to grow as fast and as large as possible. These firms are the most dynamic job generators in the economy.[8]

One of the major mistakes aspiring entrepreneurs make when starting out is *not* to closely question what they want to be "when they grow up." Choosing the path of a lifestyle company creates certain advantages and disadvantages that must be carefully considered. If the goal is to employ maybe twenty or thirty people, to create a comfortable lifestyle for yourself and family members, and to retain control of the company, then the lifestyle path is for you. However, this imposes certain limitations on how you can fund the company. This path eliminates the possibility of selling part of the company for cash to pay for growth. A lifestyle company will not provide a way for investors to get a return on their investments through the sale of their ownership positions in the company. Not being honest with yourself at an early stage about the control and lifestyle issues will lead to serious and unpleasant conflicts with investors if you take money from them and do not provide them a way to "exit" their investment.

ROADMAP

IN ACTION

The ambitions of entrepreneurs vary widely in scope. Understand your personal aims before embarking on an entrepreneurial journey.

Growth entrepreneurs, on the other hand, are much less driven by control or lifestyle. They recognize that to grow quickly, they will have to sell parts of their companies to raise cash. These investors will apply various levels of control. The aspirations of the founder and the investors are aligned; they both want to build a valuable company and sell it either to an established company or to the public via an IPO (initial public offering). The entrepreneur is willing to trade control for growth and wealth creation.

There is a third route, however—a lifestyle company that manages to grow fairly rapidly without taking in outside investors. These companies are a hybrid between the lifestyle company and the high-growth equity-financed company. We call these "growth bootstrapped" companies. In most cases entrepreneurs do not plan it this way. They may start off as a lifestyle company and find that they can generate enough interest for their products or services that they can grow using the cash that they generate from sales. Or they may be in a place where there is little or no access to equity funds or their business does not match the industry knowledge and interests of investors.

It is important for you to think carefully as you decide if control and lifestyle are what drive you or if it is growth, visibility, wealth, or perhaps fame that fuels your ambition. Moving between these two different paths is difficult for reasons explored further in Chapters 7 and 8.

THE NEED TO CONTROL

The first decision that an entrepreneur should make is whether personal lifestyle and control are more important than growth and eventual wealth creation. If you believe that the idea for a new business is "your baby," identify with it, believe you are the best person to grow the opportunity, and cannot conceive of handing the reins over to someone else, then a lifestyle choice is best. On the other hand, if you wish to grow the opportunity into something that is "going to change the world" and share the responsibility rather than control the venture, then a different set of options are open. Understanding how important control is will affect your willingness to share the management responsibilities and fundamentally impact your financial options.

ROADMAP

IN ACTION

Many problems that occur in entrepreneurial companies can be traced to conflicts over who controls what. Be completely honest with yourself on this issue *before* involving others.

Partners: Many well-known and highly successful companies were started by two or more partners: Jobs/Wozniak at Apple, Hewlett/Packard at HP, Brin/Page at Google, Allen/Gates at Microsoft, and others. Studying successful companies shows that there is a lower chance of failure when there is more than one founding partner. This is not surprising, as one person is unlikely to have all the experience or personal attributes that are required to meet all the challenges. As we will see in the Neoforma master-case, Wayne and Jeff complement each other in ways that enable them to weather some heavy storms. On the other hand, having a partner who turns out to be incompatible can be fatal to the company. Also, right from the beginning, any value that is created is immediately halved if there are two founders. There is a balance between increased likelihood of success and dividing the eventual wealth or cash flow. You should carefully consider on which side of this divide you feel more comfortable. Exercises at the end of this chapter and Chapter 7 will help you think through this process. If you feel that sharing the opportunity with a partner is best, you must carefully consider what personal values and ambitions are needed in a partner. Once an outline profile is prepared, the chances of meeting the right partner increase.

Hired Managers: Unfortunately, many companies fail because the founders do not confront their management limitations. It is one thing to have an idea, a passion, and the ability to get to the first sale of a product; it is another to build a strong organization with all the trappings of a larger company—human resources policies, structured training, international cash management, distribution channel development, and so on. The personal attributes of those who create the original idea and have the risk profile and passion to get a company off the ground are usually very different from the skills that are required as the company matures. It is rare indeed to find a first-time entrepreneur who can take it all the way. It is so rare, in fact, that most venture capitalists refuse to invest in companies where the founder is not open to the idea of stepping aside at the appropriate time. You need to be brutally honest about your own limitations. First-time entrepreneurs have little or no experience and are often too optimistic about their own capabilities. In many cases they can provide the vision and passion for a new opportunity but soon become overwhelmed as the company begins to take control of them, rather than the other way around. Bringing in new managers with more experience can often be a painful but necessary step; learn when to hand over to others before it is too late.

In the master-case, Wayne and Jeff accept from the very start that they are not the ones to take it all the way and, in fact, work hard to find their replacement. Even so, they have a really hard time handing "their baby" over to a stranger. There are two issues here: (1) Can you personally accept that it is time to step aside? and (2) Can you do this without undermining your replacement? We have seen many companies fail from the inability of the entrepreneur to confront these issues. They take the company down with them still in the captain's cabin.[9] Certainly, if you are someone wanting to retain control, you should pay careful attention to your abilities to manage growth and seek guidance when the time calls for it.

Financing Options: If control is more important to you than wealth creation through sharing, you will have to limit your financing options to so-called bootstrapping methods and bank loans and forgo using true investors to provide funding for your company. This limitation may well restrict the growth rate of your business but can retain your ability to make all the key decisions, both good and bad. These two fundamentally different financing options are so important that we devote two chapters, 7 and 8, to them.

Opportunity Selection: If control of your own company is important to you and you are somewhat risk averse, you would be better off starting with a smaller opportunity. If, on the other hand, you are someone who is comfortable with sharing decisions and ownership, you may follow a more ambitious plan where you intend to grow your company quickly with the help of one or more partners, outside investors, and advisers.

ENTREPRENEURSHIP ROLLER COASTER

Of course, life is not so predictable that you can follow each step in this book without being confronted with surprises, challenges, and disappointments. Indeed, one of the most important attributes of a successful entrepreneur is the ability to keep going under duress. Figure 1-1, adapted from *Commercializing New Technologies* by V. K. Jolly[10] from an original chart from R. J. Skaldic, shows the ups and downs typical of a start-up from the original vision or idea through to commercial success. The challenge for the entrepreneur is to manage the periods of despair as well as celebrate the ecstatic events. As you follow the Neoforma story, you will be able to clearly identify many "ups and downs."

ROADMAP

IN ACTION

The entrepreneurial life is unpredictable, challenging, and often stressful. Practice how to handle uncertainty effectively.

SO WHY BECOME AN ENTREPRENEUR?

With such a roller-coaster life, you might ask, "Why undertake such an uncertain journey?" People become entrepreneurs for many reasons. Some people are attracted to the perceived independence and freedom from the politics and restrictions of corporations. Being able "to do your own thing," make your own decisions, and exert greater control over your working environment are attractive alternatives to the

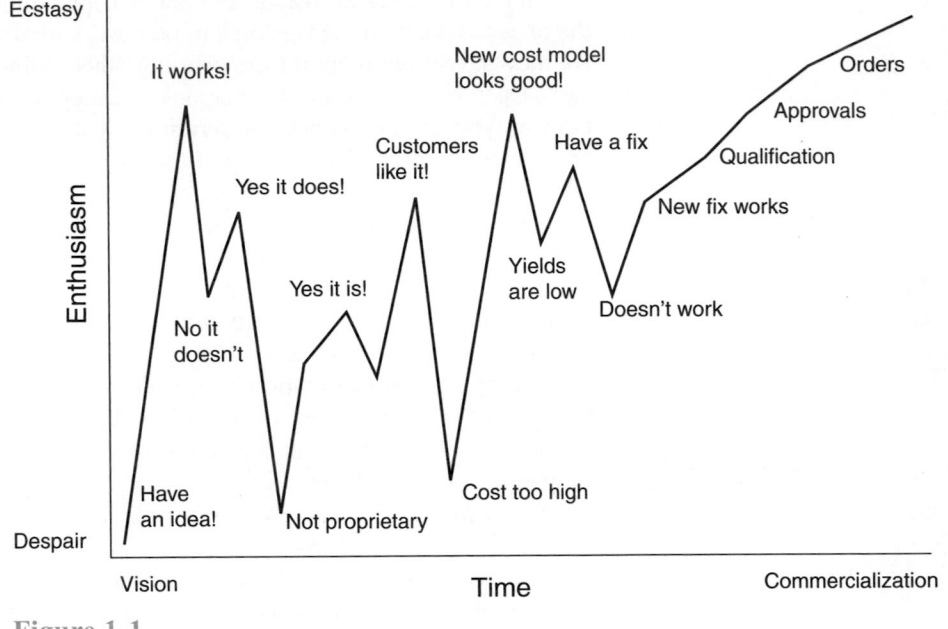

Figure 1-1

conformity—real or imagined—associated with life in a big company. Some may hit a plateau, see that they are blocked from further promotions, or recognize that they are not progressing as rapidly as they would like, and these conditions become motivating factors. We even tell our students that they should view being fired not as a negative, but as the trigger to start something exciting. Other people believe that building a company can provide them with opportunities for sustained growth and mobility. For others, starting their own company provides them with the flexibility they seek in their lives. And of course, for many, entrepreneurship offers a vehicle for creating huge financial rewards.

USE THE MASTER-CASE TO DEVELOP MANAGEMENT SKILLS

The failure rate of start-ups is very high. According to Timmons and others[11] the failure rate of new companies is 24 percent within the first two years and 80–90 percent within the first ten years. However, most companies fail not from focusing on a bad idea or even having insufficient funds; they fail because the founders are confronting complex management decisions without experience or knowledge of the tools to make them. Throughout the book we include sections on management issues that are aimed at providing you with an understanding of the unique personal challenges that an entrepreneur faces, especially in their first company adventure. You will examine your own strengths and, yes, weaknesses and learn management skills to deal with the major decisions you will have to make.

Starting a company can be very stressful, with tremendous demands on your time and energy. This can take a toll on your personal life and affect friends and family in ways that are painful. You need to be honest with yourself and those near you so the appropriate balance between your personal lifestyle and your new company can be struck.

You will acquire key management skills by studying the master-case for this book and working on exercises. The appendix to this chapter provides a brief synopsis of the master-case.

SUMMARY

The definition of an entrepreneur has evolved over time as the surrounding economic structures have become more complex. Today *entrepreneurship* is defined as the process of creating something different by devoting the necessary time and effort; assuming the accompanying financial, psychic, and social risks; and receiving the resulting monetary rewards and personal satisfaction. Entrepreneurs can be classified as *aspiring, lifestyle,* or *growth*. Different personal values, ambitions, and attributes separate these classes, yet there is a set of personal attributes that seem to be common to all types. Before embarking on an entrepreneurial journey, you should take some time to reflect on your own attributes, particularly your need to be in control. This will help you identify an opportunity and create a plan of action that is suited to you and increase the likelihood of success.

STUDY QUESTIONS

1. What are the three types of entrepreneurs? With which do you most identify?
2. Describe five common entrepreneurial personal attributes.
3. Name four reasons to choose an entrepreneurial career. What is your main one?
4. If you start a company, will you expect to always be in control, or will you be willing to share control with others if that will help the company grow and make all the participants wealthier? Describe your reasons for your choice.

EXERCISES

1. Some argue that entrepreneurship is largely based on chance and many people do not become entrepreneurs because they are never lucky enough to be in the right place at the right time. Alternatively, entrepreneurs are believed to *create* their opportunities by engineering situations that heighten the chance they find an opportunity. What is your view? Give examples to illustrate your answer.

2. Entrepreneurs often use networks to extend their "opportunity space." You never know when and how a network will be valuable or what sort of network you might need. Indeed valuable networks can be created only when you are not looking for immediate benefit. How can you develop your own network *before* it may be useful?

3. Incompatible partners can destroy a company, yet good partners are invaluable. Taking a partner as an equal when you start a company immediately halves your potential upside. Is this worth it? You are considering starting a company. How would you find the ideal partner, and what would be his or her experience, personality, ambitions, and values?

Master-Case Exercises: Read the appendix to this chapter and go to the book's Web site to read the diary entries Prequel and Months 0, 2, 19, 29, 57 and view the first video selection, "The Mindset, the Passion: Do You Have What It Takes?"

Either as a team or individually, produce a presentation on each of the following questions for class discussion. Only one or two slides for each are required to state the key points, which will then be expanded in the class.

Master-case Q 1: There are two well-known theories of entrepreneurship. Schumpeter postulated that entrepreneurs strive to "creatively destroy" the status quo; any company that does not continually innovate will eventually be destroyed by someone who is more "entrepreneurial." Kirzner, on the other hand, claims that there are always disequilibria in markets. Entrepreneurs are good at uncovering and exploiting these. Did Neoforma fit one of these theories better than the other, or can both be invoked when trying to understand this company?

Master-case Q 2: Entrepreneurship is sometimes discussed as the ability to deal with these apparent conflicts:

- **Ambiguity—Planning.** Start-up companies are usually exploring new opportunities where data, details, and the environment may be largely unknown. Yet without a plan, managers do not have a basis on which to make decisions. The discipline of a business plan is required yet is rarely followed.
- **Creativity—Discipline.** Many, though not all, start-up companies are based on a new idea or an innovative solution to an existing need. However, if everyone is creating new things all the time, then nothing will actually get done.
- **Urgency—Patience.** Entrepreneurs are driven people. Yet real advances take longer than planned—always.
- **Flexibility—Organization.** The need to respond rapidly to changing circumstances, new ideas, opportunities, and threats with limited resources requires a great deal of flexibility and the ability to change direction quickly. But as the start-up grows, it is impossible for the founders to control everything and make all the decisions. An organizational structure must be put in place, which inevitably begins to prevent just the flexibility that is needed for success.

- **Risk Taking—Risk Management.** Entrepreneurs are usually risk takers, yet too much risk does not create a successful organization and certainly may turn away investors.
- **Short Term—Long Term.** Every day presents a new challenge and possible change of direction, yet you must not lose sight of the ultimate goal.

How did the managers at Neoforma resolve these paradoxes?

Master-case Q 3: Managing a start-up requires a broad range of personal attributes, different from and more diverse than in a larger, more structured company. An entrepreneur must balance these often conflicting skills and traits. Pick eight from the list and show, with examples, how they were exhibited by Wayne and Jeff.

- **Creativity**
- **Analytical Ability**
- **Imagination**
- **Networking**
- **Risk Taking**
- **Motivation to Achieve**
- **High Autonomy**
- **Leadership**
- **Persuasiveness**
- **Initiative Taking**
- **Commitment and Tenacity**
- **Tolerance for Ambiguity**
- **Unconventional**
- **Optimism**
- **Intuition**
- **Passionate in Enjoyment of Life**
- **High Energy**

INTERACTIVE LEARNING ON THE WEB

Test your knowledge of the chapter using the book's interactive Web site.

APPENDIX: THE MASTER-CASE, NEOFORMA, INC.

Wayne McVicker kept a diary recording in great detail the management issues that he confronted in forming, growing, and eventually giving up control of Neoforma. The full diary can be found in McVicker's book, *Starting Something.* An edited version is also on the Web site for this textbook. Wayne has agreed that we can use selections from his book to help you explore key management issues. He also graciously allowed us to interview the main players in and around Neoforma concerning the tough decisions that the management team had to confront. These filmed interviews can be accessed on the book's Web site. You will be asked to analyze their decisions and reach your own conclusions. As our students state, "It's like actually being in the company and having the responsibility to resolve major conflicts, stresses, and make tough decisions." The master-case is revisited in later chapters where specific management issues related to the chapter content arise. You will get to know the major players in and around Neoforma, identify closely with them, and anguish over the challenges the founders had to confront. Apart from actually starting your own company, there is no better way to experience the subtle management threats common to all new companies. This experience will undoubtedly increase your own odds for success.

The story of Neoforma, Inc., as reported by Wayne McVicker, is richly endowed with examples of many management issues that we will introduce throughout the book. We have found in our classes that students are better prepared for digging deeper into the master-case if they are acquainted with the story and many of the participants first. So here is a brief summary of the company's history.

NEOFORMA—A SUMMARY OF THE MASTER-CASE

YEAR MINUS NINE: Wayne McVicker was trained as an architect. He never really had a career plan, working on and off for a large architectural practice where he was considered rather unconventional. A self-taught computer geek, he was frustrated by the lack of interest in technology in the office. One day he got a call from Dwight, a longtime architect friend. Dwight headed the planning department at Varian, a large, successful public company that made huge medical equipment such as radiotherapy machines for cancer treatment. They were looking to add some "technology" into their marketing department by using three-dimensional modeling of hospital facilities to show how their machines could be installed. Wayne was intrigued and decided to take the job.

YEAR MINUS FIVE: Jeff Kleck joined Varian and was not immediately impressed with Wayne's work; there was some antipathy. Gradually, however, they gained mutual respect and developed a friendship that changed both their lives. Egging each other on, their software took on a life of its own as they expanded the concepts, usefulness, and capabilities. They even wanted to model competitors' products too, thinking that would showcase Varian's offerings in a better light.

YEAR ZERO: Eventually they questioned whether their software could become a profitable product in its own right—maybe even the basis for a new company. Realizing that Wayne's boss, Evelyn, would block the idea of Wayne and Jeff doing something on their own, they went around her to Ed, the president of the division. Eventually he supported their idea to spin out the software into a new company, providing Wayne and Jeff would continue to work for Varian for one year.

MONTH THREE: Under pressure to find a senior marketing executive, Wayne hired a friend, Cassandra, who turned out to be not quite what was expected. After agonizing over what became an embarrassing and untenable situation, Wayne fired her and lost a friend forever. He then hired Isaac, who quit on the first day because "there's too much to do here," before finally hooking Dante, who turned out just fantastic.

MONTH TEN: Wayne and Jeff looked for a lawyer to draw up the legal documents. That's how they found Jack Russo. Jack was a local attorney who had decided to leave the "big partnership" world of lawyering and started his own firm, specializing in start-up companies. Meeting Jack was fortunate for Wayne and Jeff as, in his new role, Jack got to know all the key people in Silicon Valley who were involved in some way or another with small companies. Jack worked with Wayne and Jeff to help them figure out what their business was actually going to do and coached them on how to present the opportunity to potential investors, mentoring them for several years. But finding investors and actually getting them to write checks took a long time, so in the meantime, Wayne and Jeff continued working at Varian, going to Neoforma's new offices early in the morning, after supper in the evenings, and on the weekends. Family members were also involved in the company in different ways. Anni, Wayne's wife, named the company and designed PR materials; Wayne's son stuffed envelopes; Anni's father lent the company some money.

At that time, the Internet was just emerging, so Neoforma's first software product was mailed out on a CD-ROM. The company needed extra help on the software code and decided to subcontract some of the work to software developer Galatia, Linda's company.

MONTH ELEVEN: Neoforma's software, as it migrated to the Internet, created a much more transparent marketplace for medical equipment and supplies. It made product and price comparisons much easier. This was seen as a threat by the powerful medical product suppliers and their large customers, the GPOs (Group Purchasing Organizations) that act on behalf of hospitals and clinics. Neoforma was shining an unwelcome light on the cozy relationships that existed between them.

MONTH TWELVE: After one year the stress of doing two jobs was too much, and the founders left Varian, taking a significant salary cut. They had to tap their home equity and children's college funds to sustain them.

MONTH FIFTEEN: Jack felt they were ready for outside investment. He tapped his network and brought in Shawn and Wally, who helped them with a check for $25,000 to get started. After a few months, though, they both seemed to cool on the idea of investing, and again Neoforma was short of cash.

MONTH EIGHTEEN: Jack brought in Alexander and JP, two rather flamboyant, rich private investors. After a rocky start resulting from understating the opportunity, both investors got excited but, for some vague reason, disappeared from the scene, again putting more financial pressure on the company. This coincided with Anni's father getting nervous and asking for his loan to be paid back, so Wayne cashed in his retirement savings, which triggered a large and unexpected tax bill.

MONTH TWENTY-THREE: Jack introduced Wayne and Jeff to Denis Coleman, the founder of Symantec and several other companies. Denis suggests that Neoforma hires Sasa, a Stanford MBA, to write a "professional" business plan. Together with Wally, who came back onto the scene, they made an investment in Neoforma, not a moment too soon.

Just as things were looking good and Neoforma was about to sign an important contract with Baxter Healthcare, they were named in a frivolous lawsuit against Baxter, which destroyed the opportunity.

MONTH TWENTY-SIX: Suddenly Alexander and JP jumped back into the scene as Neoforma began to position itself as an e-commerce B2B company in the large health-care space. They smelled a big opportunity with a lot of the risk already removed and, together with some of their network including Bret Emery, quickly invested a million dollars in Neoforma. They promised to introduce the company to top-tier venture capital firms they knew. They convinced Venrock, a New York–based venture capital firm, to invest, and Bret joined the board of Neoforma as their representative. Denis and Jack left, and Denis warned Wayne and Jeff of the negative effect on both management and culture that Bret was likely to bring.

MONTH TWENTY-SEVEN: Wayne was burning out. He hired Larry to take over his responsibilities for software development and Emma to expand the Web site content. Wayne had difficulties delegating his work, which created tension between him and Jeff, which they eventually resolved.

MONTH THIRTY: In order to hire more software developers, Wayne went to Buck's café in Silicon Valley, where much of the local networking was done over coffee. He managed to coax Dave, Mitch, and Apar, part of a high-level team, to join Neoforma.

MONTH THIRTY-TWO: Alexander hired Lori, a flamboyant PR executive, without informing Wayne. Lori suggested that Wayne move into the background and Jeff should be the sole public figure for Neoforma.

MONTH THIRTY-THREE: Wayne went into a deep depression, concerned about the viability of Neoforma and the risk that he was imposing on his family. His relationship with Anni had become distant. By chance he found an "executive coach," George Brodsky, who saw him through the bad patch and remained a mentor to Wayne for more than a year.

MONTH THIRTY-SIX: Alexander and Bret raised some more funds for Neoforma under terms that significantly reduced the ownership and possible payout for the early angel investors, as well as for both Jeff and Wayne. Jeff was outraged at Wayne for giving in to the terms. The investors suggested that Wayne take over the company. That almost destroyed the founders' friendship.

MONTH THIRTY-NINE: Realizing that they had gone beyond their management competence and the company was getting out of control, Jeff and Wayne hired a headhunter to find an experienced CEO. With great persistence, they coaxed Bob Zollars to join Neoforma to take over leadership.

MONTH FORTY: Sensing that the window of opportunity to sell the company was closing and at the urging of the board, Bob started preparing Neoforma for an initial public offering. Bob hired Dan to be head of business development, and Dan's ex-employer immediately sued Neoforma. The courts imposed a restriction on Dan. Jeff had to spend much of his time resolving that unexpected situation. Bob also hired Ajit, an experienced medical products engineer, to head that function.

MONTH FORTY-ONE: Neoforma bought GAR, headed by Gino, a flamboyant used medical equipment trader. The cultures were incompatible, and Neoforma later sold GAR. Wayne found Pharos, a small, high-tech company, and Neoforma bought it. The cultures matched and the acquisition worked well.

MONTH FORTY-TWO: The board suggested that some corporate investors would enhance the perceived value of the company prior to going public. Bret offered to negotiate those deals but asked for extra shares for doing so. That enraged Jeff, who refused to agree and was willing to have the company fail rather than give in to Bret's demands. The board again suggested Wayne take over Jeff's position but he refused. Bob stepped in and calmed the situation at the last minute. Several of the large companies cooled off during the negotiations, and there was concern that they were just trying to learn more, but they really wanted Neoforma to fail as it was viewed as a threat rather than an opportunity.

Neoforma appointed Merrill-Lynch as its investment banker.

MONTH FORTY-SIX: Despite a number of last-minute problems, Neoforma started trading publicly on NASDAQ. The stock surged from $13 to $52 on the first day of trading.

MONTH FORTY-NINE: Neoforma's stock declined significantly based on a failed merger and nervousness regarding the dot.com bubble. Tensions grew in Neoforma.

MONTH FIFTY: Neoforma cut costs and Wayne made difficult firing decisions.

MONTH FIFTY-FOUR: Wayne and Jeff felt like strangers in their own company and decided to sell some stock and leave.

MONTH FIFTY-SEVEN: After a rest from the stress, Wayne and Jeff decided to go back to the original dream of Neoforma, raised some angel money, and formed Attainia—"to do it right this time."

FOUR YEARS LATER: After struggling for a few years under the careful management of Bob, during which the larger companies tried to undermine Neoforma, the company was finally purchased by Global Healthcare Exchange, a consortium of major firms. Bob left Neoforma.

Players. (Those marked with * were interviewed for the video materials accompanying this book; those in bolded type are the most important.)

Founders:

Wayne McVicker*: architect, author, software engineer, and cofounder of Neoforma

Jeff Kleck*: marketing manager at Varian and cofounder of Neoforma

Executives at Varian:

Dwight: Head of the planning department at Varian, manufacturer of medical equipment

Evelyn: Wayne's immediate boss at Varian

Ed: president of Wayne and Jeff's business unit at Varian

Mentors and Investors:

Jack Russo*: Neoforma's first attorney, investor, and mentor

Wally*: heart surgeon, entrepreneur, and angel investor in Neoforma

Alexander: private investor in Neoforma

JP: Alexander's partner, investor in Neoforma

Shawn: successful software entrepreneur and angel investor

Denis Coleman*: founder of Symantec, investor in Neoforma

Bret Emery: private investor in Neoforma, partner in Venrock Venture Capital

Neoforma Employees and Subcontractors:

Cassandra: Wayne's friend, a problem hire

Linda*: CEO of Galatia, a software development subcontractor for Neoforma

Isaac: employee for less than a day

Dante*: early and great hire (known as Chuey in the video clips)

Larry*: software engineer and Olympic coach hired by Wayne to manage development

Emma: liberal arts graduate and ex-Oracle employee hired to improve Web content and quality

Dave*: Mitch, and Apar; software team hired by Wayne

Lori: PR executive hired by Alexander to promote Neoforma

George Brodsky: Wayne's executive coach

Bob Zollars*: later CEO of Neoforma

Dan*: senior executive hired by Bob to strengthen the management team

Ajit*: senior executive hired by Bob to strengthen the management team

Sasa: business plan writer

Family Members:

Anni*: Wayne's wife

Anni's father: lender to Neoforma

ADDITIONAL RESOURCES

Kauffman Center for Entrepreneurial Leadership at the Ewing Marion Kauffman Foundation

Ewing Marion Kauffman established the Ewing Marion Kauffman Foundation to pursue a vision of self-sufficient people in healthy communities. The foundation, with an endowment of more than $2 billion, is based in Kansas City, Missouri. It directs and supports innovative programs and initiatives that merge the social and economic dimensions of philanthropy locally and nationally.

For more information, visit the center's Web site at www.entrepreneurship.org.

National Dialogue on Entrepreneurship

In the summer of 2003, the Public Forum Institute began work under a grant from the Ewing Marion Kauffman Foundation to develop a National Dialogue on Entrepreneurship (NDE) to improve awareness of the value of entrepreneurship. The project is building on the forum's extensive background in national dialogues on economic issues and, in particular, a series of events and activities since 2000 focusing on women and entrepreneurship.

For more information and to sign up for the newsletter, visit the Web site at www.publicforuminstitute.org.

Resource Conference Centers and Research Facilitators

American Women's Economic Development Corporation (AWED), New York. AWED, a premier national not-for-profit organization, is committed to helping entrepreneurial women start and grow their own businesses. Based in New York City, AWED also has offices in southern California, Connecticut, and Washington, D.C. It has served more than 150,000 women entrepreneurs through courses, conferences, seminars, and one-on-one counseling provided by a faculty of expert executives and entrepreneurs.

Catalyst,   New York. This national nonprofit research and advisory organization founded in 1962 has a dual mission: (1) to help women in business and the professions achieve their maximum potential, and (2) to help employers capitalize on the talents of women. Under the leadership of Sheila W. Wellington, president, the Catalyst library at 120 Wall Street offers resources on women for background research.

The National Association of Women Business Owners   (NAWBO), Washington, D.C. NAWBO propels women entrepreneurs into economic, social, and political spheres of power worldwide. NAWBO offers assistance in securing access to financial opportunities to meet, exchange ideas, and establish business ventures; educational programs, seminars, and leadership training; chapter programs, regional meetings, and national conferences; discounts on products and services; an international network of business contacts; visibility and clout in political arenas; and procurement opportunities.

www.wiley.com/college/kaplan

ROADMAP for

PATTERNS OF ENTREPRENEURSHIP
Getting Started as an Entrepreneur

- [ ] An Entrepreneurial Perspective
- [ ] Commonly Shared Entrepreneurial Characteristics
- [ ] Types of Entrepreneurs
- [ ] The Need to Control
- [ ] Entrepreneurship Roller Coaster
- [ ] So Why Become an Entrepreneur?
- [x] The Spiderweb Model
- [x] Finding Early Mentors
- [x] Managing Stress
- [x] The Five-stage Entrepreneurial Process
- [x] The Growth of Entrepreneurial Companies
- [x] The Growth Period
- [ ] Why Innovation Is Important
- [ ] Definition and Types of Innovation
- [ ] Frameworks for Learning Innovation Skills
- [ ] Finding and Assessing Ideas
- [ ] Converting an Idea into an Opportunity
- [ ] Opportunity: Five Phases to Success
- [ ] Formulating a Successful Marketing Plan
- [ ] Preparing the Marketing Analysis and Plan
- [ ] Defining the Market Segmentation
- [ ] Conducting a Competitive Analysis
- [ ] Preparing the Pricing and Sales Strategy
- [ ] Penetrating the Market and Setting up Sales Channels
- [ ] The Value of a Business Plan
- [ ] Setting Goals and Objectives
- [ ] Starting the Process to Write the Plan: Five Steps
- [ ] Determining What Type of Business Plan Is Best
- [ ] A Typical Business Plan Format and Content
- [ ] Understanding Why Business Plans Fail
- [ ] Identifying What Form of Ownership Is Best
- [ ] Forms of Doing Business
- [ ] Sole Proprietorship
- [ ] C-corporation
- [ ] S-corporation
- [ ] Partnership
- [ ] Limited Liability Company
- [ ] Business Start-up Checklist

CHAPTER 2

THE ENTREPRENEURIAL PROCESS

"Education is not filling a bucket, but lighting a fire."
WILLIAM KEATS

OBJECTIVES

- Understand the spiderweb model for small companies.
- Learn how to network and use mentors.
- Learn how to contain stress.
- Describe the five stages in the entrepreneurial process from opportunity analysis to scaling the venture.
- Learn the key growth issues for an entrepreneur.

CHAPTER OUTLINE

Introduction

Profile: Ted Graef and Scott Johnson—Getting Started with an Off-the-Shelf Idea

The Spiderweb Model

Finding Early Mentors

Managing Stress

The Five-stage Entrepreneurial Process

The Growth of Entrepreneurial Companies

The Growth Period

Summary

Study Questions

Exercises

Interactive Learning on the Web

Additional Resources

INTRODUCTION

In the first chapter, we learned what differentiates an entrepreneur from others and how the early stages of a new company can be extremely uncertain and turbulent. We also hinted that the management skills needed in a small company are very different from those in a more established corporation. How does a first-time entrepreneur cope with what is seemingly an ever-changing, almost chaotic environment with little experience and insufficient resources to fall back on? Well, it helps to have a framework to understand what is actually occurring and a fundamental roadmap and tools to navigate the rough seas. This chapter provides the models and frameworks to chart a course through the different stages of building a new company.

We start with a conceptual model of a small company, followed by some guidelines for personal behavior that will help on a day-to-day basis. Finally we lay out the five-stage roadmap that every entrepreneurial start-up must navigate before success is achieved. Often it is difficult to even see the road, let alone know where you are. But keeping the roadmap in mind will help you in your decision-making along the way.

PROFILE[1]: TED GRAEF AND SCOTT JOHNSON—GETTING STARTED WITH AN OFF-THE-SHELF IDEA

When Ted Graef and Scott Johnson left college, they were determined to start their own company. They started networking in their local community and were directed to inventor Ernest Merz, who had been trying to create a business around his patents for one-handed joysticks for industrial equipment. Until Merz's ideas were implemented, controlling a crane, for example, would require the user to manipulate several control handles for each direction of movement. That could easily lead to accidents, and Ted and Scott immediately saw the advantages in many applications. They agreed with Merz to get rights to the inventions and formed a company, Intuitive Controls Inc. They created a range of products around the inventions. To sell the products, they entered into an agreement with a major supplier of control systems, and sales started trickling in. They obtained a few hundred thousand dollars from a local group of angels (see Chapter 8 for more on this topic) to sustain the business until sales were sufficient. Then the economy took a downturn, the marketing partner reduced its efforts to sell the products, and the company hit a brick wall. As Ted relates, "There are two sides to having a large company market your products: you do not have to pay for your own salesforce, which is a major cost saving, but if things do not go according to plan, you have no way to contact potential customers to generate sales or to learn of the needs." However, the experience was not a complete waste. They had learned a lot about safety products during their first attempt, and they had learned about "points of pain" for users of electronic speed monitors and traffic control equipment. After talking with potential customers, such as police chiefs and township engineers; analyzing the shortcomings of existing products; and applying their hard-won philosophy of "intuitive controls," Ted and Scott developed a range of traffic management products and restarted their company in a new direction. Their new products, which include a service component in speed control systems, created a stir in the market. Now a police chief can monitor his or her jurisdiction in real time, over the Internet, and determine where it would be most effective to deploy patrols and place resources, making enforcement much more efficient and streets safer.

THE SPIDERWEB MODEL

The skills needed to run a small company with few resources are completely different from those required in a larger firm. In the early stages, the organization is more like a fragile spider's web; an attack that breaks one or two of the supporting threads could be fatal. An established company is more like a fortress with many specialized and organized troops ready to defend the enterprise, but a start-up has no legal department to deal with lawsuits, no head office to write checks, no cleaning service to clear the drains, and so on. The entrepreneur has to do it all, particularly in the first attempt, with no experience of being a multitasking, always-on-duty spider!

Figure 2-1

FINDING EARLY MENTORS

If the entrepreneur has limited experience and limited internal resources, then help from outside is necessary. Entrepreneurs must learn to be good listeners and find some good advisers who can help make difficult decisions. Entrepreneurs need to develop networking skills and uncover and penetrate networks of possible partners, mentors, customers, investors, and others. Of course, the Internet has become a great place to immerse yourself into social networks through such Web sites as MySpace, FaceBook, and LinkedIn. However, the interactions that such virtual media elicit tend to be rather superficial and lack some important factors required to establish personal business networks. Networks function largely on trust, which takes time to develop and often requires lengthy, face-to-face discourse in a variety of situations. This trust becomes one of your personal assets and can be used to navigate networks through recommendations.

IN ACTION

Entrepreneurs require good mentors, who are best found through networking. Identify highly connected people, and build trust with them.

There has been a lot of interest over the past few years in trying to understand the dynamics of network growth. Much of this work has been triggered by the Internet, which has fundamentally changed the way interconnectivity operates. The concept of "scale-free networks" has evolved.[2,3] In order to understand the implications of this concept, consider the following pair of easily recognized maps:

 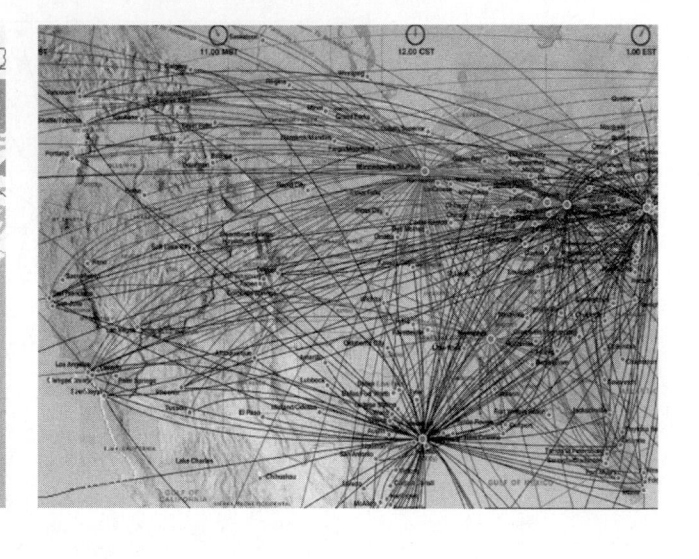

Figure 2-2

The interstate roadmap is typical of a network where connectivity is made only to nearest neighbors. It grows steadily because each link is a link between more or less equal intersections. The airline map is fundamentally different. Although having a similar number of nodes, some, the hubs, have a much higher connectivity than others. If I wanted to meet someone by chance, then standing at any of the interstate intersections would have a nearly equal probability. However, the chances are very different between, say, the airport concourses in Atlanta, Georgia, and College Station, Texas. Networks that are characterized by a few nodes with very high interactivity and many that are not often visited are referred to as scale free. The Internet is one such network. Certain Web addresses, such as Yahoo!, MSN, Google, and Amazon, are hubs; nearly everywhere else is "remote." Scale-free networks can be very powerful tools for developing new ideas and markets, a topic we will return to in Chapter 11.

Entrepreneurs who wish to access know-how and help can apply these valuable concepts. As you will see in the master-case, Wayne and Jeff used networking extensively when they were getting started. They learned that there are certain people who are "hublike," whose business life depends critically on personal connectivity. Professions such as attorneys, accountants, bankers, salespersons, and venture capitalists all depend on their network to find opportunities. Farmers, teachers, and shop owners do not. Therefore, you should identify the "connectors" in your field and locality and arrange to meet and talk to them about your plans. Start very early because you need time to build trust and respect before they are likely to devote much time to helping you directly or recommending you to their own network. You will be surprised how often people are willing to help you if you are open and honest with them. You should not seek mentors who always agree with you. Make sure you have one or two who challenge your decisions constructively.

MANAGING STRESS

Being a 24-7 spider running from one broken thread to another can easily distract you from making rational decisions. You become emotional rather than practical when choosing your actions. This is not helped by the fact that starting a company is not just a job; it is a passion, a dedication, even a life. The company can easily become all consuming, the only thing you think about, day and night. The swings from ecstasy to despair come all too often and unexpectedly. Not surprisingly, therefore, every entrepreneur—without exception—has experienced conflicts between his or her personal life and the company. It is too easy to become so completely engrossed in the venture that you neglect your friends and family and your own physical and mental health. This is dangerous as you lose balance in your judgments, forget to seek ideas and mental stimulation except within the confines of the company, and allow emotion rather than logic to guide decisions. In the worst case, you bury yourself in an isolated cocoon away from the social comforts that could actually help you through the periods of stress. You need some tools to help you avoid this common trap:

- Before taking action, ask yourself, "How can I work smarter, not harder?"
- Get advice on time-management techniques.
- Plan some personal time with friends and family and stick to them.
- Try to have your workplace at least twenty minutes from home. This seems to be the right time span for you to mentally unlatch yourself from the company.
- Find someone you trust who is not inside the company who you can discuss stressful situations with to help you tone down emotional content.
- If you have a business partner, work on ways you can help each other through the tough times. Take time to talk before the relationship breaks down.
- Think about your own behavioral patterns, and build in some slack time just to think.
- Force yourself to listen to friends and family about their lives too; don't talk about just the company all the time. They may have interesting things to talk about too.
- Delegate whenever possible, even if you think you are the only person in the world able to do the work.
- Try to see the funny side when things look really bad.

Contact your local chapter of SCORE (www.score.org) to find a retired, experienced executive who will help you on many of these issues for free and plug you into a valuable network. Balancing your personal and business lives is like walking a tightrope, and it is very easy to fall off.

ROADMAP

IN ACTION   An entrepreneurial life is inevitably stressful. Manage the different sources of stress effectively.

THE FIVE-STAGE ENTREPRENEURIAL PROCESS

Entrepreneurs can increase their chances of success if they understand, follow, and implement the basic five-stage entrepreneurial process described in this section. These five stages, summarized in Figure 2-3, form the backbone of the entrepreneurial process. Each of the key stages includes a main focus activity, discusses tactics for completing tasks, and identifies the estimated amount of time required for each stage. Costs are provided for each activity, which can be used to plan budgets.

Stage 1 **Conducting Opportunity Analysis** **(Chapters 3 and 4)**	• Innovate and create the vision • Conduct market analysis and research • Evaluate the competition • Research pricing and sales strategies
Stage 2 **Developing the Plan and Setting** **up the Company** **(Chapters 5 and 6)**	• Set goals and objectives • Start writing the plan • Investigate new processes and technologies • Determine pricing, market, and distribution channels • Prepare a full business plan
Stage 3 **Acquiring Financial Partners/Sources** **of Funding** **(Chapters 7 and 8)**	• "Bootstrap" the company • Secure early-stage funding • Secure growth funding
Stage 4 **Determining the Resources Required** **and Implementing the Plan** **(Chapters 9, 10, 11, and 12)**	• Manage the finances • Determine value of licenses, patents and copyrights • Develop a business model to maximize value retention • Prepare the organization for growth

Stage 5
Scaling and Harvesting the Venture
(Chapters 13 and 14)
	• Communicate the opportunity
	• Discuss options and alternatives
	  - Sell or merge
	  - Go public
	  - Form a strategic alliance

Figure 2-3   The Five-stage Entrepreneurial Process.

We'll also analyze the risks inherent in each stage and make suggestions for reducing potential problems.

Stage 1: Conducting Opportunity Analysis

The basic objective of this stage is to define the criteria that would make a business opportunity worthwhile. In this stage the founder identifies the opportunity and creates a *vision for the company*. If there is no vision for the venture, the new idea is just a dream. Chapter 3 discusses the role of innovation in the economy and how entrepreneurs can learn to innovate new business concepts, as well as how you screen these business ideas and opportunities. We'll also discuss various techniques that are used to evaluate the different categories of opportunities. Specifically, we'll look at the following:

● Evaluating business ideas (determining the idea's value and relevant factors, as discussed in Chapter 3)

● Protecting the idea (screening questions for patent protection and using an appropriate legal contract, as shown in Chapter 10)

● Building the vision, conducting market analysis to sustain a competitive advantage, and learning how to "think big"

● Preparing a competitive analysis (as described in Chapter 4)

This stage usually takes at least a year because it details the pricing and sales strategies required. For example, Bill Gates and Paul Allen were in college when they saw a computer on the cover of *Popular Mechanics* magazine, which set their plan in motion. It took them more than two years to complete the business planning process that led to the creation of Microsoft, an undeniably successful venture.

Stage 2: Developing the Plan and Setting up the Company

In this stage, ideas are discarded and strategies are documented and converted to an outlined business plan. The focus at this stage is not on producing a fully fledged business plan, but on documenting the main concepts for the company and the route planned for its growth. A full business plan is a vital yet dynamic document for the company; however, rarely does a newly formed company precisely follow its original plan. In addition, any plan must be tailored for the audience for which it is intended. For example, when raising money from investors or banks, one version might be required; when selling the company either to another corporation or to the public, other versions are needed; and of course, a plan is needed to guide your management team as the company grows. Because the business plan is such a vital tool for the entrepreneur, we have devoted a full chapter to just this topic (Chapter 5).

Chapter 4 describes how to undertake competitive analyses, determine marketing strategies, and develop a pricing scheme for your products or services.

Chapter 6 describes how many entrepreneurs dedicate thought and planning to starting their businesses and determining the structures of the companies. Others establish their companies without much regard to how the business should be structured. Regardless of the amount of forethought, one of the most important decisions to make is how to legally structure a business. The legal form of the business proprietorship—C-corporation, S-corporation, partnership, or limited liability company (LLC)—should be determined in light of the business's short- and long-term needs. We'll examine the pros and cons of each of these business structures as well as how to prepare a checklist to start a business.

Stage 3: Acquiring Financial Partners/Sources of Funding

Armed with a well-conceived plan, the next challenge is to focus on acquiring financial investors and partners. In most cases entrepreneurs may not be aware of the many financing options available that would best meet the needs of the business. Therefore, it is important to know the expectations and requirements of various sources of funds.

The two chapters that deal with this subject each address one of the two fundamentally different types of companies. Chapter 7 focuses entirely on funding a closely held company in which the founder(s) wish to remain fully in control of the company. Control restricts the company from certain sources of money, and the entrepreneur must creatively "bootstrap" the company to keep ownership positions from outsiders. Bootstrapping is a vital skill for all entrepreneurs; therefore, this chapter is also valuable even if the intention is to seek outside owners by selling equity, or shares, in the company. This second form of financing is discussed in detail in Chapter 8.

Early-stage funding sources include self-funding, family and friends, angels, banks, and government sources. We'll discuss these and other options used to raise capital in both chapters. Each potential source has certain criteria for providing financing, and these criteria are the focus of this stage. To increase the chances of success, we'll specify what sources are available for early-stage funding and discuss the requirements of financial partners. Chapter 8 also discusses sources for growth funding. We'll look at using private placements, attracting venture capital, and securing sources of debt financing, as well as examples of valuation of deals. The chapter describes the different valuation methods and how much of the company to sell, at what price, and for what percentage of the deal. We'll also explain the risks involved in financing in terms of timing and the emotional stress and patience required.

Stage 4: Determining the Resources Required and Implementing the Plan

> "Don't give up. Don't ever give up. And when things look worst, just don't give up."
>
> RICHARD FOREMAN
> *Former President &*
> *CEO—Register.com*

Chapter 10 explores the value of intellectual property and how to file patents, trademarks, and copyrights to gain a competitive advantage in the marketplace. The chapter provides an explanation of these forms of intellectual property (IP) and guides you toward effectively developing, protecting, and promoting your own IP.

All entrepreneurs must create a business model or framework that enables the new company to retain the value of its efforts. Otherwise, they can be quickly eroded by competition such that profits decline. Using a number of stimulating examples, Chapter 11 illustrates how it is possible to apply innovation to the overall business, not just to new products or services, and how to create a sustainable, highly profitable business that will retain its value and be an attractive opportunity for investors and, eventually, purchasers. In this chapter we show how the Internet can be used to build value and how information on customers' behaviors can be mined to build barriers to competitors.

Entrepreneurs are asked to plan operations and evaluate decisions using financial accounting information. An understanding of managing financial operations will contribute to the success of the entrepreneurial business. Chapter 9 discusses financial statements; how to analyze these statements; and how to prepare budgets, ratios, and cash flow forecasts.

Stage 5: Scaling and Harvesting the Venture

Chapter 14 highlights the methodology, procedures, and options available for entrepreneurs to scale the venture or consider an exit strategy. We'll discuss how to sell an equity stake to a partner, sell the business, merge with another company, and implement a leveraged buyout. We'll also discuss planning for a public offering that offers an option to sell a portion of the venture and scale the business for growth. The objective of this chapter is to help entrepreneurs identify the best exit plan and be in a strong position to manage the process.

Chapter 5 covers all aspects of the business plan. The plan pulls together all the topics covered in the other sections of the book. As we mentioned earlier, the plan is valid only on the day it is completed, and it must be continually updated as you learn more about your business, its customers, and its competitors. Also, when seeking funding, selecting partners, or selling your company, the plan must be tailored for the targeted audience.

Chapter 13 provides you with a vital skill that all entrepreneurs need, namely, how to communicate an opportunity concisely and compellingly to new employees, investors, partners, and customers. An idea has no value unless others understand its potential, become excited about being involved, and are willing to participate enthusiastically in the venture. Here you will learn about the different forms of communications, how to prepare for a presentation, and what is expected at each stage of relationship development.

Also, in Chapter 14, we tie together each of the issues covered in the book to show how they interact holistically in an actual company with tools and examples for you to learn true CEO skills.

THE GROWTH OF ENTREPRENEURIAL COMPANIES

Despite the growing prominence of entrepreneurship, understanding its key features and development stages lags. Mainstream media coverage frequently emphasizes the most unusual successes, creating misconceptions about the nature and evolution of most successful entrepreneurial firms. In theory, entrepreneurship includes several subdisciplines, including small business, businesses owned by women, high-technology start-ups, home-based businesses, and family-owned businesses. Businesses in these groupings have received the most intensive study.

Relatively little research has been done, however, on the distinctive features of growth companies. This is an important point because in many respects, entrepreneurial companies are indistinguishable from small businesses until they enter a "growth" phase, during which they are transformed into an almost entirely different entity. An entrepreneurial firm is one that grows large enough to influence the environment and, thus, become a pacesetter. Yet we cannot use growth alone to evaluate the real pacesetters, as 86.7 percent of all U.S. businesses employ twenty or fewer people.[4] The past fifteen years have been years of tremendous growth for entrepreneurial companies and for the individuals who make them thrive. During this time, entrepreneurs such as Bill Gates, Andy Grove, Steve Jobs, Meg Whitman, and Jeff Bezos have captured the public imagination and dominated the business news.

The reasons for this trend in entrepreneurship are clear. Each year at least 700,000 new businesses are started in the United States, and of these, a small portion turn out to be the fast-growth companies that propel the economy forward. Each year, this small set of businesses creates a disproportionate share of the new jobs and fuels the economy in numerous ways.

THE GROWTH PERIOD

Most businesses "start small and stay small." On the one hand, the business may not offer any productivity improvement and, therefore, may have no significant potential for entrepreneurial growth. On the other hand, even if they do have growth potential, the business owner may prefer to grow the business to only a certain point. As we mentioned above, not all entrepreneurs want to grow their businesses. Many entrepreneurs work toward the goal of growing the business to a certain level to provide a relatively steady stream of income and employment. The true challenges for these entrepreneurs and small-business owners are to avoid burnout from the daily operations and keep the entrepreneurial spirit that drove them into business in the first place.[5]

What distinguishes an entrepreneurial company from a small business is the ability of the venture owner to maneuver successfully through the transition stages necessary to handle distinctive periods of growth. In many cases the growth period comes right from the start and is part of the initial vision for the company. In other cases the growth period comes later or appears to arrive out of the blue. Each year a certain number of small businesses make the transition to become entrepreneurial growth companies. One thing these growth companies usually have in common is an entrepreneurial mindset.[6]

SUMMARY

> "In my view, entrepreneurs capitalize on uncertainty rather than avoid it, they create simplicity, where others see complexity, and they embrace the learning that comes from taking calculated risks."
>
> RITA G. MCGRATH
> *Columbia Business School*

The definition of an entrepreneur has evolved over time as the surrounding economic structures have become more complex. Today *entrepreneurship* is defined as the process of creating something different by devoting the necessary time and effort; assuming the accompanying financial, psychic, and social risks; and receiving the resulting monetary rewards and personal satisfaction.

The entrepreneurial process consists of five stages: (1) conducting opportunity analysis, (2) developing the plan and setting up the company, (3) acquiring financial partners and sources of funding, (4) determining the resources required and implementing the plan, and (5) scaling and harvesting the venture.

The study of entrepreneurship has relevance today not just because it helps entrepreneurs better fulfill their personal needs, but because of the economic function of new ventures. More than increasing national income by creating new jobs, entrepreneurship acts as a positive force in economic growth by serving as the bridge between innovation and application.

STUDY QUESTIONS

1. What is the spiderweb model? How does it apply to start-up companies?
2. What is the difference between a near-neighbor network and a scale-free one? How is this relevant to an entrepreneur?
3. What four mechanisms would you choose to manage personal stress?
4. What are the five stages of the entrepreneurial process?
5. What can you learn from the profile of Ted Graef and Scott Johnson? Give special attention to the following topics: (a) willingness to give up on an idea that is not working, (b) getting started and learning as you go, (c) the advantages of being in contact with the end-users of your products, and (d) the value of "sleeping" patents, or those that are not being used by existing businesses.
6. What are the growth issues entrepreneurial companies face?

EXERCISES

1. What is/was your best business idea/opportunity?
2. Who are/were the participants?
   - The person with the idea _____
   - Family _____
   - Friends _____
   - Other _____
   Explain.
3. What are/were the main risks?
4. What is the current status of your idea?
   - On hold _____
   - Abandoned _____
   - Continuing _____
   Explain.

Master-Case Exercises: If you have not yet read the appendix in Chapter 1, do so. Then go to the book's Web site and read the diary entries Months 14, 15, 18, 23, 24, 26, 30, 33, and 39 and view the video selection, "Seven Degrees of Separation?"

Either as a team or individually, produce a presentation on each of the following questions for class discussion. Only one or two slides for each are required to state the key points, which will then be expanded in the class.

Master-case Q 1: Map the networks that Wayne and Jeff had, starting from how they met, found investors, grew the company, and started again. How does your personal network link to them? Could you use this network?

Master-case Q 2: Despite the Internet, networks seem to require proximity and an entrepreneurial infrastructure. Why do you think this is so? Why are places such as Buck's found in entrepreneurial infrastructures. Do you know places such as this? How would you uncover them?

On the book's Web site read diary entries Prequel and Months 0, 21, 23, 24, 33, 45, and 46 and view the video selection, "Balance: Your Business or Your Life?"

Master-case Q 3: This was an extremely stressful and risky period for Wayne and Jeff as well as for the other key members of Neoforma. Why would you go through this again? Would you classify Wayne, Jeff, and Denis as "serial entrepreneurs." Why do you think such persons repeatedly subject themselves to the uncertainties and the stress of starting companies? (Hint: See W. Baumol's views on entrepreneurs at www.sba.gov/advo/decjan06.pdf.)

Master-case Q 4: Anni and Wayne started out with a dream that nearly became a nightmare for their family. Chart the key events in the story of Neoforma that threatened their relationship. What lessons can be learned from these events regarding how to balance work passion and personal lives?

INTERACTIVE LEARNING ON THE WEB

Test your knowledge of the chapter using the book's interactive Web site.

ADDITIONAL RESOURCES

Kauffman Center for Entrepreneurial Leadership at the Ewing Marion Kauffman Foundation

Ewing Marion Kauffman established the Ewing Marion Kauffman Foundation to pursue a vision of self-sufficient people in healthy communities. The foundation, with an endowment of more than $2 billion, is based in Kansas City, Missouri. It directs and supports innovative programs and initiatives that merge the social and economic dimensions of philanthropy locally and nationally.

The foundation's mission is to research and identify the unfulfilled needs of society and to develop, implement, and/or fund breakthrough solutions that have a lasting impact and give people a choice and hope for the future. In pursuit of its vision and mission, the foundation works to help youth become productive members of society and to accelerate entrepreneurship in America.

Inspired by his passion to provide opportunity for other entrepreneurs, Ewing Marion Kauffman launched the Kauffman Center for Entrepreneurial Leadership, the largest organization focused solely on entrepreneurial success at all levels, from elementary students to high-growth entrepreneurs. The center takes an innovative approach to accelerating entrepreneurship through educational programming and research. The center's entrepreneurial activities are organized around three primary areas:

1. It develops and disseminates innovative, effective, and comprehensive curricula and support systems for adult entrepreneurs, from aspiring to high growth.

2. Its youth entrepreneurship efforts focus on creative initiatives for enhancing entrepreneurship awareness, readiness, and application experiences for K–12 youth and community college students.

3. It also promotes entrepreneurship with public policymakers, not-for-profit leaders, and in urban and rural communities of need.[3]

For more information, visit the center's Web site at www.entrepreneurship.org.

Resource Conference Centers and Research Facilitators

American Women's Economic Development Corporation   (AWED), New York. AWED, a premier national not-for-profit organization, is committed to helping entrepreneurial women start and grow their own businesses. Based in New York City, AWED also has offices in southern California, Connecticut, and Washington, D.C. It has served more than 150,000 women entrepreneurs through courses, conferences, seminars, and one-on-one counseling provided by a faculty of expert executives and entrepreneurs.

Global Consortium of Entrepreneurship Centers, (GCEC)   The Global Consortium of Entrepreneurship Centers (GCEC), formerly the National Consortium of Entrepreneurship Centers (NCEC), was founded in 1996. The intent of the organization is to provide a coordinated vehicle through which participating members can collaborate and communicate on the specific issues and challenges confronting university-based entrepreneurship centers. The GCEC current membership totals 200 university based entrepreneurship centers ranging in age from well established and nationally ranked to new and emerging centers. Most of these centers have an outreach program to help budding entrepreneurs and are an excellent starting point to learn about support systems in their regions as well as being a place for resources and guidance materials. More information can be found at http://www.nationalconsortium.org

The National Association of Women Business Owners   (NAWBO), Washington, D.C. NAWBO propels women entrepreneurs into economic, social, and political spheres of power worldwide. NAWBO offers assistance in securing access to financial opportunities to meet, exchange ideas, and establish business ventures; educational programs, seminars, and leadership training; chapter programs, regional meetings, and national conferences; discounts on products and services; an international network of business contacts; visibility and clout in political arenas; and procurement opportunities.

The Small Business Administration

This Federal Agency has a number of planning tools and links to resources at its web-site www.sba.org

Additional Cases for Reading

There are several magazines that provide cases and tips for entrepreneurs. Stories are an excellent way of transferring knowledge, and these sources will provide you with many practical ideas to help you on your way: Entrepreneur Magazine at www.entrepreneur.com; Inc Magazine at www.inc.com; Minority Business Entrepreneur Magazine at www.mbemag.com

ROADMAP for

PATTERNS OF ENTREPRENEURSHIP
Getting Started as an Entrepreneur

- [ ] An Entrepreneurial Perspective
- [ ] Commonly Shared Entrepreneurial Characteristics
- [ ] Types of Entrepreneurs
- [ ] The Need to Control
- [ ] Entrepreneurship Roller Coaster
- [ ] So Why Become an Entrepreneur?
- [ ] The Spiderweb Model
- [ ] Finding Early Mentors
- [ ] Managing Stress
- [ ] The Five-stage Entrepreneurial Process
- [ ] The Growth of Entrepreneurial Companies
- [ ] The Growth Period
- [x] **Why Innovation Is Important**
- [x] **Definition and Types of Innovation**
- [x] **Frameworks for Learning Innovation Skills**
- [x] **Finding and Assessing Ideas**
- [x] **Converting an Idea into an Opportunity**
- [x] **Opportunity: Five Phases to Success**
- [ ] Formulating a Successful Marketing Plan
- [ ] Preparing the Marketing Analysis and Plan
- [ ] Defining the Market Segmentation
- [ ] Conducting a Competitive Analysis
- [ ] Preparing the Pricing and Sales Strategy
- [ ] Penetrating the Market and Setting up Sales Channels
- [ ] The Value of a Business Plan
- [ ] Setting Goals and Objectives
- [ ] Starting the Process to Write the Plan: Five Steps
- [ ] Determining What Type of Business Plan Is Best
- [ ] A Typical Business Plan Format and Content
- [ ] Understanding Why Business Plans Fail
- [ ] Identifying What Form of Ownership Is Best
- [ ] Forms of Doing Business
- [ ] Sole Proprietorship
- [ ] C-corporation
- [ ] S-corporation
- [ ] Partnership
- [ ] Limited Liability Company
- [ ] Business Start-up Checklist

CHAPTER 3

THE ART OF INNOVATION—DEVELOPING IDEAS AND BUSINESS OPPORTUNITIES

> "I think all great innovations are built on rejections."
>
> LOUIS-FERDINAND CÉLINE

OBJECTIVES

- Understand the changing role of innovation.
- Create frameworks for innovating.
- Source and filter ideas and build them into opportunities.
- Analyze opportunities using a five-step process.
- Use a framework to evaluate a business opportunity.

CHAPTER OUTLINE

Introduction

Profile: Becky Minard and Paal Gisholt—Finding a Point of Pain

Why Innovation Is Important

Definition and Types of Innovation

Frameworks for Learning Innovation Skills

Finding and Assessing Ideas

Converting an Idea into an Opportunity

Opportunity: Five Phases to Success

Summary

Study Questions

Exercises

Interactive Learning on the Web

Appendix: The Bayh-Dole Act

Additional Resources

INTRODUCTION

Entrepreneurs are often considered highly innovative, always coming up with unique ideas for new businesses. In fact, entrepreneurs do not have to be innovative to be successful, but they do have to understand and manage the innovation process within their companies. They may use innovations found elsewhere or use those continually

35

developed within their own companies, even when they themselves are not the source of innovation. Therefore, it is important that an entrepreneur has a grasp of the nature of innovation and how it is generated and managed.

Innovation can have many facets. For example, Michael Dell is rightly considered an extremely successful entrepreneur. Yet for many years, Dell has built products similar to its major competitors, Hewlett-Packard, Compaq, Lenovo, and so on. What is unique about Dell is the *way* that these products are sold, manufactured, and delivered to its customers. The business methods employed religiously by Dell are what make the company successful, not innovation of new products. (Chapter 11 has a more detailed discussion of Michael Dell.) In contrast, Steve Jobs of Apple fame is the driving innovator behind Apple's ability to continually come out with unique-looking and uniquely functioning products. Therefore, we cannot understand entrepreneurship without exploring the entrepreneur's relationship with innovative processes. It could be claimed, of course, that Michael Dell was innovative when he conceived the direct sale, made-to-order business model that has driven the success of his company. His competitors, after all, failed to see this model; having been caught unawares and locked into their old ways of doing things, they were unable to compete directly for a long while.

This chapter is about innovation in entrepreneurship. We begin with explaining the changing role of innovation in business, including definitions and types of innovation. We then show how you can learn to be innovative, how to seek out and screen ideas, and how to build them into creative new business opportunities.

PROFILE: BECKY MINARD AND PAAL GISHOLT—FINDING A POINT OF PAIN[1]

Becky Minard and Paal Gisholt met when they were students in the Harvard MBA program. In 1999 they formed SmartPak on Cape Cod. According to Becky, a horse lover, the company was born of necessity. "Feeding supplements was a disaster at our boarding barn. I have a horse that needs daily vitamin E, joint supplement, and a dose of daily wormer. I assumed he was generally getting his supplements. Then I noticed that the vitamin E lasted months longer than it should have. It's a white powder, so I checked his feed tub to see if it was in there. No trace of white powder. He did have a hefty dose of his daily wormer in there; maybe that would explain why I was going through it twice as fast as I should. Now it's hard to blame the barn staff since they have to feed thirty-five horses with an average of three supplements per horse. That works out to 105 supplements to be opened, measured, fed, and resealed. What a headache for them." Becky had just recognized the "point of pain" for both the horse owners and their minders.

Becky continued: "We wondered if others had the same problem, so Paal and I went out and talked to boarders, owners, and managers at other barns. All had many of the same problems. In a few cases, we found some moldy supplements or contaminated supplements (mouse droppings). We found many outdated supplements. The most consistent thing we found was that most of the feed rooms we visited had containers that had not been resealed after each use. Since then we have learned from manufacturers that oxygen, moisture, and sunlight are devastating to the potency of many supplements. Money down the drain."

These "points of pain" were solved by creating SmartPaks™. A horse owner can go to a Web site and order custom-packaged daily supplies for individual horses.

All the minder has to do is tear off the seal—similar to those used for six-packs of yogurt—and empty the different food supplements into the horse's feed. Each patented pack comes clearly labeled with the horse's name and list of additives. The owner can now rest assured that his horse is well taken care of and the barn helper's tasks are greatly simplified. SmartPak has now branched out into other pet supplies, allowing the company to grow to more than $40 million in sales.

The Changing World around Us

We often hear such broad statements as "competition is becoming brutal," "markets are global," "the Internet has changed the rules of business," and so on. Let's look at some of the facts and see how they influence an entrepreneur.[2]

The Growth of the Internet and Access to Knowledge and Ideas

Relatively recently, computers (and other digital devices) have become connected in networks, and companies such as Google have developed automated search techniques. This is resulting in a cataclysmic shift from an emphasis on local products and productivity to global knowledge sharing. We are only just beginning to understand the implications and effects of this connectivity. Although it is notoriously difficult to accurately size the Internet, any estimate provides staggering statistics. According to research from the Miniwatts Marketing Group[3] in March 2008, more than 1.4 billion people worldwide had Internet access, which equates to a 21 percent penetration rate, North America having the highest at 73 percent, and Africa, the lowest at 5.3 percent. These numbers represent an average growth of 290 percent over the period between 2000 and 2008. At the same time, the information available to these Internet users is exploding, with more than 7 million new Web pages being added *daily* to the more than 29 billion that, according to an estimate by Boutell.com[4] in February 2007, already exist on 109 million independent Web sites, up from 70 million in 2005. Google and Yahoo! claim that they regularly scan and index billions of Web pages. Now it is just as easy to find an expert at a university in Melbourne, Australia, as it is to find one in Melbourne, Florida, or a corporate partner in Cambridge, Massachusetts, as it is in Cambridge, England.

ROADMAP IN ACTION

Markets as well as competitors are now global. Recognize that opportunities are inherently larger than just ten years ago, but competitors are stronger too.

To remain competitive today, it is no longer sufficient to rely on local know-how; indeed it is vital to access the best ideas, technologies, research resources, and experts, wherever they are. For example, the networked world can support a biotech company with headquarters in Seattle; basic research undertaken at universities in San Diego, Edinburgh, and Auckland; scale-up of production in Singapore; and clinical trials in the newest members of the European Union. Its advisory board will undoubtedly be international in makeup. A management challenge—yes—but by assembling appropriate resources to compete quickly and efficiently, more certain success is in the offing. These knowledge-centered structures are variously referred to as "virtual knowledge networks" or "virtual clusters." They are fluid and may form and dissolve in short shrift when they are no longer valuable, whereas geographical-based clusters may take years to evolve with the danger of being outmoded and redundant. We can envision a world not long in the future where nearly everyone will be able to search the world's knowledge, locate experts on demand, and do this more or less for free. For an entrepreneur, this means access to more ideas, more stimulation, and more expertise when conceiving and growing a business opportunity. The Internet should be one of the entrepreneur's major tools.

The Internet and Customer Expectations

The Internet is also changing the way customers view suppliers. It enables us to find and compare products, even sometimes having the product made to order instantly; to choose when and how to have it delivered; and to decide how to pay for or finance the purchase. This is true in both business-to-business (B2B) and business-to-consumer (B2C) sales. We are being subtly educated to expect customized service and instant gratification as part of our buying experience. Products are being surrounded by service. We want *our* problems to be solved, not a standard product to buy. This shift, of course, is at the center of entrepreneurial companies such as Dell, eBay, Amazon, and Google. The lesson is this: think service, not product; personalized solution, not third-party handoff. As you will see in the many cases in this book, these ideas can be applied to the most mundane product areas.

Example: Greif Packaging (www.Greif.com)

A supplier of metal drums for shipping bulk chemicals, many of which are toxic, realized that it had no real competitive position and that profit margins were thin. An internal entrepreneur decided to listen carefully to customers. He saw there were unmet needs and new sources of value to be accessed. Customers did not want to buy and own steel drums; they just wanted to move toxic chemicals efficiently and safely. They did not want to deal with all of the details, such as finding a licensed trucker; filling in the government forms; and washing, cleaning, and refurbishing the drums. To meet its customers' actual needs, Greif converted its business model into a "trip leasing" company for specialty chemicals—the FedEx® of problem chemicals. Now it solves the total trip problem for its customers—drum supply, cleaning, refurbishing, regulatory compliance, transportation, and tracking. Greif built a new Web application and became an "Internet company." Although it subcontracts most support functions, it captures the value in the supply chain and builds long-lasting client relationships. The business model also builds barriers against competitors.

Barriers to Trade

Historical trade barriers for goods and services are rapidly being dismantled, opening up all markets to global suppliers. According to the World Trade Organization,[5] the number of international agreements signed annually to open up trade has ballooned from less than ten in 1950 to close to two hundred in 2000 and more than 250 in 2007. Any new product can be copied within days, then manufactured and shipped into most markets within a few weeks. The entrepreneur's defenses against this happening are having a sound intellectual property strategy (see below and Chapter 10) and an innovative business model that supplies more than just a product (see Chapter 11).

Access to Capital

Simultaneously with the elimination of trade barriers for goods and services, restrictions on currency trading have also been almost entirely removed. Now daily cross-border trading in currency dwarfs the value of imports and exports. Although most currency trading is on a short-term basis, the lack of restrictions in the majority of economies to inward or outward foreign investment means that funds may now seek opportunities on a global basis and firms must *compete internationally* for finance. Fully 20 percent of mutual funds managed in the United States and a mainstay of U.S. personally-managed pensions are now invested overseas.[6] Geographical location no longer provides any significant advantage for access to major sources of capital. Venture capital (VC) remains one source of funding that prefers proximity, but overall, VC funds are a very small part of total growth capital. Even venture capital is trending international. As reported recently,[7] leading "Sandhill Road" VC firms are looking to target a significant part of new funds for investment in early-stage companies in Asia, hoping to bring their startup management skills into markets where U.S.-style venture capital is little known. For the entrepreneur, this means that the competition for growth capital is becoming tougher, making the "bootstrapping" skills described in Chapter 7 important.

Technological Obsolescence

A product life cycle is the time that a product is able to command a high profit margin in the market before it becomes obsolete or develops intense competition. They are continually declining. It is much more likely to be true for fast-moving consumer products such as food and detergents and for products in which the underpinning technology is driven by Moore's law[8] or is impacted by major technological shifts. According to an internal study conducted in the mid-1990s by Hewlett-Packard (HP),[9] the average period that HP's products remained major contributors to sales had fallen from four years in 1980 to well less than two years in 1995. More recent studies[10] measure product development times that have declined from an average of 225 days three years ago to less than 200 days now. In the portable communication business sector populated by such companies as Motorola, Nokia, and Research in Motion, the maker of the BlackBerry device, market life cycles are now shorter than product development cycles; that is, it takes longer to develop a product than the time it will be successful in the market. This is a challenge to even the most efficient engineering departments, which are shifting to around-the-clock global teams. Managing such complex projects across corporate, national, and cultural boundaries requires new skills that ensure the ability to "get it right the first time."

ROADMAP

IN ACTION

No matter in which market you are operating, standing still is not an option. Adapt and take advantage of new technologies, new customers, and new partners.

Of course, in slower-moving sectors such as machine tools and locomotives, the evidence for rapidly declining product life cycles is not so obvious. However, even here, the impact of low-cost electronic computing power and the ubiquity of the Internet are accelerating the upgrades that customers expect. They want more than just a product; they anticipate nothing less than a total solution to their requirements throughout their ownership. These additional service components may cover not only financing and operator training, but also remote condition monitoring for 24-7 online support and maintenance, performance guarantees with financial penalties, and even returns of the product for recycling at the end of its life cycle. For example, Dell has recently started a recycling service for used computers. The acceleration of product life cycles changes the way that intellectual property must be managed. In the past, the seventeen to twenty years of protection afforded by a patent was often valuable over its full life. But when technology evolves rapidly, twenty years of protection loses its value. Research by one of the authors[11] shows that companies are reevaluating the ways that they protect their intellectual property and are carefully selecting areas for long-term patent coverage, usually on fundamental inventions, and are forgoing patents for trade secrets elsewhere. Patent law requires inventors to "teach" what they have done within the patent document; this inevitably exposes concepts and know-how that may be better kept secret rather than giving competitors a jump start to catch up. An agile company[12] has moved on by the time patents are issued, so the patents may be of more value to competitors than to the owner. In the new innovation model, churning out patents is replaced by including the protection of intellectual property within the overall business strategy rather than a way of protecting an invention. And when patents are filed, they are written to protect both the "hard" invention and the unique business model surrounding it.

In some sectors, of course, patents will continue to be the principal method to retain protection from competition. For example, the long and expensive development cycles and regulatory hurdles governing pharmaceutical products encourage the use of patent protection. Even here, however, careful selection of what to patent and when to retain maximum advantage after perhaps a ten-year development cycle is a challenging task.

The budding entrepreneur can learn several lessons here:

- It is becoming more and more difficult to build a company around a single product idea without strong patent protection. This is particularly true for consumer products that have a very short life cycle.
- Protective barriers must become part of any business model, whether via patents, trade secrets, uniqueness in the business model, or fast movement to market to stay ahead of competitors.
- Innovation is not a single event; one should never stop innovating.
- You should always imagine that there is someone, somewhere, having the same idea.
- The entrepreneur needs to solve customers' problems: think service, not product.

WHY INNOVATION IS IMPORTANT

So we are in a world in which access to knowledge and expertise, labor, and capital is truly global and transparently accessible, and in which technology relentlessly advances. Technical breakthroughs are no longer confined to just a few centers of excellence such as Bell Labs or MIT; the next breakthrough can just as easily occur in Bangalore, Beijing, or Brisbane as in Birmingham, Boston, or Boca Raton. Shorter product life cycles and rapid technological obsolescence make patents lose their power in monopoly preservation. In addition, companies can no longer rely on the earlier protections of trade and monetary restrictions, local labor preeminence, and cozy knowledge clusters to provide competitive advantages. The only way that sustainable advantages can be earned is through continuous innovation—innovation not only in product development, but in all aspects of business activity and at an ever-increasing rate. Of course, there has always been innovation in corporations. Indeed, William Baumol[13] argues that the unprecedented wealth generated in the major economies in the twentieth century would not have been possible without innovation. However, until relatively recently, many firms could survive and prosper without innovating: they competed in a protected environment. Now *innovation is no longer a luxury; it is a necessity.*

DEFINITION AND TYPES OF INNOVATION

Definition of Innovation

In this book we will use the following definition:

> Successful innovation is the use of new technological knowledge, and/or new market knowledge, employed within a business model that can deliver a new product and/or service to customers who will purchase at a price that will provide profits.

This definition is built on the generally accepted work of Alan Afuah.[14] In order to focus the discussion and to emphasize the new innovation, we have added the following:

"Successful…"—to emphasize that we are not interested in innovation that fails to deliver and maintain value for the innovating enterprise

"…employed within a business model…"—to stress that innovation in the business model is at least as important, as purely product or process technology. (This theme is developed further in Chapter 11.)

"…who will purchase at a price that will provide profits"—to stress that success requires that the innovator be able to extract benefit from the value created and not allow it to migrate to partners, customers, or offshore manufacturers

Types of Innovation

There are two major classes of innovation: incremental and radical. Incremental innovations are continual improvements on an existing product or service or in the ways that products are manufactured and delivered. Radical innovations are the result of major changes in the ground rules of competition, culminating in either a customer satisfying her needs in an entirely new way or in a totally new need being created through innovation.

The S-Curve is often used to illustrate the difference in which the performance achieved by a new innovation is plotted against time (see Figure 3-1). When the innovation is first made, a period of experimentation ensues in which little performance improvement is made while the innovator tries different ways of reaching goals. As learning improves with experimentation, the advances in improvements accelerate quickly until a plateau is reached, at which time major efforts are required to make minor improvements—the region of limited returns. Usually improvements can be made with *incremental* innovations, pushing the original curve higher. Then along comes a new innovation—usually from another place—which goes through

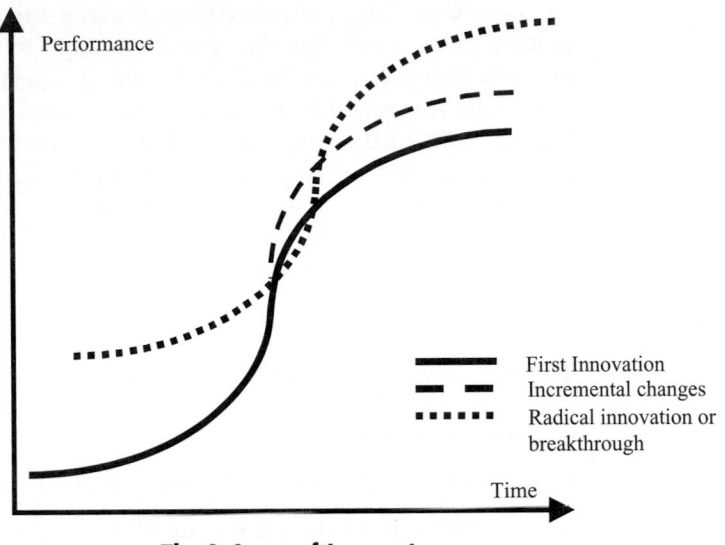

Figure 3-1 **The S-Curve of Innovations.**

the same cycle until it ends up giving a higher performance than the first idea and takes a major part of the market away from the first innovation. This is the radical change.

Example: The Evolution of Lighting

When Thomas Edison invented the incandescent lamp, it took many years before lamps were mainstream. First, he encountered difficulties in encapsulating the filament to prevent burnout, and houses had to be wired to receive electric power. But after twenty years or so, electric lighting became the preferred way. Electric lighting, a radical innovation, replaced candles. Since then, the electric lamp has undergone many incremental improvements, yet it remains fundamentally the same as Edison's original innovation. There are now only a few suppliers of lamps, and none of them makes good profits. Electric lamps are a commodity and are ripe to be replaced by the next radical innovation—solid-state diodes. We can only guess where the future may lie. For example, the glowworm's tail is a very efficient converter of electrical energy to light. With fuel costs rising rapidly, there is a big incentive to reduce energy consumption. Is the biolamp far away? The only assurance is that it will not be developed by one of the existing lamp manufacturers, for they are focused on incrementally improving the old ideas.

Edison's lamps nearly destroyed the candle industry—though not quite. There's money to be made in candles too!

Example: Blyth Candles

In 1977 Robert Groegen, an entrepreneur, bought a small, barely surviving candle company in Brooklyn, New York. At that time the company had annual sales of about $3 million. He changed the name to Blyth Candles,[15] and since then he has built the company to the point where it is the largest candle supplier in the United States, with annual sales greater than $1.1 billion. Groegen and his family members still own 29 percent of the company, which is now publicly traded, making his personal wealth in the company's stock worth $130 million—not bad for a candle maker. This has been achieved entirely via incremental innovations—perfumed candles for certain occasions and seasons, candles for outdoors, ornamental candleholders, and so on, and by buying smaller candle manufacturers that were not innovating at all.

Entrepreneurs, therefore, do not need a radical innovation to create a new, successful, and profitable company. Continuous incremental innovation can also be sufficient.

Disruptive Innovation

The term *disruptive innovation* is often used to describe innovations that *disrupt* the status quo. As companies grow, they develop cultures and procedures that create internal barriers to change. The greater the mismatch of the innovation to the current know-how and the more it threatens to destroy existing product sales, the tougher it is for a large company to respond. The change can arise from a new technology. Kodak struggled with changing from being the leading supplier of photographic film and moving to an entirely new business based on digital imaging. All of the company's chemical know-how provides no advantage in the new world, and the more digital products that Kodak sells, the faster its film business will decline. Dell entered the PC market with a new "direct to customer" business model. Google came from nowhere to threaten behemoth Microsoft. Again and again, it is entrepreneurial start-ups that can take advantage of the larger company's inability to respond to disruption. It was start-up Intel that destroyed RCA's vacuum tube business, Amazon that challenges established retail chains, and Netflix that attacks the location-based Blockbuster chain.

ROADMAP

IN ACTION

A small company, with no legacy to protect and account for, has an inherent advantage over larger enterprises, which are slow to change and adopt new ideas. Learn to swim among sharks.

To learn more about how large companies struggle with disruptive innovation, see Clayton Christensen.[16] And to learn how small entrepreneurial companies can partner with large companies, see Baumol's article on the Internet.[13] As evidence that entrepreneurs and small companies are the source of the most important innovations, see Table 3-1.

So don't be scared of those dinosaurs out there. Take advantage of their inability to respond to disruptive innovations, whether in products, services, or business models. Throughout this book you will find many examples of entrepreneurial ventures. Think about whether they are based on a disruptive innovation and how this will affect the existing larger firms. Can they respond?

FRAMEWORKS FOR LEARNING INNOVATION SKILLS

Debate continues as to whether innovators must be born or such skills can be learned. The authors' research shows that, indeed, if someone has the desire to be an entrepreneur, then innovation skills can be effectively learned. The best way to achieve

Table 3-1   Some Important Innovations by U.S. Small Firms in the Twentieth Century[17]

Air conditioning	Heart valve	Prestressed concrete
Air passenger service	Heat sensor	Prefabricated housing
Airplane	Helicopter	Pressure-sensitive tape
Articulated tractor	High-resolution CAT scanner	Programmable computer
Cellophane artificial skin	High-resolution digital X-ray	Quick-frozen food
Assembly line	High-resolution X-ray microscope	Reading machine
Audiotape recorder	Human growth hormone	Rotary oil drilling bit
Bakelite	Hydraulic brake	Safety razor
Biomagnetic imagining	Integrated circuit	Six-axis robot arm
Biosynthetic insulin	Kidney stone laser	Soft contact lens
Catalytic petroleum cracking	Large computer	Solid-fuel rocket engine
Computerized blood pressure controller	Link trainer	Stereoscopic map scanner
Continuous casting	Microprocessor	Strain gauge
Cotton picker	Nuclear magnetic resonance scanner	Strobe lights
Defibrillator	Optical scanner	Supercomputer
DNA fingerprinting	Oral contraceptives	Two-armed mobile robot
Double-knit fabric	Outboard engine	Vacuum tube
Electronic spreadsheet	Overnight national delivery	Variable output transformer
Freewing aircraft	Pacemaker	Vascular lesion laser
FM radio	Personal computer	Xerography
Front-end loader	Photo typesetting	X-ray telescope
Geodesic dome	Polaroid camera	Zipper
Gyrocompass	Portable computer	

this expertise is by using examples and practicing the learned skills. In this section we will outline some "innovation frameworks" that will help you in this regard. These frameworks are examples, not a complete list. In fact, you may be able to develop your own frameworks that you find more suited to your own personality and style.

ROADMAP

IN ACTION

Design your own personal antenna to observe the world, analyzing situations and looking for opportunities.

Analogs

Why innovate from nothing when many ideas have already worked well? The idea of this framework is to help transfer innovations from one field to another. Chapter 13 describes LeafBusters, a company that "outsources" the leaf collection and disposal services provided by municipalities to residents annually. LeafBusters claims that it can do this more efficiently because it can use the required expensive equipment for a longer season each year by "following the weather." Where did the founders of this company get this "obvious" idea? They read an article about crews that harvest crops under contract to farmers in the Corn Belt moving southward each year. The underlying drivers for the two businesses are the same: more effective use of expensive capital equipment through "following the seasons." The trick here is to analyze existing successful businesses and to get behind the immediate product or service to examine the underpinning drivers. Then ask, "Where else can these principles be applied?"

Let us work through another analog example. Dell is now supplying printers that connect to the Internet, and the printers have built-in "ink management software." The software analyzes usage, recommending when to print in black-and-white only, when in color, and so on. When it is time to replace the ink cartridge, the printer has already forecasted the need, contacted Dell via the Internet, and had ink drop shipped on time. This is a valuable service to the consumer. It also locks in the purchasing to Dell supplies, preempting competition from low-cost refill stores. The consumer is happy, and Dell grows its revenue and profits. What other products/services could be analogous to this example?

Consider that household appliances that connect to the Internet are now also being offered.[18] Initially aimed at monitoring performance so service calls can be scheduled before the appliances break down, this feature could be used as follows. The washing machine monitors usage and injects into the wash the appropriate detergent, softener, bleach, and so on, depending on the needs for the load. Like the printer, detergent usage forecast enables a supplier to drop ship the product and place it into holders built in to the machines just in time to fulfill the consumer's needs. Currently, detergent manufacturers are not making any profits because they have to pay to have their products put on retailers' shelves and they compete in a commodity market with expensive advertising. There is little consumer loyalty; products on "special" are purchased more often. Consumers do not like carrying the heavy containers of detergent. Perhaps there is an opportunity for a new detergent manufacturer to join with an appliance manufacturer such as GE, Whirlpool, or Maytag to provide the "total washing solution." This would benefit the consumer both in service and cost, for it would no longer be necessary to advertise detergents separately or to use the inconvenient and expensive retail distribution chain.

Actually, Becky Minard and Paal Gisholt might have come up with the SmartPak idea by looking for an analog. Cardinal Health (www.cardinal.com) does the same for hospital patients by taking over the internal pharmacy role. Patients' daily medicines are delivered, clearly labeled, to the bedside, reducing potentially dangerous errors and costs by eliminating the large inventories at hospitals and consolidating suppliers at central locations rather than at individual dispensaries. Both SmartPak and Cardinal provide services around their products and solve their customers' problems.

Entrepreneurs learn to think like this: always analyzing intriguing innovations and thinking about where else the *principles of the concept,* not necessarily the details, can be applied. Get into the habit of questioning situations in this way. And don't look at only successes; often analyzing a failure can shine light on another situation where the reasons for failure may not apply.

Intersection of Technology Trends

We live in a world where technology is changing quickly. Watching cost and performance trends, particularly where they begin to intersect, can give rise to whole new innovative business opportunities. Let's consider digital photography, high-bandwidth communications, and ubiquitous wireless communications and think about some new business ideas. For example, imagine a digital camera with a wireless Internet connection. You could have your own personal Web site to which your latest pictures are uploaded as soon as you take them. E-mails can be sent to friends and relatives immediately so they can participate with you in real time. Where is the business opportunity? What an interesting upgrade of services for a professional event photographer. Now at your wedding, bar mitzvah, or the like, a photographer can post pictures as they are taken, and those friends and relatives who are unable to be there in person can enjoy the event as it happens. The photographer can also sell more pictures and albums to a wider audience because they are more likely to buy when they are closely involved in the event.

Solving "Points of Pain"

Entrepreneurs are quick to notice inefficiencies, inconveniences, and other "points of pain" and to use these to build new business opportunities.

Example: Netflix (www.Netflix.com)

Netflix provides rental DVDs through the mail rather than via the bricks-and-mortar rental outlets favored by Blockbuster. The founders of Netflix realized that Blockbuster's customers had points of pain; they had to drive to the store, search through rows of movies, often not find the one they were seeking as it was already rented out, and pay late charges if they forgot to return it on time. Netflix solved these points of pain by mailing the movies (made possible by the DVD format taking over from tapes) directly to the customer. Movies can be kept as long as a consumer wishes with no late charges. When John Antioco, CEO of Blockbuster, first encountered Netflix, he did not see it as a threat, stating, "No one will want to wait three days for a movie." In fact, having a wish list and allowing a subscriber to hold several DVDs simultaneously avoids this supposed disadvantage. And because inventory is stored centrally, a greater selection is possible. The Netflix business model innovation is "disruptive" to Blockbuster, which has invested much in stores and local inventories. It is interesting that Blockbuster did not see Amazon as an analog to Netflix, just as Barnes & Noble never saw Amazon as a threat until Amazon had taken a major share of the book market.

Entrepreneurs are continually noticing and analyzing points of pain. Practice this in your daily life and challenge yourself to find the business opportunity.

Analyzing Existing Businesses

Understanding how existing businesses work, their cost structure, and customer points of pain can lead to ideas about how they can be effectively attacked. In our classes, students usually start with thinking of business ideas related to things near and dear to their everyday experience. This is often pizza. Their business idea is to open yet another pizza parlor, with the innovation centered around new product ideas—Thai-French or Indonesian curry pizzas, for example.

Example: Pizza-on-a-Truck

After some simple research, the students expose a number of areas where the current pizza delivery services are unsatisfactory:

Customer Points of Pain	*Owner's Challenges*
Pizza arrives late	Location is bad
Pizza arrives cold	Rent is high
Phone takes forever to be answered	Labor is expensive and unreliable
Order taker is incomprehensible	It is difficult to schedule baking with deliveries
Pizza tastes of the packaging	

Digging further, an analysis of the cost of making and delivering a pizza shows that the storefront and labor overhead far outweigh the cost of food ingredients. And the customers are unhappy.

So let's think outside the pizza box, and let's think really BIG. Let's ask ourselves how we can totally restructure the pizza business on a national basis and grab the lion's share of the pizza market. Are there any technical advances that might impact the pizza business? Here you can get pretty creative. The following are some ideas culled from searching the patent database, surfing the Web, and talking to experts in a number of different fields. (Remember: Use the vast sources of information now available at your fingertips.)

- Package delivery companies such as UPS and FedEx have invested heavily in software to optimize the most efficient routes for their vehicles depending on today's delivery addresses. How can this be applied to pizza delivery?

- Cars are commonly fitted with global positioning systems (GPSs) that determine where the car is and display a map and instructions on how to get to a desired location.

- Customers are increasingly becoming accustomed to using the Internet for ordering. Can this be applied to pizza ordering?

- Because labor reliability and costs are major issues for pizza outlets, Pizza Hut has developed working prototype robots for assembling pizzas automatically based on an order input. The robots make the pizza and feed it into an oven. The time in the oven depends on the size and ingredients so a perfect pizza comes out every time.

How can all these apparently unconnected developments be combined to create an entirely new pizza business?

Think about putting the robot and oven on a truck. Pizzas are made not in the sequence of the orders as they come in directly to the truck over the wireless Internet, but in the order that optimizes delivery time based on knowledge of the location of the vehicle, the optimum routing, and the oven scheduling. Labor is reduced to one person, the driver, and there is no storefront at all. Customers are informed by e-mail or phone exactly when their pizza will be delivered, and it will always be fresh, having just come out of the oven as the driver pulls up. And there is no need for flavor-destroying packaging to keep the pizza hot for twenty minutes while the driver goes to other locations or gets lost.

The results are better service, better pizzas, lower cost of doing business. Think about starting out in one or two locations first and either raising capital to expand into other markets or using a franchising model to cover the country. (See Chapter 11 for a discussion on franchising.) Look out Domino's and Pizza Hut! This example illustrates several ways in which entrepreneurs innovate. You may be surprised that it is a largely analytical process. The situation is deconstructed, ideas for stimulation are sought on the Internet, and a synthetic process is initiated whereby the different inputs are rearranged until a possible solution emerges. Entrepreneurs are very good at synthesizing new opportunities from a collection of apparently disparate concepts. They recognize patterns that others may not find obvious. Get accustomed to looking for such patterns through analogs, technology confluences, points of pain, and the like. You will find that you will quickly get better at this, and you may even develop your own personal frameworks for innovating. And do *not* be frightened to think big; often bigger is easier than smaller.

FINDING AND ASSESSING IDEAS

The previous sections show how to create new ideas for a business within innovation frameworks. For entrepreneurs just starting out, however, it may be necessary to seek some stimulation from idea sources. The world is full of ideas, but ideas are not opportunities, and opportunities are not ready-made to build a business around. Figure 3-2 shows how many ideas are required to start one business. The rest of the chapter, therefore, looks at idea sources and at how they can be built up and analyzed as real business opportunities.

ROADMAP

IN ACTION

The world is full of wonderful and freely available ideas. Ideas, however, are not businesses. Seek ideas and turn them into opportunities to build into valuable enterprises.

"During your life, you will probably generate many ideas for potential businesses. With proper training and skill development, your creativity can flourish. The value of entrepreneurship education is that you will learn how to critically evaluate your ideas to locate the best opportunities for commercial success. The pursuit of these opportunities will require significant work on your part, but the rewards are limitless."

SANFORD B. EHRLICH,
QUALCOMM Executive Director of Entrepreneurship and Associate Professor of Management, San Diego State University Entrepreneurial Management Center

Maybe you have some starting concepts but question how original they are. You may be surprised to hear that not all entrepreneurs come up with unique ideas. You can be innovative without that initial generative impulse. Here are five ways to build upon already existing material and still provide a profit-driven concept:

1. Develop ideas as an extension or redesign an existing service (Marriott Senior Living Services; Sam's Club—an extension of Wal-Mart).
2. Resegment and create an improved service (overnight delivery, such as FedEx, or buying cheaper airline tickets from Priceline.com).
3. Redifferentiate and market the product at a lower price (Internet shopping, Sam's Club).
4. Add value to an existing product or service (linked brands, such as PCs just for the Internet).
5. Develop or redesign a new version of an existing product (Snapple Iced Tea, fresh-baked chocolate chip cookies, and Krispy Kreme doughnuts).

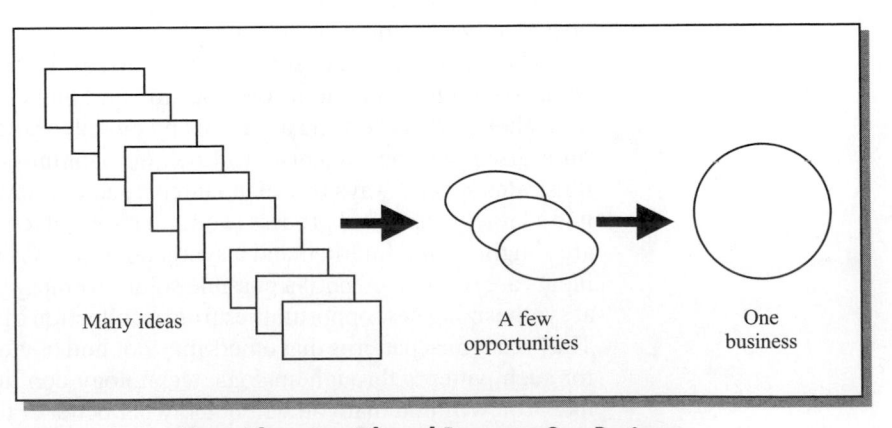

Many ideas   A few opportunities   One business

Figure 3-2   Many Ideas Are Filtered Down to One Business.

Idea Assessment

The first step for any entrepreneur is to generate an idea for a new business. The entrepreneur must then assess the opportunities available for putting the idea into practice. Is this something that has been overdone? Has it been executed poorly in the past? Has anyone else thought of it? In short, is the idea a potential dead end, a niche on an existing opportunity, or an entirely unexplored chance to create a business?

There are many sources for ideas. The Internet has made idea searching much faster and broader, and it also makes it easy to check whether an idea has already been discovered and put into a business. Entrepreneurs source ideas from many places.

To get you started, we have assembled a "starter kit" of twenty-seven general idea sourcing Web sites. The full list can be found on the book's Web site at www.wiley.com/college/kaplan. The sites range from a pure list of ideas to franchising opportunities, patent auction sites, and sites committed to global scanning of new ideas. Take a look at some of the sites and use a search engine such as Google to start searching on your own. You will be amazed at the wealth and breadth of idea triggers that will get you thinking.

Probably the most underutilized sources for ideas are the U.S. and foreign patent databases. Chapter 10 deals with protecting your own ideas using patents. Here we discuss patents as *sources* of ideas. There are more than 7 million patents issued in the United States. These can be searched by key words, owners, dates, and so on at the U.S. patent Web site, www.uspto.gov, or at a private patent database site, www.delphion.com. Many patents, of course, are filed to protect deep technology know-how. However, often forgotten are the simpler product ideas that their inventors may not have exploited for a number of reasons; perhaps they did not have the money or did not know how to develop a market, or perhaps the idea was "before its time" either because the market was not ready or the means of making them practical were not yet available. Also, every patent has to describe why the invention is important, including prior ideas, and why the idea is useful. What a great place to pick others' brains. In fact, only about 10 percent of existing patents have actually been commercialized; the remainder are still potential opportunities.

CONVERTING AN IDEA INTO AN OPPORTUNITY

Many new companies are built around a radical or breakthrough technology. As we explained earlier, major corporations are surprisingly bad at exploiting "disruptive" innovations. Indeed, as Table 3-1 shows, many of the major breakthroughs are discovered and taken to market by small firms. Of course, many of these breakthroughs are good enough that the small company grows into a large firm. Remember that all large firms started small. The important point to grasp is that breakthroughs are more likely to be conceived and developed in small companies. An entrepreneur need not be the developer of the technology. In fact, small companies can access a wealth of new technologies from a variety of sources such as universities, government-funded research laboratories, and the companies that the government funds to carry out research and development (R & D). In fact, these sources are mandated by law to make the results of their research available to companies. (See the Bayh-Dole Act in the end-of-chapter appendix.)

We have created two long lists of Web sites that you can visit to browse the technological inventions that are available, one for universities and the other from U.S. government sources. These lists can be found at the book's Web site, www.wiley.com/college/kaplan.

The Evaluation Process

The entrepreneur will unquestionably need plenty of encouragement and support while developing a business idea. But in turning this idea into a concrete business, the entrepreneur will be faced with hard facts and cold reality. Armed with information gleaned from research, the entrepreneur is positioned to legitimately decide whether to proceed with the idea and work to sustain the venture.

OPPORTUNITY: FIVE PHASES TO SUCCESS

Identifying which business ideas have real commercial potential is one of the most difficult challenges that an entrepreneur will face. This section describes a systematic approach to reducing the uncertainties. The five-step model outlined in Figure 3-3 will help entrepreneurs to know a winning business area when they see one.[19]

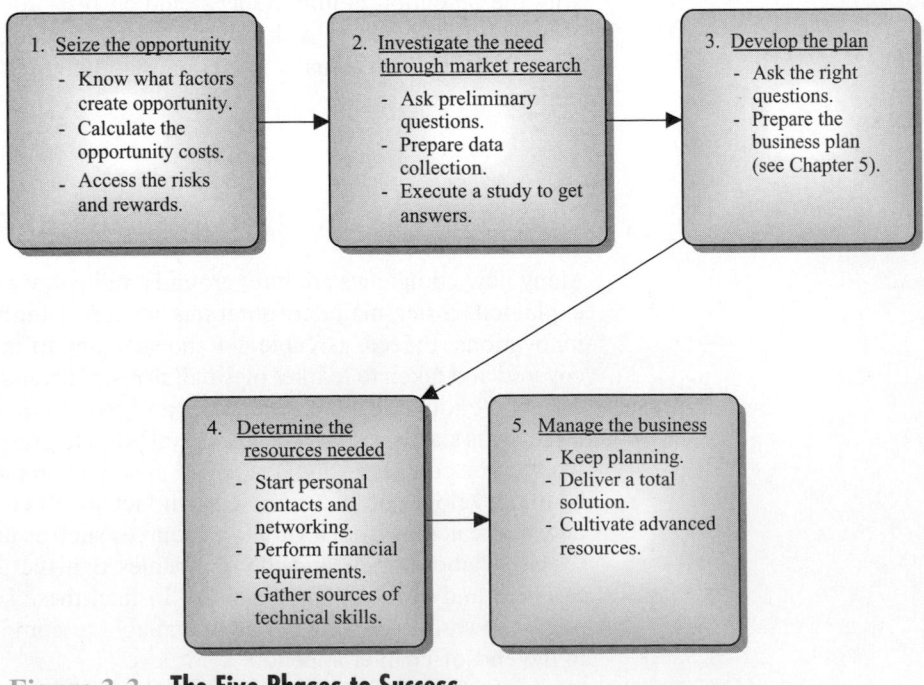

Figure 3-3   **The Five Phases to Success.**

Phase 1: Seize the Opportunity

The basic objective is to define the criteria that would make a business opportunity worthwhile to pursue. To start the process, think about how much value an opportunity can add to a business. The idea is to improve not only profits, but profitability as well. Rita McGrath's *The Entrepreneurial Mindset* describes the techniques that can be used to create an opportunity register. The register is like an inventory of opportunities. It is a list of your ideas for improving, or even completely reinventing, the current business model or going into entirely new opportunity spaces. The entrepreneur wants to store good ideas so they can be revisited to see how new ideas might fit in, determine whether the timing is right to implement older ones, or figure out what to eliminate as the direction becomes more defined. The register can take the form of a database because it is easier to review and update. The important aspect is to decide how to record and revisit ideas that are generated.[20]

To evaluate the business opportunity, review the sequence of events in Figure 3-3 and answer the following questions from the perspective of both a personal and professional experience.

- What are the indicators that lead to this idea and opportunity?
- What are the conditions that permit the opportunity to occur?
- How will the future of this new product or service change the idea?
- How great (in terms of time) is the window of opportunity?

Time Horizon

A window of opportunity is a time horizon during which opportunities exist before something else happens to eliminate them. A unique opportunity, once shown to produce wealth, will attract competitors, and if the business is easy to enter, the industry will quickly become saturated. In this situation the entrepreneur must get in quickly and be able to get out before revenues become dispersed in an overdeveloped market.[21]

The entrepreneur gains the greatest ability to maneuver at the threshold of a start-up idea by creating his or her own window of opportunity. Successful companies find and exploit markets that others have missed or that new technologies have suddenly created. For example, advertising has obviously been around for some time, but when DoubleClick started, Internet advertising was a brand-new field. Its founder helped to create a wildly successful business by taking advantage of an unforeseen opportunity. The factors that help the entrepreneur create opportunity for the business are given in Figure 3-4.

Opportunity Costs

Opportunity costs are the value of benefits lost when one decision alternative is selected over another. For example, suppose a software company refuses to deliver a software program because writing the software code will require the company to miss a major deadline for another company. The order for the software program would generate revenue of $25,000 and additional costs of $14,000. Then the opportunity cost and the net benefit lost associated with the software deadline is $11,000 (i.e., $25,000 minus $14,000).[22]

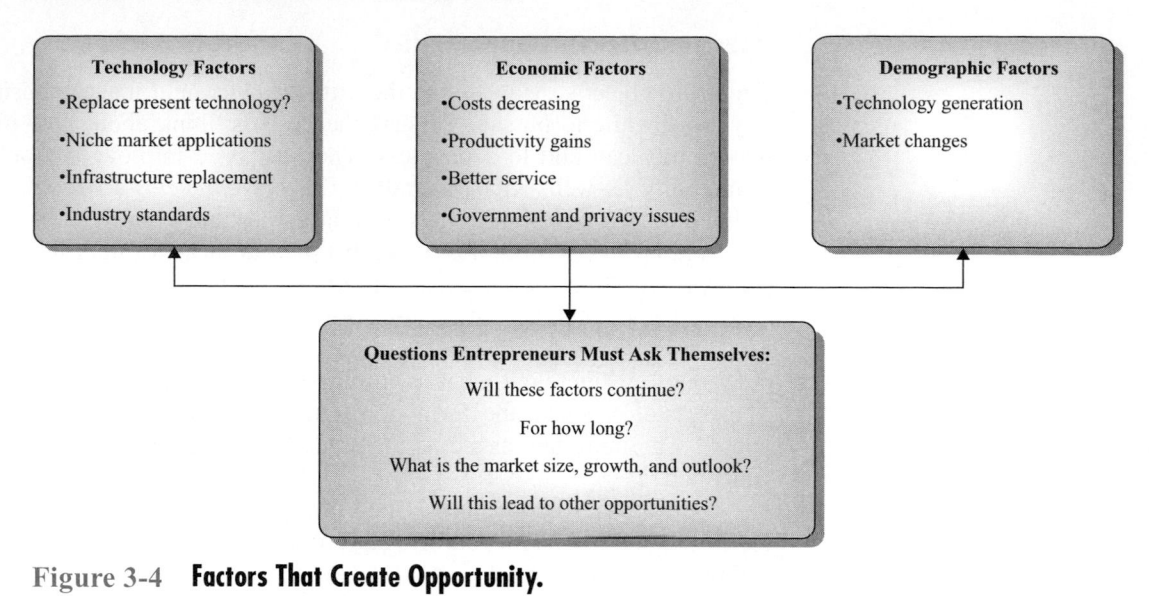

Figure 3-4 **Factors That Create Opportunity.**

Phase 2: Investigate the Need through Market Research

> "Find a need of the consumer that is currently not getting met, or inadequately met, and fill that need in a way that is appealing to the consumer and profitable for you."
>
> PAMELA POMMERENKE
> *Assistant Professor, Department of Management, Michigan State University*

The first step is to identify, measure, and document the need for the product or service. This means making a specific financial forecast of the actual potential and anticipated return for this proposed product or service. This process is not the end; it's only the beginning. The topic of marketing will be explored more fully in Chapter 4, but for now, it will be considered as it fits into the opportunity analysis.

Marketing research need not be extensive, sophisticated, or expensive but must determine what customer satisfaction means for the target market. It should also provide other critical information about the target market used to develop marketing strategies. In some cases the entrepreneur can survey the market to obtain information specifically tailored to the business's needs. However, judgment must be used to protect future marketing plans.

The questions below will assist in evaluating the actual climate surrounding the new company and preparing for the early stages of a new venture. Larger companies often outsource research to a marketing company, but this process will identify the steps and questions needed to custom-design the research and conduct it productively.

Preliminary Questions

At this point the entrepreneur needs to solidify the purpose and object of the research. Those who are developing a particular product will want to focus on questions that can tell them about product features and distribution. A more service-oriented entrepreneur will consider other inquiries, directed at identifying the sources and beneficiaries of that service. Consider the goal now; it will save time and money later on. These areas and questions are meant to guide the direction of the research.[23]

Need. Will this product/service be serving customers' real needs? What is the overall market for the business? Are there special niches that can be exploited?

Niche/Competition. What is different about the product or service that will cause the customer to choose it over the competition's product or service?

Proprietary Questions. Can the product/service be patented or copyrighted? Is it unique enough to get a significant head start on the competition? Can the process be easily copied? Will the business concept be developed and licensed to others, or developed and sold?

Cost and Manufacture. How much will the customer be willing to spend for the product/service? How much will materials and labor time cost? How much will be needed in the future? Now?

Advertisement and Packaging. What type of advertising and promotional plans will be used to market the product/service? Will the promotional methods be traditional or innovative?

Sales. What distributions and sales methods will be used? Will the reliance be on independent sales representatives, company salesforce, direct mail, door-to-door sales, supermarkets, service stations, or company-owned stores?

Transport. How will the product/service be transported—via company-owned trucks, common carriers, postal service, airfreight, or over the internet?

Employees. Can the company attract employees with the necessary skills to operate the business venture? Who are the workers? Are they dependable, competent, and readily available?

Start with Data Collection

The entrepreneur needs to find answers to the key questions, identified above, about the potential business. Data collection can come from a variety of sources. The sources to provide data collection are given in Figure 3-5. The more sources that are consulted, the more valid the results will be. However, it is not advisable to go overboard; the amount of available data can become overwhelming. Basically, the questions should be as specific as possible, the sources as relevant as possible, and the data collection as extensive as needed for the initial investment and planning to run smoothly.[24]

Experts in the field	Contact well-known entrepreneurs to get advice.
Internet searches	Visit Web sites on companies and new products or technologies.
Library research	Use college libraries to access references and specialized biographies.
Questionnaires/surveys	Use the mail, phone, Internet, or professional interviews. Write and prepare questions to make sure you collect appropriate data.
Existing research	Use investment banking firms, advisory searches, or consulting firms to gather data on existing research.
Trade associations	Visit trade shows and read trade publications.
Market research firms	Hire a firm to prepare a report or market survey for the proposed idea.

Figure 3-5   **Sources for Finding Information.**

Design and Execute a Study to Get the Answers

Once primary sources of data have been exhausted based on appropriate questions and expectations, the entrepreneur must identify secondary resources to support the preliminary research. This is the stage when the entrepreneur should consult directly with existing business owners and experts in the field and ask pertinent, key questions.

The entrepreneur should target a small number of representative businesses. First, the entrepreneur must identify companies with similar products or services and inquire as to who may be willing to give advice or provide the names of other contacts without wasting a lot of time and money. Remember that the purpose of this exercise is to start a business, not to become a research expert.

Once the participants have been identified, solicit information from them to answer the key questions, which should be based on the most unbiased model available. To eliminate receiving questionable data, certain pitfalls must be avoided.

- Ensure that all of the participants are asked the same questions in the same manner.
- Get detailed—make certain that the answers are accurate by maintaining a precise, objective method of questioning.
- Train and monitor survey recorders and telephone interviewers to ensure consistent results.

Analyze the Data

Once the primary data have been collected, they must be analyzed. What do the data reveal? How can they be interpreted? Examine the secondary sources that have been queried. How did the survey participants interpret their results? Write a final report modeled on the most thorough sources. This ensures that a record exists for the future and that others in the organization can refer to the study as necessary.

This may all sound too extensive—and expensive. Many entrepreneurs must do their market research with limited funds. Employ these cost-cutting recommendations:

- Use search engines, Web pages, and online databases.
- Use the telephone instead of mail surveys and door-to-door interviewing.
- Avoid research in high-cost cities.
- Test more than one product or service at a time.
- Avoid collecting unnecessary data.

One example of an inexpensive source is a local university. Professors and students are often involved in projects to help small companies develop marketing plans and undertake market research. Other examples include friends and relatives who own their own businesses, published interviews with successful entrepreneurs, and library resources. More detailed discussions on market research methods can be found in Chapter 4.

Phase 3: Develop the Plan

Once an opportunity has been identified, decisions must be made regarding performance and staffing. Who is going to do what? How will decisions be made? The result of the business plan should fully capitalize on all of the company's assets while maintaining flexibility. It also should be sufficiently broad to incorporate unexpected changes in the aim for success and profitability.

A business plan charts the current and future components of the business in about thirty to forty pages. Similar to a map, it should answer some basic questions. How far will the business have to go? What is the exact destination or goal? How will the destination be reached? What is the anticipated arrival time at each of the various stops or milestones? A good plan will do the following:

- Determine the viability of the business and application in selected markets
- Provide guidance in planning and organizing the activities and goals
- Serve as a vehicle to obtain financing and personnel for the business

The business plan is the backbone of the business. This single document guides the entrepreneur at three critical junctures:

1. It simplifies decision making during *times of crisis.*
2. It is the roadmap at *points of indecision.*
3. It is a motivational guide during *setbacks or downturns.*

An extremely valuable outcome of preparing and writing the plan at this stage is identifying flaws and creating contingencies. The business plan compels the entrepreneur to carefully examine the prospective venture at its initial planning stage before significant capital has been invested.

If the plan reveals insurmountable flaws, the entrepreneur may need to abandon that particular opportunity. Although it is discouraging to return to the idea stage, consider two facts:

1. The groundwork has been laid, and the initial learning curve has been completed.
2. Only a relatively small amount of time and capital have been invested.

The entrepreneur should not ignore serious misgivings. Walking away at this stage and beginning again with a new idea and a strong attitude will impress investors and others already involved with the project.

A more detailed version of the business plan is found in Chapter 5, but the entrepreneur can greatly benefit from considering these basic elements now.

Phase 4: Determine the Resources Needed

All businesses must address resource capabilities to foster venture development.[25] However, for a start-up venture that uses new technology for its service or as its product, it is crucial. The new business must have the skills to match—and triumph over—the competition. Much like Darwin's survival of the fittest, in the business world only the highly skilled will survive.

This section examines three aspects of assessing resource capabilities.

1. **Personal contacts and networking**
   Resources are needed to identify, contact, and establish a network with appropriate clients and vendors. Who will devote time to meeting people by traveling? Phone work? E-mail correspondence? Time for networking may be a daily task, high on a priority list. (Do the management exercise at the end of this chapter for more on networking.)

2. **Financing requirements**

Sufficient capital is required to sustain the company for a specific length of time, possibly a one- or two-year period. The entrepreneur must carefully consider the financial elements required for implementing the plan. Begin by answering the following questions:

How much initial capital is needed?

What resources are available for financial support?

How long can the new business be self-financed, if necessary, and still withstand initial losses?

How long will it take to make the business profitable?

What kind of profit margin will eventually result from the product or service?

How can the revenue and financial model be presented to investors for their involvement in the business?

After initial financing, new investors may be approached at a later date for further infusions of capital.

3. **Sources of technical skills**

The entrepreneur may have an idea but not possess the creative process and innovative technical skills to implement it.[26] In that case, external skilled labor is needed. This may be someone the entrepreneur already knows, such as a co-worker, or he or she might need to hire someone through want ads or an employment agency. Training costs need to be calculated into start-up costs. Furthermore, someone may be needed who can translate technical jargon to simplified terms for investors.

Phase 5: Manage the Business

So far in this chapter, we've evaluated the opportunity, begun developing the plan, and assessed resource needs. Phase 5 entails running the business, applying a specific management structure and style to any questions, and handling difficulties and roadblocks to successes that may arise. The emphasis here is on the act of investing. Substantial time, money, experience, and energy have been invested in setting up. Now the entrepreneur needs to break off from the path blazed by the most successful businesses and invest in people, operating procedures, and information technology. This involves the following two events:

1. **Deliver a Total Solution**

Traditionally, small companies have assumed unchallenged territory and special distribution channels for their products. Today, however, all companies are playing in the same markets and providing the entire range of services for their customers. Investors and customers want to buy a total solution product or service.

2. **Cultivate Advanced Resources**

The layoffs of highly skilled workers from major corporations that abound create an important opportunity for a start-up company. These trained and effective personnel are looking to apply their business skills and experiences to start-ups. The results to the business include access to small companies and major corporations, capital, and productive market knowledge.

Criterion	Stronger Opportunity	Weaker Opportunity
Need	Identified	Unclear
Customers	Reachable; receptive	Unreachable or loyalties established
Payback to user/customer	Less than one year	Three years or more
Product life cycle	Long, easier to recover investment	Short, difficult to recover investment
Industry structure	Weak or emerging competition	Aggressively competitive
Total available market	$100 million	Less than $10 million
Market growth rate	30 to 50 percent	Contracting or less than 10 percent
Gross margins	30 to 60+ percent	Less than 20 percent; volatile
Market share attainable (year 5)	20 percent or more	Less than 5 percent

Figure 3-6   Framework for Evaluating an Opportunity: Market Issues.

Consider an example of a new technology that effectively transformed day-to-day services and how a business plan was crucial in making that opportunity a business reality.

Use the Framework to Evaluate and Test the Five-Phase Opportunity Concept

Now that we have completed the five phases of the opportunity analysis, use this framework to evaluate the issues that are stronger or weaker for the market, competition, management team, and financial requirements for the new business concept.[27] Figures 3-6 to 3-9 list in greater detail the factors to be considered in each of these four categories.

The most successful entrepreneurs know where they fit in the market and where they want to be. The framework plan should account for and accommodate changes in

Criterion	Stronger Opportunity	Weaker Opportunity
Profits after tax	10 to 15 percent or more; durable	Less than 5 percent; fragile

Time to:
  Break even
  Positive cash flow
ROI potential
	Less than 2 years
	Less than 2 years
	25 percent or more per year
		More than 3 years
		More than 3 years
		Less than 15 to 20 percent per year

Value Capital requirements	High strategic value Low to moderate; fundable	Low strategic value Very high, unfundable
Exit mechanism	Present or envisioned harvest options	Undefined; illiquid investment

Figure 3-7   Framework for Evaluating an Opportunity: Financial and Harvest Issues.

Criterion	Stronger Opportunity	Weaker Opportunity
Fixed and variable costs Production, marketing distribution	Lowest	Highest
Degree of control Prices, channels of resources/distribution	Moderate to strong	Weak
Barriers to entry Proprietary protection Response/lead time	Yes 6 months to 1 year	None None
Legal contractual advantage	Proprietary or exclusivity	None
Sources of differentiation	Numerous	Few or none
Competitors' mindset and strategies	Live and let live; not self-destructive	Defensive and strongly reactive

Figure 3-8 **Framework for Evaluating an Opportunity: Competitive Advantage Issues.**

designing, testing, and marketing to prepare for the business opportunity. The issues that need to be described in more detail should include determining the improvement needed and anticipating the necessary time frames and how to remain competitive at all times.

Know How to Protect the Idea or Product

One question that might be encountered while conducting research and formulating a business plan is whether or not the idea/opportunity/product/service needs to be protected.[28] The following evaluation screening identifies those conditions whereby an idea may qualify for patent protection. See Chapter 10 for details on patent protection.

Evaluation Screening for Patent Protection

1. Is the service, product, or idea unique to get a head start on the competition?
2. Does the service or product represent a breakthrough (either high-tech or different from others)?

Criterion	Stronger Opportunity	Weaker Opportunity
Management team	Existing, strong, proven performance	Weak, inexperienced, lacking key skills
Contacts and networks	Well developed, high quality, acceptable	Crude, limited, inaccessible
Risk	Low	High
Fatal blows	None	One or more

Figure 3-9 **Framework for Evaluating an Opportunity: Management Team and Risk Issues.**

3. Is the field changing so slowly that the innovation will be valuable for at least ten years?

4. Have other, less expensive but adequate protective measures been explored?

5. Has an attorney discussed the options and recommended that a patent be pursued?

6. Is the fee for a patent search and application affordable?

If the answer to two or more of these questions was "yes," patent protection for the idea and opportunity should be seriously considered. However, if a disclosure document, which essentially protects the idea for the first two years, will suffice, then that option should be considered first. What about marketing this idea to a large company as a customer? Most companies have their own internal research and development organization dedicated to monitoring and meeting the needs of their product or service lines. The best method for submitting an idea is to contact the company and ask for its disclosure conditions to review an idea.

Some companies, however, will sign a nondisclosure form, whereas others will not. Most will have their own protection form, which essentially states that, while they may agree to review or discuss an idea, their research department may have already thought of the idea long before. Let an attorney have the last word. Get a second (or even a third) legal opinion before committing to any legal expenditure. See Chapter 12 for more on these legal issues.

SUMMARY

Every business starts from an embryonic idea that is analyzed to create an opportunity, then built up until a complete business concept has been reached. Ideas can come from many sources. They can be a result of an entrepreneur's own innovation, which is best accomplished using some simple analytical frameworks, or they can be found in searching the Internet or in observing points of pain. Some good opportunities are the result of assembling what might at first seem to be unrelated ideas. Once an entrepreneur has identified an opportunity that is worthy of further consideration, the entrepreneur must assess its potential. Often, after a market approach has been selected and the necessary research conducted, the idea may require revision, adding refinement and sophistication to the original spark of an idea.

Generally, a great deal of useful information is readily available. Often market research objectives must be modified to use available information. In some cases the entrepreneur may choose to survey the market to acquire data designed specifically to fit the project's needs. In every case the entrepreneur must apply some judgment to the data while trying to project future prospects.

Once this step is completed, the planning and developing process starts. All ideas must be screened and evaluated to determine the feasibility of the opportunity. The best ideas are evaluated through test marketing and managing the resources to successfully launch the business.

From the marketing research results, the plan must be fine-tuned. The following questions should be answered: What segment(s) of the market can it serve? What does the product or service have to offer the market? Who are the customers? How will the product or services be promoted and marketed?

The next chapter will address how to develop the marketing plan for a business.

STUDY QUESTIONS

1. Why is innovation important, and how is it changing?
2. What are the two types of innovation? Give two examples of each type.
3. What are the various ways to generate business ideas?
4. Briefly describe the various methods to research a business opportunity.
5. List the five phases to complete an opportunity analysis.
6. When does an idea need to be protected?
7. Describe the evaluation screening process.

EXERCISES

1. Finding an Idea and Turning It into an Opportunity

Go to the book's Web site, www.wiley.com/college/kaplan, and browse a number of idea source Web sites from the three lists. Use these as starters and browse until you find an idea that you think has merit for creating a business opportunity. Write a one-page synopsis of the idea, explaining why you think it is a good idea and how you would use it to build a business opportunity argument.

2. Preparing an Opportunity Cost Analysis

RJL Technologies provides custom services to its loyalty customers from Monday through Friday. David Lee, the co-owner, believes it is important for the employees to have Saturday and Sunday off to spend with their families. However, he also recognizes that this policy has implications for profitability, and he is considering staying open on Saturday.

David estimates that if the company stays open on Saturday, it can generate revenue of $2,500 each day for fifty-two days per year. The incremental daily costs will be $500 for labor, $50 for transportation, and $150 for an office manager. The costs do not include a portion of monthly rent.

David would like to know the opportunity cost of not working on Saturday. Provide an estimate of the opportunity cost, and explain why you do not have to consider rent in your estimate.

Management Exercise—Networking

If you have not read the appendix in Chapter 1, do so then go to the book's Web site and read diary entries Prequel and Months 2, 15, 18, 27, 31, 40, 41, 47, and 57 and view the video entitled "Seven Degrees of Separation." Either as a team or individually, produce a presentation on the following question for class discussion. Only one or two slides are required to state the key points, which will then be expanded in class.

Master-Case Q 1:

Trace the evolution of Neoforma's products from the earliest idea to a commercial product or service. Include the false turns and abandoned ideas. What type of innovation was employed by Neoforma? Who outside the company had a major influence on the product developments? What lessons can you learn from the Neoforma case concerning the evolution of an idea from conception to a business opportunity?

INTERACTIVE LEARNING ON THE WEB

Test your knowledge of the chapter using the book's interactive Web site.

APPENDIX: THE BAYH-DOLE ACT

For decades some universities and research institutions have retained the rights to inventions developed by their employees or professors during the course of their university-based work. Many universities routinely require faculty to file disclosures of the inventions or technologies they develop.

The 1980 Bayh-Dole Act (P.L. 96-517, Patent and Trademark Act Amendments of 1980) helped strengthen some of the university and small-business claims on inventions created by their employees. Sponsored by Senators Birch Bayh of Indiana and Robert Dole of Kansas, the act allows small businesses and nonprofit institutions, including universities, to retain the rights to inventions created with federal research funds. Since the federal government dispenses research money through thousands of programs, the act created a uniform policy for dealing with the key intellectual property rights generated in the course of federally funded research.

Under the act, universities are encouraged to file patents for the inventions they hold and to work with companies to promote the use of inventions developed with federal funds. Moreover, universities are expected to give small businesses preference in licensing new technologies and inventions.

The government retains a nonexclusive right to use or practice the patents that originated with federal funding. Critics of the act see it as a giveaway and say that the public should retain a greater share of intellectual property created with public money.

The legislation has helped create a technology transfer industry at universities around the country. The Association of University Technology Managers (AUTM), which tracks universities' commercialization efforts, reports that before the act, fewer than 250 patents per year were issued to universities and research institutions. In 1998 the 198 U.S. and Canadian universities, teaching hospitals, and nonprofit research institutes that belong to AUTM generated 4,808 new U.S. patent applications and yielded 3,668 new licenses. Those new licenses, in turn, were the foundation for 364 new companies.

Feeding that patent machine were inventions and technologies developed by faculty and employees. In 1998 university faculty declared the development of 11,784 inventions or technologies, according to AUTM.

AUTM members received $725 million in gross income from licenses and options in 1998, which was up from $611 million in gross adjusted income and options the previous year. Much of that money has been recycled back into the universities for research.

Source: Daniel E. Massing, "AUTM Licensing Survey: FY 1998" (Norwalk, CT: Association of University Licensing Managers, 1999).

ADDITIONAL RESOURCES

- **Office.com (www.office.com):** "This new way we work."
- **Digitalwork.com (www.digitalwork.com):** "Your business workshop."
- **Onvia.com (www.onvia.com):** "The premiere e-marketplace for small-businesses."
- **Ideacafe.com (www.ideacafe.com):** "A fun approach to serious business."

- **Smartonline.com (www.smartonline.com):** "Small-business answers from small-business owners."
- **Workz.com (www.workz.com):** "Helping small businesses grow and prosper online."
- **Edge.low.org (www.edge.low.org):** "A peer-learning community for growing your company."
- **Entrepreneurship (www.entrepreneurship.org):** "A world of resources for entrepreneurs."
- **Small Business Administration (www.sba.gov):** "Helping small businesses to succeed."

www.wiley.com/college/kaplan

ROADMAP for

PATTERNS OF ENTREPRENEURSHIP
Getting Started as an Entrepreneur

- ☐ An Entrepreneurial Perspective
- ☐ Commonly Shared Entrepreneurial Characteristics
- ☐ Types of Entrepreneurs
- ☐ The Need to Control
- ☐ Entrepreneurship Roller Coaster
- ☐ So Why Become an Entrepreneur?
- ☐ The Spiderweb Model
- ☐ Finding Early Mentors
- ☐ Managing Stress
- ☐ The Five-stage Entrepreneurial Process
- ☐ The Growth of Entrepreneurial Companies
- ☐ The Growth Period
- ☐ Why Innovation Is Important
- ☐ Definition and Types of Innovation
- ☐ Frameworks for Learning Innovation Skills
- ☐ Finding and Assessing Ideas
- ☐ Converting an Idea into an Opportunity
- ☐ Opportunity: Five Phases to Success
- ☑ Formulating a Successful Marketing Plan
- ☑ Preparing the Marketing Analysis and Plan
- ☑ Defining the Market Segmentation
- ☑ Conducting a Competitive Analysis
- ☑ Preparing the Pricing and Sales Strategy
- ☑ Penetrating the Market and Setting up Sales Channels
- ☐ The Value of a Business Plan
- ☐ Setting Goals and Objectives
- ☐ Starting the Process to Write the Plan: Five Steps
- ☐ Determining What Type of Business Plan Is Best
- ☐ A Typical Business Plan Format and Content
- ☐ Understanding Why Business Plans Fail
- ☐ Identifying What Form of Ownership Is Best
- ☐ Forms of Doing Business
- ☐ Sole Proprietorship
- ☐ C-corporation
- ☐ S-corporation
- ☐ Partnership
- ☐ Limited Liability Company
- ☐ Business Start-up Checklist

ANALYZING THE MARKET, CUSTOMERS, AND COMPETITION

> "The great secret of success in life is for a man to be ready when his opportunity comes."
>
> BENJAMIN DISRAELI

OBJECTIVES

- Define a successful marketing plan and its relevance to new ventures.
- Learn how entrepreneurs prepare a marketing analysis plan.
- Learn how to define market segmentation.
- Describe the methods of a competitive analysis.
- Learn the process to position a product or service.
- Describe the methods for a price and sales strategy.

CHAPTER OUTLINE

Introduction

Profile: Donn Rappaport—Marketing Visionary in Using Data

Formulating a Successful Marketing Plan

Preparing the Marketing Analysis and Plan

Defining the Market Segmentation

Conducting a Competitive Analysis

Preparing the Pricing and Sales Strategy

Penetrating the Market and Setting Up Sales Channels

Summary

Study Questions

Exercises

Interactive Learning on the Web

Case Study: Smart Card LLC Marketing Plan

Appendix: Marketing Research Techniques

Additional Resources

INTRODUCTION

In order to prepare the marketing section of the business plan, the entrepreneur must understand the customers' needs and desires, their profiles, markets, and pricing, as well as be able to plan for the company's future strategies in each of these areas. This chapter provides the information and tools needed to do just that. Throughout, the two important elements to understanding the entrepreneur's role in marketing—and the key to understanding and dominating the competition—will be explained.

A number of techniques and strategies can assist the entrepreneur in effectively analyzing a potential market. By using them, the entrepreneur can gain in-depth knowledge about the specific market and translate this knowledge into a well-formulated business plan.

This chapter addresses key issues in the marketplace and examines the major factors in marketing that entrepreneurs need to know. It also offers guidelines on attracting new marketing opportunities through e-commerce solutions. Electronic commerce is a form of marketing that is now a competitive necessity for many businesses. It can change the way an entrepreneur provides business and markets services and products. The business begins and ends with customers. Therefore, it is imperative to obtain and keep customers to sustain the business. By far the best assets for a business are its customers from which market analysis begins.

PROFILE: DONN RAPPAPORT—MARKETING VISIONARY IN USING DATA[1]

Donn Rappaport is a visionary in data marketing services and chairman and chief executive officer of American List Council. He has been the essential architect of its outstanding record of success.

ALC provides its clients with a wide range of leading-edge research, analytic, and sales and marketing capabilities specifically geared to enable them to acquire new customers profitably and to retain and maximize the value of each and every one. In addition, ALC compiles more than 25 million proprietary records each year, making it one of the industry's major independent compilers of both postal and electronic (e-mail) data. ALC's alternative media division places more than 1 billion inserts annually, and its online marketing group is breaking new ground daily in Internet and e-mail promotion.

ALC clients include the leaders in virtually every category of business, including financial services, retail and catalog marketing, magazine and book publishing, business-to-business sales, high-technology products, and nonprofit marketing.

Upon graduating from Penn State University in 1972, Donn began his career as an advertising copywriter in New York City, rising to become general manager of Schwab Beatty, the pioneering direct marketing group of Marstellar Advertising. It was there that he first perceived the need for a more sophisticated, technology-driven means of gathering, organizing, analyzing, and using marketing information. Today ALC is widely recognized as a pioneer in the innovative use of data to enable its clients to grow, increase market share, and improve profitability.

A frequent speaker and writer on direct marketing, Donn currently serves as chairman of the Direct Marketing Association (DMA) board of directors. He is a former chairman of the DMA board of directors' standing committee on ethics and privacy and a coauthor of the DMA's List Leaders Basic Training Manual. He is a past chairman of DMA List Leaders and a past chairman of List Day. As a member of the DMA Environmental Task Force, he coauthored "The DMA Environmental Resource for Direct Marketers." In 1999 he received the DMA's prestigious Leader of the Year award.

FORMULATING A SUCCESSFUL MARKETING PLAN

How can marketing techniques be used to the entrepreneur's advantage? Consider the following areas and how each question can be answered to anticipate concerns from a marketing perspective. These topics will be expanded upon later in this chapter to guide the entrepreneur in preparing a marketing plan.

1. **Set Marketing Objectives.** Marketing objectives are likely to be based on sales revenues and market share. They may also include related objectives such as sales presentations, seminars, ad placements, and proposals submitted to prospective customers.

   Remember to make all the objectives concrete and measurable. Develop the plan to be implemented, not just read. Objectives that cannot be measured, tracked, and followed up are likely to lead to implementation. The capability of plan-versus-actual analysis is essential.

   Sales are easy to track and measure. Market share is harder because it depends on market research. There are other marketing goals that are less tangible and harder to measure, such as positioning or image and awareness.

2. **Get the Product Out: Sales and Distribution.** Begin with how a business will deliver its products or services to customers. Will the business employ its own salesforce for direct marketing, or will dealers, distributors, jobbers, or perhaps partners be used? Have any of these been identified or selected? On what basis will they be chosen? How will they be compensated? If the business will rely on its own salesforce, what skills and training will that require?

3. **Set a Pricing Strategy.** Pricing should be considered part of the overall marketing strategy. Although nonprice factors have become more important in buying behavior in recent decades, price still remains one of the most important elements in determining company market share and profitability. For example, the manufacturer of women's designer apparel might pursue a high-price strategy, then discount the apparel as a means of generating sales. However, this strategy may risk weakening the image of the upscale brand.

   The entrepreneur needs to generate a rationale to explain the pricing strategy and anticipate its impact on gross profit. A detailed price list will be helpful whether the entrepreneur is handling the marketing of the product personally, getting advice from mentors, or outsourcing the marketing to a company that specializes in it.

4. **Raise Visibility: Advertising, Public Relations, and Promotion.** In many instances public relations will play an important role in attempts to generate sales. Usually the focus is on the concept and the creative content of the communications campaign, the media used, and the extent to which each will be employed.

   Many start-up or early-stage companies will not have a large advertising budget. For these companies, public relations may be the answer. Entrepreneurs may contact local media—newspapers, radio, and television—that often write or broadcast stories on new businesses in the community. A favorable response may translate into free advertising directed at a large audience. The Dyson case profile in Chapter 7 describes a novel approach using "personality marketing" for a cash-strapped company.

> "Marketing is important, but there is nothing more important to the success of most entrepreneurs than personal selling. As the expression goes, 'Nothing happens until there's a sale!'"
>
> GERALD E. HILLS
> *Coleman Foundation Chair of Entrepreneurship, University of Illinois at Chicago*

5. **Conduct a Site Analysis.** In some instances, particularly if the business has a retail focus, location must be taken into account in the marketing plan. The entrepreneur must think about the demographic and educational issues of the neighborhood, its environment, its accessibility and proximity to other businesses, and the cost of maintaining a facility there.

6. **Future Marketing Activities.** The marketing plan should consider sales strategies aimed at sustaining growth. For example, a company's immediate plans might involve penetrating only the domestic market, but in the future, the same company might consider a license for its products in some international markets or perhaps even a joint venture or partnership with a company in similar or complementary markets. The Ultrafast case history on this book's Web site illustrates how this might be achieved.

PREPARING THE MARKETING ANALYSIS AND PLAN

Marketing analysis is sometimes called a feasibility study or marketing plan. This process will help the entrepreneur develop a plan that leverages all of the strengths and accounts for any weaknesses in determining the demand for the product or service.[2]

Marketing analysis is also the process of determining a plan that provides the entrepreneur with a sense and an indication of demand. The analysis addresses the following questions: Is there a market to build a viable business? Who are the competitors? Will this venture be the first in the market or face competition? Is governmental regulation an issue? What new products are in the pipeline? How much financial support will be needed to start up? This analysis also describes the research for collecting and analyzing marketing information to make decisions about demographic and consumers' needs and buying habits.

ROADMAP

IN ACTION

When you are preparing the marketing plan, do not spend too much time describing the features and benefits of the new idea. The problem with most marketing plans is the lack of a clear description of the market, competition, and potential customers. Concentrate on the solution to how the new approach will be better for customers than the current situation.

Identifying Customers

The first step is to identify the most likely customer for the new business. Who will buy the product? Often the decision maker and the buyer are the same person, particularly with consumer product goods. A profile of the potential customer or the target audience being served should be developed.[3] This profile is usually based on the following four factors:

1. **Market Identification.** The current market and service needs are determined. How profitable are the existing company services? Which of these services offer the most potential? Which (if any) are inappropriate, and which will customers cease to need in the future?

2. **Current and Best Customers.** Identifying the company's current clients allows management to determine where to allocate resources. Defining the best customers enables management to segment this market niche more directly.

3. **Potential Customers.** By identifying potential customers, either geographically or with an industry-wide analysis of its marketing area, a company increases its ability to target this group, thus turning potential customers into current customers.

4. **Outside Factors.** Identifying the changing trends in demographics, economics, technology, cultural attitudes, and the role of governmental policy may have a substantial impact on customer needs and, consequently, expected services.

Niche or Target Markets

A niche market is a small segment of a large market ignored by other companies. For many firms, niche markets are too small to be attractive to large competitors. Yet a start-up firm can do well within them. The plan is to select a niche market in which the new business can grow and gain a competitive advantage. In the future, additional niches will open up as market efficiency improves.[4]

Target marketing is the strategy used by most successful businesses today. Usually, a company ignores segments that have limited growth because the product will not generate sufficient sales to sustain the company's profitability or allow the company to compete effectively.

ROADMAP

IN ACTION

A new venture or an early-stage business has a high degree of success in a niche market. Niche markets are too small to be attractive to large competitors. Use the marketing plan to select a niche market to grow and gain a competitive advantage.

The market segments are selected and targeted. Marketing tactics are developed for each target market, which is called *strategic market segmentation*. Once markets have been targeted, the entrepreneur should develop a marketing program for penetrating each segment. The business plan will help identify the markets and their segments. Each target market should be treated almost as a separate marketing program.

One-to-One Marketing

One-to-one marketing requires learning the profile or details about individual customers to identify which are most valuable to the company. By customizing the product or service, the value for the customer can be increased.

One-to-one marketing is rapidly becoming a competitive imperative.[5] As companies learn more about their customers, they can use this knowledge to create and sell products and services to breed loyalty. The key steps to becoming a one-to-one marketer are as follows:

- **Identify customers or get them to identify themselves.** Consider all options for collecting names: sales transactions, contests, sponsored events, frequent-buyer programs, 800 numbers, credit card records, simple survey cards, and quick one-question polls when customers call.

- **Link customers' identities to their transactions.** Credit card records are especially useful but not necessary. The best way to build individual customer transaction records is often to adopt a different business approach. Consider membership clubs to make it possible to link information about purchases with people.

- **Calculate individual customer lifetime value.** Knowing what a customer is likely to spend over time will help the entrepreneur decide which customers are most desirable (because their business is more profitable) and how much to invest in keeping them. In this light, unusual and seemingly expensive offers can make powerful economic sense.

- **Practice just-in-time marketing.** Know the purchasing cycle for the product or service, and measure it in months or years. Time the company's entry into the market to the customer's purchasing cycle. Time marketing material to meet the customer's needs rather than the company's quarterly sales goals. Send handwritten postcards or marketing materials or use a new catalog for selling.

- **Strengthen a customer-satisfaction program.** Survey questions can be tailored to a customer's wish list and buying preferences. Customize responses to meet the customer's demand.

- **Treat complaints as opportunities for additional business.** Don't ignore customer complaints; follow up with them to identify and correct the problem. By responding quickly, a disgruntled customer may turn into an advocate for the company.

- **Survey customers to find their points of pain.** Listening to customers' problems can often lead to new products, services, or business models. The Greif and SmartPak cases in Chapter 3 illustrate this point.

- **Enhance product information.** Build in some form of information that will keep customers coming back. For example, the retailer J. Crew provides a $25 electronic gift card when customers make purchases in excess of $200.[6]

The Value of Loyalty Programs

Marketing plans often place a great deal of emphasis on acquisition but not on customer loyalty. The reality is that for a start-up to survive, regardless of industry, it must not only obtain the right customers, but keep them. A widely held view is that on average it costs a firm five to six times as much to attract a new customer as to keep one.

Not all existing customer relationships are worth keeping unless you can convert them to valuable client status. Careful analysis may show that many relationships are no longer profitable for the firm because they cost more to maintain than the revenues they generate. At times firms may want to "let customers walk" if they prove unprofitable. Of course, legal and ethical considerations will influence such decisions.

In order to know how much the start-up can spend on customer loyalty, one must have a general understanding of what the customers are worth. Generally, customers are worth more with a longer relationship (although this is not always true).

The following factors often underlie hidden profit potential:

- *Profit Derived from Increased Purchases.* Individuals may buy more or consolidate their purchases.

Table 4-1   Work Sheet for Calculating the Value of a Loyal Customer

Acquisition Initial Revenue		Annual Revenues	Year 1	Year 3	Year 4	Year N*
Application Fee Initial Purchase		Annual Account Fee				
		Sales				
		Any Service Fees				
		Value of Referrals				

Total Revenues	
Discount Rate	

Initial Costs Marketing Costs Account Setup		Annual Costs Account Management				
		Cost of Sales Other				

Total Costs	

*Year N represents customer's final year with business.

Net Profit (Loss)	

Source: Christopher Lovelock, *Services Marketing* (Englewood Cliffs, NJ: Prentice Hall, 2001), p. 155.

- *Profit from Reduced Operating Costs.* As customers become more experienced, they make fewer demands on the supplier. (For example, they may call the customer service center less frequently.)
- *Profit from Referrals to Other Customers.* This saves on acquisition costs.
- *Profit from Price Premium.* Depending on the industry, new customers often benefit from introductory promotional discounts (e.g., phone service, magazine subscriptions).

Calculating the Value of a Loyal Customer

Calculating this value is an inexact science; the purpose of calculation is to ascertain which customer segments will be the most profitable and, therefore, the most viable investment.

Attempt to calculate the following revenues and costs. As the business grows and actual (rather than estimated) data become available, tweak the calculations accordingly. Table 4-1 is a work sheet to help you in this calculation.

DEFINING THE MARKET SEGMENTATION

Segmentation divides a market into workable groups or divisions. It divides a market by age, income, product needs, geography, buying patterns, eating patterns, family makeup, or other classifications. Good marketing plans rarely address the full range of possible target markets. They almost always select segments of the market. The selection allows a marketing plan to focus more effectively, to define specific messages, and to send those messages through specific channels.[7]

A market may be segmented in several different ways.

- **Demographic segmentations** are classic. This method divides the market into groups based on age, income level, and gender. Some marketing plans focus mainly on demographics because they work for strategy development. For example, video games tend to sell to adolescent males; dolls sell mainly to preadolescent females. Cadillac automobiles generally sell to older adults, while minivans sell to adults (with families) between the ages of thirty and fifty.

  Business demographics may also be valuable. Government statistics tend to divide businesses by size (in sales or number of employees) and type of industry (using industry classification systems such as SIC, the standard industrial classification). If the business is selling to companies, then the focus is on segmenting by using types of business. For example, the business may want to sell to optical stores, CPA firms, auto repair shops, or companies with more than five hundred employees.

- **Geographic segmentation,** another classic method, divides people or businesses into regional groups according to location. It is very important for retail businesses, restaurants, and services addressing their local surroundings only. In those cases, divide the market into geographic categories such as by city, ZIP code, county, state, or region. International companies frequently divide their markets by country or region.

- **Psychographic segmentation** divides customers into cultural groups, value groups, social sets, or other interesting categories that might be useful for classifying customers. For example, First Colony Mall of Sugarland, Texas, describes its local area group as "25 percent Kids & Cul-de-Sacs (upscale suburban families, affluent), 5.4 percent winner's circle (suburban executives, wealthy), 19.2 percent boomers and babies (young, white-collar suburban, upper-middle income), and 7 percent county squires (elite exurban, wealthy)."

- **Ethnic segmentations** are somewhat uncomfortable for those of us living in a country with a history of ethnic-based discrimination. Still, the segmentation by ethnic group is a powerful tool for better marketing. For example, Spanish-speaking television programming became very powerful in the United States in the 1990s. Chinese and Japanese television stations have also appeared in major metropolitan areas.

- **Combination segmentations** are also quite common. You frequently see demographic and geographic segmentations combined—population groups or business types in a specific area are an obvious example, or ethnic groups in a certain city, or "boomers and babies" within reach of a shopping center. These are all combinations of factors. For example, Apple Computer has used a combination of business and general demographics by region, segmenting the market into households, schools, small business, large business, and government. It further divides each group into countries and regional groups of countries.[8]

ROADMAP

IN ACTION

To determine the best segmentation, analyze what specific channel provides the best marketing potential. The goal is to select the right media messages and divide customers in a way that makes it easy to develop a marketing strategy and implementation plan.

Questions for Effective Segmentation

1. Do potential customer groups have different needs?
2. Does meeting customer needs require different capabilities than meeting the needs of other customers?
3. Can the customers that fit into a given segment be identified?
4. Are customers both willing and able to pay?
5. Is the segment large enough to be profitable?
6. Can the segment be reached in a cost-effective manner?
7. Can the segment be influenced to respond favorably?

Market Segmentation Factors

The nature of your industry will dictate what kind of segmentation is crucial. For some businesses it will be driven mainly by demographics (e.g., beauty products). For others, it will be driven more by psychographics (e.g., bicycles where you would want to target individuals interested in fitness or in biking).

Whereas many segmentation schemes rely on compiled demographics and psychographics, technology firms oriented to consumers need to know the propensity of potential customers to purchase their products.

If your start-up is a technology product, consider the following segmentation developed by Forrester Research, Inc.:

Segmenting Technology Customers			
	Uses		
	Career	Family	Entertainment
Optimists	**Fast Forwards**—big spenders, early adopters for all uses	**New Age Nurturers**—big spenders but for home use	**Mouse Potatoes**—like online entertainment and will spend for it
Pessimists	**Techo-Strivers**—use tech to gain career edge (cell phones, pagers)	**Digital Hopefuls**—families with limited budget but still interested in technology	**Gadget Grabbers**—like online entertainment but lack cash to spend for it
	Handshakers—older consumers who avoid computers at work	**Traditionalists**—willing to use technology but slow to upgrade	**Media Junkies**—seek entertainment but can't formulate a plan

☐ Less-affluent customers

Source: Forrester Research, Inc.; Paul Judge, "Are Tech Buyers Different?" *BusinessWeek*, January 26, 1998, 65.

CONDUCTING A COMPETITIVE ANALYSIS

Creating a competitor profile provides the entrepreneur with a detailed assessment of the competitive environment. It is helpful to know the key players, their personalities, and marketed positions in each firm with which the company will be competing. How do they compete for business in terms of product, service, location, and promotion? In many situations competitors use different methods to gain market dominance. Do the competitors vie for price? Some may pursue price-sensitive market segments, whereas others may seek the business of those who want improved service, quality, convenience, value, rapid delivery, and/or a wide selection of product options.

It is particularly important to identify which businesses will provide the most significant competition and predict what they will likely do.[9] Analyze the situation by asking the questions provided below regarding six key areas of competition.

1. **Product or Service**
   - How is the competitive product or service defined?
   - How is it similar or different?
   - Does the competition cater to a mass or targeted market?
   - What features of the product are superior?
   - What strengths or weaknesses of the competition can be exploited?

2. **Price**
   - What is the competitor's pricing strategy?
   - Is the competitor's price higher or lower?
   - What is the competitor's gross margin for similar products?
   - Does the competitor offer terms, discounts, or promotions?

3. **Industry Competitors**
   - Define the competition in terms of new, Internet, or potential threats of existing companies.
   - What are the strengths and weaknesses of each?
   - How will e-commerce companies affect the business?
   - How can the suppliers or buyers affect the competition?

4. **Selling/Promotion**
   - How do the competitors advertise? Analyze their Web sites.
   - How much do the competitors spend on advertising, Web development, and promotions?
   - What marketing vision or plan are the competitors selling?

5. **Management**
   - How strong is the competitor's management team?
   - What is the team's background or experience?
   - How does the company recruit new key employees?
   - How does the company compensate its employees?

6. Financial

- Is the competitor profitable?
- What volume are sales and market shares?
- Do they spend money for R & D, Internet, and Web development?
- Are they properly capitalized? How strong is their cash flow?

Positioning the Product or Service

Figure 4-1 highlights attributes that should be measured in a competitive analysis. The marketing plan should also specify how you will position your product. Given the competition, how will the product appeal to a specific niche market, if any? What will customers think of your product versus someone else's?

Positioning is the process of establishing and maintaining a distinctive place in the market for the start-up and/or its product offerings. Effective positioning entails that the positioning be singular, providing one simple and consistent message.

The airline industry, an overcrowded industry serving primarily a commodity service, provides fruitful examples. New entries into the industry have encountered great competition. For instance, JetBlue has positioned itself as the more youthful, playful, and fun airline with which to travel. The outcome for this section of the marketing plan should be a positioning statement. This articulates the desired position of the organization in the marketplace. The plan should also identify any competitive threats to this positioning. For example, will an existing firm copy this positioning, realizing that this is an underserviced part of the market? Will an existing competitor feel threatened by the new strategy and take steps to reposition its own service so as to compete more effectively?

To show the firm's positioning versus that of its competition, one may want to add a positioning or perceptual map to the marketing plan. A map is usually confined to two- or possibly three-dimensional attributes. This map should indicate visually any future threats. Information can be garnered from customer surveys or inferred from published information such as past surveys, reports from staff, and benchmarking. If the firm is a start-up, the entrepreneur will not yet know perceptions

Factors	Attractiveness	
	High	Low
Competition among existing firms	Competition is minimal but will become intense	The industry is declining and mature
Bargaining power of buyers	Purchase volume is high, and they are willing to negotiate pricing	The buyer can replace the service
Bargaining power of suppliers	Many substitutes and sources are available	Limited supply; products are differentiated
Internet companies	No competition defined on the Internet	Many companies are entering this market
Potential threats	Complex barriers and costs are high to enter the market	Few simple entry barriers to enter the market

Figure 4-1   Evaluating the Competition: Factors Affecting Attractiveness.

of the brand; however, for the marketing plan, complete this section for those of the competition.

PREPARING THE PRICING AND SALES STRATEGY

Once the marketing analysis and competition review are established, the entrepreneur should begin to develop the pricing and sales plan. Pricing is the key to the process of controlling costs and showing a profit. It is a very effective marketing tool that must be mastered. The price of a product or service conveys an image and affects demand. Preparing the pricing and sales strategy is also one of the most difficult tasks the entrepreneur must fulfill regarding the product or service.[10]

A number of other factors can influence the entrepreneur's ability to effectively price the product or service: notably, number of competitors, seasonal or cyclical changes in supply and demand, production and distribution costs, customer services, and markups.

Pricing procedures differ depending on the nature of the business, whether it be retail, manufacturing, or service oriented. The general methods discussed below may be applied to any type of business. They also demonstrate the basic steps in adopting a pricing system and how that system should relate to the desired pricing goals. With this general method in mind, the entrepreneur can formulate the most appropriate pricing strategy.

Pricing Methods

Value

Demonstrating value is part of pricing a new strategy. Price should not be based simply on cost plus a modest profit. Rather it should be based on the value of the product or service to the customer. If the customer does not think the price is reasonable, then the entrepreneur should consider not only a price change, but also a new image for the product or service.

Rationale

The entrepreneur must explain why his prices differ from those of the competitors.[11] For instance, does the new business perform a function faster or more efficiently? Lower prices can be justified that way. Or is the new product created with greater care and better materials? A higher cost can communicate this idea.

To determine pricing, you need to know the breakeven point, that is, the sales volume at which a product or service will be profitable. This involves dividing the total fixed and semivariable costs by the contribution obtained on each unit of service.

Example: Calculating Breakeven Points—Hotel Room Pricing

Assume a 100-room hotel

Needs to cover fixed and semivariable costs of $2 million/year

Average room is $120/night

Variable costs per room are $20/night

Average contribution per room is $100

2,000,000/100 = 20,000 room nights per year out of 36,500 capacity must be sold

If prices are cut 20% (or variable costs rise 20%), new calculation is:

2,000,000/80 = 25,000 room nights per year out of 36,500 capacity must be sold

The marketing plan should estimate the following:

- **Fixed Costs:** the overhead for the start-up; the economic costs of running the business even if no products or services are sold (e.g., rent, insurance, taxes, salaries and payroll taxes for long-term employees)
- **Variable Costs:** the economic costs associated with service for an additional customer (e.g., serving an extra hotel guest, making an additional teller transaction in a bank)
- **Semivariable Costs:** in between fixed and variable costs; represent expenses that rise or fall in stepwise fashion as the business volume increases or decreases (e.g., hiring a part-time employee to work in a restaurant on busy weekends)
- **Contribution:** difference between variable cost of selling an extra unit of service and the money received from the buyer of that service

Depending on the start-up, the ratio of fixed costs to variable will vary greatly. For example, an airline has very high fixed costs but relatively low variable costs (and airlines have reduced variable costs recently to compensate for higher fixed costs, such as oil prices). Conversely, the beverage industry would incur high variable costs (e.g., cost of can, beverage, labeling).

This ratio of fixed to variable costs has important implications for pricing. High-fixed-cost industries, such as car rental or airline, are willing to "give away" services, typically as rewards from customer loyalty programs, for many of these firms do not encounter additional costs as a result. Moreover, these industries are most likely to discount their products or services.

High-variable-cost industries cannot discount as readily, especially if their discounted price falls significantly below marginal cost or the cost of producing an extra unit.

Establishing Pricing Objectives

The marketing plan should be based on a clear understanding of the start-up's objectives. There are three basic categories of pricing objectives:

1. **Revenue oriented:** The aim is to maximize the surplus of income over expenditures.
2. **Operations oriented:** Typically, capacity-constrained organizations seek to match supply and demand to ensure optimal use of their productive capacity at any given time. (For example, hotels seek to fill rooms because an empty room is an unproductive asset; theaters want to fill seats.) When demand is low, organizations may offer special discounts. When demand exceeds capacity, these firms try to increase profits and ration demand by raising prices ("peak season" prices).
3. **Patronage oriented:** The aim is to attract customers, even at a loss, typical of grand-opening sales. For example, a theater may give away seats for an opening night of a performance to create the image of excitement and popularity.

Furthermore, if advertising is a major revenue draw, giving substantial discounts might pay off in higher advertising rates for the increased exposure.

Another concept that the marketing plan may address is price elasticity. The concept of elasticity describes how sensitive demand is to changes in price. When a small change in price has a big impact on sales, demand for that product is said to be price elastic. The converse—a small change in price having little effect on demand—is price inelastic.

Price elasticity affects different industries to varying extents. For instance, the leisure airline passenger market tends to be price elastic. For this reason airlines are always discounting prices during the off season to attract more customers. (They also must meet minimum flight capacities to stay profitable owing to their high fixed costs.) Conversely, business airline customers are far less elastic. Usually a businessperson needs to travel (to conduct important transactions or affairs) regardless of airline prices. Knowing this, some airlines discount fares far more frequently for flights with more consumer than business travelers, typically during the off season.

Here are some pricing issues to consider:

How much should be charged?

- Costs to the start-up
- Margin you are trying to achieve
- Breakeven point
- Discounts offered
- Psychological pricing points ($9.95 versus $10.00)

What is the basis of pricing?

- Execution of specific task
- Admission to service facility
- Units of time
- Physical resources consumed

How should prices be communicated to the target market?

The entrepreneur should also consider price bundling as an option. Often companies will "bundle" a core service with a supplementary one—for example, concessions at a theater and an admission ticket sold under one price. This approach works well for motivating customers to try different types of products or services in addition to those they are already buying from the company.

PENETRATING THE MARKET AND SETTING UP SALES CHANNELS

The desired market penetration determines specific methods that can be used to sell products and services to customers. Some of the selling options include the following: direct sales, sales agents, and trade shows.

Direct Salesforce

The direct salesforce is a group of salespeople who work directly for the company and are paid either straight salary, salary plus bonus, or straight commission. The advantage of a direct salesforce is that, as full-time employees, they work for the company. The entrepreneur has complete control over training them to sell, price, and service the product. The disadvantage is the added expense in maintaining a full-time salesforce. Salaries, travel expenses, office support, and benefits must be paid for each salesperson.

Sales Agents

A sales agent works as a subcontractor to sell products or services. Agents are paid by commission, which is calculated as a specified percentage of the price. They receive their commissions after the company collects from the customers. Sales agents pay for expenses such as product samples, travel, office, telephone, and supplies that are incurred in selling the product or service.

Sales agents usually work a specified territory where they can sell the product or service. In addition, they sign a performance contract, which specifies the minimum number of sales to be executed annually.

The advantage of using sales agents is that sales costs are not incurred until the product is sold. The entrepreneur can quickly build a large salesforce and sell the product or service nationwide in a relatively short period of time.

The disadvantage of using sales agents is that they usually sell other products or services as part of a complete line. They tend to push the easier-to-sell products or services and those for which they have already established a large customer following. The entrepreneur has little control over the sales agents since they are subcontractors and do not work directly for the company. Therefore, they can be extremely difficult to manage with regard to pricing, follow-up, and service.[11] An extension of the agent model is to use one or more corporate partners, where there is a closer contractual relationship. Such partners gain additional value from selling your product or service if it helps them sell more of their own products or helps them sell against their own competitors. These issues are highlighted in the Ultrafast case on the Web site associated with this book. Similar advantages and disadvantages are met in such partnerships. If you use agents or partners in this way, it is recommended that you also employ some direct selling; this retains close interaction with customers, which may identify new needs or points of pain while making you less dependent on independent sales resources.

Trade Shows

Trade shows are good places to exhibit and sell products. Many trade shows are held year-round, but finding the right one can be difficult. The entrepreneur must carefully consider which trade shows to attend to meet target customers.

Selling products at trade shows has five major advantages:

1. Many prospective customers can be identified because they come directly to the trade show booth, rather than incurring additional costs to visit each one individually.
2. It is an excellent opportunity to interact with many people in the industry who the entrepreneur might not have otherwise met.
3. The company can demonstrate the products and answer any questions from prospective customers about the product or service.

4. The company can initiate a business relationship by inviting the customer to a follow-up meeting.

5. The competition can quickly be assessed.

Prior to the trade show, the company should develop screening questions to identify solid sales leads. This is an excellent method to meet the key players in the industry and learn what is happening. The contracts that are made here can significantly increase business sales and better establish and increase market share.

Entrepreneurs should consider the variables of targeted audience, type of product, and cost to help make their choices in determining the type of advertising best suited to let potential customers know about their products or services.

Viral Marketing

The best advocate for a company's products or services is an existing customer. Viral marketing is a term used to describe mechanisms by which customers are triggered and motivated to recommend a product or service to other potential customers. These "word-of-mouth" techniques have been significantly enhanced by the growth of the internet which makes it easy for one customer to send personal recommendations to several of their contacts. The advent of internet social networking, and an understanding of how the power of the scale-free networks discussed in Chapter 1 can exponentially spread information via highly trafficked nodes, have led to a number of successful business models that capture the value of viral marketing.[12]

Example: The highly creative advertising agency "glue London"[13] created a viral campaign for the launch of the new MINI Cooper S sports car, using a library of interchangeable video clips combined with a remarkable level of personalized content. With tongue in cheek, the concept centered around the idea that men aren't real men anymore due to the onset of so-called "midlife" crisis, their target market segment. Visitors to the car web-site can nominate friends who may be jokingly demonstrating "soft" characteristics and not showing their "manliness". Using a simple Q & A interface, the visitor can create a highly personalized e-mail. The unsuspecting recipient then receives from their trusted friend a message advising them that 'someone wants to have a little word with them'. They get a personal video message from an "in-your-face" character who seems to know a lot about them including their job, partner's name and their perceived worst crimes against mankind. They are encouraged to 'sort themselves out' and enjoy the visual feast of the MINI Cooper S for inspiration. The Ad is very impactive and those that receive it typically forward it to between 5–10 of their closest male friends who automatically match the target group.

Other examples of business models designed around social networks are discussed and illustrated in Chapter 11.

SUMMARY

Writing the marketing plan is the first step in the marketing process and a vital component of a full business plan. The marketing plan is an essential of a business because it communicates most directly the nature of the intended business and the manner in which that business will be able to succeed. Specifically, the purpose of the marketing process is to explain how a prospective business intends to manipulate and react to market conditions to generate sales.

The entrepreneur must prepare a marketing plan that is both interesting and thought provoking. The plan cannot simply explain a concept; it must sell a prospective business as an attractive investment opportunity, a good credit risk, and a valued vendor of a product or service.

The degree of detail and support that should be provided may depend on the market share one requires to ensure success. If the market potential is commonly understood to be large and only a very small market share is projected, less detail and support information are needed. Conversely, this detailed information becomes more critical as relevant market share increases.

The marketing plan must establish realistic goals and objectives. The goals must address the market share, penetration, sales, and pricing strategies. Pricing strategies must consider such factors as market competition, customer demand, life cycle of products, and economic conditions.

The marketing strategy describes how the business will implement its marketing plan to achieve desired sales performance. This involves focusing attention on each salient marketing tool a company has at its disposal. Elements such as distribution, pricing strategy, advertising, promotion, site analysis, and related budgets all may merit discussion, depending on their importance in relation to the company's overall market strategy. Although meticulous detail is probably unnecessary, it is important that you gain a general understanding of how the business intends to actively market its product or service. Most important, the marketing plan should show that you have spent some time talking to actual or potential customers. This is called "primary research" and is one of the main factors that will influence your ability to raise funds to build your business. (For more details, see the appendix at the end of this chapter.) After all, there *is* no business without customers.

The plan should also detail major competitors, noting their strengths and weaknesses. For the plan to be more strategic rather than mere reporting, it should suggest how the new company will vie within the competition—how it will serve an untapped niche. Perceptual mapping can visually illustrate this in two dimensions. Furthermore, a segmentation scheme of customers can be developed with an emphasis on which customer segments the new product or service seeks to capture.

Once the marketing analysis and competition review are established, the entrepreneur can begin to develop the pricing and sales plan. The crucial step of pricing a product or service is one of the most difficult decisions a business owner must make. A number of factors can serve as guides for pricing a product or service, including the number of competitors, seasonal or cyclical changes in demand, distribution costs, customer services, and markups. The elasticity of demand, or the change in demand given an increase in price, will also influence discounting decisions. Finally, clear knowledge of the breakeven point of the business is crucial in calculating the largest discount the business can afford to give away.

With a marketing plan in place, later chapters will focus on preparing a complete business plan (Chapter 5), setting up the company (Chapter 6), accessing money (Chapters 7 and 8), and managing the company's finances and growth (Chapters 9–12).

STUDY QUESTIONS

1. What are the five steps to formulate a successful marketing plan?
2. List three kinds of segmentation. For what kinds of products or services would one kind be more important than another?
3. What is "positioning"? What is "perceptual mapping"?
4. What factors determine whether the business would offer discounts?
5. What are the three pricing objectives? Give an example of an industry that would use each.
6. You own a café in a large urban area that carries a total of $500,000 per year in fixed costs. Your café sells only coffee for $2.50 per cup. The average variable cost per cup (coffee mix, cup costs, etc.) is $1. How many cups do you need to sell per day to break even? If the price of the coffee decreased by 10 percent for a special promotion (with all other costs staying the same), how many cups would you need to sell to break even?

EXERCISES

Marketing Analysis Interview: Customer Analysis

1. Interview an entrepreneurial company and prepare the top five reasons people buy (or would buy) the product or service. Then complete the table.

Description	Importance (1–10)	Company/Product/Service Strength		
		Low	Average	High
1.				
2.				
3.				
4.				
5.				

2. When does a customer buy the product or service?

3. Describe a scenario in which a customer buys the product or service.

4. Where/how does a customer buy the product or service?

5. Describe the target customer (age, sex, income, interests, education, career, etc.).

6. How many target customers are within the geographic market (or are within reach of the distribution and marketing mechanisms)?

7. What percentage of these people would buy a product or service similar to that offered by the entrepreneurial company?

8. Do you expect this number to change? Why or why not?

9. Draw three perceptual maps (using two attributes for each map).

Marketing Analysis Interview: Competitor Analysis

1. List all of the major competitors, and complete the table with descriptions and figures.

Name	Approx. Sales	Target Market	Product/ Service	Price
1.				
2.				
3.				
4.				
5.				

Marketing Analysis Interview: Risk Questions

1. Complete the following table by describing the company's exposure to the risks listed on the left and the company's planned response or strategy should these risks be realized.

Area of Potential Risk	Company Exposure	Company Response/ Strategy
Industry Growth		
Product Liability		
Economic Changes		
Weather		
Legal and Government		

INTERACTIVE LEARNING ON THE WEB

Test your skill-builder knowledge of the chapter using the interactive Web site.

1. Self Assessment:

2. Multiple Choice:

3. Matching of Key Terms:

4. Demonstration:

5. Case:

6. Video:

CASE STUDY: SMART CARD LLC MARKETING PLAN

(This chapter does not have a management exercise based on the Neoforma master-case, so we have added this case for you to practice your marketing management skills.)

Smart Card LLC uses its expertise in smart cards and magnetic stripe technology to develop applications and solutions to meet the rapidly growing demand for marketing frequency programs. Existing and previous loyalty programs have normally been too expensive, complicated, and paper intensive, thus leading to lack of customer participation. As competition increases in retail and other industries, companies are searching for new ways to understand customers and retain them. Smart Card LLC offers a smart card solution for these companies.[14]

Smart Card LLC's strategy is focused on using smart cards for frequency programs that can benefit the customer. The company enables its clients to identify the following:

- Their most profitable customers
- What these customers purchase (how often, how much)
- Their buying preferences

Clients use these smart card solutions to better understand their customers and their purchase habits to introduce new services that create added value. Smart Card LLC also uses a marketing database to drive all aspects of the marketing mix: advertising, promotion, pricing, and site selection. Plus, it can be customized to meet the individual client's needs.

The objective is to establish an ongoing relationship with the client that will enhance the company's return on investment. Industry surveys have found that 80 percent of revenues are generated by 20 percent of customers. Smart Card LLC can help companies identify that 20 percent segment of their customers.

REVIEW OF THE PRODUCT ANALYSIS

The product's quality and features should be directly compared to those offered by competitors. Unique attributes that are important to customers should be identified and highlighted in the memory of the card. As an example, smart cards can hold one to ten pages of customer-related information.

Other important marketing characteristics for smart cards are as follows:

- *User-friendliness:* Will customers feel comfortable using the product?
- *Reliability:* Will the card work? Will the user feel 100 percent confident about the card's reliability? What backup system is in place?
- *Cost effectiveness:* How does delivery cost compare to the customer's perceived value of the service?
- *Compelling Use:* The initial application must be universal and valuable to compel a critical mass of people to accept it. Does the product fit the bill?

Figure 4-2 summarizes the marketing opportunities for smart cards, and Figure 3-3 shows the advantages of smart cards as they relate to the cardholder, merchant, and issuers.

SMART CARD MARKETING OPPORTUNITIES
• **Product**
➢ Compelling use: Application must attract critical mass of users
➢ Versatility: Multiple uses→ more value
➢ Cost effectiveness: Is service's perceived value worth the delivery cost?
• **Price**
➢ Start-up: New high-tech products command price premium
➢ Transition to maturity: Will price cover costs? Eliminate unprofitable services
➢ Maturity: Will competitive price begin cutting?
• **Selling**
➢ Direct salesforce versus distributors for selling smart cards; sale is complex, and direct sales provides better service and control
• **Promotion**
➢ Smart card's promotional issues: industry must create a need for new technology and replace existing magnetic stripe cards

Figure 4-2   **Marketing Opportunities for Smart Cards.**

Other issues the company considered were to use specialists and generalists as salespersons and to strategically assign sales territories. The number of accounts to be assigned to an individual salesperson was determined, and compensation included salary and commission.

To promote smart cards, a complex product, the company used a more sophisticated promotion approach—a combination of trade shows, press kits, Web sites, demonstrations, and other promotions.

SUMMARY OF THE COMPANY'S STRENGTHS AND WEAKNESSES

The model in Figure 4-4 measures the company's strengths and weaknesses as they relate to the factors of management financing, product sales, and marketing. The

Participant	Advantage	Description
Cardholder	Convenience	• No need for correct change • Easier than carrying cash
Merchant	Reduced costs	• Reduced cash handling • Reduced vandalism/theft
Issuer	Additional revenue	• Float/interest • Unused balances • Additional fee income • Expanded cardholder base
Acquirer	Additional revenue	• Additional merchant services charges • Expanded merchant base

Figure 4-3   **Advantages of Smart Cards.**

Factor	Attractiveness	
	High	Low
Management team	Proven	People with right skills not available
Financing	You have comfortable cushion or can raise capital if needed	You have a narrow time horizon to make money
Product development	Complete product line	One product of limited life
Salesforce	Strong contacts: specialist skills	Limited contacts: generalist skills
Marketing	Deep and tightly focused	Untargeted
Operations	Strategic alliances help improve execution	Learning in a vacuum

Figure 4-4   **Summary of Company's Strengths and Weaknesses.**

company prepared the factors that affect the business and how attractive each is in terms of high or low priorities.

CASE QUESTIONS

1. Assess the market feasibility:
  (a) Had the management team done enough research to quantify the size of the market?
  (b) How valid was their assessment of probable market acceptance of the product?
2. Assess the advantages for smart cards as listed in Figure 4-3.
3. Assess the various outside threats to the Smart Card LLC model.
4. Assume that you are a team member:
  Would you want to pursue the opportunity? Would you put your own money into it? Why or why not?

APPENDIX: MARKETING RESEARCH TECHNIQUES

Market Research to Aid Writing the Marketing Plan

Chapter 4 outlines the key parts of a marketing plan. To write a more substantial plan, the entrepreneur may consider marketing research for many purposes, including the following:

Market Dynamics

- To size up a market or industry in terms of annual sales revenue and potential for growth
- To forecast revenue and profit projections for the start-up
- To quantify the strengths and weaknesses of competitors in terms of market share and other competitive metrics
- To quantify untapped niche markets, such as underserved demographic groups, for the product or service

Consumer Behavior

- To gauge potential customers' reactions to a proposed product or service
- To test a name or concept
- To test price points
- To measure customer satisfaction with competing products or services
- To ascertain consumers' perceptions of competing products or services
- To understand customer behavior at different points in the "buying experience"
- To learn the most effective means of reaching customers
- To gain insight into which advertising appeals are most and least effective

Two Types of Market Research

Market research can be described as information gathered in order to obtain a more comprehensive understanding of an industry, product, or potential clientele. The two basic types of market research are primary and secondary.

Primary market research consists of specific information collected to answer specific questions. A few examples include user surveys, focus groups, phone interviews, and customer questionnaires. Many times specific studies are commissioned by private or public entities and are conducted for a fee by market research firms that specialize in various methods of data collection. Results are then published and may or may not be considered proprietary and, thus, may or may not be made publicly available.

Primary market research may be accessed directly from the vendor who conducted the research or via various services that collect several providers' reports, called *aggregators*. Many market research vendors, as well as aggregators, make reports and tables of contents accessible via the Internet as well as through database services such as Dialog or Profound. Entire reports can range in price from a few hundred dollars to several thousand. Many times, vendors will sell sections of various primary market research reports for much less than the entire report would cost. This is referred to as "cherry picking" and can be a cost-effective alternative to purchasing the entire report. Another cost-effective strategy can be to access the vendor's white papers, which are generally available for free at their Internet site. These are summary papers that are published when a new study is released, and many times they contain valuable bits of information. A few of the many potential sources of primary market research are listed here:

- www.mindbranch.com (MindBranch)
- www.imrmall.com (International Market Research Mall)
- www.ecnext.com (ECNext Knowledge Center)
- www.marketresearch.com (MarketResearch.com)

The dilemma for the small-business owner is that, properly done, market research is quite expensive, takes time, and requires professional expertise. Acquiring all the necessary data to reduce the risk to your venture may cost so much and take so long that you may go out of business. The answer is to find a quick and inexpensive way of getting enough data to help you make the right decision most of the time.

An entrepreneur can conduct surveys and focus groups himself or farm them out to a research firm. The cost of conducting primary research, however, may be prohibitive. Therefore, the entrepreneur may consider a "quick and dirty" study that will not be as statistically reliable but will at least provide some initial insights into the business. Two ways of conducting low-cost research are the following:

1. *Informal Focus Groups.* Gather a group of likely customers for two or three hours and ask pointed questions about the product or service. Ask open-ended questions and probe responses. Use visuals such as competitors' products to gain reactions.

2. *Online Surveys.* Write questions about potential customers' thoughts and reactions to the proposed product or service. Consider a brief consultation with a statistician to ensure that the survey has reliability. (If it were repeated, it would yield the same result.) Purchase e-mail lists of potential customers, and e-mail the survey with incentives to participate. Analyze the tabulated results for key findings. (See the reference section for more information.)

Secondary market research is information that has been gathered and repackaged from already existing sources. At one time or another in its life cycle, most marketing research has been considered primary research; someone somewhere identified the information to be gathered and contracted some entity to collect, repackage, and perhaps distribute or publish the data. Most of the information sources familiar to librarians and their patrons are considered secondary sources of market research.

Secondary market research is by far the most cost-effective information solution and generally the best place to start the information-gathering process. This information is extracted from industry studies, books, journals, and other published resources and are readily available at most public libraries. Many times, they are accessible for free via the Internet as well. You should look to both sources for a complete picture.

Information to Garner from Secondary Research

- *Basic Demographic Information.* The age, sex, geographical region, marital status, and so on of your existing and potential customers and clients. More in-depth demographic information provides details on their personal preferences and buying habits.

- *Customer Ideas and Opinions.* Information such as product quality preferences, motivators of buying decisions, and color preferences.

- *Buying Cycles or Patterns.* Do they buy weekly, monthly, yearly? Are the purchases spontaneous or planned? Is the purchase for self or a gift for others?

- *Trends for New or Improved Products and Services.* What needs do they want to have filled? What's missing in the marketplace?

- *Strategic Alliance Opportunities.* Who else is doing what you do? What companies could complement your product or service offerings if you worked together?

- *Opportunities for Beating Your Competition.* What's important to your customers? Price? Quality? Features?

ADDITIONAL RESOURCES

- **Lexis/Nexis,** Reed Elsevier, P.O. Box 933, Dayton, OH 45401; (800) 227-4908; www.lexis-nexis.com
- **Direct Marketing Association,** 1120 Avenue of the Americas, New York, NY 10036; (212) 768-7271; www.the-dma.org
- **Business Marketing Association,** 400 North Michigan Avenue, 15th Floor, Chicago, IL 60611; (800) 664-4BMA; www.marketing.org
- **Marketing Research Association,** 1344 Silas Deane Highway, Suite 306, Rocky Hill, CT 06067; www.mra-net.org

ROADMAP for

PATTERNS OF ENTREPRENEURSHIP
Getting Started as an Entrepreneur

- ☐ An Entrepreneurial Perspective
- ☐ Commonly Shared Entrepreneurial Characteristics
- ☐ Types of Entrepreneurs
- ☐ The Need to Control
- ☐ Entrepreneurship Roller Coaster
- ☐ So Why Become an Entrepreneur?
- ☐ The Spiderweb Model
- ☐ Finding Early Mentors
- ☐ Managing Stress
- ☐ The Five-stage Entrepreneurial Process
- ☐ The Growth of Entrepreneurial Companies
- ☐ The Growth Period
- ☐ Why Innovation Is Important
- ☐ Definition and Types of Innovation
- ☐ Frameworks for Learning Innovation Skills
- ☐ Finding and Assessing Ideas
- ☐ Converting an Idea into an Opportunity
- ☐ Opportunity: Five Phases to Success
- ☐ Formulating a Successful Marketing Plan
- ☐ Preparing the Marketing Analysis and Plan
- ☐ Defining the Market Segmentation
- ☐ Conducting a Competitive Analysis
- ☐ Preparing the Pricing and Sales Strategy
- ☐ Penetrating the Market and Setting up Sales Channels
- ☑ The Value of a Business Plan
- ☑ Setting Goals and Objectives
- ☑ Starting the Process to Write the Plan: Five Steps
- ☑ Determining What Type of Business Plan Is Best
- ☑ A Typical Business Plan Format and Content
- ☑ Understanding Why Business Plans Fail
- ☐ Identifying What Form of Ownership Is Best
- ☐ Forms of Doing Business
- ☐ Sole Proprietorship
- ☐ C-corporation
- ☐ S-corporation
- ☐ Partnership
- ☐ Limited Liability Company
- ☐ Business Start-up Checklist

CHAPTER 5

WRITING THE WINNING BUSINESS PLAN

"The best business plans are straightforward documents that spell out the 'who, what, where, why, and how much.'"

MICHAEL BUSCHEIT, INVESTMENT BANKER

OBJECTIVES

- Understand the value of writing a business plan.
- Explain how a business plan serves as a blueprint for building a company.
- Know the steps toward completing a business plan.
- Learn the detailed components of a business plan.
- Understand how to write a business plan so it targets investors.

CHAPTER OUTLINE

Introduction

Profile: Nikolay Shkolnik—Business Plan Turns a Dream into Reality

The Value of a Business Plan

Setting Goals and Objectives

Starting the Process to Write the Plan: Five Steps

Determining What Type of Business Plan Is Best

A Typical Business Plan Format and Content

Understanding Why Business Plans Fail

Summary

Study Questions

Exercises

Case Study: Surfparks LLC

Appendix: The Roadmap Guide for Writing A Business Plan

Interactive Learning on the Web

Additional Resources

INTRODUCTION

Smart entrepreneurs recognize the value of a business plan for securing capital and growing their businesses. Business plans are a vital mode of communication between entrepreneurs and potential investors. In addition, entrepreneurs often find that developing a business plan forces them to introduce discipline and a logical

91

thought process into all of their planning activities. In addition, a properly prepared business plan will help entrepreneurs consistently establish and meet goals and objectives for their employees, investors, and management.

In this chapter we'll establish the value of a business plan and lay out a step-by-step procedure entrepreneurs can follow to create one. We'll also discuss why certain information is required in a business plan as well as how it should be presented.

Once you decide to start a business, you understandably should have a plan to produce products or supply services and to attract the optimum marketing, operations, management team, and financing to get the business off to a good start.

It is important to realize and deal with the various "interest groups" that will be crucial to your success. Each group wants to hear something from your story that provides a comfort factor. Consider these examples:

- Financial interests want to know the risk/reward "formula" and the future "cash out/in" possibilities associated with your new venture.
- Employees want to feel secure in knowing they have not only a job with your company, but a possible career.
- Marketers need to know the product/service, pricing, placement, and positioning, ("the four Ps").
- Vendors, suppliers, and associates need to know what your operations will look like so they can plan to be part of your supply chain.
- Your partners (if any) need to codify their legal and fiduciary rights and responsibilities for their own protection and growth.
- The entrepreneur needs to place his or her ideas beside a companion roadmap to compare and contrast where the business is going to where it was supposed to go. How do you accomplish all of the above in a professional and concise manner?

PROFILE: NIKOLAY SHKOLNIK—BUSINESS PLAN TURNS A DREAM INTO REALITY[1]

Dr. Nikolay Shkolonik received an MS from Kiev Polytechnic in 1975, followed in 1984 with a doctorate from the University of Connecticut. An inveterate inventor and winner of the Motorola Award for Creativity, he is also one of a few experts in TRIZ, an analytical system for solving complex engineering problems innovatively. As a senior member of the consulting firm GEN3 Partners in Boston, he taught many companies how to innovate. At the same time, he was intrigued by the inefficiencies of internal combustion engines used in cars and elsewhere. The basic engine had not changed for more than a century, and he gradually evolved a radically new engine concept that can make a truly major improvement in fuel efficiency, a growing issue as petroleum resources decline. But for more than seven years, his ideas remained a dream until, by chance, his son Alex, studying for his doctorate at MIT, met Brian Roughan, Jennifer Andrews Burke, and Vik Sahney, three MBA students looking for some extracurricula work to hone their business planning skills. Alex introduced them to his father, and they agreed to work on a plan for a new company called Liquid Piston formed to commercialize the new engine. Initially the team, which now included Alex, thought that this would be a simple exercise, perhaps a few hours a week only, but it ended up consuming their entire lives for more than two months. According to Brian, the hardest part was identifying which markets to enter first because the engine can be configured to fit many opportunities. Indeed the team changed its market strategy many times, and this important part of the plan absorbed close to half of their effort. The team was fortunate to have Bill Frezza, an MIT alum and a partner in the VC firm Adams Capital, as a mentor during the process. (You can see Bill talking about business planning on the book's Web site.) Finally they were ready to enter the annual MIT $50K business planning competition, where they took second place. The prize money of $10,000 was used to file the first patents for the company. The team also won $12,500 in the MIT Enterprise Forum Competition and was in the top four in the GE & Dow Jones ECOnomics Business Plan Competition in 2006. The next year the company was awarded $75,000 in an SBIR grant competition. Meanwhile the team was making many presentations to venture capitalists. Did anyone really read the plan from cover to cover? Well, perhaps not. But according to Brian, going through the rigorous process of writing a full plan prepared everyone to answer any tough questions that were thrown at them, first by the judges and later by investors. Nik saw the creation of the plan not just as the production of the final document to be put on a shelf, but as a process through which his dreams of many years finally took shape and became reality. The efforts were rewarded in 2007, when the company, which had matured a lot since the first plan, was able to attract $1.5 million of seed funding from Adams Capital in Pittsburgh and Northwater Capital in Toronto to build a prototype of the engine. Now the company is working hard to fulfill the plan (www.liquidpiston.com).

THE VALUE OF A BUSINESS PLAN

The main purpose of writing a business plan is to test the viability of the business idea and set a path for the entrepreneur to follow. Writing the business plan will determine if the business has a chance of becoming successful in the following ways:

- **Test the feasibility of the business concept.** The business plan is the best way to determine if the idea for starting a business is feasible. The business plan is a safety net that can save the entrepreneur time and money if the plan reveals that the business idea is untenable. In many cases the idea for starting a business is discarded at the marketing and competitive analysis stage because the business opportunity is not viable and the competition is too severe.

- **Increase the likelihood of the venture's success.** The business plan will ensure that attention to both the broad marketing, operational, and financial objectives of the new business and the details of each section get the required attention. Taking the time to work through the process of writing a business plan will make for a smoother start-up period and fewer unforeseen problems as the business becomes established.

- **Improve your business planning process to become more manageable and effective.** A plan can help the entrepreneur develop as a manager. It can provide insight into competitive conditions that are essential in starting a business. Such insight over a period of time can increase the ability to make the right decisions. Reviewing the business plan can also help determine what goals have been accomplished, what changes need to be made, or what new directions the company's growth should take.

- **Attract bank loans and investors.** The plan allows for bank loans and investors to gain insight into the business idea and determine the financial requirements. A solid business plan is required by venture capitalists and to attract angel investors. A presentation may stimulate their interest, but a well-written document they can take away and study will determine any investment commitment. More about how a business plan fits into the range of communication methods you must use is covered in Chapter 13. Both venture capitalists and angel investors will want to conduct extensive background checks and competitive analysis to be certain that the business plan is solid and viable.

ROADMAP

IN ACTION

The term *business plan* means the development of a written document that spells out like a roadmap where you are, where you want to be, and how you want to get there.

What Is a Business Plan?

A business plan is a twenty-five- to forty-page written document that describes where a business is heading, how it hopes to achieve its goals and objectives, who is involved with the venture, why its product(s) or service(s) are needed in the marketplace, and what it will take to accomplish the business aims.

There are three essential reasons to prepare a business plan:

1. Entrepreneurs reap benefits from the planning activity itself.
2. The plan provides a basis for measuring actual performance against expected performance.
3. The plan acts as a vehicle for communicating to others what it is that the business is trying to accomplish.

SETTING GOALS AND OBJECTIVES

A business plan also serves as a blueprint for building a company. It is a vehicle for describing the goals of the business and how these goals can be reached over the coming years. A business plan provides a means to

- determine whether the business is viable.
- raise capital for the business.
- project sales, expenses, and cash flows for the business.
- explain to employees their responsibilities as well as company expectations.
- improve and assess company performance.
- plan for a new product/service development.

ROADMAP

IN ACTION

The biggest problem most business plans have is that they don't include a clear description of the market, competition, and customers. Most plans spend too much time describing the features and capabilities of the new idea rather than how this approach will be better than the current solution.

However, *the single most important reason for preparing a business plan is to secure capital.* Investors agree that an effectively prepared business plan is a requisite for obtaining funding for any business, whether it is a new business seeking start-up capital or an existing business seeking financing for expansion.[2]

The bottom line is business plans help to define **the who, what, why, when, and how of the business.**

Investors need to know parameters, timetables, and expected future revenue streams. Thus, the business plan needs to set goals, but it must be realistic in doing so.

A business plan is a first attempt at strategic planning. The entrepreneur should use it as a tool for establishing the direction of the company and for establishing the action steps that will guide the company through the start-up period.

Many entrepreneurs say that the pressure of the day-to-day management of a company leaves them little time for planning. However, without a business plan, managers run the risk of proceeding blindly through a rapidly changing business environment.

Writing a business plan does not guarantee that problems will not come up. Managers who have a well-thought-out process in place will be better able to anticipate and handle any problems that occur. In addition, a well-constructed business plan can help managers avoid certain problems altogether. This is especially true for entrepreneurs and start-up companies.[3]

Setting Performance Benchmarks

Entrepreneurs can also use a business plan to establish goals and document milestones along the business's path to success. Entrepreneurs often find that it is difficult for them to look objectively at the business's day-to-day performance. A business plan provides an objective basis for determining whether the business is viable and can meet established goals and objectives.[4]

STARTING THE PROCESS TO WRITE THE PLAN: FIVE STEPS

As entrepreneurs are bound to discover, they must tell and retell their business's story countless times to prospective investors, new employees, outside advisers, and potential customers. The most important part of the business's story is about its future—the part featured in a business plan. Thus, the business plan should show how all the pieces of the company fit together to create a viable organization capable of meeting its goals and objectives. The business plan must also communicate the company's distinctive competence to anyone who might have an interest. But how does an entrepreneur write a business plan that accomplishes these goals? Let's look at the five steps involved in this process.

Step 1: Identify the Objectives

Determine who your audience is, what they want to know, and how they will use the information you are imparting to them. For example, if the business plan's audience is a group of investors, they will review the plan to gain a better understanding of the business objectives and to determine whether an investment is worth the risk. Entrepreneurs should use the business plan as an opportunity to develop as managers.

As they create the business plan, they should think about competitive conditions, new opportunities, and situations that are advantageous to the business. The plan is also an important tool entrepreneurs can use to familiarize sales reps, suppliers, and others with the company's operational goals.

Step 2: Draft the Outline

Once the objectives have been identified, the entrepreneur must prepare an outline for the business plan. The outline should provide enough detail to be useful to both the entrepreneur and his or her audience. A sample business plan outline is listed later in this chapter in the appendix, "The Roadmap Guide for Writing a Business Plan." The information shown is included in most effective business plans.

Step 3: Review the Outline

Next the entrepreneur should review the outline to identify areas that should be presented in even greater detail. While doing the draft outline, follow up with research on areas for which you did not have sufficient information. Detailed support for any assumptions and assertions made in the business plan should also be available.

Step 4: Draft the Plan

The entrepreneur will probably need to conduct a great deal of research before there is enough information to start drafting the business plan. Most entrepreneurs begin by collecting historical financial information about their companies and/or industries and by conducting market research (refer to Chapter 4). After they have completed their initial research, they prepare initial drafts of proposed financial statements and projections. By preparing these statements, the entrepreneur will know which strategies will work from a financial perspective before investing many hours in writing a detailed description.

In the financial section of the business plan, the entrepreneur demonstrates the viability of the business; the plan should show first-year projections by each month and quarterly projections for the next two to three years. According to Ralph Subbinono, partner at Ernst & Young, the biggest problem with most business plans is that they contain unrealistic financial projections. Thus, an entrepreneur should carefully rethink the projected performance and make necessary changes before passing the plan on to others. The entrepreneur should also keep detailed notes on the assumptions being made in the business plan draft so footnotes to accompany the statements can be added later.

The last element to be prepared is the *executive summary*. Because this is a summary of the entire business plan, its contents are contingent on the rest of the document; thus, it cannot be finished until the other components of the plan are essentially complete. As each section is written, entrepreneurs should refer to the detailed outline included later in this chapter to make sure they have covered each area adequately.

The executive summary consists of:

1. **Business Concept.** This section describes the business, its products or services, and the market it will serve. It should point out exactly what will be sold, to whom, and why the business will have a competitive advantage.

2. **Success Factors.** This section details any developments within the company that are essential to its success. It includes patents, prototypes, location of a facility, any crucial contracts that need to be in place for product or service development, and results from any test marketing that has been conducted.

3. **Current Position.** This section supplies relevant information about the company, its legal form of operation, the year it was formed, the principal owners, and key personnel.

4. **Financial Features.** This section highlights the important financial information about the business, including its sales, profits, cash flow, and return on investment. (Refer to Chapter 9 for more details.)

Step 5: Have the Plan Reviewed and Updated

Once the entrepreneur has completed a draft of the business plan, he or she should have an independent professional review it for completeness and effectiveness. The plan must then be updated at least every six months and as objectives change. A business plan is not a static document that will sit on your shelf, but one that is continually reviewed and updated. In fact, it is rare that the original plan used to start the business is the one eventually followed. However, without a sound starting plan, an entrepreneur will be unable to acquire a bank loan or any equity investors or have a template against which deviations, both internally or externally from the plan, can be judged and taken into account.

DETERMINING WHAT TYPE OF BUSINESS PLAN IS BEST

What type of plan should entrepreneurs prepare to meet their requirements? Three major types of plans exist:[5]

1. **Full Business Plan**

   An entrepreneur should use a full business plan when he or she needs to describe the business in detail to attract potential investors, strategic partners, or buyers.

2. **Executive Summary Plan**

   An executive summary plan is a two- to five-page document that contains the most important information about the business and its direction. It is often used to gauge investor interest and to find strategic partners. It can also be used to attract key employees and to persuade friends to invest in the business.

3. **Action Plan**

   An implementation or action plan is a document the management team uses to implement the plan. It consists of a timetable and a list of tasks that should be accomplished within a certain time frame.

Targeting the Plan to Selected Groups

A business plan could be the perfect tool to reach the target groups listed below.[6] Some investors invest in only certain types of businesses, such as technology, health care, or financial services. Therefore, entrepreneurs must consider which investors

"When I judge the business plan competition at Columbia Business School, I first read the executive summary followed by the financial section. Only if the concept is intriguing will I spend more time reading the entire plan. We perpetually review about one hundred plans, and it's quite difficult to read them all. For those plans that capture my attention to receive funding, usually about 5 percent, there is a well-conceived, detailed plan."

CLIFFORD SCHORER
Entrepreneur in Residence, The Eugene Lang Center for Entrepreneurship, Columbia University Business School

or groups are relevant to their needs and send a plan to only the appropriate groups. These can include the following:

- Bankers—to provide loans for expansion and equipment purchases
- Business brokers—to sell the business
- New and potential employees—to learn about the company
- Investors—to invest in the company
- The Small Business Administration (SBA)—to approve business loans
- Investment bankers—to prepare a prospectus for an IPO
- Suppliers—to establish credit for purchases

How Long Will the Preparation Take?

A general rule of thumb is that it takes twice as long to write a good plan as foreseen. A useful benchmark is that it will take at least two hundred hours of dedicated effort to produce a good plan. The best way to reduce this burden is to begin drafting out initial ideas, sections where you have some good input, background information, and so on, before there is an urgent need for a full plan to present to outsiders. This is much easier than sitting down with the aim of writing a full plan in a short period, say two weeks. Our experience with many entrepreneurs indicates that a sound, well-thought-through, well-researched plan that can be defended under intense questioning will take at least eight to twelve weeks to produce. This assumes that the writing is not continuous, but time is allotted for thinking, discussing alternatives with advisers, and obtaining missing information. Sometimes entrepreneurs use consultants to help write the plan. While this can be of value and reduce the personal load, particularly for the first attempt, remember that the plan is yours, not the consultants'. If you cannot fully identify with the plan and defend each and every point and claim in the due diligence process, this will be detected by bankers and investors, who will then doubt your ability to lead the venture.

Writing the Business Plan

An effective and complete business plan should answer the following questions:

1. What is the primary product or service?
2. Is there a market for the product or service? Has the opportunity been well defined?
3. Who are the target customers for the product or service, and what value do you provide them?
4. What is the pricing structure?
5. Who is the competition, and what are the barriers to entry?
6. What risks and market constraints are involved?
7. What sales distribution channels will be needed to sell the product or service?
8. Who is the management team, and what are their specific talents?
9. What is the current financial cash flow and breakeven plan?
10. What are the immediate financial needs of the business?
11. What are the future financial goals for the business and its founder?

A TYPICAL BUSINESS PLAN FORMAT AND CONTENT

Examples of business plans and executive summaries can be found on the book's Web site.

Creating the Title Page and Table of Contents

The title page includes the name, address, and phone number of the company and the CEO. The table of contents provides a sequential list of the business plan sections as well as their corresponding pages.

I. Writing the Executive Summary

As we noted earlier, the executive summary must be able to stand on its own. It should serve as a synopsis of the business plan. Investors may read only the executive summary; therefore, it must be comprehensive and well written to gain the investors' confidence.

The executive summary should be no more than two to three pages long and should convince the reader that the business will succeed. An example of a targeted executive summary can be found for Leafbusters Inc. in Chapter 13.

II. Writing the Overview of the Company, Industry, Products, and Services

The company description provides an overview of how all of the elements of the business fit together. This section should not go into detail, however, since most of the subjects will be covered in depth elsewhere.

The section begins with a general description of the legal form of the company, which should take no more than one paragraph. It should present the fundamental activities and nature of the business. This section addresses questions such as What is the business? What customers will it serve? Where is it located, and where will it do business?

Some further insight should also be offered as to what stage the company has reached. Is it a "seed"-stage company without a fully developed product line? Has it developed a product line but not yet begun to market it? Or is it already marketing its products and anxious to expand its scale of activity?

III. Compiling the Marketing Analysis

The marketing analysis section should describe how the business will react to market conditions and generate sales to ensure its success. It should explain why the business is a good investment. Keep in mind that overcoming marketing challenges is critical to a company's success. Therefore, potential investors pay a lot of attention to the marketing analysis section. In fact, venture capitalists say that the most important criteria for predicting the success of a new company are those factors that establish the demand for the product or service. If a real market need is not presented, all of the talent and financing in the world will not make a company successful.

Some of the most important issues to address in the marketing analysis section include:

Market Opportunity: The marketing section must establish a demand or need for the product or service and should define both the market and the opportunity.

The secondary target market should also be addressed. You should quantify the size of the market as well. Investors like to see a large total available market (TAM), which is the size in dollars if you were able to capture 100 percent of the opportunity.

Competition: The marketing section should describe the market conditions that exist in the business, including the degree of competition and what impact this competition is likely to have on the business. It is also important to address other forces, such as government regulations and outside influences.

Marketing Strategy: The marketing section should define how the business will use its marketing tools. This can include factors such as distribution, advertising and promotion, pricing, and selling incentives. The mission and vision will vary depending on the stage of development.

Market Research: The marketing section should document market research as a part of the marketing plan or in a section by itself. Of most value are data obtained from primary market research, for this is the best evidence showing that, if the venture can offer a product of service at the price used in the financial projections, then there are actual customers who will buy from the company. Bankers and investors like to talk to potential customers when undertaking due diligence, and positive responses go a long way to establishing confidence in the business.

Sales Forecasts: Usually financial projections are presented in the financial section of a business plan. However, it is useful to present sales projections in the marketing section. These forecasts might include projected sales growth, market share, and sales by customer.

Support Material: Include in the appendix materials that will make the plan more credible, such as industry studies, letters of support, brochures, and reviews or articles related to the product or service.

While there is a great deal of flexibility in the writing of the marketing section, the plan should be focused to fit the characteristics of the proposed business.

The *products and services* section of the business plan describes the characteristics and appeal of the products or services. This section may include a prototype, sample, or demonstration of how the products work. The section should include the following:

Physical Description: A description of the physical characteristics of a product usually includes photographs, drawings, or brochures. In the case of a service, a diagram sometimes helps to convey what service the business is providing.

Statement Regarding Use and Appeal: The entrepreneur should comment on the nature of the product or the service's various uses and what constitutes its appeal. This is an opportunity to emphasize the unique features of the product or service, the value proposition to customers, and thereby establish the potential of the business.

Statement Regarding Stage of Development: This is a description of the stage of development (prototype design, quality testing, implementation, and so on) of the product or service that the entrepreneur plans to introduce into the marketplace.

Testimonials: Entrepreneurs can include a list of experts or prior users who are familiar with the products or services and who will comment favorably on them. Such testimonials may be included in letter or report form in an appendix.

The company description should detail the objectives of the business opportunity. Perhaps the business is seeking a certain level of sales or geographic distribution. Will it become a publicly traded company in a few years when revenues reach a certain level, or will it become an attractive acquisition candidate? A statement of such objectives is important and may succeed in generating significant interest.

IV. Describing the Marketing and Sales Plans

The marketing and sales strategy section of the business plan describes how the business will implement the marketing plan to achieve expected sales performance. This analysis will guide the entrepreneur in establishing pricing, distribution, and promotional strategies that will enable the company to become profitable within a competitive environment.

Pricing Strategy and Plan

As we mentioned earlier in the book, pricing is an important element in the marketing strategy because it has a direct impact on the business's success. The marketing and sales strategy section of the business plan should address policies regarding discounting and price changes as well as their impact on gross profit (revenue less cost of goods sold). When considering what price to charge, it is important to realize that price should not be based entirely on cost plus some profit. Consider these pricing methods to generate the necessary profits for the business.

Cost-Plus Pricing: All costs, both fixed and variable, are included, and a profit percentage is added on.

Demand Pricing: The business sells the products or services based on demand or whatever the market will bear.

Value Pricing: The business sells its products/services to capture a major part of the overall value that is created for the customer.

Competitive Pricing: The company enters a market where there is an established price and where it is difficult to differentiate one product from another. In this situation, there is limited flexibility to make price adjustments.

Markup Pricing: The price is calculated by adding the estimated profit to the cost of the product. In some industries, such as cosmetics and health care, profit levels may be higher than in others, such as automotive components.

Entrepreneurs should analyze competitors' distribution channels before deciding to use similar channels or alternatives. Distribution channels include the following:

Direct Sales: Products and services are sold directly to the end user. This is the most effective distribution channel.

Original Equipment Manufacturer (OEM) Sales: An OEM will often bundle or promote its products with yours or pay a royalty on each product sold.

Manufacturer's Representatives: These individuals handle an assortment of products and divide their time based on the products that sell the best.

Brokers: These individuals buy products, often overseas, directly from the distributor and sell them to retailers or end users.

Web E-commerce: Products and services are sold through a Web site or through Internet partner alliances.

Advertising, Public Relations, and Promotion Strategies

The purpose of this section in the plan is to describe how you will tell potential customers that you have a product or service that can satisfy their demands, to convince those customers to buy from you, and to successfully compete with similar businesses.

Many start-up companies feel they are unable to pursue advertising, public relations, or promotion strategies until they are more established and have generated significant revenues. However, public relations companies are becoming more willing to partner with start-up companies. Instead of the usual retainer that public relations firms request, they are willing to work on an hourly or budget basis.

Other Elements

The marketing and sales strategy section should also include PowerPoint pie charts, graphs, tables, and other graphics that effectively show how the marketing effort will be organized and business resources will be allocated among various marketing tools. "A picture is worth a thousand words" also applies to business plans.

V. Describing Operations

The operations section of the business plan provides a detailed, in-depth operational plan. Creating this part of the plan gives entrepreneurs an opportunity to work out potential problems on paper before beginning operations. The importance of creating an operations plan will depend on the nature of the business. An e-commerce production site will probably require significant attention to operational issues. In contrast, most retail businesses and some service businesses will probably have less operational complexity. Issues addressed in this section of the business plan include the following:

Product/Service Development: It is not unusual to prepare a business plan before a business's full range of products and services is developed. This is especially true of start-up companies. Even after the product has been developed, it is often necessary to continue developing it to maintain a competitive position. It is usually worthwhile to present a summary of the development activities that the company will undertake.

Manufacturing: In the case of a production facility, it is important to discuss the process by which a company will manufacture its products. This usually involves some description of the plant, equipment, material, and labor requirements.

Entrepreneurs should also include a description of the techniques they may employ in combining these resources, including assembly lines and robotics, as well as the production rates and constraints on production capabilities. If some or all of the operations will be outsourced, then details of the subcontractors should be supplied.

Maintenance and Support: The plan should address the level of support a company will provide after a customer has purchased a product or service. This is particularly important in the case of a software or technical product.

VI. Describing the Management Team

The management team's talents and skills should be detailed in the management team section of the business plan. If the business plan is being used to attract investors, this section should emphasize the team's talents and indicate why management will help the company have a distinctive competitive advantage. Entrepreneurs should keep in mind that individuals invest in people, not ideas. Issues that should be addressed in this section include the following:

Management Talents and Skills: Detail the expertise, skills, and related work experience of the proposed management team and the backgrounds of those individuals expected to play key roles in the venture. These include investors, members of the board of directors, key employees, advisers, and strategic partners.

Organizational Chart: After introducing the key participants, it is appropriate to offer an organizational chart that presents the relationships and divisions of responsibility within the organization. In some instances a brief narrative instead of, or in addition to, a chart may be helpful in providing further detail.

Policy and Strategy for Employees: Include a statement as to how employees will be selected, trained, and rewarded. Such background can be important for investors to give them a feel for the company's culture. A brief reference to the type of benefits and incentives planned may further help define the company's spirit.

Board of Directors and Advisory Board: Describe the number of directors that will comprise the board of directors for the company. The directors can be founders of the company, individuals, or venture capitalists who invested financially or who bring specific business experience to the management team.

VII. Describing the Financial Plan

The financial plan section of the business plan should formulate a credible, comprehensive set of projections reflecting the business's anticipated financial performance. If these projections are carefully prepared and convincingly supported, they become one of the most critical yardsticks by which the business's attractiveness is measured.[7]

While the overall business plan communicates a basic understanding of the nature of the business, projected financial performance directly addresses bottom-line interests. This is where the investor discovers the return on investment, performance measures, and exit plans.

The financial plan is the least flexible part of a business plan in terms of format. While actual numbers will vary, each plan should contain similar statements—or schedules—and each statement should be presented in a conventional manner. There should be enough information in these statistics to know not only the business, but also how it relates to similar businesses. In general, the following information should be presented:

Set of Assumptions: The set of assumptions on which projections are based should be clearly and concisely presented. Numbers without these assumptions will have little meaning. Only after carefully considering such assumptions can investors assess the validity of financial projections.

Projected Income Statements: These statements most often reflect at least quarterly performance for the first year, while annual statements are provided for years 2 through 5.

Projected Cash Flow Statements: Such statements should be developed in as great a level of detail as possible for the first two years. Quarterly or annual cash flows, corresponding to the period used for the income statements, are sufficient for years 3 through 5.

Current Balance Sheet: This should reflect the company's financial position at its inception. Projected year-end balance sheets, typically for two years, should also be included.

Other Financial Projections: This may include a breakeven analysis that will demonstrate the level of sales required to break even at a given time.

This section should not contain every line item in the financial pro formas; these are better confined to an appendix. Judicial use of charts and graphs can make this section easier to read.

VIII. Establishing the Amount of Funds Required

The funds required and uses section of the business plan should describe how much money is required to finance the business, where these funds will be spent, and when they will be needed. To determine financing requirements, entrepreneurs must evaluate and estimate the funds needed for (but not limited to) research and development, purchases of equipment and assets, and working capital. For example, to finance research and development of a product, entrepreneurs might experience a long delay between incurring research expenses and actually generating sales. Thus, it may be appropriate to fund these expenses with long-term financing.[8]

Exhibits (Typical)

Census data and other population statistics

Market potential

Process flow (operations)

Detailed financials

ROADMAP

IN ACTION   Visit the book's Web site to view sample business plans in different markets.

UNDERSTANDING WHY BUSINESS PLANS FAIL

The authors have reviewed hundreds of business plans from entrepreneurs seeking advice or funding and, in so doing, have compiled the following list of factors that differentiate a successful plan from those that fail to attract investments or loans. Remember that there are far more inadequate business plans floating around than good business opportunities. Therefore, any reviewer will try to find a quick reason to *not* read your plan and reject it. You have to find a way to sustain interest and to get your plan to the top of the reviewer's pile. Any one of the following factors is likely to trigger a "no thanks" note from a banker, angel, VC investor, or corporate partner.[9]

- The executive summary is unclear, not concise, and not specifically targeted to the intended audience.
- The basic concept of the business has not been researched and validated.
- The business is "so unique that there are no competitors." There are always competitors. They may not be obvious, but they are waiting out there to attack your business.
- The entrepreneur has never spoken to a potential customer. "I will build a new mousetrap, and they will come."
- The financial projections are far too optimistic. Sales and cash flow follow a "hockey stick" curve, with the company turning cash positive after eighteen months of operations and growing at an annual rate of 200 percent thereafter.
- There is no discussion of either how a loan will be repaid or how an investor will get his cash out with a satisfactory return.
- The entrepreneur signals that she wants to remain in control come whatever. One indicator of this is not mentioning how a board will be constructed with "arm's length" experts who may challenge the entrepreneur.
- The stated valuation of the company is outrageously high and unrealistic.
- If the company depends on intellectual property to retain its competitiveness, there is no mention of any IP search showing that there is no conflict with other companies or inventors.
- The management section refers to a group of résumés that turn out to be friends or merely acquaintances who are not really suitable for the positions but have been included because this is required in the plan. Often these résumés are barely readable and are in different formats. It is better to be open about the positions that will need to be filled and how this will be accomplished.[10]
- The financials are heavy on irrelevant details, such as weekly postage costs each month for ten years, but have fundamental flaws in the most important assumptions, such as sales and distribution costs or overly high compensation for the founder.
- There is a fact in the plan that can easily be checked independently, and it turns out that the entrepreneur has not been completely honest in the document. Nobody wants to invest in, lend to, or partner with someone they cannot fully trust.

ROADMAP

IN ACTION

Investors will ask the following questions: Will I get my money back before the entrepreneur? Will I have the right to invest in future rounds? What role will I play in the company? Have clear answers.

SUMMARY

This chapter has established the value of a business plan and the step-by-step procedure involved in its preparation. A start-up company's business plan is usually its first attempt at strategic planning. An entrepreneur can use the business plan as a guide for establishing the direction of the company and the action steps needed in obtaining funding.

Before drafting the plan, the entrepreneur will need to collect information on the market and manufacturing operations as well as financial estimates. This information should be evaluated based on the goals and objectives of the company, which provide a framework for writing the plan. The executive summary, a part of the business plan, must be able to stand on its own. It should describe the customers, financial requirements, and the expected payback.

The marketing section of the business plan must establish the demand for the product or service and the potential for the business. This section typically includes a summary of the business's growth potential, the sources of demand, and the ways in which the demand is satisfied.

The company description section of the business plan begins with a brief, general description of the company. This section should present the fundamental activities and nature of the company. A fine level of detail is not appropriate in this section because it is included in other sections.

The marketing and sales strategy section of the business plan describes how the business will implement the marketing plan to achieve expected sales performance. In this section the entrepreneur establishes pricing, distribution, and promotional strategies that will allow the business to succeed in a competitive environment.

The operations section of the business plan presents the potential problems and the ways in which these problems can be resolved. The importance of creating an operations plan will depend on the nature of the business. An e-commerce production site will probably require significant attention to operational issues. In contrast, most retail businesses and some service businesses will probably have less operational complexity.

The management team section of the business plan details the management team's talents and skills. If the business plan is being used to attract investors, this section should emphasize the management's talents and indicate why they will help the company have a distinctive competitive advantage. Investors always look for a strong management team before making investments. Many businesses fail because the proper talent has not been assembled. This issue is addressed by describing the objective assessment of the team's strengths and weaknesses as well as the company's requirements for growth. It includes how employees are selected, trained, and rewarded.

The financial plan section of the business plan should formulate a credible, comprehensive set of projections reflecting the business's anticipated financial performance. If these projections are carefully prepared and convincingly supported, they become one of the most critical yardsticks by which the business's attractiveness is measured.

As is often the case in the preparation of a business plan, the quality of information included is dependent on the amount of energy devoted to gathering it. Good sources for such data include trade associations, trade literature, industry studies, and industry experts. Your business plan will be competing with many others to get attention from bankers, investors, partners, suppliers, customers, and employees, so the document must be clear, concise, reasonable, realistic, honest, and compelling.

The business plan is essential in launching a new business. The product of many hours of preparation will be a concise yet comprehensive, well-written, well-organized, and attractive document that will serve as a guide and an instrument for the entrepreneur to raise necessary capital and funding.

STUDY QUESTIONS

1. What are the benefits of preparing a written business plan?
2. What are the components of a business plan?
3. How long does it take to write a business plan?
4. Why do business plans fail?
5. Why should the executive summary be written last?

EXERCISES

Please circle the correct answer, either true (T) or false (F) for each question. Visit the book's Web site to review your answers.

1. Many small companies do not prepare a formal business plan because the major benefit of a business plan is the discussions that occur during its preparation. Therefore, in the absence of adequate resources or time, an oral plan is adequate. (T) or (F)

2. List in order of importance the following four purposes of a business plan.
   (a) explain new technologies
   (b) guide the entrepreneur
   (c) avoid competitors
   (d) provide a historical perspective of the business

3. Business plans are planning documents. As a result, they are frequently optimistic and should not be used to assist management in operating the business, nor should they be used as the basis for performance evaluation. (T) or (F)

4. Companies need *not* produce a business plan if
   (a) they lack the necessary planning department. (T) or (F)
   (b) there is insufficient time and money to develop a meaningful plan. (T) or (F)
   (c) management does not know how to prepare a plan and is not aware of the benefits that can be derived from it. (T) or (F)
   (d) annual sales are less than $50 million. (T) or (F)

5. Financial statements are an important part of the business planning process because

   (a) the planning process relates primarily to the financial function of the company. (T) or (F)
   (b) after completing the business plan, the next step is to develop financial projections. (T) or (F)
   (c) financial statements are commonly used to express business expectations and results of performance. (T) or (F)

6. Business planning is primarily a financial activity; therefore, top managers from departments other than finance need not be involved in the preparation of the business plan. (T) or (F)

7. Because an outsider would be unfamiliar with a given business, entrepreneurs should not expect a business plan to be meaningful to such outsiders. (T) or (F)

8. Review the business plan for Railway Innovation Technologies on the book's Web site and answer the following questions:
   (a) What was the intended purpose for this plan?
   (b) What four things do you like best about this plan? Why?
   (c) What four areas require improvement and why?

Master-Case Exercises: If you have not read the appendix to Chapter 1, do so. Then go to the book's Web site and read diary entry Month 23.

Master-case Q 1: Neoforma had only a rough business plan when they met Jack and the first investors. Later, to raise more money from more ambitious investors, they were persuaded to use a professional business plan writer, Sasa. What are the advantages and disadvantages of using a consultant to write your business plan?

CASE STUDY: SURFPARKS LLC

This business plan case study was prepared by James Meiselman, Columbia MBA 2002, under the supervision of Professor Jack M. Kaplan as the basis for class discussion on the subject of business plans. Copyright © 2002 by the Lang Center for Entrepreneurship, Graduate School of Business, Columbia University, 317 Uris Hall, 3022 Broadway, New York, NY 10027.
Note: For competitive reasons, some financial figures—specifically, financial costs and marketing figures—have been altered or fabricated.

INTRODUCTION

The purpose of this case study is to evaluate the business plan of Surfparks LLC. The mission of the venture is to create and operate/franchise the world's first surfing-specific wave pools, targeted primarily at the rapidly growing surfer population. Read the case carefully then prepare answers to the following questions:

1. Does the executive summary describe key elements of marketing, company services, current position, and financial features?

2. Is the proposed offer well written and concise, and are key data included?

3. Where would you place the technology overview section?

4. Are the sections in the business plan listed in the right order?

5. What are the important marketing issues and competitive advantages that should be described in the marketing section?

6. Does the financing section address the funding requirements and how the capital will be used?

7. What are your recommendations for revising the plan to attract needed capital?

SECTION 1
EXECUTIVE SUMMARY

The World's First Surf Pools

Surfparks LLC was formed to market and manage a global franchise of surfing-specific wave pools. While crude technology to generate surfing waves in a large pool has existed for nearly twenty years, stand-alone surfing pools were considered infeasible due to high energy costs, slow wave intervals, and poor wave quality.

Surfparks' innovative business model, combined with newly patented technology in both wave generation and pool shape, has now made the perfect surfing wave both technically feasible and economically viable. The new technology generates perfect waves up to eight feet high with rides up to seventy-five yards long. Wave height and shape have near infinite variability due to a computer-controlled wave-making system and a padded adjustable "reef" lining the pool floor.

Surfparks LLC has formalized a partnership with the developers of this technology: Aquatic Development Group (ADG) and ASR Ltd. (ASR). The partnership grants Surfparks exclusive license and preferential pricing on their current and future Surf Pool technology.

The Pilot Surfpark Facility

Surfparks LLC is currently seeking partners to finance construction of the pilot Surfpark. Total required start-up capital ranges from $6 million to $8 million, depending on land costs and the extent of site preparation. Surfparks has already secured financing for an aggressive prelaunch marketing campaign for this facility. Surfparks LLC will manage and market this facility for its owners in exchange for a management fee and/or share of ownership.

Optimal sites for a pilot Surfpark include Orange County, California; Brevard County, Florida; and Monmouth County, New Jersey. Appropriate sites have been found in each location. Each of these selected locations combines a large existing surfer population with poor and/or terribly overcrowded natural surfing conditions, making them ideal candidates for a Surfpark.

In addition to the large Surf Pool, the pilot Surfpark will include a small "training pool" for beginner lessons, a Wahoo's Fish Taco restaurant, a full-service surf shop, a board demo/rental center, party rooms, and shower/changing facilities. The marketing plan includes an aggressive member acquisition strategy using highly targeted direct mailings (via merging of *Surfer Magazine/Surfing Magazine* and Surfline/SWELL.com's subscriber database), surf-shop sponsored trips, and a national/regional PR and advertising campaign. Regularly scheduled contests, lessons, camps, and other special events encourage customer retention.

Market Demand

A rapidly increasing global surfer population, combined with a severe shortage of high-quality natural surfing venues, has raised demand for supplemental surfing facilities to a critical level. **According to the sports market research company Broadtrak, the active U.S. surfer population was 2.6 million in 2002 and increases by at least 10% per year. Worldwide, according to "Surfing Australia," over 17 million people surf at least once per year.** (*Source:* American Sports Data). Global surfer population (currently 17 million) is rising at similar or even higher rates. At this point, the surfing community is not asking *if* surfing pools will be built; they are asking *how soon* they will be built and *who* will build them.

Specific market research reinforces that this demand exists. A recent Surfparks-sponsored Web survey of 2,200 surfers gauged price sensitivity and interest in a surfing pool. At the proposed session price of $25 for twenty waves, **nearly 50 percent of the respondents said they would use a Surfpark at least once per week, and 91 percent said they would use it at least once per month.**

Surfpark Pro Forma Highlights

The breakeven point to achieve positive cash flow is between 10 and 15 percent use of the pool. This translates to about 25,000 individual pool users per year, each purchasing a block of 20 waves per session, or 69 visitors per day, based on 360 operating days per year. This is the equivalent to filling approximately two full 36-surfer sessions per day. By contrast, 100 percent use of the big pool equals approximately 214,000 individual visits per year, or 594 visitors per day. Revenue at 100 percent use would exceed $10 million, with earnings before interest, taxes, and depreciation allowances (EBITDA) more than $5 million and investors recouping

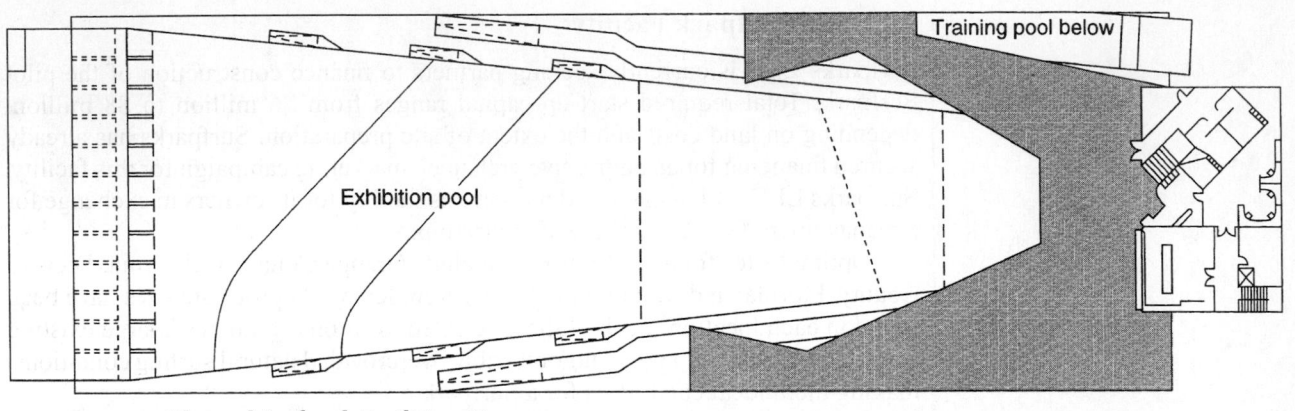

Figure 5-1 **Planned Surfpark Facilities Diagram.**

their full investment in less than two years. At a more conservative use of 35 percent, investors will recoup their full investment in three to four years.

Expansion Plans

An aggressive global rollout of Surfpark franchises is planned. Based on existing Web and print PR, Surfparks is already receiving multiple inquiries per week from parties around the world interested in operating a Surfpark facility. Hundreds of suitable locations, both coastal and inland, have been identified for continued growth. With proximity to the ocean no longer a requirement, a Surfpark brings the wave-riding experience to a huge, currently untapped inland market. Investors in the pilot facility will have preferential rights to invest in these future facilities. Figure 5-1 shows a Surfpark diagram of a planned franchise.

The Surfparks Management Team

James A. Meiselman: Founder, Chairman, and CEO

- 10+ years action sports (surf, skateboard, snowboard) sales and product management experience
- Managing Editor, *TransWorld Snowboarding, Snowboarding Business,* and *Skateboarding Business* magazines
- General Manager, Generics & Blax Snowboarding, USA
- Category Manager, Boots, Burton Snowboards
- BA Dartmouth College; MBA (Finance, Entrepreneurship) Columbia University

Nick P.: Founding Partner, CMO

- Director, New Media, National Basketball Association
- Director, Business Development, *Sports Illustrated*
- VP, Business Development, ESPN.com
- BA Connecticut College; MBA NYU Stern School of Business

Bill T.: Partner, Director of Development

- Co-owner, Del Rey Properties (commercial/residential developer, manager, construction company)

- Owns/manages L.A. Equestrian Center, 350,000 square feet of commercial space and 300 multifamily housing units
- Del Rey has built more than $100 million in commercial real estate projects

Doug S.: East Coast Marketing/Promotions

- 15-year director, East Coast Marketing/Promotions, Quiksilver, Inc.
- Producer, Quiksilver East Coast Surf Camps and "King of the Peak" pro surf contest
- Owner, Kechele Surfboards and X-Trak promotions

SECTION 2
THE SURFPARK CONCEPT

Market Opportunity

All surfers dream of riding a perfect wave. Unfortunately, the perfect surfing wave requires a precise mix of wind, swell, tide, and seafloor contour, and these elements can be found in only a handful of locations around the world. In spite of its elusive playing field, surfing has undergone explosive growth in the past decade. With participation rates increasing at more than 10 percent per year for the past three years, there are now an estimated 2.6 million surfers in the United States, and 17 million surfers in the world. Currently, all but the most remote world-class surf breaks are dangerously overcrowded. It is not uncommon to see more than one hundred surfers at a single surf spot.

This capacity problem, coupled with inconvenient ocean access for inlanders and the intimidating ocean environment, has actually restrained the potential growth and size of the surfing population. The mass appeal of the surfing lifestyle is well documented in mainstream media and proven by the fact that the surf *clothing* industry is more than ten times the size of the surf *equipment* industry.

The Solution

A solution to this surf scarcity is to create artificial waves. Artificial reefs have recently been designed and installed in select locations, but these reefs still rely on the presence of optimal swell, wind, and tide to break suitably. For reliable wave quality, a safe learning environment, and increased access for inlanders, all of these factors must be controlled. This is the idea behind Surfparks: **perfect surfing waves in a controlled pool environment.**

Hundreds of wave pools exist in the world today, but every one of those pools has been built as an extension of a water park or resort, targeted for casual recreational use. As a result, the wave quality in these pools has been designed for safety and maximum capacity. While crude technology to generate surfing waves in a large pool has existed for nearly twenty years, stand-alone surfing pools were considered infeasible due to high energy costs, slow wave intervals, and poor wave quality.

Surfparks LLC's unique business model, combined with newly patented technology in both wave generation and pool shape, has now made the perfect surfing wave technically feasible and economically viable.

The Surfpark can be an indoor or outdoor facility, depending on climate. The centerpiece of each Surfpark facility is the full-sized Surf Pool, suitable for intermediate to pro-level surfers and bodyboarders. In addition to the big pool, each facility includes a small "training pool" for beginner lessons, a Wahoo's Fish Taco restaurant, a full-service surf shop, a board demo/rental center, a board shaping/glassing facility, party rooms, and shower/changing facilities.

Competition and Market Positioning

Since no surf-specific pools have ever been built, Surfparks' only direct competitor is the ocean. On its best days, the ocean is a tough competitor, but ninety-nine days out of one hundred, waves at a Surfpark are superior to those in the ocean. In addition, the structured operating model at a Surfpark ensures that each surfer rides a wave alone, removing the common frustration of being cut off or outmaneuvered by aggressive or inexperienced surfers.

Surfparks understands that no matter how good the wave, surfing in a pool can never replace the benefits of the ocean. It is not our intention to make ocean surfing obsolete. Rather, we aim to be an enjoyable, productive supplement to the natural surfing experience. A Surfpark acts as a consistent, entertaining training facility, much like a golf driving range complements a golf course. With this in mind, we target locations with subpar, nonexistent, or overcrowded wave conditions where surfers have a difficult time logging quality water time.

Surfparks aims to make this surf experience affordable, variable, and exciting enough to warrant frequent return visits. To keep the experience fresh, the wave generator can produce a wide range of wave heights, and the pool has a computer-controlled reef that allows wave shape, peeling speed, and direction (left/right) to be altered at frequent intervals. Salt water will be used to simulate the buoyancy, smell, and feel of ocean water.

Competitive Insulation

Armed with proprietary technology, perpetual R & D resources, and an optimized business model, Surfparks aims to establish the first and dominant global brand of wave-riding facilities. We will develop a captive customer base through our membership program. Surfpark members will have privileges at an ever-increasing network of franchised facilities, increasing loyalty and raising switching costs. High upfront capital costs and a captive Surfpark membership base will discourage potential competitors from entering the marketplace.

Surfparks franchises will benefit from a global brand marketing campaign, constant improvement in operational efficiency, and access to continual technological innovation from the R & D team. The R & D focuses on improvement in both product quality and operational efficiency. Our current technology is by far the most efficient method of creating a high-quality eight-foot surfing wave in a pool, and Surfparks will strive to maintain its lead in quality, efficiency, and intellectual property.

SECTION 3
TECHNOLOGY OVERVIEW

Existing Wave-generation Technology

There are two commercialized technologies used to create artificial waves: pneumatic and hydraulic. Pneumatic systems utilize large fans to create small (up to six-foot) energy-efficient, high-frequency waves. Such pneumatic systems are used in the majority of recreational wave pools. Hydraulic systems drop a large quantity of water into the back end of the pool, displacing the pool water into a large (up to eight-foot) moving linear swell. Disney World's Typhoon Lagoon, for example, uses a hydraulic system and is thus suitable for surfing. However, the Typhoon Lagoon system is capable of producing only one wave every ninety seconds. Similar to a toilet, large storage tanks must refill before a new wave can be produced. Higher wave frequency from such a system would require additional horsepower to pump water into the chambers at a faster rate, crippling the energy efficiency of the equipment.

Surfparks' Wave-generation Technology

At Surfparks' request, WaveTek engineers have developed a new wave-generation system that combines the frequency/efficiency of pneumatic systems with the wave quality of hydraulic systems. This wave-generation system is capable of producing up to eight-foot waves in six- to thirty-second intervals. Wave size is adjustable, from three to eight feet, via computer interface.

WaveTek wave-generation machines have proven to be reliable in more than 350 installations worldwide. The machines require no significant maintenance and are backed up with twenty-four-hour technical support. The partnership agreement with ADG/WaveTek grants Surfparks global exclusivity and preferred pricing for this technology.

Pool/Reef Design

Once a swell has been generated, its breaking characteristics are determined by the pool shape and pool floor contour. Surfparks' partner ASR has developed a patent-pending pool/reef design that maximizes ride length, wave quality, safety, and operational efficiency in a minimum pool area. The pool design simulates a wide channel with converging walls (like a tapered pant leg). Waves are generated in the wide end of the pool, and they travel down the length of the pool, maintaining size, shape, and energy as the converging walls compact the swell. Salt water will be used in the pool to mimic the buoyancy and feel of ocean water.

To maintain variety in the surfing experience, ASR and WaveTek have developed a computer-controlled modular reef system. The shape of the pool bottom can be changed by raising or lowering padded reef sections via computer-controlled winches. Entirely new breaks can be created in a few minutes with the press of a button. ASR has charted the reef/bottom contour of more than forty of the world's best surfing breaks. With this database, it is possible to re-create world-class breaks in the Surfparks pool. Enticing promotions such as "Malibu Mondays" or "Teahupo'o Tuesdays" can offer challenge and variety to all skill levels and ensure regular visits.

SECTION 4
SURFPARK BUSINESS MODEL

Facility operations are divided into two basic processes: the registration process and the actual surf-session pool operation. Surfparks encourages repeat usage via a membership model. Membership benefits include reduced-rate waves, express check-in, priority reservation status, and surf shop discounts.

Registration Process

Entering the front door in street clothes, members and nonmembers with reservations proceed directly to the clothes/board checkroom. A self-service kiosk allows members to swipe their card through a magnetic reader, which dispenses a barcoded, waterproof wristband. The bar code contains information regarding the session time and the number of waves remaining in the account. Nonmembers with reservations receive this wristband from the check-in personnel at the clothes/board checkroom. Nonmembers without reservations must check in at the front desk to sign waivers and receive their wristbands before proceeding to the clothes/board checkroom.

Once the customer has received a wristband, he hands his board (if he brought one) to the clothes/board checkroom attendant, and the attendant will hand him a clothes bin and direct him to the changing room. The customer then changes into his swimsuit, returns his clothes/valuables to the attendant, and receives his board back. The attendant stores the clothes and valuables safely behind the counter and marks the customer's bin number on his wristband. If the customer did not bring his own board, he can proceed to the board rental/demo center to choose an appropriate board. Once the customer is changed into his swimsuit, has a wristband, and has a board, he proceeds to the Surf Pool area. Showers are located near the "beach" area, where surfers can rinse off before and after surfing.

Pool Operations

Surf sessions are booked in two-hour increments, and beginners/novices are segregated from intermediates/experts. In an "intermediate" or "expert" session, surfers wait in a queue on the side of the deep end of the pool. During a fifteen-second lull in wave action, a group of six surfers enters the pool via a stairway. As surfers enter the pool, a staffmember scans their bar-coded wristbands, deducting one wave from each surfer's account. After the fifteen-second lull, a set of six waves comes in nine-second intervals. Each of the six surfers takes a wave to himself or herself. The surfer rides toward the shoreward end of the pool until the wave "closes out" for a final move at the end of the pool. If any surfer fails to catch his/her allocated wave, he or she remains in the pool and gets a second chance during the next set.

The wave generator and reef design are flexible enough to host advanced and intermediate surfers in the same session. Scale model tests show a single reef design capable of producing an eight-foot tubing wave for experts and a slower, four-foot wave for intermediates/novices. In this arrangement, advanced surfers queue at the stairs closest to the back of the pool and intermediate surfers queue at the stairs forty feet closer to the front.

A complete ride takes approximately ten to fifteen seconds, depending on wave size (bigger waves move faster). From the zero-depth "beach," the surfer can exit the pool and walk back to the queue or paddle back in a current-assisted "lazy river" that runs parallel to the pool. Each surfer will ride ten to twenty waves in this two-hour period.

Additional Facilities

Mexican Restaurant/Observation Deck

To increase revenue and desirability of the wave pool, an informal southern California–style Mexican restaurant will be positioned on the second floor of the main building and will have an "observation deck" view of the entire pool. Wooden support pilings will extend downward from the deck to create a pierlike effect. The restaurant serves pool patrons but will also be marketed to the general public, who will be attracted to the unique "surfside" views and elusive southern California fish tacos. The restaurant/observation deck is designed to be a comfortable place for surfers to relax before or after a session or for friends and family to watch the action in the pool.

Surfparks has secured a commitment from Wahoo's Fish Taco to lease the restaurant space in all facilities. Wahoo's will serve breakfast, lunch, dinner, snacks, soft drinks, and beer. For authenticity, exotic beers will be imported from various famous surf locations, including Mexico, Indonesia, Costa Rica, Tahiti, and Australia. This atmosphere will provide a perfect complement to the surf theme.

Pro Shop

A pro shop, located in the reception area, will be the source for last-minute surf accessories (wax, leashes, traction pads, fins, swimsuits, rash guards, and so on) and will stock a large selection of surf- and bodyboards. It is not our intention to be a direct competitor with local surf shops, as these surf shops will act as our best promoters, organizing group trips and funneling lessons to the Surfparks facility. To maintain this symbiotic relationship with all surf shops, Surfparks must carry a strategic product mix and create an atmosphere that enhances sales at *all* surf shops.

"Pay-per-Wave" Membership/Pricing Structure

1. Surfers pay a yearly membership fee in twelve monthly installments (billed automatically to a credit card).
2. Four membership levels are available: Platinum, Gold, Silver, and Bronze.
3. Members receive a specified number of "waves" in their accounts. A wave is deducted each time a surfer enters the pool. The exact number of waves deducted depends on whether the session was standard, peak, or off-peak.
4. All waves in an account expire one year from sign-up date.
5. Nonmembers purchase lower-quantity bunches of waves at higher rates.

A summary of the membership levels and pricing structure is as follows:

Membership Level	Monthly Installment	Waves/Year	Avg. $ Per Wave
Platinum	$200	2,400	$1.00
Gold	$150	1,440	$1.25
Silver	$100	800	$1.50
Bronze	$ 50	300	$2.00

Nonmembers	Cost per Bunch		Avg. $ Per Wave
100 Waves	$225		$2.25
20 Waves	$ 50		$2.50

SECTION 5
SURF MARKET ANALYSIS

The following are highlights of demographic research conducted for Surfparks LLC:

- American Sports Data claims there were 2.25 million "active" surfers in the United States in 2000, a 25 percent increase from 1999. One million of these surfers are based on the East Coast, 1 million on the West Coast, and 250,000 in Hawaii.

- Based on surf shop and magazine distribution, approximately 750,000 surfers live in southern California (San Diego to Santa Barbara).

- Of the 1 million East Coast surfers, half live between North Carolina and Maine; half live between South Carolina and Florida.

- American Sports Data defines "very active" (significantly more than four surfs per year) surf population as 20 percent of the above figures. Using the 20 percent formula, adjusted numbers would be 200,000 "very active" surfers on the East Coast.

Surfpark Comparables

Disney World's Typhoon Lagoon Wave Pool

Surfers will pay a premium to ride a decent wave, especially when conditions in their region don't cooperate. An example of this demand is seen at Typhoon Lagoon, the wave pool in Disney World in Orlando, Florida. For the past decade, Disney has been renting the pool to private parties before and after regular park hours. The wave was designed for recreational use and is judged by surfers as mediocre at best but is often the only alternative to the flat conditions on Florida's Atlantic and Gulf coasts (about an hour's drive in either direction from Orlando).

Current pool rental rates are between $1,000 to $1,500 for one hundred waves. Thus, each individual in a group of ten surfers pays $100 to $150 to ride ten short waves. This kind of expense is for the seriously wave-deprived and can be justified only a few times per year. Interestingly enough, the sea of desperation is pretty large, as the pool is booked solid up to six months in advance, attracting users from as far as New Jersey.

Vans Skateparks

Action sports footwear company Vans, Inc., is operating skate parks in eleven locations throughout the United States. The skate parks act as a facility for Vans' target market to practice this sport in a safe facility. From a marketing perspective, the parks are a vehicle to incubate, maintain, and foster growth of this target market.

The Vans Skateparks are also an important revenue source. The parks have construction costs of about $3 million each. Yearly membership fees are $50, with session fees (for two-hour sessions) ranging from $7 to $9 for members and $11 to $14 for nonmembers. Park capacity is approximately two hundred people per two-hour session.

Each park has operating costs of approximately $700,000 per year and revenue of approximately $3.3 million per year. Retail and concessions make up nearly half the park revenue. Approximately 10 percent of the park's customers visit more than once per week. Each park sells approximately 120,000 sessions per year. The

Vans Skatepark customer (ten- to twenty-year-old male) is almost identical to the younger Surfparks customer, an indication of customers' financial resources and willingness to spend these resources on their favorite pastime.

Golf Domes

Another operation worth examining is the Golden Bear Golf Dome near Albany, New York. The privately owned Golf Dome has a nearly identical physical structure to the proposed Surfparks facility. A large, air-supported dome houses an indoor driving range, and an attached permanent structure contains a restaurant, pro shop, and restrooms. The Golf Dome currently attracts 700 to 800 customers on weekdays and 1,300 to 1,400 customers on weekends. There are several dozen Golf Dome–type facilities in the northern United States and Canada. The success of these operations displays the viability of the dome-type structure. Air domes have proven themselves the most cost effective and aesthetically pleasing structure for indoor sports.

Marketing Plan

The goal of the Surfparks marketing plan is simple: to establish Surfparks as a viable and enjoyable supplement to the ocean wave-riding experience. There are several strategies to achieve this goal:

- Gain allegiance to Surfparks with the core target market (current active surfers/bodyboarders).
- Establish legitimacy of Surfparks through pro surfer endorsements.
- Foster development of new surfboard/bodyboard customers.
- Optimize access to a Surfparks facility, especially for younger (<17) customers.
- Promote the membership program.
- Maximize global exposure of Surfparks through a multichannel PR campaign.
- Gain global exposure to ready future markets for expansion.

An essential component to the marketing plan is Surfpark LLC's marketing partnership with the leading U.S. Surfing media properties: *Surfer Magazine, Surfing Magazine,* and Surfline/SWELL.com. This partnership gives Surfparks access to a highly targeted database of subscribers/Swell customers, exceeding 250,000 U.S. surfers.

As a part of this partnership, these media partners will provide a variety of marketing tools, including Internet and subscriber mailings for the Surfparks membership drive, ongoing Internet/mail/editorial promotions, and Web site hosting and design.

The marketing plan is divided into two parts: prelaunch and ongoing. The following is a summary of key components.

Prelaunch Marketing Activities

ISO "Initial Surf Offering" When the first shovel hits the dirt, an ISO (Initial Surf Offering) pamphlet will be sent out to a group of several thousand surf VIPs (Surfrider Foundation members, surf shop owners/employees, magazine subscribers). The pamphlet will present a thorough explanation of Surfparks and offer discounted memberships for those who sign up before the grand opening. The early membership also allows an individual to reserve optimum pool space before the general public gets a chance. There is no risk to ISO members. They will not pay membership dues until the park opens, and there is a satisfaction guarantee on the wave quality. Once the Surfpark opens, they will be billed monthly for their membership dues. The purpose of the ISO is to ensure that Surfparks is operating as close to capacity as possible from opening day onward.

Web Site/Construction Cam   To ensure customers that Surfparks is not a pipe dream, a construction cam on the Surfparks Web site will monitor the progress of park construction. Customers can watch from their computers as the park takes shape. The Web site will also allow users to make online reservations and purchase memberships. The site will provide a full explanation of the Surfparks concept, updated news stories, an e-mail/phone contact for further information, and a chat room to monitor public discussion and sentiment about the project.

Advertising   A kickoff advertising campaign will begin approximately two months after the ISO and four months before the grand opening. The campaign will run in all national surfing/bodyboarding magazines *(Surfing Magazine, Surfer Magazine, Bodyboarding Magazine, TWSurf Magazine)* in addition to the more specifically targeted *Eastern Surf Magazine.* Ads will also appear on more popular surf-related Web sites (SWELL.com, Surfinfo.com, Surfline.com). Poster-style ads will also appear in all surf shops within a three hundred-mile radius of the park. The ads will encourage membership, foster interaction via the Web site/cam, and promote the grand opening contest/party.

Press Conference   A press conference will be held prior to the grand opening at a major national surf trade show. Ideally the conference will include a live-remote hookup to the pool (via Web or "staged" videotape) with pro surfers in action. This builds credibility of Surfparks with the surf industry, increases media exposure, and establishes momentum for the grand opening contest/party.

Media Sneak Previews   To increase media exposure and buildup, select surf and mainstream media will be allowed to shoot photos and write "sneak preview" stories before the official park opening. Action Sports TV shows will also be contacted for the opportunity to film preopening activities.

Ongoing Marketing Activities
Web Site   Integrated into SWELL.com, the Surfparks Web site will continue to offer a live pool cam so surf sessions can be viewed remotely. The site will also offer a monthly calendar, listing special events and operation hours. Reservations can also be made online.

Possible humorous Web site features include a "Surf Forecast" (which is always the same, because it's a wave pool) and the ability to place bets (for fun) on the surfers. The best surfer in a session gets a "Web Surf Contest Winner" T-shirt or the like. Surfers could tell their friends/family that they'll be surfing at X o'clock, and they can log on, watch the action, and score their favorite surfer. Camera-shy surfers may also request the Web cam be turned off.

To increase Web site traffic, links to popular surf/sports-related Web sites (SWELL.com, Surfline.com, Surfinfo.com) will be purchased or traded.

Regional radio advertisements will also be scheduled, with an on-air "surf report" a possibility to promote Surfparks.

Lessons To attract new customers and increase retention, surfing and bodyboarding lessons will be available to all ability levels. Resident pros will teach private and group lessons. In addition, "guest pros" will also teach lessons during scheduled promotions. The lessons will be promoted through area surf shops and Surfparks' magazine/Web/local newspaper/radio advertising. The pool will have regularly scheduled "lesson blocks" used exclusively for lessons. Board rental and video analysis will be included as part of the program. A partnership with renowned women's surf instruction company Surf Divas is also being discussed, where a Surf Divas affiliate would be based at Surfparks.

SECTION 6
START-UP COSTS

The largest capital expenditures for a Surfparks facility will be for installation of the pool, reef, and wave-generation equipment. Wave machine/pool/filtration construction would comprise approximately two-thirds of the start-up costs. As an equity holder in Surfparks LLC, ADG/WaveTek is providing wave-related equipment at a small margin above cost and giving Surfparks exclusive rights to the technology.

Research on land and building costs has been conducted as well. Several specific properties, with favorable zoning and town/county support, have been identified in all three pilot locations. Land costs range from $125,000 to $850,000. Total start-up construction costs are highly dependent on how much utility, site work, and other infrastructure preparation would be required. For example, building the facility next to an existing water park, ski area, or other recreational facility could reduce start-up costs by up to $3 million compared to a stand-alone facility. Start-to-finish construction time would be approximately six months. A late spring/early summer opening would be preferred. Complete start-up capital requirements are outlined below. More specific costing data is available in the pro forma appendixes.

Construction	Cost (in $)
Land Acquisition (Incl. Legal/Permits)	500,000
Architecture & Engineering	250,000
General Conditions	180,620
Site Work	524,475
Landscape/Irrigation	50,000
Electric	286,500
Utilities	162,500
Parking Lot/Driveways	118,750
Fencing/Barriers	65,750
Wave Pool/Equipment Buildings	1,606,700
Wave-generation Equipment	1,160,000
Filtration/Misc.	255,000
Dome/Shelter	800,000
Variable Reef/Wall Padding	920,000
Main Building (Inc. Pier)	576,000
FF&E	250,000
Contingency	300,000
Total Start-up Construction	**$8,006,295**

These figures represent the estimate for a stand-alone facility requiring a significant amount of site work, utility, and infrastructure installation.

Surfparks LLC has secured financing to cover an aggressive marketing campaign leading up to the opening of the pilot facility.

SECTION 7
POOL USAGE AND CASH FLOW FORECAST

Based on the established pricing/membership structures, we have assembled a model to demonstrate the earnings before interest, taxes, and depreciation allowances (EBITDA) from the pool in a fiscal year at a Surfparks facility. Because members pay as low as $1 per wave and nonmembers pay as much as $2.50 per wave, revenue forecasts are highly dependent on the ratio of member uses to nonmember uses. Below is a sensitivity table that shows the forecast Year 1 (for the EBITDA) based on pool use ranging from 10 percent to 100 percent and average pool revenue per customer (twenty waves) of $37.50. This analysis also includes additional capacity gained from a water park location, where water park customers can purchase shorter half-hour sessions for $20.

Sensitivity Analysis

Pool Use	Year 1 EBITDA	Total Visits	Visits per Day
10%	(184,536)	21,384	59
15%	111,552	32,076	89
20%	407,639	42,768	119
25%	703,727	53,460	149
30%	999,814	64,152	178
35%	1,295,902	74,844	208
40%	1,591,989	85,536	238
45%	1,888,077	96,228	267
50%	2,184,164	106,920	297
55%	2,480,252	117,612	327
60%	2,776,339	128,304	356
65%	3,072,427	138,996	386
70%	3,368,514	149,688	416
75%	3,664,602	160,380	446
80%	3,960,689	171,072	475
85%	4,256,777	181,764	505
90%	4,552,865	192,456	535
95%	4,848,952	203,148	564
100%	5,145,040	213,840	594

As the table indicates, the EBITDA breakeven point lies between 10 percent and 15 percent use of the pool. This translates to about 25,000 individual pool uses per year, or 69 visits per day, based on 360 operating days per year. This is the equivalent to filling less than two full 36-surfer sessions per day. This attendance level is the equivalent of 1 in 30 southern California surfers attending one time per year.

By contrast, 100 percent use of the pool equals approximately 214,000 individual visits per year, or 594 visitors per day. Keep in mind that at full capacity, only 1 in 3 southern California surfers would need to attend once per year. Recall that Surfparks' market research revealed that 51 percent of the surveyed surfers would use a Surfpark once *per week.*

APPENDIX: THE ROADMAP GUIDE FOR WRITING A BUSINESS PLAN

The roadmap guide leads you through a detailed table of contents for preparing a business plan and a framework, which provides the guidelines for writing the sections in the plan. This business plan table of contents was developed by Clifford Schorer at Columbia Business School's Eugene M. Lang Center for Entrepreneurship. Schorer has more than fifteen years of experience working with students and venture capitalists in evaluating business plans. There is no one way to write a business plan, and there are many ways to approach the preparation for and the writing of a business plan. Entrepreneurs will probably find it necessary to research many areas before they have enough information to start writing. Most begin by collecting historical financial information about their company and/or industry and completing their market research before beginning to write any one part.

Initial drafts of proposed financial statements and projections are often prepared next, after the basic market research and analysis are completed. By preparing these statements, the entrepreneur knows which strategies will work from a financial perspective before investing many hours in writing a detailed description. Entrepreneurs should keep detailed notes on their assumptions so later they can include footnotes with their statements.

The business plan framework provides a three-step process to help identify ideas, issues, and research needed to complete the seven sections included in a business plan. The guide is based on the five-phase opportunity analysis described in Chapter 3 and assumes that you have completed preparing the marketing analysis and competition section in Chapter 4.

The following is a sample table of contents that details the eight sections for the business plan.

BUSINESS PLAN

Table of Contents

Section I. Executive Summary (usually 1–2 pages)

A. The Business Opportunity and Vision

B. The Market and Projections

C. The Competitive Advantages

D. The Management Team

E. The Offering

Section II. The Company, Industry, and Product(s) and/or Service(s)

A. The Company

B. The Industry

C. The Product(s) and/or Service(s)

D. The Growth Plan

Section III. Market Analysis

A. Market Size and Trends

B. Target Customers

C. Competition

Section IV. Marketing and Sales Plan

A. Marketing Strategy

B. Pricing

C. Sales Plan

D. Advertising and Promotion

E. Channels of Distribution

F. Operations Plan

Section V. Operating Plan

A. Product Development

B. Manufacturing Plan

C. Maintenance and Support

Section VI. Management Team

A. Organization Chart

B. Key Management Personnel

C. Policy and Strategy for Employees

D. Board of Directors

E. Advisory Board

Section VII. The Financial Plan

A. Actual Income Statements and Balance Sheets

B. Pro Forma Income Statements

C. Pro Forma Balance Sheets

D. Pro Forma Cash Flow Analysis

Section VIII. Funds Required and Uses

A. Financial Required

B. Amounts, Timing, and Terms

C. Use of Funds—Capital Expenditures, Working Capital

Appendixes

Financial Data Assumptions

Exhibits and Appendixes

BUSINESS PLAN FRAMEWORK

The following framework and worksheets will assist entrepreneurs in preparing and writing their business plans by helping them gather their ideas, list the research needed, and identify issues and questions they must address in the key sections in the plan.

Step 1. Business Plan Preparation

Step 2. Business Plan Worksheet

Step 3. Business Plan Financial Planning

The worksheets can also be downloaded from the Web site www.wiley.com/college/kaplan. Entrepreneurs can review the business plans on the Web site to determine the worksheet that best fits their individual needs.

Step 1. Business Plan Preparation

The business plan preparation framework identifies the market need, competitive advantages, management team, and growth guidelines that should be emphasized in the plan.

Guidelines	List	Questions

1. Focus on Market-Driven Opportunities

- Demonstrate how product/service meets market needs for the venture.
- Establish the size of the market for the product or service, and define the specific buyers.
- Analyze the competition and the competitive environment.

2. Stress Competitive Advantages

- Demonstrate the distinct competence that the business will provide.
- How substantial is your advantage in the marketplace?

Step 1. Business Plan Preparation (*Continued*)

Guidelines	List	Questions

3. Describe the Management Team

- List the talents, skills, and experience of the management team.
- List how the team will be retained and what incentives will be provided for employees.

4. Support Projections for Growth

- Analyze the market structure and industry.
- Identify the growth rate for the product or service.
- Validate the results of your research by showing the total revenue expended for the business and the total number of current and potential customers.

Step 2. Business Plan Worksheet

The business plan worksheet details helpful tips, research needed, and further questions that need to be addressed. The following are tips to help the entrepreneur get started and make the writing of the business plan easier:

Guidelines	List	Questions

1. Executive Summary

- Make sure that the executive summary isn't more than three pages long.
- Make sure that the executive summary captures the reader's interest.
- Quickly and concisely establish what, how, why, where, when, and so on.
- Complete the executive summary after all other sections have been written.

2. Company Overview Section

- Describe the business's name.
- Include background of the industry as well as a brief history of the company.
- Define the potential of the new venture, and list key customers, major products, and applications.
- Spell out any unique or distinctive features of the venture.

3. Marketing Analysis Section

- Convince investors that sales projections can be met.
- Use and disclose market studies.
- Identify a target market and market share.
- Evaluate all competition and specifically explain why and how this business will be better than the competition.
- Describe the pricing strategy that will be used to penetrate and maintain a market share.
- Identify advertising plans with cost estimates to validate the proposed strategy.

Step 2. Business Plan Worksheet (*Continued*)

Guidelines	List	Questions

4. Marketing and Sales Plan Section

- Describe the features and benefits of the services or products.
- Describe in detail the current stage of development.

5. Research, Design, and Development Segment Section

- State the costs involved in research, testing, and development.
- Explain carefully what has already been accomplished (prototype, lab testing, early development, and so on).
- Mention any research or technical assistance that has been provided.

6. Operations Segment Section

- Describe the advantages of the business's location (such as zoning, tax laws, and wage rates).
- List the production needs in terms of facilities (plant, storage, office space) and equipment (machinery, furnishings, supplies).
- Describe the access to transportation (for shipping and receiving).
- Explain the proximity to the business's suppliers.
- Describe the availability of labor in the business's location.

7. Management Section

- Provide résumés or curricula vitae of all key management personnel.
- Carefully describe the legal structure (sole proprietorship, partnership, S-corporation, LLC, or C-corporation) of the business.
- Describe any expected added assistance by advisors, consultants, and directors.
- Provide information on current ownership and options for an exit strategy such as selling the business or going public.

Step 3. Business Plan Financial Planning

Guidelines	List	Questions

1. Financial Section

- Convince investors that the business makes sense from a financial standpoint.
- Prepare three- to five-year financial projections.
- Prepare first-year projections by month.
- Prepare second-year projections by quarter.
- Include an income statement and balance sheet.
- Include a cash flow statement for years 1 and 2.
- Include a three-year annual forecast.

Step 3. Business Plan Financial Planning (*Continued*)

Guidelines	List	Questions

2. Selling the Plan
- Prepare financial presentation.
- Seek assistance of *outside* experts.
- Identify funding sources.
- Schedule meeting for funding.
- Get started and introductions.

INTERACTIVE LEARNING ON THE WEB

Test your knowledge of the chapter using the book's interactive Web site.

ADDITIONAL RESOURCES

- **Biz Plan Software,**   www.jian.com
- **Biz Women,**   www.bizwomen.com
- **Business Plans,**   www.bplans.com
- **Business Plans Made Easy,**   www.entrepreneur.com
- **Entrepreneurship,**   www.entrepreneurship.com
- **Small Business Advancement National Center,**   http://sbaer.uca.edu
- **Student Guide to Business Presentations,**   www.ideapitch.smeal.psu.edu

www.wiley.com/college/kaplan

ROADMAP for
PATTERNS OF ENTREPRENEURSHIP
Getting Started as an Entrepreneur

- ☐ An Entrepreneurial Perspective
- ☐ Commonly Shared Entrepreneurial Characteristics
- ☐ Types of Entrepreneurs
- ☐ The Need to Control
- ☐ Entrepreneurship Roller Coaster
- ☐ So Why Become an Entrepreneur?
- ☐ The Spiderweb Model
- ☐ Finding Early Mentors
- ☐ Managing Stress
- ☐ The Five-stage Entrepreneurial Process
- ☐ The Growth of Entrepreneurial Companies
- ☐ The Growth Period
- ☐ Why Innovation Is Important
- ☐ Definition and Types of Innovation
- ☐ Frameworks for Learning Innovation Skills
- ☐ Finding and Assessing Ideas
- ☐ Converting an Idea into an Opportunity
- ☐ Opportunity: Five Phases to Success
- ☐ Formulating a Successful Marketing Plan
- ☐ Preparing the Marketing Analysis and Plan
- ☐ Defining the Market Segmentation
- ☐ Conducting a Competitive Analysis
- ☐ Preparing the Pricing and Sales Strategy
- ☐ Penetrating the Market and Setting up Sales Channels
- ☐ The Value of a Business Plan
- ☐ Setting Goals and Objectives
- ☐ Starting the Process to Write the Plan: Five Steps
- ☐ Determining What Type of Business Plan Is Best
- ☐ A Typical Business Plan Format and Content
- ☐ Understanding Why Business Plans Fail
- ☑ Identifying What Form of Ownership Is Best
- ☑ Forms of Doing Business
- ☑ Sole Proprietorship
- ☑ C-corporation
- ☑ S-corporation
- ☑ Partnership
- ☑ Limited Liability Company
- ☑ Business Start-up Checklist

CHAPTER 6
SETTING UP THE COMPANY

"The ladder of success doesn't care who climbs it."

FRANK TYGER

OBJECTIVES

- Assess the factors in deciding which form of ownership is best suited for a potential business.
- Outline the advantages and disadvantages of a sole proprietorship and partnership.
- Explain the corporate form of ownership and describe how a business is incorporated.
- Understand the S-corporation and the limited liability company (LLC).
- Understand how to register a business with government entities.
- Learn how to choose an attorney.

CHAPTER OUTLINE

Introduction

Profile: Ethan Wendle and Matt Chverchko—When to Convert from an S- to a C-corporation

Identifying What Form of Ownership Is Best

Forms of Doing Business

Sole Proprietorship

C-corporation

S-corporation

Partnership

Limited Liability Company

Business Start-up Checklist

Summary

Study Questions

Exercises

Interactive Learning on the Web

INTRODUCTION

Some entrepreneurs start businesses and determine the structure of the company with lots of thought and planning. Others find themselves establishing a company without much regard to how the business should be structured. However, one of the most important decisions to make is how to legally structure a business.[1]

Before deciding how to organize a company, the entrepreneur needs to identify the legal structure that will best meet the requirements of the business. This is due to the tax laws, liability situation, and ways to attract capital.

Many companies provide added incentives for keeping key employees by offering an ownership or equity interest in the company. This is usually in the form

127

of common stock or options to acquire common stock. In Chapter 12 we will discuss in some detail how companies should establish a qualified stock option plan and how selected employees receive options to purchase stock in the company.

The legal form of the business—sole proprietorship, C-corporation, S-corporation, partnership, or LLC—should be determined in light of the business's short- and long-term needs. In this chapter we will examine the pros and cons of each of these forms and how to prepare a checklist to start the business. The entrepreneur's specific situation, circumstances, and issues will determine the choice.

PROFILE: ETHAN WENDLE AND MATT CHVERCHKO[2]—WHEN TO CONVERT FROM AN S- TO A C-CORPORATION

Matt and Ethan met while still undergraduate students in Penn State's College of Engineering, Matt specializing in mechanical and Ethan in civil engineering. Matt is an avid hunter and realized that there was a need for hunters to have a dual carrying capability with their pickup trucks— a lockable section for valuable equipment and a large load carrying area for hauling large game, ATVs, or other equipment. To meet this need, he designed a unique truck cover that could be retrofitted onto existing trucks, and the prototype won the "best product" award in his class's final year design competition. Based on this success, Matt and Ethan decided to start a company and formed Diamondback Truck Accessories Inc. (www.diamondbackcovers.com) as an S-corporation in 2003 ready to sell their first commercial product. The S structure was chosen for simplicity and provided the founders the advantage of a single taxation level. Word of mouth soon created a demand for the company's products, and they turned to friends and family to help out with cash in the form of a 20 percent membership interest for Ethan's father coupled with a small loan. The partners also received $140,000 from the Ben Franklin Technology Partnership, an economic development agency in Pennsylvania, and other help from the commonwealth for locating in a targeted development region in Clearfield. In 2005 the company received its first patent (6883855) and substantially expanded its manufacturing facilities.

As the company grew and moved into new, larger markets such as off-road vehicle transportation systems and building contractors, it needed more working capital. Using their links to Penn State, the founders approached the student-managed Garber Venture Fund, which agreed to invest $350,000 in two stages in the form of a convertible preferred class of stock. However, this created a problem for the university in two regards. First, as a public nonprofit entity, the university cannot participate in a structure that would provide it possible tax advantages. Second, membership in an S-corporation may, under certain situations, imply a liability on its members; in any case, the university could participate at only full-arm's length as a passive investor, not even taking a board seat. The Diamondback board decided to convert to a C status, even though this removed the personal tax advantages for the founders, required a forfeit of tax losses carried forward, and required badly needed cash for the legal fees to make the changes. However, the long-term aim of the company is to create an exit for its shareholders, which will be easier under a C-corporation umbrella. In 2007 the company posted its first profitable year and growth of more than 35 percent. Over 2007 and 2008, the company has established itself as a major industry player in truck cover manufacturing and has procured key partnerships with many large industry leaders including A.R.E., LINE-X, and HUMMER. As the company has continued to grow, so have its financial and corporate structures needed to grow and change. While an S-corp or LLC may have suited the small start-up firm, the C-corp status positions the company for future merger or acquisition opportunities and better reflects the current size of the business.

IDENTIFYING WHAT FORM OF OWNERSHIP IS BEST

In choosing a form of ownership, entrepreneurs must remember that there is no single "best" form; what is best depends on the individual's circumstances. To determine the form of ownership, be prepared to address the following issues.[3]

- How big can this business potentially become?
- How much control do you need in the decision-making process of the company? Are you willing to share ideas and the business's potential profits with others who can help build a more successful business?
- How much capital is needed to start the business?
- What tax considerations are important? What sources of income are there, and how are they to be sheltered?
- In case of failure, to what extent are you willing to be personally responsible for debts created by the business?
- Is it important that the business continue in case of owner incapacity or death?
- Who will be the sole or major beneficiary of the business success? Is the owner the type of person who doesn't mind taking all the risks but expects to reap all the benefits if successful?
- Can you put up with the time-consuming bureaucratic red tape associated with more complicated forms of ownership? What is your emotional reaction to government regulations and their accompanying paperwork requirements?

FORMS OF DOING BUSINESS

The legal form of business (sole proprietorship, C-corporation, S-corporation, partnership, or LLC) should be carefully considered to ensure that the form chosen best meets the short and long term requirements as well as the significant tax and non-tax differences. A brief analysis of each form is presented. Because there are significant tax and nontax differences among the forms, the results and requirements of each form should be carefully considered to ensure that the business form chosen best meets the requirements.

SOLE PROPRIETORSHIP

A sole proprietorship is a form of business in which a single owner does business himself or herself and requires only a business license to open. If the plan is to operate a business under a name other than that of the owner, the business name must be filed as a "doing business as" registration with a state and/or local filing authority (e.g., Jack Smith doing business as Jack's SmartCard Consulting). The business can be terminated at any time and always ends with the death of the owner.

The sole owner has the right to make all the decisions for the business. However, the owner is personally liable for all debts and contracts of the business. Because there is no distinction between personal and business debts, if the business cannot pay its bills, the creditors can sue to collect from the owner's personal assets. In matters dealing with taxes, profits and losses from the business flow directly to the owner and are taxed at individual income tax rates on the owner's personal tax return. If the owner does not plan to take a salary, income is the profits of the business. There is no carryback or carryforward of losses for tax-reporting purposes.

Advantages of a Sole Proprietorship

Sole proprietorships are popular because they have a number of attractive features:[4]

- *Simple to Initiate Business.* One of the most attractive features of sole proprietorships is how fast and simple it is to begin operations. If a proprietor wishes to operate the business under his or her own name, one simply obtains the necessary license(s), if any, and begins operations. In a sole proprietorship, the proprietor is the business. It is not difficult to start up a proprietorship in a single day if the business is simple.

- *Low Start-up Fees.* In addition to being easy to begin, the proprietorship is generally the least expensive form of ownership to establish. Legal papers do not need to be created to start the business. Rather, if required, the proprietor goes to the appropriate state and/or county government office and states the nature of the new business in his or her license application. The government assesses the appropriate fees and license costs. Once these fees are paid, the owner is allowed to conduct business.

  If the proprietorship is to do business under a trade name, a Certificate of Doing Business under an Assumed Name must be filed with the state and/or county in which the business will operate. The fee for filing the certificate is usually nominal. Acquiring this certificate involves conducting a name search of previously filed names to determine that the name to be used is not already registered as the name of another business or as a trademark or service mark for another business.

Entrepreneurs have a number of legal forms of business to choose from, including sole proprietorship, C-corporation, S-corporation, partnership, or LLC. Entrepreneurs should determine which business form is best for their short- and long-term needs. In choosing a form of ownership, entrepreneurs must remember that there is no single "best" form; what is best depends on the individual's circumstances.

- *Profit Incentive.* One major advantage of the proprietorship is that after all the debts are paid, the owner receives all the profits (less taxes, of course). Profits represent an excellent scorecard of success.

- *Total Decision-making Authority.* Because the sole proprietor is in total control of operations and can respond quickly to changes, this becomes an asset in rapidly shifting markets. The freedom to set the company's course of action is another major motivation for selecting this ownership form. For the individual who thrives on the enjoyment of seeking new opportunities and modifies the business as needed, the free, unimpeded decision making of the sole proprietorship is a must.

- *No Special Legal Restrictions.* The proprietorship is the least regulated form of business ownership. In a time when government requests for information seem never ending, this feature has much merit.

- *Easy to Discontinue.* When an owner cannot continue operations, he or she can terminate the business quickly, even though such persons will still be liable for all outstanding debts and obligations of the business.

Disadvantages of a Sole Proprietorship

As advantageous as the sole proprietorship form of ownership is, it does have its disadvantages:

- *Unlimited Personal Liability.* The greatest disadvantage of a sole proprietorship is unlimited personal liability; that is, the sole proprietor is personally liable for all business debts. The proprietor owns all the assets of the business. If the business fails, these assets can be sold to cover debts. If there are still unpaid debts, creditors can seize and sell the owner's personal assets to cover the remaining debts. Failure of the business can ruin the owner financially. Because the law views the proprietor and the business as one and the same, the debts of the business are considered the owner's personal debts. Laws protecting an individual's personal assets to some degree may vary from one state to another. Most states require creditors to leave the failed business owner a minimum amount of equity in a home, a car, and some personal items. The new Federal Bankruptcy Law protects retirement assets from creditors. Bankruptcy or other insolvency protection may be needed to protect a failed business owner. Because laws vary, picking the proper jurisdiction in which to do business is critical.

- *Limited Skills and Capabilities of the Sole Owner.* The owner may not have the needed skills to run a successful business. Each individual has skills and talents reflective of education, training, and work experience. However, the lack of skills and knowledge in other areas is what often causes failure. If an owner is not familiar with an area such as finance, accounting, or law, he or she will tend to gloss over these areas, thinking that they do not seriously impact his or her business or that this is a way to save money by ignoring these services even when needed. The sole owner who fails may have been successful if he or she had had previous knowledge of possible problems in one or more of these areas and had obtained good, timely advice. Sole owners need to recognize their shortcomings and find help in those areas in which they are not proficient.

- *Limited Access to Capital.* For a business to grow and expand, a sole proprietor generally needs financial resources. Many proprietors put all they have into their businesses and often use their personal resources as collateral on existing loans. In short, proprietors, unless they have great personal wealth, find it difficult to raise additional money while maintaining sole ownership. The business may be sound in the long run, but short-term cash flow difficulties can cause financial headaches. Most banks and lending institutions have well-defined formulas for borrower's eligibility. As a result, a proprietor may not be able to obtain the funds needed to operate the business, especially in difficult times.

- *Lack of Continuity for the Business.* Lack of continuity is inherent in a sole proprietorship. If the proprietor dies or becomes incapacitated, the business automatically terminates. Unless a family member or employee can effectively take over, the business could be in jeopardy. If no one is trained to run the business, creditors can petition the courts to liquidate the assets of the dissolved business and the estate of the proprietor to pay outstanding debts.

C-CORPORATION

The C-corporation is the most common form of business ownership. A corporation is a separate legal entity apart from its owners and may engage in business, issue contracts, sue and be sued, and pay taxes. The owners of a corporation hold stock in the corporation. Each share of stock represents a percentage of ownership. The actual business of the corporation is conducted by the directors and officers of the corporation.

When a corporation is founded, it accepts the regulations and restrictions of the state in which it is incorporated and of each state in which it does business. Corporations doing business in the state in which they are incorporated are domestic corporations. When they conduct business in another state, that state considers them to be foreign corporations. Corporations that are formed in other countries but do business in the United States are alien corporations. Where and how a corporation does business has an impact on its ability to operate and its tax liability. Also, a corporation may be taxed in every jurisdiction where it is incorporated or doing business.

Generally, the corporation must annually file in its state of incorporation and in every state in which it is doing business. These reports become public record. If the corporation's stock is sold in more than one state, the corporation must comply with federal and state regulations governing the sale of corporate securities.[5] For most small businesses, the selling of stock will not involve registering the stock as a security. However, the law may require the filing of reports showing a registration exemption.

A corporation has three primary sections: the stockholders, the board of directors, and the officers. It is important to understand the specific functions of each section.

The stockholders are the owners of the business.

When a corporation is established, its equity is divided among a number of shares of stock that are issued to the investors in proportion to their investment in the corporation. A general protocol for the company's operations, called the "by-laws," is adopted by the stockholders. Sometimes these by-laws can be amended or changed by the board of directors, sometimes by only the stockholders. The ultimate power and control of every corporation lies in the hands of the stockholders.

The board of directors has responsibility for the overall operation of the company.

The stockholders elect the board and have the power to remove board members. The board establishes the general policies of the company and, to a greater or lesser extent depending on the particular corporation, can become involved in various details of the operating procedures. The board of directors elects the officers of the corporation to handle the day-to-day affairs.

The usual officers in a corporation are president, secretary (or "clerk" in some states), and treasurer.

The functions of each officer are defined by the board of directors. The president is in charge of day-to-day operations under the directives of the board of directors. The secretary is charged with handling the paperwork of the corporation, such as preparing minutes of stockholder and directors' meetings, sending out notices, and preparing stock certificates. The treasurer is charged with guardianship of the corporate finances. However, there are differences in the functions of the officers among different corporations.

Additional officers may include vice presidents, who are sometimes charged with a specific aspect of operations such as engineering, finance, production, or sales. There may also be assistants for each of the offices, such as assistant secretary and assistant treasurer.

You do not need the services of an attorney to set up and maintain a corporation. The days when a corporation was a rigid structure with reams of rules for the precise keeping of records and holdings of meetings are gone. The various states have revised the corporate laws to allow great flexibility in creating and maintaining a corporation. Nevertheless, if you wish to have the benefits offered by a corporation, you must treat the business as a corporation, not as a proprietorship. We'll say more about this presently.

The specific requirements for forming a corporation vary from state to state. The easiest way to start is to request information and forms from the office of your local secretary of state. This will tell you the fees and generally how to prepare the papers for filing.

What State to Register In

Delaware is a popular state for incorporation, so we will use that as a practical example.[6] If you are not a resident of Delaware, you must have an agent in the state who is empowered to accept service in the event the corporation is sued. In other words, if you incorporate in a particular state, the corporation can be sued in that state even if you conduct no other activities there. Such agents represent the corporation for a relatively modest annual fee. A list of acceptable agents in Delaware can be obtained by writing to the Department of State, Division of Corporations, P.O. Box 898, Dover, DE 19901. Similar lists for other states are available from the secretary of state in that state. After obtaining the list of agents, you can then write to them to inquire about their annual fees and the "extra" fees for performing additional special functions.

After selecting a local agent, the next step is to select the corporate name. The name must include an indication that the entity is a corporation. In many states you could not, for example, call your corporation "The SMITH Company." You could call it "The SMITH Company, Inc." or "the SMITH Company Corp." You should find out just what corporate indicators are required in your state of incorporation. In Delaware the permitted corporate indicators are *Association, Club, Company, Corporation, Foundation, Fund, Incorporated, Institute, Limited, Society, Syndicate, Union,* and any of these abbreviations: *Co., Corp., Inc.,* or *Ltd.*

You can ask your agent to check on the availability of the name; this can usually be done by telephone. If the name is available, it can be reserved for thirty days without charge. "Availability" means that no other corporation has a prior registration of the same name or one sufficiently similar that it might cause confusion. If

"SMITH Incorporated" is already incorporated in your state, you cannot use the name "SMITH" even if you change the other parts of the name. You can still incorporate in another state where the name has not been used, but this is not likely to be a practical solution because before a foreign corporation (a corporation formed in another state) can do business in your state, it must register there as a foreign corporation. This will not be permitted if another local or foreign corporation has the same or a confusingly similar name.

The next step is to prepare the Certificate of Incorporation (sometimes the Articles of Incorporation). The following is a typical form ready for forwarding to the agent, along with the filing fee and the first annual charge for the agent:

> "To raise capital for early-stage companies, a C-corporation is preferred and provides the most flexible structures for various rounds of private equity investments."
>
> MICHAEL BUCHEIST
> *Managing Partner, Advanced Infrastructure Ventures*

CERTIFICATE OF INCORPORATION OF SMITH INCORPORATED

A Corporation

First: The name of this corporation is SMITH Incorporated

Second: Its registered office in the State of Delaware is to be located at (here insert the address of the Delaware agent you have selected). The name of the registered agent is (name of registered agent).

Third: The nature of the business, and the objects and purposes proposed to be transacted and carried on, are to engage in any lawful act or activity for which corporations may be organized under the General Corporation Law of Delaware.

Fourth: The amount of total authorized capital stock of the corporation is divided into 3,000 shares of no-par common (the maximum number of shares with minimum tax).

Fifth: The name and address of the incorporator is:
Jane Vista
345 Boulder
Austin, TX 29555

Sixth: The powers of the incorporator are to terminate upon the filing of the Certificate of Incorporation. The name and mailing addresses of the persons who are to serve as directors until their successors are elected are as follows:
Jane Vista
345 Boulder
Austin, TX 29555

Seventh: All of the issued stock of the corporation, exclusive of treasury shares, shall be held of record of not more than thirty (30) persons.

Eighth: All of the issued stock of all classes shall be subject to the following restriction on transfer permitted by Section 202 of the General Corporation Law.

Ninth: The corporation shall make no offering of any of its stock of any class which would constitute a "public offering" within the meaning of the United States Securities Act of 1933, as amended.

Tenth: Directors of the corporation shall not be liable to either the corporation or to its stockholders for monetary damages for a breach of fiduciary duties unless the breach involves: (1) a director's duty of loyalty to the corporation or its stockholders; (2) acts or omissions not in good faith or which involve intentional misconduct or a knowing violation of law; (3) liability for unlawful payments of dividends or unlawful stock purchases or redemption by the corporation; or (4) a transaction from which the director derived an improper personal benefit.

> ## CERTIFICATE OF INCORPORATION OF SMITH INCORPORATED (cont.)
>
> I, the undersigned, for the purpose of forming a corporation under the laws of the state of Delaware do make, file, and record this Certificate, and do certify that the facts stated herein are true and I have accordingly set my hand.
> Dated:
> _____ Incorporator

Corporate Stock

The ownership of a corporation lies in the stockholders and is evidenced by stock certificates issued to the shareholders. There may be several classes of stock. The most usual is no-par-value common stock. Common stock most often has voting power equal to one vote per share. However, there may be more than one class of common stock. For example, a Class A stock may have voting rights, while Class B stockholders own, say, 95 percent of the corporation, but the entire corporation is controlled by the 5 percent of the outstanding stock held by the Class A stockholders.

A specific number of shares of each class are authorized in the Articles of Incorporation, and more than that amount may not be issued without first amending them. Provision may be made for converting one class of stock into another. For example, Class B stock might be convertible, at the option of the holder, into Class A stock on a share-for-share basis or any other specified ratio.

Another class of stock is called "preferred" because it usually has a preferred position with respect to dividends or receiving distributions should the company go into bankruptcy. More about different classes of stock is covered in Chapter 8.

There is great flexibility in establishing classes of stock, voting rights, and rights to dividends, so you can tailor your corporation to best meet the needs of your particular situation.

"Par value" is an archaic concept that is still applied to stocks; it is the monetary value assigned to each share of stock in the Articles of Incorporation. Such stock must be issued for an amount of money, or other property, equal to at least the par value of the stock. If par value stock is issued by the corporation without such remuneration, the stockholder could be liable to creditors for the difference between the par value and the amount actually paid. Once the stock is issued, the par value of the stock bears no relationship to its actual value. "No par value" common stock has no stated valuation in the corporate charter. In practical terms, the difference between par-value stock and no-par-value stock lies in the tax area. In some states, as in Delaware, the corporate tax may be less for par-value stock than for no-par-value stock.

Taxes

Annual taxes are usually based on the number of shares of authorized stock and on whether the stock has a par value. Currently in Delaware, the minimum annual tax on a company with 500,000 shares of authorized no-par-value common stock is almost $1,770.55. If the stock has a par value, the minimum tax on the same amount of par-value stock may be as little as $40.00. Before sending in your annual corporate tax to the state of incorporation, read the tax law carefully because the rules can be somewhat misleading. Delaware, for example, sends the company with 500,000 shares of authorized stock having a par value of $0.01 per share an official notice in which the tax is calculated as $1,770.55. The busy businessperson might just send a check for the full amount. However, the fine print on subsequent pages of the tax notice describes a rather complex method of computing an alternate tax based on the assets of the corporation. If the corporation has few assets, the actual tax due may be only the minimum of $40.00. If you inadvertently pay the larger sum to the state of Delaware, you can, with some red tape, likely recover the overpayment.

Shares Authorized and Issued

The number of shares you will want to authorize depends on the particular circumstances. Suppose only one or a few people are to be stockholders, then 10 or 100 shares might be sufficient. Usually, some number of shares can be authorized at the minimum tax rate. In Delaware it is 3,000. The maximum might as well be authorized, so if needed in the future, additional shares can be issued without amending the Certificate of Incorporation.

There may be other reasons for authorizing more shares. If a corporation, for example, intends to issue stock options available to its employees or executives and has only 100 shares issued, an employee getting an option for an amount of stock representing 1 percent ownership of the company receives an option for one share, which doesn't sound like much. If the ownership of the corporation is represented by 2 million shares, then 1 percent ownership is represented by 20,000 shares. There is, of course, no difference, but many individuals may not be aware of that. Even if one does know the difference, one might still rather show 100,000 shares in her portfolio than only one.

Issued Shares

Issued shares are the stock that a company sells to investors to generate capital. It also includes stock given to insiders as part of their compensation packages. Shares that are held as treasury stock, are not included in this figure. The amount of issued shares can be all or part of the total amount of authorized shares of a corporation.

The total number of issued shares outstanding in a company is most often shown in the annual report.

Advantages of a C-corporation

- *Limited Liability of the Stockholders.* The corporation allows investors to limit their liability to the total amount of their investment in the corporation if they adhere to the terms of the Certificate of Incorporation and by-laws. A corporation cannot just be set up and run as if it were a sole proprietorship. Business must be conducted in the name of the board of directors through the officers using books and records separate from those of the shareholders. This legal protection of personal assets beyond the business is of critical concern to many potential investors. Because start-up companies are so risky, lenders and other creditors often require the owners to personally guarantee loans made to the corporation. By making these guarantees, owners are putting their personal assets at risk (just as in a sole proprietorship), despite choosing the corporate form of ownership. However, it is possible to limit the scope of a guaranty so not all assets of a person may be at risk.

- *Ability to Attract Capital.* Based on the protection of limited liability, the corporation has proved to be the most effective form of ownership to accumulate large amounts of capital. Limited by only the number of shares authorized in its charter (which can be amended) and subject to the laws on registration of securities, the corporation can raise money to begin business and expand as opportunity dictates. Professional or "institutional" investors such as venture capitalists (Chapter 8) demand this form of incorporation.

- *Ability of the Corporation to Continue Indefinitely.* Unless limited by its charter, the corporation as a separate legal entity theoretically can continue indefinitely. The existence of the corporation does not depend on any single individual.

- *Transferable Ownership.* If stockholders in a corporation are displeased with the progress of the business, they can sell their shares to another individual, subject to only restrictions on transfer of shares. Stocks can be transferred through inheritance to a new generation of owners. If any person wishes to own some shares in a firm and there is someone who would like to sell his or her interest in that firm, an exchange is possible. During all this change of ownership, the business continues.

- *Skills, Expertise, and Knowledge.* Unlike the sole proprietor who is often the only active member of management, the corporation can draw on the skills, expertise, and knowledge of its officers and board of directors and people whose knowledge and experience can be used to shape the direction of the firm. In many cases the board members act as advisers, giving the stockholders the advantage of their years of experience.

Disadvantages of a C-corporation

- *Cost and Time Involved in the Incorporation Process.* Corporations can be costly and time consuming to establish. The owners are creating an artificial legal entity, and the start-up period can be prolonged for the novice. In some states an attorney must handle the incorporation, but in most cases entrepreneurs can complete the requirements. However, the complexity of the requirements leads many entrepreneurs to employ an attorney even in states where one is not required so one does not go afoul of the legal and registration requirements. Failure to properly register and follow the corporate form may cause loss of the ability to limit shareholder liability.

- *Double Taxation.* Corporations are taxed on their profits. Rates range up to 35 percent. In addition, when shareholders are distributed profit in the form of a dividend, taxes on the dividend up to 35 percent may be incurred.

SETTING UP A C-CORPORATION

SUMMARY OF PROS AND CONS

- Separate legal and tax entity
- Shareholder liability limited to invested capital
- Existence continues after shareholder's death
- Easier to raise equity capital

SETTING UP A C-CORPORATION (cont.)

PROS

- Limited liability
- Most appropriate structure for an IPO
- Tax benefits such as loss carryforwards and easy-to-set-up stock option plans
- Ease of transferability of interests
- Structure that a venture capitalist requires

CONS

- Double taxation
- High administration compliance costs
- Directors held accountable
- Well-defined corporate governance rules and laws to follow

ROADMAP

IN ACTION

Corporations offer limited liability to the owner, which means owners cannot be sued for the debts of the business unless they have personally guaranteed those debts. Therefore, the potential loss for owners is limited to the capital they have invested.

S-CORPORATION

The S-corporation, often referred to as a sub-S corporation, is a corporation that elects under federal and state tax laws to be taxed like a partnership. Its profits and losses are recognized for tax purposes at the individual shareholder level. It is the shareholder's responsibility to report the profits or losses on his or her individual income tax returns. To become an S-corporation, the following must occur:[7]

- The company must be a domestic company.
- Only one class of stock is allowed.
- Only individuals and certain trusts may own stock.
- Shareholders cannot be nonresident aliens.
- There can be a maximum of only 100 shareholders.
- The shareholders must elect to become an S-corporation at the federal and state levels.

Advantages of an S-corporation

The S-corporation retains all the advantages of a regular corporation, such as continuity of existence, transferability of ownership, and limited personal liability. The most notable provision of the S-corporation is that it avoids the corporate income tax (and the resulting double taxation) and enables the business to pass operating profits or losses on to shareholders. In effect, the tax status of an S-corporation is similar to that of a sole proprietorship or partnership.

Entrepreneur Fanny Chin, who launched Creative Calendar in 1998 as an S-corporation, maintains that form of ownership today. "Since there were no shareholders except me, I didn't see any advantage to C-corporation status since my earnings would have been taxed twice."

Disadvantages of an S-corporation

An S-corporation has restrictions on use of its losses and tax recognition on sales of its assets different from those of a C-corporation. These may be disadvantages to the owners. Thus, although one may face double taxation as a C-corporation, the loss of flexibility on the sale of assets or stock of the corporation may require one to remain a C-corporation and ultimately gain the most profit upon the sale of a business. In addition, if the entrepreneur's intention is to raise capital from third parties, such as venture capitalists, the company will have to be restructured into a C-corporation before this can occur.

SETTING UP AN S-CORPORATION

SUMMARY OF PROS AND CONS

- Corporation but with "flow through" tax benefits
- Limited liability for owners and stockholders
- Limited to only 100 owners, one class of stock, and domestic shareholders

PROS

- Offers liability protection
- Enjoys corporation status, but owners pay the taxes

CONS

- Stringent rules to maintain S-corporation status; breaking them can lead to disastrous tax consequences
- Qualification requirements necessitate administrative and cost burdens
- Not eligible for qualified employee stock options
- Investors cannot receive preferred shares, as in a C-corporation

When Is the S-corporation a Wise Choice?

Choosing the S-corporation status is usually beneficial to start-up companies anticipating net losses and to highly profitable firms with substantial dividends to pay out to shareholders. In these cases the owner can use the loss to offset other income, or the owner is personally in a lower tax bracket than the corporation, thus saving money in the long run.

Small companies with the following characteristics, however, are not likely to benefit from S-corporation status:

- Highly profitable personal service companies with large numbers of shareholders, in which most of the profits are passed on to shareholders as compensation or retirement benefits
- Corporations in which the loss of fringe benefits to shareholders exceeds tax savings
- Corporations with sizable net operating losses that cannot be used against S-corporation earnings

PARTNERSHIP

A partnership is usually defined as an association of two or more people carrying on as co-owners of a business for profit. There are typically two types of partnerships. The first type, a general partnership, requires that each partner participate in all profits and losses equally or to some previously agreed upon ratio. Normally, a general partner has unlimited liability, which includes personally owned assets outside the business association. A partnership can be created either by a formal agreement or an oral understanding. In addition, it must be banded together for profit-producing motives and is generally not considered a legal entity separate from the partners. A general partnership may not sue or be sued in the firm's name. Each partner shares potential "joint and several" liabilities.

The second type of partnership, a limited partnership, limits the liability of the partners to the extent of their capital contributions. A limited partnership must have at least one general partner so at least one person or entity's personal assets must be at stake. In many instances the general partner is a corporation so only the corporate assets are at stake.[8]

Advantages of a Partnership

- *(General Partnership) Easy to Establish.* Like the sole proprietorship, the general partnership is easy and inexpensive to establish. The partners must obtain the necessary business license and submit a minimal number of forms. In most states, partners must file a Certificate for Conducting Business as Partners if the business is run under a trade name. Limited partnerships require registration to be official.
- *Complementary Skills of Partners.* In a sole proprietorship, the owner must wear many different hats, and not all of them will fit well. In successful partnerships the parties' skills usually complement one another. For example, one partner in a software firm says, "My co-owner provides the vision, energy, and enthusiasm needed in a deal situation. I am more negative and careful. Together we're a solid team."
- *Division of Profits.* There are no restrictions on how profits must be distributed as long as they are consistent with the partnership agreement and do not violate the rights of any partner.
- *Larger Pool of Capital.* The partnership form of ownership can significantly broaden the pool of capital available to the business. Each partner's asset base

improves the ability of the business to borrow needed funds. Therefore, each individual has more to contribute in equity capital, and together their personal assets will support a larger borrowing capacity.

- *Ability to Attract Limited Partners.* There can be any number of limited partners as long as there is at least one general partner. A partnership can attract investors who, with limited liability, still can realize a substantial return on their investment if the business is successful. A great many individuals find it very profitable to invest as limited partners in high-potential small businesses.

- *Flexibility.* Although not as flexible as a sole proprietorship, the partnership can generally react quickly to changing market conditions because its organizational structure does not stifle its quick and creative responses to new opportunities.

- *Taxation.* The partnership itself is not subject to federal taxation. Its net income is distributed directly to the partners as personal income, which they pay taxes on. General partners are allowed to use partnership losses on their personal returns. The partnership, like the sole proprietorship, avoids the double taxation applicable to the corporate form of ownership.

Disadvantages of a Partnership

- *Unlimited Liability of at Least One Partner.* At least one member of every partnership must be a general partner. The general partner has unlimited personal liability.

- *Capital Accumulation.* Although the partnership is superior to the proprietorship in its ability to attract capital, it is generally not as effective as the corporate form of ownership. This is because the partnership usually has limitations and restriction to raising capital.

- *Restrictions of Elimination for the General Partnership.* Most partnership agreements restrict how partners can dispose of their shares of the business. It is common to find that partners are required to sell their interest to the remaining partners. But even if the original agreement contains such a requirement and clearly delineates how the value of each partner's ownership will be determined, there is no guarantee that the other partner(s) will have the financial resources to buy the seller's interest. When the money is not available to purchase a partner's interest, the other partner(s) may be forced either to accept a new partner who purchases the partner's interest or to dissolve the partnership, distribute the remaining assets, and begin again. When a general partner dies, becomes incompetent, or withdraws from the business, the partnership automatically dissolves, although it may not terminate. Even when there are numerous partners, if one wishes to disassociate his or her name from the business, the remaining partners will probably form a new partnership.

- *Lack of Continuity for the General Partnership.* If one partner dies, complications arise. Partnership interest is often nontransferable through inheritance because the remaining partner(s) may not wish to be in partnership with the person who inherits the deceased partner's interest. Partners can make provisions in the partnership agreement to avoid dissolution due to death if all parties agree to accept as partners those who inherit the deceased's interest.

- *Potential for Personality and Authority Conflicts.* Friction among partners is inevitable and difficult to control. Disagreements over what should be done or what was done have dissolved many a partnership. For example, when the cofounders of a successful communications company got into a dispute over its future direction, the firm lost its edge and momentum in the market. While the partners fought over buyout terms, the business floundered. Ultimately, the business was sold at a very low price.

LIMITED LIABILITY COMPANY

A limited liability company (LLC) is a blend of some of the best characteristics of corporations, partnerships, and sole proprietorships. It is a separate legal entity like a corporation, but it is entitled to be treated as either a sole proprietorship or a partnership for tax purposes, depending on whether there are one or more members. Therefore, it carries with it the "flow through" or "transparent" tax benefits that corporations do not have. It is very flexible and simple to run. As long as the terms of the governing document, called the Operating Agreement, are adhered to, the LLC may be operated more like a sole proprietorship or a partnership than a corporation.

The owners are called members, who can be individuals (residents or foreigners), corporations, other LLCs, trusts, pension plans, and so on.

An LLC is formed by filing an Article of Organization form with a secretary of state and signing an LLC Operating Agreement. The corporation division of most secretary of state offices handles the filing of LLC papers. Most states require that an annual report be filed to keep them apprised of the current status of an LLC. The LLC is not a tax-paying entity. Profits, losses, and the like flow directly through and are reported on the individual member's tax returns unless the members make an election to be taxed as a corporation.

Advantages of an LLC

- Owners do not assume liabilities for debt.
- They may offer different classes of memberships.
- There are no restrictions on the number and types of owners.

Disadvantages of an LLC

- There may be difficulty in business expansion out of state.
- Transferring ownership is restricted. Requirements are different for each state.

SETTING UP A LIMITED LIABILITY CORPORATION

SUMMARY OF PROS AND CONS

- Owned by "members," not shareholders
- A combination of characteristics of corporations, partnerships, and sole proprietorships

SETTING UP A LIMITED LIABILITY CORPORATION (cont.)

PROS

- Liability protection (a separate legal entity as in a C-corporation)
- Not a tax-paying entity (tax benefits to members)
- Statutory meetings are not required

CONS

- Unlikely that a venture capitalist would invest in an LLC
- Cannot take the company public
- Different shareholder interests result in complex operating agreements
- Restrictions on transfer of ownership
- Management and member rules different in each state

ROADMAP

IN ACTION

Different forms of company registration match various stages of development and aims of the founders. Know how and when to change the form as the company grows.

Business Organizational Structure Comparison Chart

Characteristic	C-corp	S-corp	LLC
Limited liability for all owners	Yes	Yes	Yes
Owners can participate in management without losing liability protection	Yes	Yes	Yes
Easy to form and maintain without extensive records	No	No	Yes
Number of owners	1 or more	1–100	1 or more
Restrictions on ownership	No	Yes	No
Double tax	Yes	No	Maybe
Able to deduct business loss on individual return	No	Yes	Maybe
Basis for loss includes owner's share of company debt in owner's tax return	No	Yes	Maybe
Can increase basis by "step-up" election	Yes	Yes	Yes
Can specially allocate terms of income and expense	Yes	Yes	Yes
Contributes and distributes property tax free	Yes	No	Yes

BUSINESS START-UP CHECKLIST

Now that you are beginning to understand the legal forms of the organization, a business start-up checklist is presented.[9] This checklist will be your guide for the first thirty days, sixty days, and year-end activities.

This list may seem a little daunting, so you can break it down into monthly tasks as follows:

First 30 Days

Do a name search in location state to determine if the name is available on Clerks Commission Web site. Check whether a web-name is available that matches the name. It may be necessary to purchase the web address from a web-name trader. You may have to modify the company name until you find one that is both available to register and you can file the web-address.

Determine if company will be a C-corp, S-corp, or LLC.

- In Delaware: https://sos-res.state.de.us/tin/GINameSearch.jsp
- For reference in VA: http://www.state.va.us/scc/division/clk/

Obtain an Employer Identification Number from the IRS by completing federal form SS4.

- Select a lawyer.
- Select an accountant.

Need to show:

- business license #, federal ID, 2 current IDs for each person authorized, signed corporate resolution allowing for certain persons to make withdrawals, sign checks.
- SSN's, household location for business owners
- Business tax ID and SIC code.
- Date business established
- Business location address
- Sales and profit for last fiscal year
- Prepare a business plan. This Plan will define the operational details of the Company and will include, but not be limited to, items such as: budgets, forecasts, capital expenditures, salaries and wages, hours of operation, market information (products, services, pricing, discounts, etc). The Plan will serve the purpose of giving management direction as to the day-to-day operation of the Company.
- Select a banker or banking institution.
- Select an insurance agent.
- Obtain business insurance.
- Order business cards and letterhead.
- Obtain a business license or permit from the city hall or county office.
- Establish bank accounts.
- Establish Merchant Credit Card Service allowing your business to accept major credit cards (if applicable).
- Pick a year-end date.
- Corporations hold an organizational meeting where:
- By-laws are adopted.

1. A Board of Directors is elected.
2. Share certificates should be distributed to shareholders once purchased, and these transactions should be recorded on the corporation's stock ledger.
3. Company members and/or managers and officers are elected.
4. Any corporate business that needs immediate attention is addressed.

- An LLC should have an organizational meeting where:

5. An operating agreement is adopted.
6. Membership certificates are distributed.
7. Company members and/or managers are elected.
8. In some states, publishing is required of your operation or an LLC.

First 60 Days

- Establish presence on Internet with at least a home page using the url that you have registered or acquired.
- Contact suppliers.
- If selecting S-Corporation status, file Form 2553 within 75 days.
- Obtain business insurance (liability, health and dental, workers' compensation, etc.).
- Join a professional organization.
- Some states such as Nevada require a list of officers and directors to be filed with the state.

By First Year End

- Obtain federal tax forms.
- Obtain state tax forms.
- Pay corporate franchise tax or annual state fees.
- Secure first round of financing from friends/family or angel investors.
- Establish a relationship with a bank in order to acquire a line of credit in the near term.

Selecting Your Attorney

The legal requirements for setting up a company can vary greatly from state to state. An attorney should be consulted to ensure you meet the legal requirements facing the business. An attorney can provide assistance in formatting the business; filing necessary documents with appropriate governmental authorities; and preparing employment contracts, stock ownership agreements, and other documents for equity holders. An attorney can also assist in preparing documents for the hiring of employees and independent contractors (confidentiality agreements, work-for-hire agreements, noncompetition agreements, nonsolicitation agreements, etc.) and those required for raising capital.[10]

In selecting an attorney, the most important element is finding one that can competently meet your needs. Selecting an attorney based on price is not a good idea. The intricacies of forming and operating a business require that an attorney be knowledgeable in corporate law, securities law, taxation, contract law, employment law, and license and trademark law. Therefore, one should find out how experienced an attorney is in rendering services for a business. One should also get recommendations from other business owners and consult guides that list attorney credentials and rate their abilities. An attorney should always be interviewed before being engaged for his or her services. A competent attorney should be able to answer all of your questions in your initial interview. The attorney should also be able to give an estimate of cost for establishing a business. If you are not satisfied with the answers received, then you should consult another attorney. As you grow your business, you are likely to need additional legal advice in specialist areas such as exporting, franchising, and patenting. Ask your first corporate attorney what affiliations he or she has with specialist legal offices.

Selecting Your Accountant

The accountant should be a practical business adviser who can set up a total financial control system for the business and render sound financial advice. At the outset, the accountant should work to establish accounting and reporting systems, cash projections, financing strategies, and tax planning. In addition, as the company matures, the following services can be provided:[11]

- Vendor services and payment options
- Cash management or fiscal accounting
- Cost-reduction planning using invoices
- Compensation plan for employees
- Merger, acquisition, and appraisal assistance
- Management information systems to determine the accounting software requirements

Name Registration

A business that adopts an assumed business name must register the name with the state of incorporation and with each state in which the business is doing business. This should be done before taking any other steps to do business in the state. The registration will protect the name from infringement. The amount of registration fee varies by state.

In most states a corporation's name must include the word *corporation, company, incorporated, limited,* or an abbreviation of one of these words. Limited liability companies must include *LLC* as part of their names. A competent attorney can assist with this phase of establishing a new business.

Federal Identification Number

A business must obtain an identification number from the Internal Revenue Service, except for a sole proprietorship that has no employees other than the owner. An identification number can be obtained by using Form SS-4, "Application for Employer Identification Number."[12] One may get an Employer Identification Number (EIN) by calling the IRS or going online.

Insurance Issues

Most businesses require insurance of one form or another. In addition, state law may require some forms, such as workers' compensation. The entrepreneur should shop around to find the insurer who offers the best combination of coverage, service, and price. Trade associations often offer special rates and policies to their members.[13]

Even though not required by law, the entrepreneur should consider the following forms of insurance to protect the business:

- Fire
- Employee health and life
- Crime coverage, which reimburses the employer for robbery, burglary, and vandalism losses
- Business interruption, which compensates the business for revenue lost during a temporary halt in business caused by fire, theft, or illness
- Key man insurance, which compensates the business for the death or disability of a key partner or manager
- Liability, which protects the business from claims of bodily injury, property damage, and malpractice
- Product liability

Other issues the entrepreneur should address in the business are as follows:

- Directors and officers insurance may be required as the company grows to protect against personal lawsuits associated with the company's business activities
- State registration
- Most state taxing authorities require a business, whatever its form, to register. The purpose of this registration is to receive sales tax registration numbers or exemptions and to receive the proper forms for filing wage withholding. Each state in which an entity does business must be contacted to determine how to do this registration
- Web site registration
- Domain name registration is a separate form of registration from registering a business name with a government entity. One should register a domain name as soon as possible. If a name is already registered, a business cannot use it on the Internet. Domain names can be bought and sold. This is an expensive alternative to direct registration. One should "reserve" one's domain name prior to filing with any government authority. This will prevent the costly process of changing the name on government registrations to the domain name after one has registered with government authorities.

SUMMARY

This chapter provides a good beginning for understanding the legal forms of the organization. It presents guidelines on the best legal form most appropriate for a particular situation.

In choosing a form of ownership, entrepreneurs must remember that there is no single "best" form; what is best depends on the individual's circumstances. Ask the questions that will help determine which form of ownership is best:

- How big can this business potentially become?
- How much control do you need in the decision-making process of the company? Are you willing to share ideas and the business's potential profits with others who can help build a more successful business?
- How much capital is needed to start the business?

A sole proprietorship is a form of business that has a single owner and requires only a business license to open. If the plan is to start a business under a name other than that of the owner, one must file a name to operate as "doing business as" (e.g., Jack's SmartCard Consulting). The business can be dissolved or closed at any time, and it always ends upon the death of the owner.

The C-corporation is the most common form of business ownership. It is a separate entity apart from its owners, and it may engage in business, issue contracts, sue and be sued, and pay taxes. When a corporation is founded, it accepts the regulations and restrictions of the state in which it is incorporated.

The S-corporation is a corporation that is treated like a partnership for tax purposes in that profits and losses are typically taxed directly to the individual shareholders. It is the owner's responsibility to report the gains or losses on individual income tax returns.

A partnership is usually defined as an association of two or more people carrying on as co-owners of a business for profit. A general partnership requires that each partner participate in all profits and losses equally or to some previously agreed upon ratio. A limited partnership limits the partners' liability to the extent of their capital contributions. Both types of partnership must have a general partner whose liability is unlimited.

An LLC is a blend of some characteristics of corporations, partnerships, and sole proprietorships. It is a separate legal entity like a corporation, but it is entitled to be treated as a sole proprietorship or a partnership for tax purposes and, therefore, carries with it the "flow through" or "transparent" tax benefits that corporations do not have. It is very flexible and simple to run, and, like a sole proprietorship, there is no statutory necessity to keep minutes, hold meetings, or make resolutions, which can trip up many corporations' owners.

The chapter summarizes the major forms of the legal business organization. The advantages and disadvantages of each are discussed, and a list of questions are highlighted to help you decide which form of ownership is best for you. In addition, a checklist has been prepared to assist you in the first thirty-day, sixty-day, and year-end periods to maximize the best performance for the business.

You should also seek legal advice to assist in preparing charters, name registration, and other documents to ensure the proper registration of the form of business.

STUDY QUESTIONS

1. What are the factors in deciding what form of ownership is best suited for the potential business?

2. Briefly describe the advantages and disadvantages of a sole proprietorship and partnership.

3. Explain the corporate form of ownership and how a business is incorporated.

4. List the differences between the S-corporation and the limited liability company.

EXERCISES

There is no master-case exercise associated with this chapter. We have, therefore, created this case for study.

Starting a New Health Care Service Company

In the fall of September 2006, Peter, the chief technology officer for a health-care technology company, resigned from his position. He then contacted Jennifer, who was a hospital's director of marketing, in charge of advertising and promotions. Both discussed an idea to start a company that offered health-care providers claim-processing services. Peter and Jennifer committed to start a new company called New Health Claim Processing. This name was important, for it would carry great weight in the industry. Peter and Jennifer had developed a unique business model to process claims at a very low cost while providing a high degree of customer service. The company would lease all the back-end hardware and write the software necessary to operate the business. The company would also provide all implementation, maintenance, and other ongoing support that would be required to use the service.

Peter and Jennifer invited Andy and Grace to join their effort. The four had met in Professor Jack Kaplan's entrepreneurship course at Columbia Business School. They were all technologically savvy and had outstanding grades and extensive relevant work experiences. Their credentials would look good for raising capital. This core group of four refined Peter and Jennifer's initial ideas and started drafting a business plan.

As part of the business plan, the group decided that they needed a CEO to attract the venture capital they believed they needed. Before the business plan was complete, they called their friend Michael with a proposition. They promised that they would make it worth his while if he would lead the company as the CEO. Two months later, the business plan was complete. The group of five was very excited as Michael took the lead in seeking funding for the venture. Michael's early contacts were successful. Within weeks of completing the business plan, he had scheduled an appointment to present the business plan to a venture capital firm.

During the presentation, the venture partners became interested in the company's vision and strategy and in the business processes for delivering customer service. However, as the due diligence questions got around to organization, Michael became quiet as the partners asked him about the type of company formed and the ownership of the business. A moment of silence occurred when one partner asked who owned the company. Michael had not yet settled how the ownership would be divided.

At the end of the all-day session, one of the venture partners told Michael in frank terms that he had handled the ownership questions poorly. He referred Michael to Cathy, a partner at a local law firm who was a close friend of his. Michael immediately made an appointment with her for the next day.

Cathy was an expert in organization and stock option incentives programs. She began by asking Michael for a retainer, which he paid out of his personal funds. Michael gave her a brief overview of the situation and arranged to bring all members for questioning.

Cathy soon uncovered the following:

- Jennifer had left her previous company three months ago but did not tell him that she was still on retainer. She had also signed a nondisclosure agreement on the day she left.
- Peter had taken from his previous job his client list and index of all his personal contacts. He also took a notebook and articles on health-care products. Peter had received a letter from his previous company stating, "It has come to our attention that you may have in your possession confidential documents belonging to the company."

Based on the foregoing information, please answer the following questions:

1. Identify the legal structure and issues involved in starting the business.

_____

_____

_____

_____

2. Identify the issues raised by the conduct of the start-up team.

_____

_____

_____

_____

3. Identify three ethical business issues presented in the case.

_____

_____

_____

4. What is your decision: to proceed or not to proceed?

_____

_____

_____

_____

INTERACTIVE LEARNING ON THE WEB

Test your knowledge of the chapter using the book's interactive Web site.

www.wiley.com/college/kaplan

PART TWO

MONEY SOURCES—FINDING AND MANAGING FUNDS

Part Two, "Money Sources—Finding and Managing Funds," focuses on one of the key resources of a company, cash. Without it, a company cannot survive, grow, and prosper. These three chapters teach an entrepreneur without financial training the fundamentals of entrepreneurial finance. This is substantially different from techniques and methods taught in more conventional corporate finance courses. The chapters deal with the sources of early and growth financing as well as the key factors employed in managing the cash and financial structure of a growing company. Chapter 7 covers methods of financing that are more applicable to early-stage companies before they are ready for major infusions of funds. It also examines techniques for growing a closely held company—one in which the founders retain control. These techniques are often referred to as *bootstrapping*. Chapter 8 addresses growth funding sources such as angel investors and venture capitalists, including how to find investors, preparation of the deal, valuation of the business, and guides for working with investors to establish terms and conditions. Chapter 9 is concerned with financial management and the controls that must be embedded in the company to monitor its progress and forecast funding needs.

CHAPTER 7: BOOTSTRAPPING AND FINANCING THE CLOSELY HELD COMPANY

CHAPTER 8: EQUITY FINANCING FOR HIGH GROWTH

CHAPTER 9: MANAGING THE MONEY

ROADMAP for

PATTERNS OF ENTREPRENEURSHIP
Money Sources— Finding and Managing Funds

- ☑ **Securing Early-stage Funding**
- ☑ **Self-funding**
- ☑ **Family and Friends**
- ☑ **Using Factoring and Bank Loans as a Source of Cash**
- ☑ **How to Use Commercial Banks**
- ☑ **Using Government Sources of Funding**
- ☐ **Equity Investment Fundamentals**
- ☐ **Angel Investors**
- ☐ **"Microequity"—Little Money with a Lot of Mentoring**
- ☐ **Understanding the Venture Capital Process**
- ☐ **Guide to Selecting a Venture Capitalist**
- ☐ **Private Placements**
- ☐ **Strategic Partnerships and Corporate Investments**
- ☐ **Learning How to Value a Business**
- ☐ **The Value of the Balance Sheet**
- ☐ **Review and Analysis of the Balance Sheet**
- ☐ **The Value of an Income Statement**
- ☐ **How to Use Ratios for Profitability**
- ☐ **The Value of the Statement of Cash Flows**
- ☐ **Understanding Footnotes to Financial Statements**
- ☐ **Preparing Financial Projections**
- ☐ **Preparing a Cash Flow Forecast**
- ☐ **Preparing a Breakeven Analysis**
- ☐ **Analyzing an Investment Decision**
- ☐ **Taxes and Filing**
- ☐ **The Stresses of Managing Money**

CHAPTER 7

BOOTSTRAPPING AND FINANCING THE CLOSELY HELD COMPANY

"Very early on, the founders of start-ups make an important choice. Do they want success or control? Neither is bad so long as the choice is explicit."

JOE KRAUSE, FOUNDER OF EXCITE AND JOTSPOT

OBJECTIVES

- Understand bootstrapping and its importance.
- Identify the different methods of early-stage funding and access other resources.
- Learn the problems and issues in raising capital from friends and family.
- Learn how to use commercial banks to acquire a loan.
- Learn how to prepare and apply for a loan.
- Build a relationship with a banker.
- Identify government financing programs.

CHAPTER OUTLINE

Introduction

Profile: James Dyson—Bootstrapping out of Necessity

Securing Early-stage Funding

Self-funding

Family and Friends

Using Factoring and Bank Loans as a Source of Cash

How to Use Commercial Banks

Using Government Sources of Funding

Summary

Study Questions

Exercises

Interactive Learning on the Web

Appendix: Start-up Entrepreneurs and Business Incubators

Additional Resources

INTRODUCTION

Chapter 1 discusses the personal attributes of entrepreneurs and the management skills that need to be developed within the context of a new business. Therefore, it is important that every entrepreneur examine at the outset and choose one of two fundamentally different routes for the proposed company. If control and remaining the chief executive of the company is of paramount personal importance, then the company should in no way seek funding by selling part ownership to outside investors. This way of raising money is called equity investment. Equity investors provide money to companies in exchange for part ownership in the form of shares to get a financial return on their money. Early-stage companies are risky investments, and investors typically seek an annual return on equity investments of 30 percent at a minimum. This is clearly well more than the 5 percent or so they can earn by putting their money into Treasury Notes or bank CDs.

To provide investors with a return on their investments, the company must create a "liquidity event." Otherwise its money stays locked up in the company and is "illiquid." To unlock the value, the stock of the company must be purchased by another company through an acquisition (the most usual way), by a sale of stock to the public through an initial public offering (IPO). In very rare cases, the company is generating so much cash that there is enough left after internal funding requirements that it can afford to buy back the stock from outside investors. If the founders wish to retain control of the company, they have no incentive to create such a liquidity event and, therefore, are unable to provide a real return to their investors. This misalignment of objectives between founders and investors is the principal reason that start-up companies end up with major conflict problems. If control is the prime objective, then equity financing should not be pursued. In this case, other means of attracting resources, both financial and otherwise, are required. The techniques for doing this are broadly referred as *bootstrapping*—a term deriving from "pulling oneself up by the bootstraps."

ROADMAP

IN ACTION

Before starting a company, be completely honest with yourself. How much personal risk will you take? Are you building a lifestyle? Do you wish to remain the chief executive, or are you willing to forgo some control if it means greater wealth in the long run?

If, on the hand, an entrepreneur is comfortable with trading control with an interest in acquiring significant personal wealth, then seeking outside investors should be considered. This may even lead to stepping aside as CEO, should the entrepreneur not have the appropriate skills to manage hectic growth. Raising outside equity investment is the subject of the next chapter.

Even if the eventual aim is to seek equity investment, however, the contents of this chapter are highly relevant. The further a start-up company has progressed successfully with its plans before selling stock, the higher the value of the company is likely to be and, therefore, the lower the percentage of the company that must be sold to raise an equivalent amount of money. Typical milestones that can trigger a jump in the value of the company include developing a working prototype, gaining a few paying customers, having a patent awarded, receiving a government grant, and signing up a larger company to test the results of the development. Therefore, it nearly always makes sense for entrepreneurs who plan on seeking outside investors to delay this event until as late as possible. Also, investors like to see that entrepreneurs are not totally dependent on their funding but know how to complement their money with other resources. Every entrepreneur, therefore, needs to learn how to bootstrap her company whether for reasons of control retention, increasing valuation before taking in equity investments, or perhaps out of necessity.

We will examine a number of options in this chapter, including self-funding, various forms of bootstrapping, family and friends, early-stage loans, and government sources such as the Small Business Administration and Small Business Innovation Research Program. Finding the source that is best will depend on many different factors, including the amount of funding required, when it is needed, and how long and when it can be repaid. It is important to remember to plan ahead and not let financial requirements be a surprise. Arranging financing takes time, and rushing decisions can be costly to the entrepreneur and his new venture. Running out of money is the most common reason for small companies to fail. Generally speaking, it takes twice as long as anticipated to raise money. Forecasting cash requirements is, therefore, very important and is dealt with in detail in Chapter 9. Starting early to make sure that the funds are available when they are needed and having contingencies in place are extremely important considerations and cannot be overemphasized.

PROFILE: JAMES DYSON—BOOTSTRAPPING OUT OF NECESSITY

James Dyson[1] studied at the Royal College of Arts in England, where he focused on furniture design. While still at college, he invented several new products such as the Ballbarrow and the SeaTruck boat (see www.dyson.com). His first and only job was as a sales manager for a small company in the west of England called Rotork (www.rotork.com). He rose rapidly to become a director of this small engineering firm, where he furthered his skills in product engineering. Yet he felt confined in this position and left the company in 1978 to branch out on his own, using some cash that he had earned from his first ideas. While vacuuming his old cottage in the bucolic Cotswold Hills, he noticed that the sucking power was quickly lost as the paper bag filled. He had observed a point of pain and decided to tackle the problem of making a bagless cleaner. His idea was to spin the air flowing through the cleaner, throwing the dirt to the outside, where it could be collected. He built exactly 5,127 prototypes in his basement workshop before he felt he had reached a satisfactory outcome. Now was the time to cash in on these efforts, so he filed a number of patents on the invention. His initial business model (refer to Chapter 11 for more discussion on this topic) was to license his ideas, and he took to the road, providing demonstrations to all of the existing vacuum cleaner companies around the world. He thought they would readily grab the opportunity to make and sell his "much better"–performing products. After two years and no interest, he decided to start manufacturing and selling his products. He was unable to raise any venture funding, however. The idea of breaking into a well-established but dull market dominated by large companies with deep pockets was hardly alluring to venture capitalists when there was a lot more fun to be had with high-tech "dot.com" start-ups, which were in fashion at that time. Moreover, Dyson did not match the profile of a super-techie high-flyer living in one of the start-up hotbed regions of the United Kingdom. He was simply seen as a "country boy" inventor playing around with vacuum cleaners.

The constant process of learning and refining led to several cash shortages before the product was launched in the UK in 1993, forcing Dyson to sell the patent rights in Japan for just $70,000 in 1986 and the U.S. rights for $100,000 in 1988. He later bought back the rights for both countries but at vastly inflated prices. Dyson paid $2 million in 2002 to buy back the U.S. rights after having success in the UK market. With little money left, he had to be creative in how he introduced the first "cyclone" product to the market in 1993. A combination of cameo appearances on popular television programs such as *Friends,* combined with what Dyson describes as word-of-mouth recommendations, helped to raise sales. He also decided to price the product well above the entrenched competition that on average sell for $150; Dyson's cleaners sell in the range of $399 to $1,500. The distinctive bagless vacuum cleaner has managed to grab a 20.7 percent share of the $2.3 billion U.S. market in just more than two years, leaving Hoover trailing with only a 15.6 percent share at the end of 2004. In 2003 Dyson had only a 4.5 percent share of the U.S. market, but sales of 891,000 units—a threefold increase—over the next year catapulted it to the top. These strong U.S. sales, which now make up 40 percent of worldwide revenue, helped Dyson to more than double profit from $70 million to $185 million, while sales grew by 54 percent. To date, more than $10 billion worth of Dyson's cleaners have been sold worldwide.

So why didn't one of the existing companies take up the offer when Dyson was just starting out? Perhaps their reticence had something to do with the large profits they were making on the disposable bags, which, without any marketing or selling expenditure, provided revenues of $500 million every year. Hoover was locked into a business model that prevented it from responding. According to Mike Dutter, a Hoover executive, "I do regret that Hoover did not take the product technology off Dyson; [in our hands] it would have lain on the shelf and not been used." As Dyson states, "Hoover wouldn't give me the time of the day. They laughed at it. They said, 'Bags are best. Bags will always be best.' Then they copied it." This copying, which came after Hoover realized that this little start-up was beginning to take away its market and profits, forced Dyson to sue for infringement of his patents. Again straining his cash for payment of legal fees, he won the case after eighteen months of litigation.

Dyson is not satisfied yet with his success. With the cash now coming in, he has repurchased the Japanese business, which, as in the United States, has also accelerated sales in Asia. Sales in 2004, which were running at 14,000 units a month there, rose fourfold. Expansion in Japan demonstrates Dyson's continued focus on research and his ability to shape his technologies to new markets. Since Japanese apartments tend to be smaller than those in the United Kingdom or United States, his team has devised a compact vacuum cleaner that uses a digital motor rather than a traditional mechanical one. The resulting machine is not only half the weight and size and more powerful than its larger contemporaries, but the digital technology allows customers who have problems with the unit to hold the machine up to the phone and have faults diagnosed online. In this way, Dyson is embedding services into his products. If sales increase, the company is hoping to make a mark in China. As Dyson says: "It may be taking coals to Newcastle, but it is the biggest market in the world for domestic appliances." The company is also planning to launch a new washing machine. Dyson is now working on another point of pain. It takes a few minutes to wash by hand, so why must it take longer than an hour for a washing machine to do the same thing? Watch out, Maytag, Whirlpool, and GE! And his company has recently introduced a radically new, low-energy hand dryer.

Dyson's company, which he and his family still own completely, employs twelve hundred people in Malmesbury, Wiltshire, UK. Recently Dyson paid himself and his wife approximately $30 million, a prize worth waiting for after facing bankruptcy on more than one occasion.

There are many ways of accessing resources, including cash, without taking major risks or selling part of your company. Be creative to find ways to bootstrap. Take the company as far as you can before bringing in investors or putting your personal assets at high risk.[2]

- Self-funding
  - Moonlighting
  - Bootstrapping
- Family and friends
- Bank loans
- Government programs

Figure 7-1 **Sources of Nonequity Funding.**

SECURING EARLY-STAGE FUNDING

Most entrepreneurs and business owners know when the company requires financing. However, it is much more difficult for entrepreneurs to judge what type of financing is appropriate and realistic for the business. In addition, after a string of record-breaking years in which public and private companies have created high wealth, investor interest in entrepreneurial companies was at its height in the early years of this century. Bank lending was readily available and affordable. Now with the capital and debt markets being highly uncertain, what are the best financing prospects for entrepreneurial companies? Raising funds can be confusing, so careful review and analysis are necessary to learn the process.

The various nonequity sources of funding available to the entrepreneur are listed in Figure 7-1.

In contrast, Figure 7-2 lists sources of funding[3] using other and later-stage sources for growth. (These sources are covered in detail in the next chapter.)

SELF-FUNDING

This form of financing is usually available to entrepreneurs who are highly motivated and committed to using personal resources to launch a venture. The majority of new

- Angels
- Institutional venture capital
- Private placements
- Other debt funding sources: factoring, asset-based lending
- Strategic partnerships/joint ventures as an equity partner

Figure 7-2 **Equity and Later-stage Funding Sources.**

businesses are usually started with funds that come from personal savings or various forms of personal equity of the founder(s). This form of capital reflects the business founder's degree of motivation, commitment, and belief. Personal investment can also include what is called *sweat equity,* where owners either donate their time or provide it at below market value to help the business get established. Sometimes it is possible to pay the first hires with some ownership in the company rather than with a salary. However, it is important that the aspirations of these hires be in line with those of the founder(s); otherwise a conflict may arise later similar to that which arises when investors seek an exit. Also, in some cases, entrepreneurs use profits from previous endeavors to invest in their new enterprises.

When considering self-funding, carefully decide how much financial risk you are willing to take. This is a very personal decision and should involve other family members. Some entrepreneurs will stretch themselves to the limit and use every cent they have, including pledging all of their assets—their house as well—to the bank. Others are much more cautious. However, investors and lenders alike expect entrepreneurs to put some of their own assets at risk, so entrepreneurs must learn to be comfortable with this scenario.

Moonlighting and Part-time Consulting

Many businesses are begun while the founder is still working a full-time job. The income from the job can both help support the owner during negative or low cash flow and provide working capital to augment the business's cash flow. Usually, when the business begins paying as well or better than the regular job, the entrepreneur can leave the job and devote all her time to building the new business.

Similarly, most people have skills that are valuable to existing companies on a part-time basis, perhaps as an advisory expert. Skills can include deep technical knowledge, design skills, the ability to write computer code, or the like, which are currently in demand on a part-time basis. Perhaps the existing employer is willing to have the work performed for six months or so in a part-time capacity, continuing the current work while a replacement is found. This may be a better solution for both parties than just leaving the company. Having a source of "survival" income while the company is getting started removes a lot of stress and improves the chance of success. If a technical consulting assignment is available, the entrepreneur must make it clear who owns the result of the work—usually the client. Therefore, document what areas are considered the property of the entrepreneur, so the future opportunity is not stymied due to questionable ownership of the intellectual property.

"Entrepreneurship is creating something of value from practically nothing."
The late JEFFRY TIMMONS
Franklin W. Olin Distinguished Professor of Entrepreneurship, Babson College, MA

Bootstrapping

Bootstrapping, a type of self-funding often applied in a current business, can reduce costs from the current operation and overhead.[2] It is usually overlooked as a source to business owners. The process of analyzing the operation to save and improve efficiencies will also allow the entrepreneur to learn more about the company. By becoming more efficient and cost conscious, the entrepreneur will be in a stronger position to qualify for additional financing. A multitude of bootstrapping techniques is available, and it is not possible to catalog all of them. Indeed, an entrepreneur can be just as innovative in developing his own methods as in developing the original business opportunity. The following discussion describes some bootstrapping techniques that may suit your own and your company's needs.

No or Low Rent. Start by using a residence for office and workspace. Paying extra rent to a landlord takes away cash that can go directly into the company. The term *garage start-up* is not a myth. Hewlett-Packard was started by two fresh graduates in a now-famous garage in Silicon Valley. When it comes time to move out and have a separate location for the business, avoid signing long-term leases in expensive locations. Often incubator space is available, which may be subsidized by an economic development grant for just this intermediate phase. Incubators usually have shared services too, so money need not be spent on copiers, conference room furniture, and full-time office support staff since they are shared with other start-ups (see the appendix to this chapter for more details on incubators). Investors and lenders like to see that "unproductive overhead" spending is being kept to a minimum. Unless the business is a beauty parlor or a wealth management consulting firm, opulence is usually a waste of hard-to-find funds. If a lease for more space is signed, make sure subletting is available to offset some of the costs.

Bartering for Goods and Services. Perhaps you can trade some Web site development work with a local small engineering firm in exchange for their machining the first prototypes of a product—or the other way around. (Note: Some bartering activities may have tax implications).

Trading Intellectual Property Rights. Dyson traded international rights when he desperately needed cash. At that stage in his company, he could not enter overseas markets anyway, so using these "sleeping assets" was one way to continue. Alternatively, you may be developing technology that has multiple applications, perhaps a new glue for rapidly assembling metal parts. Your interest may lie in the high-value but smaller aircraft market. You could sell the rights for the automotive sector to an existing company to fund your field of interest. The Ultrafast case in Chapter 10 provides another example of this method.

Renting or Leasing Equipment. Often an expensive piece of equipment may be needed in only the start-up phase. Rather than buy, rent or lease the equipment only while it is needed.

Used Equipment. Usually the latest high-speed machines are not needed in the early stages of manufacturing and test marketing. It is often possible to find a piece of used equipment, often at a scrap price, that with a little work will fill short-term needs. The same applies to office furniture. Look for large companies that are moving or companies in bankruptcy; they will often give away or sell for a song perfectly good furniture they no longer need.

Access to Expensive Equipment. Check out universities and government labs. They often have programs to help small companies and may allow access to equipment that an entrepreneur could only dream of owning.

Suppliers' and Customers' Help. Suppliers may be willing to help in many ways with the hope that, in the future, a new company will become a major customer. Help may include access to experts, supplies of test materials, introduction into their supplier and customer networks, technical support, sharing of market data and reports, and perhaps even an option to license some of their proprietary know-how. They may also be willing to help with funding inventory until you have been able to receive payment from your customers. Establishing a close and honest relationship with suppliers will help.

Similarly, engaging with customers early on can provide a range of benefits, even financial, by prepaying on a future delivery or paying for product development work to meet their specific needs. Also, a purchase order from a large company in good standing, even if it is contingent on delivery of product or service to a defined specification, may help in securing a working capital loan.

Cooperative Purchases. As companies begin to scale up, often they can find ways to work with other small companies to create a buyers' club. The first area to look at is health insurance costs, which are exploding. Often professional society membership can provide access to reduced costs in a range of areas.

Outsourcing. A new, growing company will need a number of professional services that are not required full time and, indeed, may make sense to outsource entirely. These include payroll services, bookkeeping, and tax return preparation, which can usually be found as a service or by using part-time workers. Legal, accounting, and other consulting services will always be purchased as needed. These professions are usually accommodating with regard to payment schedules. Find more about outsourcing in Chapter 11.

Contingent Litigation. A small company does not usually have the financial resources to fight a major lawsuit against a large infringer of its patent rights, such as James Dyson faced. If the case looks as if there is a good chance of prevailing, then there are some patent law firms that will take the case "on contingency" whereby the settlement, if the case is won, is shared by the legal team and the company filing the case. Some major law firms specialize in such cases, and just signing up with them can send a strong message to the alleged infringer, perhaps prompting an early settlement.

Example: Ron Chasteen and John Balch Fight for Their Rights

Ron Chasteen[4] was awarded a patent for a fuel-injection system for snowmobiles in the late 1980s. He and his partner, John Balch, approached Polaris Industries in Minnesota about a possible supply agreement. "When we first met with their chief engineer, he told us we had made a massive leap in technology," states Chasteen. Initially, Polaris wanted to buy rights to the system outright. But Chasteen didn't want to sell. Eventually, a deal was struck, and Polaris agreed to purchase the system. After about a year of collaboration, Polaris claimed it was not going to proceed in selling fuel-injected snowmobiles, and so the relationship ended.

Chasteen was shocked when, soon after, Polaris launched a fuel-injected snowmobile. Examination of the product immediately showed that the snowmobile was very similar to the product Chasteen had developed. "We were furious; they'd simply cloned ours." Chasteen and Balch decided to sue not only Polaris, but their component supplier, Fuji Heavy Industries. It took several years, a lot of money, and five different patent law firms before they found one that agreed to take the case on a contingent-fee basis. "They were all happy to just take our money with no end in sight," Chasteen says. "We got nowhere, just a lot of bills." The case was eventually taken by the Chicago law firm of Niro, Scavone, Haller & Niro. According to Joe Hosteny, a partner at the firm, "Contingent-fee litigation is for individual inventors and small- to medium-size businesses which would have trouble affording normal patent or trade-secret litigation. Without contingent-fee litigation, big corporations could steal solo inventors' ideas with no one to stop them."

After almost eleven years, Chasteen and Balch finally got their justice—a check for $70 million. Other well-known cases include $120 million paid by Microsoft for using the "Stacker" data[5] compression software developed by Stac Electronics and a payment of more than $10 million from Ford Motor Company to Robert Kearns, an individual inventor, for infringing on his patent on intermittent windshield wipers.[6]

Credit Cards. Credit cards have always been a source of funding for a new venture. If the options of equity or bank loans are not available, the entrepreneur may contact all the major credit card suppliers to compare prices and options. As with a bank, the entrepreneur should ensure that there are opportunities to increase the borrowing limit (and add on other financing sources, such as equipment leasing) as necessary, once the company has proven to be a good customer. Credit card funding is quick funding of the business and is more viable now than ever before. MasterCard or Visa cardholders with good credit now often receive credit limits of at least $10,000. By carrying more than one credit card, the entrepreneur can considerably boost the total amount tapped into at any given time. Entrepreneurs may also take advantage of the regular offers of "no interest for six months" and keep rolling over their credit.

Unfortunately, use of credit cards in this way can adversely affect personal credit ratings if done too often. Credit card interest rates on cash advances vary considerably, from as high as 21 percent to 10 percent or lower. Annual fees can also range from more than $50 down to zero. Therefore, when obtaining credit cards, it is wise to investigate getting the best deal. It may be advantageous to cancel one or more of the high-interest cards and transfer the balances to lower-cost credit cards. The disadvantage is that it costs much more to obtain funds through credit cards than through bank loans. If the enterprise is not successful, the credit card payments will continue and may place the entrepreneur in a personal financial squeeze.[7]

The above is a short list of the many bootstrapping techniques entrepreneurs use to get through their early stages either to defer the search for equity funding or to retain control of the company.

FAMILY AND FRIENDS

Friends and family members are a very popular source for start-up capital because they are not as worried about quick profits as are professional investors. However, there are problems associated with this method. Usually friends and family do not investigate the business very well and are not familiar with all the risks of the business. In many cases friends and family accept the word of the entrepreneur without any analysis or detailed review of the business venture. To guard against the risks of failure and to avoid being blamed for not disclosing all the important information about the proposed venture, the best method is to provide the same disclosure to a friend or relative that would be provided to the most sophisticated investors. Entrepreneurs should always resist the temptation to keep the venture on an informal basis and not document the details of the company's risks and financial requirements.[8]

USING FACTORING AND BANK LOANS AS A SOURCE OF CASH

It is important to understand debt financing and its appropriateness for the business. The primary advantage of debt financing is that the entrepreneur does not have to give up any part of ownership to receive the funds. However, the loan has to be paid back with interest and may require the entrepreneur to personally guarantee part or all of the money. In addition, many loans have certain conditions ("covenants") that come with them. Often these conditions are tied to certain milestones or events that the company must make in order for the loan to remain in place and not be recalled. These covenants are not so different from conditions that might be applied by equity investors, and therefore, they often remove some control of the company from the founders until the loan is repaid. Bank loans are more suitable for companies that have a track record of sales and growth. For the formative stages of a company, before any substantial sales, an entrepreneur will most likely have to secure the loan with personal assets or seek out loan programs underwritten by federal, state, or local economic development agencies.

Bank loans, commercial banks, loan proposals, and *government sources* are some of the major terms used in the search for debt capital. This section outlines a range of credit options regarding debt financing from a commercial lending institution. Not all of these sources are equally favorable. From a bank's perspective, the most important consideration is the degree of certainty that a loan will be paid back on the agreed schedule of intent and timing. In addition, we describe what lenders look for in preparing a loan proposal and the guidelines to improve the entrepreneur's chances for a loan approval.[9]

Factoring

This is an alternative to conventional bank loans. As we shall see, bank loans usually require some form of guarantee based on personal quantifiable assets or cash flow in the company. If you are unable to provide such guarantees but you have purchase orders from reputable customers, it may be possible to use these orders to secure funding from so-called factors. These are private lenders that provide funds for your operations using purchase orders as security for the loan. They lend only a percentage of the sales orders and charge very high interest rates. The payment goes directly from your customers to them before they provide you with any cash that may be left over after their fees and any interest payments are paid. The profile of Alvin Katz in Chapter 9 illustrates the value of factoring to raise cash in tight situations.

Bank Loans

Many companies depend on bank loans, and according to the Small Business Administration, in the past few years, both the number and the amount of bank loans to small companies has increased, topping $500 billion annually with average loan amounts near $100,000.

HOW TO USE COMMERCIAL BANKS

Most commercial loans are made to small businesses and can be either unsecured or secured. An unsecured loan is a personal or signature loan that requires no collateral; it is granted on the background and strength of the borrower's reputation. Such loans are made at fair market interest rates if the borrower can demonstrate that the business is sound. To most banks, that will mean having an operating history of at least two or three years. Banks often require that the borrower maintain appropriate deposits with them. In addition, most banks will require personal guarantees for newer companies.

Table 7-1   Small Business Loan Data

Total number of bank loans of less than $1 million (in millions)

2006	21.3	10%
2007	24.5	growth

Total amount of loans of less than $1 million

2006...$624 billion

2007...$684 billion

Average amount of each loan (rounded)

2006...$44,000

2007...$24,900

Source: Small Business Administration, 2008.

Secured loans are those with security pledged to the bank that the loans will be paid. Several types of security and collateral are used in loans:

Comaker: person who signs as secondary principal

Endorser: person who pledges to back loan

Guarantor: person who personally guarantees loan

Real property: real estate, leaseholds, and land

Securities: stocks and bonds that can be pledged

Equipment: capital assets that include machinery, computers, and instrumentation

Inventory: usually finished goods

Accounts receivable: items receipted as sold with verifiable credit outstanding

Insurance policies: cash surrender value of policies

Not all commercial banks are willing to grant loans to early-stage businesses.[10] In most instances the entrepreneur must seek loans through community banks that make it their business to serve the small-business sector. Talk to the owners of other small companies locally to learn about the most receptive banks for small companies and to get an introduction if possible.

Community banks are independently chartered and serve local clients; consequently, they thrive on small businesses. The entrepreneur should first find out which banks are most active in making loans in state. If no local institutions are available, reference the Small Business Administration (SBA) publication for friendly, out-of-state banks. Many of the 567 banks that make business loans of less than $100,000 cross the state lines in the process. Also, the entrepreneur should reference the SBA's report on small-business lending in the United States, which ranks about nine thousand commercial banks by state based on their lending practices. Other reports are available at www.sba.gov or at (800) 827-5722. The entrepreneur may also want to visit www.entrepreneur.com/bestbanks for a recent listing of the banks friendlier to small businesses.

Managing Personal Credit Ratings

When an entrepreneur applies to a bank to acquire a loan for a business that has few or no assets as collateral, the banker will turn to the credit history of the founder as an indication of the likelihood that the loan will be secure. A track record of meeting personal financial obligations, although not being sufficient to secure a loan, will help considerably in the application. It is, therefore, important that an entrepreneur establishes a sound credit record with a score greater than 700 well before any loans either personally or for a business are contemplated. This is achieved by paying all bills on or before due dates, keeping any borrowing levels down to less than around 50 percent of established borrowing limits, and refraining from continually changing sources of credit such as credit cards. Long, stable records count for a lot. There are three major personal credit rating agencies in the United States: Equifax, Experian, and TransUnion. Under the Federal FACTA ACT of 2003, everyone has the right to access their credit ratings from each of these companies annually for free through the Web site www.annualcreditreport.com. You should monitor your ratings every four months by rotating the free requests and correcting any habits that are impacting your rating. Additionally, if you have credit refused at any time, make sure that you follow up to determine the reason; often mistakes are made in data entry, such as an incorrect address record, that can seriously impact your rating unwittingly.

Preparing a Loan Proposal

A loan proposal consists of six key parts, not unlike the structure of a business plan covered in Chapter 5:

- *Summary.* State your name and title, company name and address, nature of business, amount sought, purpose, and source of repayment.
- *Management Team Profiles.* Bankers seek their ultimate security in experienced management, so provide the backgrounds and history of the key managers.
- *Business Description.* The products and markets as well as customers and competitors should be defined, along with the inventory in terms of size, rate of turnover, and market ability. The status of your accounts receivable and accounts payable should also be reported with a list of fixed assets.
- *Financial Projections.* Include forecasts for the next three years with fallback plans. Bankers judge plans and goals in terms of the industry's practices and trends.
- *Financial Statements.* Include a balance sheet and income statement for the past three years (if available). Bankers are more comfortable with audited statements. If the entrepreneur cannot afford a full audit, he or she should ask the accountant for a financial "review." Two sets of projected balance sheets as well as income and cash flow statements should also be prepared, one predicated on receiving the loan and the other on proceeding without it. Bankers match projections against published industry standards, searching for padded earnings and meager cost estimates. Personal financial statements, including tax returns for the past three years, must also be submitted because the entrepreneur's own net worth is a factor. Bankers check the entrepreneur's personal credit rating in addition to the company's.

- *Amount and Purpose.* Bankers want to know how much you're asking for and why. Detail how the funds will be used.

- *Repayment Plans.* Show how you will generate the cash to provide payments of both the interest and principal.

The Four Cs of Lending

Lenders are looking for a company's ability to repay its debt. No matter how successful a company is, usually a lender has only the promise of being rewarded with steady payments of principal and interest. Although a borrower may become a better customer of the bank as the business grows, the bank will not necessarily prosper in direct proportion to the company's success. When lenders consider a loan request, they concentrate on what are sometimes referred to as the "four Cs" of credit: character, cash flow, collateral, and (equity) contribution.[11]

Character

The lender must have confidence in the individual he or she is dealing with, or the lender will not proceed with the venture. Such traits as talent, reliability, and honesty are used to describe character.

One aspect of character that is always used is credit history. Credit history in terms of a commercial loan is a one-way street. A bad credit rating will often eliminate the potential for a new business to obtain credit. A good credit history, on the other hand, has little upside. In the final analysis, even with a positive credit history, a banker's decision comes down to intuition: How capable is this individual? Will he or she run the business ethically and keep the bank honestly apprised of the real status of the business? How much faith can the bank have that this individual can successfully run a business and pay the monthly debt service?

Cash Flow

Banks need to be satisfied that cash flow will be adequate to cover debt service throughout the term of the obligation. Most loans are structured with interest payments due every month beginning in month 1, and principal payments also due, usually beginning in month 1. In some instances, principal payments can be deferred but usually no more than a year.

The business must be solid to meet debt service and operating obligations and still have enough available cash to address uncertainties. The entrepreneur must remember that projections are imperfect and must, therefore, provide for deviations. Lenders will want to be assured that the margin of error has been considered and provided for amply.

Collateral

No good lender will make a decision to loan money based solely on strong collateral. But every good lender will try to get the best collateral possible on the loan. This normally involves securing the lender's interest by liens or mortgages against tangible assets such as real estate or equipment. In addition, most lenders will require the entrepreneur's personal signature as evidence of the borrower's real commitment to the business.

As an example, one may keep personal assets in the name of other family members, most often a spouse or child. Also, a lender cannot take assets held jointly by spouses unless the lender has both spouses' signatures on the note. Incidentally, most lenders will ask for both signatures if the collateral is insufficient. The issues related to personal liability and loan repayment are complex, and it is often important to have advice from a lawyer when making borrowing arrangements.

ROADMAP
IN ACTION

The entrepreneur will generally be required to have some type of collateral to support a loan. The types of securities used for collateral include endorsers or cosigners, accounts receivables, real estate, stocks and bonds, and personal savings.

Contribution

Almost all lenders require a significant commitment by the entrepreneur to ensure the success of the financing. The commitment also serves to reduce the lender's exposure relative to the deal's total size, providing a cushion to allow the lender to come out "whole" in the event of default.

In addition, different industries customarily have different ratios of debt to equity, commonly known as leverage. Some industries have traditionally been highly leveraged with debt three to four times greater than equity, often because of high success rates and good collateral. The real estate and apparel industries are good examples of highly leveraged businesses. An unusually high failure rate or poor-quality collateral may result in relatively low leverage in an industry, as exemplified by the restaurant business. Because of these varieties, it is difficult to generalize as to how much the entrepreneur must contribute to a venture.

Establishing the Terms of Debt

The term of the debt (the length of time over which the obligation is amortized or paid off) usually depends on the life of the asset financed. If a lender really wants to make a deal, he or she can give some latitude to structure the debt in a way that makes sense economically and so cash flow is sufficient to amortize the debt. Working capital loans are usually paid off over the shortest periods of time, and real estate loans are usually paid off over the longest. Remember: the longer the term is, the lower the monthly payment (principal and interest) will be, but there will be more monthly payments, more interest accruing, and more money paid in total to meet the debt requirements. Failure to meet interest payment typically constitutes loan default. Normally, on default, the entire principal amount outstanding becomes immediately due.

Rates

Most business debt today is provided at a variable interest rate, usually fluctuating with the prime rate (the rate banks charge their "best" customers). This rate is usually quoted as "prime plus" multiplied by percentage points, often 0.5 to 2 percent, but it can be as much as 3 or even 4 percent greater than prime, depending on risk and other variables that motivate the lender. This rate can change as often as the prime rate changes; therefore, each monthly payment can be different.

There will also be other covenants, rules, and restrictions to the loan, which may constrain the entrepreneur's management freedom. This can include not giving raises to senior management without the lender's approval or obtaining further financing or reaching certain sales milestones.

Debtors can sue only the business and can claim only the assets of the business. For this reason, banks will usually require business owners to sign or guarantee any loans.

Building a Relationship with a Banker

Setting up a checking account at a bank is one of the first steps in building a relationship with a lending institution. It will provide the opportunity to meet a loan officer, who can be crucial in developing the business. The best borrowing relationships often depend on a loan officer who knows the business and will take a personal interest in the entrepreneur and his or her company. The entrepreneur should consider the following questions before making a choice:[11]

- How much lending authority does the banker have, and what is the approval process?
- Can the banker understand the business? Is there any personal excitement about the business potential?
- What experience does the banker have with similar companies?

USING GOVERNMENT SOURCES OF FUNDING

Many sources of financing are available to small businesses from federal, state, and local governments. The main source of funding from the federal government is the Small Business Administration. Many state governments provide funding for businesses through their state departments of commerce, economic development, trade, or industry development. Local resources include city governments and regional authorities anxious to further economic growth in their area.

Consider using government sourcing as a method for financing a venture. Review federal and local government options and the Small Business Administration. Also, state governments provided funding for businesses through their state departments.

Federal Sources of Funding

The major source of government financing available to small businesses is the Small Business Administration. The SBA was established in 1953 to "aid, counsel, and protect the interests of the Nation's small business community." The agency works with intermediaries, banks, and other lending institutions to provide loans and

Table 7-2   SBA Small Business Size Standards (2008)

Industry	Size (revenues/employees)
Retail and service	$7.0 to $35.5 million
Construction	$7.0 to $35.5 million
Agriculture	$.75 to $12.5 million
Wholesale	No more than 100 employees
Manufacturing	500 to 1,500 employees

venture capital financing to small businesses unable to secure financing through normal lending channels.

Many other federal programs are operated through government departments and agencies. The Small Business Innovation Research (SBIR) program and the Advanced Technology Program (ATP) are among other federal programs that provide funds to small businesses to develop new technologies.

Small Business Administration Programs

The Small Business Administration was established by an act of Congress in 1953; in 1957, four years after its setup, the SBA was granted permanent status.

The SBA is involved in several aspects of small-business financing. There are financial programs whereby the SBA guarantees loans for small businesses to help them get financing when they cannot meet normal bank conditions. The SBA runs an investment program—the Small Business Investment Company. The SBA also assists small businesses in obtaining government procurement contracts. Counseling and development services are offered to small businesses from several sources, including SCORE (Service Corps of Retired Executives), and many programs are designed to assist minority-owned businesses. The fifty-seven Small Business Development Centers across the country, with a network of more than one thousand service locations, provide advice and training to new and existing business owners.[12]

For a business that is looking for start-up funds, applying for an SBA loan is considered an alternative approach. The first step in obtaining SBA financing is to

Table 7-3   The SBA Loan Application

1. Applicant Information	Names of owners, background, addresses, business name, date started, and other statement of business
2. Use of Loan Proceeds	Description of how the loan will be used in business operations
3. Collateral Pledged	List of all business and personal assets to secure the loan
4. Disclosures	List existing or previous government financing, personal and business debts, bankruptcies, and lawsuits
5. Personal Balance Sheet	Balance sheet on borrower(s)
6. Financial Statements	Cash flow, income, and use-of-funds statements

locate a commercial or savings bank that is a certified SBA lender. The SBA does not directly fund the loan. What it does is guarantee up to 85 percent of the loan for the lending institution. The key advantage is to repay the note over an extended period of time. The SBA is not in the business of guaranteeing bad loans. Once the institution accepts the credit, it recommends the company to the SBA. As the types and sizes of loans change regularly, you should refer to the SBA Web site for the latest opportunities.

Small Business Innovation Research Program

One of the best opportunities for obtaining early-stage funding is participation in the federally funded SBIR Program. This program allocates in excess of $1 billion annually to businesses with proposals for developing scientific innovation, and it has three phases:[13]

Phase I: There is a grant award up to $150,000 for the purpose of investigating the feasibility of an innovation. The award recipient has six months to prepare a feasibility plan that includes prototypes, market research, and report development.

Phase II: The report is reviewed, and if feasible, grant of up to $1 million can be awarded for operating expenses. There is a two-year deadline to complete this phase, which can include further testing and market research. A report must be prepared to review the results that were achieved and how the funds were spent.

Phase III: This is not a funded stage of the program but includes selling the developed products or services to a federal government agency. Funding for development and commercialization must be obtained through private financing, which may be helped by having on hand a purchase order from a creditworthy customer.

How to Qualify

To begin the process, the entrepreneur should remember that the SBIR receives more than eight thousand proposals each year with fewer than one thousand grants being approved. Under the Small Business Innovation Development Act, applicants must be independently owned companies with five hundred or fewer employees and be able to demonstrate the capability for scientific or technological research. Through the first eight years of SBIR grants, award recipients have had, on average, fewer than thirty-five employees, with nearly half of all initial Phase I grants awarded to companies with fewer than ten employees. The SBIR grant program provides operating money to companies and is not a loan. There is no assumption to repay the amount of the grant. One problem the SBIR Program presents for entrepreneurs is the time it may take for the relevant agency to make a decision on grants, leaving a gap in cash flow. For more information on the SBIR Program, contact:

Small Business Administration
Office of Innovation Research and Technology
1441 L Street, NW
Washington, D.C. 20416
(202) 653-6458

Small Business Technology Transfer Program

The Small Business Technology Transfer (STTR) Program[13] is similar to the SBIR Program in that it fosters R & D by small businesses. The major difference between the programs is that funding from STTR is provided to joint ventures or partnerships between nonprofit research institutions and small businesses. Like the SBIR, the STTR Program has three phases. An award of $100,000 is made during the year-long Phase I. Phase II awards are up to $500,000 in a two-year expansion of Phase I results. Funds for Phase III of STTR must be found outside the STTR Program. By this time, however, the research project should be ready for commercialization. The STTR Program began making awards in fiscal year 1994.

Financing for Minorities and Women

The definition of a minority-owned business is one that is 51 percent or more owned by one or more owners who are either minorities or women. Federal assistance is available, for example, to Native American–owned businesses and programs that promote the business and economic development of reservations.

The SBA division of the Office of Minority Enterprise Development (MED) assists certain business owners. The act provides assistance, through the Division of Management and Technical Assistance, to "socially and economically disadvantaged individuals and firms owned by such individuals, businesses located in areas of low income or high unemployment, and firms owned by low-income individuals."

Other federal offices and agencies that give assistance to minority firms and individuals for business expansion and development are the Bureau of Indian Affairs, the Office of Small and Disadvantaged Business Utilization, and the Minority Business Development Agency.

State and Local Small-business Financing Initiatives

Most states have programs that provide financial assistance or incentives to small businesses. Such programs are administered by departments and agencies within state and local governments. Many different programs are available in each state, but most states have a department of trade or commerce that runs loan assistance, investment, procurement, and other programs. Small-business assistance at the state level can be in the form of direct financial assistance, tax benefits, technical assistance, or small-business incubators.

Contact city and county or township governments for assistance. In many areas local development authorities can also be useful resources in locating financing for new or existing businesses.

SUMMARY

Depending on funding needs, the entrepreneur faces a number of options. To increase the chances of success, the entrepreneur must know what sources are available and understand the requirements of the financial partners. Preparing a business and financial plan before beginning the search helps the entrepreneur determine which sources would be most likely to assist in capitalizing the business.

This chapter examined the many sources of nonequity early-stage capital. Determining which source is best will depend on many different factors, including amount required, when it is needed and for how long, and when it can be repaid. The development stage for the company and the goals and objectives must be considered. Entrepreneurs become expert at using a range of bootstrapping methods to bridge the gap from starting the company to the stage where either they can acquire equity or bank loan funding for growth or the company becomes self-financing through retained profits from sales.

Most commercial loans are made to small businesses and are either unsecured or secured. An unsecured loan is a personal or signature loan that requires no collateral. The loan is granted on the background and strength of the entrepreneur's reputation. Such loans are made at fair market interest rates if the entrepreneur can demonstrate that the business is sound. To most banks, that will mean having an operating history of at least two or three years. Banks often require that the borrower maintain appropriate deposits with them. In addition, most banks will require personal guarantees for newer companies. In either case, banks tend to be cautious about lending and carefully weigh the four Cs of lending: character, cash flow, collateral, and contribution.

Lenders are looking for the ability of a company to repay its debt. No matter how successful a company is, usually a lender has only the promise of being rewarded with steady payments of principal and interest. An idea for a great product or service is meaningless without a solid marketing plan. The entrepreneur must include a customer-focused marketing plan as part of the loan request. The plan must explain how the entrepreneur plans to sell the product, how the product will be priced, to whom it will be sold, and why they will want to buy it.

Every banker would rather see a strong, experienced team of managers working together to make a company successful than a strong entrepreneur trying to do everything all alone. A solid business plan is essential, but the entrepreneur must have the management team to implement it.

The Small Business Administration is the most active federal agency in assisting small businesses. Loans guaranteed by the SBA (up to 80 percent) are the prevalent means of obtaining government support, but direct loan assistance is available under certain programs.

The Small Business Innovation Research Program provides direct grants to businesses engaged in scientific development. With an SBIR Phase I grant, entrepreneurs are provided up to $100,000 for development feasibility plans; Phase II grants can be as much as $1 million for commercialization of their innovations.

STUDY QUESTIONS

1. What sources of funding are available to entrepreneurs at the early stage of the company?
2. What are the major techniques for bootstrapping?
3. Why is bootstrapping important for (a) closely held companies and (b) early-stage, high-growth companies that plan to seek equity investors?
4. What is meant by factoring of purchase orders?
5. What steps should entrepreneurs take to prepare a loan proposal?
6. Describe how you would build a relationship with a loan officer.
7. Describe government funding programs.

EXERCISES

1. Refer to the Dyson profile in this chapter and consider the following questions:
   (a) What personal attributes led to Dyson's success?
   (b) Give three reasons you think Hoover rejected Dyson's offer of a license.
   (c) Describe three ways that Dyson creatively bootstrapped his company when he did not have enough cash to proceed.
   (d) Name two other large consumer companies with household brand names that are still privately owned and were, therefore, bootstrapped from their very beginning.

2. With regard to establishing early-stage funding:
   (a) Select and briefly describe a business idea that will require early-stage funds to get started.
   (b) Establish the amount of start-up capital needed to fund the venture for one year.
   (c) Describe where the venture will get sources of funding and other resources it may need. Use a mix of personal funds, family, friends, bank loans, and creative bootstrapping.
   (d) Prepare an oral presentation to bankers for any loans you seek.

Master-case Exercises: If you have not already read the appendix in Chapter 1, do so. Then go to the book's Web site and read the diary entries Months 0, 2, 12, 15, 18, and 21 and view the video selection, "Your Money, My Life: the Pros and Cons of Bootstrapping."

Either as a team or individually, produce a short presentation on each of these questions for discussion. Only one or two slides for each are required to state the key points.

Master-case Q 1: Bootstrapping allows founders to have more control and give up less of their company to investors. Yet in a rapidly changing world, living on limited resources and continually worrying about money can slow the growth of a company. What are the pros and cons of bootstrapping generally (include control issues, lifestyle questions, dilution in ownership, speed to market, habit forming, personal risk taking, etc.)?

Master-case Q 2: List the range of bootstrapping methods used by Wayne and Jeff. What were the pros and cons for each of these?

Master-case Q 3: Linda chose to retain control of her company for personal reasons, whereas Jeff and Wayne were willing to give up control. Who do you most identify with and why?

INTERACTIVE LEARNING ON THE WEB

Test your knowledge of the chapter using the book's interactive Web site.

APPENDIX: START-UP ENTREPRENEURS AND BUSINESS INCUBATORS

Business incubators are organizations designed to assist and accelerate the growth of small business. They typically provide business assistance in the form of coaching and training, access to investors, and access to office services and space on flexible terms. Incubators are short-term assistance programs. They are designed to provide concentrated critical resources during the key development period. Most incubators have time limits ranging from six months to three years. Business incubators have become one of the most concentrated and useful methods for obtaining business assistance.

TYPES OF INCUBATORS

Incubators have been around for about forty years and have helped produce more than twenty thousand successful businesses. Today there are more than eight hundred in the United States and another two thousand worldwide. The U.S.-based incubators are divided into three types based on their sponsorship and objectives:

1. **Publicly sponsored (45 percent of U.S. incubators)**
   These incubators are organized through city economic development departments, urban renewal authorities, or regional planning and development commissions. Job creation is the major objective of publicly sponsored incubators.

2. **University related (27 percent of U.S. incubators)**
   Most of these incubators are focused on science and technology companies. Many of them develop business based on research started at the university. The major goals of this type of incubators are technology commercialization and return on investment.

3. **For-profit incubators (33 percent of U.S. incubators)**
   These incubators are organized and managed by investors with the goal of receiving a return on their investment. A recent study by Harvard Business School found that most of the for-profit incubators were investor led, focused on the Internet, and designed to accelerate the speed and size of the start-up.

The study identified 345 for-profit incubators worldwide; 58 percent were new organizations founded by investors to maximize investment return, 31 percent were operated as part of a venture capital firm.

Incubators give entrepreneurs the opportunity to focus on business creation activities while providing essential equipment at cost and time savings.

INCUBATOR SERVICES AND ADVANTAGES

Flexible Space and Flexible Leases

Most incubators provide facilities for start-up companies. The biggest advantage they offer is flexibility in committing to space based on the growth of the business. Traditionally incubators provide space at below-market rates. Many incubators are now pricing at the market and are focusing on business assistance services as a major value offering.

Administrative Services

Look closely at the services an incubator offers. Most incubators (88 percent) provide shared copiers, fax machines, telephone systems, computers, and high-speed Internet access. Access to equipment is a big time saver. Many incubators also provide administrative staff assistance such as answering telephones and clerical support.

Management Help

Management help can be the most important service you receive. It often begins with a consultation to help you evaluate the concept or growth prospects for a going concern, and it continues with regular reviews of the business. Incubators typically provide support on business basics such as developing business plans, refining the business concept, and marketing assistance. Roughly 75 percent of all U.S. incubators also provide help with accounting and financial management services.

Expert Advice

Expert advice from university business professors, other business owners, lenders, and accountants can help keep your business on track.

Specialization

Some incubators are industry specific (e.g., food service, software, biotech, Internet, art, or ceramics). Others focus on service businesses or specific social goals. For example, Entergy Arts Business Center in New Orleans started as an incubator specifically for individual artists and arts-related businesses. Other incubators serve specific groups, such as women or minority business owners. For example, the San Francisco–based Women's Technology Cluster is a high-tech incubator for women entrepreneurs. The Cluster helps start-ups get off the ground, hosts weekly seminars on business basics, and offers services such as help with hiring, finances, public relations, sales, and Web design.

Increased Credibility

Acceptance represents a kind of *Good Housekeeping* Seal of Approval. Most incubators are highly selective about who they admit. High-quality meeting rooms, professional telephone coverage, and reception areas all improve a start-up's image.

Easy Networking

This includes opportunities to chat with other tenants or make formal presentations to potential investors. It's often easier to get your phone calls returned when you are physically located at a known incubator in a normal business building.

Funding

Funding is not usually available directly from incubators, but many will help arrange meetings with potential investors. A few public incubators will provide funds to get you started. For example, the Austin incubator, housed in the University of Texas, will provide $500,000 in seed money. For-profit incubators usually provide investments but take on average 45 percent equity versus the 2 to 5 percent common in nonprofit incubators. For-profit incubators differ from venture capitalists in that they are willing to fund small seed rounds (those below the VC radar screen), they take a more active role, and they usually are willing to stay in longer.

GUIDELINES FOR SELECTING AN INCUBATION PROGRAM

TRACK RECORD

- How well is the program performing?
- How long has the program been operating?

GUIDELINES FOR SELECTING AN INCUBATION PROGRAM (cont.)

- Does it have any successful graduate companies, and if so, how long have they been in business independent from the incubator?
- What do other clients and graduates think of the program?

GRADUATION POLICY

- What is the program's graduation policy; that is, what are the incubator's exit criteria?
- How flexible is the policy?
- How long, on average, have clients remained in the program? (Incubators typically graduate companies within three years.)

QUALIFICATIONS OF MANAGER AND STAFF

- How long has the current staff been with the program?
- How much time does the staff spend on-site?
- Have they had any entrepreneurial successes of their own? Do they actively engage in professional development activities, or are they a member of a professional/trade association to keep them up to date on the latest in incubation best practices?

FOR MORE INFORMATION

Information about Joining an Incubator

The National Business Incubator Association's web-site has resources to help you manage an incubator, or to become an incubator tenant. This site will also help you find an incubator near you. See www.nbia.org/

Additional tips can be found at www.smallbusinessnotes.com/

A wealth of valuable information, directories and links to incubators is found at www.1000ventures.com/business_guide/business_incubators_main.html

For information on a network of incubators focusing entirely on renewable energy companies see www.nrel.gov/technologytransfer/entrepreneurs/inc.html

A number of research reports on business incubators can be found at www.kauffman.org/

WEB SITES OF LEADING FOR-PROFIT INCUBATORS

CMGI: www.cmgi.com
IdeaLab: www.idealab.com/

Research Articles

Dina Adkins, Chuck Wolfe, and Hugh Sherman, *Best Practices in Business Incubation* (2000). Study performed for the Maryland Technology Development Corporation (TEDCO). www.marylandtedco.org.

David S. Chappell and Hugh Sherman, "Methodological Challenges in Evaluating Business Incubator Outcomes," *Economic Development Quarterly* 14 (1998).

Morten Hansen, Henry Chesbrough, Nitin Nohria, and Donald Sull, "Networked Incubators: Hothouses of the New Economy," *Harvard Business Review,* September 1 (2000).

Susie McKinnon and Sally Hayhow, *State of the Business Incubation Industry* (Ohio: NBIA Publications, 1998).

Lawrence A. Molnar, Donald R. Grimes, and Jack Edelstein, *Business Incubation Works* (Ohio: NBIA Publications, 1997).

ADDITIONAL RESOURCES

There are many articles and case reports of entrepreneurs' bootstrapping ideas published by popular magazines. You can search for articles for ideas and tips at the following sites:

www.entrepreneur.com

www.inc.com

www.fastcompany.com

The following Web sites provide further information about certain aspects of government grants:

www.nttc.edu/ has details of all ten units of SBIR and five units of STTR sources.

www.winbmdo.com lists all contact information, has links to relevant Web sites, and so on. This agency, now known as MDA, has traditionally funded riskier projects.

www.grants.gov/Applicants/index.html lists all active federal grants programs.

www.acq.osd.mil/sadbu/sbir/overview/index.htm covers most SBIR and STTR documents.

www.acq.osd.mil/sadbu/sbir/solicitations/sttr04/index.htm lists solicitations from the DOD, which includes Army, Navy, Air Force, DARPA, and MDA with contact information. The DOD constitutes about 50 percent of the total SBIR/STTR funding, more than $500 million.

grants1.nih.gov/grants/oer.htm is a link to grant opportunity, policy and guidelines, and contact information for the National Institutes of Health, the second largest funding source. At this site, click on "Small Business Funding Opportunities."

www.nsf.gov/funding/ is a link to grant opportunity at the National Science Foundation.

www.nsa.gov/msp00002.cfm refers to the National Security Agency Mathematical Sciences Program, which funds high-quality mathematical research in the areas of algebra, number theory, discrete mathematics, probability, statistics, and cryptology.

A particularly useful source is an up-to-date reference book on *all* federal R & D funding programs entitled *Federal Technology Funding Guide, 2008–2009*. It can be downloaded free at: www.larta.org/media/pdf/FTFG/pdf

For finding technologies available at government labs, see www.nttc.edu/

USING UNIVERSITY OUTREACH PROGRAMS

Certain business schools have venture funds that review opportunities for investment presented by students and outside entrepreneurs. We give two examples here from the authors' universities. These resources may also provide more than access to funding; they may provide student teams to work with start-ups to help them evaluate various options for their businesses. They are typical of resources that can be found at leading business schools. A list of contacts can be found at the Global Consortium of Entrepreneurship Centers Web site, www.nationalconsortium.org.

Columbia Business School—Eugene Lang Entrepreneurial Initiative Fund

Purpose and History

The Eugene Lang Entrepreneurial Initiative Fund was established in 1996 by an initial gift of $1 million from Eugene Lang, founder and chairman emeritus of REFAC Technology Development Corporation. Its objective is to foster an entrepreneurial environment at Columbia Business School by providing students who conceive qualified business initiatives with seed capital for carrying them out after graduation. It also seeks to provide the business school with the opportunity to share in the success of funded ventures through negotiated equity or other participation.

Eligibility

All students enrolled in Columbia Business School's MBA program are eligible to submit business plans for funding consideration in accordance with specified procedures. Students may work individually or with a partner.

Criteria

Proposals for all types of enterprises—small- or large-scale; high- or low-tech; start-ups or acquisitions; service, manufacturing, or retail operations—will be given consideration in relation to the following criteria:

- Feasibility of the proposed venture and its prospects for success
- Strength of the student's commitment to the venture and his or her qualifications to make it succeed
- Prospects for raising additional funding as may be required
- Technical or conceptual originality or social value

Mentoring and Assistance

Students will have a variety of resources available to them to assist with the development of their proposals. These include the school's entrepreneurship courses, faculty advisers, the Lang Fund Advisory Panel, volunteer mentors and relevant external sources, and the Lang Fund board of directors.

For further information, visit the Web site: www4.gsb.columbia.edu/.

Eugene M. Lang Center for Entrepreneurship
3022 Broadway
317 Uris Hall
New York, NY 10027
Phone: (212) 854-3244
Fax: (212) 280-4329

Smeal College of Business, Pennsylvania State University—Bette and John Garber Venture Capital Center

Purpose and History

The fund, established in 1999 through a $5 million commitment from Penn State Alumnus Dr. John Garber and his wife, Bette, brings reality to the teaching of entrepreneurship and venture capital by enabling MBA students to become actively involved in the process of equity investment and new ventures. Students examine current investment opportunities and decide whether to invest from the fund in a particular transaction. Interaction with external private equity groups provides an opportunity for students to experience the complexities and pressures of the volatile private equity sector and to link applicant companies to other sources of help and funding.

Eligibility

Any early-stage company seeking help and investment can apply for analysis by teams of students within the Smeal College MBA program. To request consideration, nonconfidential outlines should initially be sent to fcfe@smeal.psu.edu.

Criteria

Proposals for all types of enterprises from entrepreneurs within the United States will be given consideration, provided that the following apply:

- The entrepreneur is in an early stage of building an investment and is seeking no more than $500,000 in this round.
- The entrepreneur is willing to make an investor's presentation and interact with a student team for several weeks.
- The business is sufficiently challenging that it can provide a learning experience.

Mentoring and Assistance

Students, themselves mentored by experienced faculty within the Smeal College, work closely with the entrepreneur, providing valuable input.

For further information, visit the Web site: www.smeal.psu.edu/fcfe/garber.

www.wiley.com/college/kaplan

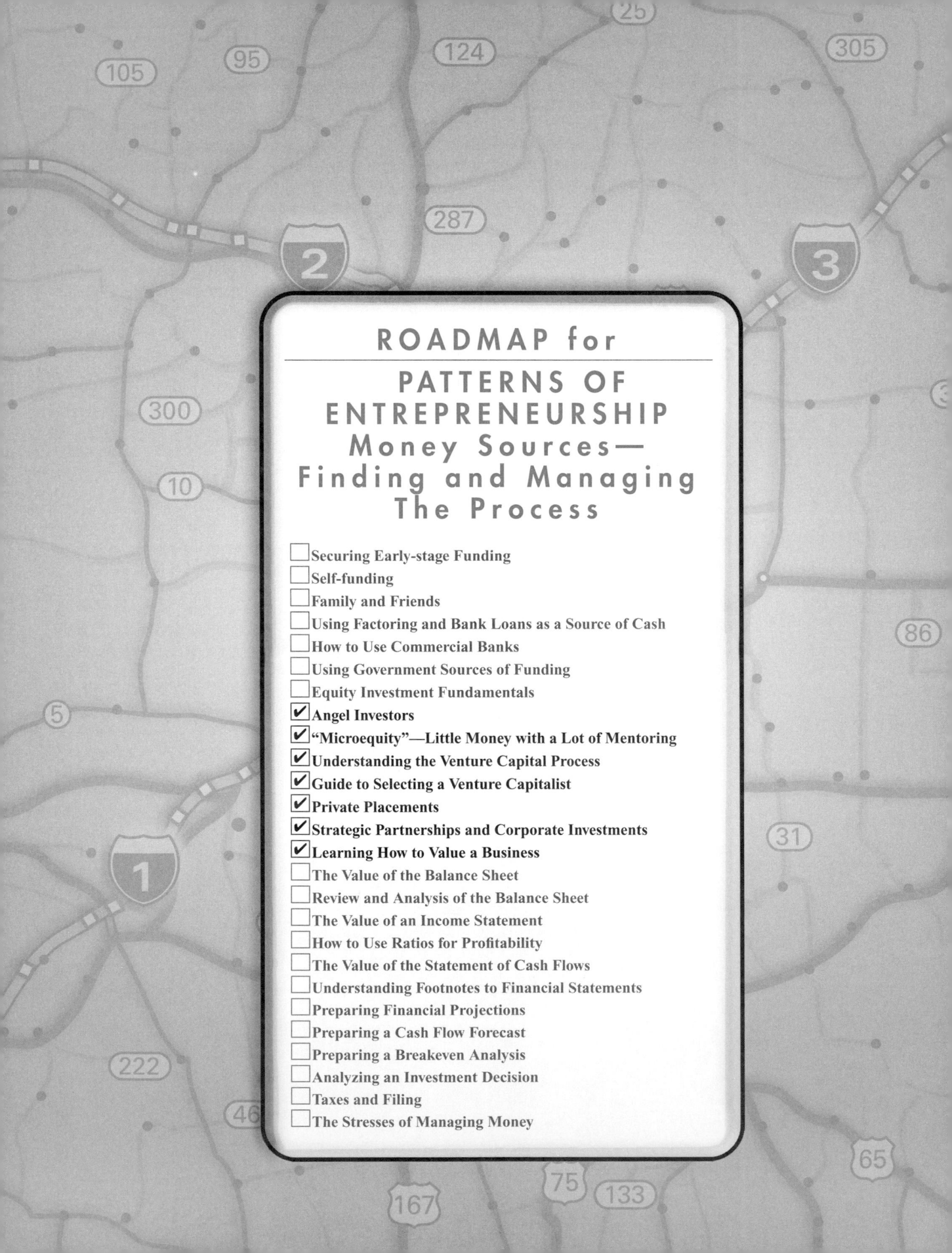

ROADMAP for

PATTERNS OF ENTREPRENEURSHIP
Money Sources—
Finding and Managing
The Process

☐ **Securing Early-stage Funding**
☐ **Self-funding**
☐ **Family and Friends**
☐ **Using Factoring and Bank Loans as a Source of Cash**
☐ **How to Use Commercial Banks**
☐ **Using Government Sources of Funding**
☐ **Equity Investment Fundamentals**
☑ **Angel Investors**
☑ **"Microequity"—Little Money with a Lot of Mentoring**
☑ **Understanding the Venture Capital Process**
☑ **Guide to Selecting a Venture Capitalist**
☑ **Private Placements**
☑ **Strategic Partnerships and Corporate Investments**
☑ **Learning How to Value a Business**
☐ **The Value of the Balance Sheet**
☐ **Review and Analysis of the Balance Sheet**
☐ **The Value of an Income Statement**
☐ **How to Use Ratios for Profitability**
☐ **The Value of the Statement of Cash Flows**
☐ **Understanding Footnotes to Financial Statements**
☐ **Preparing Financial Projections**
☐ **Preparing a Cash Flow Forecast**
☐ **Preparing a Breakeven Analysis**
☐ **Analyzing an Investment Decision**
☐ **Taxes and Filing**
☐ **The Stresses of Managing Money**

CHAPTER 8

EQUITY FINANCING FOR HIGH GROWTH

"The most important thing for a young man is to establish credit—a reputation, character."

JOHN D. ROCKEFELLER

OBJECTIVES

- Learn when and how to attract angel investors.
- Describe how to attract venture capital financing and use a private placement.
- Learn the process of finding investors and targeting the right firm.
- Prepare a term sheet.
- Learn the different methods to value a business.

CHAPTER OUTLINE

Introduction

Profile: Matt Brezina—Staged Investments

Equity Investment Fundamentals

Angel Investors

"Microequity"—Little Money with a Lot of Mentoring

Understanding the Venture Capital Process

Guide to Selecting a Venture Capitalist

Private Placements

Strategic Partnerships and Corporate Investments

Learning How to Value a Business

Summary

Study Questions

Exercises

Case Study: CoreTek, Inc.

Interactive Learning on the Web

Additional Resources

Appendix 1: Due Diligence Checklist

Appendix 2: Model Venture Capital Term Sheet—Series A Preferred Stock

INTRODUCTION

This chapter describes the financing options for private entrepreneurial companies that are anticipating fast growth. The first sections describe the three main sources of attracting equity funding, namely angels, "institutionalized" venture capital (VC), and formal private placements of stock. Equity funding means selling part of the

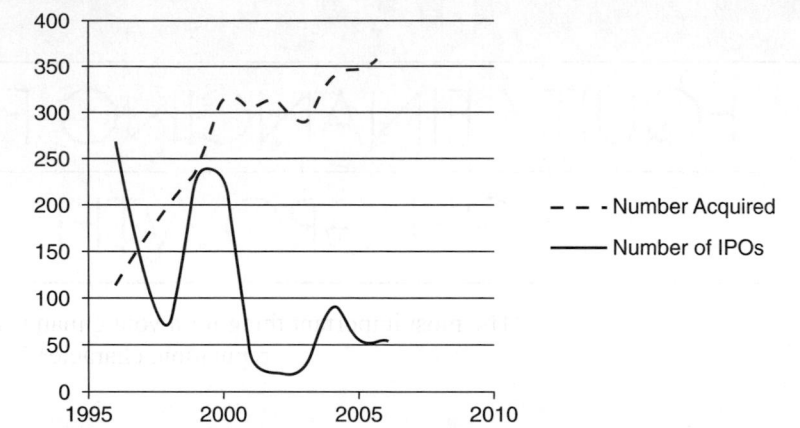

Figure 8-1 Comparison between Exit Methods for VC-backed Companies, 1996–2006. *Source:* **National Venture Capital Association**

ownership of the company to investors through the purchase of shares. Once an entrepreneur sells part of her company, her life fundamentally changes. Outside shareholders' primary objective is to earn a substantial return on their investment. The anticipated return will depend on the stage of the company when the investment is taken; usually the earlier the investment, the riskier the venture and, therefore, the higher the expected returns. Investors can derive the benefit of their investment only when a liquidity event occurs and an exit strategy is fulfilled. This means that a new entity agrees to buy the stock in the company held by the current shareholders. The most common way for this to happen is for the company to be sold to a larger firm.

Alternatively, the company may be sold to the public via an initial public offering, or IPO, although this is relatively rare. Figure 8-1 compares the occurrences of these two types of "exits." In 2008 the number of IPO's was in the single digits. The master-case company for this book, Neoforma, provides a good example of a company that first managed to have an IPO when the public markets were buoyant but was eventually sold to a larger company.

Clearly, if the founders' intention is to retain control of the company and manage it for their own benefit and lifestyle, there will be a fundamental conflict of interest between the inside entrepreneurs and the external shareholders. So the golden rule is *do not take cash from external shareholders unless you intend to build the company for sale.* Note that this is irrespective of *how much* of the company you sell; sale of only 1 percent of the company fundamentally changes the way the company must be run. Many entrepreneurs starting out make the mistake of thinking that if they sell less than 50 percent of the company, they are still in control. As we shall see, investors with a minority interest can still determine how the company is run.

IN ACTION

Entrepreneurs wishing to retain control of their company, come what may, should not accept equity financing from outsiders.

In the second part of the chapter, we look at how a company is valued using the different methods such as earnings and asset valuation, adjusted book value, discounted cash flow comparatives, and market valuation. A discussion for evaluating investment opportunities using the time value of money that addresses net present value and internal rate of return are also presented. The chapter closes with structuring a strategic partnership or joint venture as an alternative to seeking a private equity investment.

PROFILE: MATT BREZINA — STAGED INVESTMENTS[1]

Matt Brezina graduated from Penn State in electrical engineering in 2003 and moved to the University of Maryland with a scholarship for an engineering masters program. By chance he met Adam Smith, a computer graduate student at MIT. They first made contact on the Internet while Matt was searching for a summer roommate on craigslist. One day he received a call from Adam, who was excited about starting a company "doing something in e-mail" thinking that "there were a lot of folks out there that were not so happy with the current products." Although Matt did not initially think that he could add much to the software development, Adam convinced him to join him as a partner. Matt dropped out from his program in Maryland and moved into Adam's dorm room to work on some possible innovative ideas with him. Adam had already contacted the Boston office of YCombinator, a new form of very-early-stage angel network (see below), and the pair received $12,000 to help them live for a few months while they worked on their ideas. Matt supplemented this by working as an engineering consultant with the Naval Research Lab for a few days a month. After the three-month program, YCombinator suggested that they move to California, where they were promptly immersed in the local advisers' network. After six months of living on a shoestring, they were ready to make a presentation to a group of more substantial angel investors, and they quickly raised $80,000. This allowed them to create a very good demonstration of their e-mail management software, and after another six months, they were ready to present to institutional venture capitalists, raising a further $4 million led by Khosla Ventures.[2] According to Matt, "Without YCombinator's mentoring and investing network, Xobni[3] would not exist." The $4 million allowed the company to launch its product to much public enthusiasm from notables such as Bill Gates. Having money in the bank has also helped in hiring great people, including Jeff Bonforte, who joined them from Yahoo! to take up the CEO's role. "We realized we needed really good operational management skills, with which neither Adam nor I had much experience." Within two years, Adam and Matt had built a fifteen-person company; raised more than $4 million in investment; hired top talent away from leading companies such as Google and Yahoo!; built a product used by thousands of people; appeared in *Newsweek,* the *Wall Street Journal,* and *Entrepreneur* magazine; and struck a partnering relationship with LinkedIn. Early in 2008 Microsoft offered them approximately $20 million for their company, which they felt was too low.

EQUITY INVESTMENT FUNDAMENTALS

Public Stock

There are two basic classes of ownership in companies. The first, with which most people are familiar, is by holding shares in publicly traded companies. Usually associated with larger, well-known corporations such as Ford Motor, Johnson & Johnson, and Citibank, public companies trade freely on stock exchanges, such as the New York Stock Exchange and NASDAQ, both of which are designed for trading the stock easily and transparently. In fact, many smaller companies also trade on these exchanges, which provide a "liquid market" in their stocks. Any member of the public can buy and sell these shares in this type of company. This liquidity enables inside shareholders to turn their shares into cash. When a privately held company "goes public," several benefits result. The private stock can now be traded openly, and insiders can convert their illiquid assets into cash. The company can also sell some of its own stock to raise further money for growth and acquisitions. This also provides an easy way to later, should more cash be required, sell more stock in a secondary offering. No wonder most entrepreneurs dream of going public.

As we saw above, not many of these dreams come true. Going public requires a significant amount of expensive legal work to prepare the company for such an event. Timing is critical. The stock market is very volatile, and synchronizing an IPO for a particular company with the right market timing is extremely difficult and uncertain. Often an IPO is withdrawn on the day prior to the event because there is not enough public demand at the price the company finds attractive. The public is fickle and follows fads, as was clear during the dot.com boom. After the bust, it was impossible to take an Internet company public for several years, even if it was potentially a great company.

Private Equity

In contrast to public stock, the term *private equity* actually covers a broad range of investment categories that come into play at different stages of a company's and even an industry's, life cycles.

- **Venture capital** is a broad subcategory of private equity that refers to equity investments made, typically in less mature companies, for the launch, early development, or expansion of a business. Venture capital is often subdivided by the stage of development of the company, ranging from early-stage capital used for the launch of start-up companies to late-stage and growth capital that is often used to fund the expansion of an existing business that is generating revenue but may not yet be profitable or wants to generate cash flow to fund future growth.

- **Leveraged buyout,** also known as **LBO** or **buyout,** refers to a strategy of making equity investments as part of a transaction in which a company, business unit, or business assets are acquired from the current shareholders, typically with the use of financial leverage. The companies involved in these transactions are typically more mature and generate operating cash flows.

- **Growth capital** refers to equity investments, most often minority investments, in more mature companies that are looking for capital to expand or restructure operations, enter new markets, or finance a major acquisition without a change of control of the business.

- **Distressed,** or **special, situations** refers to investments in equity or debt securities of a distressed company, or a company where value can be unlocked as a result of a one-time opportunity (e.g., a change in government regulations or market dislocation).

- **Mezzanine capital** refers to subordinated debt or preferred equity securities that often represent the most junior portion of a company's capital structure that is senior to the company's common equity.

Here are two examples of industry-specific investments that have emerged recently:

1. **Infrastructure** investments in various public works (e.g., bridges, tunnels, toll roads, airports, public transportation, and other public works) are made typically as part of a privatization initiative on the part of a government entity.
2. **Energy** and **power** investments are made in a wide variety of companies (rather than assets) engaged in the production and sale of energy, including fuel extraction, manufacturing, refining, and distribution (energy), or companies engaged in the production or transmission of electrical power (power).

Private equity firms generally receive a return on their investments through one of the following avenues:

- *Initial Public Offering.* Shares of the company are offered to the public, typically providing a partial immediate realization to the financial sponsor as well as a public market into which it can later sell additional shares.
- *Merger* or *Acquisition.* The company is sold for either cash or shares in another company.
- *Recapitalization.* Cash is distributed to the shareholders (in this case, the financial sponsor) and its private equity funds from either cash flow generated by the company or raising debt or other securities to fund the distribution.

The category that is of most interest to an entrepreneur, at least at the early stages of the company, is venture capital. When an entrepreneur starts a company, he and perhaps a few other cofounders agree how the company should be owned and issue stock in the company (see Chapter 6). They own private equity in their company, usually in the form of common stock, or participate as members in a partnership or LLC. For brevity, this is now referred to as private equity.

When a company is founded, legal contracts called membership or shareholders' agreements must be in existence as soon as there is more than one owner. An attorney should be hired for preparing these contracts. They should clearly state how ownership can be transferred under different situations and how the company will be valued in these cases. For example, if one of the owners should die, there must be a way that the ownership position can be valued both for probate reasons and to set a price for which this ownership can be bought back by the company or other designated shareholders.

Private equity has limited liquidity. Trading is usually confined to the existing shareholders of the company, and this internal trading may also have restrictions. So ownership in a private company has real value only when a liquidity event occurs.

Using Private Equity for Raising Funds

One way that a privately held company can acquire funds for its operations and growth is to sell an ownership position in the company to willing investors. Usually a company will not need all the money to reach its goals immediately, and therefore, investments are divided into "rounds." The entrepreneur and investors have to balance several factors in choosing the size and timing of each round.

- The earlier in the company's life that the investment is sought, usually the less a company is worth. Therefore, to raise, say, $250,000 when there is little more than an idea and a business plan could cost the founder 50 percent of the company, for the idea at this stage is worth only $500,000. Clearly using the bootstrapping techniques described in the previous chapter to move the company further along its development path will reduce this early loss of ownership. This loss in percentage ownership is called "dilution." In this case, the entrepreneur will have "suffered a 50 percent dilution on the first round."

- This dilution will discourage the entrepreneur from asking for more funding, even if the plan really needs $1 million to reach a key milestone.

- On the other hand, raising very small amounts of money in dribs and drabs can be a tremendous drain on the founder's time, leaving little time to actually build the company.

- Not raising enough money in the first round and, therefore, being unable to meet a key milestone could actually damage the company's reputation and make it even more difficult to raise in the next round. In fact, it is not unusual in these cases that the investors demand a "down" round—that is, one in which the company's value is lower than in the previous round. This, of course, creates an even greater dilution of the ownership for the company's founder, who can end up with little ownership if things go wrong.

- The investor may not insist on too low a valuation, however, because once the ownership position of the founder is diluted down to a few percentage points, then there is no motivation left for the insiders to work hard to create value, little of which they will ever see. Smart investors are careful to leave "enough on the table" for the entrepreneur(s) so there is enough alignment of objectives left for both parties.

These complex forces are at play every time an entrepreneur raises equity finance, and it is advisable, if possible, until sufficient experience is gained, to find a trusted adviser who has gone through the process several times to guide the negotiations.

Before seeking private investments, it is vital that a sound business plan as outlined in Chapter 5, has been prepared, stating clearly when funds are required, the key milestones, and how the funds will be used. This enables the entrepreneur to determine the right time, amount, and potential sources for the funds.

Table 8-1 shows the likely targets for investors at different stages of a company's growth.

The fewer rounds of investment that a company must go through prior to exit, the less dilution both the founders and the early-stage investors will experience. If the company needs large amounts of capital to fulfill its plans, different investors will likely be required for later stages. It is usual for investors to work together to share the risk if the cash demands get too high for their risk profile. This is called syndicating. Investors like to choose their own syndicating partners and usually have relationships in place for this role. Entrepreneurs should question potential investors about their own "appetites" for funding and their access to syndicating partners if this is required in later rounds.

Table 8-1   **Rounds of Equity Finance**

Round	Status	Likely Sources of Funds	Expected IRR
Preseed	Barely an idea, rough business plan	Friends/family, bootstrapping, grants, and microequity funds	1–40%
Seed	Prototype or proof of principle, no sales	Angels, grants, possibly a local VC firm	20–40%
A Round	Development nearly complete, first trials with customers	Angels, early-stage VC	30%+
B Round	Customers, first growth phase	VC or other institutional sources of funds	30%+
C/D Rounds	Sufficient to get to cash flow neutrality or exit	Late-stage VCs in syndicate	20%+
Mezzanine	Prepare for sale or IPO, acquisitions	Large private equity funds	15–20%

The table indicates that friends and family are usually undemanding on the annual return (internal rate of return, or IRR) that they expect. They are usually helping out for personal, not financial, reasons. It is rare, however, that they have deep enough pockets to see the whole venture through. Other professional investors expect high rates of returns for the risk they are taking.

Classes of Stock

Once an entrepreneur seeks equity funding beyond his or her close friends and family, the structure of the investment becomes more formal. Any professional investor will require that an LLC or partnership is converted into a full corporation, usually a C-corporation. The founders and any employees who own stock will have common shares that carry few rights except their ownership position. Investors will demand a different class of stock, preferred stock. These shares carry with them certain preferences, the most important of which is "preference on liquidation." This means that if the company is sold at a low price or files for bankruptcy, once any debt is paid off, the preferred shareholders receive their investment back before any distribution to the founders holding common stock. Different classes of stock may also have different voting right powers.

Another form of investment often used is convertible preferred. In this case the initial investment is made in the form of a loan sometimes referred to as a debenture. This loan will carry interest, typically a few percentage points above the current prime rate. The interest is normally accrued and not paid to the investors but, of course, increases the debt owed by the company. The loan can be converted at the investor's option to a defined class of preferred stock within a given time and at a valuation of the company that has normally been agreed to beforehand; the interest becomes part of the debt that is converted to equity at the time the option is taken. If the conversion is not requested, then the investor usually has the right to recall the loan plus interest. This gives the investor greater flexibility. If the company does not appear to be meeting its growth objectives and moving toward a liquidity event, then the investor can get the original sum plus interest out of the company. This is also a protection for the investor in the case that the founding entrepreneur(s) run the company as a "lifestyle" business. Calling the loan can effectively give the investor control should this happen, for it is unlikely that the company is financially strong enough to pay back the full sum owed.

As the company moves forward, additional rounds of investment will likely be required. The first investors will have insisted that they have the first right to make investments in subsequent rounds. Thus, the entrepreneur will enter into a negotiation before the funds are needed to try to reach mutually agreeable terms. This can result in the following scenarios:

- The investors are pleased with how the company is developing and wish to take all of the next round of investment. In this case it is usually easy to reach satisfactory terms. However, the entrepreneur also has the right to find other investors who might be willing to invest at a higher valuation of the company, thereby reducing the dilution experienced by the existing shareholders. The existing investors are entitled to be informed of this intention and meet the terms that the entrepreneur finds. It is important to be open and retain a good relationship with the current investors.

- The investors do not want to make the full investment in the next round but are willing to coinvest with new sources of funds. Coinvestment is common in later rounds and is called "syndication." It allows investors to diversify their risk portfolio much in the same way that individual investors are advised to do for their retirement funds. In this case the entrepreneur should negotiate the terms of the next round and approach other investors to see if they wish to participate on these terms or perhaps better terms. Asking the existing investors to find other sources of funds through their own networks is by far the best approach here.

- The investors decline to invest in the next round. It is important to understand the reasons for this decision. If they do not have sufficient funds to go to the next level or their investment objectives are not to invest at later stages, then having them talk to new investors can help raise the next round; there are legitimate reasons for no further participation. On the other hand, if they are dissatisfied with the company's performance, the entrepreneur may have difficulty attracting further investments. Any new investor will insist on talking to the existing external shareholders, and this will make them very cautious in making an investment. In this case any new investor will likely view this as high risk, and the round will be at a lower valuation than the previous round. This will significantly dilute all the old shareholders, and the new money will dictate the terms of the deal. Often, in this case, the earlier investors will lose their preferences and downgrade to a common stock ownership position. Clearly this is a bad situation for the entrepreneur and is to be avoided if at all possible.

Warrants

Investors may also negotiate to receive warrants when making an investment. Warrants convey a right to purchase a certain number of shares, common or preferred as defined, within a given time period and at a stated price. The exercise of the warrants is at the option of the investor, not the company. For example, assume that an investor purchases 10 percent of a company for $1 million by buying 100,000 preferred shares at $10 each. Each share purchased may have an attached warrant to allow the investor to buy one-half of an additional share of common stock for $6.00 within two years from the original investment. Within a two-year period, the investor may exercise all or part of this right and buy more of the company at a slightly higher valuation than the original investment—$12.00 a share rather than $10.00. In this case this new stock is common rather than preferred, and therefore, the investor will have to feel pretty confident about the company's progress to buy it. On the other hand, he or she has two years to watch the company before this decision is made. If the company is not doing well, the investor is unlikely to come up with the extra funds and the warrants will run out.

Note: "How much more is a preferred share worth than a common share?" This question is often asked. The answer depends on the actual preference terms and the health and stage of the company's development. As a rule of thumb, in the very early and uncertain stages, the ratio can be as high as ten times. As the company approaches a suitable exit point for investors, this ratio approaches unity. Thus, in the warrant case above, the investor would take into account how far the company had moved forward toward an exit plan before exercising the warrants. If there was little progress, then the warrants would be worth as little as $1.20 a common share, and the purchase of the warrants would not be attractive. The company may have to raise money in a down round, which would be a better opportunity for the investor's participation.

Pre- and Postmoney Valuation

Pre- and postmoney valuation are commonly used at the time an equity investment is made. The premoney valuation is the value that the entrepreneur and the investor agree the company is worth prior to any investment. The postmoney is the valuation of the company immediately after the investment is made. The simplest way to reconcile these two numbers is just to add the premoney valuation to the amount of the investment. For example, a company that is valued at $10 million just before receiving $5 million in equity investment will now be worth $15 million—the original company plus the $5 million cash now in the company's bank account. Of course, now that the money is in the bank, other possibilities for the company have opened up, and the postmoney valuation may be considered higher than this number for various reasons. However, the simple calculation is a good guideline to use in most cases.

ROADMAP

IN ACTION

Investors will undertake a detailed analysis of your company before providing any cash. Reduce the chance of future antipathy by being completely open with them and carefully checking out whether they are the best partners for you.

Due Diligence

The term *due diligence* refers to the investigative process that prospective investors undertake prior to making an investment. This is usually broken down into at least two phases. The first is a quick evaluation on key claims made by the entrepreneur. Investors are loath to spend significant efforts until they have made some checks to see whether there are any obvious showstoppers. They may want to do some background checks on the principals, make sure they own title to any intellectual property, do a short analysis of existing and potential competitors, and talk to some existing or future customers. If these check out, then they will start a complete and detailed investigation on all aspects of your business and plans. Appendix 1 at the end of this chapter shows a due diligence checklist that is typical for a professional investor. (A similar list may be used by a bank before approving a loan.) It is broad and thorough. It is mandatory that the entrepreneur provides full and complete access to this information and offers any other information that may be relevant. This is called "full disclosure," and it is a legal responsibility imposed on anyone seeking funds from an investor or bank. (The ethical importance of disclosure is discussed in Chapter 12).

In addition, the entrepreneur should undertake due diligence on the potential investor(s) to make sure that the deal is a good fit to their investment criteria, that they have deep knowledge in the business area, that they will take an active role to help and be there for a follow-up round or can provide access to a network of future investors, and most important, that they will be easy to work with during times of stress. There will be such times for sure, and investors should be good partners, not enemies, when this happens. The best way to check this is to call the CEOs of companies who have already received investment from the investors and question them on the quality of the relationship. Poor due diligence and an entrepreneur's unrealistic expectations when seeking equity investment are common causes of future conflict. Building a company is difficult enough in any case; doing it with misunderstanding and with a misalignment of objectives between an entrepreneur and investors makes it impossible.

Bridge Financing

Timing investments to match a company's plans is extremely difficult. In today's climate the time between identifying the need for additional funds and actually getting money in the bank can range from a minimum of six months to more than a year. There is always the danger, therefore, that a company fails to raise the funds needed before running out of cash. In this case it may be appropriate to seek "bridge" funding. Remember, a bridge spans the area between two places and does not hang in midair. Bridge deals require an event to happen that terminates the interim financing. A well-known example is a bridge loan that allows someone to own two homes at the same time during a move. If there is a contract to purchase your original home from a qualified buyer, then the bank will provide bridge financing for the period between buying the new home and selling the first home. The bridge loan is secured by the first house, and the loan is repaid precisely when the first home is sold. Bridge loans are expensive but convenient. For a company strapped for cash, current investors may agree to provide enough funding until the company has closed a new round of funding. The bridge financier must be relatively confident that the new money will be secured, so the bridge money can be extracted or at least the investor made safe.

As expressed in the bridge loan offer in Table 8-2, the current investor, BVP, is not willing to continue to fully fund this company, which requires $16 million of additional financing. It is willing to invest a maximum of $7 million. In order to bridge the company to its next "C" round, it will lend the company an interest-bearing sum of $4 million in stages. In addition to the interest, which will be paid in stock and not cash, the company will have a right to further invest at a very low rate for five years by exercising warrants. Both of these terms significantly dilute the ownership of the founders. The loan is secured by all of the company's assets. BVP will, however, commit to providing nearly half of the next round, which will greatly help the company raise the rest of the money. Clearly the company has not

Table 8-2   **Bridge Loan Example**
Terms for $4 Million Bridge Loan for Acme Inc.

Amount	A total of up to $4 million to be done in an initial closing of $1 million and a secondary closing of $1 million and, if necessary, a third closing of $2 million
Institutional support	Beta Venture Partners LLC
Interest rate	6% simple interest to be paid in stock
Repayment	At the earlier of Series C close or December 31, 2008
Security interest	UCC filings on all assets (and if applicable in the Patent and Trademark Office)
Warrant coverage	Note holders will receive a warrant to purchase one share of common stock for every $2.50 invested in the bridge note
Warrant term	5 years
Warrant exercise price	$0.01
Commitment to Class C Round	BVP will commit $7 million to the Series C financing and will work with management to secure the $9 million follow-on financing to fill out a $16 million Class C round
Conditions of closing	Satisfactory completion of customer reference checks
Date of closing	The date of the first closing will be August 15, 2007, the date of the second closing will be October 1, 2007, and the date of the third closing, if necessary, will be November 1, 2007, unless otherwise agreed upon by the company and BVP

achieved its expectations, and the deal is punitive for the company and the founders. However, they have little alternative at this stage.

Preferences and Covenants

The terms negotiated by investors when making an investment will contain several conditions that provide certain advantages over the common stockholders and certain rights to protect their interests. Private equity investment terms can become rather complicated, and the company will require the services of an attorney specializing in venture investments to guide it through the negotiations and contracts. The following list describes some of the more important terms that are encountered.

- *Board Membership.* Investors usually request a board seat in the company. If several investor groups or VCs participate (i.e., the deal is syndicated), then one investor will be the lead. This means that they will negotiate the terms of the investment, agree on it with the coinvestors, and usually take on the board representation. Investors look for a balanced board, not control of the board. Other investors might request "board visitation rights," which enables them to observe but not participate in board meetings or have voting rights.

- *Management Decisions.* Investors owning preferred stock may request a right to change the management team if certain conditions are not met. This is often an emotional topic. However, it offers a wonderful chance for each party to understand its objectives. A smart entrepreneur will know whether she is the right leader to take it all the way, or her management skills will be sorely tested once the company reaches fifty employees, for example. Often it is better to step aside for more seasoned management to be brought in with mutual consent and take on a chairperson or technology officer role. Remember, control is not equivalent to ownership or wealth creation. Have this discussion up front, before the investment is made. It will avoid major problems later.

- *Registration Rights.* Investors will insist on having registration rights should the company go public. This means that, in this event, their shares will convert automatically to common shares and have the same rights to be included in the public offer.

- *Later Rounds.* A right of first refusal to participate in future investment rounds is granted. Investors fear that they will be diluted out of the company ownership or the company will bring in investors that the original investors do not like or trust.

- *Antidilution Rights.* Antidilution provisions protect an investor from the company not meeting its objectives and from a subsequent round of investment being made at a lower valuation (i.e., a down round). In this case the investors are freely issued an amount of common stock to bring their ownership position back up to their original stake so they do not suffer dilution. The dilution in this case then falls onto the shoulders of the founders. This arrangement is also referred to as a *ratchet* clause.

- *Forcing Exit.* The investors may request a *forced buyout* term, which means that if the company has not created a liquidity event within a stated time frame, the investors can take independent action and find a buyer and impose it on the board of the company. This is intended to protect investors from the founding entrepreneurs wishing to preserve the company as a lifestyle firm and not to lose their perceived control. If this clause is invoked, then clearly there is significant animosity between the insiders and the investors. A similar clause, called "demand registration rights," allows the investors to force an IPO on the company by an agreed-upon date. These clauses are rarely exercised in full as the ability to create a viable exit may depend more on externalities. However, the existence of these clauses does enable investors to force the board to take action.

- *Piggybacking.* This gives all shareholders holding such rights to sell their stock at an IPO. An IPO may be used to sell the company's stock (treasury stock) only in order to raise further funding for the company. It is not automatic that shareholders can offer their stock at the same time. Normally the investment banker managing the IPO makes these decisions.

These terms and conditions may sound very complicated; indeed, they can be. However, there is one guiding principle in private equity financing that must be remembered: at each new round, *everything* can and usually is renegotiated. For example, if an investor in an "A" round does not have enough capital to invest when the company looks for a "B" round investment, the new investor will often require the first investor to forgo all of their preferences and rights, converting their shares to common. In the parlance of private equity, "last money in calls the shots." If the company is exceeding everyone's expectations, then the entrepreneur may be in a good position to negotiate great terms on later rounds. Unfortunately, this is not usually the case, and the entrepreneur takes the brunt of the dilution and loss of rights before any investor.

This happens for the following reason. To get investors to finance the company, an entrepreneur, always the optimist, will write a business plan that looks fantastic—*if* everything goes according to plan. The financial forecasts will have a hockey-stick sudden rise in sales and positive cash flow in year 2. If the plan is not so aggressive, then it is unlikely to attract investment. The entrepreneur knows this, but so do the investors. They are already discounting the plan when they evaluate the investment. The overenthusiastic plan, therefore, can be used to the detriment of the entrepreneur when the company does not reach its goals by the time the next round of investment is required—usually earlier than planned. A better approach is to have a conservative plan as well as a more aggressive plan, which the company can follow if things go better than expected. Funding should be sought for only the first phase of the more conservative plan. This leaves space for slippage, and yet the situation has been set up for raising more capital at a much higher valuation should things really take off. Investors are always ready to continue funding if an entrepreneur is exceeding the plan. Start-up companies rarely, if ever, follow their business plans; they will change direction many times as they learn about their environment and understand more about the opportunities they are creating. Investors welcome this flexibility, as can be reflected in the structure of the capital raising.

ANGEL INVESTORS

Angels[4] are an excellent source of raising capital and sometimes represent the best method for the entrepreneur to pursue when self-funding and friends are not a viable option. Angels are high-net-worth individuals who have some funds they are willing to risk in start-up companies. They usually invest locally because they like to have personal interaction with the entrepreneur. Often they look for investments in areas that they know well, which could range from retail stores to health products, from real estate management to high-tech manufacturing. They may have a social agenda attached to their investments. For example, one group in Pennsylvania has invested in a chain of drug rehabilitation centers and a company that provides software for school districts to help the No Child Left Behind Program. They are often willing to become actively involved, and they are usually well networked into the local professional service firms. They may operate individually; more often they work as an investment partnership. Angels are usually less rigorous in their due diligence and their push to reach an exit strategy. However, as the VCs are moving to later-stage investment and angels take over more of the earlier-stage funding, they are themselves becoming more professional and demanding in their style and governance.

Angels are sufficiently different from venture capitalists in that they invest their own money, in the range of $50,000 to $500,000 that companies need to get started. However, as a group, the investments are significantly higher. VCs, by contrast, invest institutional funds, and typically they are likely to invest later in a company's life, supplying $1 million or more to both early-stage and mid-stage companies. Angels always review potential deals carefully. They review business plans, require a strong management team, and perform financial review and analysis. Angels also expect the companies they invest in to go public or to be acquired in five to seven years, not

Table 8-3 **Typical Profile of Angels Investors**

Average number of members in an angel group	10–25
Average group investment per year	$2 million to $5 million
Average group investment in a start-up	$350,000
Percentage of companies funded, out of all that presented	33 percent
Estimated total invested per year by angels	$54 billion

one to two years. Angels require an equity stake and a return of 20 to 35 percent on their investments, and some require a seat on the board of directors.[5]

The best method to locate angel investors is through word of mouth. It is best to come recommended or to seek a referral from a friend or business associate. Another option is to receive an invitation to present to a local angel group. Angel groups offer an opportunity to present the company to a group of angels in one session and determine the financial viability quickly. Entrepreneurs should explore friends, acquaintances, chambers of commerce, and any entrepreneurial groups in the state. Angel networks and matchmaking services set up by universities and state development agencies are other sources.[6] Sometimes for a small fee ranging from $100 to $300, your company can be listed in the organization database. (Investor contacts and angel networks are listed in the resource section at the end of this chapter.) Angels are always looking for new deal opportunities, called "sourcing." The best angels are those that can bring contacts, experience, and long-term financing. Contacts means helping the company find customers, employees, and partners. For experience, the angel should understand the business and be able to assist the company in deals and important issues. The financing of the business may require additional funds in the future; the ideal angel will have the financial wherewithal to continue to support the company.[4]

The number of angel investors grew 60 percent during the stock market boom years, but since then they have become more reticent in investing as their own net worths have significantly declined with the public stock markets' fall. Nevertheless they are still an exceedingly important source of funds, many times larger in aggregate than professional venture capital firms.

"MICROEQUITY"—LITTLE MONEY WITH A LOT OF MENTORING

A relatively new form of help organization for entrepreneurs has emerged over the past few years. Recognizing the tremendous value that mentors can provide to young founders, angel investors are banding together and creating regional networks of advisers. Two examples are YCombinator with offices in Boston, Massachusetts, and Mountain View, California, and DreamIt based in Philadelphia, Pennsylvania. Without a full-blown business plan, an entrepreneur can submit an idea on the Web sites of these "microinvestment" organizations. For a small percentage ownership of your company, typically 4 percent of common stock, they will provide you with sufficient cash to live for a few months near their offices. During this period the team can develop plans and work on a prototype. Most important, the entrepreneur will be introduced into their network of entrepreneurs, potential employees, angel investors, attorneys, bankers, and venture capitalists who will meet the entrepreneur on a regular basis to prepare him for his first round of investment. The profile at the beginning of this chapter relates to one successful case using this process.

UNDERSTANDING THE VENTURE CAPITAL PROCESS

How VC Firms Work

Nearly all venture capital firms are organized as partnerships.[7] A group of professional managers gets together to manage high-risk private equity investments for investors who wish to participate in this sector of the investment market. The managers form a legal partnership and assume the role of general partners. This means that they have the authority to make decisions on investments that the partnership makes. The partners prepare a prospectus describing in detail how much money they are trying to raise for their VC fund and how the money will be used. It also details how the profits from the fund will be distributed back to the limited partner investors. A typical VC fund has a defined life, typically ten years; this is called a "closed-end fund." At the end of this period, all the assets held by the partnership must be converted into liquid assets and the proceeds distributed according to the terms of the partnership agreement. There may be a provision by which certain assets can be held for up to, say, three years further to create a higher value for the fund, but after ten years, no further investments can be made.

The general partners use the prospectus to solicit commitments to their funds. Typical sources of money are corporate, state, and university pension funds and endowments; high-net-worth individuals; and large funds under management by other money managers. All of these sources of money are looking to diversify their own investments by putting a small percentage of their cash into a high-risk, high-gain fund managed by professionals who understand the small-company environment. The size of funds raised has grown significantly, and now a fund of $500 million would be considered a small to mid-sized fund. As the size of funds has grown, it has resulted in VC investments moving toward later-stage opportunities. This is a direct result of the difficulty of putting so much money to work; it takes just as long to undertake due diligence for a $250,000 investment as for a $10 million investment. If the partnership has raised $500 million, then there is just not enough partner time to make many small investments and sit on a myriad of boards. Thus, these funds look to put a total investment of more than $10 million into one opportunity, even if it is in two or three rounds.

Once the partnership has commitments for the amount it was seeking by having sufficient subscription agreements signed, the partners then actively look for opportunities for investment. Usually any VC firm is very focused on what sort of companies it seeks. When an opportunity is found, one or two of the partners undertake a full due diligence exercise, perhaps taking several months, before an investment decision is made. (See Appendix 1 at the end of this chapter for a complete due diligence checklist.) Prior to making this large investment in time and resources, the VCs agree on the terms of a possible investment, which is memorialized in a "term sheet." Although this is a good faith rather than a binding document, it does restrict the entrepreneur in seeking other investors during the period of the agreement. Most VC firms use a standard form of term sheet. A typical pro forma is shown in Appendix 2 at the end of this chapter. If the due diligence meets the partners' requirements, a vote is taken; usually a majority or sometimes a unanimous agreement is sought before the investment is made. Attorneys then draft the final shareholders' agreement, and the investment is made. The VC general partner makes a call for funds on the limited partners, who have a short time to transfer the funds to the company. Should they default, they lose all rights, including the value of the investments in which they may already have participated. At the same time, each general partner is usually required to invest personally alongside the limited partners, thus aligning their interests and making sure they "have some skin in the game."

In order to pay for the running of the VC office, including partners' salaries and expenses, the investors pay a fee of typically 2.5 percent of funds invested annually. When a liquidity event occurs and one of the investments is turned into cash, the distribution agreement determines how the proceeds will be used. Typically, the limited partners receive all of their investment back first; then the rest is split 80:20 between the limited partners and the general partners. As an example, let us assume that an investment of $10 million has been made in Acme Inc. and the company is sold, returning $100 million to the VCs. Then the limited partner investors would receive $10 million "off the top" and $72 million of the remainder. The general partners would share $18 million among them.

The most important thing for an entrepreneur to understand about a VC firm is that all interests are focused to maximize the return on investment; there is no other agenda. If the company is successful and achieves a high value upon exit, then everyone wins. If the VC firm fails to help the company and does not make sure that the management is well motivated, they and their investors lose too. So negotiating with a VC firm becomes easier if the entrepreneur understands these motivations and realizes that the aim is to make the pie bigger for everyone rather than to make the entrepreneur's slice smaller.

Venture capital firms look for generally larger deals and more impressive returns than do angel investors. Also, angels will invest in the early stages of a company, whereas venture capitalists usually do not invest until a product or service can be demonstrated or a prototype is ready for commercialization. Some venture capital firms specialize in very-early-stage funding, but this is the exception rather than the rule. Many venture capital firms want to invest where the time horizon is relatively short, since they must liquidate their investments and provide cash returns to their investors over a comparatively short period of time. Some venture capital firms focus on specific industries or stages of investment, such as bridge financing. In addition to raising capital, venture capitalists can be a valuable asset to the company in terms of their contacts, market expertise, and business strategy. As with angels, it is imperative to locate potential investors whose skills, experience, and reputation complement the entrepreneur and the company. The most critical element in a successful venture capital relationship is the close alignment of the entrepreneurs' objectives with those of the venture capitalists. The entrepreneur should reach agreement on several key aspects when negotiating a deal with venture capitalists, including the following: What are the investment objectives? How much control will be given up? And are the entrepreneur's needs compatible with the venture capitalists' for a successful result?

The factors that might influence a venture capital firm's funding decisions are as follows:

- **Specialized Industries for the Venture**
  Many venture capitalists specialize in a narrow set of industries. Some specialize in semiconductors, others in health-care devices, biotech, or Internet services. Still others invest in "low-tech" businesses such as retail stores and service businesses. Knowing what industries a venture capital firm invests in will help in locating appropriate funding and demonstrate past performance in similar cases.

● **The Location of the Venture**

Some venture capitalists are located in Silicon Valley, California, because traditionally, a large number of technology start-ups began in this geographic area. Others are located in large cities. This does not mean the firm will invest in only their area. Although venture capital firms prefer to invest in companies that are located near them, others have a national or global scope. However, entrepreneurs will fare better if they are located within two hours' driving time of the VC head office, for they are likely to receive more help and attention from the senior partners than from more junior staff.

● **Stage of Fund**

In a ten-year life fund, investments made early on have a longer time to mature to an exit, and the VC firm will have more patience. As the fund nears the termination date, it is unable to make longer-term investments. This would not be a good fit with, say, an early-stage biotech opportunity that may take ten years of patient investment to reach an exit. However, late-stage funds may be suitable for a short bridge finance.

● **Stage of Development**

Although some firms like to invest in a start-up company, others like to invest in later stages of development. The key stages of development that venture firms consider are divided into three sectors—early stage, expansion, and acquisitions/buyout—and are based on the type of financing each requires. The following details each of these stages.

Early-stage Financing

– Seed financing is the initial investment required to prove a concept (e.g., to build a prototype or conduct market research) and qualify for start-up financing.

– Start-up financing is typically required to build a management team and bring a product or service to market.

– First-stage financing is often needed when start-up financing is depleted and a company needs to expand its marketing and/or sales capabilities to grow the business.

Expansion Financing

– Second-stage financing is used by companies that are shipping products (or delivering services) but need additional funds for working capital requirements and to grow faster than internal cash flow will allow.

– Mezzanine financing is typically used to fund substantial growth and/or expansion of companies that are up and running and are beyond breakeven volumes. Capital to fund a plant expansion or to move into a new geographic market is often categorized within this class of funding.

– Bridge financing is sometimes needed when a company is about to go public and requires capital until the IPO event. Usually bridge financing is short term and is repaid with proceeds from the public offering. This form of bridge financing is less burdensome than that taken when the company is under duress.

Acquisitions/Buyouts Financing

– This type of financing is used to fund the acquisitions or buyouts of existing businesses. In many cases these are mature businesses that are funded with a large component of debt or equity capital (leveraged buyouts). The KKR

Table 8-4   **Recent U.S. Venture Capital Statistics[7]**

Year	Total Investment ($ bn)	Number of Deals
1997	14.87	3155
1998	21.08	3647
1999	54.05	5502
2000	204.77	7900
2001	40.58	4484
2002	22.01	3102
2003	19.78	2944
2004	22.47	3093
2005	23.17	3155
2206	26.74	3675
2007	30.88	3952
2008	28.30	3868

(Kohlberg Kravis Roberts & Co., www.kkr.com) acquisition of RJR/Nabisco was one of the more famous (and large) examples of this type of transaction.

ROADMAP

IN ACTION

Venture capitalists can also be a valuable asset to the company in terms of their network of personal contacts to attract customers, assist in building partners, and as board members to participate in business strategy. Make sure to find potential investors whose experience and reputation complement the venture.

Note that angels actually invest *more* than professional VC firms. Together, however, they represent only a minority of the funding accessed by early-stage companies, indicating the importance of the financing methods discussed in Chapter 7.

As can be seen in Table 8-4, in recent years the U.S. VC industry has been shrinking both as a lingering result of the dot.com bubble in 2000 and then the 2008 global economic crisis. The number of U.S.-based VC partnerships fell by 5% to 850 in 2006 and we can anticipate more going out of business in the next few years. A survey by the National Venture Capital Association late in 2008 predicted a fall in the level of VC investment in small companies by at least 10% in 2009 to less than $27 billion. The percentage drop is much higher at the seed and earlier stages of a start-up's development. This is mainly because any remaining funds are being used to keep existing portfolio companies alive until an exit opportunity, either through a sale of the company or an IPO, emerges. Existing VC partnerships are also having difficulty in raising additional funds from their traditional sources, which does not bode well for small companies finding growth capital for some time. This downward trend emphasizes a greater need for the bootstrapping skills described in Chapter 7.

GUIDE TO SELECTING A VENTURE CAPITALIST

1. *Scrutinize your business with a critical eye.* Can the business give the returns that a venture capitalist demands? Work out solid financial projections to prove the results to the venture capitalist.

> "The single best thing any start-up can do is to find a beta customer or a customer sponsor as early as possible. This immediately gives you legitimacy in that you have moved from a business concept in a plan to solving a real problem. It also makes you smarter about what real customers want and will pay for. Ideally these beta sites become references and sources of funding."
>
> JAMES B. SANDERS
> *President, Columbia Group,
> investor and consultant to
> high-tech start-ups; adjunct
> professor of entrepreneurship,
> University of Maryland*

2. *Beef up management.* Venture capitalists invest in start-ups, but they usually don't want unseasoned executives. Everyone has strengths and weaknesses. Hire staffers who can make up the deficits.

3. *Keep a high profile so the VCs will visit.* For example, Edison Venture Fund, a venture capital firm in Lawrenceville, New Jersey, initiates contact with about 35 percent of the companies it funds. "We've already heard good things about the company and have researched their potential," says managing partner John Martinson, who also serves as chairman of the National Association of Venture Capitalists.

4. *Target the search.* Look for firms that specialize in the industry and the size of investment.

5. *Keep a lookout.* Look for smaller VC firms that may be more flexible and more receptive to investing in a company.

6. *Investigate possible venture partners.* One should treat the method of locating venture capitalists as though they were a customer. Find out what the needs are for the venture capitalist so when a visit is made, the meeting can be more successful.

Venture capitalists like to invest in companies that include some bootstrapping techniques in their plans as a way of reducing their investment and risks.

IN ACTION

A private placement memorandum is another alternative for raising capital. A business plan and a prospectus explaining the risks, issues, and procedures of the investment are offered. Private placements should be done with the advice of an attorney who knows the federal laws as well as those of the state in which the business will operate.

PRIVATE PLACEMENTS

A private placement involves selling stock in a private company to investors. Federal and state laws regulate these activities and determine how the offerings are made. The investors are solicited with a private placement memorandum that involves a business plan and a prospectus explaining the risks, issues, and procedures of the investment. Private placements should be done with the advice of an attorney who knows the federal laws as well as the laws of the state in which the new business will be run. Private placements are less expensive and take less time to achieve than a public offering. Each state has standardized disclosure and offering documents that must be followed. Some states require a registration process, and others do not. Also, private placements are not exempt from the issue of antifraud provisions. This means that the company must give potential investors the information they need to make a well-informed decision.[8]

The Securities Act of 1933 states that securities may not be issued unless they are registered or an exemption from registration is available. The typical exemption would be Regulation D, adopted by the SEC in 1982. This details the SEC rules governing the exemptions from registration for private placements and limited offerings. The intent was to make capital markets more accessible to businesses and to simplify the private offering process for investors who met the requirements. The exemptions under Regulation D used for a private placement are commonly referred to by their rule number as follows:

Rule 504: Sell up to a $1 million limit in twelve months' time to a number of investors, whether or not they are sophisticated. No requirement of disclosure and no advertising restrictions on resale of stock are required. *Sophisticated* refers to investors who have a net worth of at least $1 million or salaries greater than $250,000 annually for the previous two years.

Rule 505: Sell up to $5 million in twelve months of unregistered securities. There can be no more than thirty-five non-accredited investors, no requirement of disclosure to accredited investors but disclosure to non-accredited investors, no advertising, or restrictions on resale.

Rule 506: There is no limitation to selling stock. There is a maximum of thirty-five non-accredited investors (non-accredited investors must be able to evaluate merits and risks), and there is no requirement of disclosure to accredited investors.

ROADMAP
IN ACTION

Another method to secure capital or debt financing is to structure a strategic partnership that may include an equity investment. When the entrepreneur is rejected from traditional financing methods or is unwilling to accept the equity valuations assigned by potential investors, this option is often used.

STRATEGIC PARTNERSHIPS AND CORPORATE INVESTMENTS

Structuring a strategic partnership that includes an equity investment is an excellent alternative for many companies to raise equity funds. This usually occurs when ventures find that they are rejected from traditional financing methods or are unwilling to accept the equity valuations assigned by potential investors. Funding associated with strategic partnerships is usually at a more attractive valuation than it might have been with a traditional financing deal. A strategic partner assigns other nonfinancial values to the transaction that relate to the impact on its own operations and competitive positioning.

Although any financial equity structure is possible, a typical strategic partnership involves the sale of a minority interest in the business to a larger company. In addition to the partner providing equity, the partner may also expect to benefit from the entrepreneurial venture itself. The partner might gain access to technology, add a new product to its product line, or profit from a business opportunity that is identified. From the small company's perspective, such an arrangement can provide access to resources such as development facilities, complementary technologies, fast access to the market, and reputation. An investment from a corporation may make it easier to attract VC funding in parallel.

There may be significant downsides too as the objectives of the small company, the VC investors, and the larger corporation might not coincide.

Here are some points to consider:

- The corporation is usually seeking only access to intellectual property and know-how rather than a direct return on the investment it makes in the entrepreneur's company.

- The corporation may perceive that the small company is financially weak and use this fact to take advantage (refer to the Chasteen case on contingent litigation in Chapter 7).

- The relationship may *reduce* the chance of receiving VC funding, particularly if the corporate investor is considered to be a prime target to buy the company later. The value may be depressed as the ability to have an auction to gain the highest price could be compromised.

- Corporations are usually slow in making decisions and may hinder the growth of the smaller firm.

- Corporate management often changes, and the champion supporting the relationship may suddenly disappear or be moved to another position. This can be disastrous for the smaller firm. Always have numerous contact points at different levels to mitigate against this common problem.

On the other hand, many VCs are comfortable with coinvesting with a corporate partner, realizing that they can bring value other than just the funding. Balance is required, however, and an entrepreneur should enter into relationships with major corporations being aware of the downside. The best solution is to have a VC lead the investment round, take a board seat, and negotiate the relationship with a known and trusted corporate partner. Many corporate VC funds welcome this arrangement, not wishing to be the lead investor. Examples include the internal venture funds of Dow Chemical and Intel. Establishing an expression of strategic interest with such a fund may lead to the introduction to VC partnerships with which they have already coinvested.

A minority investment by a larger company is only one way to structure a strategic alliance. Other forms of such alliances include setting up a separate legal entity (joint venture), establishing cooperative arrangements (e.g., to fund research and development or to exploit an idea or strategy), and instituting a variety of cross-licensing or cross-distribution agreements.

Such relationships can ease cash flow constraints and lower the amount of funding the venture must obtain from other sources. Some examples of such relationships are described in Chapter 11.

Unfortunately, in many cases, large companies make uncomfortable partners as their objectives and decision-making methods may not align closely with the faster-moving, innovative, smaller firm, so the relationship usually requires a lot of skilled management time. The master-case has many instances where these issues occur, and there are management exercises based on this topic at the end of Chapter 11.

Investments from larger firms usually fall in the range of two to twenty-five million dollars, gaining ownership of up to 25 percent. UPS, for example, has established a venture fund and receives more than one hundred plans a year to review; no more than 5 percent receive any funding. The investments are strategic; UPS invested in Vidco networks, a digital document security company, a clear fit to UPS's core business. As with the case for venture capitalists, approach a corporate investment office only if your business has a clear strategic fit to the company.

LEARNING HOW TO VALUE A BUSINESS

Any private equity investment requires that the entrepreneur and the investors reach an agreement on the premoney value of the company, for this determines how much of the company the investors will own on closing the transaction. A number of valuation methods can be applied. The later the stage of the investment round, when there is likely to be a history of sales and operations and it is easier to predict future performance, the more precise the valuation. In this case financial analytical techniques can be used. However, in early rounds, when there is little history on which to base future performance and there are still many unknowns to be explored, it is much harder to establish a valuation. This section describes the various valuation methods and when they are applied.

Early-stage Investments—the Venture Capital Model

The first step taken by investors looking at a seed or early-stage company is to estimate the company's future value at the planned exit date of usually three to five years. Remember outside shareholders can make a return on their money only when the company is sold or a liquidity event occurs. There are two fundamental ways of making this calculation:

1. *Cash Flow Estimates.* By looking at forecasted earnings (profits) and multiplying those earnings by a factor that is relevant to the industry, a value can be computed. In growth industries, such as computing or telecommunications, investors might use an earnings multiple between 15 and 25. In a consumer-oriented business, a multiple of 2 to 10 might be used. For example, a health-care company forecast annual sales of $3 million at the end of three years, with a profit of just greater than $1 million. Multiplying the forecasted profit by 10 yields an estimated value of $10 million. This is the value one could assume for a company if it went public or were offered for sale.

2. *Strategic Sale.* For the same strategic reasons major corporations make investments in small companies, they also purchase later-stage companies. They will often pay a premium price if they think that the acquisition will have a major effect on their competitive position. Indeed the company may have little or no positive cash flow now or in the foreseeable future, and the first method is not applicable at all. In this case the valuation has little or nothing to do with cash flow and much more to do with the potential impact on market share, perceived stock market price, competitive positioning, and other aspects of the acquirer. Estimates of values that might be attained in a strategic acquisition are usually calculated on the basis of comparison with other purchases that have taken place recently in the same industry sector.

Whichever method is used, investors use the potential exit values to indicate whether a company will be large enough someday to make their investment worthwhile and to determine whether their percentage of ownership in the company would be commensurate with the amount of their investment.[9] Taking the health-care company as an example, assume the investor seeks a compound annual internal rate of return of 30 percent after three years. This is equivalent to an increase in value of 2.2 times over this period. Thus, the present value of the company to provide this level of return is $4.55 million, post investment. If the investors provide $1 million for the company now, they need to own 22 percent of the company to meet their goal. This calculation provides the investor with a starting point for negotiating the value. However, they will discount the exit value, knowing that the company will probably fall short of its plans, which are optimistic. Therefore, the exit may be later than anticipated and the amount of ownership demanded commensurately higher. More details on how to calculate an internal rate of return are covered later in this chapter.

The investors will consider other factors regarding exit valuation. As illustrated in the CoreTek case at the end of the chapter, the valuation at exit of $1.35 billion was high not because of any earnings forecast, but because the oligarchical structure of the market sector drove the value up. An everyday analogy is the price that an owner of a key piece of real estate might capture if it is the last house blocking a large subdivision development by a major real estate investor. The value is related to the overall project and not the simple value of the house as a dwelling. Thus, an investor is likely to look at the structure and dynamics of the industry sector targeted for an exit to determine whether this might provide a premium over a purely financially driven sale. Concentrated markets where there are well-defined and intense competitive forces produce higher valuations than unstructured sectors where there are no clear competitive factors at play. Investors will also look for similar transactions ("comps") where a comparable company in the same field has recently been acquired or been taken public and can be used to benchmark a potential exit price. Entrepreneurs must also realize that certain fields become "hot" when valuations greatly exceed any that can reasonably be quantified on purely financial calculations. This was certainly the case with the dot.com bubble, where companies with no believable plans to ever be profitable still attracted enormous valuations in what is termed a "feeding frenzy" by investors and acquirers. We are now well past this phase, and valuations have returned to levels that can be more soundly justified based on purely financial grounds.

In the end, all of the valuation methods, though helpful in establishing a basis for discussions, are overridden by the negotiations between the company's board and the investors where other factors come into play.

ROADMAP

IN ACTION

At later stages in the company's growth, the major factor that determines the value of a business is the cash flow and generation of profits in the marketplace. Other valuation factors include the history, characteristics, and industry in which the business operates as well as the strength and weakness of the management team and risks in investing in the business.

Motivational Issues

Investors must take into account the need to maintain the enthusiasm and drive of the key persons in the company. Entrepreneurial founders seeking equity finance expect to create a significant amount of personal wealth by building their dream company. In this regard they are aligned with the investors. However, if the investors, in order to get a high return, insist on taking too much of the company, this may demotivate the insiders, reducing the company's passion to succeed. This hurts everyone, and investors, especially at the earlier rounds of investment, are wise to accept a somewhat higher valuation. They are, after all, receiving preferred stock, which protects their investment to some extent, and they are in a position to readjust their ownership position during subsequent rounds, where there are more data available to establish a firmer valuation. Entrepreneurs usually have an inflated view of what the company is worth in the first round of investment and may have to accept a valuation well less than their expectations. They should not base the decision solely on the valuation offered, but on whether they believe the investors are acting as partners and will help to grow the company. A good rule for any negotiation in business is if both parties feel that they did not get what they hoped for but feel that they can live with the deal and are keen to proceed, then the chance of a solid, lasting partnership is high. If one party believes that it "got one over" on the other, there is a high chance that the partnership will hit rough water later when the going gets tough.

Later-stage Valuation: Later Rounds or Exit

Valuation skills to guide entrepreneurs for business decisions are prerequisites for success in today's competitive environment. For example, the key issue companies confront when raising equity funds or going public with an IPO is determining a valuation for the company and how much the new investors will receive for funding the company. Business valuations should always be considered as a starting point for the buyer and seller.[10] The goal is to determine a working valuation from which one can negotiate a fair price. The key factor in the value of any later-stage business is the focus on the company's cash flow and its ability to generate consistent profits in the marketplace. Other valuation factors include the history, characteristics, and industry in which the business operates; the strengths and weaknesses of the management team; the growth trajectory of the company; and risks in investing in the business. Another financial factor to consider in the analysis is comparing the company to other companies in the industry and the stock price of similar companies in the industry. This can include the price-to-earnings ratio of similar companies and understanding the company's financial condition. The master-case and readings provide some real insight into the IPO process and the dynamics of pricing the stock in a volatile public market.

ROADMAP

IN ACTION

The valuation process involves trial and error; there is no single best method. The best is a combination of valuation methods that may apply to a given situation.

Earnings Valuation

This approach is more suitable for a company with an established track record and involves valuing the business based on the following:[11]

- Historical earnings: valuation based on how profitable the business has been in the past
- Future earnings: the most widely used method of valuing a business, which provides the investor with the best estimate of the probable return on investment

Once the buyer or seller has decided on the time frame (i.e., historical versus future earnings), the earnings figure must be multiplied by a factor to determine its value. Generally, a price/earnings (P/E) multiple is used. For example, if the company is expected to have earnings of $1.5 million in five years and if similar companies are likely to go public at a price-to-earnings ratio of 10, the company is projected to be worth $15 million five years from now.

The appropriate price/earnings multiple is selected based on norms of the industry and the investment risk. The search for a similar company must be classified in the same industry; the company should share similar markets and have similar products and earnings. A higher multiple is used for a high-risk business and a lower multiple for a low-risk business. Higher multiples are typically applied to companies with higher earnings growth. Growth is directly tied to multiples. Higher-growth companies receive higher market multiples (e.g., high-tech, etc.), and lower-growth companies or cyclical companies, whose earnings have peaked, typically receive lower multiples (e.g., basic industry or airlines). For example, a low-risk business in an industry with a five times earning multiple would be valued at $7.5 million in the above example.

The P/E ratio is also used to value both publicly traded corporations and privately held companies.[10] To value a private company in a particular industry, research a set of comparable publicly traded companies, or comps, to benchmark the private company. Compute the P/E and other valuation ratios for the public comparables. After comparing many financial measures and growth prospects of the private company versus the public company, choose an appropriate P/E multiple based on the public company's P/Es. This multiple chosen for the private company is the estimate of the P/E that the market would apply to this company if it were public. This is basically the same process that investment bankers and underwriters undertake for a public company. Also, valuation is determined by dividing the market price of the common stock by the earnings per share. As an example, for a company with 300,000 shares of common stock, trading at $5 per share and net income of $1 share, the P/E would be $5 ($5 divided by $1). In addition, since the company has 300,000 shares of common stock, the valuation of the enterprise would now be $1.5 million (300,000 shares × $5).

Asset Valuation

This method is based on the worth of the business's assets. This is a useful starting point for negotiations, for it constitutes the *minimum* value of the business. It would not be appropriate to value most companies using an asset-based approach, especially in the case where the company is a typical earnings-based concern with few fixed assets, such as a software company, or its assets are largely intangible, such as a portfolio of patents. Indeed even for the S & P 500, the largest 500 companies in the United States, the average market valuation is approximately three times their asset value. Shareholders place significant value on so-called intangible assets and other factors. The asset approach is most appropriate when used in a liquidation scenario and/or in valuing an asset-based company such as a real estate holding company or investment holding company. Assets can be valued as follows:

- *Book value* equals the total net worth or stockholders' equity of the company, as reflected on the balance sheet.
- *Adjusted book value* adjusts for discrepancies between the stated book value and the actual market value of assets, such as machinery and equipment—which have depreciated; or land—which has appreciated the book value.

- *Liquidation value* adjusts for the value of assets if the company had to dispose of those assets in a "quick sale." Liquidation value is the amount that can be realized if the company's operations cease and the assets are sold over a reasonable period of time, with the company receiving an auction price for each asset. The first step is to determine the value of the assets and deduct the liabilities to arrive at the adjusted net assets of the company. The next step is to determine the cost associated with the sale of the assets; legal, accounting, and administrative expenses must be deducted. Let's look at an adjusted book value example, as shown in the following table:

Assets	Book Value	Market Value
Liquid assets	$53,429	$53,429
Receivables	$622,000	$573,983
Inventory	$422,000	$468,184
Real property	$250,000	$425,000
Other property	$17,000	$17,000
Liabilities		
Short-term liabilities	$644,140	$644,140
Long-term liabilities	$501,106	$501,106
Net book value	$283,438	
Adjusted book value		$486,663

Now let's look at an example of liquidation value:

Assets	Liquidation	Book Value	Value
Cash	100%	$ 7,000	$ 7,000
Accounts receivable	70%	200,000	140,000
Inventories/computers	50%	100,000	50,000
Land and buildings	100%	250,000	250,000
Equipment	80%	100,000	80,000
Other assets	50%	80,000	40,000
Total		$ 800,000	$630,000
Less: liabilities			$(400,000)
Cost of liquidation, commissions			$(30,000)
Net liquidation value			$200,000

Discounted Cash Flow Valuation[12,13]

The real value of any ongoing business is its future earning power.[11] Accordingly, this approach is most often used to value a business. The discounted cash flow method projects future earnings over a three- or five-year period then calculates their present value using a certain discount or present value rate (e.g., 15 percent). The total of each year's projected earnings is the company's value. The basic principle underlying this method is that a dollar earned in the future is worth less than a dollar earned today. Thus, it is not only the amount of projected income (or net cash flow) that a company is expected to generate that determines its value, but also the timing of that income. This method can be used for companies at any stage, but for an early-stage company, where greater uncertainty is attributed to future cash flow forecasts, a higher discount rate is used to account for the larger risk and uncertainty.

In discounted cash flow valuation, the value of a company is the present value of the expected cash flows that will be generated by the company's assets. Every asset has an intrinsic value that can be estimated, based on its characteristics in terms of cash flows, growth, and risk that it can generate.

Information that is needed to use discounted cash flow valuation includes data on the estimated life of the asset, the cash flow forecasts during the life of the asset, and the discount rate to apply to these cash flows. The present value is then calculated according to the following formula:

$$\text{Value} = \sum_{t=1}^{T=CF} \frac{t}{(t+r)t}$$

where CF is the cash flow in period t, r is the discount rate appropriate given the riskiness of the cash flow, and t is the life of the asset. For an asset to have value, the expected cash flows have to be positive sometime over the life of the asset. Assets that generate cash flows early in their life will be worth more than assets that generate cash flows later; the latter may, however, have greater growth and higher cash flows to compensate.

The Steps Involved in Discounted Cash Flow

First, estimate the discount rate or rates to use in the valuation. Discount rate can be in nominal terms or real terms, depending on whether the cash flows are nominal or real. Discount rate can vary across time. Discounts are higher when there is a greater uncertainty in future cash flows.

Next, estimate the current earnings and cash flows of the company to either equity investors or stakeholders. Estimate the future earnings and cash flows on the asset being valued, generally by estimating an expected growth rate in earnings. Finally, estimate when the firm will reach "stable growth" and what characteristics it will have when it does. Now calculate and value the discounted cash flow (DCF).

When using this approach in valuing a company, one must decide how to value the cash flows after the forecast period is over. If you were to limit your DCF calculation to just the three or five years in the forecast, you would omit any value that would accrue from year 6 and beyond. The way this value is typically captured, as discussed earlier, is by using some P/E to indicate what the selling value of the business would be after year 6, for example.

Let's assume that you will receive $100,000 today and $100,000 a year over the next four years. What is today's value (present value) of the total $500,000 income stream? To determine the value of the transaction, you must use present-value factors. Now let's construct a table that would show you how the total $500,000 payments would be valued today and over the next four years. To compute the value, indicate the amounts by year and apply an 18 percent present-value factor to each amount.

Today's Value of Income

Year	Inflow	18% PV Factor	Value Today
Today	$100,000	1.000	$100,000
1	100,000	0.847	84,700
2	100,000	0.718	71,800
3	100,000	0.609	60,900
4	100,000	0.516	51,600
	$500,000	3.690	$369,000

As shown, the total income of $500,000 over five years is worth (today) $369,000. This is called the net present value (NPV) of the cash flow. That represents 30 percent less than the $500,000 you thought you were going to receive over the five-year period. This method can be used to value a company when you have a high confidence in future cash flows.

SUMMARY

Entrepreneurs seeking significant funds for growth may seek out investors who wish to purchase an ownership position in the company. Recognizing that this implies giving up some control in the company, you should not approach investors unless

Table 8-5   **Present Value of 1 Due in _n_ Periods**

	6%	7%	8%	9%	10%	11%	12%	13%	14%	15%	16%	20%	30%
1	0.9434	0.9346	0.9259	0.9174	0.9091	0.9009	0.8929	0.8850	0.8772	0.8696	0.8621	0.8333	0.7692
2	0.8900	0.8734	0.8573	0.8417	0.8264	0.8116	0.7972	0.7831	0.7695	0.7561	0.7432	0.6944	0.5917
3	0.8396	0.8163	0.7938	0.7722	0.7513	0.7312	0.7118	0.6931	0.6750	0.6575	0.6407	0.5787	0.4552
4	0.7921	0.7629	0.7350	0.7084	0.6830	0.6587	0.6355	0.6133	0.5921	0.5718	0.5523	0.4823	0.3501
5	0.7473	0.7130	0.6806	0.6499	0.6309	0.5935	0.5674	0.5428	0.5194	0.4972	0.4761	0.4019	0.2693
6	0.7050	0.6663	0.6302	0.5963	0.5645	0.5346	0.5066	0.4803	0.4556	0.4323	0.4104	0.3349	0.2072
7	0.6651	0.6227	0.5835	0.5470	0.5132	0.4817	0.4523	0.4251	0.3996	0.3759	0.3538	0.2791	0.1594
8	0.6274	0.5820	0.5403	0.5019	0.4665	0.4339	0.4039	0.3762	0.3506	0.3269	0.3050	0.2326	0.1226
9	0.5919	0.5439	0.5002	0.4604	0.4241	0.3909	0.3606	0.3329	0.3075	0.2843	0.2630	0.1938	0.0943
10	0.5584	0.5083	0.4632	0.4224	0.3855	0.3522	0.3220	0.2943	0.2697	0.2472	0.2267	0.1615	0.0725
11	0.5268	0.4751	0.4289	0.3875	0.3505	0.3173	0.2875	0.2607	0.2366	0.2149	0.1954	0.1346	0.0558
12	0.4970	0.4440	0.3971	0.3555	0.3186	0.2858	0.2567	0.2307	0.2076	0.1869	0.1685	0.1122	0.0429
13	0.4688	0.415	0.3677	0.3262	0.2897	0.2575	0.2292	0.2042	0.1821	0.1625	0.1452	0.0935	0.0330
14	0.4423	0.3878	0.3405	0.2992	0.2633	0.2320	0.2046	0.1807	0.1597	0.1413	0.1252	0.0779	0.0254
15	0.4173	0.3624	0.3152	0.2745	0.2394	0.2090	0.1827	0.1599	0.1401	0.1229	0.1079	0.0649	0.0195
16	0.3936	0.3387	0.2919	0.2519	0.2176	0.1883	0.1631	0.1415	0.1229	0.1069	0.0930	0.0541	0.0150
17	0.3714	0.3166	0.2311	0.2311	0.1978	0.1696	0.1456	0.1252	0.1078	0.0929	0.0802	0.0451	0.0116
18	0.3503	0.2959	0.2120	0.2120	0.1799	0.1528	0.1300	0.1108	0.0946	0.0808	0.0691	0.0376	0.0089
19	0.3305	0.2765	0.1945	0.1945	0.1635	0.1377	0.1161	0.0981	0.0829	0.0703	0.0596	0.0313	0.0068
20	0.3118	0.2584	0.2145	0.1784	0.1486	0.1240	0.1037	0.0868	0.0728	0.0611	0.0514	0.0261	0.0053

you intend to create a liquidity event for them to give a cash return on their investment. Selling equity dilutes the ownership for the entrepreneur; combining sale of stock with the bootstrapping and debt financing methods of the previous chapter can reduce the dilution. There are many different types of investors, and they must be carefully matched to the company business, needs, stage of investment, and personal chemistry. The entrepreneur should research sources of funds and approach only investors that are a good fit. Angel investors are typically less demanding than venture capital and other institutional professional investors. They are more patient and less demanding as to terms. However, they may not have sufficient funds to take you all the way. Other alternatives include selling stock to accredited investors using a private placement, or attracting corporate partners. In every case a valuation of the company must be agreed to prior to the investment. This valuation can be calculated in several ways. At the earliest stages of a company, it is usual to base today's value by discounting a future exit value at a rate equal to the internal rate of return that the investor is seeking. More mature companies may be valued using more exact methods based on assets, earnings, or future cash flow. However, in the end, it comes down to negotiating a satisfactory deal depending on the current investment market for your type of opportunity. Valuation is only one part of the transaction, and often it may be better to accept a lower current valuation in exchange for a better long-term relationship with investors. Investors will undertake detailed due diligence prior to making an investment after the terms of a transaction have been agreed to and memorialized in a term sheet. An entrepreneur should also thoroughly research investors prior to accepting their money.

STUDY QUESTIONS

1. What are various sources of equity investment?
2. What are the main differences between an angel and a VC investor?
3. What are the main ways an entrepreneur can value a business?
4. What guidelines should entrepreneurs follow when they are selecting a venture capitalist?
5. What is a private placement?
6. What are the advantages and disadvantages of corporate investors?
7. What is the difference between the earnings valuation approach and the asset valuation approach?

EXERCISES

1. Calculate the net present value using Table 8-5, "Present Value of $1 Due in *n* Periods." What is the present value of $100 received at the end of seven years if the required return is 12 percent?

2. Examine Table 8-5, "Present Value of $1 Due in *n* Periods." Discuss why the numbers decrease as you move from left to right and why the numbers decrease as you move from top to bottom in a given column.

3. Assume you will receive $300 per year for the next three years plus an extra $300 payment at the end of the three years. Determine how much this prospect is worth today if the required rate of return is 12 percent.

4. Value a stock in a company of your choice using a discounted cash flow model. List the key drivers of value for the company. (Identify the key assumption or variable that you would focus on in doing a discounted cash flow valuation. Examples would include the growth rate

assumption, the growth period assumption, and the net capital expenditure assumption.)

5. Prepare a list of comparable companies, using criteria you think are appropriate. Choose a multiple that you will use in comparing firms across the group. (You might have to try out a number of multiples before making this choice.) Evaluate the company against the comparable firms using the multiple that you have chosen for your valuation. Determine if the company is under- or over-valued.

Master-case Exercises:

If you have not yet read the appendix in Chapter 1, do so. Then go to the book's Web site and read the diary entries Months 14, 15, 18, 19, 23, 24, 25, 26, 36, and 42 and view the video selections, "Angels, More than Just Investors" and "VCs and Investment Bankers: When the Stakes Get High, the Ethics Get Low."

Either as a team or individually, produce a short presentation on each of these questions for discussion. Only one or two slides for each are required to state the key points.

Master-Case Q 1: Money and/or advice, is there a trade-off? Angels provide funding *and* mentoring. Is one fine without the other? What are the most important factors that you should take into account when (a) finding and (b) working with angel investors? Include networking, champions, deep pockets, and others in your discussions.

Master-Case Q 2: VCs need deal flow, which often comes from angel investors. Yet they often abuse the very people who are providing them with opportunities. Discuss the reasons for potential conflicts between angel investors and institutional VC firms. How can these impact (a) the start-up investment field and (b) the operations of a start-up company.

Master-Case Q 3: VCs benefit by creating the highest value for the companies they invest in. However, they often act as if they are willing to destroy the company. Was Venrock working in its best interests in driving a wedge between Wayne and Jeff? State your reasons.

CASE STUDY: CORETEK, INC.[14]

A physicist by training, Dr. Parviz Tayebati received a B.Sc. with first-class honors from the University of Birmingham, England, in 1982, followed by a master's degree from the University of Cambridge in theoretical physics and a Ph.D. in quantum electronics from the University of Southern California in 1989. Parviz then joined Foster-Miller, Inc., near Boston, a small firm that in the past had derived much of its revenues by undertaking government-funded research using the SBIR Programs (see Chapter 7).[15] While there, Parviz led research in optical computing and, most important, learned much about the process for winning technology development awards from the federal government.

Throughout the 1990s, Internet bandwidth and information applications grew dramatically in a kind of "virtuous circle," with more bandwidth making new applications practical and acceptance of these new applications driving demand for even more bandwidth. Recognizing the opportunity to apply his technical and management skills to this area, Parviz formed CoreTek, Inc., in 1994 with the vision of developing truly innovative, enabling technologies to support this growth. Continued expansion of the Internet required components and architectures enabling bandwidth to grow faster than costs. CoreTek's tunable laser technology was important because it could address cost growth in two ways: it reduced manufacturing and inventory costs for the source lasers, and it provided an essential element of the wavelength-managed network, which promised to reduce costs by dramatically increasing network use and efficiency. He initially secured government funds for the development of what was viewed as a speculative technology. Between founding the company and 1998, CoreTek received more than $5.5 million in SBIR grants, nine Phase One awards, and five Phase Two awards.

Parviz soon realized that to make his dream come true in this fast-moving field, he would have to accelerate his development program. Therefore, in 1999,

CoreTek raised $6 million in an "A" round of preferred stock from a syndicate of three VC firms, led by Adams Capital Management (www.acm.com), valuing the company at $11.5 million prior to the investment. The VCs were attracted by the fact that the company was in a hot field and was able to secure significant amounts of government funding. For his part, Parviz chose this investor group not only on the attractive deal that he was offered (in fact, another group of VCs offered a higher valuation), but by witnessing the speed with which they could make decisions and their deep knowledge of the telecommunications industry, the fit was excellent. Parviz and his team were now working 24-7. The development proceeded rapidly, as CoreTek built its first manufacturing line. But the money was still not enough, and only nine months later, the company closed on a "B" round of $20.5 million at a premoney valuation of more than $52.5 million from an extended syndicate of four VC firms. In 2000 a number of the major telecommunication giants expressed an interest in acquiring CoreTek. At that time, the telecommunications industry was anticipating major growth, and technologies such as that developed by CoreTek were seen as vital for them to reach their targets. The oligarchical structure of the industry worked to CoreTek's advantage—a breakthrough in cost/performance in components could radically shift market share. Finally, in June 2001 Nortel Networks purchased CoreTek for $1.35 billion paid in Nortel's publicly traded stock. Parviz joined Nortel as vice president of business development. At that time, Parviz and the other insiders of the company still owned approximately 30 percent of the company.

CASE STUDY QUESTIONS

1. Why did the VC firms like the fact that the company had received significant government grants? Assume that this had not happened and that all the funding for the company had come from VCs. Add an earlier seed round to replace the government funds, and make an estimate of the dilution that Parviz and the founders would have had to take in this case if the VCs were to retain their IRR. Approximately how much less would the founders have in their pockets when the company was sold?

2. Draft a short term sheet (no more than two pages) for each investment round under the new circumstances of question 1.

3. Give three reasons Adams Capital Management, the lead VC firm, was a good fit to this opportunity.

INTERACTIVE LEARNING ON THE WEB

Test your knowledge of the chapter using the book's interactive Web site.

ADDITIONAL RESOURCES

Banking References

American Banker's Association   1120 Connecticut Avenue, NW, Washington, D.C. 20036; (800) 338-0626

National Association of Small Business Investment Companies   666 11th Street, NW, Suite 700, Washington, D.C. 20001; (202) 628-5055

Annual Statement Studies   Robert Morris Associates, 1650 Market Street, Suite 2300, Philadelphia, PA 19103; (800) 677-7621

Polk World Bank Directory, Polk Bank Services   Thompson Financial Services, 1321 Murfreeboro Road, Nashville, TN 37217; (615) 889-3350

Dun & Bradstreet Corp.   3 Silvan Way, Parsippany, NJ 07054; (973) 605-6000; www.DNB.com

Thompson Bank Directory   Thompson Financial Services, 4709 W. Golf Road, 6th Floor, Skokie, IL 60076-1253; (847) 676-9600

Venture Capital Guides

Accel Partners   One Palmer Square, Princeton, NJ 08542; (609) 683-4500

Association of Venture Capital Clubs   P.O. Box 3358, Salt Lake City, UT 84110; (801) 364-1100

The Capital Network, Inc.   3925 West Braker Lane, Suite 406, Austin, TX 78759; (512) 305-0826

National Venture Capital Assoc.   1655 N. Fort Meyer Drive, Suite 400, Arlington, VA 22209; (703) 351-5269

New York Venture Group, Inc.   (212) 832-NYVG (6984)

"Pratt's Guide to Venture Capital Sources"   Published annually by Venture Economics Inc. Wellesley, Mass.

Seed-Capital Network, Inc.   8905 Kingston Pike, Suite 12, Knoxville, TN 37923; (423) 573-4655

WEB RESOURCES

Companies looking for funding or ways to attract the attention of venture capitalists have plenty of places to look on the Internet. For starters, bookmark these sites:

- www.vfinance.com   A comprehensive venture capital resource library
- www.redherring.com   Site for *Red Herring,* which covers high-tech venture capital networks; online material is tailored toward the venture capital community itself
- www.nvca.org   Headquarters for the National Venture Capital Association
- www.techcapital.com   Online magazine dealing with venture capital
- www.garage.com   Assists start-ups wishing to acquire funding

NETWORKS

Many angel and VC investors participate in networks. Here are some of them. You can find others through your local chambers of commerce or by searching on the Internet.

The Kauffman Foundation in Kansas City has several programs to help entrepreneurs and also undertakes research on matters affecting start-up companies. For example, a 2002 report on Business Angels has valuable information for entrepreneurs seeking angel investments. Web links into the Kauffman Network can be found at www.kauffman.org and www.entrepreneurship.org.

Georgia Capital Network	(404) 894-5344
Investors' Circle	(708) 876-1101
L.A. Venture Network	(310) 450-9544
Mid-Atlantic Investment Network	(301) 681-0162
Northwest Capital Network (serves only businesses located in Oregon)	(503) 282-6273
Pacific Venture Capital Network	(714) 856-8366
Seed Capital Network, Inc.	(615) 573-4655
Technology Capital Network (formerly the Venture Capital Network at MIT)	(617) 253-7163
Texas Capital Network	(512) 794-9398
Venture Capital Network of Minnesota	(612) 223-8663
Venture Line	(518) 486-5438
Washington Investment Network	(206) 389-2559

Venture Clubs

Arizona
Enterprise Network Inc.
Tempe
(602) 804-0012

California
American Venture Capital
  Exchange
San Jose and Bay Area
(800) 292-1993

Greenhouse Venture Group
Bay Area
(415) 401-0577

Los Angeles Venture Assoc.
Los Angeles
(310) 450-9544

MIT Enterprise Forum
San Diego
(619) 236-9400

No. California Venture Forum
San Francisco
(415) 296-2519

San Diego Venture Group
San Diego
(619) 272-1985

Colorado
Rockies Venture Group
Denver
(303) 831-4174

Connecticut
Connecticut Venture Group
Fairfield
(203) 333-3284

MIT Enterprise Forum of
  Connecticut
Hartford
(860) 275-0294

Delaware
Delaware Entrepreneurs Forum
Wilmington
(302) 652-4241

Florida
Central Florida Venture Capital
  Network
Orlando
(407) 277-5411

North Florida Venture Capital
  Network
Jacksonville
(904) 642-4840

Gold Coast Venture Capital Club
Boca Raton
(561) 488-4505

Hawaii
Hawaii Venture Capital Assoc.
Kailua
(802) 262-7329

Illinois
Midwest Entrepreneur Forum
Chicago
(312) 857-0301

Indiana
Venture Club of Indiana
Indianapolis
(317) 253-1244

Private Investors Network
Bloomington
(812) 339-8937

Michiana Venture Network
South Bend
(219) 282-4350

Kentucky
Kentucky Investment Capital
  Network
Frankfort
(502) 564-2064

Venture Club of Louisville
Louisville
(502) 589-6868

Massachusetts
Technology Capital Network at
  MIT
Cambridge
(617) 253-2337

Maryland/Virginia/D.C.
Dingman Center for
  Entrepreneurship
College Park, MD
(301) 405-2144

MIT Enterprise Forum of
  Baltimore/Washington
Arlington
(703) 758-4021, www.mitef.org

Michigan
Southeastern Michigan Venture
  Club
Southfield
(313) 884-2727

New Enterprise Forum
Ann Arbor
(313) 665-4433

Travis Bay Enterprise Forum Traverse City (616) 947-5075	New Jersey Entrepreneurs Forum Morristown (908) 789-3424	Greater Cincinnati Venture Association Cincinnati (513) 686-2946	**Virginia** Charlottesville Venture Group Charlottesville (804) 979-7259
Minnesota New Venture Collaborative Minneapolis (612) 338-3828	**New York** Long Island Venture Group Hempsted (516) 463-6326	**Oregon** Oregon Entrepreneurs Forum Portland (503) 222-2270	**Washington** Northwest Venture Group Bellevue (425) 746-1973

Missouri
Missouri Venture Forum
St. Louis
(314) 241-2683
	New York Venture Group
	New York City
	(212) 832-6984
		Pennsylvania
		Greater Philadelphia Venture
		  Group
		Philadelphia
		(215) 790-3660
			MIT Enterprise Forum of the
			  Northwest
			Seattle
			(206) 283-9595, www.mitwa.org

Montana High Plains Venture Group Great Falls (406) 454-1934	Capital Region Tech. Dev. Albany (518) 465-8975	**Texas** MIT Enterprise Forum of Texas Houston	**Wisconsin** Wisconsin Venture Network Milwaukee Contact:
New Mexico New Mexico Private Investors Albuquerque (505) 856-0245	Silicon Alley Breakfast Club Scarsdale (800) 273-2832 **Ohio**	(713) 651-5529 MIT Enterprise Forum of Texas Austin	Mr. Paul Sweeney P.O. Box 92093 Milwaukee, WI 53202-0093
New Jersey Venture Assoc. of New Jersey	Ohio Venture Association Cleveland (216) 566-8884	(512) 342-0010 **Utah**	(414) 224-7070 **Canada**
Morristown (973) 631-5680	Miami Valley Venture Assoc. Dayton (937) 228-1141	Mountain West Venture Group Salt Lake City (801) 595-1141	MIT Enterprise Forum Toronto, Ontario (416) 736-5708

APPENDIX 1: DUE DILIGENCE CHECKLIST[16]

Corporate Documents

- ☐ Complete record of all charter documents of the company since inception
- ☐ Current by-laws of the company
- ☐ List of states in which the company is authorized to transact business
- ☐ Schedule of all subsidiaries
- ☐ Charter and by-laws of all subsidiaries
- ☐ List of states in which each subsidiary is authorized to transact business
- ☐ Minutes of the proceedings of meetings of the stockholders of the company and each subsidiary since inception
- ☐ Agreements relating to any acquisition or disposition since inception or that is currently planned

Securities Matters

- ☐ List of current stockholders
- ☐ Stock books and/or ledger of the company and of each subsidiary since inception (including originals or canceled certificates and copies of outstanding certificates)
- ☐ Schedule of outstanding options, warrants, or any other commitments or promises, oral or written, with respect to the issuance of the company securities (including where applicable dates of issuance, exercise price, vesting term, etc.)

☐ Voting trust agreements, redemption agreements, stockholder agreements, registration rights agreements, restrictive agreements, and other similar agreements, contracts, or commitments

☐ Agreements for the purchase of shares from the company

☐ All private placement memoranda since inception

☐ Copies of all federal and state securities filings since inception and of all correspondence relating thereto

Financings

☐ Documents and agreements evidencing borrowings, whether secured or unsecured, other indebtedness (long term or short term), including indentures, credit or loan agreements, commitments letters, and so on relating to any outstanding or available long-term or short-term debt, including amendments thereto and any relating instruments granting security interests

☐ All documents and agreements evidencing other material financing arrangements, including sale and leaseback arrangements, installment purchases, and so on

☐ Schedule of all liens and encumbrances against any of the company's assets or stock (whether or not of public record)

Employee Relations

☐ All employee benefit plans and policies, including salary policies, stock option plans, stock option agreements, stock purchase plans, retirement plans, pension plans, and bonus and incentive compensation plans; provide details with respect to cost of plans and sources of coverage

☐ All audit reports covering retirement, pension, or employee benefit plans of the company and its subsidiaries since inception

☐ Management, executive, and other employment contracts and agreements not to compete

☐ Management organization chart, including descriptions of job responsibilities

Management/Directors

☐ Résumés or detailed biographies for senior management team, including approximate dates of employment

☐ Reference list for officers

☐ Social Security numbers and addresses for officers and permission to do background checks (employment check, record search)

☐ Description of any outstanding management loans and transactions with affiliates

☐ Description of director compensation

Insiders

☐ Details of all board and/or management perquisites and arrangements

☐ Contracts or agreements (including employment agreements) with or pertaining to the company or any of its subsidiaries and to which directors, officers, stockholders, or any affiliate of the foregoing are parties

☐ All documents pertaining to any receivables from or payable to any director, officer, stockholder, or any affiliate of the foregoing

☐ Documents relating to any other transactions between the company and directors, officers, stockholders, or any affiliate of the foregoing

Agreements

☐ Contracts for the sale of the company's products or services

☐ Licensing agreements

☐ Product maintenance/warranty/service agreements

☐ All government contracts

☐ Supply contracts

☐ Joint venture and partnership agreements to which the company or any of its subsidiaries is a party

☐ Equipment and other leases

☐ Any other contracts relating to the products, services, or business of the company

Real Property Matters

☐ List and descriptions of owned realty

☐ Deeds and options to purchase or sell real property

☐ Real property leases (plant and office) in which the company is lessee or lessor

☐ Easements, licenses, and restrictions on use relating to real property

☐ Schedule and a copy of title insurance policies

☐ Copies of any environmental studies relating to property owned/leased by the company or any of its subsidiaries

Sales and Marketing

☐ Customer list (prior and current) and contacts for reference, listing corresponding revenue

☐ Current customer pipeline/backline

☐ Copies of marketing material (e.g., brochures)

Trade/Analyst Reports

☐ Industry information

☐ Competitor analysis

☐ Names and phone numbers for industry analysts whom you have talked with

Technology Matters

☐ Schedule of U.S. and foreign patents, trademarks, service marks, and copyrights, including pending applications of the company and its subsidiaries

☐ Documents issued by PTO or relative foreign organization

☐ Licensing agreements to which the company or any subsidiary is a party, whether as licensor or licensee, including research and development, manufacturing, distribution, or marketing agreements

☐ Copies of all notices and correspondence relating to allegations of infringement of rights of third parties by the company or any subsidiary or of the company's or any subsidiary's rights by third parties

☐ Copy of the company's policies or written summary or oral policies regarding the protection of trade secret and other proprietary information

☐ Copy of the company's policies or written summary of oral policies regarding information brought with them by employees from former employers

☐ Assignment agreements with employees and with other persons, with respect to proprietary information

☐ Confidentiality/nondisclosure agreements with employees and with any other persons with respect to proprietary information

☐ Agreements with independent contractors for the development of products for use or sale by the company or any of its subsidiaries

Governmental Licenses

☐ U.S. federal licenses and permits

☐ All state, county, city, and local licenses, including vendor's and building permits and environment-related permits

☐ Foreign licenses and permits

Insurance

☐ Copies of all insurance policies

☐ Schedule and description of all insurance policies

Litigation and Regulatory Compliance

☐ Schedule and brief description of all pending, potential, threatened, or recently resolved legal proceedings or investigations (including claims covered by insurance) to which the company or any subsidiary is subject together, in each case, with the name of the court or agency before which the proceedings are pending, the date instituted, principal parties thereto, a description of factual basis alleged to underlie the proceedings, and relief sought, together with copies of all pleadings and other records relating to such proceedings

☐ Consent decrees, judgments, other decrees or orders, settlement agreements, and other agreements to which the company or any subsidiary is a party or is bound, requiring or prohibiting any future activities

☐ Schedule of contingent liabilities, including any guaranties, indemnification, or other agreements whereby the company or any subsidiary is responsible for the obligations of another party

☐ Copies of all reports, notices, or correspondence relating to any violation or infringement of government regulations, and copies of all other correspondence with all federal, state, local, or foreign authorities with which the company has filed for approval to transact or conduct its business and with any other federal, state, local, or foreign regulatory agency to which the company is subject

☐ All material correspondence with, reports of or to, filings with, or other material information with respect to any administrative or regulatory bodies that regulate the company's or its subsidiaries' businesses

Tax

☐ Copies of all federal, state, local, and (if applicable) foreign tax returns for the current and the past three years, together with the most recent revenue agent's report

☐ Copies of memoranda and other material documentation relating to the company's income or other tax liability or prepared in connection with any tax problems affecting the company, its stockholders, or its subsidiaries since inception or that may arise in the future

☐ Copies of all state sales and use tax reports and returns for the current and the past three years

☐ A schedule describing any ongoing tax disputes together with copies of reports, correspondence, and so on with respect to pending federal, state, local, or foreign tax proceedings with regard to open years or items

Financial/Accounting

☐ Audited financials for the past two years

☐ Copies of operating budget for the current year and estimated operating budget for next year

☐ Summary of capital expenditures since inception and of anticipated capital expenditures for this year and next

☐ Accounts receivable and accounts payable agings

☐ Any internal financial projections and any records regarding any backlog or orders for the company's services, including a list of the backlog of contracts for the company's services

☐ Historic revenue breakdown by customer

☐ Monthly financial packages (including management commentary), if any

☐ Any waivers or agreements canceling claims or rights of substantial value other than in the ordinary course of business or any documents relating to write-downs and write-offs other than in the ordinary course of business

☐ Auditors' opinions and review letters as to financial statements since inception

☐ Auditors' management letters as to internal controls and related correspondence since inception (annual and updating letters)

☐ Lawyers' letters to auditors regarding contingent liabilities since inception

☐ List of accounts payable exceeding $10,000 each, by age

☐ Copies of all asset appraisals

☐ Status of any unreported liabilities (e.g., medical claims, pension, past employment)

☐ Copies of any analyses pertaining to the potential effects of recent and proposed changes in accounting rules

☐ Summary of pension fund asset and liability balances and a copy of the most recent actuarial report prepared by the company

Miscellaneous

☐ Schedule of bank accounts and authorized signatures with respect to each account

☐ Any other documents or information that, in the judgment of officers of the company, are significant with respect to the business of the company

APPENDIX 2: MODEL VENTURE CAPITAL TERM SHEET—SERIES A PREFERRED STOCK[17]

(*Note:* This is a checklist for the VC firm to make sure that *all* issues have been considered when drafting a term sheet. In most cases many of its provisions are not included in the actual terms. Nevertheless, the entrepreneur must be prepared to negotiate each term in this list; many of them can be denied, but most VCs will have those that they insist on keeping.)

Investors/Amount of Investment

The investor group will purchase ____ shares at a per-share price of $__, of a new class of securities, Series A Convertible Preferred Stock ("Series A Preferred"). Total investment from all investors ("Investors") will be $__. Premoney valuation will be $__. The Investors group will own __ percent of the company, on a fully diluted basis (after all securities, options, warrants, and other rights have been converted or exercised). Funds managed by Acme VC ("AVC"), its affiliates, partners, and/or consultants will own __ percent. AVC has the right to assign any portion of its investment to its affiliates, partners, and/or consultants.

Closing Date _____

Use of Proceeds/Milestones

Describe intended use of proceeds and milestones for investment, if any.

Capitalization after the Financing

Following the purchase of Series A Preferred, company's equity capitalization shall be:

Owner	Security Type	Shares	Percentage
Founders Shares			
AVC			
Other Series A Investors			
Stock Option Plan			
Warrants (if applicable)			
Total Equity			

Using this capitalization, the postinvestment valuation of the company is $__.

Other Securities

[Address warrant coverage, if any, stating percentage of warrants, exercise price, exercise term, and whether common stock or preferred stock.] If debt securities constitute all or part of the investment (including bridge loans), the following terms should be addressed:

Term of debt (e.g., demand note or fixed payment date or combination)

Interest rate

Whether debt is subordinate to third-party debt (existing and/or future)

Specify what, if any, assets will secure debt (security agreement and filing of UCCs)

Whether debt may be prepaid (at option of company or Investors)

Specify that AVC is agent for lenders and what percent of Investors/Lenders may authorize actions or amendments

Events of default (e.g., failure to pay principal or interest, assignment for benefit of creditors, commencement of bankruptcy or insolvency proceedings, assignment of note by company, failure to perform obligations, or breach of a representation or warranty under loan agreement, note or security agreement, dissolution of company, etc.)

Note assignable by Investor/Lender without consent of company

Warrants, if any

Protective Provisions

The consent of a majority (or __ percent) of the holders of Series A Preferred, voting separately as a single class, shall be necessary to authorize the following actions (any exceptions should be noted):

1. Any Liquidation Event as described under Liquidation

2. The alteration of the rights, preferences, or privileges of the Series A Preferred

3. The creation of a new class of equity or debt having parity with or preferences over the Series A Preferred

4. An increase in the authorized number of shares of Series A Preferred or common stock

5. An increase in the number of shares of common stock or the number of options in the Stock Option Plan

6. The issuance of debt of more than, singly or in aggregate, $__, *[Optional: other than debt incurred in the normal course of business for the purpose of financing receivables, and financial purchase or lease commitments of greater than $__ that are other than those approved annually by the board of directors as part of the annual budget and capital plan,]* or the issuance of any debt with equity conversion provisions or warrants, or the guarantee, directly or indirectly, of any indebtedness.

7. Any action that reclassifies any outstanding shares into shares having preferences or priority as to dividend, liquidation, assets, voting, or redemption senior to or on a parity with the Series A Preferred.

8. Amend, repeal, or waive any provision of the company's Articles of Incorporation or by-laws.

9. The declaration or payment of a dividend on the common stock (other than a dividend payable solely in shares of common stock).

10. Increase or decrease the size of the board of directors.

11. Engage in any line of business other than that engaged in by the company on the date of the first sale of Series A Preferred.

12. Redeem or acquire any equity securities of the company other than repurchases from employees, directors, and consultants pursuant to agreements where the company has the option of repurchase upon the occurrence of certain events, such as termination of employment.

13. Any material related to third-party transactions except as approved by the board of directors.

14. The acquisition of stock or assets of any other entity.

INVESTORS RIGHTS

Conversion

The Series A Preferred holders shall have the right to convert, at the then applicable conversion rate, Series A Preferred into shares of common stock at any time and from time to time. Each share of Series A Preferred shall initially be convertible into __ share(s) of common stock.

Automatic Conversion

The Series A Preferred will automatically convert into common stock, at the then applicable conversion price, in the event of a consummation of a public offering that results in aggregate gross proceeds to the company in excess of $__, and at a per-share price of at least __ times the Series A Preferred purchase price. *[Optional: or state specific price per share as adjusted for any subsequent stock dividends, stock splits or recapitalizations.]* Automatic conversion may also be initiated with the consent of __ percent of the Series A Preferred holders.

Antidilution

The Series A Preferred shall have weighted average dilution protection in the event of a financing at an equivalent price per share, adjusted for splits and the like, of less than the original Series A Preferred price. *[Optional: as an alternative to weighted average antidilution protection, use full-racket antidilution protection.]*

   The antidilution formula shall have the customary carve-outs for employee stock options and restricted stock grants of up to __ shares in the aggregate, shares issued in connection with mergers, stock-for-stock acquisitions, and an initial public offering (IPO), each of which must be approved by the board of directors. *[Optional: carve-outs may also include shares issued in connection with joint ventures, R & D, and licensing arrangements and technology transfers approved by the board of directors.]*

Redemption

If securities are subject to redemption, the following terms should be addressed:

Whether redemption is optional or mandatory
Time(s) of redemption (5–7 years)
Redemption price

Liquidation

A liquidation event ("Liquidation Event") shall occur in the event (i) that the company is wound up or liquidated, whether voluntarily or otherwise, (ii) of a sale of all or substantially all of the assets or stock of the company, (iii) of a sale of 51 percent of the company's outstanding stock or assets (by merger, consolidation, or otherwise) in a transaction or a series of related transactions, or (iv) of a dissolution of the company.

Upon the occurrence of a Liquidation Event, the holders of Series A Preferred shall receive, in preference to the holders of common stock, $__ per share plus all accrued but unpaid dividends.

[Optional: After receiving the liquidation preference, the holders of Series A Preferred shall share proceeds on a pro rata basis with the holders of common stock until the holders of Series A Preferred have received__ times the price of the Series A Preferred.]

[Alternative: Upon the occurrence of a Liquidation Event, the holders of Series A Preferred shall receive, in preference to the holders of common stock, an amount equal to __ times the price of the Series A Preferred plus all accrued but unpaid dividends.]

Dividends

Series A Preferred shall be entitled to noncumulative dividends at the rate of __ percent annually ("Dividends"). Dividends shall have priority over common stock. Dividends shall not have a current pay effect but shall be payable only upon liquidation *[and conversion],* as described in this term sheet. The issuance of Dividends may be delayed or waived, in whole or in part, with the consent of __ percent of the holders of Series A Preferred.

[Alternative: Dividends shall be cumulative and shall accrue, without interest, from the date of issuance of shares of Series A Preferred.]

[Optional: After the payment of the Dividends to holders of Series A Preferred, for any additional dividend, the Series A Preferred will participate with the common stock on an as-converted basis.]

[Optional: In the event of an IPO or a Liquidation Event, holders of Series A Preferred may elect, in their sole discretion, to be paid any Dividends by accepting shares of common stock whose aggregate value is equivalent to the dollar value of such Dividends. The number of shares of common stock shall be determined by dividing the dollar value of the Dividends by the price per share to be paid in connection with the IPO or Liquidation Event.]

Voting

On all matters submitted to a vote of the common stockholders, the holders of Series A Preferred shall be entitled to vote on an as-converted basis.

Registration

The Series A Preferred shall have the following registration rights:

Demand Registration—If, at any time, after the IPO or __ years after the closing, holders of __ percent or more of the Series A Preferred may request that company file a registration statement for an offering of at least $__, and company shall use its best efforts to cause such shares to be registered. Company shall not be obligated to cause more than two demand registrations and shall be entitled to reduce the number of shares to be registered based on the advice of the underwriters; provided, however, that employees, directors, officers, and Founders must be cut back before the holders of registrable securities may be cut back. The company shall not be required to effect more than one demand registration in any six-month period.

Form S-3 Registration—At any time after company becomes eligible to file a registration statement on Form S-3 (or any successor form relating to secondary offerings), holders of Series A Preferred may request company to effect the registration on Form S-3 (or any successor form) of shares owned by holders of Series A Preferred having an aggregate net offering price of at least $__ (based upon the then current market price or fair value). Company will not be required to effect more than one such registration in any six-month period.

Piggyback Registrations—The Series A Preferred holders shall be entitled to unlimited "piggyback" registration rights. Company shall be entitled to limit the number of shares to be registered based on the advice of its underwriters, including exclusion of piggyback registration rights from an IPO; provided, however, that the registration must include at least __ percent of the shares requested to be included by the holders of registrable securities *[Optional:, and employees, directors, officers, and Founders must be cut back before the holders of registrable securities may be cut back]*.

Registration Expenses—The registration expenses, excluding underwriting discounts and commissions, but including a single counsel representing the selling Series A Preferred holders in each of the two demand registrations and all S-3 and piggyback registrations shall be borne by company.

Customary Provisions—Customary provisions, including cross-indemnification, push back, underwriting arrangements, and the like, shall be included in the Rights Agreement.

Market Stand-off—Each Investor shall upon notice by the company and the managing underwriter, be subject to a 180-day lock-up agreement following the company's IPO, during which period Investor may not sell or transfer shares of the company's stock, other than those registered in such offering, those purchased by the Investor in the IPO and those purchased by the Investor in the open market following the IPO. All officers, directors, Founders and owners of __ percent or more of the common stock shall be subject to the same lock-up agreement.

Transfer of Rights—The registration rights may be transferred to a transferee who acquires at least __ percent of the outstanding shares of the preferred stock (or common stock issued upon conversion). Transfer of registration rights to a partner or affiliate of the Investors will be without restrictions as to minimum shareholdings.

Right of First Refusal/Co-Sale/IPO

Company and all common and Series A Preferred holders who own more than __ percent of company's equity on a fully diluted basis and future executives who are appointed as corporate officers, will enter into a right of first refusal and cosale agreement, providing that any of these stockholders (other than Series A Preferred holders) who proposes to sell all or a portion of his shares to a third party must permit the company, then the Series A Preferred holders, at their option (i) to purchase such stock on the same terms as the proposed transferee or (ii) with respect to the holders of Series A Preferred only, to sell a proportionate part of their shares on the same terms offered by the proposed transferee. Series A Preferred holders will be a party to the Agreement but their stock will not be subject to the right of first refusal or cosale rights.

Right of First Offer

Series A Preferred holders shall have the right, but not the obligation, to participate in subsequent rounds of financing for an amount that will maintain their pro-rata interest in the company, on a fully diluted basis. Failure to exercise this right will not preclude any Series A Preferred holder from participating in future rounds. Such equity shall not include shares issued as part of an approved Stock Option Plan up to an aggregate of __ shares, shares issued as part of an acquisition of another company approved by the board, or shares offered in an approved and underwritten public offering, in each case approved by the board of directors.

IPO Participation

The Investors will have a right, subject to compliance with applicable securities laws, to purchase their pro-rata share of __ percent of the shares offered in the company's IPO (to be accomplished through a private offering to the Investors completed, subject to the closing of the IPO, prior to the company's first filing of a registration statement with the SEC).

Information Rights

Series A Preferred holders shall receive the following information:

1. *[For start-up companies with no business plan: Business Plan—__ months after the closing of this transaction, company shall complete and have approved by the board a business plan that includes a product roadmap, operating plan, financing plan, marketing plan, and personnel development and recruiting plan that will serve as the basis for the next round of financing.]*

2. Business Plan—Prior to the beginning of each fiscal year, the company shall complete and have approved by the board an annual business plan that includes financial statements on a monthly basis and operating goals for each functional unit.

3. Monthly Unaudited Results—Company shall provide either monthly unaudited financial statements or a CEO letter summarizing relevant company developments no later than thirty days after the close of each month.

4. Quarterly Unaudited Results—Company shall provide unaudited quarterly financial statements within forty-five days after the end of each fiscal quarter.

5. Annual Audited Financial Statements—Company shall provide annual audited financial statements within ninety days after the end of each fiscal year *[Optional: to all shareholders]*.

6. An annual budget at least thirty days prior to the end of each fiscal year.

7. Other Management Information—Company shall provide other materials customarily made available to directors.

Qualified Small-business Stock/Parachute Payments

Company shall make reasonable efforts to ensure that the Series A Preferred constitutes qualified small-business stock within the meaning of Section 1202(c) of the Internal Revenue Code and shall make all filings required under Section 1202(d)(1)(c) of the Internal Revenue Code and related Treasury regulations.

In compliance with Rule 280G ("Golden Parachute"), company shall ensure that there is a vote held of the qualified preferred stockholders (as defined under Rule 280G) at the time of a change of control or other event that might result in the application of Rule 280G, such that in compliance with Rule 280G a vote of 75 percent of the qualified shareholders as defined thereunder can alter the applicability of the "golden parachute tax."

BOARD OF DIRECTORS

The company's Articles of Incorporation and by-laws shall provide for a board of __ directors. The number of directors may not be changed except by amendment.

Upon the closing, the board shall be composed of __ directors as follows:

Director	Nominated By	Affiliation
	AVC	Series A

All directors shall be reelected annually. In addition to the directors, the board may elect to have other representatives as observers with the approval of AVC.

Committees

The board may create committees to conduct such business as may properly come before them. A director representing AVC shall have the right, but not the obligation, to be elected to any committee constituted by the board.

Expenses

Company shall reimburse directors for reasonable out-of-pocket expenses incurred while attending board meetings or committee meetings, or while on company-approved business.

OTHER AGREEMENTS

Nondisclosure and Proprietary Rights

All current and future employees and consultants shall enter into nondisclosure and proprietary rights agreements that are in a form and substance satisfactory to the Investors.

Stock Option Plan

The company's Stock Option Plan shall be in a form and substance satisfactory to Investors. On a fully diluted basis, the Stock Option Plan shall represent __ percent of company's fully diluted equity at closing. The board, or a duly constituted compensation committee, shall determine the price and other terms of options at the time of award.

All stock and stock equivalents issued after the closing to employees, directors, consultants, and any additional new stock options offered to founders, shall be subject to vesting as follows: __ percent to vest at the end of the __ year with the remaining to vest monthly thereafter.

[Optional: Vesting of new employee stock options shall be accelerated by one year upon a change of control.] The board, or a duly constituted compensation committee, shall determine the price and other terms of options at the time of award.

Stock Purchase Agreement

The purchase of Series A Preferred shall be made upon completion of an executed Stock Purchase Agreement, which shall contain representations and warranties made by the company as to its assets, liabilities, corporate authority, litigation, and similar matters as are customarily given by a seller of securities to a purchaser, including an opinion of company's counsel acceptable to the Series A Preferred Investors.

Founders' Buyback Agreements

The Buyback Agreements shall provide for reverse vesting of __ of the Founders' common stock on a __ basis over a __ year period. The Agreements shall further provide for all remaining unvested shares to vest if a Liquidation Event occurs or if the Founders are terminated without cause during the term of the Agreement. Vesting shall not be accelerated in the event of an IPO.

PRECONDITIONS TO INVESTMENT

Completion of Diligence

The Investors shall complete their due diligence to their individual satisfaction. Such diligence includes, but is not limited to, the items listed in this section.

Intellectual Property Review

Company will reimburse the investors for the cost of the intellectual property review up to $__. *[Optional: If the investment is not consummated, the Investors will pay for the review.]*

Intellectual Property Agreement with XYZ Company (if applicable)

Prior to the closing, the company and __ will have entered into a written agreement that in effect transfers the ownership of and the proceeds associated with licensing or commercialization of agreed-upon patents, issued and pending, to the company, on terms acceptable to the Series A Preferred holders.

Corporate and Stockholder Agreements

Company's Articles of Incorporation, By-laws, Shareholder's Agreements, Intellectual Property Agreements, and the like shall be in form and substance satisfactory to the Investors.

Key Manager Insurance

Company shall carry Key Manager Insurance with a value of $__, payable to company, on __. The company shall have such policy in place within forty-five days of closing.

Opinion of Counsel

Receipt of an opinion of counsel to the company as to customary matters.

Material Changes

Representation by company that no material adverse change in the company's business conditions or prospects from what has been reported to the Investors has occurred.

Directors and Officers Insurance

The company shall maintain Directors and Officers Indemnity Insurance, with a face value of $__ and customary terms, in force while it is privately held. The company shall increase the minimum face value of the policy to $__ prior to an IPO.

EXPENSES

Company shall bear its own legal and other expenses with respect to the transaction. Company will pay the investor's reasonable auditing, legal, background check, and closing expenses, which shall not exceed a total of $__ without company's approval.

PREPARATION OF DOCUMENTS

The operative documents for the Series A Preferred financing shall be prepared by counsel for ACM.

CLOSING

The closing is expected to occur __ days after company executes this Term Sheet *[Optional: Additional closings may be held at the option of the Investor Group within __ days of the initial closing, whereby total proceeds shall not exceed $__.]*

CONFIDENTIALITY

The company and AVC each agree not to disclose the terms or conditions of this Term Sheet, including the valuation, to a nonaffiliated third party other than potential investors in this financing. Notwithstanding the foregoing, the parties hereto may disclose such information to their respective boards of directors, attorneys, accountants, and other consultants as part of the due diligence process and the consummation of the financing as may be reasonably required and engage in such other discussions as may be required by law.

STANDSTILL

Company agrees that, upon signing of this Term Sheet, AVC will have __ days to complete their diligence and fund the investment as described. Company further agrees that it will use its best efforts to immediately and fully inform AVC if company is contacted by, or intends to begin negotiations regarding investment in, or acquisition of, the company in whole or part during this period.

[Alternative: Company agrees that it will not solicit, negotiate, or otherwise encourage or accept any other offers to purchase company's securities (other than employee options) until this transaction is closed unless (i) AVC so consents in writing in advance or (ii) this transaction has not closed on or before___.]

NONBINDING EFFECT

Except for the "Standstill" clause above, this Term Sheet is not intended to create any legally binding obligations on either party, and no such obligation shall be created unless and until the parties enter into definitive documents.

EXPIRATION

This Term Sheet shall expire if not signed by company on or before __.

SIGNATURES

www.wiley.com/college/kaplan

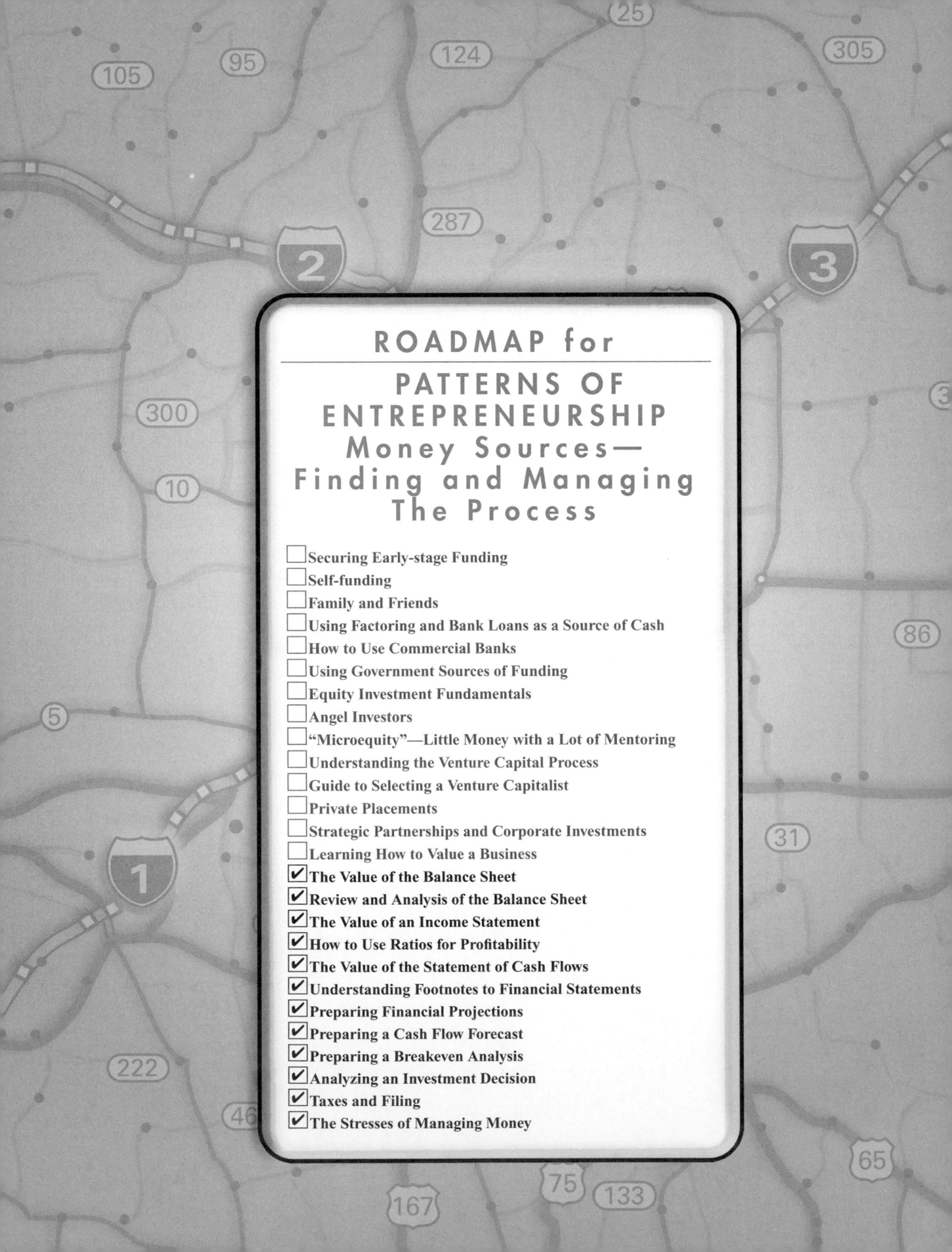

ROADMAP for

PATTERNS OF ENTREPRENEURSHIP
Money Sources—
Finding and Managing
The Process

- ☐ Securing Early-stage Funding
- ☐ Self-funding
- ☐ Family and Friends
- ☐ Using Factoring and Bank Loans as a Source of Cash
- ☐ How to Use Commercial Banks
- ☐ Using Government Sources of Funding
- ☐ Equity Investment Fundamentals
- ☐ Angel Investors
- ☐ "Microequity"—Little Money with a Lot of Mentoring
- ☐ Understanding the Venture Capital Process
- ☐ Guide to Selecting a Venture Capitalist
- ☐ Private Placements
- ☐ Strategic Partnerships and Corporate Investments
- ☐ Learning How to Value a Business
- ☑ The Value of the Balance Sheet
- ☑ Review and Analysis of the Balance Sheet
- ☑ The Value of an Income Statement
- ☑ How to Use Ratios for Profitability
- ☑ The Value of the Statement of Cash Flows
- ☑ Understanding Footnotes to Financial Statements
- ☑ Preparing Financial Projections
- ☑ Preparing a Cash Flow Forecast
- ☑ Preparing a Breakeven Analysis
- ☑ Analyzing an Investment Decision
- ☑ Taxes and Filing
- ☑ The Stresses of Managing Money

CHAPTER 9

MANAGING THE MONEY

"The secret of success in life is known only to those who have not succeeded."
J. CHURTON COLLINS

OBJECTIVES

- Understand financial statements.
- Use ratios to calculate solvency and profitability.
- Prepare financial projections such as the budget, cash flow forecast, and burn rate.
- Calculate and interpret return on investment.
- Prepare a breakeven analysis.
- Analyze an investment decision.
- Calculate the lifetime value of a customer.
- Manage the timing and stresses of fund-raising.

CHAPTER OUTLINE

Introduction

Profile: Alvin Katz—Managing Cash in Tight Situations

The Value of the Balance Sheet

Review and Analysis of the Balance Sheet

The Value of an Income Statement

How to Use Ratios for Profitability

The Value of the Statement of Cash Flows

Understanding Footnotes to Financial Statements

Preparing Financial Projections

Preparing a Cash Flow Forecast

Preparing a Breakeven Analysis

Analyzing an Investment Decision

Taxes and Filing

The Stresses of Managing Money

Summary

Study Questions

Exercises

Interactive Learning on the Web

Additional Resources

INTRODUCTION

This chapter provides you the tools to analyze a company's performance, to manage the day-to-day activities, and to prepare financial statements for investors and lenders.

The financial statements are the tools through which the company communicates its financial condition to others. Financial statements include the balance sheet, financial performance for a given period (income statement and statement of cash flows), and supplemental financial information.

Financial statements should reflect the operation of the business in the same way that management views its business. When these statements are used to forecast what the business would look like given certain events, they are referred to as "pro forma statements."[1]

PRO FORMA

A Latin term that translates into "for the sake of form." In the investing world, the term describes a method of calculating financial results to emphasize either current or projected figures.

Pro forma financial statements could be designed to reflect a proposed change, such as a merger or acquisition, or to emphasize certain figures when a company issues an earnings announcement to the public.

Investors should use caution when reading a company's pro forma financial statements because the figures may not comply with generally accepted accounting principles (GAAP). In some cases the pro forma figures may differ greatly from those derived from GAAP.[2]

Most businesses use the following basic financial documents:

- The balance sheet (also called the statement of financial position)
- The income statement or profit-and-loss (P&L) statement
- The statement of cash flows (also called source and use of funds)

PROFILE: ALVIN KATZ—MANAGING CASH IN TIGHT SITUATIONS[3]

Alvin Katz had always been in the lighting industry. While a six-term house member in the Pennsylvania Legislature, he had supplemented his income by first acting as a manufacturer's representative, then starting his own lighting company. Finally he decided to get out of politics and build his own company but ran into cash flow difficulties, avoiding bankruptcy only through a bailout from his brother. After a number of unfortunate business ups and downs brought by circumstances out of his control, he found himself at the age of sixty-two with just more than $200,000 in a bedroom closet and only Social Security checks and a small state pension to support himself and his wife.

Faced with a tough decision for his future, he decided to start a new lighting company in Santa Ana, California. Best Lighting Products manufactured recessed lighting fixtures. He and his partner were unable to get a bank loan, so they used a factoring company, Altrez Inc., in Salt Lake City, Utah, to finance the purchase of components for assembly. As discussed in Chapter 7, factors operate by providing finance secured by purchase orders. When the cash from the sale comes in directly to them, they take 10 percent and send the remainder on to the company. With no personal credit or a sound company balance sheet, this was the only financing source Alvin could find.

The company had just enough money to rent a 1,000-square-foot warehouse, which was far too small to move inventory around as orders came in. So each day the partners moved products onto the sidewalk to make space; if it rained, they had to move them back in and delay shipping until the weather improved, often forcing them to work eighteen hours a day.

Gradually the sales climbed. The first full year's sales of $450,000 grew to $2.6 million the following year. This level of business allowed Alvin to move from the punitive factor financing to a more conventional bank loan. However, this was not sufficient to buy new equipment to diversify into the growing market for emergency lighting for commercial buildings. The cost would be greater than $200,000. He was fortunate to find a small tool-making company that was willing to defer payment for the tooling for two years in order to obtain the sale. This so-called vendor financing avoided the need for Katz's company to find capital which would have further damaged the already weak balance sheet. The partners could now hire a few workers, move to a larger warehouse, and open a 17,000-square-foot manufacturing plant.

Competitive pressures on prices forced the company first to move its production to Las Vegas and finally to source components from overseas. To finance the rapid growth that the business could generate, Alvin eventually managed to find Asian suppliers that would give the company an unlimited line of credit for product purchases with a 150-day payment cycle, which allowed the company to receive payment from customers *before* they had to pay their suppliers. This strategy used suppliers' cash to fund the growth of the company. This supplier-financed model really allowed Best Lighting to take off, and nine years after signing the lease on the tiny warehouse in Santa Ana, an investment firm out of New York City called Waffra purchased 60 percent of the company from the founders for $31 million, which equated to a value of 7.2 times annual sales. The founders will also receive an extra $5 million if they stay on as managers for a further five years.

Looking back at his difficult decision at age 62, Alvin did not view putting all his savings into a new venture as a risk: "I really had no other choice than to use my extensive knowledge in lighting and give it one last shot, and when you are absolutely confident in your ability to succeed, it never seems like a risk." Alvin and his partner are still active in the company but are living on more than Social Security! All this was possible through creative management of the cash resources of the company that carried it through difficult times.

THE VALUE OF THE BALANCE SHEET

The balance sheet provides a picture of the business's financial position at a particular point in time—generally at the end of a financial period (e.g., month, quarter, or year). It is essentially a snapshot of a company's resulting financial position, encompassing everything the company owns (assets) or owes (liabilities), as well as the investments into the company by its owners and the accumulated earnings or losses of the company (equity).

The balance sheet equation is

$$\text{Assets} = \text{Liabilities} + \text{Shareholder equity}$$

Assets are current if they can be converted into cash within one year; liabilities are current if they must be paid off within one year; otherwise they are considered long term. Inventory is considered current because it is sold within one year from

Table 9-1　**Sample Pro Forma Balance Sheet (in $,000's)**

Pro Forma	Year 1	Year 2	Year 3	Year 4	Year 5	Comments
Balance sheet						
Assets						
Cash	$ 33.0	$ 39.9	$ 47.9	$ 57.5	$ 69.0	% of Sales
Accounts receivable	180.7	174.2	209.1	250.9	301.1	% of Sales
Inventories	168.6	158.6	190.3	228.3	274.0	% of CoGS
Current assets	382.3	372.7	447.3	536.7	644.1	
Net fixed assets	107.6	130.1	156.1	187.3	248.8	% of CoGS
Other	16.1	18.2	21.8	26.1	31.4	% of Sales
Total assets	$ 506.0	$ 521.0	$ 625.2	$ 750.2	$ 900.2	
Liabilities & Net worth						
Notes payable, banks	$ 209.7	$ 169.0	$ 202.0	$ 237.0	$ 281.0	% increase in NP
Accounts payable	53.7	61.0	73.2	87.8	105.4	% of CoGS
Accrued expenses	24.4	28.5	34.2	41.0	49.2	% of CoGS
Current portion, LTD	1.0	1.0	1.0	1.0	1.0	
Current liabilities	288.8	259.4	310.3	366.8	436.6	
Long-term debt	5.0	4.0	3.0	2.0	1.0	
Convertible debt	30.0	30.0	30.0	-	-	
Net worth	182.2	227.5	281.8	381.4	462.6	

date of receipt; however, certain business inventories can be further segregated into work-in-process (WIP), raw materials, or finished goods inventories.

The sample pro forma balance sheet in Table 9-1 shows shareholders' equity, or the net worth of the company projected to be $182,200 in year 1 and $462,600 by year 5. Equity is calculated by subtracting the total liabilities of $323,800 (year 1) from the total assets of $506,000 (year 1).

REVIEW AND ANALYSIS OF THE BALANCE SHEET

When analyzing a company's balance sheet, managers and investors alike must view it in terms of its type of business. For example, one would expect to see that fixed assets accounted for a greater percentage of total assets in a manufacturing operation as opposed to a distributor or professional services company. In addition, the balance sheet should be analyzed with respect to the volume of the company's business. For instance, receivables should be compared to sales to determine how quickly the company collects its cash, or current liabilities compared to expenses to see if the company is paying its short-term obligations in a timely fashion.

Book Value

Book value is derived through an analysis of the *balance sheet:* totaling up the tangible assets then subtracting all the liabilities. Whatever is left is the book value. Divide the book value by the number of shares outstanding, and you'll know the value each share would have were the company to go out of business. Some companies, such as Amazon.com, have negative book values and can be risky investment propositions. But if a company is trading for less than its book value, its stock might be a bargain for an acquirer or an investor. Book value does not include intangible assets such as patents and intellectual property, and it does not take into account the value of a company's business relationships, or *going-concern value.*

When a firm is acquired, the difference between its book value and its going-concern value is called *goodwill.* Goodwill includes factors that add value but cannot be easily liquidated or sold, such as brand, market share, the "learning curve," and human capital.

Note: The Financial Accounting Standards Board (FASB) Rule 142 of 2001 changed the GAAP treatment of goodwill. It is no longer amortized; rather, it is written down when "impaired." The FASB issued SFAS 142, Goodwill and Other Intangible Assets, in June 2001. See below for further details.

The Burn Rate aka "How Long Can the Entrepreneur Keep It Going?"

The burn rate is the rate at which a new company uses up its cash to finance overhead before generating positive cash flow from operations. In other words, it's a measure of negative cash flow. Burn rate is usually quoted in terms of cash spent per month.

$$(COH + I)/BR = MO$$

Where COH is the cash on hand, I is the income from all sources, BR is the monthly burn rate, and MO is the remaining months of operation.

COH is the cash in all bank accounts *plus* expected cash from customers, suppliers, and other accounts. If the business intends to borrow to access cash (e.g., bank credit line or revolving fund), be sure to include the cost of this debt in the burn rate. Additional considerations include quarterly or semiannual payments, such as tax installments or advertising. Include a pro rata of these expenses in the calculation. The burn rate is determined by looking at the cash flow statement. The cash flow statement reports the *change* in the firm's cash position from one period to the next by accounting for the cash flows from operations, investment activities, and financing activities. Compared to the amount of cash a company has on hand, the burn rate gives investors a sense of how much time is left before the company runs out of cash—assuming no change in the burn rate. This time period is called the "runway."

Time left before cash runs out = Cash reserves/Burn rate

If you want to know if a company is really in trouble, compare its burn rate with the working capital measured over the same time period. The burn rate is important for two reasons:

1. It provides the business manager with a financial picture of where the company is going and what needs to be done *before* cash becomes a problem.
2. It allows management to dynamically analyze the financial position of the business and determine how long the business can operate if changes are not made to its operations.

Example of Measuring Burn Rate

Refer to the cash flow forecast in Table 9-2. Net cash from operating activities was negative $382,771 for the year. This means that the core business operations burned cash at a rate of about $31,898 per month, largely due to continuing net losses.

Table 9-2   A Typical Cash Flow Statement

Statement of Cash Flows

Year Ended December 31, 2008

Cash Flows from Operating Activities	
Net income (loss)	($262,381)
Adjustments to reconcile net income (loss to net)	
Cash provided by (used in) operating activities	
Depreciation	99,182
Issuance of common stock in lieu of compensation	0
Bad debts	14,875
Deferred taxes	(241,800)
	(390,124)
Changes in Operating Assets and Liabilities	
Accounts receivable	(12,387)
Loan receivable, employee	0
Prepaid expenses and other current assets	(32,213)
Accounts payable and accrued expenses	56,845
Income taxes payable	(4,892)
Net Cash Provided by (Used in) Operating Activities	(382,771)
Cash Flows from Investing Activities	
Purchases of certificates of deposit	(250,000)
Purchases of property and equipment	(59,158)
Net Cash Used in Investing Activities	(309,158)
Cash Flows from Financing Activities	
Repayment of loan	(14,644)
Issuance of common stock	6,423
Issuance of preferred stock	2,500,000
Acquisition of treasury stock	(363,398)
Net Cash Provided by (Used in) Financing Activities	2,128,381
Net Increase (or Decrease) in Cash	1,436,452
Cash, beginning of period	48,021
Cash, End of Year	$1,484,473
Supplemental Disclosures of Cash Flow Information	
Cash paid during the period for:	
Interest	$380
Income taxes	$0

The net cash flow from investing was also negative, owing primarily to purchases of certificates of deposit (CDs). The negative cash flow was $309,158, which represents another big use of cash. Indeed, the net cash burned by operations and investing amounted to greater than $691,929—a burn rate of almost $57,661 per month.

Finally, the cash flow from financing was positive, but it was due primarily to the issuance of $2.5 million worth of preferred stock.

This illustration demonstrates the primary importance of knowing a company's burn rate. The bottom line: Is the company staying in business because it's "burning cash," that is, using debt and shareholder equity to remain viable, or is the company generating enough cash from operations to sustain its expense structure?

The various financial metrics and exhibits introduced in this chapter are designed to optimize learning. It is important to develop a comfortable working knowledge of financial statement analysis, for these skills are a critical tool for the successful entrepreneur. We recommend a three-step approach to the study of financial analysis: (1) skim the chapter for a quick overview; (2) read the chapter carefully and pay attention to the formulas and statement analysis; and (3) test your knowledge using the interactive Web site to practice reviewing financial operations.

Accounting Treatment of Goodwill

As mentioned above, in 2001 the FASB made two major changes to goodwill accounting:

1. Amortization of *all* goodwill ceased, regardless of when it originated. Goodwill is now carried as an asset without reduction for periodic amortization.
2. Companies are to assess goodwill for impairment at least annually. If goodwill is impaired, its carrying amount is reduced and an impairment loss is recognized.

Sarbanes-Oxley Act of 2002

The Sarbanes-Oxley Act (SOX) was passed by the U.S. Congress to protect investors from the possibility of fraudulent accounting activities by corporations. It was triggered by a number of major cases of alleged fraudulent accounting methods exposed in major public companies. The rules and enforcement policies outlined by SOX amend or supplement existing legislation dealing with security regulations. Although the requirements are targeted to public companies, private companies should try to follow the principles outlined in the legislation for several reasons: (1) the rules provide sensible guidelines for sound accounting practice; (2) corporate partnering is playing a larger role in the business models of smaller companies (see Chapter 14) and large companies often require their smaller partners follow these rules to avoid liability for themselves; and (3) if the intent is to create an exit strategy either by a sale to a public company or through an IPO, meeting the requirements of SOX will be a necessity. Although full compliance with the act by small companies would be too arduous a task in most cases, you should at least operate under the general meaning and intent of SOX so moving to full compliance when required will be relatively painless.

Sarbanes-Oxley contains eleven titles that describe specific mandates and requirements for financial reporting. Each title consists of several sections, summarized below.

1. **Public Company Accounting Oversight Board (PCAOB)**
   This title consists of nine sections and establishes the Public Company Accounting Oversight Board to provide independent oversight of public accounting firms providing audit services ("auditors"). It also creates a central oversight board tasked with registering auditors, defining the specific processes and procedures for compliance audits, inspecting and policing conduct and quality control, and enforcing compliance with the specific mandates of SOX.

2. **Auditor Independence**

   This title consists of nine sections and establishes standards for external auditor independence to limit conflicts of interest. It also addresses new auditor approval requirements, audit partner rotation policy, conflict-of-interest issues, and auditor reporting requirements. Section 201 of this title restricts auditing companies from doing other kinds of business apart from auditing with their auditing clients.

3. **Corporate Responsibility**

   These eight sections mandate that senior executives take individual responsibility for the accuracy and completeness of corporate financial reports. It defines the interaction of external auditors and corporate audit committees and specifies the responsibility of corporate officers for the accuracy and validity of corporate financial reports. For example, company board members, chief executive officer, and chief financial officer should certify and approve the integrity of their company financial reports quarterly to establish accountability.

4. **Enhanced Financial Disclosures**

   Consisting of nine sections, this title describes enhanced reporting requirements for financial transactions, including off-balance-sheet transactions, pro-forma figures, and stock transactions of corporate officers. It requires internal controls for assuring the accuracy of financial reports and disclosures and mandates both audits and reports on those controls. It also requires timely reporting of material changes in financial condition and specific enhanced reviews of corporate reports by the SEC or its agents.

5. **Analyst Conflicts of Interest**

   This title has only one section, which includes measures designed to help restore investor confidence in the reporting of securities analysts. It defines the codes of conduct for securities analysts and requires disclosure of knowable conflicts of interest.

6. **Commission Resources and Authority**

   This title consists of four sections and defines practices to restore investor confidence in securities analysts. It also defines the SEC's authority to censure or bar securities professionals from practice and defines conditions under which a person can be barred from practicing as a broker, adviser, or dealer.

7. **Studies and Reports**

   These five sections are concerned with conducting research for enforcing actions against violations by the SEC registrants (companies) and auditors. Studies and reports include the effects of consolidation of public accounting firms, the role of credit rating agencies in the operation of securities markets, securities violations, and enforcement actions.

8. **Corporate and Criminal Fraud Accountability**

   The seven sections in this title, also referred to as the "Corporate and Criminal Fraud Act of 2002," describe specific criminal penalties for fraud by manipulation, destruction, or alteration of financial records or other interference with investigations, while providing certain protections for whistle-blowers.

9. **White-collar Crime Penalty Enhancement**

   This title, also called the "White-collar Crime Penalty Enhancement Act of 2002," consists of two sections that increase the criminal penalties associated with white-collar crimes and conspiracies. It recommends stronger sentencing guidelines and specifically adds failure to certify corporate financial reports as a criminal offense.

10. Corporate Tax Returns

The single section in this title states that the chief executive officer should sign the company tax return.

11. Corporate Fraud Accountability

Consisting of seven sections, this title is referred to as the "Corporate Fraud Accountability Act of 2002." It identifies corporate fraud and records tampering as criminal offenses and joins those offenses to specific penalties. It also revises sentencing guidelines and strengthens their penalties. This enables the SEC to temporarily freeze large or unusual payments.

ROADMAP

IN ACTION

The entrepreneur must be able to apply financial ratios to address financial condition. Ratios can also be used to analyze a balance sheet. *Current ratio* is the total current asset divided by the total current liabilities. *Quick ratio,* or *acid-test ratio,* is very similar to the current ratio but includes only cash and accounts receivable.

How to Use Ratios for Financial Analysis

Ratios can also be used to analyze a balance sheet. The following solvency ratios are the most commonly used by entrepreneurs for financial analysis.[4]

Current Ratio

This is the total current assets divided by the total current liabilities. Current assets and liabilities are those items expected to generate cash or require the disbursement of cash within the next year. The current ratio indicates the company's ability to meet its obligations for the next year. The higher the ratio, the greater the liquidity. A low ratio indicates a lack of liquidity and a potential problem in meeting maturing obligations. Table 9-3 shows a list of current ratios by industry.

Quick Ratio

Also called the acid-test ratio, this ratio is very similar to the current ratio except that it includes only those current assets—cash and accounts receivable—that can be most readily used to pay bills today. The quick ratio excludes inventory, which

Table 9-3   Ratios by Industry

Current Ratios by Industry

Construction	1.5	Manufacturing:	
Finance (banks)	0.9	Food and retail	1.1
Services (hotels)	0.8	Apparel	1.9
(personal)	1.9	Printing and publishing	1.3
Retail (restaurants)	1.0	Motor vehicles	0.9
General merchandise	1.4	Grocery stores	1.2
Furniture	1.9	Insurance agents	1.3

Source: BizStats.com.

must first be sold and the cash collected before it can be used to pay liabilities. It also excludes current assets such as prepaid expenses, which are never converted to cash (they are simply assets paid for in advance). As a result, the quick ratio is a good indication of how well the company is able to meet current liabilities in a crunch situation. In general, the entrepreneur should try to maintain a quick ratio of 1:1, which means that $1 worth of cash and accounts receivable is on hand for every $1 of total current liabilities.[5]

Rules and Examples

Although a satisfactory value for a current ratio varies from industry to industry, a general rule of thumb is that a current ratio of 2:1 or greater is fairly healthy. In terms of dollars, a 2:1 ratio means that there exists $2 of current assets from which to pay every $1 of current bills. A smaller current ratio may mean that the company has successfully negotiated to pay its suppliers later than the usual thirty days, which essentially gives the company an interest-free source of cash. Let's say current assets are $15,000 and current liabilities are $10,000, yielding a current ratio of 1.5:1. In this scenario, the entrepreneur could improve the current ratio to 2:1 by paying $5,000 of the current liabilities with the current assets, thereby reducing both by $5,000 (i.e., $10,000 divided by $5,000 = 2:1). If, however, the suppliers were willing to wait for payment without charging interest, this would probably be a bad idea (unless a financing agreement required the company to maintain a current ratio of 2:1).

Solvency Ratios

Debt management ratios can help the entrepreneur evaluate the business liabilities. Since debt is associated with risk, the greater the debt, the higher the return rate will be. If the liabilities are large compared to equity or assets, potential lenders and investors may feel that the company is already too indebted and is not a good investment risk. Other solvency ratios include the following:

- Current liabilities to net worth
- Total liabilities to net worth
- Fixed assets to net worth
- Debt-to-worth ratio

Current-liabilities-to-net-worth Ratio The current-liabilities-to-net-worth ratio is calculated by dividing current liabilities by net worth. This ratio contrasts the funds that creditors are temporarily risking with the funds invested by the stockholders or owners. The smaller the ratio, the more secure the creditors.

Total-liabilities-to-net-worth (Debt-to-equity) Ratio The total-liabilities-to-net-worth ratio is calculated by dividing total liabilities by net worth. This ratio expresses the relationship between capital contributed by creditors and capital contributed by owners. It expresses the degree of protection provided the creditors by the owners. The higher the ratio, the higher the risk being borne by the creditors.

A business with low debt-to-equity ratios usually has more borrowing power and longer-term financial security. The ratio indicates how highly leveraged the business is. Lower is usually better.

Fixed-assets-to-net-worth Ratio The fixed-assets-to-net-worth ratio is calculated by dividing fixed assets by net worth. This ratio shows to what extent the owner's equity has been invested in fixed assets. Lower ratios show a proportionally smaller investment in fixed assets in relation to net worth. A lower ratio indicates that the business has a better cushion for short-term cash needs or in case of a sudden liquidation. A high ratio indicates that the business may be too heavily invested in fixed assets (plant, equipment, autos, etc.) and may be strangling its supply of working capital.

Debt-to-worth Ratio   The debt-to-worth ratio is calculated by dividing total liabilities by net worth. Also called debt to owners' equity, this ratio compares the total liabilities of the business to the total owners' equity or net worth (the value of the total assets minus the total liabilities from the balance sheet). This ratio gives insight into whether the company's previous funding has been through equity (sales of stock) or debt. The higher the ratio, the higher the risk borne by creditors. A low debt ratio usually means more borrowing power and financial security.

This discussion of ratios is not meant to be all inclusive. Each industry and business will have a set of ratios that is especially pertinent. The point to remember is that ratios are nothing more than a comparison of two numbers. So if the entrepreneur finds a particular ratio that is helpful in the financial management of the firm, then by all means, it should be used.[6]

ROADMAP

IN ACTION

The entrepreneur should also use the income statement to evaluate the business's financial condition. The income statement shows how the business made a profit by displaying how much money it generated in sales and how much money it cost to run the business.

THE VALUE OF AN INCOME STATEMENT

The statement of operations, also known as the income statement, profit-and-loss statement, or P&L statement, summarizes the revenue (or income) and expenses of a company on a monthly basis for one year or on an annual basis for several years. It divides expenses into broad categories, such as cost of goods sold and operating expenses. The cost of goods sold would represent the resources that went into production of the products ultimately recognized as sales. These costs would include materials, labor, and manufacturing expenses. Two more terms for costs of goods sold are shown here:

1. *Inventory costs*—costs that are assigned to inventory before being sold

2. *Production costs*—costs that are identified with the product

Operating expenses are costs that are not identified with the product. The major categories include research and development, sales and marketing, general and administration (SG&A), and financial expenses.

The income statement in Table 9-4 shows how the business made a profit by displaying how much money it generated in sales and how much money it cost to run the business. The equation used to determine net profit or loss is

$$\text{Net profit (or loss)} = \text{Gross sales} - \text{Total expenses}$$

The entrepreneur should be aware that operating income is not the same as net profit. Operating income is determined by subtracting costs from sales and does not

Table 9-4   **Income Statement Pro Forma (in $,000's)**

Pro Forma Income Statement	Year 1	Year 2	Year 3	Year 4	Year 5	Comments
Sales	$ 605.0	$ 726.0	$ 871.2	$ 1,045.4	$ 1,254.5	% increase in Sales
Cost of goods sold	349.5	406.6	487.9	585.4	702.5	% of Sales
Gross profit	255.5	319.4	383.3	460.0	552.0	
Research & development	100.4	108.9	130.7	156.8	188.2	% of Sales
General & administration	106.9	123.4	148.1	177.7	213.3	% of Sales
Income from operations	48.2	87.1	104.5	125.5	150.5	
Interest expense	19.7	19.0	20.0	21.0	23.0	% of Debt
Profit before taxes	28.5	68.1	84.5	104.5	127.5	
Taxes	10.0	23.8	29.6	36.6	44.6	Income Tax Rate

include taxes or interest charges. Operating income is the amount the business earns after expenses but before taxes and other income, such as interest. It is sometimes referred to as EBIT (earnings before interest and taxes). The ratio of EBIT to interest is used to show how many times earnings cover interest.

The EBIT-to-interest ratio is calculated by dividing the EBIT by the interest. For example, if operating profits were $10,000 and interest was $10,000, the business would break even. This is risky, as a slight downturn in sales or an increase in interest rate would cause losses.

A Rule of Thumb: The ratio should be at least 3:1. Monthly trends might fluctuate (building up inventory for seasonal fluctuations, awaiting payment on large receivables, etc.), but in the long term, it is important that this ratio hover in the 2.5+ range.

HOW TO USE RATIOS FOR PROFITABILITY

When analyzing the income statement, the entrepreneur must view it in terms of the type of business and how long the company has been involved in its current operations. Many companies change their type of business over time through acquisitions, divestitures, or diversification. Ratios can also be used to analyze the statement of operations. The four most commonly used are described here.

1. **Return on Investment (ROI).** This ratio compares the net profit of the business to the investment (net worth) of the business. It is calculated as net income after taxes (from the income statement) divided by total owners' equity (from the balance sheet).

$$\text{Return on investment} = \frac{\text{Net income}}{\text{Shareholders' equity}}$$

To relate return on investment to the debt-to-worth ratio, remember that given a fixed total asset figure, the greater the debt, the lower the net worth. Therefore, given two companies of identical asset size and profitability, the company with the higher debt-to-worth ratio will also have a higher return-on-equity ratio. When potential leaders and investors consider the risk of investing in the business, they will look at the return-on-equity ratio.

2. **Level of Reliability of ROI.** Return on investment is not a totally reliable measure of financial performance for the following reasons:

- Returns are examined without the risk factors of the business.
- The assessment is measured in an annual time frame, and long-term decisions may not be reflected.
- Book value rather than market value is used for shareholders' equity.

Therefore, return on investment should be examined in relationship to the business and environment rather than just mechanically.

3. **Return on Total Assets.** This measures how efficiently the business is using the assets in negotiating net income. This is calculated as the net income after taxes (from the income statement) divided by the total assets (from the balance sheet). Assets are used to generate profits. Therefore, the return on total assets is a measure of how effectively the entrepreneur is employing the assets of the business.

Understanding the Terms *Gross Profit Margin, Operating Profit Margin,* and *Net Profit Margin*

Gross profit margin (or percentage) is the ratio of gross profit (gross sales minus the cost of goods sold) divided by gross sales, expressed as a percentage. High gross margins are usually a sign that the company is in a strong competitive position. As a benchmark, venture capital investors may look for high gross margin projections (60 percent or more) when investing so they can create a high valuation when it's time to "exit" the investment. All three percentages should be included on the income statements. To analyze the profitability, compare these percentages to the industry's averages or those of the immediate competitors (if this information can be obtained). Of course, the entrepreneur will always want to compare the current year's profitability percentages to the percentages from the company's previous years to determine the progress of the company.

ROADMAP

IN ACTION

When analyzing cash flows, the entrepreneur needs to determine if the numbers are positive or negative. Examine the relationship between cash available through operations and cash from investment. Examine whether growth in receivables is due to increased sales or poor collection results. Is an increase in debt matched with fixed assets, or is the debt being used to fund operations? The statement of cash flows is usually overlooked by investors, but it can frequently disclose information about how a company manages its cash.

THE VALUE OF THE STATEMENT OF CASH FLOWS

The statement of cash flows (SCF) summarizes where cash comes from and how it is used over a period of time. The SCF is divided into three parts: cash from operations, cash from financing activities, and cash from investing activities. The SCF begins with the net income sourced from the income statement. It then shows adjustments for items that do not involve cash (such as payables and depreciation), other nonoperational sources, and uses of cash (such as fixed asset purchases, financing proceeds, and vendor payments). Finally, the increase or decrease in net cash balance is calculated. The statement shows the movement of funds through a business over

Table 9-5   **Statement of Cash Flows**

Year Ended December 31, 2008

Cash Flows from Operating Activities

Net income (loss)	($262,381)
Adjustments to reconcile net income (loss to net)	
Cash provided by (used in) operating activities	
Depreciation	99,182
Issuance of common stock in lieu of compensation	0
Bad debts	14,875
Deferred taxes	(241,800)
	(390,124)

Changes in Operating Assets and Liabilities	
Accounts receivable	(12,387)
Loan receivable, employee	0
Prepaid expenses and other current assets	(32,213)
Accounts payable and accrued expenses	56,845
Income taxes payable	(4,892)
Net Cash Provided by (Used in) Operating Activities	(382,771)

Cash Flows from Investing Activities	
Purchases of certificates of deposit	(250,000)
Purchases of property and equipment	(59,158)
Net Cash Used in Investing Activities	(309,158)

Cash Flows from Financing Activities	
Repayment of loan	(14,644)
Issuance of common stock	6,423
Issuance of preferred stock	2,500,000
Acquisition of treasury stock	(363,398)
Net Cash Provided by (Used in) Financing Activities	2,128,381

Net Increase (or Decrease) in Cash	1,436,452
Cash, beginning of period	48,021
Cash, End of Year	$1,484,473
Supplemental Disclosures of Cash Flow Information	
Cash paid during the period for:	
Interest	$380
Income taxes	$0

time. The format used in Table 9-5 shows how the sources of funds are accumulated. This includes changes in operations, new sources of capital such as debt and equity, the sale of fixed assets, and all the uses of the company's funds. The bottom line is the net change in working capital.

UNDERSTANDING FOOTNOTES TO FINANCIAL STATEMENTS

Financial statements are usually accompanied by footnotes. As with the statement of cash flows, these footnotes are often overlooked but contain valuable information. Certain footnotes are especially important, as shown by the following six.[7]

1. **General Description of Business.** The first footnote usually includes a general description of the company's business and a recent history, often detailing any

events that have a material impact on the company's current financial statements, such as an acquisition or increased competition.

2. **Acquisitions and Divestitures/Discontinued Operations.** If the company has acquired or sold either the assets or stock of a company, the details of the transactions will be included in this footnote. In addition, if a company has discontinued a material segment of its business, the details of the discontinuance will be included.

3. **Intangible Assets.** This footnote details any intangible assets the company has on the balance sheet, such as goodwill, capitalized patents, or capitalized research and development. The viewer should make note of how much the company capitalized during the year and how quickly it is being amortized.

4. **Debt.** The debt footnote will classify the debt on the balance sheet by loan instrument and by the bank. It will also include the current interest rates and may disclose how much financing is available in the future as well as the payoff schedule of the company's present debt.

5. **Legal Proceedings.** This footnote must disclose any material legal proceedings either by or against the company. This should always be reviewed to determine if any legal proceedings could significantly affect the company's financial viability.

6. **Subsequent Events.** This footnote details any unusual and material events that have occurred after the date of but before the issuance of the financial statement.

PREPARING FINANCIAL PROJECTIONS

Entrepreneurs need to be able to plan operations and evaluate decisions using financial accounting information. Budgets, cash flow forecasts, and breakeven analyses are not only important management tools, but they are also usually required information for potential investors or lenders.

One of the first steps in any business is to establish a financial plan to measure financial performance. There are three widely used methods of measuring financial performance.

1. **Measuring sales volume.** The first perspective is to view performance in terms of sales, such as percentage of increased sales or new business. Many Internet companies measure success in terms of increased sales volume. However, if the expectation is that additional sales means higher profits, which may not always be the case, certainly increasing sales is a part of the financial plan. But to stop at that point is shortsighted.

2. **Measuring profits.** The second perspective is to measure profits, that is, the difference between revenues and expenses as reported in the income statements. Sales must be profitable for the business to succeed. A firm can determine the profitability of either products or customers. It can also provide incentives to its salesforce to encourage more profitable sales.

3. **Measuring cash generated.** Just because a company has an income statement that shows it is profitable does not necessarily mean it is generating cash. If the company uses accrual accounting, a sale is recognized when, as an example, a customer takes title to the product, even though the cash may not be collected for some time. Accrual accounting does not recognize that cash may have been required to purchase materials, labor, and other resources in advance of the sale.

Frequently businesses, though profitable, run out of cash because when a sale occurs, the cash from the sale is not collected until a later date. It is important, especially for undercapitalized companies, to project cash flow and to note any periods where it will have inadequate cash, so the company can secure outside financing; otherwise the company may be forced into bankruptcy. A major cause of failure of start-up companies is poor cash management rather than a lack of customers willing to pay.

These financial methods give the entrepreneur an idea of the nature of financial goals that may be set for her company. Obviously, how high the goals are set depends on the nature of the business, the opportunities available, and management's decisions.

How to Prepare an Annual Budget

The annual budget presents a month-by-month projection of revenues and expenses over a one-year period. The budget is the foundation for projecting the other financial statements. It presents a more detailed accounting of expenses than does the income statement. In a budget, expense details are usually grouped by department or functional area, such as general, administrative, and research and development. The details of a standard budget are divided into eleven major categories:[8]

1. **Sales.** The budget detail should include all or some of the following: sales by product line and by customer, geographical region, and goals for each sales representative.
2. **Cost of Goods Sold.** The detail should include both materials and shipping costs, as well as any allocated overhead if the company is a manufacturer. If sales are identified by product line, the cost of goods sold for each product line should be calculated to determine gross profit by product line.
3. **Gross Profit.** The detail should include, where possible, the gross profit by whatever categories the sales are classified (e.g., product line, geographical region). Gross profit is defined as sales less those costs directly incurred to achieve the sales (such as component pieces and assembly labor in the sale of a computer).
4. **Operating Expenses.** The detail should classify expenses by research and development, sales and marketing, and general administrative. Within these categories the detail should reflect the budgeted expenses by category, such as salary, benefits, rent, and telephone. Some expenses should be further categorized by such items as salary by employee and allocation of rent expenses.
5. **Operating Profit/Loss.** If operating expenses can be identified by sales category, an operating profit/loss for each sales category should be calculated.
6. **Other Income and Expenses.** This category usually includes interest expense, which should be detailed by each type of debt (e.g., leases for computers and copying equipment, lines of personal credit, and bank loans), and other income and expenses not related to the normal operations of the business, such as a legal settlement or loss due to fire.
7. **Pretax Income.** Income before taxes is calculated by taking operating profit and factoring in other income and expenses. It denotes the income that will be subject to corporate income tax.
8. **Income Taxes.** This is management's estimate of what taxes will be owed on its earnings. Detail should reflect amounts owed for federal and state taxes.

9. **Net Income.** This is the amount available for dividends or reinvestment in the company.

10. **EBIT.** This is the earnings (net income) before interest expense, interest income, and income taxes. It measures the profitability of the company's current operations as if it had no debt or investments.

11. **EBITDA.** This is the earnings before interest expense, interest income, income taxes, depreciation, and amortization. It measures the profitability of a company's operations without the impact of its debt, investments, and long-term assets.

The sample budget in Table 9-6 shows a projection of the first five months of the company's fiscal year. An actual budget would include all twelve months and a column totaling the months. It could also include a column after the total column showing the previous year's activity for comparison purposes.

Table 9-6   Preparing Budget Projections

Five Months Sample

Company X
Budget for 2008

	January	February	March	April	May
Income Statement					
Sales					
Product A	1,000,000	1,040,000	1,080,000	1,120,000	1,160,000
Product B	525,000	565,000	605,000	645,000	685,000
Product C	300,000	340,000	380,000	420,000	460,000
Total Sales	1,825,000	1,945,000	2,065,000	2,185,000	2,305,000
Cost of Goods Sold					
Product A	500,000	520,000	540,000	560,000	580,000
Product B	262,500	282,500	302,500	322,500	342,500
Product C	150,000	170,000	190,000	210,000	230,000
Total Cost of Goods Sold	912,500	972,500	1,032,500	1,092,500	1,152,500
Gross Profit					
Product A—Profit	500,000	520,000	540,000	560,000	580,000
Product A—Margin	50.0%	50.0%	50.0%	50.0%	50.0%
Product B—Profit	262,500	282,500	302,500	322,500	342,500
Product B—Margin	50.0%	50.0%	50.0%	50.0%	50.0%
Product C—Profit	150,000	170,000	190,000	210,000	230,000
Product C—Margin	50.0%	50.0%	50.0%	50.0%	50.0%
Total Gross Profit	912,500	972,500	1,032,500	1,092,500	1,152,500
Total Gross Margin	50.0%	50.0%	50.0%	50.0%	50.0%
Operating Expenses					
Research and Development	90,000	90,000	90,000	90,000	90,000
Sales and Marketing	125,000	125,000	125,000	125,000	125,000
General and Administrative	215,000	215,000	215,000	215,000	215,000
Total Operating Expenses	430,000	430,000	430,000	430,000	430,000

(Continued)

Table 9-6   *Continued*

	January	February	March	April	May
Operating Profit	482,500	542,500	602,500	662,500	722,500
Operating Margin	26.4%	27.9%	29.2%	30.3%	31.3%
Other Expense					
Interest Expense	40,000	37,500	35,000	32,500	30,000
Total Expense	40,000	37,500	35,000	32,500	30,000
Income before Income Tax	442,500	505,000	567,500	630,000	692,500
Provision for Income Taxes					
Federal	177,000	202,000	227,000	252,000	277,000
State	44,250	50,500	56,750	63,000	69,250
Total Taxes	221,250	252,500	283,750	315,000	346,250
Net Income	221,250	252,500	283,750	315,000	346,250
Sales Detail					
Product A					
Eastern Region	400,000	425,000	450,000	475,000	500,000
Central Region	320,000	325,000	330,000	335,000	340,000
Western Region	280,000	290,000	300,000	310,000	320,000
Total Sales of Product A	1,000,000	1,040,000	1,080,000	1,120,000	1,160,000
Product B					
Eastern Region	105,000	120,000	135,000	150,000	165,000
Central Region	320,000	340,000	360,000	380,000	400,000
Western Region	100,000	105,000	110,000	115,000	120,000
Total Sales of Product B	525,000	565,000	605,000	645,000	685,000
Product C					
Eastern Region	110,000	125,000	140,000	155,000	170,000
Central Region	30,000	40,000	50,000	60,000	70,000
Western Region	160,000	175,000	190,000	205,000	220,000
Total Sales of Product C	300,000	340,000	380,000	420,000	460,000
Costs of Goods Sold Detail					
Product A					
Parts	200,000	208,000	216,000	224,000	232,000
Assembly Labor	200,000	208,000	216,000	224,000	232,000
Factory Overhead	100,000	104,000	108,000	112,000	116,000
Total CoGS Product A	500,000	520,000	540,000	560,000	580,000
Product B					
Parts	105,000	113,000	121,000	129,000	137,000
Assembly Labor	105,000	113,000	121,000	129,000	137,000
Factory Overhead	52,500	56,500	60,500	64,500	68,500
Total CoGS Product B	262,500	282,500	302,500	322,500	342,500

(*Continued*)

Table 9-6   **Continued**

	January	February	March	April	May
Product C					
Parts	60,000	68,000	76,000	84,000	92,000
Assembly Labor	60,000	68,000	76,000	84,000	92,000
Factory Overhead	30,000	34,000	38,000	42,000	46,000
Total CoGS Product C	150,000	170,000	190,000	210,000	230,000
Operating Expenses Detail					
Research and Development					
Salary and Payroll Tax	33,000	33,000	33,000	33,000	33,000
Benefits	7,000	7,000	7,000	7,000	7,000
Rent	12,000	12,000	12,000	12,000	12,000
Office Expense	5,000	5,000	5,000	5,000	5,000
Telephone	10,000	10,000	10,000	10,000	10,000
Consulting	15,000	15,000	15,000	15,000	15,000
Insurance	7,000	7,000	7,000	7,000	7,000
Miscellaneous	1,000	1,000	1,000	1,000	1,000
Total R & D	90,000	90,000	90,000	90,000	90,000
Selling and Marketing					
Salary and Payroll Tax	42,000	42,000	42,000	42,000	42,000
Benefits	10,000	10,000	10,000	10,000	10,000
Rent	15,000	15,000	15,000	15,000	15,000
Office Expense	7,500	7,500	7,500	7,500	7,500
Telephone	14,500	14,500	14,500	14,500	14,500
Commissions	25,000	25,000	25,000	25,000	25,000
Insurance	9,000	9,000	9,000	9,000	9,000
Miscellaneous	2,000	2,000	2,000	2,000	2,000
Total S & M	125,000	125,000	125,000	125,000	125,000
General and Administrative					
Salary and Payroll Tax	65,000	65,000	65,000	65,000	65,000
Benefits	20,000	20,000	20,000	20,000	20,000
Rent	25,000	25,000	25,000	25,000	25,000
Office Expense	10,000	10,000	10,000	10,000	10,000
Telephone	20,000	20,000	20,000	20,000	20,000
Legal	55,000	55,000	55,000	55,000	55,000
Insurance	15,000	15,000	15,000	15,000	15,000
Miscellaneous	5,000	5,000	5,000	5,000	5,000
Total G & A	215,000	215,000	215,000	215,000	215,000

PREPARING A CASH FLOW FORECAST

Reasons to Prepare a Cash Flow Forecast

As stated earlier, one of the major problems that start-up companies face is cash flow. Lack of cash is one reason that profitable companies fail. Cash managers can anticipate temporary cash shortfalls and have sufficient time to arrange short-term loans if needed.

A cash flow forecast shows the amount of cash coming in (receivables) and cash going out (payables) during a certain month. The forecast also shows a bank loan officer (or the entrepreneur) what additional working capital, if any, the business may need. In addition, it provides evidence that there will be sufficient cash on hand to make the interest payments on a revolving line of credit or to cover the shortfalls when payables exceed receivables.

Computer spreadsheet programs such as Microsoft Excel or any variety of full-faceted business software can be very useful for generating a cash flow worksheet. Reliable cash flow projections can bring a sense of order, well-being, and security to a business. The most important tool that owners and/or managers have available to control the financial liquidity of their businesses is the cash flow worksheet.

Getting Started

Step One: Consider Cash Flow Revenues

Find a realistic basis for estimating sales each month. For a start-up company, the basis can be the average monthly sales of a similarly sized competitor's operation, which is operating in a similar market. Be sure to reduce your figures by a start-up year factor of about 50 percent a month for the start-up months. Libraries and bookstores offer publications that discuss methods of sales forecasting.

For an existing company, sales revenues from the same month in the previous year make a good basis for forecasting sales for that month in the succeeding year. For example, if the trend in the industry predicts a general growth of 4 percent for the next year, it will be entirely acceptable to show each month's projected sales at 4 percent higher than the actual sales the previous year. Include notes to the cash flow to explain any unusual variations from the previous year's numbers.

Step Two: Consider Cash Flow Disbursements

Project each of the various expense categories (normally shown in your ledger) beginning with a summary for each month of the cash payments to suppliers as well as wages, rent, and equipment costs (accounts payable).

Each month shows only the cash that is expected to be paid that month to the suppliers. For example, if suppliers' invoices are paid in thirty days, the cash payoffs for January's purchases will be shown in February. If longer terms are obtained for trade credit, then cash outlays will appear two or even three months after the stock purchase has been received and invoiced.

An example of a different type of expense is insurance expenditure. Commercial insurance premiums may be $2,400 annually. Normally, this would be treated as a $200 monthly expense. However, it will not be recorded this way on the cash flow statement. Rather, the cash flow records show how it will be paid. If it is to be paid in two installments, $1,200 in January and $1,200 in July, then that is how it must be entered on the cash flow worksheet. The same principle applies to all cash flow expense items.

Step Three: Reconcile the Revenues and Disbursements

The reconciliation section of the cash flow worksheet begins by showing the balance carried over from the previous month's operations. To this, the net inflows/outflows or current month's receipts and disbursements will be added. This adjusted balance will be carried forward to the first line of the reconciliation portion of the next month's entry to become the base to which the next month's cash flow activity will be added or subtracted.

Making the Best Use of the Cash Flow Statement

Cash flow statements must constantly be modified as new things are learned about the business and paying vendors. Since this cash flow forecast will be used regularly to compare each month's projected figures with each month's actual performance figures, it will be useful to have a second column for the actual performance figures alongside each of the "planned" columns in the cash flow worksheet. Look for significant discrepancies between the planned and actual figures.

For example, if the business's actual figures are failing to meet cash receipt projections over a three-month period, this is a signal that it is time to revise the year's projections. It may be necessary to apply to the bank to increase the upper limit of a revolving line of credit. Approaching the bank to increase an operating loan should be done well in advance of the date when the additional funds are required. Do not leave cash inflow to chance.

Designing a Cash Flow Worksheet

A cash flow forecast can be presented in a variety of ways. The best way is to show only revenues from operations and the proceeds from sales.

The format should be a double-width column along the left side of the page for the account headings and two side-by-side vertical columns for each month of the year, beginning from the planned opening month (e.g., the first dual column might be labeled *April Planned* and *April Actual*). (See Table 9-7.)

From there, the cash flow worksheet is divided into three distinctive sections. The first section (at the top left portion of the worksheet, starting below and to the left of the month names) is headed *cash revenues* (or *cash in*). The second section, just below it, is headed *cash disbursements* (or *cash out*). The final section below that is headed *reconciliation of cash flow*.

Table 9-7   Sample Cash Flow—Planned versus Actual

Item	April Planned	April Actual	May Planned	May Actual
Cash revenues/cash in	$22,000	$18,500	$24,000	$22,500
Cash disbursements/cash out				
Wages	$10,000	$11,500	$11,000	$12,000
Commissions	$ 2,000	$ 1,500	$ 2,000	$ 2,000
Rent	$ 3,500	$ 3,500	$ 3,500	$ 3,500
Equipment payment/computers	$12,000	$12,000	$12,000	$12,000
Total cash out	$27,500	$28,500	$28,500	$29,500
Reconciliation of cash flow				
Opening cash balance	$ 5,000	$ 5,000	($500)	($5,000)
Add: Total cash revenues in	$22,000	$18,500	$24,000	$22,500
Deduct: Total cash disbursements out	$27,500	$28,500	$28,500	$29,500
Closing cash balance				
(Carry forward to next month)	($500)	($5,000)	($5,000)	($12,000)

ROADMAP

IN ACTION

The entrepreneur should use the breakeven technique as a decision-making model to determine whether a certain volume of output will result in a profit or loss and to measure the profit associated with a given level of output. To use this technique, one needs only three types of information: fixed costs of operation, variable costs of production, and price per unit.

PREPARING A BREAKEVEN ANALYSIS

The breakeven technique is a decision-making model that helps the entrepreneur determine whether a certain volume of output will result in a profit or loss. The point at which breaking even occurs is the volume of output at which total revenues equal total costs. The technique can be further used to answer the question, "What is the profit associated with a given level of output?" To use this technique, you need only know the fixed costs of operation, variable costs of production, and price per unit.

Fixed costs are expenses that do not change in the short run, no matter the levels of production and sales. Variable costs differ according to the volume produced; they are usually expressed in terms of per-unit variable costs. Total costs are the sum of fixed and variable costs. Price is the total amount received from the sale of one unit of the product. Multiplying the price by the number of units sold yields the amount, which is revenue. Profit is what remains when the total costs are subtracted from the total revenues. The breakeven point is the level of output or sales at which total profit is zero—in other words, where total revenues equal costs.

Example 1

Suppose the company spent $10,250 of variable material cost and $20,000 of variable labor cost in the prior month when the company sold 10,000 units. How much variable cost should the company plan on for the current month if it is expected to increase by 20 percent? Assume costs change in proportion to changes in activity.

Note that although the total variable cost increases from $30,250 to $36,300 when production changes from 10,000 to 12,000 units, the variable cost per unit does not change. It remains $3.02 per unit. With variable cost of $3.02 per unit, variable cost increases by $6,050 (i.e., $3.025 × 2,000) when production increases by 2,000 units.

	Prior Month		Current Month	
Units	10,000	Per Unit	12,000	Per Unit
Variable costs				
Direct material	$10,250	$1.025	$12,300	$1.025
Direct labor	20,000	2.000	24,000	2.000
Total variable costs	$30,250	$3.025	$36,300	$3.025

Example 2

Suppose that in the prior month the company incurred $22,500 of fixed costs, including $10,000 of depreciation, $7,500 of rent, and $5,000 of other fixed costs. If the company increases production to 12,000 in the current month, the levels of depreciation, rent, and other fixed costs incurred should remain the same as when it was only 10,000 units. However, with fixed costs, the cost per unit does change when there are changes. When production increases, the constant amount of fixed cost is spread over a larger number of units. This drives down the fixed cost per unit. With an increase in production from 10,000 to 12,000 units, total fixed cost remains $22,500. Note, however, that fixed cost per unit decreases from $2.250 per unit to $1.874 per unit.

Month	Prior Month		Current Month	
Units	10,000	Per Unit	12,000	Per Unit
Fixed costs				
Depreciation	$10,000	$1.000	$12,300	$0.833
Rent	7,500	0.750	7,500	0.625
Direct labor	5,000	0.500	5,000	0.416
Total variable costs	$22,500	$2.250	$22,500	$1.874

Using the Breakeven Formula

A quick way to calculate the breakeven point is to use the following formula. The price per unit (P) multiplied by the number of units sold (X) is equal to the fixed costs (F) plus the variable costs (V) multiplied by the number of units produced expressed as the following formula:

$$P(X) = F + V(X)$$

As an example, if fixed costs are $40,000, the variable costs per unit are $15, and the price per unit is $20, the breakeven point can be calculated by plugging these values into the equation:

$$20(X) = 40,000 + 15(X)$$
$$20X - 15X = 40,000$$
$$5X = 40,000$$
$$X = 80,000 \text{ units}$$

The breakeven point is one measurement of your business's "time to profitability." This measurement can be used in different ways during, for example, the start-up phase or the expansion phase. What if the business wants to expand its production? We can readily calculate the additional capital needed to fund this expansion, but a few very important questions must be asked: "Are the customers there, and what will it cost to capture them?" "If I can capture these new customers, will it be profitable?" These questions can be answered by employing a second measurement of viability—the lifetime value of a customer (LVC).

The LVC is the net profit customers generate over their lifecycle. You should not spend more to get customers than their lifetime value, or you might lose money.

Example

When many businesses look at customers, they see the value of the first sale. If Jeffrey bought a product worth $99, many companies would see Jeffrey as being worth $99 in revenue. Then if, and only if, later on Jeffrey buys another $99 product will he be seen as worth $198 in revenue. Let's assume X Company looks at customer value this way.

A better approach would be to let the above model also reflect the element of the time value of money. The true value of Jeffrey is the value of all the purchases he has made plus the value of all the purchases he is likely to make in the future (discounted to the present). This is called the lifetime value.

Do not be afraid to spend more than the profit on the first sale to acquire a customer, however. As long as your cash flow is healthy enough to support it, spend whatever you need to acquire that customer, as long as it is less than the average lifetime profit plus your current customer acquisition cost.

Increasing the lifetime value of your customers comes down to three objectives: increasing the length of time a customer buys from you, increasing the amount customers spend on each purchase, and decreasing the time between purchases.

ANALYZING AN INVESTMENT DECISION

In evaluating whether to make an investment, for example, in a piece of expensive equipment, an entrepreneur must consider not only how much cash the company must give out, but also whether the investment will earn a suitable return for the company. The *time value of money* approach recognizes that it is better to receive a dollar today than it is to receive a dollar next year or any other time in the future. This is because the dollar received today can be invested so at the end of the year, it amounts to more than a dollar. It also considers the decrease in the value of a dollar over time due to inflation.

In making an investment, a company invests money today in the hopes of receiving more money in the future. Obviously, a company would not invest money in a project unless it expected the total amount of funds received in the future to exceed the amount of the original investment. But by how much must the future cash flows exceed the original investment? Because money in the future is not equivalent to money today, we must develop a way of converting future dollars into their equivalent current, or present, value.

Net Present Value Method

The net present value (NPV) method is an alternative method for determining whether to make an investment.[8] It is usually applied to later-stage investments or in making investment decisions within a company on whether to undertake a planned project or purchase a piece of machinery. To illustrate the method, let us evaluate an investment opportunity using the NPV method. A trucking company wants to purchase engine testing equipment. The equipment will have a five-year life. Each year it will save the company $2,000 in wasted current operation, and it will also reduce labor costs by $20,000. It is estimated that the engine equipment will require maintenance costs of $1,000 per year. The equipment costs $70,000, and it is expected to have a residual value of $5,000 at the end of five years. Management has determined that the rate of return required on any new initiative is 12 percent. Should the company invest in the new equipment?

The Steps Involved in the Net Present Value Method

The first step in using the net present value method is to identify the amount and time period of each cash flow associated with a potential investment. Investment projects have both cash inflows (which are positive) and cash outflows (which are negative).

The second step is to equate or discount the cash flows to their present values using a required rate of return, which is the minimum return that management wants to earn on investments.

The third and final step is to evaluate the net present value. The sum of the present values of all cash flows (inflows and outflows) is the NPV of the investment. If the NPV is zero, the investment is generating a rate of return exactly equal to the required rate of return. Thus, the investment should be undertaken. If the NPV is positive, it should also be undertaken because it is generating a rate of return that is even greater than the required rate of return. Investment opportunities that have a negative NPV are not accepted because their rate of return is less than the required rate of return.

Refer to Table 8-5 which shows the present value (PV) for each year cash flow total. Consider first the $70,000 cash outflow created by purchase of the equipment. Note that the present value factor associated with the $70,000 purchase price is 1.0000. Because this amount is going to be spent immediately, it is already expressed in terms of its present value. Now consider the cash flows in year 1. In this year, the net cash inflow is $21,000. The present value factor for an amount received at the end of year 1 using a 12 percent rate of return is 0.8929 (see Table 8-5 in Chapter 8 showing the present value of $1). Multiplying the present value factor by the cash inflow of $21,000 indicates that the present value of the net cash inflow in year 1 is $18,751. The net present value of the investment in testing engine equipment is found by summing the present values of the cash flows in each year. This amounts to $8,538. Because the net present value is positive, the company should go ahead with plans to purchase the equipment.

Internal Rate of Return

An alternate way of analyzing internal investments is using the internal rate of return (IRR) method. This is the rate of return that equates the present value of future cash flows to the investment outlay. If the IRR of a potential investment is equal to or greater than the required rate of return, the investment should be undertaken. Like net present value, it takes into account the time value of money.

Consider a simple case where $100 is invested to yield $60 at the end of year 1 and $60 at the end of year 2. What rate of return equates the two-year, $60 annuity to $100? Recall that when we performed present value analysis for previous annuities, we multiplied a present value factor by the annuity to solve for a present value. Because the $60 is to be received in each of two years, we use the annuity table to look up the internal rate of return. In the row for two periods in the following table, we find a present value factor of 1.6681 (very close to 1.6667) in the column, for a 13 percent rate of return. Thus, the IRR on this investment is approximately 13 percent. If the required rate of return is 13 percent or less, the investment should be undertaken.

EVALUATING COMPANY STATEMENTS

The Securities and Exchange Commission requires already public companies and those applying to go public to file a variety of forms quarterly, annually, or on an as-needed basis. The SEC also requires independent audits of companies' financial statements. Learn how to determine a business's basic financial health

EVALUATING COMPANY STATEMENTS (cont.)

by reviewing some of the following documents, which can be accessed on the Internet.[9]

- *S-1: The Prospectus.* Companies must file this form before selling shares to the public. It contains details of the company's operations, including recent quarterly results. Check the "Competitors" section as well as "Risk Factors" to determine the risks.

- *10-Q: The Quarterly Report.* This contains a company's balance sheet, its income statement, and an accounting of its cash flow. Check the "Management Discussion" section for developments such as acquisitions, new customers, and unexpected losses.

- *10-K: The Annual Report.* Current shareholders receive this report by mail. The 10-K includes employment details and credit and lease agreements and often lists pending legal actions.

- *8-K: The Current Report.* Companies have filed more of these forms as a result of the SEC's Regulation FD (fair disclosure). The regulation requires that companies reveal any material information to all investors simultaneously, instead of feeding it first to Wall Street analysts.

- *144: Insider Trades.* When officers, board members, or major shareholders want to buy or sell stock, they must first register their intent with the SEC under Form 144.

- *13D: Beneficial Ownership.* Any individual or company that acquires more than 5 percent of another company's shares is required to report this fact to the SEC.

- *DEF-14A: Proxy Statement.* This document, issued before a company's annual meeting, details directors' compensation and insiders' shareholdings as well as proposed changes in corporate governance.

FINANCIAL ACCOUNTING STANDARDS BOARD

The FASB is a powerful institution, even though, as a nongovernmental, not-for-profit body, it doesn't wield the might of the SEC. By defining generally accepted accounting principles (GAAP), the FASB plays a big part in making sure the numbers companies report accurately reflect their business performance.[10]

TAXES AND FILING

The entrepreneur is required to withhold federal and state taxes from employees. Each month or quarter (depending on the size of the payroll), deposits or payments need to be made for funds withheld from wages. Generally, federal taxes, state taxes, Social Security, and Medicare are withheld from employees' salaries and are deposited later. If payments are late, high interest and penalties will be assessed. In addition to withholding taxes, the company may be required to pay a number of taxes, such as state and federal unemployment taxes, a matching FICA and Medicare tax, and other business taxes. These taxes will need to be part of the plan since they will affect cash flow and profits.

The federal and state governments also require the company to file end-of-year returns of the business, regardless of whether it earned a profit. A tax accountant should be consulted for advice on handling these expenses. The accountant can also assist in planning or budgeting appropriate funds to meet any of these expenses.[11]

THE STRESSES OF MANAGING MONEY

The topics covered in this chapter are, for the non-financially trained entrepreneur, rather complex. Yet managing the money is one of the most important aspects in building a company securely. As early as possible in the activities of the company, you must engage a financial adviser who you can trust to help you set up the systems *before* it is too late. Not knowing precisely whether you have sufficient funds to execute your plans is one of the most stressful and dangerous threats to a company. As we learned in Chapters 7 and 8, raising money whether from banks, investors, corporate partners, or getting paid by customers *always* takes longer than anticipated. Yet your employees and suppliers expect to get paid promptly. Sound financial accounting systems and forecasting can help manage these stresses. Highly profitable and fast-growing companies can go bankrupt from not managing money carefully. As you can observe in the master-case, making sure that Neoforma had sufficient access to cash, particularly in the earliest stages, put enormous strain on the founders and their families.

SUMMARY

An entrepreneur should examine financial statements, including the balance sheet, profit and loss statement, and cash flows, which can help analyze and monitor overall performance. These important accounting statements show the company's financial picture either at a given time or for a given period. The balance sheet itemizes assets, liabilities, and shareholders' equity at a given time and gives a detailed picture of where a company stands. The income statement is an itemized statement of revenues and expenses during an accounting period. It basically shows revenues, minus expenditures, resulting in income or loss. The cash flow statement is an itemized statement of receipts and expenditures, resulting in increased or decreased cash. Both the income and cash flow statements uncover important trends and overall performance, giving management direction as to what adjustments need to be made to the business's operations.

Another effective approach for checking overall performance is the use of financial ratios. Ratios indicate strengths and weaknesses in the business expectations. Entrepreneurs must also value different groups of customers to determine how much should be invested in procuring and managing them over time. Financial management is a key attribute of an entrepreneur and one that is often underestimated. Too many good companies fail because the founding entrepreneur was not adequately concerned with managing cash, assets, and profits. Budgets, projections of cash flow, and breakeven analyses must be monitored on a regular basis and evaluated when changes occur.

Launching a successful business requires an entrepreneur to create a solid financial plan. Such a plan is not only an important tool in raising the capital needed to get a company off the ground, but also an essential ingredient in managing a growing business. Not paying attention to managing money can place enormous stresses on entrepreneurs and lead to the failure of potentially highly successful enterprises.

STUDY QUESTIONS

1. What financial measurements should be prepared to measure performance?
2. What are the categories and steps in preparing a financial budget?
3. What are the major categories and steps in preparing the projected cash activity?
4. Describe the differences among quick ratio, debt ratio, and current ratio.
5. Describe the breakeven technique in the decision-making model to determine profit and loss.
6. Why are some customers more valuable than others? How can these differences be measured and used for decision making?

EXERCISES

1. List four items that entrepreneurial companies should show on a balance sheet.

2. Ratios are important in analyzing a balance sheet; list those most commonly used by entrepreneurs for financial analysis.

3. Prepare a breakeven analysis for the following example. David Falk, the vice president of business development, wants to determine the breakeven point for the company's gift card product. The analysis will help David determine the possibility of incurring a loss for the product. The company will sell the product for $200 per customer. Variable costs are estimated at $185,000 per month, composed of $95,000 for producing the product and $65,000 for fixed selling and administrative costs. How many units must be sold to break even?

4. Calculate the pretax income and the return on investment for a company with sales and expenses as follows:

Sales	$40,000,000
Cost of goods sold	25,000,000
Selling and administrative expense	5,000,000
Interest expense	1,000,000
Income taxes	5,850,000
Shareholders' equity	$800,000

Comment on the company's profitability.

5. Joe Flicek of SIP Commendations is considering investing $79,137 in a computer storage room. He will rent space to customers and expects to generate $22,500 annually (rental charges less miscellaneous expenses other than depreciation).

(a) Assuming Joe wishes to evaluate the project with a five-year time horizon, what is the internal rate of return on the investment (ignore taxes)?

(b) Should Joe make the investment if his required rate of return is 12 percent?

Master-case Exercises: If you have not yet read the appendix in Chapter 1, do so. Then go to the book's Website and read the diary entries Months 0, 14, 15, 18, 21, 23, 26, 36, 42, 46, and Four Years Later and view the video selection, "Balance Your Business or Your Life."

Either as a team or individually, produce a presentation on each of the following questions for class discussion. Only one or two slides for each are required to state the key points, which will then be expanded in the class.

Master-case Q 1: List the sources of funds that Wayne and Jeff used to finance Neoforma. How long after the anticipated date were each of these funds actually received? Why was this in each case?

Master-case Q 2: Anni and Wayne started out with a dream that nearly became a nightmare for their family. Chart the key stressful events in the story of Neoforma that threatened their relationship. What lessons can be learned from these events regarding how to balance work passion and personal lives?

INTERACTIVE LEARNING ON THE WEB

Test your knowledge of the chapter using the book's interactive Web site.

ADDITIONAL RESOURCES

- **Dun and Bradstreet Information Services** www.dnb.com
- **Hoover's Corporate Information** www.hoovers.com
- **NASDAQ** www.nasdaq.com
- **Small Business Advisor** www.isquare.com
- **Thomas Net Register of American Manufacturers** www.thomasnet.com

www.wiley.com/college/kaplan

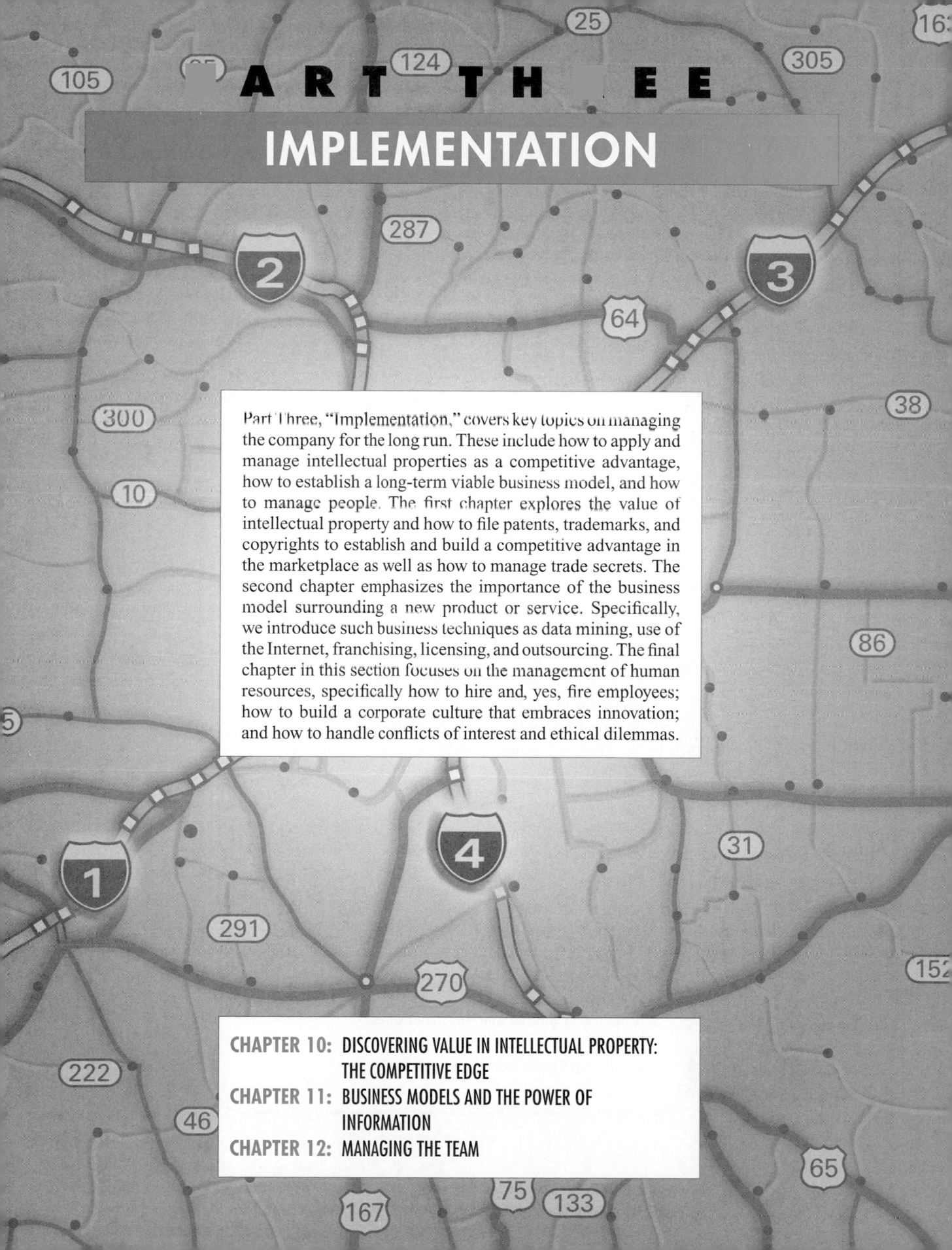

PART THREE

IMPLEMENTATION

Part Three, "Implementation," covers key topics on managing the company for the long run. These include how to apply and manage intellectual properties as a competitive advantage, how to establish a long-term viable business model, and how to manage people. The first chapter explores the value of intellectual property and how to file patents, trademarks, and copyrights to establish and build a competitive advantage in the marketplace as well as how to manage trade secrets. The second chapter emphasizes the importance of the business model surrounding a new product or service. Specifically, we introduce such business techniques as data mining, use of the Internet, franchising, licensing, and outsourcing. The final chapter in this section focuses on the management of human resources, specifically how to hire and, yes, fire employees; how to build a corporate culture that embraces innovation; and how to handle conflicts of interest and ethical dilemmas.

CHAPTER 10: DISCOVERING VALUE IN INTELLECTUAL PROPERTY: THE COMPETITIVE EDGE

CHAPTER 11: BUSINESS MODELS AND THE POWER OF INFORMATION

CHAPTER 12: MANAGING THE TEAM

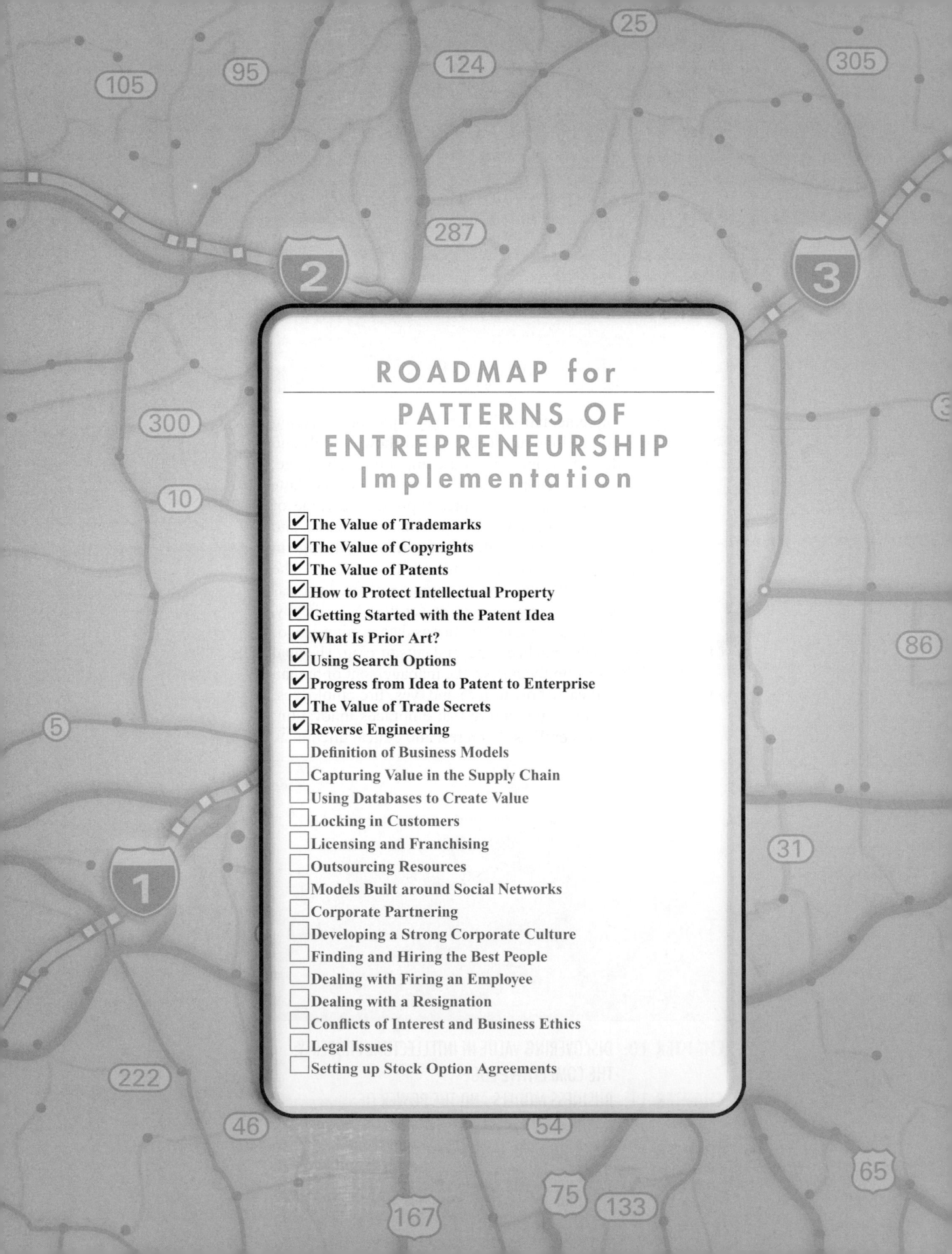

ROADMAP for

PATTERNS OF ENTREPRENEURSHIP
Implementation

- ☑ **The Value of Trademarks**
- ☑ **The Value of Copyrights**
- ☑ **The Value of Patents**
- ☑ **How to Protect Intellectual Property**
- ☑ **Getting Started with the Patent Idea**
- ☑ **What Is Prior Art?**
- ☑ **Using Search Options**
- ☑ **Progress from Idea to Patent to Enterprise**
- ☑ **The Value of Trade Secrets**
- ☑ **Reverse Engineering**
- ☐ **Definition of Business Models**
- ☐ **Capturing Value in the Supply Chain**
- ☐ **Using Databases to Create Value**
- ☐ **Locking in Customers**
- ☐ **Licensing and Franchising**
- ☐ **Outsourcing Resources**
- ☐ **Models Built around Social Networks**
- ☐ **Corporate Partnering**
- ☐ **Developing a Strong Corporate Culture**
- ☐ **Finding and Hiring the Best People**
- ☐ **Dealing with Firing an Employee**
- ☐ **Dealing with a Resignation**
- ☐ **Conflicts of Interest and Business Ethics**
- ☐ **Legal Issues**
- ☐ **Setting up Stock Option Agreements**

CHAPTER 10

DISCOVERING VALUE IN INTELLECTUAL PROPERTY: THE COMPETITIVE EDGE

"Property is an intellectual production. The game requires coolness, right reasoning, promptness, and patience in the players."

RALPH WALDO EMERSON

OBJECTIVES

- Know the different forms of intellectual property and how they differ.
- Learn the purpose and value of trademarks, copyrights, and patents.
- Learn how to obtain a copyright.
- Learn the process from creating an idea to patent approval.
- Know the guidelines for selecting professional assistance, such as legal services, in pursuing intellectual property rights.
- Discover the important roles of reverse engineering and trade secrets in intellectual property.

CHAPTER OUTLINE

Introduction

Profile: Ian Kibblewhite—An Integrated IP Strategy

The Value of Trademarks

The Value of Copyrights

The Value of Patents

How to Protect Intellectual Property

Getting Started with the Patent Idea

What Is Prior Art?

Using Search Options

Progress from Idea to Patent to Enterprise

The Value of Trade Secrets

Reverse Engineering

Summary

Study Questions

Exercises

Interactive Learning on the Web

Internet IP Source Sites

Additional Resources

INTRODUCTION

The realm of intellectual property (IP) deals with a range of usually legally defensible rights conferred upon individuals and companies that have produced original work of some potential value. The forms of intellectual property protection are defined as trademark, copyright, and patent. Another form of intellectual property is a trade secret. Trade secrets are not afforded the same assurance of legal protection as their counterparts (laws vary from state to state) but are sometimes a more effective way of securing property rights.

This chapter explains these forms of IP and guides you toward effectively developing, protecting, and promoting your IP. A variety of tools and resources can be found throughout the chapter and in the additional resources offered at the end of this text.

Before going any further, it is important to point out that the laws governing intellectual property are complex and frequently subject to change. It is advised that entrepreneurs pursuing the advancement of their IP consult the appropriate code early in their endeavors to minimize the possibility of wasted time and effort, especially given the importance of timely registration in seeking competitive IP rights. Professional legal advice and assistance may constitute the most appropriate means for efficiently pursuing IP rights for many entrepreneurs.

PROFILE: IAN KIBBLEWHITE—AN INTEGRATED IP STRATEGY[1]

Kibblewhite is the founder of Ultrafast Inc., a company which is the subject of a more complete case on the book's Web site. For the purpose of this chapter, we confine ourselves to the intellectual property strategy and issues that Ultrafast confronted as the company developed.

Kibblewhite was educated as an engineer and joined SPS Technologies Inc., a publicly traded company manufacturing a range of industrial threaded fasteners mainly for the automotive and aerospace markets. After several years, Kibblewhite attained a senior position in the engineering development department and was responsible for new innovations. During that time he tried to improve the accuracy of assembly methods in manufacturing. A key invention was to glue onto the head of a bolt a special piece of plastic film that acted as a way of sensing how tight the bolt was as it was tightened. The film was contacted with a special probe attached to an electronic control and software system. This idea increased the accuracy of automated assembly over the conventional "torque wrench" method by three times or more. Over a period of nearly ten years, Kibblewhite applied for and was issued seven U.S. patents and several foreign patents on the idea. These patents were assigned to SPS under the employment agreement with Kibblewhite.

When there was a downturn in the economy, SPS decided to reduce its expenditure on long-term research and development and Kibblewhite left. He had always wanted to start his own company, and this triggered him into action. Looking around for something to do, he stumbled on some research work at Penn State that allowed him to replace the glued-on film with a vacuum-deposited hard film, similar to that seen on architectural glass. This would work better and have many other advantages such as stability and lower cost. Using money obtained from NASA under the SBIR program, he paid Penn State under a work-for-hire contract to supply his first "proof of principle" products.

He had learned the patenting process while at SPS and at one time had interacted with Ratner and Prestia, a large and highly regarded patent firm near Philadelphia. SPS had decided to take its patent work inside the company, which freed Ratner and Prestia to undertake work in the fastener field without having a client conflict. Kibblewhite knew the partner there and asked him to file patents on his new invention, which he assigned to his new firm, Ultrafast Inc. Over a period of eight years, Kibblewhite was granted five new patents for his company. SPS challenged Ultrafast on these new patents, claiming that the ideas were developed while Kibblewhite was working for them and there was nothing unique in the new patents not covered in the SPS patents. SPS's arguments did not hold water as Kibblewhite with his attorneys were able to convince them that the word *film* had two entirely different meanings: a plastic film that was largely impractical and a vacuum-deposited film, which was an entirely new concept and circumvents the early inventions. They might have been chalk and cheese. While searching the U.S. patent database, Kibblewhite uncovered a patent issued to Albert Holt in California. Use of this patent (4602511) could improve the Ultrafast system even more, and Ultrafast contacted Holt and purchased rights to this patent, thereby building a patent portfolio.

ROADMAP

IN ACTION

Understand how intellectual property is important to the entrepreneur because it can generate profits and create a competitive advantage.

There were three different parts to the tightening systems that Ultrafast developed: the threaded fasteners with the film on them, the electronic controllers, and the software to manage the controllers in different installations. The company's business model was to license the patents and software to manufacturers of industrial assembly systems. Ultrafast then purchased standard fasteners and applied the film to them in an automated plant, shipping them directly to the automobile or plane factories that had installed licensed assembly systems. The patents, therefore, were written to protect not only the technology and products, but also the *use* of the technology in fastening tools and systems.

These claims in the patent enabled Ultrafast to license its patents for tools only, which was a valuable source of early bootstrapped funds. Included in these licenses were rights to the software, which was protected via a copyright.

Ultrafast was concerned about other companies supplying treated bolts once the products were in use. It protected against this in several ways in addition to patents. Every bolt had an embossed Ultrafast trademark, shown in Figure 10-1, on the head, made at little cost during the bolt's normal manufacture. This made it easy for end users to trace false parts if they worried about safety and liability, and Ultrafast could then challenge the supplier.

In addition, the software needed access to a proprietary database of all allowed parts and their tightening protocols in each application. Controllers could not run accurately without having access to this database, which was jealously guarded as a trade secret. Also the Ultrafast coating plant was open to personnel on only a "need to know" basis, so it would be difficult for a competitor to provide bolts with the same performance and accuracy.

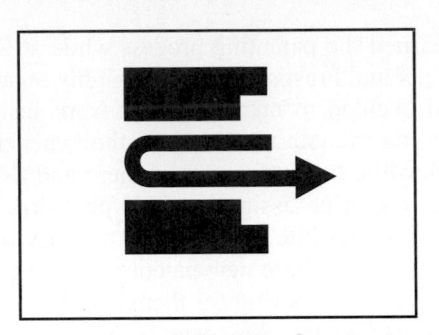

Figure 10-1   **The Ultrafast Registered Trademark.**

THE VALUE OF TRADEMARKS

A trademark can take a number or some combination of forms, including name, symbol, motto, or jingle, just to name a few, and represents a company and/or product with which it is associated.[2] The red triangle on a bottle of Bass Ale is a trademark for the Bass Brewing Company. The slogan "Quality is Job #1" is one of Ford Motor Company's trademarks. The three-note call sign of the National Broadcasting Company (NBC) is a well-known example of a trademark in the form of sound.

A lesser-known cousin of the trademark is the service mark, which differs only by way of applying to services and their sources rather than to products.[3] Other lesser-known marks include the collective mark, which organizations often use to designate membership but is also used in commerce, and the certification mark, which is used by entities other than the owner of the mark but with the owner's permission. Because of its association with nonowner entities, the certification mark may be indicative of their identities and the attributes of the products, such as elements of quality and composition.

The key to trademarks is the association they render in the mind of the consumer. They are important forms of intellectual property affecting decisions in the minds of consumers or users. Based on personal experience, word of mouth, advertising, and other means of acquaintance, consumers form impressions about different products or services offered. Those impressions guide the consumer in making decisions about spending time and money when given a choice between competing products or services. Trademarks protect a word, name, symbol, motto, or other distinctive form of identification associated with a product or service. Examples include Coca-Cola in script form, the name Windex, Band-Aid, and the Intel Inside symbol.

Even a catchy jingle or attractive design used as a trademark is unlikely to provide a business entity with much value unless that entity takes steps to create the positive associations described. Such associations are initially built with good advertising and promotional trials and are reinforced by such practices as providing good quality, value, user-friendliness, and customer service. To achieve the favorable trademark awareness it needs, a business entity will likely have to invest a substantial amount of capital, effort, and time in development. Once a trademark has been reliably established, it can be a highly effective tool for communicating a broad amount of information at a glance and for promoting use among consumers.

How Are Trademarks Registered?

Simply by using a mark in the course of public commerce, the entrepreneur establishes a "common-law" right to that mark and may be considered its legal owner.

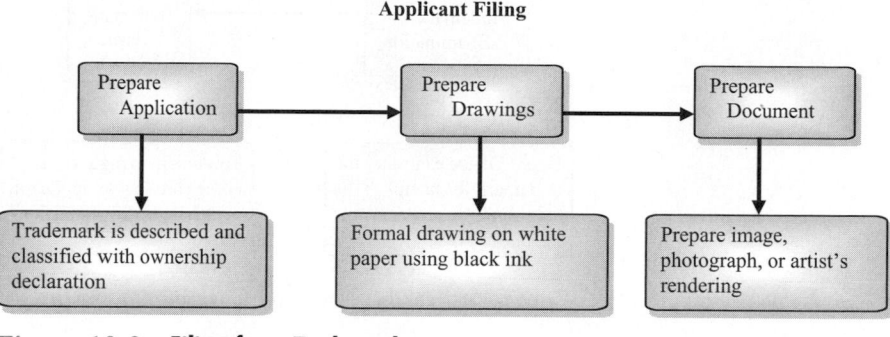

Figure 10-2   **Filing for a Trademark.**

Nonetheless, given the potential for different parties to concurrently use the same or similar mark, the challenge to one's common-law right to a mark has the potential to surface and interfere with some or all future rights associated with its use. In order to safeguard one's trademark rights, it is recommended that the user of a mark apply to have it registered with the U.S. Patent and Trademark Office (USPTO) in Washington, D.C.[4,5] Figure 10-2 depicts the process involved with filing for a trademark.

Only the owner of a trademark may apply for registration, although an attorney may initiate the application on behalf of an owner. Attorneys are not essential to this process, but they can provide invaluable guidance to the aspiring trademark registrant for avoiding pitfalls and safeguarding the fruit of labor. The owner must submit an application along with supporting documentation. If the applicant's mark is already in commercial use, you must submit a use application that includes a drawing of the trademark on a separate sheet of paper, a filing fee corresponding with the class of product to which the trademark applies, and three specimens of the trademark. Where possible, specimens ought to be actual commercial-grade material bearing the trademark. Where specimens are impractically unwieldy, $8\frac{1}{2} \times 11''$ photostats or photographs of actual specimens may be supplied instead.

When an applicant's trademark is not yet in commercial use at the time of application, an intent-to-use application must be filed. Submit a drawing of the trademark on a separate sheet of paper with a filing fee corresponding to the class of product to which the trademark applies. Also send either an amendment to allege use or a statement of use, depending on whether the trademark has been published in some form and issued a notice of allowance by the USPTO. Owners filing an amendment to allege use form must also file an additional request for an extension of time to file a statement of use if the trademark is not used within the six months following their submission of application. Failure to make commercial use of the mark without an extension filing will result in the USPTO's disavowal of the application.

Applications should be sent to:

Assistant Commissioner for Trademarks
Box New App/Fee
2900 Crystal Drive
Arlington, VA 22202-3513
Fees are about $325 online and $375 by mail.

Figure 10-3 depicts the actions taken in the Patent Office when registering a trademark.

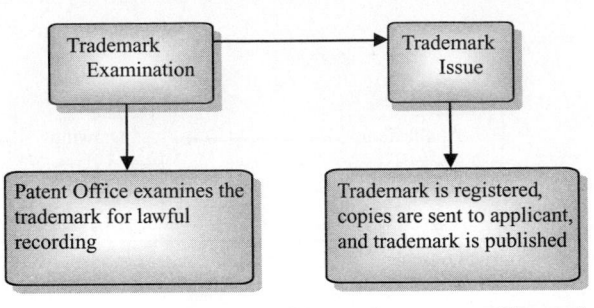

Figure 10-3   Actions Taken in the Patent Office When Registering a Trademark.

The USPTO also offers the Trademark Electronic Application System (TEAS) for easy online application or printing that can be sent to the above address via mail.

The USPTO will grant registration approval to the first party to commercially use or file an intent-to-use application (see below for more information). Because registration of a trademark with the USPTO confers upon the registrant particular legal privileges, it is recommended that entrepreneurs seek registration as early as possible.

Applicants should expect it to take approximately one year until receiving registration approval for the trademark. During this period, the application is reviewed by one of the USPTO's trademark attorneys and evaluated for its compliance with regulations and for potential conflict with existing registered marks. Having passed such tests, a trademark will subsequently be published in the USPTO's *Gazette* for review and possible challenge by competitive parties.

What Are the Benefits of Trademark Registration?

Federal registration of a trademark grants the owner a competitive advantage in the use of the mark.[6] In addition to nationwide public notice of the legal claim being made, the owner has the benefit of legal appeal in federal court concerning matters of dispute and infringement. National evidence of ownership can provide a basis for achieving international registration of the trademark and for preventing importation of international goods, which infringe on the registrant's rights in the United States.

How Are Trademarks Enforced?

Once a trademark is registered with the USPTO, the owner of the mark may use the federal registration symbol (®) in association with its mark. This will inform others of the exclusive rights afforded by the mark. Until such time as official registration occurs, it is a good idea to use the ™ symbol as a way of notifying others that rights are claimed in association with use of your mark. The ˢᴹ symbol may be used in the case of service marks.

Even when properly registered and kept in constant use, there is no guarantee that others will not infringe on the trademark. Where infringement is deemed to have taken place, the USPTO should be notified. A decision to pursue legal recourse for damages should hinge on the existence of actual or potential financial loss as a result of the infringement, although owners of marks are entitled to file suit even where no such losses are readily apparent.[7] In cases where injury is minimal, it may make more sense simply to notify the infringing party of infringement, providing records of your rights and a request to terminate usage of the mark. Document this

Until such time as one's trademark can officially be registered with the USPTO, the trademark symbol should be used in conjunction with a mark as a way of notifying others that rights are claimed in association with use of the mark.

The federal registration symbol may be used in association with any mark officially registered with the USPTO. Use of the symbol informs others of the exclusive rights afforded the owner of the registered mark.

Figure 10-4   The Trademark and Registered Symbols.

action so you can use it in future prosecution should the infringing party fail to comply. Where compliance is not observed or where significant financial interests are at stake, a qualified attorney should be contracted to perform prosecution.

IN ACTION

A trademark infringement does not have to be identical to that used by the infringed party. If a trademark is similar and is likely to cause confusion, this is sufficient grounds for infringement.

In order for infringement to exist, a mark need not be identical to that used by the infringed party, only similar enough to be likely to cause confusion. Similar marks are more likely to infringe on one another when used in the same or similar businesses. Furthermore, infringement need not be intentional for damages to be awarded. It is the obligation of any party employing a mark to be certain that its use is unrestricted. Nonetheless, determination of intent can strengthen a case against an infringing party and result in the award of greater damages than in cases where intent does not exist.[8]

THE VALUE OF COPYRIGHTS

Copyrights are instruments of legal protection given to authors of original works of writing, art, musical composition, photography, and architectural design, to name a few creative areas.[9,10] Material protected by copyright includes books, plays, musical

Notice of copyright is not required under U.S. law, as ownership rights exist concurrently with creation of a given work. Nevertheless, use of the copyright symbol or the abbreviation "Copr." serves as public notice of the special status afforded a copyrighted work. Furthermore, when proper notice of copyright is given on any work, owners of copyright are entitled to full damages against infringing parties, which might claim innocent infringement for not realizing that the work was copyrighted. Proper copyright notice should include the symbol © or the abbreviation "Copr.," the date of first publication, and the author's name(s). Example: © 2000 Eric Hirsch.

Figure 10-5 **Copyright Symbol.**

composition, works of art, architectural plans, and computer programs. With rare exceptions, names may not be copyrighted. The same is true of titles, slogans, and short phrases, all of which are potentially protectable by trademark. One exception to this rule is representations of names, titles, and the like presented in a sufficiently original style or manner. Where the name for a band might not be copyrighted (remember that trademark protection is available for such protection), and if that name is rendered in an original manner with sufficient artistic content, for example, it may be copyrighted in that particular form. As is the case with all copyrighted work, it is not the idea per se that is copyrighted, but the original expression of that idea.[11] Figure 10-5 depicts the copyright symbol.

How Do Entrepreneurs Obtain a Copyright?

In most cases the author of a work owns the copyright at the moment of its creation. The only exception is in the case of a work made for hire. Work for hire is defined as work not owned by the author or work performed in some other salaried or compensated capacity. An example of a work made for hire could be an article written by an individual author freelancing for a magazine or employed by the same.

Figure 10-6 **Obtaining a Copyright.**

In the case of a work made for hire, copyright ownership is again present at the moment of a work's creation but is the intellectual property of the party employing or otherwise compensating the actual author. (Consulting or "work-for-hire" contracts are discussed in more detail in Chapter 12).

ROADMAP

IN ACTION

Entrepreneurs who own a copyright have the exclusive right to reproduce, distribute, sell, and display their protected work. Persons other than the owner of a copyright who want to use the protected work must receive permission from the copyright owner to do so.

The U.S. Copyright Office makes it very easy for authors of original works meeting the copyright criteria to register their works federally. A payment of $35 if applied for online and $45 if applied for by mail must be sent along with a simple application form and nonreturnable copies of the work. Once registered, an author will receive a certificate of registration for his work; his copyright will be part of the public record and may become part of the collection at the Library of Congress. Registration typically takes approximately eight months but may take as long as a year.[12] Unlike trademarks, copyrights must be renewed to remain in force. The USCO's *Circular 15* and *15a* should be consulted for detailed renewal conditions and benefits. Upon expiration of the copyright, the work becomes a part of the public domain.

To contact the USCO by mail, write to U.S. Copyright Office, 101 Independence Avenue, 4th floor Washington, D.C. 20559-6000. To contact the USCO by phone, call Public Information (202) 707-3000.

How Are Copyrights Protected and Enforced?

As mentioned above, original works are considered copyrighted at their moment of creation. Nonetheless, copyright infringement is a widespread problem that has become more complex in recent years owing to the novel nature of electronic forms of authorship found in software and on the Internet.

To protect their works from copyright infringement, copyright holders must provide a comprehensive notice of their copyrights. This notice must include the following, typically in the order listed.

1. The term *copyright* or a derivative thereof, such as the abbreviation "copr." or the © symbol (For original sound recordings, a symbol with a *P* in a circle is sometimes used instead.)
2. The year of the first production
3. The name of the author, or copyright owner, if different

In some countries outside of the United States, including the clause "all rights reserved" may provide additional protection. It should be noted that international copyright protection differs from country to country and may be nonexistent in many.

Another easy step for an author is to send a copy of the copyrighted work to himself or herself via registered mail as early as possible in order to establish a date of earliest production. Once received, the envelopes should be kept sealed and in a safe place.

The most formal and important step to take in protecting one's copyrighted IP is to properly register it with the U.S. Copyright Office as outlined above. Although property rights and ownership exist at the moment of creation, taking steps to register copyrighted material provides stronger legal remedies to owners and makes cases of copyright infringement easier to prove.[13]

Because of the relative ease and cost of registration, it is recommended that all authors take the steps necessary to register their original works with the USCO. Nonetheless, it is recognized that a significant portion of original work is created specifically for private use. For entrepreneurs, the importance of notification and registration increases in relation to the commercial value of any given work of authorship. Similarly, in cases of copyright infringement, the damages afforded in a lawsuit increase in proportion to the value of the copyrighted material and to the actual or potential damages resulting from infringement. Such damages may result even in cases where copyrighted work is reproduced and distributed free of charge, as such infringement can, for example, have a real impact on an author's ability to charge for use of his work in the future.

THE VALUE OF PATENTS

The U.S. government originally established patents as a way to encourage invention and technological progress by granting inventors rights from which they could gain personally. In exchange for this benefit, inventors must fully disclose their invention, and "teach" others how to replicate in detail the invention for themselves. In this way, the know-how is made available to others for them to build upon in their own inventions. However, if their inventions embody the actual claimed novelty of the original patent, they are allowed to market products with their improvements only by gaining rights to the first patent.

U.S. patents are issued by the U.S. Patent and Trademark Office (USPTO) in Washington, D.C. In most cases a patent grants the inventor (or his or her heirs or assignees) specific property rights for a term of twenty years from the date the patent application is filed. In cases where a patent application refers to an earlier filing, the twenty-year period shall extend from the date of the earliest referenced filing. The rights granted the inventor apply only within the United States and its territories and possessions. Inventors concerned about securing their rights outside the United States need to file additional foreign patent applications to do so.

In the United States, a patent grants its holder the right to exclude others from making, using, selling, or offering for sale the patented invention. For the value of a patent to be realized, the patent must be exercised to yield the patent holder competitive advantages from which to profit or present financial compensation for allowing others to participate in the activities otherwise restricted by the patent.

A patent is good for protecting a business model from new competition, extracting rents (royalties) from competitors already using the invention, earning an additional return from other entrepreneurs (sale or royalty) from your sunk R & D cost, potential for collateral for borrowing, and increasing the value of the enterprise.

What Is a Patent Portfolio?

A patent portfolio is all of the patents owned by a venture and may contain some or all of the following items in addition to the actual patents that are approved and issued:

- All pending applications for additional patents

- Rights gained through foreign counterparts that may be in alliance with your venture to file overseas for joint benefit
- Licenses, both exclusive and nonexclusive, to others' patents that will generate revenue for the venture

A patent portfolio has the potential to be a major asset of the venture in negotiations with other companies that would like to license or form alliances with the venture. However, remember that patents are not visible on the balance sheet and do not appear there with any value. (Licensing as part of a business model is dealt with in the next chapter.)

The value of the portfolio, however, can be shown as goodwill when demonstrating the venture's value proposition. The actual valuation of the portfolio is normally a task for experts or lawyers or companies specializing in patent valuation.

Acquiring patents from companies or individuals that are not using them as there is value in sheer numbers that can impact in the following ways:

- Cross-license negotiations often start with answering the question, "Whose portfolio is bigger?"
- When a large number of patents are asserted against an infringer, contesting the assertion takes time and money as the number of patents increases. These costs may appear daunting and lead to an early settlement.
- A weakness in the history or claims of one patent can be addressed in other members of the portfolio.
- You never know when a "dark horse" or so-called sleeping patent will surprisingly become valuable, but this can be an expensive practice if carried too far. Remember that at least 95 percent of all issued patents are worthless.

What Are the Various Patent Classifications? How Do They Differ?

The following are the various patent classifications available:

- *Design patents* are issued to individuals who have created a novel ornamental design. A design patent does not include the elements of structure and function.[14]
- *Plant patents* are issued to individuals who have invented or discovered a novel type of plant and who have been able to reproduce that plant asexually. Plant patents are not issued for either tuber-propagated or uncultivated plant varieties.
- *Utility patents* are issued to individuals who have invented novel processes, machines, and compositions of concern matter or improvements thereof. Most of the following discussion concerns utility patents—the most common but most complex of all patents issued.

Asking the Right Questions about Patents

Before embarking on an expensive patenting process, you should consider the following questions to determine (1) whether it is worth patenting the invention(s), (2) the possible value of the patent, and (3) how best to position the patent for revenue growth and competitive advantage.

- What is the size of the market affected by the invention?

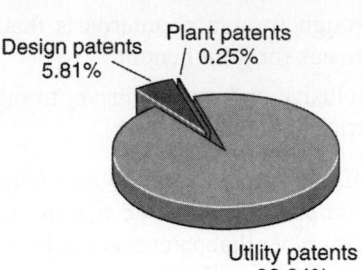

Design patents
5.81%

Plant patents
0.25%

Utility patents
93.94%

Figure 10-7   **New Patent Applications in the United States, 2001.**

- What resources would it take for the venture or a licensee to commercialize the invention in terms of money, time, and know-how?
- What is the novelty of the technical field covered? Is this a small improvement or a radical and broadly impacting invention?
- How central is the invention to products that may be expected to use it?
- What is the scope of claims that you anticipate?
- How easily can the use of the invention be detected? Companies often do not patent processes for manufacturing as it may not be possible to detect *how* a product is being made after the fact, and filing the patent means that you will be telling your competitors exactly what to do. This is usually a case to use trade secrets for protection.
- How easy is it to avoid using the *patented* invention? (See the Datamark case at the end of this chapter for an example.)
- What percentage of companies in the field may use the invention?
- What users of products or services will benefit from the invention?
- Can you afford to sue a large company that is infringing your patent? A patent is only as strong as the defense you can bring to bear. (See the Chasteen example in Chapter 7). If the answer is no, then perhaps using trade secrets and being fastest to market is a better strategy.

What Are the Qualifications for a Patent to Be Granted?

The U.S. patent law has very specific rules for patenting a particular invention. Broadly speaking, all inventions must meet three major categories of requirements

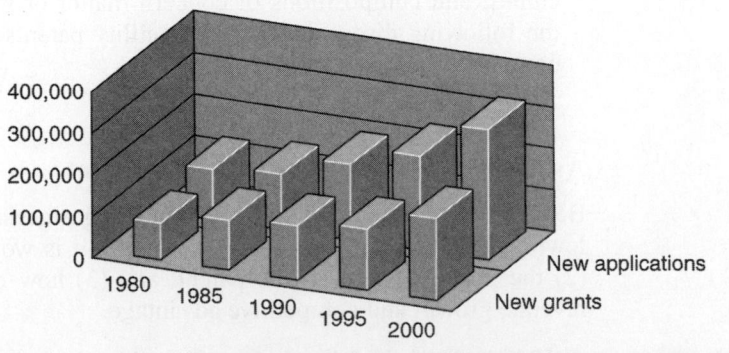

400,000
300,000
200,000
100,000
0

1980   1985   1990   1995   2000

New applications
New grants

Figure 10-8   **New Patent Activity in the United States, 1980–2000.**

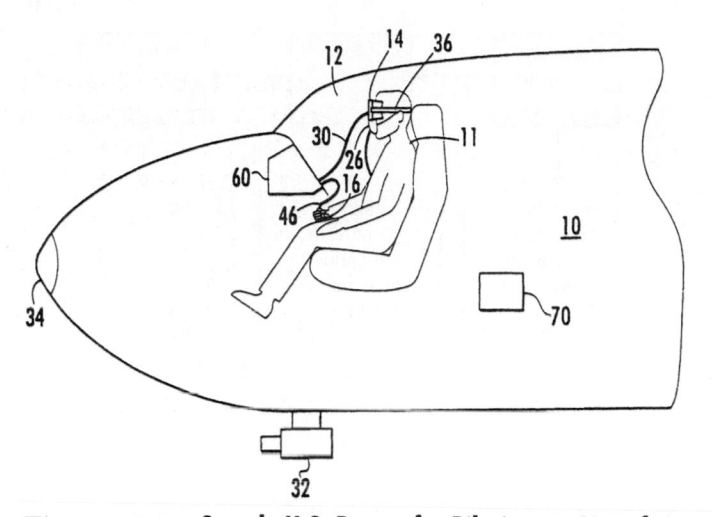

Figure 10-9   **Sample U.S. Patent for Piloting an Aircraft in a Smoke-filled Cockpit.**

if they are to be considered patentable. An invention must have **utility and novelty** and must be **nonobvious.**

Among the things that may not be patented are naturally occurring objects, entities, laws, and phenomena, as well as abstract ideas. Some types of plant may be patented, but only when the DNA has been genetically manipulated in a unique way, which may yield some novel and useful benefit.

- **Utility:** Nonuseful inventions may not be patented. Any useful machine, process, composition of matter, or improvement on the same may be patented, provided that said machine, process, and so on, is not disclosed in the prior art. The Supreme Court has broadly interpreted the utility requirement to include anything manmade, including genetically altered cells and animals.

- **Novelty:** For an invention to qualify as novel, a number of very specific conditions must be met. Novelty requires that the original invention predate knowledge and use or sale of the invention by others within the United States or any foreign country. The application must also be submitted within one year of the applicant's public use or sale of the invention in the United States.

- **Nonobviousness:** If an invention is judged to have been obvious to any person of ordinary skill in the field relating to the invention, it may be barred from receiving patent approval.

Figure 10-10 depicts the patent process from document disclosure to patent grant.

Is the Patent Obvious?

- To be patentable, your invention must give new and nonobvious results when compared to known approaches. Ordinary differences in size, materials, or other obvious modifications are generally not patentable.

- Even if the invention is new, it may be obvious. The test of obviousness is whether or not the invention is obvious to a "person of ordinary skill in the art."

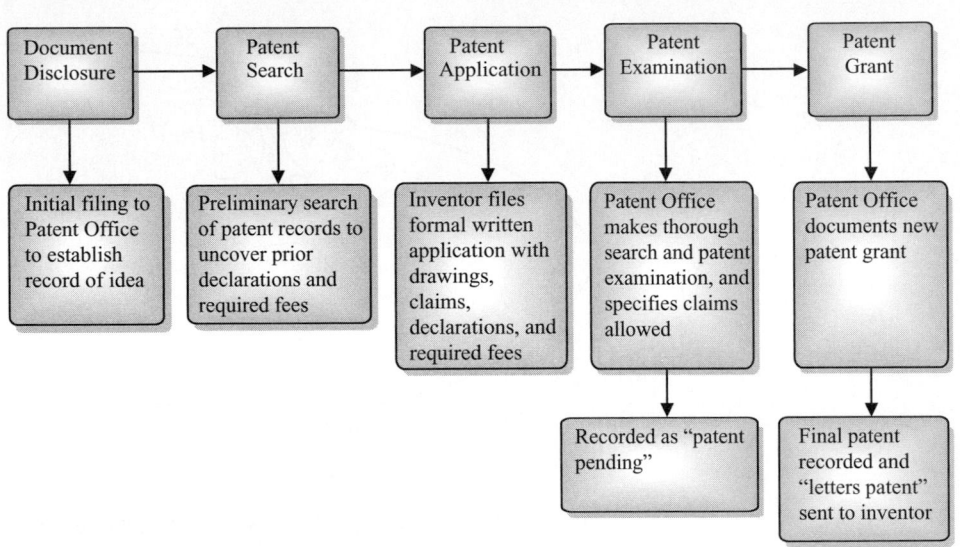

Figure 10-10 **The Patent Process.**

- Patent examiners will often reject an application on the grounds of obviousness. It is a challenge for the inventor(s) and his attorneys to anticipate this in their specification, and it is not always easy.

- Of course, obviousness is a subjective matter. In the final analysis, however, a patent examiner will have to be convinced, so it is necessary to give the matter some thought. A strong argument for nonobviousness is that no one has thought of your invention before, but you will have a better case if you can demonstrate that someone ordinarily skilled in the art lacks some particular knowledge or skill that you have. For example, a chemist might be able to synthesize a new optical material, but he might not have the skill or knowledge that allowed you to tailor that material to have novel electronic properties.

Is There Potentially Invalidating Prior Art?

- Inventor(s) are the primary source for relevant "prior art," such as publications and patents, that may have contributed to their original conception and so forth. When you submit this disclosure, you are not expected to have carried out an exhaustive search. Such a search can be expensive and may not be necessary. At the outset you should be able to list the nearest prior art of which you are aware. This will help reviewers decide whether to accept your assertion about novelty. More important, if a detailed search is needed, this listing of prior art will enable the professional search agent to use her time most economically and effectively.

- One can do a simple search by going to Delphion (www.delphion.com) and doing an advanced search on some of the key words describing one's invention.

- Ordinarily, a combination of known things is not patentable if the combination does not confer a novel, nonobvious benefit. For example, you would have a problem patenting a car with a radio since the radio in the car does the same things it does anywhere else. On the other hand, a car with a GPS receiver might have patentable features if, for example, the position data was in some way combined with the direction of the vehicle (i.e., autopilot). Combinations are hard to patent; if your

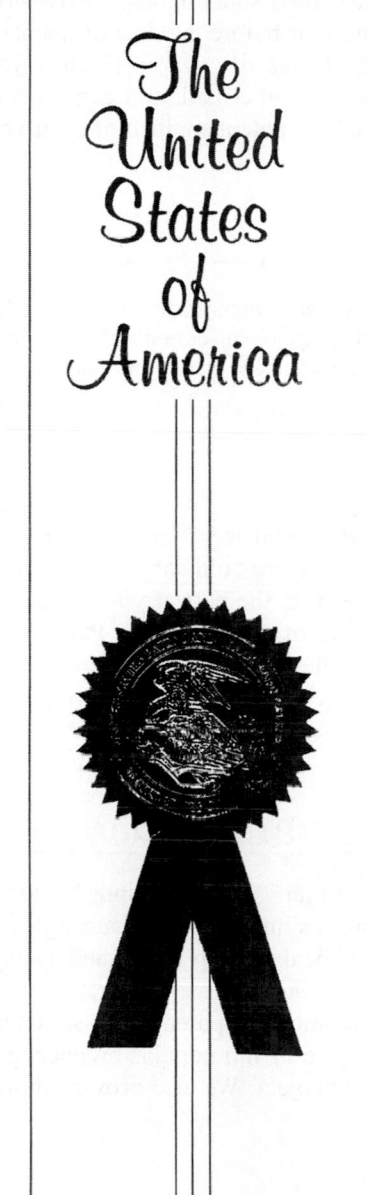

The Director of the United States Patent and Trademark Office

Has received an application for a patent for a new and useful invention. The title and description of the invention are enclosed. The requirements of law have been complied with, and it has been determined that a patent on the invention shall be granted under the law.

Therefore, this

United States Patent

Grants to the person(s) having title to this patent the right to exclude others from making, using, offering for sale, or selling the invention throughout the United States of America or importing the invention into the United States of America for the term set forth below, subject to the payment of maintenance fees as provided by law.

If this application was filed prior to June 8, 1995, the term of this patent is the longer of seventeen years from the date of grant of this patent or twenty years from the earliest effective U.S. filing date of the application, subject to any statutory extension.

If this application was filed on or after June 8, 1995, the term of this patent is twenty years from the U.S. filing date, subject to any statutory extension. If the application contains a specific reference to an earlier filed application or applications under 35 U.S.C. 120, 121 or 365(c), the term of the patent is twenty years from the date on which the earliest application was filed, subject to any statutory extensions.

Nicholas P. Godici

Acting Director of the United States Patent and Trademark Office

Q. M. Person

Attest

Figure 10-11   Sample Letter on Receiving a Patent.

invention might be perceived as some combination, carefully explain where the unexpected use arises.

Is the Invention Novel?

● Has the invention been anticipated by another patent (anywhere in the world, to the best of your knowledge)? Is it described in the scientific or technical literature? Is it embodied in a product or service that is currently available for sale?

● To be patentable, an invention must be new. If it has been publicly known, used, or sold anywhere in the United States or described in printed material anywhere in the world more than one year before the date of the patent application, the invention cannot be patented. *A note of caution:* Even if you yourself use the invention publicly or describe it in an e-mail, at a conference, or in published form more than one year before your patent application, you've likely worked yourself out of a patent.

ROADMAP

IN ACTION

The entrepreneur is careful about how much involvement others are allowed in developing an idea. If assistance from others is needed, prepare an agreement specifying the precise nature of any compensation due and make sure to retain ownership and control of the ideas and any invention involved.

● In spite of this fundamental legal requirement, unfortunately some patents are issued for inventions that are "old hat" to people skilled in the art. Your accurate answer to this question, to the best of your knowledge, is nevertheless key. If an inventor withholds information from the Patent Office, this can be fraud, and a patent obtained fraudulently is invalid.

● There is no guarantee that an issued patent will be able to withstand a legal challenge.

HOW TO PROTECT INTELLECTUAL PROPERTY

If an idea truly has potential value, it is important to begin some form of protection and to act with caution. A simple nondisclosure agreement (NDA) or confidentiality agreement (CA) should be drawn up and signed by any person with whom the ideas are discussed before any substantive conversation takes place.[15] Where the costs of having such an agreement prepared professionally are of concern, the inventor may wish to review some of the popular prepackaged legal software available in stores or books on the subject. We also provide more information and samples in Chapter 12.

Registered Patent Agents

Patent agents are not attorneys at law, yet they are specially registered to practice patent law by and before the U.S. Patent and Trademark Office.[16] Although the range of duties these individuals are legally authorized to perform is not as extensive as that of patent attorneys, patent agents are generally equally qualified to perform all of the basic work that many inventors will require in obtaining patents for their inventions. Patent agents generally have an advanced degree or work experience suiting them to their legal function. In addition, any agent who has not served for at least four years as an examiner within the USPTO must pass a special exam to guarantee competence in the field of work. These individuals do not work for the government but may be found in private organizations that serve the needs of inventors.

Registered Patent Attorneys

Registered patent attorneys must successfully complete the same exam issued to individuals wishing to become patent agents, but they hold higher credentials that allow them to perform legal services above and beyond those executed by patent agents. Most important, patent attorneys, by virtue of their juris doctorates, are authorized to litigate in matters of patent law in any state in which they are licensed to practice law. Having been admitted to the Bar Association, attorneys are bound by a code of ethics. Even if they fail to adhere to the ethics they pledged to uphold, their qualifications also permit them to be sued, should a lawsuit become necessary.

Choosing Your Representative

Generally speaking, one should expect to pay more for the services of a patent attorney, who is licensed to litigate over matters of intellectual property, than for the services of a patent agent, who is not licensed to litigate over such matters. Fees for professional services vary substantially between agents and attorneys, and among the members of the groups themselves. However, considering what many inventors have at stake, the cost of even highly priced professional services may be indispensable. It is advised that total fees be determined before entering into a binding contract with any agent or attorney because many of the "flat rates" quoted by attorneys and agents do not actually cover work required after submission of an application. For convenience, the accompanying table provides a starting point with some average figures obtained from a selection of professionals. The rates apply to small entities; large corporations will pay much more for comparable services.

Service Description	Agent	Attorney
Initial Consultation	Free	Free
Hourly Rate[17]	$300	$450
Preparation and Submission	$5,000	$7,500
Expected Total Costs	$6,500–7,500	$8,000–12,000

These figures apply most specifically to utility patent applications. Design applications can cost far less, sometimes half the amount of a utility application, and plant patent applications usually cost somewhere between design and utility. Office actions taken by the USPTO require responses from inventors, and rejected applications will require additional capital outlays in order to be disputed. Agents and attorneys may charge by the hour for such work, or these costs may be included in a fixed rate. Many agents and attorneys give inventors the option of paying flat fees, hourly rates, or some combination of the two. Again, the above figures are rough averages only. Inventors can expect to find costs varying considerably, given such factors as the complexity of their inventions.

The most important criterion for selecting a representative will be the relative amount and quality of experience in practicing patent law. You will also want to learn what sorts of activity the representative has regularly engaged in and his or her success. Were any complaints registered? Each of these questions must be answered, and you must weigh your answers carefully in your decision.

Whenever possible, use an agent or attorney who specializes or has knowledge in the scientific or technical field pertaining to your invention. You can search the patent database and find patent attorneys who have written strong and important patents in your field. The added insight that comes with such an understanding can be especially helpful in guiding development in the most appropriate manner possible.

Finally, it should be noted that nonregistered agents, attorneys, organizations, and the like do not practice within the USPTO's jurisdiction, so they fall outside the realm of regulation that the USPTO has over registered professionals. This will be a key consideration to inventors who may have grievances with their attorney, agent, or other representative.

GETTING STARTED WITH THE PATENT IDEA

The U.S. government gives rights to the first person who conceives an idea, provided that it can be proven. Therefore, it is very important to keep a well-documented account of the invention's development wherever possible. This may very well be the most important step an inventor can take in protecting IP rights.

The Disclosure Document Program

Send a document disclosing the invention; this document must contain a comprehensive explanation of the invention and how it is produced and used. Where applicable, drawings should be included as well. Furthermore, a disclosure should be made as to the purpose of the invention and what makes it "novel." For the sake of efficiency, the USPTO mandates a specific format for disclosure documents. Contact the USPTO for details on the latest requirements and fees.

The Patent and Trademark Office will keep the disclosure document for a period of two years. During that time, the document will be considered evidence of the earliest date of conception for the invention. If no official patent application is filed before the end of this initial two-year period, the disclosure documents will be destroyed. It is incumbent upon the inventor to proceed with the patent process in as expeditious a manner as possible to fulfill the intended purpose of safeguarding the origination date of property rights.

Upon receipt of the successfully completed disclosure document, the USPTO will return a receipt form identifying the date of receipt and providing an identification code for the document. Remember that specific reference must be made to the original disclosure document date of receipt and identification number at any such time as further documents, such as an official patent application, are submitted to the USPTO.

WHAT IS PRIOR ART?

Before beginning the often lengthy and expensive campaign to get one's idea or invention patented, it is highly advisable that one conduct a search for prior art. The term *prior art* refers to all subjects that do not meet the condition of novelty, as explained earlier in the section on patent qualifications.

The USPTO examiner's first step in evaluating a patent application is to review the prior art. Discovery of the existence of prior art will immediately nullify any possibility of the application's approval. Consequently, it ought to be clear that beginning the patent process without having conducted a prior art search may very well be an exercise in futility.

USING SEARCH OPTIONS

Since professionals usually charge between $1,000 and $2,500 for a simple prior art search, most inventors should initially explore prior art on their own. While there's no way one can be sure how long the search will take, it is easily possible that the invention may be already disclosed in the prior art within just the first few minutes of searching. A variety of tools, including the Internet, can help the inventor discover the prior art status.

Internet Searching

The most easily accessible tool is the World Wide Web. By performing even simple searches on Internet search engines, the inventor will find hundreds of sites devoted to intellectual property, ranging from university programs to law firms. For best results, you should try using search terms related to your topic such as *intellectual property* and *patent*. The USPTO's own home page, located at www.uspto.gov, is perhaps the most indispensable Internet site, replete with all of the information needed to successfully patent a qualifying invention. The additional sources appended to this chapter present numerous other sites worth visiting.

Agencies and Organizations

In addition to the Internet, several public and private agencies may assist the inventor in discovering prior art. The costs of employing them can vary considerably, but so does the effectiveness of each organization's searching capabilities. Inventors choosing to use professional assistance should research the firms, agents, and attorneys they're dealing with before entering into any binding agreements. Look for a track record of success, among other things.

Government Resources

The U.S. Patent and Trademark Office
Crystal Plaza 3
2021 Jefferson Davis Hwy
Arlington, VA 20231

The USPTO provides physical facilities that the general public can use in pursuing intellectual property research.

Some Words of Caution

Before using the services of any organizations, check with the local Better Business Bureau to see if any complaints have been lodged. Be particularly wary of services that ask for up-front fees to promote your invention. The USPTO issues a warning on its Web site about "inventor services." It states, "there are many firms who prey on small inventors"; they essentially start with a small fee and grossly escalate charges while providing little in the way of substantive assistance. The Federal Trade Commission (FTC) is currently conducting an operation investigating such companies. Any inventor considering using an unfamiliar firm should contact the FTC for more information. Should an inventor already be mired in a troublesome relationship, it is wise to seek assistance from the FTC. Poor quality of work done for the inventor can actually do more harm than good to the long-term intellectual property rights. This is not to say that all such firms are untrustworthy, but forewarned is forearmed.

What Is the Patent Application Process?

Generally, only the inventor himself may apply for a patent.[18] In cases where more than one inventor are responsible for generating the idea, inventors must file jointly. Only in cases of insanity or death may a person other than the inventor legally apply. Exceptions are when an inventor declines to apply or is unable to apply, in which case some person with an exclusive interest in the intellectual property may apply on an inventor's behalf.

The USPTO offers a choice of two patent applications, depending on what state of development an inventor's subject is in at the time application is made. Essentially, the inventor with a complete concept who is fully prepared to submit a comprehensive case for patentability will submit a nonprovisional application. Inventors who want to establish a filing date but are not prepared can file a provisional application giving them one full year from the date of filing to complete development of the invention. Concerns regarding marketability, licensing, capital requirements, and the like should also be included. Only inventors seeking design patents are limited to use of the nonprovisional application form. Inventors seeking utility or plant patents may use either form.

Provisional Application

Since June 8, 1995, the USPTO has offered inventors the option of filing a provisional application for patents, which was designed to provide a lower-cost first patent filing in the United States. Applicants are entitled to claim the benefit of a provisional application filed not later than twelve months after the provisional application filing date. Under the provisions the corresponding nonprovisional application would benefit in three ways:

1. Patentability would be evaluated as though filed on the earlier provisional application filing date.
2. The twenty-year patent term would be measured from the later nonprovisional application filing date. The domestic applicants are placed on equal footing with foreign applicants with respect to the patent term. Inventors may file U.S. provisional applications regardless of citizenship.

To be complete, a provisional application must include the filing fee and a cover sheet identifying the following:

- The application as a provisional application for patent
- The name(s) of all inventors
- Inventor residence(s)
- Title of the invention
- Name and registration number of attorney or agent and docket number (if applicable)
- Correspondence address
- Any U.S. government agency that has a property interest in the application

Forms are available on the printable forms page of the USPTO Web site at www.uspto.gov/web/forms/index.html and may be used as the cover sheet for a provisional application.

Nonprovisional Application

The nonprovisional application is the more complete of the two application forms offered by the USPTO. Submission of a nonprovisional application will initiate the process of examination leading to a USPTO judgment on patentability.

The nonprovisional patent application must include the following:

- A specification—a written description of the invention that makes at least one specific claim
- An oath or declaration
- A drawing in cases where it is necessary
- A fee (consult the USPTO or updated fee schedule for current fees)

The claims must be as comprehensive as possible. They will form the basis for an invention's patentability and serve to settle legal considerations concerning infringement after such time as a patent might be issued.

How Are Claims Drawn?

Claims are the most important element of the patent application. They officially designate the property boundaries of the invention. In a very real sense, the claim defines the intellectual property. If the claim is too broad, it may be invalid, and if the claim is too narrow, it may be infringed by a copier. Drafting claims is where patent lawyers earn their fees. Follow these guidelines:

- A patent covers what is taught in the specification. Legally, however, you own only what you claim and (in principle) nothing more. There have been many inventions that have been on their face not very interesting but that, thanks to creative claims, have reaped tens of millions of dollars for their inventors. In contrast, there are many inventions that, because of incomplete or sloppy claims, were in the end worthless. You should do some homework on claims. Although your attorney will do the drafting, it is the inventor who will enable him to reach for a broader claim, to grab a bigger piece of the potential user space.
- The patent law recognizes many different kinds of claims. There are material structures (chemical compounds and molecules), physical structures (devices, mechanisms), uses (you can claim both a material or structure and its use), methods (you can also claim the way it is used), software, algorithms, and since 1998 ways of doing business. If your invention looks to you like a way of using molasses for some purpose, you would be lucky if you got a claim on a "fluid" or, if not an abstract fluid, at least a "high-viscosity fluid." Your patent will probably be worth a lot less if your broadest claim is limited to "molasses." This is not idle semantics; it is where your patent develops true value.
- Look at some patents on the U.S. Patent and Trademark Office Web site or Delphion.com to see some examples. Although when it comes to claims, the broader the better, a good attorney can get at least a narrow claim on almost any useful invention.

The Patent Review Process

Once the completed nonprovisional application has been filed with the USPTO, it will be assigned to a specific examination group knowledgeable in the realm of technology where the invention falls. From within this group, a particular examiner will take up the review. Reviews are conducted in the order in which patents are filed, or as otherwise prescribed by the commissioner of patents and trademarks. Inventors who wish to make a case for special consideration, including early review, must have appeals approved directly by the commissioner.

What Does "Patent Pending" Mean?

Inventors who want to engage in the production and/or sale of any article for which they've already submitted an application for patent may elect to mark these articles with the term *patent pending.* Doing so will serve notice to others that they may be in violation of patent infringement should they choose to engage in competitive production or sale of such articles or those that are substantially similar. No actual infringement can occur unless patent status has already been granted. Hence, the *patent pending* mark carries no legal weight. Nonetheless, the term may prove an effective deterrent to potential competitors. If for no other reason, it might be used on this merit. The *patent pending* mark may appear on the article itself, its packaging, in materials promoting the article, or in any other appropriate and relevant way.

What Financial Considerations Should Entrepreneurs Keep in Mind?

Although receiving a patent is an accomplishment, it is worthless if it is not used. A patent simply gives its holder a "negative right" to prevent others from using the idea or infringing on rights in some other way. In order to make the patent and its related work and costs worthwhile, you must capitalize on the opportunity the patent presents. Doing so need not entail actually taking the idea and putting it into practice, although this is the option of choice for many entrepreneurs. As the owner of a patent, you may choose for a variety of reasons to employ any number of different avenues to realize some of the potential rewards available. Your decision either to start a business or use the competitive benefits offered by the patent to sell or license will include your risk preference, personal and professional constraints, and money consideration.

How Are Patents Licensed?

To license a patent, the owner authorizes a person or business to engage in activity that would otherwise infringe on the patent. In consideration for this benefit, the licensee will typically pay some kind of up-front fee, ongoing royalty, or both to the owner of the patent. The decision to license one's patent for use by another need not exclude the owner of the patent from using it independently. Some inventors prefer simply to create and to leave more commercial endeavors to others. Having a revenue stream from up-front fees and ongoing royalties can help to finance the development and patenting of future inventions. Others simply don't have the time or finances to start a business built on the inventions. Even where time and finances might not be of concern, the licensing option can be a highly attractive alternative.

The subject of licensing is dealt with in more detail in Chapter 11 in the context of using it as an ingredient of a business model.

PROGRESS FROM IDEA TO PATENT TO ENTERPRISE

The following are the steps entrepreneurs must take to go from idea to patent to enterprise:

1. Conceive an idea and perform a preliminary analysis of the market and patent potential. Take preparatory steps to protect your idea, limiting exposure and documenting carefully.

2. Document a brief, descriptive record of the idea. Define what is being protected. There are numerous forms of protection, and each may vary from a single attribute or range of services. Product features or an entire line of products may be included.

3. Select an intellectual property law firm. Consider the firm's success in handling applications and its experience with the technology related to the patent. Visit the firm for an initial consultation, which is usually provided free of charge. It might be helpful to compare the services and costs of using registered agents and attorneys.

4. Conduct preliminary research. Depending on your financial position, you or your attorney should perform the initial prior art search. This search may be done using the online resources of the USPTO or with on-site computers dedicated for this purpose. Attorneys and agents will have their own resources with which to perform this search. If no prior art is discovered, you may proceed to the next step.

5. Perform a detailed search. Conduct an in-depth review to identify and review related patents. This research must be disclosed to the patent office. If there are no conflicting patents, you can proceed to the next step.

6. Prepare the patent application using diagrams and flow charts. File the patent with a law firm and receive filing data from the patent office.

7. Expect a waiting period. It takes approximately nine to twelve months to get a response from the patent office in the form of an Office Action letter. More than one such letter may require a response.

8. Respond to the Office Action letter. This is your opportunity to address any objections or issues raised by the USPTO with regard to the application.

9. Wait some more. For the next four to six months, wait to hear if the patent is accepted or rejected. It may happen that only part of the patent or claims is accepted. If you and your representatives have done a good job, however, the entire application will be approved.

10. Look for notice that the patent is accepted and that a patent number has been issued.

11. Embark on your new enterprise. Options may include licensing the patent for use by others. Ultimately, an exit strategy involving the sale of the patent can also be considered.

12. Maintain vigilance and safeguard your rights by searching for patent infringement and prosecuting appropriately.

THE VALUE OF TRADE SECRETS

In the realm of intellectual property, at times information is best left undisclosed, even if disclosure and registration with the federal government would afford a measure of legal protection. Vital information not shared with the general public but valuable to the success of an entrepreneurial entity may fall within the realm of trade secrets.

Modern trade secret law dates back to the Industrial Revolution in England, but its precedent goes back much further to ancient Roman law, which imposed punishment for persons found guilty of impelling others to disclose secrets of trade. In the United States, the Uniform Trade Secrets Act (UTSA) was drafted by the National Conference of Commissioners on Uniform State Laws. Because the protection of trade secrets differs from state to state, entrepreneurs need to familiarize themselves fully to best safeguard trade secrets.

Broadly speaking, a trade secret may constitute any manner or form of information that, by way of its secrecy, yields its user potential or actual economic value and economic and/or competitive advantage over others. For a trade secret to be legally defended as such, its "owner" must take reasonable steps to ensure its secrecy. Information subject to common knowledge may not be protected as a trade secret, but trade secrets needn't be complex or novel in order to qualify as such. Among the many forms a trade secret may take are those of formula, pattern, device, and process. Even a customer list may serve as a trade secret when meeting the above requirements. In some cases such trade secrets are more appropriately referred to as "business secrets."

What Are the Advantages and Disadvantages of Trade Secrets?

The trade secret's greatest advantage over other forms of intellectual property may be in the potentially limitless duration of its value and service to its owner. Coca-Cola is an oft-quoted example of a company that has maintained a trade secret for more than one hundred years and continues to enjoy the economic benefit of such.[19] Coke claims that it has been successful in keeping the formula for its popular soft drink secure from outside discovery. However, this trade secret could probably be broken using the most modern methods of chemical analysis, but it would be to little avail. The years of withholding the recipe allowed the company to build such a powerful brand that, even if you could duplicate the product, no one would accept that it was identical!

There is a danger, however, in relying totally on trade secrets. Any formulation, process, or other form of IP maintained as a trade secret by one party can be lawfully employed by an outside party if development is done independently and without any infringement. Because the value of a trade secret may be compromised even under the best cases of internal protection, the decision to maintain some IP as a trade secret rather than filing and registering for a patent, for instance, must be weighed carefully. To help make such a decision, consider whether disclosing the details in a patent or just making it public would give your competitors a valuable head start to develop a competing idea. Also, if you patent a process, for example, a way to mix paints, it may not be possible to determine if the paint on sale was actually mixed the same way. In fact, in this case, it may be impossible to police whether someone else is using your invention. This is not true for a physical product, say a new type of pen, for this can readily be detected as soon as it is offered for sale. For this reason, many companies do not patent processes but take careful steps to retain them as secrets.

How Are Trade Secrets Protected?

One of the most effective ways of maintaining a trade secret is to limit disclosure. The smaller the number of persons exposed to a trade secret, the lower the likelihood that it will fall into the hands of competition. Where possible, it is a good idea to expose only part of a trade secret to any given individual in whom some trust must be placed (such as a worker required for completing only part of a process).

An even more important consideration than the number of persons exposed is the *nature* of the persons exposed. It is better to place faith in a large number of individuals who can be relied upon to maintain the secrecy of some information than in just one who cannot. Members of a venture who have a vested interest in maintaining trade secrecy are naturally more likely to be reliable in terms of not disclosing key knowledge. Keep the trade secret disclosure on a need-to-know basis, and in all cases make sure that some form of CA, NDA, or other employment agreement is filled out and kept safe as early as possible.

REVERSE ENGINEERING

Reverse engineering[20] is a process whereby an existing system of structure, design, code, or otherwise is analyzed and broken down with the purpose of understanding the system and how it functions, and it is then reproduced or improved upon. Commercially, reverse engineering is used principally in the study of high-tech systems such as those found in software and robotics.

How Can Reverse Engineering Benefit the Entrepreneur?

Provided that IP protection regarding patents, trademarks, and copyrights is not violated, this method can be a highly effective tool in building improved products. Given the enormous costs and great deal of time often required to bring new and competitive products to market, the advantages of reverse engineering should not be overlooked. However, reverse engineering can be an extremely expensive undertaking. Conditions such as market maturity, demand, product lifespan, and consumer loyalty (to existing competitors' products) should all be carefully weighed in any decision to reverse engineer, for they will factor strongly in the profitability of any reverse engineering venture.

SUMMARY

The United States and most foreign governments make provisions for protecting intellectual property. Among these provisions are copyright, trademark, patent, and trade secret. The government's purpose in granting protection for IP is to encourage the advancement of "science and the useful arts" by offering rewards to those who make such advancements. Intellectual property is important to the entrepreneur because it provides profit or other form of competitive advantage. Intellectual property possesses many of the same characteristics as other forms of property. It may be used, bought and sold, licensed, or otherwise transferred.

The development and protection of intellectual property can be a painstaking and costly process. Many tools exist to assist entrepreneurs in pursuing IP rights, some of which can add significantly to the costs involved but can prove invaluable to doing the job right. The government agencies responsible for the oversight and administration of IP matters are among the most accessible, inexpensive, and useful resources available to entrepreneurs. In addition, a variety of public and private organizations are available for hire in pursuing IP rights. Registered patent agents and attorneys may be the most qualified to help entrepreneurs. In spite of the higher fees charged by agents and attorneys, their qualifications and expertise can help overcome the complex hurdles encountered in the pursuit of IP rights.

Each form of IP offers different levels of legal protection by the federal government. Protection for IP differs widely internationally and in the case of trade secrets may even vary from state to state within the United States. Promoting and protecting IP is an active process. Specific steps can and should be taken to achieve these ends. It is equally important to defend one's IP as it is to avoid infringing on another's. Particular care should be given to avoid infringement in reverse engineering. Infringement can be extremely costly and may prove the downfall of even the most well-planned venture. However, if done right, reverse engineering can prove instrumental in advancing an endeavor. If you are involved in IP infringement, a cost-benefit analysis should be employed in determining what legal remedies, if any, to employ. The costs of prosecution can be daunting and may not prove worthwhile unless real financial gain is at stake. Where significant value may be in jeopardy, it is recommended that entrepreneurs engage legal counsel.

The field of law pertaining to intellectual property is complex and in constant flux. Recent developments in technology have only added to the complexity of IP law. It is recommended that the entrepreneur stay abreast of current developments and consult early with professionals in the field. The way entrepreneurs handle the development, protection, enforcement, and prosecution of intellectual property can make or break any enterprise. It also can be of particular consequence to start-up companies with less experience and fewer resources. Conscientious attention to detail and commitment to one's project are vital to ensuring the success of an IP-based enterprise.

STUDY QUESTIONS

1. What are the different forms of intellectual property, and how do they differ?
2. What is the purpose of trademarks, and how are they registered and protected?
3. What is the copyright process, and why is it important?
4. What are the various forms of patents, and what is the patent application process?
5. What qualifications must be met for a patent to be granted?
6. When does an idea need to be protected?
7. What steps would you take to choose a patent attorney?
8. What is the disclosure document, and how is prior art defined in the patent process?
9. What are the twelve steps to create a patent from idea to completion?
10. What are the advantages and disadvantages of trade secrets?

EXERCISES

As the management of intellectual property was not a key issue for Neoforma in the master-case, we provide two cases here to explore key management issues surrounding the topic.

Case 1: Ultrafast

Read the Ian Kibblewhite profile in this chapter and answer the following questions:

1. What different intellectual property protection mechanisms did Ultrafast use? What was the specific purpose of each?

2. Why did Ultrafast choose Ratner and Prestia as its patent firm?

3. Explain why the claims of a patent should be written to protect not only the actual invention, but also how the invention is used?

4. Why is the choice of language in a patent very important?

5. Find patents 4899591 and 5131276. Why are the dates of filing relevant? Note the use of the word *film* in each case. In retrospect, how could the second patent have avoided the confusion around this word?

Case 2: Datamark Patent

How to Read but Not to Write a Patent

The way a patent is written can be extremely important in protecting a company's intellectual property. This case will show you how to read a patent and test whether you can find a way to get around the claims.

Background

Datamark's original business idea was to create a new credit card format that would allow a consumer the benefit of having to carry only one credit card rather than the pocketful with which we are all burdened. In order to get into this business, one of Datamark's employees, Doug Taylor, filed a patent to cover the concept using a well-known firm of patent attorneys. It was recognized that without a patent, once the idea was known, any of the large banks or credit card companies could copy the idea and put small Datamark out of business.

Patent Filing

The patent was filed in February 1995 and issued in November 1996, U.S. patent number 5,578,808. Go to the U.S. patent site, www.uspto.gov, and find this patent. Briefly scan it. After the abstract, you will find the list of prior knowledge and the claims. After the claims, the patent gives the background to the invention including a discussion of prior art—that is, what is already known and the benefits. The inventor must demonstrate a need and uniqueness beyond what anyone else has done. The next section tells the reader how the invention can actually be made. Again, to get a patent, the inventor must describe the "how-to." This is because patents are granted in order to increase the spread of ideas for the benefit of all; the trade-off for the inventor is, therefore, between publishing know-how against gaining a market monopoly for many years.

Now turn to the claims and note the following points:

- There are only four claims, and three of them depend on the first claim. Usually there are more claims than this in a patent including more "primary claims." Check out some other patents to see how many claims they have.
- The first claim begins with the words "A smart card. . ."
- The fourth claim lists four groups of applications that can be carried out by the card.

It should not be too difficult for you to see how to get around these claims. Focus on claims 1 and 4 and see if you can think of a card format that would meet the original concept for "one card does all" but is *not* covered by Datamark's claims.

INTERACTIVE LEARNING ON THE WEB

Test your knowledge of the chapter using the book's interactive Web site.

INTERNET IP SOURCE SITES

- U.S. Patent and Trademark Office: www.uspto.gov
- U.S. Copyright Office: www.loc.gov/copyright
- Delphion Intellectual Property Network: www.delphion.com
- Gibbs Group's Inventors Resource Homepage: www.productbuilders.com
- Hoover's Corporate Information: www.hoovers.com
- ThomasNet Register of American Manufacturers: www.thomasnet.com
- Licensing Executives Society International: www.lesi.org
- American Intellectual Property Law Association: www.aipla.org
- Franklin Pierce Law Center: www.piercelaw.edu
- Inventors' Alliance: www.inventorsalliance.org

ADDITIONAL RESOURCES

Avoiding Patent, Trademark, and Copyright Problems　U.S. Small Business Administration Publications, P.O. Box 30, Denver, CO 80201-0030

The Complete Copyright Protection Kit　Intellain, Inc., 1992, P.O. Box 6492, Denver, CO 80206

Inventors Clubs of America　Alexander T. Marinaccio, P.O. Box 450621, Atlanta, GA 31145-0261 (800) 336-0169

***The Inventor's Notebook,* 2nd Edition**　Fred Grissom and David Pressman, Nolo Press, 950 Parker Street, Berkley, CA 94710 (800) 955-4775 or (510) 5410-1976

Licensing Industry Merchandisers' Association　350 5th Avenue, Suite 2309, New York, NY 10118 (212) 244-1944

NASA Tech Briefs　Associated Business Publications, Inc., 317 Madison Avenue, New York, NY 10017 (212) 490-3999

National Technical Information Service Center　Center for Utilization of Federal Technology, U.S. Department of Commerce, 5285 Court Royal Road, P.O. Box 1423, Springfield, VA 22151 (703) 487-4600

Patent It Yourself　David Pressman, Nolo Press, 950 Parker Street, Berkley, CA 94710 (800) 955-4775 or (510) 5410-1976

ROADMAP for

PATTERNS OF ENTREPRENEURSHIP
Implementation

☐ The Value of Trademarks
☐ The Value of Copyrights
☐ The Value of Patents
☐ How to Protect Intellectual Property
☐ Getting Started with the Patent Idea
☐ What Is Prior Art?
☐ Using Search Options
☐ Progress from Idea to Patent to Enterprise
☐ The Value of Trade Secrets
☐ Reverse Engineering
☑ **Definition of Business Models**
☑ **Capturing Value in the Supply Chain**
☑ **Using Databases to Create Value**
☑ **Locking in Customers**
☑ **Licensing and Franchising**
☑ **Outsourcing Resources**
☑ **Models Built around Social Networks**
☑ **Corporate Partnering**
☐ Developing a Strong Corporate Culture
☐ Finding and Hiring the Best People
☐ Dealing with Firing an Employee
☐ Dealing with a Resignation
☐ Conflicts of Interest and Business Ethics
☐ Legal Issues
☐ Setting up Stock Option Agreements

CHAPTER 11

BUSINESS MODELS AND THE POWER OF INFORMATION

"Someday, on the corporate balance sheet, there will be an entry which reads, 'Information'; for in most cases, the information is more valuable than the hardware which processes it."

GRACE MURRAY HOPPER

OBJECTIVES

- Learn the importance of business models.
- Understand the five components of innovative business models.
- Uncover value in supply chains.
- Use databases to engage and lock in customers.
- Compare licensing and franchising.
- Learn about outsource services.
- Understand network models.
- Explore corporate partnering.

CHAPTER OUTLINE

Introduction

Profile: Neal DeAngelo—Using Data Collection

Definition of Business Models

Capturing Value in the Supply Chain

Using Databases to Create Value

Locking in Customers

Licensing and Franchising

Outsourcing Resources

Models Built around Social Networks

Corporate Partnering

Summary

Study Questions

Exercises

Interactive Learning on the Web

Additional Resources

INTRODUCTION

As we saw in Chapter 3, the environment in which a new company finds itself is increasingly competitive, with pressures not only from local firms, but from overseas competitors as well. Moreover, technological advances are accelerating, customers are becoming more informed, and new products and services are being generated at a breathtaking pace. No longer is it sufficient to build a company around just one new product or service idea. Something more is needed if profits are to be sustained. As your company grows, you will need to explore ways to retain its competitive position against challenges from existing and new market entrants. The frameworks in which a sustainable, high-profit company is constructed are called *business models*. This chapter explores this relatively new way of thinking about how companies are designed using innovations not just in the products and services that are sold, but also in the *ways* they are offered.

A new company will start with an initial concept of how it will be structured to serve its customers, work with suppliers, and evolve. As the company begins to grow, the entrepreneur will uncover knowledge about the company's environment that may not have been obvious at the outset. This new information must be fed into the company's plans to stimulate innovation not only in products and services, but in the very fabric of how the company will operate within a unique business model.

Creation of a powerful business model, as we shall see, requires blending all the aspects of the business into an integrated operating system where manufacturing, marketing, information, suppliers and customers, product development, and so on become one. This is not easy and requires the entrepreneur to build a way of thinking into the company—its culture—so continuous innovation becomes a daily routine. (How to build such a culture is dealt with in Chapter 12).

This chapter covers a number of topics related to business model design and implementation. We rely heavily on examples to help you understand what is meant by an innovative business model. Because there are almost as many novel business models as there are companies, rather than try to catalog them, we will present examples that will stimulate you as you plan your own company for growth. We will introduce different ideas that can be incorporated into a business model, such as using information to lock in customers, learning how to capture value from suppliers, deciding when to use licensing or franchising, recognizing when to outsource activities to consultants or other companies, and using the power of networks and corporate partners.

PROFILE: NEAL DEANGELO—USING DATA COLLECTION[1]

When Neal DeAngelo and his brother Paul left school in 1978, they decided to start their own company. Using a truck bought for them by their father and some standard mowing equipment, the two brothers provided services in "vegetation management" to businesses rather than homeowners. This choice of customer segment turned out to be the right one; businesses were more stable, and as the company, DBI Services, soon learned by listening carefully to them, businesses have greater and more complex needs than do homeowners. For example, "Class I" railroads are regulated by the federal government on the amount of vegetation that may grow on their rights of way. This, for example, mitigates against fire hazards and ensures a clear line of sight at crossings for safety. DBI realized that the *value proposition* for these customers was focused not on low cost but on the reliability and speed with which a service provider could treat the vegetation growing along the tracks. If any equipment breaks down on the railroad, the loss of income from trains not being able to run will greatly surpass any small cost savings for the service.

Understanding the customers' true needs has enabled DBI to build a dominant position in this sector by designing and building its own vegetation treatment road/rail vehicles. These vehicles rapidly mount the track and detect the location and type of vegetation along the line, mix optimized herbicides in real time, and spot-spray using robot arms on the truck. This minimizes the amount of chemical carried and used, limiting any environmental damage and coincidentally reducing the time needed to refill the containers with herbicides. By mapping the exact location of every plant using on-board GPS technology, the company ensures that its next service run can be accomplished in minimum time, with highly efficient use of chemicals and equipment. The proprietary data that the company collects on its clients' unique situations are a major competitive advantage, making it exceedingly difficult for a competitor to bid accurately on a contract and to compete in service. DBI has no patents but protects its know-how and data through trade secrets and works with universities to augment its own science and technology. Neal and Paul have now bootstrapped their business to more than $80 million in sales, using only bank loans to finance the growth. Their business model is based on the principles of providing business customers with reliable and customized services supported by proprietary information systems. Many students earn summer money by cutting grass; few grow a large and successful company from such a humble start. (Neal can be seen talking about DBI on the book's Web site.)

Example: The Dell Business Model[2]

In 1984 Michael Dell, while an undergraduate at the University of Texas, formed a company called PCs Limited to sell IBM-compatible computers assembled from standard components.

In 1985 PCs Limited made its first in-house-designed computer using an Intel 8088-compatible processor running at 8 MHz. These "Turbo PCs" were sold directly to customers via advertising in computer magazines. Each computer was custom built from a selection of options, thus providing a combination of prices lower than retail brands and greater convenience than assembling from kits. Dell dropped out of school to run the business full time; he made more than $6 million in sales the first year.

In 1988 the company was renamed Dell Computer Corporation, and in 1992 *Fortune* magazine included the company in its list of the world's 500 largest companies.

In 1999 Dell surpassed Compaq to become the largest seller of personal computers in the United States and since then has remained among the leaders with sales growing to $61 billion in 2008 with net income of $2.6 billion. Despite some setbacks in an increasingly competitive marketplace, Dell has continued to succeed where others have failed. Indeed IBM gave up the fight by selling its PC business to Lenovo in China. After just twenty-five years, Michael Dell's "direct model" had created a company worth $50 billion.

Dell Computer Company's ability to succeed while others failed is a result of its powerful business model and the company's passion in execution of the model—not its ability to conceive and develop novel products.

The four concepts behind the direct model that enabled Dell to grow so rapidly and establish a leading brand are as follows:

1. **One-to-one customer contact.** Dell believes that the most efficient path to the customer is through a direct relationship, with no intermediaries to add confusion and cost. The company is organized around groups of customers with similar needs, removing inefficient translation of customers' requirements by resellers.

This approach also reduces the costs to the customer by taking out at least one level of distribution expenditure, which can amount to up to 30 percent of the retail price.

2. **Accountability.** Dell recognizes that technology can be complex. By making the company the single point of accountability, resources necessary to meet customer needs can be easily marshaled in support of complex challenges.

3. **Made to order.** Dell provides customers exactly what they want in their computer systems through easy custom configuration and ordering. "Build to order" means that Dell need not hold months of aging and expensive inventory. This concept is deeply embodied within the day-to-day operations of the company, with sometimes surprising innovations. For example, Dell does not take ownership of microprocessors until just before they are inserted into the circuit boards; they remain the property of their suppliers, such as Intel, right up to this moment. This reduces not only Dell's inventory costs, but also insurance and quality management expenses. If components are shipped by plane from Asia, the suppliers must provide their own transportation on a regular just-in-time schedule at their own cost. The supply of parts is so lean at Dell that the company pays for its inventory *after* the customer has actually purchased the product, thereby removing the need to have cash reserves to hold inventory. If the inventory on hand does not align precisely with demand, then Dell is ready with special-offer advertising programs that immediately redress the balance. Dell also allows customers to configure their own products at their Web site. The real-time data collected from this site feed directly into the supply chain information system that communicates directly with Dell's component suppliers. It also reduces the cost of selling by removing labor costs of salespersons. Everyone at Dell is looking to improve on these ideas every day they go to work.

4. **Nonunique products.** Dell uses standard technology as a key to providing customers with relevant, high-value products and services. Focusing on standards gives customers the benefit of extensive research and development from not only Dell, but an entire industry. Unlike proprietary technologies, standards give customers flexibility and choice. This concept also reduces Dell's research expenditures to much less than those of any of its competitors. Unique first-to-market products are not the reason for Dell's success; a rigorous focus on the direct business model is.

The Dell business model seems so obvious and easy to replicate. So why have the competitors not been able to follow? First, the old model of selling through distributors and retail outlets was established by Compaq and IBM before Dell came on the scene. For these competitors to switch to a direct model, they would have to tear down their existing distribution network. This cannot be done overnight, and setting up a direct sales channel would compete with their existing resellers. This action might prompt a mass exodus of these independent partners, say to a competitor's products, destroying overnight the major sales capability before a direct sales model could be built up. Customers would also be confused by two price levels for the same product and would be unsure where they should go for customer support. A local distributor would hardly welcome customers asking for support after they had purchased their computer online at a lower price. The difficulty of switching from a legacy retail distribution model to a direct model is a major reason for the inability of the competitors to follow Dell. Also, Dell established a "monoculture" built around its business model; every employee and partner focused on its execution and continual improvement. The competitors, caught between conflicting business models, were initially unable to perform either one effectively to compete in a very cost-conscious market. It took Dell's competitors longer than twenty years to duplicate the Dell model. Now Dell has been forced into some limited retail sales outlets to maintain its market share. It remains to be seen which companies can manage an emerging dual-channel model more effectively.

DEFINITION OF BUSINESS MODELS

A business model provides a framework in which entrepreneurs can examine their business plans and explore alternative ways for their companies to function and grow profitably while building barriers to ward off competitors. It is more than a business strategy, for it describes how the different functions within a company work harmoniously together to build "more than the sum of the parts." The following definition captures the meaning: "A business model is a description of how your company intends to create value in the marketplace. It includes that unique combination of products, services, image, and distribution that your company carries forward. It also includes the underlying organization of people, and the operational infrastructure that they use to accomplish their work."[3] If you read the Dell example again, you will see how all of these factors work together to construct the unique business model pioneered by Dell.

A more concise summary definition can be stated as follows: "A business model is the way a company applies knowledge to capture value."[4] Note the emphasis on *capturing value*. Establishing value for your customers, and suppliers too, and building a company that can hold on to this value are key to optimizing your business model. The greatest inventions may not be able to retain the value that they can provide. For example, imagine that you have invented a simple instrument, costing less than a thousand dollars, to detect the early stages of Alzheimer's disease long before symptoms are detectable. Your test can enable preventive medication to be used to delay major patient needs for care and support for up to ten years. The value of this is clearly enormous, not only in financial terms, but in social benefits too. Ten years of *not* requiring full support could easily add up to hundreds of thousands of dollars. Yet who will pay you for your invention at a price that will reflect a major part of the value you are promising: patients, doctors, pharmaceutical companies, family members, health insurers, and the government? None of these potential customers has a way of paying you for the value you can provide, and it requires a really novel business model to do so. Perhaps you have some ideas on how to do this. When you review the examples in this chapter, think about how the companies have designed their businesses to both capture value and protect themselves against competitive attacks.

ROADMAP
IN ACTION

Learn to question why some businesses are much more successful than others. Ask whether they have a unique business model that prevents competitors from taking away their customers. What is unique about what they do? Why do other companies have a problem competing? Try to see how their ideas might translate into your business.

Analyzing five vital components helps us construct a unique business model.[5]

1. Articulate the *value proposition,* that is, the value created for the user of the product or service. Sometimes the value may not be created for the most obvious user. For example, the value of the Alzheimer's test may be for the health insurers rather than the patients or their caregivers. Such insights can trigger ideas for business models. Also, the value may not be obvious; talking to different users may highlight hidden values (see the DBI and Greif cases in this book).

2. Identify a *market segment,* that is, users to whom the product or service is useful and for what purpose; specify how this will generate revenues for the firm. This will help you focus your marketing messages and sales resources so they deliver the highest and most profitable sales. This focus is particularly important during the early stages of building a company, when resources are limited.

3. Define the structure of the *value chain* in which the firm operates, and define the assets that are needed for the firm to function in this environment. Dell provides value to its direct customers and its suppliers. The Greif case presented in Chapter 3 illustrates how value can be created in several parts of a *value* or *supply* chain. Suppliers, customers, and other stakeholders operate more and more in *value networks*. Competitors may also be customers. The more you understand where your company fits in these networks, the better you can create a viable business model.

4. Estimate the *cost structure* and *profit potential* of delivering the product or service given the value proposition and value chain. Having great products and services in a fast-growing firm yet selling them at a loss does not constitute a sustainable business model.

5. Formulate the *competitive strategy* by which the innovating firm will gain and hold advantage over rivals. This summarizes how all the other attributes fit together in a model that both captures value and builds competitive barriers.

The rest of the chapter relies heavily on examples of different business models. In each case, you should analyze the models using these five attributes. In this way, you will gain valuable insights into how sustainable business models are constructed and followed. In particular, note how in most cases they are innovative and not immediately obvious. Innovation in business models is becoming a key skill in the entrepreneur's toolkit. The following sections describe business models built around supply chains, databases, customer lock-in, licensing and franchising, outsourcing, networking, and partnering. These examples can be applied individually or in combination to design your own unique business model.

ROADMAP

IN ACTION

Every business exists within a network of suppliers, customers, competitors, and other companies, all vying to capture as much value as possible. Ask how you can capture some of the value that they currently provide, or add more value for your customers through innovation.

CAPTURING VALUE IN THE SUPPLY CHAIN

Any company finds itself in a supply chain. No company undertakes all of the functions required to deliver an end product from soup to nuts. Intel, for example, does not mine and refine the sand for making the silicon wafers for microprocessors. Rather, it purchases raw materials and manufacturing equipment from other firms. Neither does it sell computers or other electronic products. It focuses on what it does best: developing new silicon integrated circuits for use in the products of other companies such as Dell. Intel relies on other companies in the supply chain and focuses on extracting value from microprocessors, leaving the computer value to others. Intel's business model is structured to maximize its retention of value in what it offers in this supply chain. If you are opening a restaurant, you will require fresh ingredients from the markets, tableware, kitchen equipment, and staff. All these are components of your supply chain. You will also have to advertise, create promotional programs, and the like, all of which are your bought-in services. Every business is continually trying to maximize the value it can command and retain in its own supply chain or network. Sometimes the business model to achieve this goal is not obvious. Return to the Greif example in Chapter 3, and think about the move from being a commodity supplier of metal drums to a value-added service provider of "trip leasing."

USING DATABASES TO CREATE VALUE

Selling snowblowers is a tough business. The majority of blowers are bought on impulse a day or two before a major snowstorm lands. And these storms are difficult to forecast. Competing for a last-minute sale of a snowblower requires that a potential customer has *your* product in mind when she goes to the store just before the snow hits. Toro greatly improved its efficiency in this regard by building a software program that took into account several independent weather forecasts, had local advertisements ready to go into local print and radio media, and tied its own supply network and dealers together so they could get products into appropriate local outlets. This innovative combination of externally and internally created data helped the company capture greater market share from its competitors and reduce its cost of inventory that sat in stores where the sun was shining. Or consider Wal-Mart's vaunted supply chain software system, which detected a sudden upsurge in the sale of flags on September 12, 2001. Its purchasing department immediately contacted its suppliers and tied up nearly all of the short-term supply of U.S. flags worldwide, enabling Wal-Mart to be the sole source of flags for the next few weeks and bringing more customers into its stores.

ROADMAP

IN ACTION

We live in the information age. Data are being collected daily about nearly everything. Much of these data are freely available. Think how you can use data combinations creatively to generate greater value for your customers and sustain your competitive position. How much of these data must you generate yourself, and how much are free?

The fall in price of computers and data storage devices, coupled with the Internet, have made the use of digital information as a competitive weapon no longer the domain of just larger companies. Start-up companies can now harvest information technology to provide their customers with greater value and to create subtle barriers to competition. Indeed, this new low-cost digital freedom may even give smaller companies advantages over larger firms, which are encumbered by legacy data systems and cultures, freezing them in outdated business models. It was, after all, Amazon and eBay that pioneered online bookstores and auctions rather than Barnes & Noble and Sotheby's.

Capturing data on customer requirements and using it to create unique services or products can be a powerful way of adding value and keeping out competitors. Recall the case of Netflix in Chapter 3; that company changed the way consumers rent movies. The power of the Netflix business model derives not only from the convenience, but also the ability to mine the data obtained by combining information from *all* customers nationwide. This enables the company to make suggestions on what you might like to rent based on not only your past rentals, but also on matching your behavior with that of others with similar tastes. This ability is termed *collaborative filtering*. In addition, by getting instant feedback from their database (customers provide long lists of future wants), Netflix can balance its inventory centrally to meet both current and anticipated customer requirements, something that cannot be done on a local basis. Using this novel database structure, Netflix is able to provide its customers with a convenient, personalized service as it continually optimizes its own supply chain. Amazon, Netflix, and the iTunes store are just three examples of what Chris Anderson[6] refers to as "mining the long-tail." The long-tail consists of those products that appeal to only a few customers, are specialized, and are uneconomic to be placed in local stores or warehouses. Combining powerful search tools with collaborative filtering enables customers to find and access little-known books, movies, or music hidden in the long-tails yet fit their personal taste. Retail stores are unable from both physical and financial constraints to store such large inventories or provide a customer an easy way to find what he wants. What other fragmented and specialist markets can be attacked using these concepts?

LOCKING IN CUSTOMERS

Netflix and the DeAngelo brothers use customer data to provide superior services, making them tough competitors. This can be taken a step further. Information can be shared between customers and suppliers, so the one is closely locked into the other as business partners. A business model based on information sharing can provide high barriers against competitors because the costs involved in integrating incompatible data and computer systems can be prohibitive. On the other hand, the entrepreneur must be aware of becoming too dependent on one supplier or customer when the "lock-in" can become disadvantageous. A sound business model using data lock-in will have multiple partners so the dependence on one partner is reduced.

Data lock-ins inhibiting a move to a competitor can be found in e-mail services, banking, insurance, and health-care services. Such lock-ins can also occur between businesses.

Gaining customers costs five times as much as retaining them. What information can you share with your customers that would provide benefit to both of you? Will this bind you together such that it would be difficult for your customers to change suppliers? In so doing, can you perform higher-value services that would make it even more difficult for a split?

Example: General Fasteners

For years suppliers of components to the major automotive companies have been squeezed more and more on price as the global competition in this sector has become increasingly tough. Even if a supplier has some proprietary technology, the large buyers such as GM and Ford are so powerful that they insist that their suppliers share their unique know-how so they can play multiple competing suppliers against each other. Life is particularly tough when the component is simple to make, the product is not proprietary, and there is an oversupply. Faced with these daunting pressures on profits, General Fasteners (GF),[7] a manufacturer of bolts and other metal fasteners for the automotive industry, looked for an innovative business model to change its competitive status. It started by undertaking the engineering design for new car "platforms," taking responsibility for how the car would be reliably assembled. This requires special, hard-to-come-by engineering skills. GF then contracted to supply the car company with just-in-time components directly to the production lines, with 100 percent quality inspection and guarantees. GF either uses fasteners that are made in its own plants or purchases them from other suppliers. It manages an integrated supply chain from design to final assembly. This requires GF's computer systems to seamlessly integrate with car plants exchanging data in real time. They are "locked in" to their customers in both design and operations, making it difficult for competitors to displace them. They provide both products and services. In addition, by taking over the front-end skilled design work, their customers have no need to retain these expensive skills in-house for occasional use and, therefore, become more dependent on their supplier when they are ready to design a new family of cars.

ROADMAP

IN ACTION

Sharing your business with others can accelerate your own growth pathway and reduce your need for cash. Rather than selling part of the company to stockholders, you can use licensing or franchising. Is your idea a match to these methods as either a part or even the core of your business model?

LICENSING AND FRANCHISING

Licensing and franchising can be valuable components of a business model. They are often confused. This section describes their similarities and differences and explores when they are best employed as the basis or as a part of a business model.

Licensing and franchising refer to types of contracts between an "issuing" entity (the licensor or franchisor) and a "receiving" entity (the licensee or franchisee). These contracts grant the receivers certain rights to access certain intellectual properties, such as patents, trademarks, trade secrets, and copyrights, as discussed in Chapter 10.

The License Agreement and How to Use It

A license agreement allows a licensee to use intellectual property under certain conditions as spelled out in the agreement. A license agreement usually includes the following key topics:[8]

- The licensor and licensee are identified together on the basis of their reasons for entering into the agreement. This helps ensure that there are no misunderstandings between the two parties.

- The licensed intellectual property (IP) is precisely defined. This may give patent numbers, trademarks, and lists of trade secrets, together with a description of the products, services, and processes covered by the IP. The agreement also clearly states whether the licensor and licensee have any rights to improvements that either of them make in the future. It is usual for the licensor to have rights to any improvements made by the licensee; if not, then the licensor could find itself blocked by new inventions made by the licensee.

- The granted rights to the IP are carefully defined. Licensees may have a great deal of freedom, or they may be limited to selling products, making and not selling, and so on. Any limitations to rights are also stated here. For example, if the licensee is not allowed to further license the IP (referred to as sublicensing), this requirement is clearly stated. On the other hand, if sublicensing is allowed, then the terms of this stipulation must be clearly defined.

- The "territory" allowed for practice of the rights is defined. For example, if a licensee has a marketing presence in only one country, then the territories can be divided among several licensees. The Dyson case presented in Chapter 7 illustrates how breaking IP into territories can be used to bootstrap financing creatively. The company sold rights to regions where it had no presence in order to finance the home markets. Only later did Dyson repurchase these rights. If the IP covers several different applications, then an entrepreneur can license rights in market sectors where it does *not* intend to operate, using the proceeds to fund its core business.

- The level of exclusivity is defined. An exclusive license provides just one licensee the rights stated in the agreement. Of course, if there are licensees for different products, territories, or markets, each of these may or may not be exclusive. A nonexclusive license means that the licensor can enter into as many licenses as it wishes even if the rights are identical. For example, when you use Microsoft software, you are actually doing so under a license agreement. You do not expect this right to be exclusive, and Microsoft issues unlimited licenses to its products. It is also possible to offer limited exclusivity. For a small company, it is important to examine the advantages of these different strategies. Giving one large company exclusive rights to an important piece of intellectual property may give too much control to a powerful outsider. On the other hand, granting unlimited licenses provides little competitive advantage to any one licensee. This should be considered only if the license is to the ultimate "end user," as is the case for the Microsoft Office^{TM} suite of software. We usually recommend that a small company restrict the number of licenses it issues to two or three competitors. In this way, each has some advantages, yet not too much control is taken away from the entrepreneur.

- In exchange for gaining certain rights, the licensee pays fees to the licensor. These fees can be of several types. An *up-front* fee may be paid to initiate the contract. This fee can be very helpful to an early-stage company as a form of bootstrap funding. *Running royalties* are paid as a percentage of net sales of products or services. The percentage rate can range from 1 percent in the case of a simple product to 10 percent for a pharmaceutical formula once it has been approved for sale. *Advances* or *minimums* may be paid periodically to maintain the rights before royalty income is received. Minimums may prevent a licensee from just sitting on the rights and not trying to generate sales.

- Other terms include such items as term of the agreement; treatment of confidentiality; payment scheduling and licensor's ability to audit sales; treatment of breaches of contract; any warranties, liabilities, and indemnifications offered by either party; and other general legal requirements.

Licenses can be a key component of a business model. For example, an entrepreneur could license the rights to *market and sell* its products in certain markets while restricting any manufacturing. This strategy provides several benefits: the company needs less cash to develop its sales organization; partnering with a larger company can provide reputation and customer confidence, which is invaluable to an unknown company; and the income from the license can be used to fund other development activity. The Ultrafast case on the Web site associated with this book describes how a small company supplying the car industry used licensing of non-core products to develop foreign markets; gain reputation; and provide early-stage, nonequity financing.

At the other end of the spectrum, some companies base their business models entirely on licensing and have no intention of producing or selling any product. For example, Intertrust Inc. in California[9] owns thirty-seven patents with another one hundred filed worldwide in the field of digital rights management, or DRM. DRM is software that protects the copyrights of composers, writers, filmmakers, and software producers when the results of their efforts are transmitted electronically over the Internet. Intertrust recognized early on that this would be an important area for creating patents, which was borne out by the developments of such companies as Napster and the emergence of a number of high-profile lawsuits between copyright producers and users of their output. Intertrust's business model is to "stake out" the field by acquiring or developing a large portfolio of patents, then requiring purveyors of digital media to license these if they wish to continue to operate using technology and processes covered by the patents. License fees in this area can top $1 million up front, with continuing royalties based on sales.

Other companies use a business model in which more than just rights to IP are provided to their licensees. For example, Amberwave Inc.[10] in New Hampshire has developed a way of greatly improving the performance of the microprocessors found in every personal computer by modifying the properties of the basic silicon semiconductor "wafer" that are the foundation of most integrated circuits. Amberwave was started by Dr. Gene Fitzgerald, a professor at MIT. He undertook the original research there, and in fact, the company initially licensed technology *from* MIT before developing the concepts further. Amberwave now owns or has exclusive rights to more than one hundred patents issued or filed in the area of strained silicon. The company offers its licensees much more than just rights to these patents. Amberwave has invested heavily in developing the processes for using its IP, including building a complete semiconductor processing plant. This has created vast amounts of detailed know-how or trade secrets that would take any licensee many years and considerable investment to replicate. Amberwave, therefore, offers as part of its license agreements a program of "technology transfer" in which the licensee is taught the know-how existing within Amberwave and how to apply it to its own processes and products.

The Franchise Agreement and How to Use It

A franchise[11] is defined as a "legal and commercial relationship between the owner (franchisor) of a trademark, service mark, trade name, or advertising symbol and an individual or group (franchisee) wishing to use that identification in a business." In this case the franchisor is viewed as providing a "starting kit" for a new business, which enables the franchisee to create a new business with lower risk and costs than developing a business from scratch. Franchisors can grow their businesses into many locations without needing to raise the cash to do so, giving up total ownership of all the opportunity, while gaining some revenue in the form of fees to compensate giving up this upside. In exchange for lowering risk, the franchisee pays some profits to the franchisor but gains from national advertising, centralized product/service development, and reputation derived from a national or even an international reputation and image.

Probably the best-known franchise organization is McDonald's™. Each location is owned by a franchisee committed to funding the facility and start-up costs but benefiting from a large and powerful central resource and strong brand. The franchisor has strict requirements regarding menus, quality, training, hygiene, facility design, and the like because any single bad franchise can seriously damage the value of all other local franchise holders. Such items as opening hours may also be required but may be left to the local owner. However, there are many other franchised organizations, and you can see the enormous variety at such Web sites as www.franchiseworks.com, where many new franchise opportunities are offered.

An entrepreneur should not seek to be a franchisee or build a business as a franchisor without seeking competent legal advice. The field is littered with embittered partners, which can lead to expensive legal cases for resolution. These cases often arise because local conditions are highly diverse, whereas the franchise is based on creating uniformity across markets. Thus, a hairdressing franchisor may spend a lot on advertising the latest chic, short-haired styles from Europe, which may play well in New York or San Francisco but perhaps not so well in the Midwest. Sales may fall in one location and rise in another, leading to obvious concerns on fair use of fees. In contrast to licensing agreements, the federal government has issued regulations that require franchisors to prepare an extensive disclosure document called the Uniform Franchise Offering Circular (UFOC).[12] A copy of this document must be given to any prospective franchise purchaser before he or she buys a franchise. This law arose partly because of the concern that many potential franchisees did not understand the complexities and dangers of a franchise agreement, which ultimately led to legal wrangling and personal bankruptcies.

The franchise agreement allows a franchisee to participate in building a business together with other franchisees, under the rules stipulated by the franchisor and under certain conditions spelled out in the agreement. The agreement usually includes the following key topics:

- The franchisor and franchisee are defined together for the reason that they are entering into the agreement.
- The business of the franchise is stated, and the deliverables that the franchisor must provide to the franchisee are specified. These deliverables may vary considerably depending on the business type. They may include use of intellectual property,

trademarks and names, recipes, formulas, training and training manuals, design rules for facilities, promotional materials, operations manuals, forms of advertising, products or ingredients that must or may be bought from the franchisee, identification of a suitable site, and so on. It is important that these specifications be as complete as possible to avoid future disagreements. The limitations of the franchisee's business are defined. Usually this entails a location or region of activities. There may be "area development rights," which are optional rights to develop multiple individual franchises in a specific geographic area.

The limitations may also spell out precisely what the franchisee may offer to its customers. Significant problems may arise in this area. For example, a restaurant franchisor based in California may stipulate that only organic health products are used in the foods sold; a franchisee in West Texas may find little market for this locally and wish to add barbecued meat products to the menu. The franchisor will argue that this devalues the franchise for everyone else by diluting the brand message, whereas the franchisee will claim that she cannot prosper when there is little market for organic health foods locally.

- The franchisor may offer to fund part or all of the start-up costs. This may be an option or mandatory. Usually, the franchisee must show that it has access to a sufficient amount of cash to fund the start-up.

- The commitments of the franchisee are defined. Again these may be very broad and include such items as the minimum investment in the business, local advertising expenditures, meeting quality requirements, purchasing from approved suppliers, sharing new ideas with the franchisor, and using common software systems.

- In exchange for entering into the agreement and receiving support from the franchisor, the franchisee pays fees to the franchisor. These fees can be of several types. An *up-front* fee may be paid to initiate the contract. There is usually an advertising fee of up to 3 percent of net sales due to the franchisor and a royalty on net sales of several percent. The franchisee may also be obligated to purchase certain supplies from the franchisor or from "designated suppliers."

- There may also be items stating under what terms a franchisee can sell its business, including, for example, an option for the franchisor to purchase the business and make it a franchise-owned property. In this way, an entrepreneur can view franchising as an alternative route to building a large, wholly owned company using franchisees' funds for the growth phase. Franchisees may welcome this built-in exit strategy, giving them a fair return on their own investment and efforts.

- Other terms include such items as length of the agreement and conditions for renewal (the initial period agreed upon is typically around seven years), treatment of confidentiality, payment scheduling, and franchisor's ability to audit sales, treatment of breaches of contract, any warranties, liabilities and indemnifications offered by either party, and other general legal requirements, including a noncompete stipulation.

Unlike licensing, which is often only a small, if important, part of a business model, franchising is usually the core of a business model. However, even within the confines of a standard franchise agreement, entrepreneurs have managed to innovate powerful new business models.

Example: ChemStation's Franchise Model

George Homan founded ChemStation in 1983, after he had spent some years as a distributor of industrial cleaning chemicals.[13] His close contact to customers led him to recognize that businesses do not want to handle bulky containers of cleaning chemicals. George saw an opportunity to provide a better service by offering custom-formulated, environmentally friendly industrial cleaning and process chemicals delivered to proprietary refillable containers, which are placed free of charge at customer facilities. ChemStation has used a franchise business model to expand rapidly nationally without the need for the founding entrepreneur to raise any external capital. ChemStation has used its franchisee network very effectively to get tremendous reach within the U.S. market. The first franchise was given in 1985, and since then forty-eight franchises have been awarded. Today there are fifty units operating in the United States, of which only two are company owned. George's elegant business model is depicted in Figure 11-1.

The franchisor's headquarters are based in Ohio, which also serves some local customers and uses its buying power to purchase cleaning chemicals at a price lower than small competitors can get. The headquarters also holds the secure and coded database of proprietary cleaning formulas for specific customer needs, whether to clean egg-packing equipment or the floors of a car-assembly plant. A franchisee is granted a region to service and funds the local marketing, sales, and delivery services after paying an entry fee of about $1 million to ChemStation. In exchange, the franchisee gets access to the database on demand when a customer need is defined. This provides the formula for the optimum cleaner components and the usage instructions. In this way, the franchisee can provide customers with an immediate, proven solution to their cleaning problems.

In addition, if a major national company, for example, a rental car firm, would like every car to be cleaned the same way and have a distinctive, brand-building aroma, ChemStation can provide the formula to every franchisee for delivery to local offices. A small local firm is unable to guarantee this service. In the event

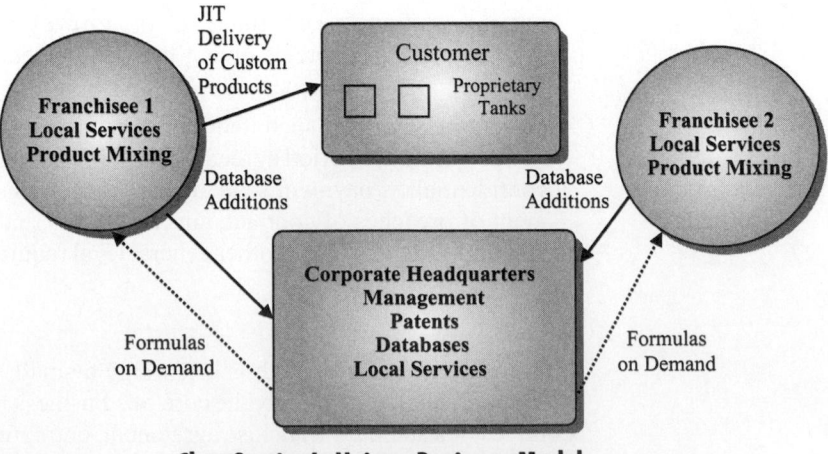

Figure 11-1   **ChemStation's Unique Business Model.**

that no solution for a customer's new problem can be found in the database and the franchisee develops the answer, then the franchise agreement commits them to submit the answer to the central database, where it becomes available to all franchisees and adds to ChemStation's intellectual assets. In this way, the franchise model is enhanced by the continual building of a proprietary database of customer solutions, adding greater value to both the franchisor and franchisees.

Whatever problems are solved at a franchisee's location are fed into the software package that has been devised by ChemStation, and the new solution becomes an integral part of the ChemStation database. The sharing of such information by the franchisees with headquarters is mandated by a written agreement between ChemStation and its franchisees. The database is a key asset for ChemStation, and it has the necessary software and framework in place to interpret the results and distribute the data. The database also builds barriers against competition. For example, ChemStation solved a cleaning problem at a Harley-Davidson plant within its shock absorbers manufacturing division, which resulted in using one cleaning solution on one line and another solution for the adjacent sister line. This subtle know-how becomes part of ChemStation's data bank. Such captured knowledge helps to lock in customers and prevents competitors from gaining the account. Since its founding, ChemStation has captured, in less than ten years, around 25 percent of the $300 million U.S. industrial cleaner market from local "mom 'n' pop" suppliers. It has done so by providing customized cleaning solutions in an innovative business model, which includes elements of franchising, data mining of customer information, and customer lock-in.

OUTSOURCING RESOURCES

Every company, large or small, is now contemplating "outsourcing" some or even most of its functions for several reasons.[14,15]

- The costs associated with certain activities are much lower in certain parts of the world than in others. This is particularly true for the manufacture of high-volume consumer products and garments; staffing of call centers; and more recently, software production.

- Certain functions may not be core to the business, and experts who focus on just one thing, say Web site design, can usually be more effective as a supplier to you than as an in-house employee, particularly if you need these resources for only a certain time.

- Some routine activities such as payroll management, Internet services, and health-care management need either large investments in hardware or very specialized databases. By outsourcing such functions, a company can gain from economies of scale without having to make a large investment. The third-party investment is spread over many customers.

- Small companies are always short of management time and skills. These should not be wasted on noncore functions.

- Knowledge is becoming more specialized. Even large companies cannot afford to have a deeply knowledgeable expert sitting around, waiting for the day that her know-how will be needed.

Start-up companies are strapped for resources. If there is someone who can do something better and faster than you can and it is not core to the company's business, then you should seriously consider outsourcing the work.

Outsourcing can be a viable option for many functions, such as payroll, accounting, manufacturing, delivery, customer service, employee training, property management, and computer services. The key advantage of outsourcing is that it enables you to invest your resources in more profitable activities. Companies, however, should be careful not to outsource functions that appear negligible but that are actually essential, such as customer service operations in a small business that wishes to build rapport with a loyal customer base.

Outsourcing functions range from use of individual specialist consultants and focused service providers to full manufacturing facilities and large software program developers. Small companies, in particular, are nearly always stretched for resources, and careful use of outsourcing should be part of their business models. Use the following checklist to test whether you should outsource a task:

- Is the activity central to the company's success? (For example, will you lose close contact with your customers, or will you not be able to control later versions of your products?)
- Can the outsourcing lead to a loss of intellectual property rights or leakage of valuable trade secrets to competitors or their suppliers? (For example, outsourcing the engineering of a piece of manufacturing equipment tailored to your proprietary products might leak to a competitor using the same engineering contractor, providing valuable knowledge about your business.)
- Is the task routine and wasteful of your staff's time? (For example, payroll tax calculations, payments of regular bills.)
- Is this a one-off or periodical need? (For example, building a stand for a trade fair or managing relationships with the media.)
- Is it less expensive to have an outsider do it rather than handling it in-house? (For example, writing routine software or staffing a call center.)
- Alternatively, will the task cost less in-house *but* use resources that are more valuable elsewhere? (For example, building ten extra prototypes of a new product for customer trials when you need your designers to work on the *next* product.)
- Is the skill so specialized that it's impractical to have a full-time employee provide the best input? (For example, you need to know how to do accelerated sunlight aging tests on a new fabric you plan to use in a planned range of women's coats. Don't balk at paying a high fee for the best consultant. One full day's briefing from an expert, even if it costs you $5,000, can save you many times that by avoiding mistakes.)

If none of these questions elicits concern, you should consider outsourcing the task. Here are some tips for finding and working with an external consultant or company.

- Ask around in your field for recommendations on good outsourcing firms or consultants. Search the Internet to expand the list. Ask the companies or consultants to give you references, and interview their clients to find out how reliable and flexible service providers are or how knowledgeable the expert consultants were. Unless the references are stellar, do not proceed. This is a case of "when in doubt, don't." A small company does not have the luxury of making a bad decision. You must feel entirely comfortable with the provider.

- Choose a company that understands *your* needs and can meet them. Devise a contract that allows you to adjust the terms of the agreement to suit unpredictable changes. An arrangement that's satisfactory now might not work in the future as your company expands or competition increases. For example, Intuitive Controls/ All TrafficSolutions, described in Chapter 2, outsourced all of its manufacturing for the first four years to another small firm that was very supportive, including being generous in delaying collection of payments when Intuitive Controls was short of cash. They provided supplier's funding. Now that sales are accelerating, Intuitive Controls is bringing its manufacturing in-house as it is generating sufficient cash to support these activities and the associated inventory. At the same time, their operating margins are increasing.

- Outsourcing implies loss of direct control and supervision, so communicate clearly the performance standards you expect. Record these standards in the contract in detail, include a "right to inspect" clause, and check up periodically to make sure your standards are being met.

- Schedule regular meetings with your staff member who is managing the outsourcing and discuss any day-to-day problems encountered. Staying abreast of what's going on will prevent potential problems from getting out of hand.

- Always make sure you have a backup in place in the event that the outsourcing company cannot complete its tasks. A call center, for example, should provide you with a regular electronic log of all calls; a manufacturer should provide a copy of drawings of any equipment made for your project, together with an operating manual, quality control procedures and data, and these should be kept in a secure location.

Example: Outsourcing Application Service Providers

Entrepreneurs can outsource critical software applications rather than deploy them in-house. Using an application service provider (ASP) to host an application can save time and money, especially if the business does not have the necessary technical expertise. An ASP is any company that remotely hosts a software application on a recurring-fee basis. ASPs are often able to provide entrepreneurs with software tools that are equal or even better than those that have been developed in-house by large corporations. ASPs provide a number of advantages:

- Applications can be up and running quickly with low up-front costs.
- Ongoing operational, maintenance, and continual product improvement headaches are removed from the company.
- Outsourcing frees capital and personnel resources that can be used for more important tasks.

For example, Schoolwires Inc.[16] hosts Internet portal software for school districts. This enables students, teachers, parents, and the community to interact on the Internet without the schools having to develop their own software or in-house skills for managing their Web sites. Schoolwires is an ASP serving the education sector. The company uses two sales channels for its products and services. It maintains a direct salesforce for certain regions as the company wishes to hear directly from customers about new features they are seeking. These ideas are vital to the company as it continually enhances its products. However, developing a national salesforce would be too costly for the company; therefore, it also works through resellers in many of its markets. Efficiently managing such a complex sales distribution network also requires specialist software. Therefore, Schoolwires itself purchases this function from another ASP, www.salesforce.com, preferring to devote its in-house computer experts to building its own proprietary software.

MODELS BUILT AROUND SOCIAL NETWORKS

The Internet has evolved to offering more than a static connection between a user and a Web site. So-called Web 2.0 [17] technologies have emerged that enable more complex and dynamic interactions. We have seen such companies as LinkedIn, Facebook, and MySpace grow rapidly as social networking portals that enable individuals to create and manage their own social networks. While these businesses are intriguing in themselves as an entirely new form of business, it is interesting to consider how such social networking concepts can be applied to entirely new businesses that do more than just manage personal networks. Here are some examples to stimulate your thoughts.

Threadless.com sells T-shirts that are designed by customers. The best design each month is chosen by the customers. Threadless does not produce products unless they are highly rated by customers. Thus the company gets free designs, free market research, and distribution via its popular Web site. Designers are willing to enter the competition as winning a Threadless competition comes with personal fame and peer recognition. Threadless makes money by selling award-winning clothes.

Syndicom.com, in contrast, builds extremely focused professional communities in the health-care industry. These communities consist of people who wish to help each other in their daily practice and to contribute to important innovations. The company's first community was for spine surgeons, and more than 70 percent of the U.S.-based surgeons have freely joined this online community. Syndicom makes money by providing major companies access to these highly specialized communities for tasks such as market research, clinical trials, and product innovations.

Go2Athlete.com, started by two Penn State students, builds and manages three converging networks surrounding college athletes—present and past athletes, college administrators, and potential recruiters. The company makes money in several ways by providing value to all three constituents and the advertisers who wish to reach a very targeted and potentially affluent customer group.

Other interesting examples emerge daily. For example, specialist social networks can be created to get input from your most important customers on new products and ideas. P&G created Vocalpoint[18] which is a network of mothers with young children that are themselves actively involved in talking to other mothers. By spreading the word about new products, providing reviews of planned products, and making suggestions, this community of "opted-in" mothers receives free samples and notices of new products in the pipeline. They can also share ideas and tips with other mothers. P&G realizes that engaging highly motivated and active mothers can increase the rate that new product sales grow by establishing a "buzz" around the product and spreading the news by word of mouth, so-called viral marketing. Think how you can build social networks into your business as a way of getting sales leads and new ideas for products or services from your customers.

CORPORATE PARTNERING

We briefly introduced the concept of small companies partnering with larger corporations in Chapter 8, where we focused primarily on corporate investing. However, there are many other forms of relationships that can exist between small and large companies that can be mutually beneficial.[19] As we saw in Chapter 1, we live in a global economy where changes occur rapidly, even in the most stable of industries. Often a small company may not have the resources or time to gain a share of a new market before its products, services, or even business models have become obsolete. Partnering with large companies may accelerate your growth. There are many different forms of corporate partnering. Here are some examples that illustrate the range of involvements that may occur.

- The large firm may make an investment in a smaller firm for reasons that are described in Chapter 8. For example NewsCorp made an investment in NewsStand,[20] which has developed novel ways of processing books and articles for publishing on the Internet. NewsCorp sees ways of both protecting the copyright of materials that it owns and creating new revenue streams by "slicing and dicing" content to provide greater value to customers.
- A large firm has both reputation and networks that it can employ to help a small company. In the NewsStand case, NewsCorp wants the company to be successful, so it is using its contacts to promote the company and its services. This is not a conflict as everyone benefits from the development of digital delivery of content.
- A large corporation can license rights to a small company's intellectual property. When the license aids rather than competes with the smaller company, multiple benefits accrue. The Ultrafast case on the book's Web site provides an excellent example to explore. A large licensee may also be effective in bringing in other licensees to expand the market further.
- Large companies have extensive sales networks that can be used by a smaller company, perhaps in regions where it would be too expensive to establish a salesforce. Chapter 12 returns to this topic with an example of a marketing agreement to penetrate the Canadian market in this way.
- Large companies may have a complementary product or service that can be sold alongside a small company's product for mutual benefit. For example, a company that is interested in selling industrial gases can benefit from selling an entrepreneur's proprietary equipment that would use its gases. This builds on existing customer relationships and reputation and deals with such issues as stability, safety, and quality control methods that are usually not developed in a small firm.

Despite the obvious benefits from partnerships between small innovative companies, and larger corporations that have resources, contacts, reputation, and other things, often the relationships can become tense as cultural issues become dominant.[21] The master-case has several examples of difficult relationships between Neoforma and the large health-care suppliers that saw the upstart initially as a threat before eventually buying the company at a much later stage.

SUMMARY

This chapter extends the ideas on innovation raised in Chapter 3. No longer is it sufficient to build a company around a single product or service; equal attention must be given to innovation of a business model that can capture and retain value against current and future competitors. We defined a business model and listed the five key components that it must support. Frameworks to stimulate business model innovations include capturing more value in the supply chain; using proprietary data; finding ways to lock in customers; and embodying licensing, franchising, and outsourcing as components when constructing a model. The Internet has created new ways of using virtual social networks as business models in their own right or, perhaps more sustainable in the longer term, embedding these networks within a more traditional framework. Corporate networks can also play a significant role in business model development in a wide range of ways.

STUDY QUESTIONS

1. What definition of *business model* do you find most useful and why? What are the four basic components of Dell's business model?

2. What are the five factors to consider when analyzing a business model?

3. Refer to the Greif case in Chapter 3. Why was Greif able to capture more of the value in the supply chain? Where did the extra value come from, and were there others who lost the value they were selling?

4. What is digital collaborative filtering? Name three companies that are successfully using this technique in their business models. Can you think of other businesses that might employ this technique in their business models? (*Hint:* Think of media companies and retail stores.)

5. What do you understand by the term *long-tail* as applied to markets? Give three examples of current businesses that exploit long-tails. Think of a new one that might be an opportunity for a new business.

6. What do you find most innovative about the DBI business model? Can you think of similar examples where these concepts might be used?

7. Name three similarities and three differences between a franchise and a license.

8. Name six factors that make outsourcing attractive.

9. List four types of corporate partnering with the advantages and potential disadvantages to both the large and small companies.

EXERCISES

1. Why do you think Dell was successful when other companies trying the same model failed?

2. Think of a possible idea for a franchise business model. You can search the Internet for ideas if you wish. In this case, would you rather be the franchisee or the franchisor? Why?

3. Think of an example where Internet social networking has enhanced an existing business. Propose a new business idea based on the concept of social networking by thinking of a unique network of people with a common interest that could be accessed and motivated somehow using the Internet. What would be the sources of revenue?

Master-Case Exercises: If you have not yet read the appendix in Chapter 1, do so. Then go to the book's Web site and read the diary entries Prequel, Months 11, 12,

25, 40, 42, 47, 49, 57, and Four Years Later and view the video selection, "Large Corporations. David vs. Goliath: Dealing with Big Corporations."

Either as a team or individually, produce a short presentation on each of these questions for discussion. Only one or two slides for each are required to state the key points.

Master-case Q 1: Why is it difficult for large companies to embrace change? Relate this to the reaction by the major companies to Neoforma's rise and the increasing power of the GPOs.

Master-case Q 2: If you were the founder of a small company, what procedures would you use to develop and manage partnerships with larger companies?

Management Case Study: DBI

Go back and read the profile of Neal DeAngelo, then watch the four video sequences of Neal DeAngelo on the book's Web site. Also visit the company's Web site. Consider the following questions:

1. Do you feel that Neal has a passion for what he and his brother are building? Are you willing to work as hard in the early years and take the personal risks?

2. DBI serves both private and government clients. In some cases customers are mandated by law to take the lowest bid. How does DBI manage this situation? What sort of relationships does DBI have with its customers? How do these relationships shape the company's business model?

3. DBI has grown rapidly and has several locations. Does Neal think about forming a unique culture for the company, and if so, how can this be accomplished? Do you think the company has a clear plan?

4. DBI is still owned by the DeAngelo family members. Is the company a lifestyle company? What specific issues does this private, family-owned structure raise with regard to financing growth, management succession, and eventual "cashing out" of the value that has been built?

5. Why does DBI outsource some research tasks to universities? What are the dangers in doing so?

Management Case Study: Ultrafast

We have created a case study for this chapter on the book's Web site. It concerns a company started and grown by an entrepreneur after recognizing a point of pain when working for a larger company. The founder used licensing and government grants to bootstrap the company, retaining control before the company actually went bankrupt—however, not before building a complete manufacturing plant to supply the car industry. We chose this case because failures often provide insights that are not seen in stories of success. Go to the book's Web site at www.wiley.com/college/kaplan and watch the video sequence on the Ultrafast case related by one of the authors.

1. Describe how the company used licensing to accelerate its development. What advantages and disadvantages did this strategy have for the company in the short and long terms and for the tool licensees, Bosch and Atlas Copco?

2. Draw a diagram of all different types of companies in the supply chain that Ultrafast found itself, including bolt manufacturers, suppliers of automatic assembly equipment, hand tools used in repair workshops, companies that chemically treat car components, and the car manufacturers themselves. How do these relate to each other? What value did each of these supply to their customers *before* Ultrafast came on the scene? How is the value distribution changed when the Ultrafast method is proven and enters the market? Which companies can gain most from Ultrafast, and which can suffer? Is the business model followed by the company the best one for capturing the value from the invention?

3. Using licenses and government grants to bootstrap the company, the founding entrepreneur managed to retain full control of the company right to the end. Was this ultimately the best thing for him or the company? If not, why not? What lessons on ownership and personal ambitions can you gain from this example?

4. Imagine that you had started this company. What would you have done differently?

INTERACTIVE LEARNING ON THE WEB

Test your knowledge of the chapter using the book's interactive Web site.

ADDITIONAL RESOURCES

The Licensing Executives Society is a professional organization for those practicing licensing and technology transfer. Their Web site (www.usa-canada.les.org) provides information about licensing and has many links to other sites of interest on this topic.

For access to articles and advice on franchising, visit www.franchisefoundations.com. Although this is a commercial site offering consulting advice to potential franchisors and franchisees, there are excellent references and links to a number of valuable articles and learning tools.

To access a variety of articles and cases on building organizational culture, refer to www.business.com/directory/management/organization_development/corporate_culture.

www.wiley.com/college/kaplan

ROADMAP for

PATTERNS OF ENTREPRENEURSHIP
Implementation

- ☐ The Value of Trademarks
- ☐ The Value of Copyrights
- ☐ The Value of Patents
- ☐ How to Protect Intellectual Property
- ☐ Getting Started with the Patent Idea
- ☐ What Is Prior Art?
- ☐ Using Search Options
- ☐ Progress from Idea to Patent to Enterprise
- ☐ The Value of Trade Secrets
- ☐ Reverse Engineering
- ☐ Definition of Business Models
- ☐ Capturing Value in the Supply Chain
- ☐ Using Databases to Create Value
- ☐ Locking in Customers
- ☐ Licensing and Franchising
- ☐ Outsourcing Resources
- ☐ Models Built around Social Networks
- ☐ Corporate Partnering
- ☑ Developing a Strong Corporate Culture
- ☑ Finding and Hiring the Best People
- ☑ Dealing with Firing an Employee
- ☑ Dealing with a Resignation
- ☑ Conflicts of Interest and Business Ethics
- ☑ Legal Issues
- ☑ Setting up Stock Option Agreements

CHAPTER 12

MANAGING THE TEAM

"It appears to me that almost any man may, like the spider, spin from his own inwards his own airy citadel."

JOHN KEATS

OBJECTIVES

- Understand the importance of managing the team every day.
- Learn how to build a strong creative culture.
- Learn how to hire and fire employees.
- Know how to deal with a resignation.
- Create frameworks for dealing with ethical conflicts.
- Learn basic legal requirements.

CHAPTER OUTLINE

Introduction

Profile: Paul Silvis—Building an Embracing Culture

Developing a Strong Corporate Culture

Finding and Hiring the Best People

Dealing with Firing an Employee

Dealing with a Resignation

Conflicts of Interest and Business Ethics

Legal Issues

Setting up Stock-Option Agreements

Summary

Study Questions

Exercises

Interactive Learning on the Web

Appendix: Legal Document Templates

INTRODUCTION

We started this book by emphasizing the importance of learning management skills to become a successful entrepreneur. One of the greatest challenges entrepreneurs face is the day-to-day management of human resources. A young company is not a set of independent activities, such as marketing and sales, money management, or product development, but a complex and changing interplay among all functions made more complicated by the individual aspirations and behaviors of creative, high-energy employees. The company is more like a fragile spider's web than a solid building supported on individual pillars. This chapter details how to manage, on a daily basis, the ever-changing and unpredictable events met when hiring and motivating employees. Of course, we cannot foresee all the challenges that one might encounter, but by introducing some key concepts and tools, illustrated with examples, entrepreneurs can gain confidence to guide a team through the inevitable stormy seas.

Often an entrepreneur will feel overwhelmed by the seemingly unending and unpredictable problems he must face. But these must be tackled and the sooner, the better. Letting things slide by hiding will only make things worse. Prioritize them and deal with them promptly, seeking help from mentors if necessary. The stress to manage the business every day will be reduced by creating a supporting culture and employee expectations that in many cases will actually deflect problems before they develop. One of the most important leadership tasks, therefore, is to create an organization in which everyone understands the core values that underpin decision making in the organization.

PROFILE: PAUL SILVIS — BUILDING AN EMBRACING CULTURE[1]

Before founding Restek in 1985, Paul Silvis worked at Supelco, Inc., as supervisor of the capillary research group and for the federal government's Mining and Safety Enforcement Agency. He received a B.S. in chemistry/life science from the University of Pittsburgh in 1977 and later took chemical engineering courses at Penn State. Not satisfied with just working for a company, Paul decided that he had some ideas for a new business. He took the plunge in 1985 and started Restek Corporation in State College, Pennsylvania. At the outset, Paul had a modest target of reaching $3 million in sales in five years. However, the company continually innovated new products and was able to finance its growth from the retained funds from sales of products. During this time, Paul kept control of the company as he wanted to grow a "family" and not just personal wealth. Restek (www.restek.com) is now a leading manufacturer of chromatography laboratory supplies with annual sales of greater than $40 million and offices and distribution centers in more than sixty countries.

Paul's title, head coach (rather than president or CEO), reflects his leadership philosophy. "The head coach puts the right players in the right positions; provides training, tools, and opportunities for them to become star players; encourages an atmosphere of support and honesty; helps to define the team's strategy for winning— all for the sake of creating a championship team of which each member can be proud!"

Restek has grown every year since its formation and has always been profitable. It has been ranked among the top fifteen companies in the United States to work for by the *Wall Street Journal*. Paul sends clear messages to his top managers regarding hiring and firing which is consensus driven. "Hire the best, even if you have to pay them more than yourself. Intensively mentor new hires to assimilate them into the culture. Always give someone help to improve their performance before firing them—give them a chance, help them if they have to leave, and make sure everyone's self-esteem is preserved. Celebrate when you lose someone that you want to retain and tell them that they will always be welcome back." These clear statements from the top of the organization have enabled Restek to establish an embracing culture in which everyone pulls together, works hard, and is ready to give that little extra when the inevitable problems arise. Paul has elected to sell the company to the employees using an ESOP (see Chapter 14) in order to preserve this unique culture and not have it threatened by being acquired by a larger company. Paul uses the sports metaphor often: "Embracing problems and overcoming insurmountable obstacles is the key to any successful venture. Envision 'problems' like a track and field event, in which the relay team that jumps hurdles faster than the competitor wins the race. It is not the number or magnitude of the problems you have, but how fast you can jump over them and embrace the next one that wins the race."

DEVELOPING A STRONG CORPORATE CULTURE

A successful entrepreneur must demonstrate strong leadership skills and the ability to engage everyone in pulling together toward a single defined goal. As we have seen, innovation, not only in products and services, but also in the all-encompassing business model, is an important factor for success. Companies with seemingly identical financial assets, products, brand recognition, and the like may perform entirely differently—one is highly successful; the other gradually declines. The successful one is judged as innovative, motivating, and exciting; the other, dull and unable to get its innovative ideas executed smoothly. Why is this? Michael Dell was not the first person to experiment with the direct model for computers. Why did he succeed where others failed for more than twenty years? The ability to lead an organization on a mission where everyone is involved every day in moving toward clearly defined goals makes the difference between success and failure.

ROADMAP

IN ACTION

Two companies competing in the same markets with the same resources may have very different success rates. Learn how to develop a corporate culture to provide the key advantage.

Much research has been done in this area, and many business books have been written about the field. On one point at least there seems to be consensus. A culture supporting innovation requires leadership from the very top of an enterprise. It is never too early to start, and this section will provide guidance in shaping a winning culture for the company. Getting it right from the start is *much* easier than trying to change an old, unsuitable, and deeply embedded culture.

We have narrowed the leadership attributes down to ten factors, which should be practiced and demonstrated *in nearly everything that is done.* We have tried to make these factors largely independent of each other so areas can be identified to improve a management style without concerns that changes in one area will create other problems.

Table 12-1 provides definitions of these ten cultural attributes,[2] together with illustrative statements that might be casually overheard within a company. We suggest that you review these factors and ask yourself whether your leadership style exhibits these attributes. Imagine what you might hear if you could be a fly on the wall in the offices of a company you are leading. If you cannot imagine hearing these statements, start modifying your behavior and adopt a leadership style in which such factors would become more evident. This will help you build a flexible, innovative organization where everyone is valued and willing to contribute their utmost efforts daily.

It is easy to imagine successful entrepreneurs encouraging these behaviors. When you next see or read an interview with a successful entrepreneur, you will not

Table 12-1   Cultural Attributes of a Successful Innovative Company

Attribute	Definition	Example Statements
Honesty	The degree to which each employee has total confidence in the integrity, ability, good character of others, and the organization, regardless of role	"I trust the people I work with. I find it easy to be open and honest with people from other departments."
Alignment	The degree to which the interests and actions of each employee support the clearly stated and communicated key goals of the organization	"We have clear aims and objectives, which everyone understands. We build consensus around key objectives. We recognize and reward loyalty."
Risk	The degree to which the organization, employees, and managers take risks	"I am encouraged to experiment. We take calculated risks. We encourage trial and error."
Teams	The degree to which team performance is emphasized over individual performance	"We promote teamwork; it is the center of everything that we do. There are usually people from other departments in my team. We have both problem-solvers and 'out of the box' thinkers in our teams."
Empowerment	The degree to which each employee feels empowered by managers and the organization	"As a manager, I am expected to delegate. We have a 'no blame' culture. We allow staff to make decisions."
Freedom	The degree to which self-initiated and unofficial activities are tolerated and approved throughout the organization	"I am allowed to do my own thing. We encourage people to take initiative. We recognize the individual."
Support	The degree to which new ideas from all sources are welcomed and responded to promptly and appropriately	"We encourage fresh ideas and new approaches. We reward innovative individuals and teams."
Engagement	The degree to which all levels of the organization are engaged with the customer and the operations of the organization	"Management understands the operations of the company. I can share problems with my managers. I know why my job is important."
Stimuli	The degree to which it is understood that unrelated knowledge can impact product, service, and operations improvements	"I am encouraged to search externally for information and obtain data from many sources. We listen to suppliers' suggestions."
Communication	The degree to which there is both planned and random interaction between functions and divisions at all levels of the organization	"I am kept in the loop about how we are performing. We have excellent formal channels of communication. We use best practice knowledge transfer between departments. We actively manage our intellectual assets."

find it difficult to imagine how she would have run her own organization along the lines of these attributes.

We now turn to three key functions of a founding entrepreneur: hiring, firing, and dealing with employee resignations. The way that you carry out these vital tasks will clearly demonstrate to the world what your personal and, hence, corporate values are.

FINDING AND HIRING THE BEST PEOPLE

It is easier to build an exciting, trusting, and supportive corporate culture if the people you hire have personal values that match. In a small company, one bad hire can do a lot of damage quickly. There is no room for misfits, so the hiring practices need to be excellent. Here are some guidelines that will help you in this important task:

- *Searching:* Look for people in places where you might expect their personal values to match the company's culture. Personal networks and recommendations are best. However, be careful when bringing friends into the company. Of course, you are more likely to know their values and skills, but the personal relationship may cloud your judgment, send the wrong messages to the company, and if things don't work out, you will have a tough decision to make. For very key positions, it may pay to use a professional recruiter. These tend to be expensive, but remember, a bad hire can be fatal. If you advertise, choose the appropriate medium and make sure the copy clearly reflects the values of the company. Don't have a stodgy ad if you are seeking creative people who are interested in a real challenge. For example, here is an ad that Neoforma might have placed to attract two key hires:

NEOFORMA, INC.

You've heard the buzz; now join an exciting, energetic company that is changing the way that lives are saved.

We are seeking ambitious self-starters to join our management team as we move into the next phase of our rapid growth. If you have strong leadership skills, are not afraid of hard work, and enjoy intense teamwork, then we may be the place to save you from boredom.

Specifically we are looking for:

Sales Leader: Someone who can establish high-level relationships with the top suppliers and purchasers in the health-care industry and convince them that the Neoforma Web-based marketplace is *the* future in health-care supply chains. You must be passionate about improving access to affordable health care anywhere in the world and believe that the latest technology is the means to achieve this. Ability to succeed in adverse situations, create your own opportunities, and earn the respect of your fellows in more important than direct experience in the health sector—*if* you are a quick learner.

Operations Leader: Neoforma is one of the fastest-growing companies in the Valley. Our management structure and organization is always trying to keep up with our unbounded acceleration. If you think you can grab a raging bull by the horns and tame it into a behaved beast, you may be the person to manage the company to its next platform of success and beyond. The ability to work

NEOFORMA, INC. (cont.)

with some of the most creative and passionate folks on earth, providing them the infrastructure that supports, not hinders, them in their quest for the best is more important than being a number-cruncher or form-filler. Show us how you can achieve the impossible and join us on the ride to fame and, yes, fortune.

These positions are not for the faint-hearted. There are generous benefits for those who can stand above the rest, including a stock-option pool, free health care, and much more.

Neoforma is a privately held Internet marketplace that removes the inefficiencies from the health-care supply chain to bring quality and affordable health care to everyone. We are partnered with several major companies and funded by the best of Silicon Valley's VC firms.

For more information, call Wayne or Jeff at 1-800-NEOFORMA anytime.

- Once you have a short list, you will need to interview the candidates. Do not treat this lightly; it is a difficult skill that will take time to learn. Hire for cultural fit if the other skills are good. Err toward culture if in doubt. Skills can largely be trained; values cannot. If in doubt, don't hire even if under pressure to fill a position. Table 12-1 provides a useful guide to the interview process.

You will probably need a second interview with someone you would like to make an offer to. A more relaxed environment, say over dinner, may be more appropriate. Ask for and check references. Then reach a decision as quickly as possible and make an offer. In a small company that is usually short of cash, it is customary to keep salaries as low as possible and enroll key employees in a stock-option program. (See the legal section of this chapter for further details.) Options provide the owner the right to purchase stock at an agreed-on price, usually current or even below current price, over some future time period, typically ten years. Any appreciation of the value of the company allows the option owners to exercise their rights and buy stock at a low price and sell it to a buyer at a much higher price. The company often retains the right to be first in line to buy these shares. Stock options then allow an employee to become a shareholder in the company over time. Indeed investors usually welcome these programs, allotting a certain amount of shares to be in the "option pool" for motivating and retaining key people. These plans, if managed correctly, can be an excellent way of building a strong culture and team values. Typically the pool will be between ten and twenty percent of the total equity of the company. New hires do not get all of their options at once, but earn them over a vesting period, say three years, based on their performance. They may get some options issued as a joining bonus, but these can be taken back if they are fired within a certain time for nonperformance or real cause. In addition, certain positions, such as sales manager, may have part of the compensation based on measurable performance.

- Once you have reached an agreement on compensation and role, you will execute the appropriate legal documents (see this chapter's section on legal issues) and set up a starting date.

- Mentoring and assimilation into the culture is an important part of the hiring process. On the first day, make sure you take the time to introduce the new person to everyone and put a plan in place to train and support the new hire. Over the first few months, it is a good idea to set up a regular time each week, even if for

Table 12-2   **Interview Guide**

Establish culture	The way you interview reflects on the culture of your company.
Have a two-way dialogue	Taking a new position is just as important a decision to the interviewee as to you. Create a level playing field.
Be punctual	Stop whatever you are doing at least fifteen minutes before the scheduled time, review the applicant's background, and think through carefully what you are looking for and how you are going to learn about the fit. Be overly prepared. It is an insult to an applicant if you are late and you have not read their résumé and background.
Be prepared	If more than one person is going to interview the applicant, say you and your partner, then agree beforehand on the areas that each of you are going to explore. It is insulting to be asked the same questions twice and indicates poor internal communications.
Relax	Start the interview by talking about the company, your background, and what excites you about being there. This allows the interviewees to relax, so they can more easily open up later in the discussions.
Invite input	Ask them to tell you a little about themselves and what attracts them to the position. If they know little about the company and have done no research, it is a bad sign. A great candidate should tell you something about your company, markets, competitors, and/or trends that is new to you.
Explore values	Most candidates rehearse standard questions such as "Tell me about something in your past work that you are really proud of." This will allow them to be expansive. Follow this up with a question such as "And what are you are less proud of, what did you learn from it, and what would you do this time around?" Such questions highlight personal values (do they blame others, do they think they are perfect, etc.). Other pairs of such questions are: "What do you most like doing when at work, and what do you least like doing?" "If you go home at the end of the day feeling on top of the world, what might have happened, and if you feel really down at the end of the day. . .?"
Explore creativity	Pose a real challenge you are confronting. How they would tackle it?
Explore ambitions	Where do you see yourself in three years?" "Would you like my job?" You should be hiring to grow, and you need to delegate.
Now ask me	Prompt their questions. These will be rehearsed, so use them to probe. "How many weeks' vacation?" or "What is the pay?" may indicate misaligned values for a small company.
Summarize	Be clear at the end of the interview what the process is and how quickly you will get back to them with an indication of the next steps.
Record	Write your notes on the meeting immediately after the interview, and compare these as soon as possible with the other interviewers.
Act	If turning someone down, do it quickly, be honest, and preserve their self-esteem; create ambassadors, not enemies.

only fifteen minutes, to review progress and to deal with any misunderstandings or emergent problems.

DEALING WITH FIRING AN EMPLOYEE

Unfortunately, it is highly likely that you will have to terminate the employment of one or possibly several employees as the company evolves. The reasons for this decision fall into the categories described in Table 12-3.

Table 12-3   **Reasons for Terminating an Employee**

Funding shortage	The business is suffering a downturn and you do not have sufficient funds to pay all salaries. This could be from failure to raise sufficient funding using the various sources described in Chapters 7 and 8, a loss of a major customer, a costly lawsuit, the emergence of a strong competitor putting pressure on prices, and so on. You have to trim down your payroll to match the lower income or cash reserves.
Change of direction	The company needs new skills and experience as it matures. Some of the early-stage employees are no longer needed and are to be replaced by new hires.
Performance	The employee is not performing adequately and needs to be replaced.
Disruptive	The employee is disruptive and possibly untrustworthy.
Cause	The employee has broken a contract or behaved illegally in some way.

All good companies mishire; all great companies correct their mistakes quickly. The way that someone is terminated is a strong indicator of the company's culture. Not taking appropriate action promptly is bad for the company *and* the employee. In all cases terminating the employment of someone you have hired is one of the most difficult tasks for any manager. According to Paul Silvis of Restek Inc.,[3] "The day that you enjoy firing someone is the day you should leave the company." Here are some guidelines to help with this task:

- Implement a system for catching problems early and working with the employee to correct them. If possible, it is better to help someone perform better, perhaps in a different role, than to have him leave and risk hiring an inappropriate new person. Give feedback early; provide timelines for improvement and keep to them. But when it is clear that it is not going to work out, make the decision to end the relationship.

- In all circumstances it is vital that employees retain their self-esteem. Give the reasons for the decision, and provide guidance and help if possible. If the company can afford it, be generous in benefits to soften the financial impact on the employee.

- Do not allow anyone you have decided to fire to remain on the company's premises. Make the break clean. Make a final payment contingent on the former employee not causing any disruption or maligning the company to third parties.

- Remind the employee of her continuing contractual obligations to the company regarding the protection of confidential information. If a noncompete contract is in place, agree on the companies, customers, and/or others to which it applies. Do not be overrestrictive.

- Keep discussions professional and try to maintain a level of trust between you. Remember, it is to the company's benefit too if the former employees believe they were treated fairly and with respect. It is best if they tell others that the company has great values and that any grudge that may be there dissipates quickly.

DEALING WITH A RESIGNATION

An entrepreneur will likely have to deal with a situation in which one of the most important employees decides to leave and join another company. First try to convince her to stay, but do not enter into a bidding war with the new company regarding compensation. There may be some small adjustments that can be made, but being held hostage will lead to many problems later. Once it is clear that the employee cannot be convinced to stay, follow the steps outlined in Table 12-4, trying to make the process as open and as painless as possible for everyone involved.

Table 12-4   **Handling a Resignation**

Agree on procedures	If there is a notice period, then insist that this is respected and do not pay any outstanding benefits if it is not met.
Keep door open	If the company would really like the employee to come back if things do not work out, then make this clear. Do not let a feeling of betrayal prevent rational thinking.
Celebrate	Have an office party to celebrate moving on and treat her like a star.
Conduct exit interview	Learn why he made the decision. Ask for honest feedback. Take this opportunity to explain ongoing legal obligations with regard to confidential information and any noncompete conditions. Ask the employee where he is going. If he declines to tell, indicate that he should inform his new employer of these obligations. If he does disclose this information, write to the new company, complementing them on a good hire and stating the ongoing constraints that apply to the move.
Analyze	What triggered the move? A good leader knows if someone is unhappy *before* he starts looking around.

ROADMAP
IN ACTION

Understand how to analyze conflicts of interest and ethical dilemmas and deal with them clearly and fairly.

CONFLICTS OF INTEREST AND BUSINESS ETHICS

We all find it difficult sometimes to know what is right and wrong, particularly when the boundaries are not clearly drawn and the situation is complex and perhaps ambiguous. There seems to be a gray area where we can tread a path that allows us to "have it both ways." These situations abound in the business world, and it is important for you to have some guidelines that help you analyze such issues so they do not get out of control and begin to undermine your personal values and the culture of the company that you are building. Let us consider a case that could relate directly to this course.

Mini-case: Teachers Helping Students outside of Class[4]

In your entrepreneurship class, you and two team members come up with a great idea for a new business. In fact, the whole class and your professor urge you not to wait but to start a company and work on its development while still at college. You really value the experience of your teacher so you approach her and ask whether she would act as a mentor. Of course, you have no money to pay her, so you decide to offer five percent of the equity of the company to pay for the extra time that you are demanding. Should she accept this offer? Before jumping to a conclusion, consider some of the issues involved here:

- She is already being compensated by the college for performing her duties as a teacher of entrepreneurship.
- At the end of the course, she is required to give you a grade for your work. Will a deeper involvement in your project bias her in this regard?
- Will the extra work that she undertakes to help your team take away from efforts that should be devoted to other class members who are entitled to equal attention?
- Does it make a difference if only two of the three team members want to participate in the new company? How would you handle this?
- What policies are in place at the college to govern such issues? For example, it is common for professors to agree in their employment contract that any invention that they make while in employment will be the property of the college. What if she invents something valuable while in the role of company mentor? Who owns it? Some colleges allow professors to consult for up to one day a week for extra compensation. Would this case come under this arrangement? Does it make a difference if the class has ended and grades have been submitted, or must the students in the team have graduated fully from college?

As you see, the picture is rather more complicated than it first appears. There are a number of conflicts of interest between different groups of stakeholders—those with some interest in any decision that is made. These include teammates, classmates, the college, and individual teachers. There may be contractual agreements in place, and college policies that must be taken into account. For example, professors at Columbia University may be compensated to help students in company formation once course grades are entered, whereas at Penn State, the students must have graduated from the university.

Let us now take this a step further. As before, you have decided with your teammates to actually form a company to take your class idea further and you indicate this to your teacher. She then asks to see you after class and indicates that she can help you but only if you are willing to allot 10 percent of the shares of the company to her. You would certainly value the input, and you are worried that if you refuse, then this might adversely affect your grade. How do you respond?

The case has taken on a rather more serious tone. Whereas before you have to decide how to avoid conflicts of interest, now you are faced with an ethical issue in addition. You have the gut feeling that this is not appropriate, but you are caught in a dilemma. If you flatly turn down the offer, then you may suffer repercussions; if you accept, then you may be breaking rules and even existing contracts. You like the teacher, and feel that she, herself, may not be aware of all the issues that come into play in this situation.

This is the time to invoke the "full disclosure" principle.[5] If you sense that everything is not in order, then you must disclose it fully and honestly to *all* the key stakeholders and ask for their comments. Failure to fully disclose makes you a party to unethical behavior. So in this case, you could raise your concerns with the teacher and ask her for the mechanisms for full disclosure of the situation. If she understands the issues, she is likely to withdraw her offer and help you anyway. If not, she can take it to the appropriate authority in your college, perhaps the dean, who will clarify the situation and make sure that the conflicts of interest are resolved.

The Three Principles to Resolve Ethical Dilemmas

1. **The Gut-feel Test.** We all know the feeling when we sense something is wrong about an action. If you get this feeling, then most likely there is something amiss. Don't ignore it; stop and consider the issues surrounding the problem. Ask yourself, "If one of the stakeholders finds out later what happened, could this be embarrassing or worse, create serious problems, even legal repercussions?"

2. **Analysis of Conflicts.** As we saw in the case above, things are not quite as they seem at first blush. There can be multiple levels of interests from a range of stakeholders. You must find out who they are, what their interests are, how they are governed, what rules apply, and what contracts may be in place. Only when you have these data can you actually draw out the lines between the stakeholders and expose all the real or potential conflicts of interests.

3. **Full Disclosure.** Once you understand the complexities of the conflicts of interest together with the ethical and legal issues, you will be able to determine who you should inform about the situation and its potential outcomes. This is called full disclosure. You should not edit or color your disclosures; overdisclosing is far better than restricting information. Let the interested recipients tell you what the problems might be.

With these three principles, you will find it easier to spot and resolve ethical issues quickly.

LEGAL ISSUES

Unfortunately, you will not be able to grow your company without dealing with some basic legal issues. Indeed, failure to manage the legal affairs of your company can result in serious consequences. In Chapter 6 we dealt with the formation of the company and in Chapter 10 you learned about the management of your intellectual property; here we address the day-to-day management of your legal affairs. You should incorporate these procedures from the first day. Correcting mistakes after they occur may be costly or even impossible. We provide templates for legal documents in the appendix to this chapter. (In each case, NUCO is the name used for the issuing company.) These will enable you to become acquainted with the way that these documents are framed. However, you should always check with the company's legal counsel before issuing and signing anything. Laws and their interpretations change over time and will certainly differ depending on location. Here we describe the basic legal documents that you will require for any company.

- **Employment Agreement.** It is important to establish employment agreements for your management team and key employees in the company. The agreement describes the obligations of the employer and employee and varies widely among companies and even among employees within the same company. Usual provisions included in the agreement should emphasize the following employee issues[6]:

  – They cannot disclose any confidential information about the company either during or subsequent to employment.

  – They must return all materials that belong to the company at the time of termination of employment.

  – They cannot engage in a new business during the period of employment without the consent of the employer.

  – They will not compete with the company for a period of time subsequent to employment.

  – They will disclose and assign to the company all inventions during their employment.

ROADMAP

IN ACTION

The best employment agreement serves as an incentive for the employee and provides protection against the employee damaging the company subsequent to employment. The incentives may include stock options, payments for inventions, or bonuses.

Employment agreements can present an element of coercion. The employee may assume that because he is given the agreement for signature, the employee has little choice but to sign it or seek employment elsewhere. If the employer tries to enforce an agreement, the sympathies of the court usually lie with the employee. Seldom will a court enforce an employment agreement if it deprives the ex-employee of the means of making a living. For these reasons, employment agreements should be drafted, read, and agreed to prior to actual employment.

- **Consulting Agreement.** You are likely to use consultants for certain tasks as you build the company. These should be subject to a work-for-hire agreement. Without such an agreement, the work that the consultant does would become their property. For example, you might be paying for someone to design a Web site. Without such an agreement, they would own the site and its content.

- **Separation Agreement.** It is important when someone leaves the company, voluntarily or otherwise, that the conditions and expectations of their leaving are clearly laid out and understood. These agreements usually contain a "general release" protecting your company against later legal actions.

- **Sales and Marketing Agreement.** A growing company may not have the resources to reach all markets simultaneously, and entering into an agreement with a marketing partner is a common alternative. It is important to specify the responsibilities of both parties. The example we provide relates to a U.S. firm partnering with a Canadian company.

- **Confidentiality Agreement.** You will need to enter into exploratory discussions with third parties before any definitive agreement is made. To protect the disclosures that you make, you must execute this agreement. These can be one-way or perhaps two-way agreements if there is a need for both parties to protect against disclosure of confidential information.[7]

SETTING UP STOCK-OPTION AGREEMENTS

Many young companies provide added incentives for keeping key employees by providing an ownership or equity interest in the company. This is usually in the form of common stock or options to acquire common stock. Companies should consider establishing an incentive stock option plan under which selected employees receive options to purchase stock in the company. Incentive stock options are restricted to employees and are not available to others. The incentive stock option and nonqualified stock option are used in the following manners.

1. **Incentive stock option (ISO)** is a type of stock that qualifies for preferential tax treatment provided that the option holder holds the stock for one year and one day after exercise and two years after the date of any renewal, whichever is later. Under current tax laws, the employee pays no taxes at exercise and will be subject to capital gains tax if the holding requirements are met. Exercise of ISOs may subject the employee to alternative minimum tax (AMT). The company does not receive a tax deduction for this form of compensation. Incentive stock options are for the holder only and cannot be transferred.[8]

2. **Nonqualified stock option (NQSO)** is an option that does not receive preferential tax treatment and is considered the equivalent of cash compensation. The option holders pay payroll and income taxes at the time of exercise and, if they hold on to the stock, are subject to capital gains treatment when the stock is sold. The company takes a tax deduction on the difference between the grant price and the fair market value upon exercise.[9]

Any plan must be adopted by the board of directors and approved by the stockholders of the company and can be effective from the next annual shareholders' meeting or within twelve months.

The plan must state the aggregate number of shares being set aside for the options and the employees or class of employees (e.g., "key employees") for which options will be made available. The option cannot be transferable.[10] When setting up a plan, you should consult with an expert in the field as there are complex legal and tax issues to consider.[11,12]

SUMMARY

A company is not an assembly of individual functions, such as marketing or human resources, to which you can turn your attention when needed, but a complex and ever-changing interplay between many activities that continually combine in new ways. Just as a conductor guides an orchestra through a symphony, an entrepreneur must lead and impose personal values on the organization every day. In this way, a collective culture can be created, one which is able to deal with adversity and respond to new opportunities without the need for micromanagement.

Guidelines and procedures for hiring, firing, and dealing with conflicts of interest and ethical transgressions all help to build and sustain such a culture. These must be underpinned with a basic set of legal documents and contracts that provide a firm foundation on which to build. Without these basic structures in place, it is too easy for things to get out of control and overly stressful, leading to chaos.

STUDY QUESTIONS

1. Why is building a corporate culture to match a company's mission important?
2. Name three important factors that you must take into account when hiring key people.
3. Name three important factors that you must take into account when firing key people.
4. How do you treat someone who resigns from the company?
5. What are the three principles for resolving conflicts of interest and ethical problems?
6. What are the five basic legal agreements needed for day-to-day management? What are the key features of each?
7. What is a qualified stock-option plan, and what is its purpose?

EXERCISES

Master-case Exercises

Corporate Culture If you have not yet read the appendix in Chapter 1, do so. Then go to the book's Web site and read the diary entries Months 4, 27, 29, 31, 37, 39, 40, 50, and 52 and view the video selection, "Culture: Invisible, Intangible, Important."

Either as a team or individually, produce presentations to address the following questions for class discussion (refer to Table 12-1 as needed).

Master-case Q 1: How do you maintain a vibrant and successful culture as the company grows rapidly and the founders have no time to engender new employees with the value systems that they consider important. Consider the following attributes often referred to by the managers in Neoforma: honesty, freedom, and empowerment. Which attributes were most prevalent earlier in the company, and which became important later?

Master-case Q 2: A great corporate culture seems to just happen; forcing it is counterproductive. How was the unique culture of Neoforma developed? Despite coming under stress due to fast growth and mistakes in hiring, it seemed to survive and be almost indestructible. Why do you think this is? What other culture threats can you name? Put them in the order of most potential culture damage, and argue why you chose this order. If you were a manager, what would you do to embed a great culture and mitigate against its erosion?

Master-case Q 3: Companies use acquisitions to accelerate growth and gain skills. Yet acquisitions rarely meet their expectations because of "culture clash." Was Linda right in not selling her company to Neoforma? After all, Neoforma survived, and Galatia did not. Why did she choose to remain separate? Did Neoforma make the right decisions regarding GAR and Pharos? Why?

Master-case Q 4: Using the culture table, compare Varian and Neoforma.

Conflicts of Interest and Ethics

If you have not yet read the appendix in Chapter 1, do so. Then go to the book's Web site and read the diary entries Months 18, 25, 26, 26–36, 42, and 46 and view the video selection, "VCs & Investment Bankers: When the Stakes Get High, Ethics Get Low."

Either as a team or individually, produce short presentations to address the following questions for class discussion.

Master-case Q 5: Do you consider Bret's behavior reasonable? Ethical? Defensible? Argue for your position. If you were Wayne in this situation, what steps would you have taken to resolve the conflicts? (*Hint:* Refer to the three principles in the section on ethical dilemmas.)

Master-case Q 6: An IPO is often priced low by the underwriters so there is an immediate rise in value even though this hurts the company. When Neoforma went public, the stock price went from $13 to $52 on the first day of trading. Why did Merrill Lynch price the offering so far below the market demand price? This resulted in less money going into the company and the internal shareholders suffering more dilution. Discuss the ethical issues concerning this "bounce" in the first day of trading.

Hiring and Firing If you have not yet read the appendix in Chapter 1, do so. Then go to the book's Web site and read the diary entries Months 3, 5, 27, 31, 32, 39, 40, and 50 and view the video selection, "Hiring and Firing: Using Your Head and Trusting Your Gut."

Either as a team or individually, produce short presentations to address the following questions for class discussion.

Master-case Q 7: Is it better to hire someone you know than a total stranger? How do you avoid the "Cassandra Problem" when you are under pressure to hire quickly?

Master-case Q 8: Imagine you are Jeff and Wayne. Create an interview guideline for *each* founder separately for hiring key people. What will each explore? How will you cross-check? How do you test for tenacity, honesty, values, and innovativeness?

Master-case Q 9: Paradox: you hired all good people, so how do you choose which to fire? Do you think Wayne did the right thing regarding the firing of Thalia over Sheila? Give your reasons.

INTERACTIVE LEARNING ON THE WEB

Test your knowledge of the chapter using the book's interactive Web site.

APPENDIX: LEGAL DOCUMENT TEMPLATES

1. Employment Agreement

NUCO INC.: EMPLOYEE AGREEMENT

_____ agrees to be an employee of NUCO INC. under the following terms and conditions:

1. My employment by NUCO INC. will not violate any other obligation I have (such as an obligation not to compete with a former employer or client). I will not bring to or use in my work for NUCO INC. any confidential documents, software, or other information or property of any person or entity other than NUCO INC.

2. I realize that during my employment with NUCO INC. I may have been exposed or may be exposed to Confidential Information of NUCO INC., including, without limitation, Confidential Information of clients of either entity. "Confidential Information" means all information that NUCO INC. treated or NUCO INC. treats as confidential, even if that information is not a "trade secret" as defined by law. I agree that

   • I will not disclose any Confidential Information to any person or entity other than employees or agents of NUCO INC. who need to know the Confidential Information to do their jobs for NUCO INC. and who are bound by nondisclosure obligations consistent with this paragraph 2.

- I will not use the Confidential Information for any purpose other than to do my own job for NUCO INC.

- I will safeguard the confidentiality of the Confidential Information by taking all precautions that NUCO INC. reasonably requires.

My obligations under this paragraph 2 will continue during my employment by NUCO INC. and for three years after such employment is over.

3. I also realize that during my employment with NUCO INC. I may have created or may create certain materials for NUCO INC. The term "Created Materials" means anything I created for NUCO INC. or create for NUCO INC. by myself or with others. Created Materials may be tangible things such as documents, reports, specifications, or software or may be intangible things such as concepts, discoveries, ideas, or information. Something is a Created Material if I created or create it during the time in which I was employed by NUCO INC. or am employed by NUCO INC., even if I created or create it only in part, or only together with other people, or out of normal business hours, so long as it was or is applicable to the business of NUCO INC. With respect to Created Materials, I agree that

- they will be the sole and exclusive property of NUCO INC., and I assign to NUCO INC. all of my rights, including, without limitation, any patent rights, in all Created Materials.

- to the extent that a copyright may be obtained in any Created Material, that Created Material will be considered a work made for hire owned by NUCO INC. under the copyright laws of the United States or if deemed by a court not to be a work made for hire owned by NUCO INC., I assign to NUCO INC. all of my rights under the copyright laws of the United States in any Created Material.

- I will sign any documents and assist NUCO INC. in any applications or proceedings that may be necessary to secure for NUCO INC. the ownership or protection of the Created Materials and any patents, copyrights, or other proprietary rights related to the Created Materials. If necessary, I will do these things even after my employment with NUCO INC. is over, provided that NUCO INC. pays me a reasonable fee for the time that I spend on its behalf and reimburses me for any ordinary and necessary out-of-pocket expenses that I incur.

- I will deliver all Created Materials to NUCO INC. when my employment with NUCO INC. is over and not keep any copies of any Created Materials without NUCO INC.'s permission.

4. During the term of my employment by NUCO INC. and for one year thereafter, I will not be employed by or act on behalf of any other person or entity that is engaged in any business or activity that is competitive with that of NUCO INC. unless such employment has been approved by NUCO INC. in advance in writing.

5. If any provision or portion of this Agreement is held to be void or unenforceable, the remaining provisions of this Agreement and the remaining portion of any provision held void or unenforceable in part shall continue in full force and effect. This Agreement may not be modified, in whole or in part, except by an agreement in writing signed by the parties hereto.

Name:
Date:

2. Consulting Agreement

NUCO INC. CONSULTING AGREEMENT

THIS CONSULTING AGREEMENT ("Agreement") is made and entered into as of DATE by and between NUCO INC., a XXX corporation, (the "Company") and Mary X. Citizen, a consultant based in State College, Pennsylvania ("Consultant").

WITNESSETH:

WHEREAS, the Company is desirous of retaining the services of Consultant as an independent contractor under the terms and conditions set forth in this Agreement and Consultant is willing to perform such services for the Company on such terms and conditions.

NOW, THEREFORE, in consideration of the mutual covenants and agreements contained in this Agreement, the parties hereto, intending to be legally bound hereby, agree as follows:

1. Consulting Duties. The Company agrees to and does hereby retain Consultant in a consulting capacity as an independent contractor to provide such consulting and advisory services as are set forth on EXHIBIT A attached hereto and made a part hereof. Consultant agrees to serve the Company in such capacity for the period commencing on the date hereof and continuing through DATE unless this Agreement is sooner terminated as set forth in Section 9.

2. Requirements. The Company acknowledges that Consultant has other clients to whom Consultant must provide services and devote time and accordingly, that Consultant may not devote time to Consultant's duties under this Agreement every day. However, Consultant agrees to devote the time and effort required to accomplish in a timely manner the services for which Consultant is responsible under this Agreement.

3. Compensation.

   (A) Consultant will be paid by the Company as set forth on EXHIBIT B attached hereto and made a part hereof.

   (B) Subject to Consultant furnishing the Company with adequate records and other documentary evidence to substantiate such expenses, within 30 days thereof, Consultant shall be entitled to reimbursement for all reasonable expenses incurred in connection with the performance of its duties hereunder.

4. Relationship of Parties.

   (A) Consultant's performance of services hereunder is as an independent contractor. The Company shall determine the work to be done by Consultant, but Consultant shall determine the means by which Consultant accomplishes the work specified by the Company. Consultant will not be considered an employee, servant, partner, or joint venturer of the Company for any reason. None of the benefits provided by the Company to its employees shall be available to Consultant or any of Consultant's employees, agents, or contractors (including, without limitation, medical insurance, life insurance, paid vacations, paid holidays, pension, profit sharing, or Social Security), and neither Consultant nor any of Consultant's employees, agents, or contractors have any express or implied right or authority to assume or create any liability, obligation, or responsibility on behalf of or in the name of the Company. In furtherance of the foregoing, Consultant acknowledges that no workmen's compensation or unemployment insurance coverage shall be provided by the Company to Consultant.

(B) Inasmuch as Consultant is entering into this Agreement as an "independent contractor" and not as an "employee" of the Company, all taxes or withholdings, including, without limiting the generality thereof, Social Security taxes, shall remain the sole responsibility of Consultant. If Consultant is deemed an employee of the Company by any taxing authority or other governmental agency, Consultant agrees to indemnify the Company for any taxes, penalties, or interest imposed upon the Company by such taxing authority or other governmental agency as a result of compromise, litigation, or consent by Consultant with the acquiescence of the Company.

5. <u>Nondisclosure of Confidential Information.</u>

(A) Consultant recognizes and acknowledges that: (i) the information developed by or communicated to Consultant in the course of Consultant's performance of its duties hereunder is of a highly confidential nature, whether or not any of such information is marked "confidential"; (ii) such information may include by way of example but not limited to, financial, technical, and business information that provides the Company with an advantage over its competitors, business strategies and plans, designs, processes, materials, inventions, improvements, writings, memoranda, reports, client and partner information, documents, equipment, computer software systems and other computer products, Internet applications, product and services information, marketing and distribution methods, information concerning the Company's portfolio companies and potential portfolio companies, and relationships between the Company and its affiliates, partners, clients, portfolio companies, and others who have business dealings with the Company, all of which is confidential and proprietary to the Company (hereinafter collectively referred to as the "Confidential Information"); (iii) the Confidential Information is the property of the Company; (iv) the use, misappropriation, or disclosure of the Confidential Information would constitute a breach of trust and could cause irreparable injury to the Company; and (v) it is essential to the protection of the Company's goodwill and to the maintenance of the Company's competitive position that the Confidential Information be kept secret and that Consultant not disclose the Confidential Information to others or use the Confidential Information to Consultant's own advantage or the advantage of others.

(B) Consultant agrees to hold and safeguard the Confidential Information in trust for the Company, its successors, and assigns, and Consultant will not, either during or at any time after the term of this Agreement, disclose any such Confidential Information to any person for any reason whatsoever, or use the Confidential Information to Consultant's own advantage or the advantage of others, except in the performance of its services under this Agreement, without the written permission of the Company, unless such information (i) has become publicly known through no wrongful act of Consultant; (ii) has been rightfully received from a third party authorized by the Company to make such disclosure without restriction; (iii) has been approved or released by written authorization of the Company; (iv) is being or has theretofore been disclosed pursuant to a valid court order after a reasonable attempt has been made to notify the Company in order to permit the Company an opportunity to respond to the order; or (v) is independently developed by Consultant without use or reference to the Company's Confidential Information, as shown by written records.

6. <u>Disclosure of Works; Inventions/Assignment.</u>

(A) Consultant shall maintain such records of its work as the Company may direct from time to time. Consultant shall promptly disclose to the Company, in writing, any and all copyrightable works, including software, and any and all discoveries, inventions, technological innovations, and improvements (hereinafter collectively referred to as "Intellectual Property"), whether patentable or not (whether it be a machine, process, apparatus, article, composition, design, software, writing, or other thing) conceived or made by Consultant, solely or jointly, during the period of this Agreement, whether or not authorized, conceived, or made during working hours or with the Company's equipment or facilities, which relates in any manner to the existing or contemplated business of the Company. Unless otherwise waived in writing by the Company, all such Intellectual Property shall be the exclusive property of the Company with respect to any and all countries in the world, and Consultant shall assign and hereby does assign all right, title, and interest thereto to the Company or its nominee.

(B) Consultant, both during the term of this Agreement and after the expiration or termination of this Agreement, shall cooperate fully with the Company in taking all actions and measures necessary for the Company to acquire and perfect its ownership of all Intellectual Property. Whenever required to do so by the Company, Consultant shall execute any and all applications, assignments, or other instruments, which the Company shall deem necessary to apply for and obtain Letters Patent or copyrights of the United States or any foreign country or to otherwise protect the Company's interest therein. Such obligations shall continue beyond the termination of this Agreement with respect to all Intellectual Property authorized, conceived, made, or reduced to practice by Consultant during the term of this Agreement and shall be binding upon Consultant's assigns, executors, administrators, and other legal representatives. In conformance with Company policy from time to time, Consultant shall be reimbursed by the Company for reasonable expenses incurred by Consultant in connection with its obligations under this Section 6(B), subject to Consultant furnishing adequate documentary evidence to substantiate such expenses.

7. <u>Return of Materials.</u> Upon the termination of this Agreement for any reason, Consultant shall promptly deliver to the Company all documents, files, computer discs and other electronic media, tools, equipment, and other property of the Company, including all correspondence, memoranda, drawings, blueprints, manuals, letters, notes, reports, flowcharts, software, training and marketing materials, and related documents, proposals, plans, and any documents concerning the Company's clients, partners, portfolio companies and affiliates, or prospective clients, partners, portfolio companies and affiliates, or concerning products or processes used or developed by the Company and, without limiting the foregoing, will promptly deliver to the Company any and all other documents or materials containing or constituting Confidential Information.

8. <u>Work Made for Hire.</u> All services and products performed or delivered by Consultant hereunder shall be considered "work made for hire" by Consultant for the Company and shall be owned by the Company. Consultant agrees that in the event of publication by Consultant of written or graphic materials, the Company will retain and own all rights in said materials, including right of copyright.

9. <u>Termination.</u> In the event of a breach of any of the terms and provisions of this Agreement by a party, this Agreement may be terminated by the nonbreaching party upon 30 days' written notice to the other party of such termination; provided, however, that the provisions of Sections 5, 6, 7, 8, and 10 shall expressly be deemed to survive such termination.

10. <u>Nonsolicitation.</u> Consultant agrees that during the term of this Agreement and for a period of one year after the termination of this Agreement, Consultant shall not, directly or indirectly, solicit the employment or engagement of, or cause the solicitation of the employment or engagement of, or engage or employ, any of the Company's employees, consultants, affiliates, or employees or consultants of the Company's portfolio companies without the prior written approval of the Company.

11. <u>Warranties.</u>

    (A) Consultant warrants and covenants that the services to be provided hereunder shall be performed in a workmanlike manner with that degree of skill and judgment normally exercised by professionals performing services of the same or substantially similar nature.

    (B) Consultant represents to the Company that its execution of this Agreement and the performance of services hereunder will not breach any obligation or agreement of Consultant to any third party, including without limitation, any agreement to keep in confidence proprietary information of a third party acquired by Consultant, or any other agreement to which Consultant is a party which may otherwise restrict its ability to perform services pursuant to this Agreement. Consultant has not entered into, and Consultant agrees not to enter into, any agreement, either written or oral, in conflict with this Agreement.

12. <u>Equitable Relief.</u>

    (A) Consultant acknowledges that the restrictions contained in this Agreement are reasonable and necessary to protect the legitimate interests of the Company and that the Company would not have entered into this Agreement in the absence of such restrictions and that any violation of these restrictions will result in irreparable injury to the Company. Consultant represents that its experience and capabilities are such that the restrictions contained in this Agreement will not prevent Consultant from earning a living. Consultant further represents and warrants that it had a full opportunity to review this Agreement prior to its execution.

    (B) Consultant agrees that the Company shall be entitled to preliminary and permanent injunctive relief, without the necessity of proving actual damages, as well as an equitable accounting of all earnings, profits, and other benefits arising from any violation of this Agreement, which rights shall be cumulative and in addition to any other rights or remedies to which the Company may be entitled. In the event that any of the provisions of this Agreement should ever be adjudicated to exceed the time, geographic, product or service, or other limitations permitted by applicable law in any jurisdiction, then such provisions shall be deemed reformed in such jurisdiction to the maximum time, geographic, product or service, or other limitations permitted by applicable law.

13. <u>Corporate Opportunities.</u> Consultant agrees that it will not take any action that might divert from the Company any opportunity, which would be within the scope of any of the present or future businesses thereof.

14. <u>Entire Agreement.</u> This Agreement sets forth the entire agreement and understanding of the parties concerning the subject matter hereof and supersedes all prior understandings between the parties hereto. No representation, promise, inducement, or statement of intention has been made by or on behalf of either party hereto that is not set forth in this Agreement. This Agreement may not be amended or modified except by written instrument executed by the parties hereto.

15. <u>Counterparts.</u> This Agreement may be executed in counterparts, each of which shall be deemed an original but all of which, taken together, constitute one and the same agreement.

16. <u>No Assignment.</u> Neither this Agreement nor any obligation or duty under this Agreement is assignable by Consultant without the prior written consent of the Company.

17. <u>Governing Law.</u> This Agreement shall be governed by and construed in accordance with the laws of the STATE.

18. <u>Binding Effect.</u> The terms and provisions of this Agreement shall be binding upon and shall inure to the benefit of the parties hereto and their permitted successors and assigns.

IN WITNESS WHEREOF, the parties hereto have caused this Agreement to be executed as of the day and year first above written.

NUCO INC.   CONSULTANT

By: _____   By: _____

Title: CEO   Mary X. Citizen

3. Separation Agreement

NUCO INC. SEPARATION AGREEMENT AND GENERAL RELEASE

1. The intent of this Separation Agreement and General Release (hereinafter "Release") is to mutually, amicably, and finally resolve and compromise all issues and claims of the employment of John Q. Public (hereinafter "Public") with NUCO INC. (hereinafter "NUCO") and the separation thereof. Public will be separated from her/his employment with NUCO effective DATE. The execution of this Release shall not in any way be considered an admission of any liability on the part of NUCO.

2. In exchange for the Release described below, NUCO will tender monies to Public fifteen days after he/she signs this agreement in the amount equivalent to two weeks' salary, less legally mandated payroll reductions and withholdings. This sum does not include any accrued, unused vacation pay, which, if due and owing, shall also be tendered to Public on DATE, less legally mandated payroll reductions and withholdings.

3. In consideration for the payments, promises, and undertakings described above, Public, his/her representative, successors, and assigns do hereby completely release and forever discharge NUCO, its shareholders, officers, partners, and all other representatives, agents, directors, employees, attorneys, successors, and assigns from all claim, rights, demands, actions, obligations, and causes of action of any and every kind, nature, and character, known or unknown, which Public may now have, or has ever had, against them arising from or in any way connected with the employment relationship between the parties, any action during the relationship, and/or the termination thereof, including, but not limited to, all "wrongful discharge" claims; and all claims relating to any contract of employment, express or implied; and covenant of good faith and fair dealing, express or implied; any tort of any nature; any federal, state, or municipal statute or ordinance; any claims under Title VII of the Civil Rights Act of 1964, the Civil Rights Act of 1991, the Age Discrimination in Employment Act, the Older Workers' Benefit Protection Act (42 USC Sec. 1981), the Employee Retirement and Income Security Act, the Americans with Disabilities Act, any labor and civil codes of the state of STATE, and any other laws and regulations relating to wages, benefits, and employment discrimination and any and all claims for attorneys' fees and costs.

4. Public agrees that the existence of this Release and the existence of and terms and conditions of this Release are strictly confidential. Public also agrees to use his/her best efforts to prevent any publicity or disclosure of the facts, terms, and/or surrounding circumstances of this Release. If asked about the matter, he/she will only state that "it was resolved."

5. Public acknowledges that he/she has had the opportunity to consult with his/her attorney prior to signing the Release. Pursuant to the Older Workers' Benefit Protection Act, Public has twenty-one (21) days in which to consider whether he/she should sign this Release; and if he/she signs this Release, he/she will have seven (7) days following the date on which he/she signs the Release to revoke it, and the Release will not be effective until after this seven-day period has lapsed.

6. In the event any controversy or dispute arises in connection with the validity, construction, application, enforcement, or breach of the Separation Agreement and General Release, any such controversy or dispute shall be submitted to final and binding arbitration pursuant to the rules of the American Arbitration Association and the Federal Arbitration Act and the parties hereto expressly waive their rights, if any, to have any such matters heard by a court or a jury, or administrative agency, whether state or federal. The arbitrator shall require the losing party to reimburse the prevailing party for reasonable attorney's fees and costs incurred in connection with arbitration. The losing party shall also be required to pay the arbitrator's fees for said arbitration.

7. This Release constitutes the entire understanding of the parties on the subjects covered. Public expressly warrants that he/she has read and fully understands this Release; that he/she has had the opportunity to consult with legal counsel of his/her own choosing and to have the terms of this Release fully explained to him/her; that he/she is not executing this Release in reliance on any promises, representations, or inducements other than those contained herein; and that he/she is executing this Release voluntarily, free of any duress or coercion.

8. This Release shall be construed and governed by the laws of the State of STATE. The parties hereto further agree that if, for any reason, any provisions hereof are unenforceable, the remainder of this Release shall nonetheless remain binding and in effect.

_____	_____
John Q. Public	Date
_____	_____
NUCO INC., Inc.	Date

4. Sales and Marketing Agreement

NUCO INC. SALES AND MARKETING AGREEMENT

This Agreement is entered into by and between NUCO Inc., a XXXX Corporation, hereinafter referred to as "NUCO," located at _____, _____, _____, and Canadian Marketing Services, Inc., hereinafter referred to as "CMS," located at _____, _____, _____, effective DATE.

WITNESSETH:

WHEREAS, NUCO is engaged in providing software systems, including, but not limited to, transaction processing for electronic gift certificates and licensing of loyalty programs for a wide range of industry clientele.

WHEREAS, CMS represents that they possess the physical resources and skills to promote the services of NUCO and is desirous of marketing such services and software within the scope of activity hereinafter defined, and

WHEREAS, NUCO is desirous of having CMS develop a demand for and to market its services and software to the Canadian marketplace on the terms and conditions set forth herein:

NOW, THEREFORE in consideration of the representation, covenants, and promises made herein, the parties agree as follows:

1. APPOINTMENT

    1.1. NUCO hereby engages CMS on an exclusive basis to market the services and software offered by NUCO to the Canadian marketplace. The U.S. marketplace will be on a nonexclusive basis and handled as a case-to-case business.

    1.2. The exclusive agreement will be based on performance criteria such as revenue projections that CMS will project on a year-by-year basis.

2. CAPACITY

    2.1. CMS agrees to comply with all federal, state, and local laws in conducting business for NUCO.

3. NUCO RESPONSIBILITIES

    3.1. NUCO shall provide CMS with information regarding NUCO's loyalty products and services and licensing arrangements such that CMS will be able to perform under this Agreement.

    3.2. NUCO shall review for acceptance all contracts submitted by CMS on a timely basis. It is agreed and acknowledged by CMS that NUCO shall have sole discretion in approving or declining each contract.

3.3. NUCO will agree on a revenue/commission structure with CMS for all marketing leads that CMS generates. Each revenue statement will include all payments received by NUCO within ten days of the end of the particular month.

3.4. CMS will have the right to review NUCO's invoicing and payment records relating to contracts for CMS clients as necessary to determine that commission payments are being made accurately and on a timely basis.

3.5. NUCO will provide CMS with marketing materials and recommend particular markets that CMS should pursue. NUCO will make joint calls with CMS when CMS recommends a qualified lead that NUCO wants to pursue.

4. CMS'S SALES AND MARKETING DUTIES

4.1. CMS shall use its best efforts in marketing NUCO's services and software and in acquiring additional clients to use the services and software now or hereafter offered by NUCO.

4.2. CMS will offer the following services as part of the loyalty program offered:

a) 800 customer service
b) VRU (voice response unit)
c) Direct marketing, mailings, promotions, etc.
d) Consulting services

4.3. CMS shall have the authority to receive monies payable to NUCO; however, under no circumstances shall CMS endorse NUCO's checks or carry bank accounts in the name of NUCO. All funds collected shall, along with a copy of the receipt and all other paperwork, be forwarded to NUCO within 48 hours of receipt.

4.4. CMS understands residual commissions originate from providing ongoing customer support for clients as may be reasonably requested, from time to time, by the client or NUCO. CMS will strive in all reasonable ways to provide for complete customer satisfaction.

5. COMMISSIONS

When a client to which CMS recommended NUCO services and software (a "Prospect") actually purchases NUCO's services and software at any time during the term of this Agreement or during the 90-day period thereafter, NUCO will pay CMS 15 percent of NUCO's net revenues received from that Prospect pursuant to a contract for NUCO's services and software (the "Commission"). In order to receive a Commission for a Prospect, CMS must register in writing with NUCO the names of Prospects to which it has recommended or intends soon thereafter to recommend NUCO's services and software. If NUCO is actively marketing its services or software to a Prospect when CMS registers the name of that Prospect with NUCO, then NUCO will so notify CMS within 15 days after it receives CMS's registration of the name of that Prospect. If that Prospect purchases NUCO's services or software, NUCO will not owe CMS any Commission for that Prospect.

6. DURATION OF AGREEMENT

This Agreement shall continue in full force and effect under the conditions contained herein for a period of one year from the date of its execution and will automatically renew for subsequent one-year periods on a year-to-year basis unless written notification of cancellation by either party to the other is provided 90 days prior to the contract renewal date. Either party may terminate this Agreement by 30 days' advance written notice to the other party if the other party is in breach of any material obligation that cannot be cured or, if the breach can be cured, the breach is not cured within 30 days after the breaching party's receipt of notice of breach and demand to cure.

7. RIGHTS UPON TERMINATION OF SALES AND MARKETING AGREEMENT

7.1. CMS will receive a vested interest in 100 percent of the residual Commissions generated by CMS during the term of this Agreement and for two years thereafter.

7.2. NUCO shall have no obligation to pay residuals on customers who discontinue to use NUCO's services or software, and NUCO does not warrant or guarantee any residuals other than those actually collected by NUCO.

8. NONCOMPETE/CONFIDENTIALITY

CMS recognizes that in performing this Agreement, NUCO may disclose to CMS confidential or proprietary information relating to NUCO's services and software, marketing methods, prices, business strategies, and other customer information (collectively, the "Confidential Information"). CMS agrees not to use or disclose to any third party any Confidential Information during the term of this Agreement and for five years thereafter. In addition, CMS agrees that it will not be employed by or act on behalf of any other person or entity, including its employees as individuals, that is engaged in any business or activity that is competitive with that of NUCO for two years after the termination of this Agreement unless such employment has been approved by NUCO in advance in writing.

9. GENERAL CLAUSES

9.1. The failure of NUCO or CMS to enforce at any time, or for any period of time, any provision of this Agreement shall not be construed as a waiver of such provisions or the right of either party, thereafter, to enforce each and every such provision.

9.2. CMS may not assign its rights and obligations hereunder, in whole or in part, without the written consent of NUCO, and any attempted or purported assignment thereof without such consent will be null and void.

9.3. Neither the making of this Agreement nor the performance of its provisions will be construed to constitute either of the parties hereto as an agent, employer, employee, partner, joint venturer, or legal representative of the other. Each party expressly acknowledges that it has no right or authority to incur or create any obligation, make any representation, or undertake any responsibility, express or implied, unless authorized in advance in writing by the other party. In no event will either party act or represent itself as an agent for the other party.

9.4. This Agreement states the entire agreement and understanding of the parties on the subject matter of this Agreement and supersedes all previous agreements, arrangements, communications, and understandings about the subject matter.

9.5. If any provision of this Agreement is held by a court of competent jurisdiction to be contrary to law or public policy or otherwise unenforceable, the remaining provisions will remain in full force and effect, and the invalid provision will remain in force as reformed by the court.

9.6. This Agreement will be governed by, and construed in accordance with, the laws of the State of STATE applicable to contracts made and to be performed wholly within such State, without reference to principles of conflicts of laws thereof. Each party hereby irrevocably and unconditionally accepts, and agrees to submit to, the exclusive jurisdiction of any state or federal court in the State of STATE in respect of any dispute arising out of, based upon, or relating to, this Agreement.

NUCO INC.		CANADIAN MARKETING SERVICES, INC.	
By:	John Smith	By:	Harry Lime
Title:	President	Title:	Vice President & Managing Director
Date: _____		Date: _____	

www.wiley.com/college/kaplan

PART FOUR
COMMUNICATING AND EXITING

Part Four, "Communicating and Exiting," covers two important aspects of interacting with third parties. Chapter 13 is concerned with why, how, and when an opportunity is presented to external stakeholders such as investors, bankers, and potential employees. Having a wonderful opportunity is a personal dream only until others who can help the dream become reality become excited and motivated to join the entrepreneurial journey. Great entrepreneurs are excellent communicators, and they use these skills every day to harness the energy of others. It takes time to develop these skills but is well worth the effort in whatever path you choose to follow. Chapter 14 deals with how companies can eventually create tangible value for the founders and investors. Of course, a lifestyle company may not plan an "exit," but eventually nearly all companies need to find a way to create tangible liquid wealth, perhaps at retirement, a family emergency, or just a desire to do something new. It is, therefore, a sound strategy to have exit options in place for just these situations, even if the original plan did not call for an "exit event."

CHAPTER 13: COMMUNICATING THE OPPORTUNITY
CHAPTER 14: SCALING AND EXITING THE VENTURE

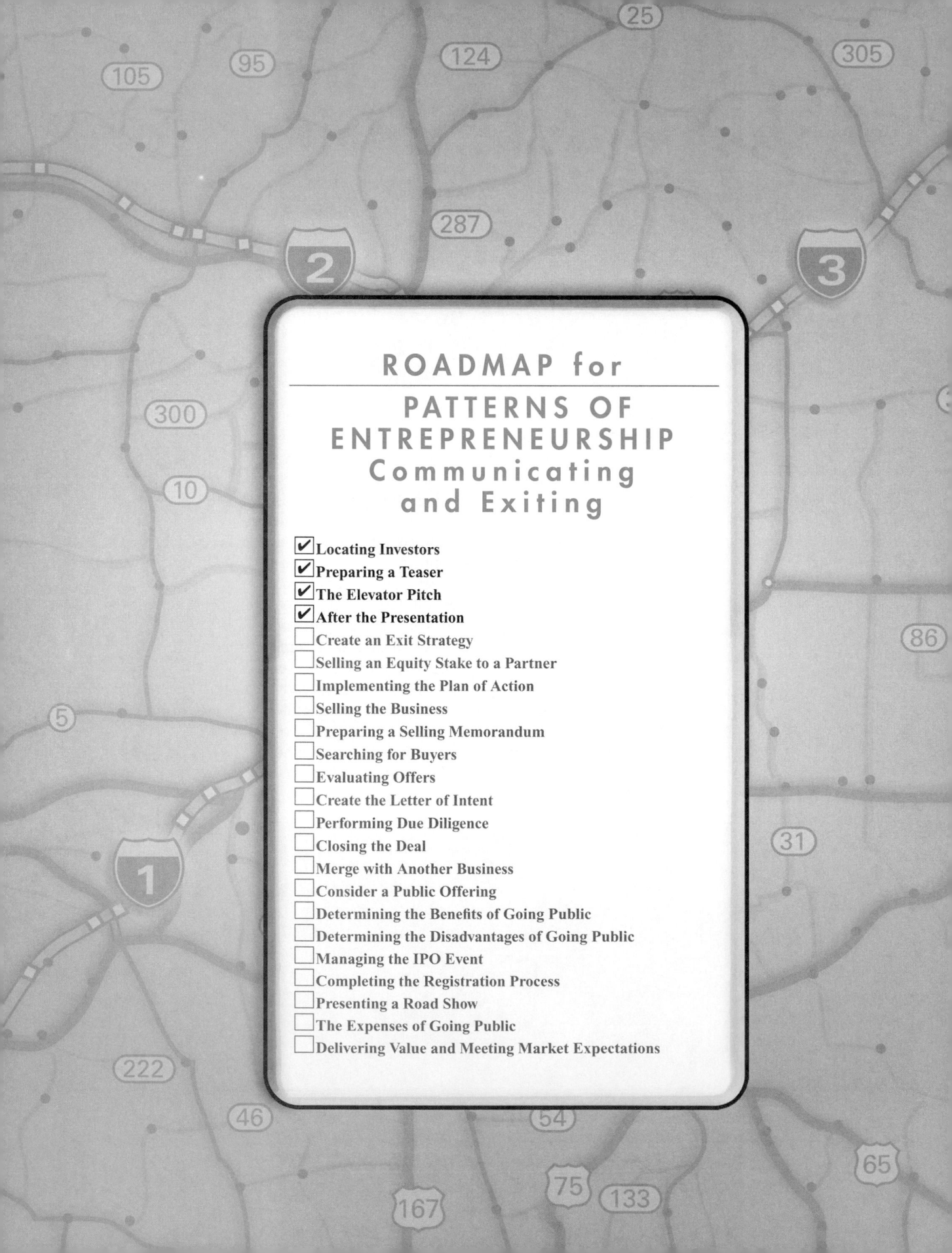

ROADMAP for

PATTERNS OF ENTREPRENEURSHIP
Communicating and Exiting

- ☑ **Locating Investors**
- ☑ **Preparing a Teaser**
- ☑ **The Elevator Pitch**
- ☑ **After the Presentation**
- ☐ Create an Exit Strategy
- ☐ Selling an Equity Stake to a Partner
- ☐ Implementing the Plan of Action
- ☐ Selling the Business
- ☐ Preparing a Selling Memorandum
- ☐ Searching for Buyers
- ☐ Evaluating Offers
- ☐ Create the Letter of Intent
- ☐ Performing Due Diligence
- ☐ Closing the Deal
- ☐ Merge with Another Business
- ☐ Consider a Public Offering
- ☐ Determining the Benefits of Going Public
- ☐ Determining the Disadvantages of Going Public
- ☐ Managing the IPO Event
- ☐ Completing the Registration Process
- ☐ Presenting a Road Show
- ☐ The Expenses of Going Public
- ☐ Delivering Value and Meeting Market Expectations

COMMUNICATING THE OPPORTUNITY

> "I have made this letter a rather long one, only because I didn't have the leisure to make it shorter."
>
> BLAISE PASCAL

OBJECTIVES

- Understand how to target the business to investors.
- Prepare oral and visual presentations to the investor.
- Learn the investor evaluation process.
- Prepare the teaser.
- Prepare the investor presentation.

CHAPTER OUTLINE

Introduction

Profile: Craig Bandes—Matching Presentations to Investors

Locating Investors

Preparing a Teaser

The Elevator Pitch

After the Presentation

Summary

Study Questions

Exercises

Interactive Learning on the Web

INTRODUCTION

No idea or company, however good it is, will attract resources to help it grow or attract purchasers unless the entrepreneur can communicate the opportunity clearly to potential stakeholders whether they are investors, bank loan officers, corporate partners, or potential acquirers. (In this chapter we use the term *investors* broadly to encompass all external stakeholders that may provide resources to help the company grow or eventually acquire it.) Communication skills are, therefore, key to successful entrepreneurship. This chapter will help you gain those skills.

These skills are necessary any time you present your company to outsiders. In this chapter we will largely focus on locating and engaging with potential investors to fund the company as it grows. In the final chapter, we will show how these skills can be extended to the case where the company is executing an exit for its shareholders.

Entrepreneurs need several prepared documents and verbal presentations to communicate their opportunities to interested parties. These are an executive summary, a full business plan, and both a short and long presentation. All of these must be adjusted to take into account the specific needs of the audience.

Any communication whether verbal or written must be customized to the target audience. One message does not fit all. For example, when seeking a bank loan, entrepreneurs have to show how the risk is minimized for the lender, whereas, if talking with a venture capitalist, the entrepreneur will need to show how the business fits with the VC's investment profile, how it can grow quickly, and how an "exit" for the investors will be created. When approaching a potential acquirer, it is necessary to show the value that can be created by the purchase.

Any commitment from an investor will not come quickly. There has to be an exploratory period during which the two parties get to know one another. This "dating" period requires different levels and types of communications as the process proceeds. The first communication should be in the form of an executive summary, or "teaser." The purpose of this short document is merely to gain the attention of the targeted audience. Most investors receive a torrent of business plans and teasers, so it is important that their attention is grabbed quickly.

The verbal equivalent of the teaser is the so-called elevator pitch. The name describes an imaginary situation in which an entrepreneur finds herself by chance in an elevator with a potential investor/lender and has his ear for just the length of the elevator ride. In the minute or two available, a crisp, compelling message that engages the recipient must be conveyed.

If the teaser is successful, it is likely that a full business plan will be requested for review. If this plan continues to appeal to the investor, the next step is usually an invitation to give a full "investors" presentation.[1]

Think of these stages of more and more engagement with potential investors as similar to trout fishing. A good angler will choose her bait carefully to match what she thinks the fish are feeding on at that moment. After setting the appropriate bait and the fish takes it, the angler "plays" the fish, gradually bringing it closer and making sure that nothing happens to allow the fish to get off the hook.

Chapter 5 has already shown you how to produce a winning business plan. Now is the time to get it in front of the right stakeholders and convince them to participate in your venture. In this chapter you will learn how to approach stakeholders, prepare the appropriate documents and presentations, and move toward closing a negotiation.

PROFILE: CRAIG BANDES—MATCHING PRESENTATIONS TO INVESTORS[2]

A graduate of Babson College, Craig Bandes now has more than seventeen years of experience as a CEO, entrepreneur, venture investor, and investment banker, building companies in the defense, telecommunications, and professional services industries with particular emphasis on raising capital and creating exit strategies. Bandes has negotiated more than $300 million in financial transactions and completed strategic partnerships in the United States, Asia, and Europe. According to Craig, "the key ingredient in raising capital is to clearly and effectively communicate the investment opportunity. I've found that the biggest mistakes most often made in an investor presentation are spending too much time on the 'widget' rather than the market strategy and not tailoring comments to the audience and what drives their ultimate investment decision." For example, when Craig was the chief financial officer for a telecommunications start-up that needed to raise at least $200 million to fund the expansion of both a nationwide network and an extensive sales force, he used a two-pronged strategy. He first approached strategic investors, both telecom equipment manufacturers and fiber cable operators, and followed that by contacting private equity sources. The providers of the equipment and the network operators had a completely different set of objectives from the private equity funds, so two very different pitches were developed. The equipment manufacturers and network providers that were targeted were asked to lend the company about $150 million to purchase hardware and network bandwidth from them in the future and invest an additional $25–$50 million in equity for working capital. What these corporations cared about was the ability for the company to pay back the debt and to buy more equipment and network resources in the future as the company grew, rather than a pure return on their investments. The presentation to them primarily focused on equipment purchase schedules and increasing bandwidth needs. The targeted private equity groups who provided the balance of the capital, cared solely about how they would gain a 30 percent rate of return on their capital and the timing of when they would realize that return. In these presentations Craig focused on revenue growth rates, when EBITDA was expected to turn positive, comparable company valuations, and expected exit strategies for them.

He knew that the strategic investors would give the private equity groups confidence because they were perceived as the experts and that the corporate investors would view the private equity fund managers as validating their assessment, both of which worked in tandem to enhance the value of the company and encourage two types of investors with very different agendas to work together.

LOCATING INVESTORS

Once the entrepreneur has prepared a business plan, a presentation that contains ten to sixteen slides (discussed in more detail later in this chapter), and an executive summary, it is time to contact potential stakeholders to see if they may be interested in funding the business. (Chapter 14 deals with the specific case of locating acquirers.)

Investors are busy people, and it is important that the entrepreneur contact only those who are likely to be interested in the opportunity. This requires some research before making an approach. One way to do this is to speak with other entrepreneurs in similar business fields who have been successful in getting investment, closing loans, or entering into a corporate partnership. The Internet is valuable here in locating and learning about the interests for different investors and finding the correct contacts.

To locate active investors, one should first look within the industry where the business is focused. Investors prefer involvement in a business they know, which will require less explaining or selling the concept. Locating the right investor can add value in a number of ways besides investment. This can include identifying and helping to recruit key management team members and providing key industry and professional contacts. The investor can serve as a mentor, confidant, and sounding board for ideas and plans to solve problems. In some cases the investor helps to establish relationships with key customers, suppliers, and potential corporate partners.

Another less obvious alternative to finding active investors is to pursue passive, or arm's-length, investors, who will have little or no involvement in the business. This could include companies that wish to diversify or groups of investors formed for tax advantage reasons. In general, this route is not recommended. "Smart money" brings not only funding, but knowledge, help, and contacts and is far more valuable. Entrepreneurs may feel that hands-off funding is preferable as they won't have interference in their businesses while growing them. This thinking is misguided, and finding sources of funding coupled with real help is *always* the best choice.

The initial conversation with the investor is to present a summary of the plan describing the business and the type of financing needed. The entrepreneur should also prepare a list of potential investors and phone them for an interview. If an investor asks for a business plan, one should explain that a meeting is preferred before handing over a formal plan. Investors invest in people, not plans. The entrepreneur should arrange to send the business plan or preferably only the executive summary prior to a face-to-face meeting. Send the plan or summary with a cover letter. One should try to be as specific as possible in the letter and refer to matters discussed in the initial telephone conversation so the letter is not perceived as a mass mailing. A follow-up call in two weeks should be made to answer any questions.

ROADMAP

IN ACTION

Entrepreneurs should use a "rifle" rather than a "shotgun" strategy for engaging with potential investors. Imagine that there are only twenty *people* (not just organizations) who might have interest. Research them and contact them after knowing precisely what is likely to interest them. Blasting your idea out to everyone wastes time and devalues your opportunity.

Here are some tips on finding the right contact:

- If an entrepreneur thinks that the opportunity is best fitted to an angel investor or angel investor group, go to any local entrepreneurs' networking function. Often angels go to these meetings to seek out new deals. Many local angel groups now have Web sites where your opportunities can be listed; these sites can easily be found by Web searching. There may be someone in the local community who has been successful in a similar field whether in retail, software, construction, or technology. He or she may be investing privately in new opportunities or know individuals who are; they are often willing to make introductions. Introductions can also be made through accountants and lawyers. As entrepreneurs build their businesses, they will need such services, and it is wise to choose professional service firms that are able to access strong local networks. Chapter 8 lists several useful places to enter the angel networks.

- If the target is a VC firm, then it is important to narrow down the targets to just a few. VC firms are usually very focused and do not look at opportunities that do not pass through their tight filters, which usually have the following important categories:

- *Stage of company.* Taking an early-stage company opportunity to an expansion-stage investor is futile.
- *Domain or field.* Many VCs invest in only businesses that sell to other businesses (B2B); others focus on retail opportunities. Others may prefer technology-based businesses, software companies, or franchises.
- *Size of investment.* If $250,000 is sought, there is no point in talking to a firm that invests only upwards of $5 million.
- *Location.* The majority of VC firms have a bias to invest in a local region, which they can reach within, say, a three-hour drive.
- *Stage of fund.* VCs usually have a ten-year horizon to invest their money. If it is getting near to the end of their fund life, it is unlikely that they will invest in a biotech firm that will take seven to eight years to mature to an exit.

A match can be found by first accessing "Pratt's Guide to Venture Capital" online or at a local library.[5] Once a short list of potential VC firms has been made, each can be researched in greater detail by visiting its Web site. VC firms are looking for matching deals and, therefore, are usually very clear in their communications as to what they are looking for. In addition, their past investments (portfolio) will be listed on their Web sites. Reviewing these will determine whether there is a good fit with your company. Calling the CEOs of the portfolio companies most closely aligned with your new opportunity can provide more insight and may lead to a personal introduction, which always helps. Venture capitalists are much more likely to review an opportunity that is referred to them by someone already in their network rather than looking at unsolicited business plans.

> "If an entrepreneur cannot locate me and send me a compelling executive summary that is a close fit to what I am looking for, then they have already failed the first test of being an entrepreneur!"[4]
>
> BILL FREZZA
> *Partner, Adams Capital Management (www.acm.com)*

- If a small-business loan is sought, then there are probably several local banks that seek such opportunities. Calling them and asking if they have a small-business loan officer can start the conversation. They may participate in the federal lending programs to support small companies.

PREPARING A TEASER

Once a target has been identified and researched, the bait needs to be set. This requires a well-written executive summary, or "teaser." This document must be impeccable in its appearance, short and to the point, clear in both the description of the opportunity and what benefit is offered to the targeted investor or partner.

ROADMAP

| IN ACTION | Writing a compelling teaser can take an experienced entrepreneur a full day. Do not underestimate either the importance or difficulty of this task. You will need help and practice. |

Writing a clear, concise, elegant, and engaging short document is extremely difficult and requires considerable practice. Although everyone has a personal approach to writing, we find that it is best to create a draft rather quickly then wait a couple of days before going back and reading it critically *as if you were the recipient.* Edit this document to a second draft and again wait. This is a good time to have someone not closely involved in the company but with business experience read the document and provide criticisms and suggestions for improvement. It must flow logically and smoothly; every sentence should be carefully constructed and grammatically correct; there must be no typos or spelling errors. Avoid repetition, long sentences, jargon, and short forms. Avoid "woolly" words such as *hopefully* and *maybe* and the conditional verb forms. Finally, go through the document with a fine-tooth comb and be ruthless in removing every word that is not absolutely necessary and could be seen as padding.

Example: LeafBusters Inc.[5]

The idea for this new business was triggered by an entrepreneur reading an article about how farmers in the Midwest do not own their own combine harvesters, but use crews with their own equipment to take in the wheat crop. These crews move from north of the Canadian border and follow the harvest time south as the climate changes. This makes sense for the farmers who cannot justify the high cost of a combine and/or do not have the skilled labor available for just a short harvest period. For the crews, the cost of the equipment can be justified much more easily as it is in use two to three months a year, not just two weeks. The entrepreneur recognized that leaf collection has much the same issues, and so she conceived a company to provide leaf-collecting services to local municipalities. After researching the opportunity and creating a business plan, the entrepreneur decided that the $3 million required to fully finance the start-up should come from two sources. Since half of the money would be for leaf-collecting equipment, a bank loan could be used for the purchases as there would be hard assets with which to secure the loan. The rest of the money would be best raised from angel investors. This size of investment would most likely require more than one angel, so an angel network was sought—one that was local to the region where the entrepreneur lived. After meeting one of the angel group members at a local networking meeting, the following teaser was supplied to the angel group for discussion.

EXECUTIVE SUMMARY

THE OPPORTUNITY

LeafBusters Inc. offers leaf collection services to municipalities in the Northeast region with a significant cost savings over their current operations. Our research has shown that municipalities use their own workforce and equipment, spending as much as $1 million per year to perform this service for residents. We estimate that our service will be able to offer municipalities a 10 to 20 percent cost reduction. Our business model has tremendous growth potential since we will be able to perform this service at a 30 to 40 percent lower cost than the municipalities can for themselves.

THE MARKET

Leaf collection is a major activity performed ten to twelve weeks every fall in virtually every town and city in the United States with hardwood trees. Municipal employees normally perform this activity with a variety of leaf-collection equipment owned by the municipalities. Our research estimates the expenditures

EXECUTIVE SUMMARY (cont.)

on leaf collection to be $250–$500 million/year throughout the United States and southern Canada. Budgets for leaf collection range from $100,000/year for small towns to $1 million/year for large suburban counties.

Municipalities are under significant pressure to reduce costs. Outsourcing of the leaf-collection process will provide them with a very attractive cost-cutting solution to their budget pressures.

THE COMPETITION

We are surprised to find that no significant business competition currently exists for this activity. Individual municipalities perform an estimated 98 percent of the leaf collection in this market with no significant sharing of resources. Small local subcontractors perform the remaining leaf collection primarily for business properties. Although we do expect our success to draw the attention of potential entrants, our business model should provide us with the flexibility and economies of scale to remain the consolidated market leader.

BUSINESS MODEL

LeafBusters Inc. intends to become the premier supplier of seasonal curbside leaf-collection services throughout the United States and Canada. All contract services will be provided from regional service centers, with more efficient collection cycles than those currently available from local municipalities. Shorter collection times will allow LeafBusters Inc. to cover more areas with less equipment and staff than are currently used. Our business model will create an outstanding opportunity for investors such as the Network Angel Group. Based on our projections, we believe that we can capture 20 percent of the market within the first five years of operations.

LeafBusters Inc. will provide the staff and equipment necessary to perform those services currently provided by local governments for curbside leaf collections. While the length of annual leaf-collection programs varies (depending on weather and the volume of leaves), the normal program length is ten to twelve weeks. Our business model involves moving leaf-collection equipment and operations from north to south, following the leaf fall patterns, which will allow us to expand the collection season. For example, the first regional rollout will begin in New England and end in North Carolina, with a total collection period of at least fourteen to sixteen weeks. Instead of the usual eight to ten hours/day staffing by most municipalities, LeafBusters Inc. will operate for approximately twenty hours each day. The goal is to use less equipment and staff to cover more areas by migrating them based on schedule collections. While the transportation of equipment is extremely important, particular care will be taken in recruiting and retaining seasonal staff. Transportation and accommodations will be provided, as well as a competitive hourly pay rate and per diem.

The collected leaves will be turned over to local recycling and composting facilities in an effort to assist communities in achieving their solid waste reduction goals.

Some optional services available from LeafBusters Inc. are scheduling services, communications services (to notify home owners of collection days and times), and compost distribution services.

EXECUTIVE SUMMARY (cont.)

OPERATING SUMMARY

During its first year of operations, LeafBusters Inc. will focus on acquiring equipment and on obtaining at least thirty contract awards for leaf collection in its first targeted region. In each ensuing year, one additional region will be added to operations until all four are operational.

The regional rollout of services will be the Northeastern states, the Midwestern states, and the West Coast, with final expansion into Canada. This approach will allow LeafBusters Inc. to properly manage growth while providing a high level of service to customers. In addition, proving our concept in stages will allow us to deliver success stories as a part of the bid submission process. We already have two orders from municipalities that we will service as soon as our financing is in place.

Although the focus during the first regional rollout will be on those municipalities that currently offer leaf-collection programs, those that do not do so will be targeted during the next phase. We intend to offer our services as a means for municipalities to save money on solid waste removal efforts and to improve their recycling efforts.

In addition, each rollout phase will include the exploration of additional lines of business such as tree-trimming services, street sweeping, solid waste removal, and composting facilities. These additional services will allow us to further utilize our seasonal staff and equipment, keeping our staff employed and improving our return on assets.

PRELIMINARY FINANCIAL SUMMARY

The following table summarizes the preliminary five-year forecast of revenue, expense, and net income for LeafBusters Inc.

ProForma Income Statement LeafBuster Inc.

(in thousand USD)

	For the Year Ending Dec. 31,					
	2007	**2008**	**2009**	**2010**	**2011**	**2012**
Revenues	$0	$6,075	$13,669	$30,755	$69,198	$107,001
Direct Labor	0	1,519	3,417	7,689	15,224	23,540
Gross Profit	0	4,556	10,252	23,066	53,974	83,461
SG&A	500	2,126	4,784	10,764	22,143	34,240
Other Expenses		911	2,050	4,613	10,380	16,050
EBIT	(500)	1,519	3,417	7,689	21,451	33,170
EBIT Margin		25.0%	25.0%	25.0%	31.0%	31.0%
Net Income	($600)	$1,063	$2,392	$5,075	$14,158	$21,892
Profit Margin		18%	18%	17%	20%	20%
Cumulative Income/(Loss)	($600)	$463	$2,855	$7,930	$22,088	$43,980

FUNDING REQUIREMENTS

LeafBusters Inc. is seeking initial financing of $2.5 million, of which $1.5 million will be a bank loan secured against equipment and $1 million will be equity in the form of preferred stock from angel investors. These funds are sufficient to initiate

EXECUTIVE SUMMARY (cont.)

the establishment of a leaf-collection fleet and begin operations. These funds will finance the equipment, marketing activities, labor expenses, organizational costs, and working capital for the first year. Since we expect that contracts will be in place for the fall 2004 season with the profitability shown above, no additional external funding will be needed after the 2005 season.

EXIT STRATEGY

There are several possible exit strategies. The most attractive option will likely be selling the business to a major municipal service company such as a solid waste removal company after three to four years of operations. We anticipate providing our first-round investors with an internal rate of return exceeding 40 percent.

For further information contact:
LeafBusters Inc.
Main Street
Any town, USA
www.leafbuster.com
1-800-Leafbust

Normally, the document would be provided with a short personal cover letter highlighting the opportunity and expected outcome. Note the following points in this document:

- The summary has a clear identity and image. It looks like something from a company, not an individual. The company has a name, relating directly to the opportunity.
- The opportunity, market size, and the customer "value proposition" are spelled out clearly at the outset.
- Competition, business model, and how the company will be operated are described.
- Six-year financial projections are summarized.
- Expectations from investors, including the expected payback and the method of achieving liquidity, are all stated unequivocally. There are no "woolly" terms such as *might, hopefully,* and *could.* Such words convey doubt and, hence, high risk; edit them out. Anything beyond this content detracts from its impact. Keep it brief and to the point.

THE ELEVATOR PITCH

An elevator pitch (so named in reference to the short time you may have to describe your opportunity during a chance meeting in an elevator) is essentially a verbal version of the teaser. For an example of an actual elevator pitch, visit www.wiley.com/college/kaplan where Ankit Patel pitches an idea for how to reduce the operating costs of major U.S. freight railroads[6]. This relates to the full business plan for Railway Innovation Technologies that you can find on the book's Web site. Again, making all the points in a one- to two-minute presentation is extremely difficult. You have time simply to state the problem you are solving and the value that your company will bring when solving that problem. It must be easy to understand with no jargon, leave no major uncertainties in the audience's mind, and show how the investor will make money; everything else must be left to later. Elevator pitches must be rehearsed, first alone, then in front of an audience. Pay attention to the following factors:

- Speak clearly, do not mumble, and do not rush. Modulate your voice and make the presentation pleasant and engaging.
- Get the audience involved and interested as early as possible. A good way of doing this is to relate your opportunity to something that the audience already knows. This is particularly important if your idea is rather obscure or highly technical.
- Be enthusiastic. If you are not excited about the opportunity, how can you expect someone else to be?
- Enthusiasm is also reflected in body language. You should be comfortable with your posture, but hands in pockets, masking your face, or other involuntary movements detract highly from the impact.
- Do not be overanxious or overact. Take some deep breaths before starting, and be determined to enjoy the experience yourself. Avoid theatrics.
- Finish on an up note, and let your closure focus on the next actions.

Get into the habit of watching professional presentations and analyzing what is powerful, natural, and engaging about them.

Investors' Presentation: Preparation for the Meeting

After reviewing the executive summary or hearing the elevator pitch, the investors, if interested, will ask for a copy of the business plan. Follow up with a phone call a few days after submitting the plan to test reactions and to deal with any immediate questions. In reality, most investors do not read business plans in detail; they read just enough to determine whether they wish to go to the next step.

NOTE ON CONFIDENTIALITY

Most investors will not sign a confidentiality agreement at this stage. Put in the plan only materials that are not considered proprietary. If the business is based on new technical inventions, the inventors are justifiably concerned about disclosing proprietary information. Indeed, doing so can jeopardize the patent filing process. On the other hand, we find that scientists and engineers are only too eager to disclose their invention in looking for professional recognition or kudos for "their baby." Remember that investors are interested in the *business* opportunity, not the invention itself. Therefore, the entrepreneur has to state only *what the invention can do*, not *how it does it*. For example, "I have invented a new fuel injector for cars that increases the efficiency of existing gasoline engines by up to 7 percent. It has been tested at an independent test facility, and I can share the results with you. The market for such a product is $900 million annually. I am willing to disclose the details of the invention with you under a confidentiality agreement at a later date should you choose to enter into full due diligence for making an investment in my company." This statement does not threaten the proprietary nature of the invention, yet it gives the potential investors comfort that, should they proceed, they will learn more but under a full confidentiality agreement.

NOTE ON CONFIDENTIALITY (cont.)

A further intermediate step can be taken to protect both parties. They can agree to let an independent third party review the invention and comment on its status, viability, originality, and so on without disclosing the invention to the investors. This is called "escrowing the IP" and is often used when investors want to get an opinion that the invention is likely to be patentable. No details are provided to the investors, only an opinion on status and likelihood of success in getting patents granted.

ROADMAP

IN ACTION

An investor's presentation is a key event. It needs extensive preparation and rehearsal. Try to think of every difficult question you are likely to be asked and prepare answers for them beforehand.

If the investors wish to proceed after a review of the plan, they will usually require the entrepreneur to make an oral presentation. This is an important event. This presentation is more formal than the teaser or elevator pitch and is normally made to a group of investors, perhaps the senior partners of a VC firm, an angel investment board, two or three loan officers at a bank, directors of a local enterprise development board, a road show before an IPO, or several executives within a corporation deciding whether to become a partner with your company. Like the teaser, it should be tailored to the audience.

It is as much about personal chemistry as the opportunity. This is the chance to establish a rapport with investors as partners in the future success of the company. At this presentation other members of the management team should be prepared to answer questions. The entrepreneur should strengthen the oral presentation with the use of presentational aids such as prototypes of products and Web sites.

Early arrival at the venue, allowing time for setup, is important. Survey the room and arrange it to suit the presentation. Start with personal introductions, exchange business cards, and some general small-talk to relax the atmosphere. Ask how long the investors have for the meeting, and tailor the presentation to allow for questions. Try to determine who the key decision influencer is in the group, and make an extra effort to answer any questions or uncertainties this key person expresses. Don't get sidetracked by questions if they are to be dealt with later in the presentation, but answer relevant questions promptly and move on. If the answer is not readily at hand, don't bluff; indicate that an answer will be provided within, say, two days. If several persons are presenting, have one "director" of questions. Avoid interrupting others on the team, and do not disagree among yourselves.

An investor's presentation will follow the same general pattern of the teaser but will fill in many of the details. You can find a comprehensive guide for the creation of your presentation at www.ideapitch.smeal.psu.edu. Your pitch should last no more than twenty minutes without questions, using about twelve to sixteen slides covering the opportunity overview, customer value proposition, market, competition, products/services, business model, management, and financials. Table 13-1 shows eleven basic slides and their contents. The topics here are typical for an early-stage

Table 13-1   Template for an Investors' Presentation

Slides	Notes on Contents
SLIDE 1: OUTLINE • Market • Product or Service • Customers • Intellectual Property • Development Plan • Distribution Plan • Team • Competition • Financial Projections • Exit Strategy	This slide provides an overall guide to your presentation and a roadmap for the audience. You can title each slide to relate to this guide.

SLIDE 2: MARKET
• What market will your company serve with its *first* product or service?
• How large is this market?
  – Is it existing or emerging?
  – Show third-party market research data: historical and forecasts
• Name entrenched or potential competitors.
• What market(s) might your company serve with potential future products or services?
	Starting with this topic will engage your audience and enable you to put your best foot forward. Describe who are you going to serve. How large is the market you are attacking? Is it mature, developing, or must you create it? Show third-party research to support your claims. Name your first product or service and how you will add to this later.

SLIDE 3: PRODUCT OR SERVICE • What product/service will your company develop and sell *first*? • What competitive advantage does your *first* product/service have over alternatives? • After the *first* product/service gains traction in the market, what future offerings will you develop and sell?	Describe in detail your first product or service. Eighty to 90 percent of your presentation should be based on this "market entry" offering as this is where you will spend your initial money. Show how you can build on this later with new products or services as a "roadmap" for expansion.

SLIDE 4: CUSTOMERS
• Who are target customers for your *first* product/service?
  – Name at least two specific prospective customers, and include contact information.
• Why will they buy from you, and how much do they say they will pay?
  – Describe your economic value proposition to these customers.
• What alternatives do your prospective customers have besides buying from you?
	Name the customers showing interest in your product/service. Name the person(s) you spoke to and describe what they said. Why are they going to buy from you, and how much are they willing to pay? Describe the value proposition of your product/service—how is the customer going to make and save money by buying from you rather than buying from someone else?

(Continued)

Table 13-1   **Continued**

Slides	Notes on Contents
SLIDE 5: INTELLECTUAL PROPERTY • State the form(s) of IP you will use (trademarks, patents, copyrights, trade secrets). • Describe the competitive benefits they will provide. • Describe how you plan to obtain, develop, expand, and protect your IP. • If your company uses new technology, give a general overview, state the stage of development, and describe any risks remaining in its implementation.	Here is an opportunity to talk about your special attributes. Keep the discussion at a high level. How are you protecting your intellectual property? Have you filed patents, or are you planning on filing patents, trademarks, etc.? How long do you think your IP will protect you from competition?

SLIDE 6: DEVELOPMENT PLAN
• Outline the timetable under which your *first* product/service will be brought to market.
• Specify the resources required and when you need them, defining milestones:
  – Personnel and materials
  – Capital equipment
  – Third-party products, services, or IP
  – Corporate partners
	How long will it take and how much is it going to cost to get your first product or service out and producing income?
	How many people is it going to take?
	Will you need to buy capital equipment?
	When do you need different amounts of funding?
	Are there third-party products/services or other partners needed for your success? Do you have a bootstrapping plan to minimize the amount of cash you will require?

SLIDE 7: DISTRIBUTION PLAN • Describe the company's business model. • Describe the company's sales model. – Direct, indirect, Web-based, IP licensing, franchising or other • Describe any partnering plans with other companies.	How are you going to sell your product/service? How are you going to get it to your customers? Will you sell direct, through distribution, use licensing or franchising, etc.? Describe your business model and how that will provide you with healthy profits.

SLIDE 8: MANAGEMENT TEAM
• Describe team members.
  – Include founders, identified or committed follow-on hires, and the advisory board.
• Describe the additional skills and key management personnel required to build a company and when you need to add them.
  – CEO, CFO or controller, VP marketing, VP sales, VP engineering, etc.
	Who are you?
	Who are the founders? Provide relevant background information on your team and their roles.
	Describe the ideal characteristics of the rest of the senior management team that you are going to have to fill as you build the company and/or get funding.

SLIDE 9: COMPETITION
• Describe incumbent competitors.
  – Number, size, market shares, growth rates, IP, product/services positioning, likely roadmap
  – Can any of these competitors be turned into customers or partners?
• Describe emerging or potential competitors.
  – Stage, backing, technology, product positioning, likely roadmap
  – Why will you be the winning start-up in your market?
	This is a very important slide. You are never unique. You will have competitors, and you must understand who they are, their strengths and weaknesses. Are they big or small companies, are they competitors you might be able to turn into a distribution partner or customer, and why. What is your strategy to win against these competitors?

(*Continued*)

Table 13-1   ***Continued***

Slides	Notes on Contents

SLIDE 10: FINANCIAL PROJECTIONS
• Describe the amount and phasing of the capital you need to raise to reach exit.
  – Are federal or state grants included?
• Show pro forma annual financials for five years.
  – Include gross margin forecasts.
• Describe the potential enterprise value of the company you hope to build.
	State how big and how fast a company you can build. Give financials at a high level by year, showing revenues, expenses, and sources of capital, highlighting the breakeven point. Show use of federal or state grants supplementing bank or equity funding. It is important to state your expected gross margins after two or three years, how the value of your company will grow, and what it might be worth when you are ready to sell it.

SLIDE 11: EXIT STRATEGY
• Is your company an IPO candidate?
  – If so, explain why and show comparables.
• Who are your likely acquirers?
  – How much might they pay, why, and when?
  – Have they completed similar acquisitions in the past?
  – What will compel them to buy you rather than see you bought by a feared competitor?
	Investors need to know not just how much money they need to put into a company, but also when they are going to get it back out with a profit. This will occur when you sell or take your company public. What companies like yours can serve as benchmarks either by looking at their public stock price or knowing how much an acquirer paid for them? Describe how, in four to six years, investors are going to earn a return on their investments.

company. However, the flow of information is similar for all stages of investment, loans, or an exit. Up to five more may be added for extra clarification. It is useful to anticipate probing questions and have backup slides that address these points. It impresses investors if they come up with a difficult question such as "Isn't Global Inc. a major competitive threat to this business?" and the presenter can immediately show an analysis of Global Inc. and illustrate the new company's advantages over that company. A well-prepared presentation of twelve to sixteen slides may have as many again anticipated backup slides. All the comments made above regarding making an elevator pitch apply here too. In addition, consider the following:

• Do not hand out copies of your presentation prior to the formal part of the meeting. Indicate that you will leave copies afterward for reference. If you fail to engage all the participants, you will be distracted by one or more reading forward from the handouts and perhaps even participating in side conversations about points that you have not yet reached. You will have lost control of the situation.

• Do not read from the slides. Use the slides to raise points and add to the content with your presentation.

• Face the audience, not the screen.

• Do not overrun your time for the formal presentation. This may leave you no time for more personal engagement, and the opportunity will be lost.

• Fewer slides are better than too many.

• Design the presentation around a clearly articulated and visual roadmap.

Since prospective investors are often taking an unsecured position in the company, the presentation must include a financial plan that describes data to make an informed decision. Sophisticated investors will rigorously evaluate the abilities of the management team, the financial strength of the company, and the commercial viability of the business. Prior to the "real event," the entrepreneur should make the presentation before several people to get feedback and to make sure a compelling case is made for the new company.

PRESENTATION TIPS

- Goal is to offer a high-level, summarized view of the company
- Presentation is not a business plan on screen
- Have only one or two speakers, no more
- Limit material to twelve to sixteen slides
- Slides should contain concise ideas, not sentences
- Use no more than five bullet points per page
- Choose Arial typeface, twelve-point font (simple, noncurlicue font)
- Dark background with white letters is easier read on the screen
- Minimize the use of bullet points, check marks, boxes, and other noninformation symbols

A full investors' presentation based on the elevator pitch and business plan for Railway Innovation Technologies referred to earlier is available at www.wiley. com/college/kaplan. The presentation is accompanied by a commentary and the slide presentation.

AFTER THE PRESENTATION

The entrepreneur should contact the investors a few days after having completed the presentation to see if additional questions need to be answered.

Create Excitement about the Investment

If investors have expressed any degree of interest, the entrepreneur should move interest into action and investment. He should set a realistic deadline for the investment and notify investors that the supply of available equity is rapidly dwindling. Once investors have put money into a company, the relationship isn't over; it's just beginning. To state the obvious, investors have a vested interest in seeing the business succeed. The company should always make a point of involving investors in the success of the business by keeping them updated on new business opportunities and sales and financial targets. Good communications are vital throughout the life of the investor-company relationship. This is particularly true when the company goes through some disappointments, as undoubtedly it will.

Learn the Investor Evaluation Process

During the evaluation period, investors analyze the business into four fundamental sections.

1. Management Team

Investors like to review the experience and previous successes of the management team and the entrepreneur. They like to know a team is in place to run the business.

The entrepreneur does not have to hire an entire team immediately, but she should indicate the types of individuals the company will hire to operate the business. In cases where the entrepreneur has been involved in previous successful ventures, investor confidence in providing immediate funding is made easier. Also, other investors, advisers, and board members who have a stake in the business are reviewed.

2. Business Model

The business model, market size, and customers are examined along with the timing of the opportunity. It is important to emphasize that the company has sales or can obtain sales through a solid sales plan. The emphasis for investors is that the longer it takes to achieve sales, the longer it will take for investors to get their money back.

3. Context

Both internal and external factors that affect the business, including customer reactions to the product, competitors, economic regulation, and the stage of technology, are analyzed.

4. The Deal

The deal and the price structure relate to the valuation. Structure refers to the terms and timing of the deal, and price is the stock, cash, or debt that will complete the transaction. This can include a silent investor, active participation, or an adviser. A final valuation is generally made three to six months following the presentation, after the investors have conducted full due diligence along the lines explored in Chapter 8.

Dealing with Rejection

The entrepreneur can view the experience of finding investments as a positive, even if the investment is rejected owing to inadequate answers regarding the risks of the business. The entrepreneur should always inquire if the investor knows another interested party or under what conditions the investor would reconsider. Therefore, the entrepreneur should always ask, "Who else may be interested?" "Do you have a contact name?" "If we do not receive funding now, can we count on you for later financing?" The entrepreneur must learn to turn negative experiences into positive opportunities.

The Financing Agreement

Once an offer is accepted, the entrepreneur will begin to negotiate the final financing agreement that includes ownership, control, and financial objectives. This is called a *term sheet* (see more on term sheets in Chapter 8), and it sets out the initial investment and understanding between the issuer and investor. The ownership for investors can range from 10 percent (profitable companies) to 90 percent (financially troubled firms). Most investors, however, do not want to own more than 50 percent of a business. Voting control usually remains with the entrepreneur and his management team. However, the investors will generally ask for representation on the board of directors to have some say in important decisions. Therefore, the actual control exercisable by the entrepreneur is usually greatly curtailed after an equity investment.

The financial objectives of the investors are either a corporate acquisition or a public stock offering within three to five years of their initial investment. These objectives are discussed when long-term financial goals are negotiated with the investors. A major concern for the investor is in determining the valuation of the business and the returns, which will be dictated by the value of the business. Investors price a business on the potential capital return in the future. The share an investor expects to gain in return for the investment depends not only on the amount of money contributed, but also on the time and opportunity costs (missing investments in other businesses). The entrepreneur wants the investor to value the company for what it will be worth in three to five years (i.e., a corporate acquisition or an initial public offering). This is important in determining how an investment today will be worth more tomorrow. Investors usually value a company at a lower price than the entrepreneur would. For example, an early-stage company has a great idea and a young management team but no sales. From the investors' viewpoint, ideas are cheap, and an inexperienced management team might not be able to execute or implement the plan. Investors are always interested in maximizing the return on their investments. See Chapter 8 for more on term sheets and deal structures and Chapter 8 for business valuations and the methods and procedures used.

ROADMAP

IN ACTION

Remember, the questions to be answered are as follows: Will the investors get their money back before the entrepreneur? Will the investors have the right to invest in future rounds? There are also the issues of what role investors will play in the company.

SUMMARY

No idea or opportunity can create value unless the entrepreneur can communicate it effectively to all classes of potential stakeholders in the venture, including investors, lenders, customers, suppliers, agents, advisers, partners, and employees. Entrepreneurs must learn to lead others so they can become as excited and driven by the opportunity as the founders themselves. Communicating, then, is vital.

Every communication medium must be tailored to fit the targeted audience. The entrepreneurs must become used to putting themselves in the role of recipient so they can craft a message that will directly appeal to the individual needs and aspirations of the audience.

Entrepreneurs use oral, written, and presentation media to communicate. The short forms of an elevator pitch, introductory letter and teaser, and executive summary require a surprising effort to make them lucid, concise, and engaging. It is often more difficult to express yourself in a limited time or space than in a full business plan or full-blown presentation. These shorter forms are used to create initial interest and must be followed up with a more detailed presentation, which highlights all the key points of a business plan. These skills need practice, and entrepreneurs should take every opportunity they have to present to an audience and to write brief summaries of their opportunities for different targeted stakeholders.

STUDY QUESTIONS

1. What are the various types of communications that an entrepreneur uses, and what are their main purposes?

2. What key points would you make in an investor's presentation to the following audiences: bankers, angel investors, VC partners, suppliers, and potential key employees?

3. What are the major content items in a teaser?

4. Name the eleven foundation slides for an investor's presentation.

5. Name five common mistakes made by entrepreneurs when making a presentation.

6. How does an entrepreneur handle the situation when an investor refuses to sign a confidentiality agreement?

EXERCISES

1. Read the SurfPark case study in Chapter 5. Prepare a teaser for this business targeted at one of the following audiences: a banker, a venture capitalist, or a corporate partner. Identify the actual entity that you are targeting and the appropriate person, by name and title, to whom you wish to send the teaser. Write a one-page accompanying letter of introduction as if you were the CEO of SurfPark.

2. Read the SurfPark case study in Chapter 5, and prepare a twelve- to sixteen-slide presentation for a group of angel investors.

3. Prepare five backup slides for difficult questions that you anticipate will be asked in the presentation referred to in question 2.

4. View Ankit Patel's elevator pitch on the book's[6] Web site. What three things do you like best about this, and why? How would you improve it?

5. View the investor's presentation by Ankit Patel for the railroad opportunity mentioned in the previous question. What are five key points that he makes? How would you improve the presentation, and why?

Management Exercise

View Denis Coleman's comments in the video on the book's Web site entitled "Angels, More Than Just Investors."

Then individually or as a team, produce a short presentation analyzing the following: "I regret I had to write you a long letter, I did not have time to write a short one." Describe an elevator pitch and explain why it is extremely important. Why is it so difficult to accomplish?

INTERACTIVE LEARNING ON THE WEB

Test your knowledge of the chapter using the book's interactive Web site.

www.wiley.com/college/kaplan

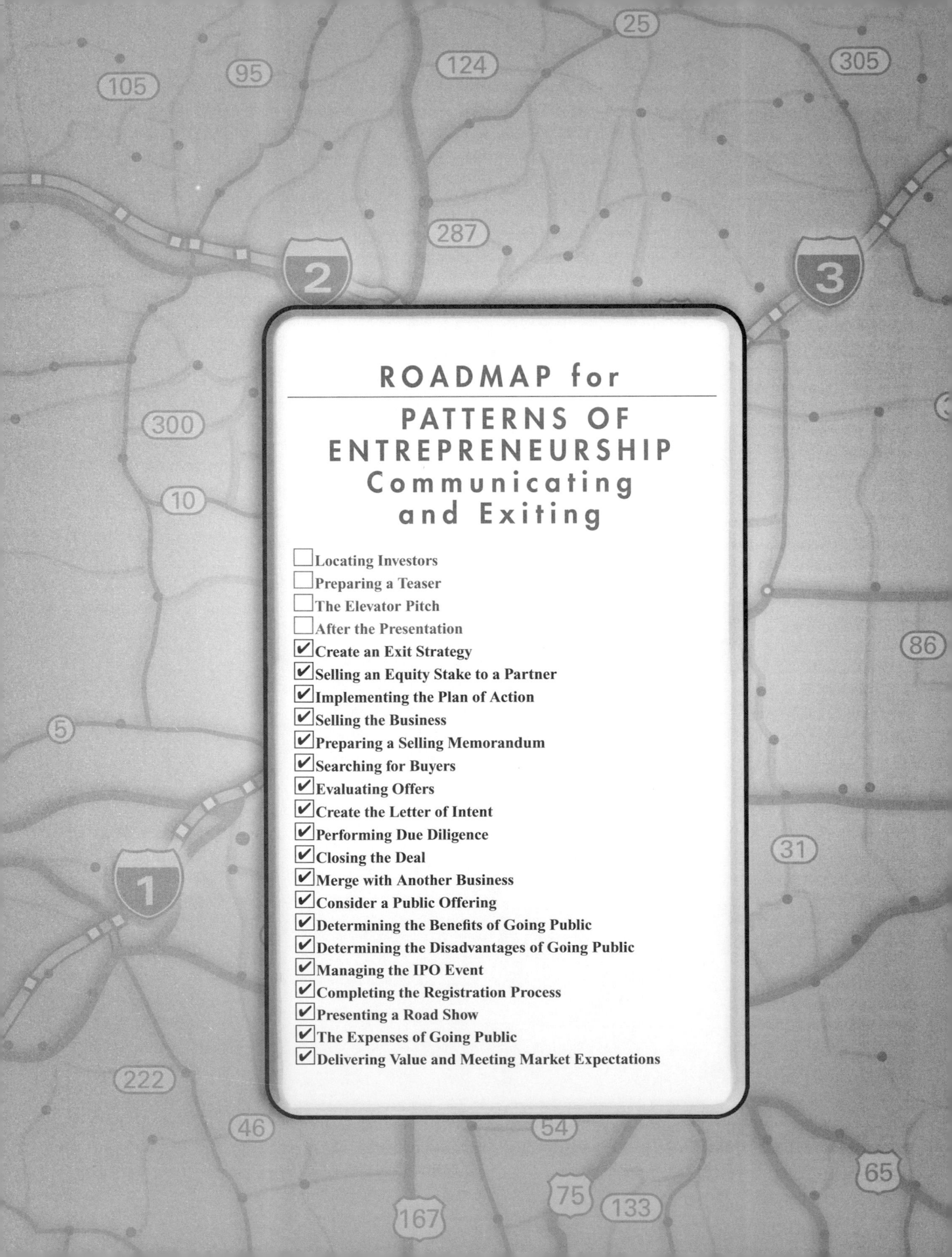

ROADMAP for

PATTERNS OF ENTREPRENEURSHIP
Communicating and Exiting

- ☐ Locating Investors
- ☐ Preparing a Teaser
- ☐ The Elevator Pitch
- ☐ After the Presentation
- ☑ Create an Exit Strategy
- ☑ Selling an Equity Stake to a Partner
- ☑ Implementing the Plan of Action
- ☑ Selling the Business
- ☑ Preparing a Selling Memorandum
- ☑ Searching for Buyers
- ☑ Evaluating Offers
- ☑ Create the Letter of Intent
- ☑ Performing Due Diligence
- ☑ Closing the Deal
- ☑ Merge with Another Business
- ☑ Consider a Public Offering
- ☑ Determining the Benefits of Going Public
- ☑ Determining the Disadvantages of Going Public
- ☑ Managing the IPO Event
- ☑ Completing the Registration Process
- ☑ Presenting a Road Show
- ☑ The Expenses of Going Public
- ☑ Delivering Value and Meeting Market Expectations

CHAPTER 14

SCALING AND EXITING THE VENTURE

"Think of yourself as on the threshold of unparalleled success, a whole clear life lies before you. Achieve. Achieve."

ANDREW CARNEGIE

OBJECTIVES

- Learn how to use alliances to sell an equity stake in the venture.
- Identify the various sources to develop an exit strategy.
- List the exit options available for entrepreneurs.
- Describe the process and sequence of events in selling a business.
- Describe the selling memorandum and its contents.
- Learn the process of launching an initial public offering.
- Understand the advantages and disadvantages of going public.

CHAPTER OUTLINE

Introduction

Profile: Alan Trefler—Private to Public Ownership

Create an Exit Strategy

Selling an Equity Stake to a Partner

Implementing the Plan of Action

Selling the Business

Preparing a Selling Memorandum

Searching for Buyers

Evaluating Offers

Create the Letter of Intent

Performing Due Diligence

Closing the Deal

Merge with Another Business

Consider a Public Offering

Determining the Benefits of Going Public

Determining the Disadvantages of Going Public

Managing the IPO Event

Completing the Registration Process

Presenting a Road Show

The Expenses of Going Public

Delivering Value and Meeting Market Expectations

Summary

Study Questions

Exercises

Interactive Learning on the Web

Additional Resources

INTRODUCTION

As we have seen, many entrepreneurs, more interested in their lifestyle, never intend to give up control of their companies. However, personal aspirations change over time, and lifestyle entrepreneurs may eventually decide to find a way to take more than just income out of the company by selling part or all of the enterprise. This chapter provides the knowledge to identify the best exit plan for the entrepreneur and the venture's shareholders and how to be in the strongest position to manage the process. Not until the shares of the company are purchased by a third party can investors sell their ownership positions and cash out, preferably at a profit. This is called a "liquidity event."

A number of techniques and strategies can help the entrepreneur develop an exit plan. This chapter highlights the methodology, procedures, and options available for entrepreneurs when considering an exit strategy. There are several ways a company can realize an exit plan from the value it has created. Described in this chapter are the most common methods, namely, to sell an equity stake to a partner, sell the business, merge with another company, implement a leveraged buyout, or sell the company to its employees. We also discuss the planning for a public offering that provides an option to sell a portion of the venture and to scale the business for growth. In all cases researching and carrying out an exit require the communication skills learned in Chapter 13.

PROFILE: ALAN TREFLER—PRIVATE TO PUBLIC OWNERSHIP[1]

Alan Trefler started playing chess at a young age and became a world-class player. He reasoned that if you could program a computer to play at that level, it should be possible to create software to make complex management decisions. So in 1983, with a loan of $500,000 from family members, he started Pegasystems Inc. The Massachusetts-based business creates software that wades through databases to help corporations capture useful information about their customers. The company grew rapidly, and he managed to pay back the loan in just four years. Back in the late 1970s, Trefler actually offered to create software for his previous employers at Citibank, but they turned him down. Ironically, the bank signed on as one of Pegasytems' first customers. Through the 1980s Trefler bootstrapped the business completely, never seeking or accepting a dime of venture capital. He eventually did something every entrepreneur dreams of but few accomplish: he took his company public in 1996 and retained more than 70 percent of the equity. Because so few people owned stock, he was free to keep a huge chunk of the outstanding shares for himself. Pegasystems has grown to more than $160 million in revenues and a market capitalization of around a billion dollars since then, leaving Trefler with a considerable fortune through his ownership, which still stands at 58 percent.

CREATE AN EXIT STRATEGY

Entrepreneurs spend so much time creating a business that many do not plan for a successful exit. The entrepreneur often sees selling the company as selling out and, in most cases, not meeting the expectations of investors or the management team. This situation can occur when new technologies impact the current product revenues or when competitors gain market share and the company loses its market position.

Usually the entrepreneur begins to develop reasons for exiting the business, including the stress level of managing the business and not finding enough time for the company because of family commitments. The opposite may also occur: the entrepreneur spends so much time on the venture that her family commitments suffer. Another first sign, which usually occurs in the early stages of growth, is the struggle for the company to stay alive. Therefore, it is important to prepare the exit plan early in the business cycle and at the right time. As discussed in Chapter 8, any entrepreneur seeking equity funding for growth must have plans for an exit prior to accepting external investors. There are several ways a company can realize an exit from the value it has created; the most common follow.

ROADMAP

IN ACTION

Entrepreneurs may want to exit the business by establishing a strategic alliance and selling an equity stake in the business. An effective equity alliance can substantially increase the value of the venture and offer an exit option at a later date.

SELLING AN EQUITY STAKE TO A PARTNER

Selling an equity stake in the business to a strategic partner can substantially increase the value of the venture and offer an exit option to the entrepreneur. However, it takes research and due diligence to sell a minority or majority equity interest in the venture to a strategic partner. Just picking up the phone and calling as many big players as possible in the hopes that they will want to buy an interest will generate lots of effort but few results. A well-researched and targeted effort is needed to determine why an alliance partner should purchase a stake and the reasons and justification for the sale. Usually, for the entrepreneur to sell an equity position, the partnership must be beneficial to all parties. In most cases an exploratory alliance is formed first. After measuring the success of the relationship, an equity position is negotiated to sell out completely or receive a minority stake in the venture. As an example, to initiate the alliance, the entrepreneur can offer the company licenses to patents, copyrights, or trade secrets, and the other company can bring a stronger marketing organization with an eye toward growing the business. When the companies have complementary skills, the alliance can accomplish tasks that neither party could do alone. This positions the relationship for equity participation. The parties can also share customer relationships and costs and reduce their individual exposure to risk. The alliance can be mutually beneficial by obtaining additional revenue from existing products, limiting the amount of capital to invest in needed capacity, and avoiding the need to add personnel. Additional benefits can increase the chances of getting into the market faster or obtaining first mover advantage and possibly gaining exclusive access or license to a product. Success in any or all of these factors of strategic alliances develops the relationship for the partners to purchase an equity stake in the venture.

"Although selling an equity stake of a business is financially attractive, entrepreneurs must consider where they are in regard to their personal plan and at what point they are willing to give up control of their business. For many entrepreneurs, the control issue is as important if not more important than the financial gain."

LIZ ELTING
President and CEO,
Transperfect Translations, Inc.

IMPLEMENTING THE PLAN OF ACTION

The first principle in positioning the alliance partner to acquire an equity stake is to know what value the partner sees in the business.[2] The most common value for most alliances is increasing the revenue or decreasing the costs of operation. Before any serious negotiation, however, this value needs to be determined, and both sides require an evaluation to quantify the present and potential market opportunities. Also, the entrepreneur needs to identify what the alliance will cost in time and money. For example, a relationship with a partner may limit the chances of selling the venture to the company's competitors. The following actions serve as a guide for establishing an alliance:

- Identify the objective of a proposed alliance. The entrepreneur should determine the time requirements and the expectations of the parties involved in the process.
- Build a target list of possible candidate companies. It is best to go after more than one possible partner, and a mixture of size and scope is important. Although it might be exciting to go after a global brand, in some instances (especially on the support and development side) finding a possible partner of like size and/or with existing industry experience and a regional player, is a smarter move. The parties will be more interested in partnering and making the relationship work.
- Research the candidates and examine the Web sites and press releases. Determine who is in charge of business development—the CEO or the president. Analyze information, including articles that mention them. The key is to find out the company's mission and focus. Build a document on each target, including contact information and phone numbers.
- Present the finding on each target to the key members of the areas that will be impacted by the relationship (e.g., software development, IT, marketing, sales) and gather their input, concerns, and interests.
- Develop a nonconfidential introduction kit and cover letter to send to possible alliance partners. (This could be an e-mail with attached document or PDF). (More about creating such a document is covered in Chapter 13.) The letter should be short and to the point, highlighting why the relationship would be of value to the partner. The goal should be an in-person meeting. It is best that the first meeting be on the potential alliance partner's terms and location. In this way you can make an on-site inspection, and they will be more comfortable and more likely to know that you are showing commitment. A sample meeting agenda should be prepared as follows.

MEETING AGENDA

Prepare an agenda with names, titles, and contact information.

State the goals and desired outcomes of the meetings.

Prepare an overview of the business and role (have hard copies, including extras).

Review the specific reason for the meeting and the driving reason for an alliance.

Prepare a general business overview.

MEETING AGENDA (cont.)

- Conduct a walk-through and tour. No matter how small an office, walk the floor and talk with people; get a sense of the environment and the culture.
- Review the level of interest and get ideas on how the two businesses would work together.
- Agree on the relationship, timing, next steps, action, and who will be the responsible persons on each side.[3]

Making an alliance work requires constant involvement and communication. The companies need to stay connected and be in constant communication. Because of this time commitment and effort, the company should target only a few key alliances. Otherwise the alliances will die off, and the cost of time, legal, and emotional investments will never be recouped.[4]

Starting the Negotiation Process

When the negotiating starts, both companies should use their best efforts to make it work. The parties should establish relationships with the highest officers and decision makers. The entrepreneur should make sure he is kept informed and does not entrust the fate of the partnership to a lower-level person. To determine the price or value as part of the negotiation, the outline of the selling memorandum shown later in this chapter will assist in maximizing efficiencies. When the contract is prepared, keep in mind that the best results for a successful alliance are the responsibility of both parties.

SELLING THE BUSINESS

Selling the business is another option in the entrepreneur's exit plan. However, in a weak economy, selling a business seems a risky option to the entrepreneur. The best plan is to build valuable assets and identify them in the selling process. The obvious assets are inventory, receivables, equipment, and real estate. If the business is a service company, the entrepreneur must become more inventive. The entrepreneur should plan to arrange long-term employment deals with his staff or sign extended contracts with customers or key suppliers. This plan can be very time consuming and be an emotionally charged experience, as it is typically one of the most significant events in an entrepreneur's business life. If you have outside investors and have added experienced board members, they can be extremely valuable in preparing and structuring a sale of the company.

After the initial assessment to sell the business, a preliminary calculation of the company's value should be determined. Selling a company is time consuming, and you will not want to proceed unless the company's value meets your own and your shareholders' expectations. However, in a tight money environment, it can take a lot of give-and-take to close a deal. Sellers may have to agree to a long-term payment for part or all of the transaction or lease high-priced equipment to the buyer.

Along with determining an acceptable price, the entrepreneur should think about what kind of compensation or payment is acceptable. Cash only? Earn-out agreements based on reaching predetermined earnings? Stock? What form of seller employment agreements and noncompete clauses? Is she willing to help the buyer finance the purchase? Although these decisions do not have to be made immediately, the entrepreneur should start to consider the alternatives. The sellers who thrive are those who are flexible in their strategies and actions, capable of moving quickly and adapting to change.

PREPARING A SELLING MEMORANDUM

Entrepreneurs should use the business plan as a marketing tool to help sell the company. In this context, the revised plan becomes the selling memorandum. The information in the business plan will be the basis for the buyer's preliminary evaluation of the company.

A selling memorandum normally includes information about the company's history, the market in which the company competes, the company's products, its operations, and its strengths. The memorandum should be a very comprehensive document because it reflects the quality of the organization. Once the selling memorandum is completed, the company is in a good position to refine the preliminary valuation and begin determining an appropriate range of selling prices.[5]

OUTLINE OF A SELLING MEMORANDUM

EXECUTIVE SUMMARY

The executive summary should explain the purpose of the memorandum and describe all the key elements of the memorandum in just a few pages. A well-written summary should convince the prospective buyer to continue reading. The summary has another important use. It can be sent separately to people who may not be serious buyers. If, after reviewing the summary, they are still interested in seeing the whole plan, the entrepreneur can release it to them after they sign a confidentiality agreement drafted by an attorney. This should help protect the confidential details of the memorandum.

PRODUCTS AND SERVICES

The memorandum should describe the company's products and services. How are they different from others on the market? Are they patented? Are there follow-on products? What R & D is required, and what technological risks exist? Include any product literature that is available.

MARKETING

Describe the market for the products and services. Explain the dynamics of the market, market size, market trends, growth potential, user demographics, and so on. What are the company's marketing strategies, pricing strategies, penetration targets, and advertising and promotional plans? Include a competitive analysis, listing direct competitors and their strengths and weaknesses, market share, financial information, and the like.

MANUFACTURING

How are the products manufactured? How will the resources be used? Describe required raw materials and their sources. Are there second sources for all critical

OUTLINE OF A SELLING MEMORANDUM (cont.)

items? Describe production facilities and capacity requirements and constraints. What warranties do the products carry? How is the service provided?

MANAGEMENT

Describe the current organization. List key personnel who will be staying with the company, and describe their positions and experience. Do not disclose their compensation, however, since this could provide recruiting information to competitors.

EMPLOYEES

Describe how the employees are compensated. What major benefits are provided? Does a union represent them? If so, what are the significant terms of the contract? How have relations been with the union?

HISTORICAL FINANCIAL STATEMENTS

Present financial statements for the most recent interim periods, including comparisons with prior years' results and with budgets. Also include statements for the past three fiscal years, including auditors' reports, if any.

FINANCIAL PROJECTIONS

Prepare financial projections for the next three to five years. Some sellers include their projections and the assumptions underlying the projections in the selling memorandum.[6]

SEARCHING FOR BUYERS

When the selling memorandum is complete, a search for potential buyers begins. Who might be interested in purchasing the company? The potential list that is prepared can include individual investors or entrepreneurs, existing management, other employee groups, competitors, customers, vendors, investment groups, and foreign investors. Each of these groups has different motivations to buy, and depending on the company's situation, some groups may be more appropriate than others as potential buyers.

ROA

IN

The most desirable way for the entrepreneur to find the right buyer is to have a file of prospective buyers who have contacted the company. In addition to personal contacts, other sources of potential buyers include trade associations, investment and commercial bankers and accountants.

Several types of professional intermediaries are available to help identify potential buyers:

- The major investment banking firms have mergers and acquisitions departments that specialize in providing a wide range of services for these types of transactions. These firms are probably the most sophisticated and generally focus on transactions where the purchase price is $25 million or more.

- Commercial banks recently have developed affiliates that provide services similar to the services of investment banking firms. As affiliates of banks, they have information about and access to the bank's client companies.

- Finally, smaller independent firms that specialize in these areas can be highly qualified intermediaries. They participate in a range of transactions from small ones to those of about $5 million, with the majority on the smaller side. There are also some intermediaries who can generate a list of sales prospectuses and aid with placing newspaper ads.

Lehman Formula Fee Schedule. The intermediary's key role is to identify potential candidates and assist both parties throughout the entire process to consummate the sale. This task is usually undertaken on an exclusive basis. Fees for bringing together the buyers and sellers are generally guaranteed by the seller, who provides an up-front retainer and a substantial amount contingent upon completion of the transaction. The total fee is often based on the "Lehman formula," which calls for fees of 5 percent of the first $1 million of purchase price, 4 percent of the second million, 3 percent of the third, 2 percent of the fourth, and 1 percent of amounts in excess of $4 million. Variations of the Lehman formula usually work well for midsize transactions. However, a different arrangement may be negotiated for very small and very large transactions.

EVALUATING OFFERS

In evaluating prospective offers, sellers should investigate the prospective buyer's (1) credentials and track record; (2) creditworthiness, especially if a portion of the purchase price is deferred or is paid in notes or stock; (3) management style; and (4) integrity.

The investigation may uncover some hidden problems with the buyer's company. The information gathered may indicate that the timing of the sale is inappropriate for business or personal reasons. More important, the research may prove that the buyer is simply the wrong party to make the purchase for any number of reasons. Discussions with some of the companies the buyer has already acquired might yield further insights.

After potential buyers are identified, the entrepreneur must determine which are financially capable of purchasing the business. The seller business should contact credit bureaus and trade journals, which can be used to rule out buyers who cannot afford the asking price. Next, determine which prospects are most likely to be interested in the company. Look at the business from each of the prospective buyers' standpoints, and determine why each one might be interested in the business.

Holding the Initial Meeting

One of the most critical steps in effecting the sale of a company is the initial meeting between the buyer and seller. Both buyer and seller will have certain objectives. The buyer will want to know the seller's motives for selling the company and how serious the seller is, as well as more detailed information about the business. The seller will also want to know how serious the buyer is, if the buyer has the financial resources necessary to purchase the company, and whether the buyer is the type of person to whom he or she wants to sell the company.

If the results of the initial meeting warrant further consideration of the deal, the buyer will next begin to evaluate the company and develop a financial structure for the proposed purchase. The buyer should hold preliminary discussions of the proposed financial structure with specific lenders and any investors to get their thoughts on the viability of the deal. As in the initial meeting with the seller, the buyer should avoid the tendency to negotiate the specific points of investor agreements and should instead concentrate on whether there is an appropriate degree of interest in the transaction.

Negotiating

Negotiations play a key role throughout the acquisition process. There is no single session of negotiations in this type of transaction; rather, negotiations will be made at every step of the process as new information becomes available and additional analyses are performed.

Volumes have been written on the art of negotiating. The key to successful negotiation is an understanding of one's objectives, needs, strengths, and weaknesses and those of the other party. In a successful negotiation, both sides feel they have won. Give-and-take is inherent in the negotiating process. Both the buyer and the seller need to be flexible and to understand which bargaining points are important to win and where compromises can be reached. The buyer should consult with key advisers to develop a negotiating strategy and should keep those people involved throughout the process.

CREATE THE LETTER OF INTENT

Before investing the time and money needed to thoroughly evaluate the target company, the buyer will want to know that the seller is interested in continuing the process. A letter of intent is often written to confirm the interests of the two parties and to outline the basic terms that have been agreed on in the initial phase of negotiation. The letter of intent is, in many ways, similar to the term sheet for venture investments discussed in detail in Chapter 8.

The letter of intent is an agreement by the parties to continue to negotiate in good faith. Generally, it contains provisions that the terms are subject to a definitive contract and proclaims the document to be only an expression of intention. The letter of intent will have many escape clauses in it to allow both parties the opportunity to withdraw from the deal at any point. Such clauses may include requirements for approval by the board of directors or by the stockholders. Certain issues related to the transaction are normally addressed at this stage, and the preliminary resolution of these issues will be contained in the letter of intent:[7]

- *The Purchase Price.* This is either its amount or an agreed-on formula for its computation.
- *What Is Being Purchased?* The general categories of assets, liabilities, and operations that are being transferred to the buyer and those being retained by the seller should be identified.
- *The Structure.* The parties need to agree about whether the sale will be a sale of assets, a sale of stock, a merger, or some other structure.
- *The Payout or Types of Compensation.* Will it be cash, notes, equity, or some combination of these?

- *Escrow for Contingencies.* The buyer may want to establish an escrow account into which a portion of the purchase price will be deposited. This escrow might cover such items as unrecorded liabilities that later surface or recorded items that are only estimates (e.g., the allowance for uncollectable accounts).

- *Other Significant Terms.* These include contingent payments, covenants not to compete, and employment contracts.

- *Other Required Agreements.* These include renegotiated leases and long-term purchase contracts.

- *The Purchase Agreement.* What is the expected timing for preparing the purchase agreement? Who will draft it? Typically, the buyer's counsel will be the drafter.

- *Due Diligence.* What are the timing and extent? What are the buyer's expectations for documentation? Are management personnel and records available? (See Chapter 8 for a complete due diligence checklist for investment and purchase transactions.)

- *Professional Fees.* Who will be responsible for the various related fees, including fees for attorneys, accountants, appraisers, and investment bankers?

- *Exclusivity Agreement.* A buyer will want to negotiate with the seller on an exclusive basis. The seller will usually grant such a right for a defined period, such as ninety or 120 days.

- *"Bust-up Fees."* It has become fairly common for the buyer to want a provision for bust-up fees if the company is ultimately sold to another bidder. The buyer will argue that, by putting the company in play (i.e., performing a valuation and beginning negotiations so other companies are aware the target company is seriously for sale) the buyer has added value to the target company. If another buyer then outbids the original buyer, the original buyer should receive a portion of the increased price as compensation for this value added. Sellers, of course, will try to avoid such a fee.

Other Conditions

The following conditions for closing will also be included in the letter of intent:

- *Applicable Law.* If the transaction involves parties located in different states, it is common to identify which state laws will govern the agreements.

- *Adjustments of Purchase Price for Interim Results.* A purchase price is usually negotiated based in part on historical financial information. The price may be adjusted for any income or losses that occur through the actual closing date.

PERFORMING DUE DILIGENCE

Both the buyer and the seller will have to perform legal due diligence. The seller and advisers will review and prepare the disclosure schedules of information that are requested by the buyer to investigate the affairs of the company. They will also perform a legal audit to render an opinion on legal contingencies and other legal issues as of the closing.[8]

The typical information requested includes all corporate records (articles of incorporation, by-laws, minutes, stock records, etc.), material contracts, loan agreements, pending or threatened litigation, royalty agreements, labor agreements, leases, commitments, employment contracts, and stockholder agreements. An increasingly important area is environmental liability, as current owners of businesses may be held responsible for cleaning up toxic chemicals left by prior owners. Also, the need for regulatory clearance relating to restriction of trade concerns may have to be identified and obtained. The seller's counsel will issue a legal opinion at the closing that generally covers (1) the legality of the transaction (i.e., the company is authorized to do it and has all the requisite approvals), (2) confirmation of capital stock information, (3) the validity and enforceability of all material contracts, and (4) knowledge and status of pending or threatened litigation.

Preparing the Purchase Agreement

As the buyer's team begins its detailed evaluation of the company, the attorneys will be preparing the purchase agreements. The drafting of the documents will give rise to rounds of negotiations to resolve some of the obstacles deferred earlier in the process and to renegotiate issues previously agreed on but modified because of information that came to light in the evaluation process.

The purchaser's attorney usually drafts the purchase agreement. Although the letter of intent will serve as the outline for this agreement, the final document will generally be quite lengthy. New issues often arise as a result of the due diligence process, and much time is spent in drafting the representations and warranties of both the buyer and the seller, as well as in drafting the indemnification provisions.

CLOSING THE DEAL

Once all these issues have been resolved and the financing commitments have been received, the deal is in condition to close; all the documents are signed, the stock or assets are transferred, and the consideration exchanges hands.

Often, certain time-consuming procedures such as obtaining a tax ruling, receiving an audited balance sheet, or perfecting the title on assets are a prerequisite to consummating the deal. Rather than wait until everything is done, the parties will agree to a deferred closing. The purchase agreement may be signed and the consideration may change hands, but the actual passage of title may occur at a later date. *Conditions* are obligations that must be met for the deal to legally close. Typical conditions include fulfillment of key employment agreements; delivery of financial statements; maintenance of minimum net worth requirements; provision of accountants' comfort letters and legal opinions; and if applicable, gaining third-party consent on the transfer of material agreements, licenses, or rights.

MERGE WITH ANOTHER BUSINESS

A merger is a transaction between two companies and is an alternative to selling the business or selling an equity stake to a strategic partner. A merger between two businesses ranges from survival to value-added services for the growth of the new venture. When a company loses its competitive advantage in the marketplace, a merger may be the only path left to follow.

On creating a merger, the entrepreneur should identify areas of similarity and differences and define the capability that shows the value of each company.

Planning a merger requires calculating the values of both the business and all existing resources. (Use Chapter 8 to determine which valuation methods are best and how to evaluate the other company's management and capabilities.) The benefits of a merger can be the route to instant product diversification and quick completion of product lines. It also can provide technical know-how, greater executive depth, economies of scale, improved access to financing, entry into otherwise closed markets, vertical integration of manufacturing operations, and new marketing strength.

CONSIDER A PUBLIC OFFERING

Entrepreneurs can realize a harvest from the value they have created by considering a public offering. In deciding whether to go ahead with a public offering, it is important that entrepreneurs remember that the initial offering (IPO) is neither more nor less important than any of the exit options we have discussed. It is usually one that a company may undertake over time. An important consideration for an IPO is the timing of the transaction, as the demand for newly issued stock can be extremely volatile. In deciding whether to do an IPO, it is always advisable to proceed with a backup plan. Even if the company is well prepared and the market is favorable, the economy can change by the date of the IPO.[8] Going public represents a rite of passage for a company and provides both benefits and obligations that should be carefully considered. The IPO process is difficult, the pitfalls are numerous, and the stakes are high. Poor market timing and inadequate planning can jeopardize an IPO. Despite initial positive performance after the offering, many companies discover that the values recede soon after going public and the company underperforms in both profits and share price.

The following questions need to be addressed in making an IPO decision:

- Are you ready to share the ownership of your company with the public?
- Are you prepared to disclose your company's most closely held secrets?
- Can you live with the continued scrutiny of investors and market analysts?
- Can you devote the required 100 percent of your time for six to eight months and pay the substantial fees that it takes for a typical IPO?
- Are you prepared to take on the issues, challenges, and responsibilities of going public?

DETERMINING THE BENEFITS OF GOING PUBLIC

The benefits of going public are many and diverse. To determine whether they outweigh the drawbacks, you must evaluate them in the context of personal, shareholder, and corporate objectives. Some of the most attractive benefits include the following:[9]

- *Improved Financial Condition.* Selling shares to the public brings equity money that does not have to be repaid, immediately improving the company's financial condition.
- *Benefits to the Shareholder/Investor.* Going public offers liquidity to existing investors despite the sales restrictions imposed on the major investors and officers and directors of the company. Underwriters will restrict founding stockholders

and management from selling their sales through lock-up agreements (normally 180 days) for a specific period of time; eventually they can convert their shares into cash. The value of the stock may increase remarkably, starting with the initial offering. Shares that are publicly traded generally command higher prices than those that are not. Investors are usually willing to pay more for public companies because of (1) the marketability of the shares, (2) the maturity/sophistication attributed to public companies, and (3) the availability of more information.

- *Diversification of Shareholder Portfolios.* Going public makes it possible for shareholders to diversify their investment portfolios. IPOs often include a secondary offering (shares owned by existing shareholders) in addition to a primary offering (previously unissued shares). The entrepreneur must ensure that potential investors and shareholders do not perceive the secondary offerings as a bailout for shareholders. Underwriters frequently restrict the number of shares that can be sold by existing shareholders in a secondary offering.

- *Access to Capital.* Accessing the public equity markets enables you to attract better valuations, accept less dilution of ownership, and raise more money. The money from an IPO can repay debt, fund special projects, and be used for acquisitions. For example, the proceeds can be used to acquire other businesses, repay debts, finance research and development projects, and acquire or modernize production facilities. Another plus is that raising equity capital through a public offering often results in a higher valuation for your company, through a higher multiple of earnings (or price-earnings ratio) as compared with many types of private financing. Thus, it often results in less dilution of ownership than with some other financing alternatives, such as venture capital. Raising capital in this way also avoids the interest costs and cash drain of debt financing.

- *Management and Employee Incentives.* The company can issue stock options to management and employees. This can be more motivating and rewarding to employees than issuing illiquid stock and will attract and retain the key executives.

- *Enhanced Corporate Reputation.* The company's public status and listing on a national exchange can provide a competitive advantage over other companies in the same industry by providing greater visibility and enhanced corporate image. This can lead to increased sales, reduced pricing from vendors, and improved service from suppliers.

- *Improved Opportunities for Future Financing.* By going public, an entrepreneurial venture usually improves its net worth and builds a larger and broader equity base. The improved debt-to-equity ratio will help the company borrow additional funds as needed or reduce the current cost of borrowing. If the stock performs well in the continuing aftermarket, the company is more likely to be able to raise additional equity capital on favorable terms. With an established market for the stock, the entrepreneur will have the flexibility to offer future investors a whole new range of securities with liquidity and an ascertainable market value.

- *A Path to Acquisitions.* Private companies often lack the financial connections and resources to assume an aggressive role in acquisitions. Well-conceived acquisitions can play a big part in corporate survival and success. Going public enhances a company's financing alternatives for acquisitions by adding two vital components to its financial resources: (1) cash derived from the IPO and (2) unissued equity shares that have a ready market. Public companies often issue stock (instead of paying cash) to acquire other businesses. The owners of an acquisition target may be more willing to accept a company's stock if it is publicly traded. The liquidity provided by the public market affords greater flexibility and ease in selling shares using shares as collateral for loans.

DETERMINING THE DISADVANTAGES OF GOING PUBLIC

The benefits of going public must be weighed against its drawbacks. Again, the entrepreneur must view the possible drawbacks in the context of personal, company, and shareholder objectives. In many cases the impact of these drawbacks can be minimized through thoughtful planning backed by the help of outside advisors.[8]

- *Loss of Control.* Depending on the proportion of shares sold to the public, the entrepreneur may be at risk of losing control of the company now or in the future. Retaining at least 51 percent of the shares will ensure control for now, but subsequent offerings and acquisitions may dilute control. However, if the stock is widely distributed, management usually can retain control even if it holds less than 50 percent of the shares. To retain voting control, it is possible to have a new class of common stock with limited voting rights. However, such stock may have limited appeal to investors and may, therefore, sell for less than ordinary common stock.

- *Sharing the Success.* Investors share the risks and successes of the new venture to which they contribute capital. If the entrepreneur realistically anticipates unusually high earnings in the next two or three years and can obtain bank or other financing, he or she may wish to temporarily defer a public offering. Then when the company does go public, the shares will, most likely, command a higher price.

- *Loss of Privacy.* Of all the changes that result when a company goes public, perhaps none is more troublesome than the loss of privacy. When a company becomes publicly held, the Securities and Exchange Commission (SEC) requires disclosure of much information about the company—information that private companies don't ordinarily disclose. Some of those disclosures contain highly sensitive information such as compensation paid to key executives and directors, special incentives for management, and many of the plans and strategies that underlie the company's operations. These disclosures rarely harm the business. For the most part, employee compensation and the prices paid for materials and received for products are governed by market forces, not by the disclosed financial results.

- *Limits on Management's Freedom to Act.* By going public, management surrenders some degree of freedom. While the management of a privately held company generally is free to act by itself, the management of a public company must obtain the approval of the board of directors on certain major matters; on special matters it must seek the consent of the shareholders. The board of directors, if kept informed on a timely basis, can usually be counted on to understand management's needs, offer support, and grant much of the desired flexibility.

- *Demands of Periodic Reporting.* Management is required to comply with SEC regulations and reporting requirements. These requirements include quarterly financial reporting (Form 10-Q), annual financial reporting (Form 10-K), and reporting of current material events (Form 8-K). Reporting the requirements of a registrant demands significant time and financial commitments. Securities analysts will also demand management's time. Recently the additional costs and personal burdens imposed by the Sarbanes-Oxley legislation for financial reporting have become a further concern to senior management.

- *Initial and Outgoing Expenses.* Going public can be costly and will result in a tremendous commitment of management's time and energy. The largest single cost in an IPO ordinarily is the underwriter's discount or commission, which generally ranges from 6 to 10 percent of the offering price. In addition, legal and accounting fees, printing costs, the underwriter's out-of-pocket expenses (generally not included in the commission), filing fees, as well as registrar and transfer agent fees can typically add another $300,000 to $500,000.

- *New Fiduciary Responsibilities.* As the owner of a private business, the money invested and risked is the owner's. However, as the manager of a public company, the money invested and risked belongs to the shareholders. The entrepreneur is accountable to them, so she must approach potential conflicts of interest with the utmost caution. It also will be necessary to work with the board of directors to help them discharge their fiduciary responsibilities when acting on corporate matters.

MANAGING THE IPO EVENT

The IPO event follows many months of careful preparation.[10] During the IPO, the president/CEO will serve as the company's major representative, delivering the company's story to the financial market. The CEO will be involved in setting the strategic direction for the SEC Registration Statement.

The IPO event usually lasts between ninety and 120 days, but some take up to six months.[11] It includes preparing and filing the Registration Statement (and one to three amendments responding to comments from the SEC), going on the road show, and the closing and buying of the company stock by the underwriting syndicate. Other events will include the first periodic reports, proxy solicitation, and dealing with restricted stock.

Example of Timetable for an IPO

Day 1	First meeting ("all hands")
Day 45	Draft of registration statement
Day 55	Second meeting—revisions and agreement
Day 60	Filing of Registration Statement with the SEC
Day 90	Receipt of SEC comment letter
Day 70–100	The road show
Day 90–110	Revisions and pricing
Day 115	Effective date
Day 120	Closing

COMPLETING THE REGISTRATION PROCESS

The registration process begins when the entrepreneur has reached an understanding with an underwriter on the proposed public offering. From this point on, he becomes subject to SEC regulations on what may or may not be done to promote the company. The center of the process is preparing the Registration Statement (S1), which includes a complete description of the company, its business, the market for its products, and the regulatory environment in which it operates. This entails establishing the appropriate internal accounting policies for the business, systems, and management and preparing the required financial data, including highlights and timing. The financial statements must be audited and should reflect income statements for the preceding three years, balance sheets for the prior two years, and interim financial statements for the applicable periods. The statement also lists the company's officers and directors, biographies, compensation, and stock ownership. Other factors to consider are employment contracts, compensation, and the board of directors.

The first step in preparing the Registration Statement is the initial meeting or "all hands," which includes company executives, attorneys, auditors, underwriters, and underwriters' attorneys. At this meeting, responsibility is assigned for gathering information and for preparing the various parts of the Registration Statement. Typically, the attorneys play a coordinating role in directing this team effort.[10]

The Registration Statement is usually approved by company counsel and has comments from the underwriter, management, and company accountants. The prospectus, which is a part of the Registration Statement, becomes the marketing document for the IPO.

THE REGISTRATION PROCESS

Example of an IPO prospectus cover.

Initial Public Offering Prospectus

TECH-DATA INCORPORATED

10,000,000 Shares of Common Stock

$5.25 per share

TECH-DATA, INC.	We sell enterprise software to companies in the United States and Canada.
Per share price $5.25	Total $52,500,000 — This is the initial public offering, and no public market currently exists for the shares.
Less Discounts	$0.525 $5,250,000
Proceeds	$4.725 $47,250,000

Proposed Trading Symbols:

The Nasdaq SmallCap Market™ — DII

This investment involves a high degree of risk. You should purchase shares only if you can afford a complete loss. See "Risk Factors."

Neither the Securities and Exchange Commission nor any state securities commission has approved or disapproved these securities or determined if this prospectus is truthful or complete. Any representiation to the contrary is a criminal offense.

LEAD UNDERWRITERS, INC.

Initial Public Offering Prospectus

Filing the Registration Statement

When outstanding issues have been resolved and the company officers and majority of the board of directors have signed the Registration Statement, it is filed with the SEC (normally electronically) on the SEC's EDGAR system. In addition to filing with the SEC, the statement is also filed with any state in which the securities will be offered and with the National Association of Securities Dealers. At closing, documents are executed and stock certificates are exchanged. Usually company officers, counsel, transfer agent, and managing underwriters attend the final closing.

The rules also require that a final prospectus be delivered to all purchasers of the company stock.

Waiting during the Quiet Period

The SEC places restrictions on what a company can do while "in registration." These restrictions apply during the "quiet period." This is defined as the time and date the company agrees with the investment firm to offer the securities to the public until twenty-five days after the securities become available to the public. During the quiet period, any publicity release can raise questions or concerns about whether the publicity is part of the selling efforts—even if the publicity does not specifically mention the public offering.[10] However, this does not preclude the normal ongoing disclosure of factual information about the company. The SEC encourages companies to continue product advertising campaigns, periodic reporting to shareholders, and press announcements on factual business and financial developments, such as new contracts and plant openings.

The company, however, can publish a limited notice of the offering, including the amount of the offering, the name of the company, and a description of the security, the offering price, and the names of the underwriters. Known as "tombstone ads" because of their stark appearance, these notices are typically published in newspapers shortly after the initial filing of the registration statement and are not considered sales literature. The accompanying exhibit shows a tombstone ad for a company's IPO.

This announcement is neither an offer to sell nor

a solicitation to buy these securities.

The offering is made only by the prospectus.

New Issue   **February 15, 2009**

10,000,000 Shares

TECH-DATA, INCORPORATED

Common Stock

Price $5.25 per Share

Copies of the prospectus may be obtained in any state in which this announcement is circulated from only such of the undersigned or other dealers or brokers as may lawfully offer these securities in such state.

PRESENTING A ROAD SHOW

After the Registration Statement has been filed, the underwriters generally will take representatives of the company on a traveling road show, also referred to as a "dog-and-pony show." These meetings give prospective members of the underwriting syndicate, institutional investors, and industry analysts an opportunity to meet the company's management team and ask questions about the offering and the company.

The participants probably will be the company's chief executive officer and chief financial officer, whose major task will be to generate interest in the investors, and the investment bankers, who will manage the tour and monitor the book, or computerized log of orders. Typically, the road show consists of five to seven back-to-back meetings every day for two weeks. The question-and-answer period is equally important and requires extensive preparation. If the entrepreneur can anticipate the most challenging questions and welcome them, she will have a chance to turn what might have been an issue into a nonissue.

ROADMAP

IN ACTION

> The road show presents the opportunity to tell the company's story to the people who will help sell the securities and influence potential investors. It will also allow the CEO to meet many of the people who will follow the company after the public offering. The show is so challenging that no one can ever be completely prepared. The plan is to present a balanced view of the business, market, and competition, and why the company will be a huge success.

The preparation of the road show to interested investors should include the following:

- Development of a precise, twenty- to twenty-five-minute slide presentation, including details of the company's business, strategy, financial history, management, growth prospects, market, and regulatory environment
- Determination of which management personnel will present material and field questions
- Education of the underwriters' team
- Dry run of the road show presentation before institutional sales and corporate finance presentations are given at selected locations

Selecting the Underwriter

The underwriter that manages the offering plays a critical role in the success of the IPO, preparing the company's Registration Statement and selling the company's securities. In selecting an underwriter, the following factors are important:

- *Experienced Industry Analyst.* The underwriter should have an analyst experienced in IPOs and the industry you are in.
- *Synergy.* The company should feel comfortable with the individual bankers. The right synergy between the bankers and management is important.
- *Distribution.* The investment bank should have the resources of a retail salesforce to sell the stock.
- *Post-IPO Support.* The underwriter should have a strong record of the post-IPO price performance of companies it has recently taken public. A solid track record will indicate how well the investment bank priced recent transactions.

THE EXPENSES OF GOING PUBLIC

Underwriters' Compensation

The underwriters will receive a discount (spread) between the price at which they buy stock and the price at which the underwriters sell the same stock to the public. The amount of the spread is negotiated based on the size and risk of the offering. A typical firm commitment–offering discount is approximately 7 percent of the public offering price of the stock.

Underwriters may also be granted warrants as partial compensation for an offering. Other compensation may include reimbursement of expenses and rights of first refusal on future underwriting, directorships, and consulting arrangements.

Accounting and Legal Fees

The lawyers' and accountants' fees depend on the amount of work involved in preparing the Registration Statement and reviewing the financial statements and other financial data. The company should endeavor to do as much of the work of preparing the Registration Statement as possible to cut costs.

Directors' and Officers' Insurance

Before going public, a company needs to take out a personal liability insurance policy that will protect the officers and directors from being held personally liable if a shareholder suit is brought based on incorrect information in the Registration Statement.

DELIVERING VALUE AND MEETING MARKET EXPECTATIONS

When the IPO is completed and finalized, the entrepreneur and the management team must begin meeting the shareholders and board of directors. Investors and shareholders are very well informed, and if the company misses earnings projections by even a small amount, the stock price can drop 10 percent or more the next day. It has been said that it can take six quarters of on-target performance to win the market back. The challenge after the IPO is to deliver the value that the company promised in the business plan and offering memorandum. Delivering the value is a balancing act that involves meeting and exceeding the expectations of the market and all the stakeholders while the company implements the strategic initiatives on time and on budget.

For the entrepreneur/CEO of a public company, credibility is important. Yet many elements cannot be controlled, such as the fluctuations of the industry, the stock market, and national and world economics. Nevertheless, the entrepreneur should continue to provide strong leadership by delivering the growth that is promised and by communicating to the stakeholders.

Meeting Expectations

The pressure most public companies face is to maintain short-term earnings growth. The financial markets generally react adversely to reports of lower earnings, even if the long-term strategic decisions from which they result are sound. Consequently, companies are often tempted to maintain share prices by sacrificing long-term profitability and growth for short-term earnings. The entrepreneur must plan and implement a business strategy that balances short- and long-term needs and communicate the plan to shareholders and the financial community.

SUMMARY

It is important to prepare an exit plan for the business to be executed at the right time. A company can realize the value it has created in several ways. The most common are selling an equity stake to a strategic partner, selling the business, merging with another business, and employing a public offering. Selling an equity stake to a strategic partner can attract needed capital from a source interested in the technology and can lead to completely selling the business at a later time. Selling the business is another option but might be risky in a weak economy. Entrepreneurs might have to agree to long-term payment plans that include a stock-for-stock exchange that may result in stock price declines. Merging with another company involves a transaction between two companies and is an alternative to growing a business. When a company loses its competitive advantage in the marketplace, this alternative can be a viable option. The founders can also sell the company, usually over time, to the management team (an MBO) or even to a broader group of employees through an ESOP[12]. The entrepreneur can also arrange an exit by going public. This option can be the most profitable strategy for the entrepreneur, but it has the disadvantages of costing a great deal of time and money and demanding significant financial commitments. Securities analysts will also demand management's time. The proceeds from an IPO can repay debt, fund special projects, and be used for acquisitions.

STUDY QUESTIONS

1. What are the various options to establish an exit strategy?

2. Briefly describe the procedures in selling a business.

3. List the major pitfalls in creating an alliance.

4. Describe the methods that make alliances successful.

5. Why should the venture consider an IPO?

EXERCISES

Develop an Exit Strategy

1. Prepare and list an entrepreneur's reasons for developing an exit strategy:

Reason for an Exit Strategy	Importance (1–10)	Company/Strengths/Weaknesses		
		Low	Average	High
1.				
2.				
3.				
4.				
5.				

2. When does an alliance start and end in selling an equity stake?

3. Describe a scenario in which an equity alliance will succeed.

Alliance Analysis

List the types of alliances and complete the table with descriptions and figures:

Name	Approx. Sales	Target Market	Type of Alliance
1.			
2.			
3.			
4.			
5.			

Selling a Company

Complete the following table by describing the company's exposure to the risks listed on the left and the company's planned response to an exit strategy:

Area of Potential Risk	Company Exposure	Exit Strategy
Industry growth		
Product technology or liability		
Financial		
Management changes		

INTERACTIVE LEARNING ON THE WEB

Test your knowledge of the chapter using the book's interactive Web site.

ADDITIONAL RESOURCES

- **AllianceStrategy.com** www.alliancestrategy.com
- **Association of Strategic Alliance Professionals** www.strategic-alliances.org
- **ReCap IT** www.recapit.com
- **Booz Allen Hamilton** www.boozallen.com

www.wiley.com/college/kaplan

THREE CASE STUDIES COVERING
THE WHOLE BOOK

These three case studies have been prepared for use toward the end of the book. They are designed to test both analytical skills and the softer, more complex management skills that every entrepreneur will meet. They establish dilemmas and paradoxes that you must confront and solve. In each case, you play the role of one of the founders of the company together with a partner. To make the cases as realistic as possible, your partner in the third question is *not* the same as in the first two. Read the questions *very* carefully several times. Make sure you consider all the points raised and that you take a holistic view of the management problems and resolutions. You might find it useful to ponder the issues for a few days before drafting your analyses. These are not cases that you can just read and immediately dash off as a final document. There are deep and dangerous waters flowing here! The questions occur in the first three stages of an entrepreneurial company—conception/existence, survival, and profitability/stabilization—as these are the phases in which an entrepreneurial management style is most required. You should look at each dilemma from several different angles: cultural, financial, ethical, legal, strategic, and personal. If you think other factors are important, state them and add them into the mix.

You should be concise, logical, and clear. No length is stipulated, but any answer that is less than one page is likely to be too thin in content. However, more than four pages per question may indicate that you haven't organized your thoughts clearly.

CASE 1: HALF MOON PRODUCTS—CONCEPTION/EXISTENCE

You have decided to start a company called Half Moon Products. You have a wonderful idea and have tested it on friends and done some preliminary market research. It looks very promising, and although you have not yet written a full business plan, you feel that you can build a company to have revenues of more than $30 million within eight years with pretty attractive profits. At this stage, like many first-time entrepreneurs, you have not really thought through "what you want to be when you grow up"; issues such as attracting different sorts of finance and, heaven forbid, selling the company have hardly crossed your mind. You have saved $200,000, and your mother has agreed to lend you $50,000 "for as long as you need it, dear," to start the company.

You think this is just enough to get you off the ground, and you might even be able to squeeze through to profitability with this injection of funds. But although you are very excited, you realize that there is lot you do not know. In talking to a number of friends, some of whom have started companies themselves, you feel that you need a partner to complement your skills, to be there when things are tough, and to share the load.

1. What is the profile of this partner, and how are you going to find and get comfortable with him or her?

2. You think that you have eventually found the ideal person, Jeb. He fits your profile, has complementary skills, and has already been number two in a successful start-up company in the same general market area. He is eager to get on board. He informs you that he will have to work part time for three months while working through his current consulting contract. Jeb indicates that he does not have any cash to bring into the company and he will need a get-by minimum salary when he comes fully on board. You really want to build a trusting partnership relationship that will last for years, but you are concerned that your new partner's suggestion of 50:50 ownership at the start is perhaps unfair. Jeb claims it would provide the right balance and equality to underpin this new partnership. How would you handle this situation? What legal, ownership, and financial structures and arrangements would you choose for your start-up? What specific terms would you insist on having in the partnership agreement?

CASE 2: HALF MOON PRODUCTS — SURVIVAL

You are now eighteen months into your new venture. You have made some mistakes, but at last you have your first satisfied customers. Some new products are nearly ready to supplement your first offerings, and you are beginning to attract the attention of the business press. Jeb has taken on more of the strategic role in the company, while you have been focusing on operations. He has convinced you that you needed to lease some expansion space to accommodate the impending growth. He happens to have an aunt who has space available that is reasonably priced, and you both have just signed a five-year lease, although you have probably taken on more space than you will need for at least two years under even the most optimistic scenario.

You both realize that you will need some more cash to fund the business; in fact, it looks as if you will need up to $1 million within six months. Jeb has spoken with the bank, which offered to provide a line of credit for half this amount if (a) you and Jeb use your houses as collateral and (b) you raise the other half of the needed cash from equity (i.e., selling a part of the company to investors). Jeb suggests that he approach his aunt again as she just might be interested in making an equity investment. You both meet with her. She is clearly a shrewd businessperson and sees that indeed the business may be an interesting investment. She immediately picks up that the weakness is the thinness of the management team and suggests you find someone with experience to take over the sales management role while you go back to doing what you are best at—product innovation and mentoring new hires. She has a close friend, Alex, who might be the perfect fit and suggests that you take a look at him for the role. Alex is the sales manager for a direct competitor in the next town. He is willing to move over to your company as he is "disenchanted with the management over there" and your company offers an upside if you are willing to provide him with some stock (ownership) rights in the company. He is willing to take a salary cut.

Jeb is enthusiastic about this hire; you feel that his judgment may be clouded a little by the need to get the funding. When you meet Alex alone, you are not entirely comfortable with him, but you cannot find any real reason why he could not do a good job, and frankly, you are getting really frazzled with the sixteen-hour days that you are putting in. Alex can relieve the stress immediately, so you and Jeb agree to hire him. Jeb's aunt is pleased and says that she will watch the company carefully for the next few months, and if all goes well, she will seriously think about investing in the company.

1. What compensation package would you offer Alex at this stage in the company?

You should consider several components here: basic salary, bonuses, and stock options. What components would you suggest, and what are the actual figures for each? In the case of stock options, how much of the company should you offer to Alex, and under what conditions could he acquire this ownership position?

Alex hits the ground running. You feel relieved and the sales really start to climb. In fact, he lands one very major customer that agrees to take one-third of your product output for the next year. After about four months, Jeb informs you that the cash is running out faster than anticipated and the company needs to get some funding within four weeks. The bank seems to be lined up, and Jeb has offered to use his new house as collateral. For the sake of the partnership, you have decided, with some trepidation, to match this with your home as an additional pledge against the loan. Your spouse is not too happy about this but agrees to go along.

You have both set up a meeting with Jeb's aunt at the end of the week to go over the progress and suggest that she now invest in the company to bring your cash reserves up to the level that is required to grow the company.

On Thursday you receive a phone call from the CEO of your competitor in the next town. She understands that you have hired Alex as your sales director. Did you know that he had signed a noncompete agreement when he left her company? Did you know that he had taken their customer list when he left the company? And did you know that your major customer was until recently her major client and Alex's breaking of the agreement had seriously damaged her company?

2. How are you going to handle this situation?

Hint: An entrepreneur views a threat as a possible opportunity. How can you use this event to clarify the situation with your partner and his aunt, Alex and the competitor?

CASE 3: MACAHULA SOFTWARE INC. — PROFITABILITY AND STABILIZATION

Your company, Macahula Software, is now nearly five years old. You have grown to around $20 million in sales, but the profitability over the past eighteen months has been falling; your products and services are becoming commoditized. You have personally given much to this company and feel very loyal to the hundred or so employees you have hired, trained, and mentored. They are "family."

As you started the company in a depressed economic area, you were able to finance the growth entirely through bank debt of $3 million, 90 percent of which was guaranteed by the State Economic Development Agency under a job creation program. In fact, you have made a major impact on this small town, there really being no other employment opportunities for your staff.

Your partner and you guaranteed the loan "as a last resort" as cosignatories, meaning that, should the company go into bankruptcy or there is a default on the loan, the state trustees can sell the assets of the company and what they do not recover must be repaid personally by the partners. The loan is joint and several, meaning that either of you is responsible for the whole loan should the other default.

When you and Jack, your partner, signed this guarantee, you were, like all first-time entrepreneurs, very optimistic about the future of the company and felt that there would always be enough retained assets to cover the guarantee. You also needed the money quickly at that time, and a low-interest state loan guarantee seemed a good deal.

Jack and you knew each other long before you got into business together. He was an attorney specializing in financial transactions and securities law; you were the one with the unique ideas for new services in the financial sector. Jack had already created substantial net worth before you got into business together, and he put $500,000 in as seed capital when you formed Macahula, although you have always been 50:50 partners. The partners' buy-back agreement states that the valuation of the company is fixed at $2 million perpetually.

At Jack's suggestion, you assembled a management board, and the current constituency is as follows:

Jack—Chairman

You—President and COO

Frank—Corporate counsel (an ex-partner in an earlier business who was brought in by Jack)

Martin—external board member and board member of two small public companies

Alicia—board member of a major public financial services company (an old acquaintance of yours)

You and your partner had been living well on the earnings of the company until the past six months, when cash flow has slowed considerably. You have both agreed to take half salaries. The company has only $80,000 in retained earnings.

You are no longer happy in the work environment. The company seems to have gone stale, you are not having any really new ideas, and you are starting to hurt financially. You and Jack hardly speak with one another. Indeed, he comes into the office perhaps only once a week. When in the office, he closes his office door and entertains visitors you do not know. When you question him about this, he says that he has always had other business interests, and he has to look after them carefully at the moment.

You are also beginning to have concerns about the $3 million guarantee. Although the loan is not yet due, you realize that there *will* be a payday and Jack and you are ultimately responsible for the funds. Certainly there are no major assets left in the company.

One Friday evening, you are feeling very depressed and Jack's personal assistant, Roger, comes into your office and asks to speak with you. His wife has landed a great job in California, and he has decided to move, leaving your company immediately. As Jack is not in this week, he would like to hand in his resignation to you.

Roger then gulps and says there is something that you ought to know. He has been afraid to bring this to you earlier, but now that he is no longer dependent on the company and his boss, he feels that he has to tell you. You should know that Jack, Frank, and Martin have set up a separate company. Roger knows this as Jack asked him to file all the legal documents. More important, the new company is based on an idea that you had proposed at an earlier management meeting but was not followed up on as the board decided that it was too risky at that stage of the company to invest in the development and marketing for a potentially highly profitable new service. Roger then hands you a folder with all of the evidence to support his claims—the legal filings, the business plan for the new company, which includes word-for-word the new service description taken directly from the meeting minutes, and some promotional materials for the new service under the name of the new firm. You thank Roger and ask him to leave after wishing him and his family every success in California.

You decide to not do anything hastily but to spend the weekend looking at the material and trying to get your thoughts in order about what this really means. On Sunday evening you decide to call Alicia. You relate the story, and she states that she is not really surprised. She had never fully trusted the other board members and had joined the board only as a favor to you. She then says that based on what you have stated, she would have to immediately resign from the board of your company. Anything that could remotely impact her reputation would seriously hurt her in her role as a board member for a major public corporation, which was currently filing for a secondary sale of stock to the public. As much as she realized what her walking away might mean to you, she had no alternative and would prefer that you did not discuss this with her any further. She would tender her resignation first thing in the morning.

What actions are you going to take?

Hint: Again, think entrepreneurially. This may seem a major threat to you personally and you will certainly feel betrayed, but perhaps it is an opportunity. First calm down and decide where you want to end up: owning and controlling your company or walking away free and clear from debt. Then decide how you are going to get to this point quickly. Put yourself in Jack's position. What is important to him personally as well as financially?

www.wiley.com/college/kaplan

NOTES

Chapter 1: What Is an Entrepreneur?

1. Findings by the Entrepreneurial Research Consortium, a publicly and privately sponsored research effort directed by Dr. Paul Reynolds at Babson College, indicate that 7 million adults are trying to start businesses in the United States at any given time. The Global Entrepreneurship Monitor, a joint research initiative by Babson College and the London Business School and sponsored by the Kauffman Center for Entrepreneurial Leadership, was launched in September 1997 to analyze entrepreneurial activity, its impact on national growth, and those factors that affect levels of entrepreneurial activity.

2. See Dale Meyer, plenary address at USASHE on February 15, 2001, "Changes in Entrepreneurship Curriculum." Courses in entrepreneurship are now taught at nearly one thousand colleges and universities. Entrepreneurship education programs for youngsters in the K–12 age range now exist in more than thirty states. The YESS!/Mini-Society entrepreneurship curriculum has been accepted by the U.S. Department of Education's National Diffusion Network as being effective in both acquiring knowledge and improving attitudes toward school and learning. In addition, according to the Global Consortium of Entrepreneurship Centers, the number of U.S. universities having such centers has grown from fifty to more than 250 in less than ten years.

3. See M. Kourilsky, "Entrepreneurship Education: Opportunity in Search of Curriculum," Kauffman Center for Entrepreneurial Leadership, 1995.

4. See *Starting Something* by Wayne McVicker, available in paperback.

5. For a more complete discussion of the evolution of the term *entrepreneur* and theories of entrepreneurship, see "Theories of Entrepreneurship: Historical Development and Critical Assessment" in *The Ox-ford Handbook of Entrepreneurship* (Oxford, U.K.: Oxford University Press, 2006), 33–56.

6. See Alex F. DeNoble, Doug I. Jung, Sanford B. Ehrlich, and Mark Butler, "A Paper on Entrepreneurial Self Efficacy: The Development of a Set of Measures and a Preliminary Test of Their Properties," Entrepreneurship Management Center, College of Business Administration, San Diego State University, 1999. Paper submitted on September 23, 2001, at Babson Research Conference.

7. See Ray Smilor, *Daring Visionaries* (Holbrook, MA: Adams Media Corporation, 2001), xxiv–xv. Smilor is the president of the Foundation for Enterprise Development and former vice president of the Kauffman Center for Entrepreneurial Leadership.

8. A breakdown of types of lifestyle entrepreneurs can be found at the U.S. Department of Commerce, "Statistical Abstract of the United States," Bureau of the Census, Washington, D.C., 2008. This report also provides a wealth of data on the state of entrepreneurship in the United States.

9. For a discussion of the problems that arise when founders are unable to give up control and hand over the reins to more experienced managers, see N. Wasserman, "The Founder's Dilemma," *Harvard Business Review* (Feb. 2008): 103–109.

10. V. K. Jolly, *Commercializing New Technologies* (Boston: Harvard Business School Press, 1997).

11. It is extremely difficult to obtain reliable data on the failure rate of start-ups for reasons discussed at www.businessweek.com/smallbiz/news/coladvice/ask/sa990930.htm. However, a good summary can be found in J. A. Timmons and S. Spinelli, *New Venture Creation,* 7th ed. (Princeton, NJ: McGrawHill/Irwin, 2006). For a more theoretical discourse on small firm failure see: R. Cressy, "Determinants of Small Firm Survival and Growth" in *The Oxford Handbook of Entrepreneurship*

(Oxford: Oxford University Press, 2006), 162–193.

Chapter 2: The Entrepreneurial Process

1. You can experience firsthand how Ted Graef and Scott Johnson redirected their business after their first idea failed by visiting their original Web site at www.intuitivecontrols.com and following the link to www.alltrafficsolutions.com.

2. Two introductory books on how social networks can enhance businesses are D. Silver, *Smart Start-Ups: How Entrepreneurs and Corporations Can Profit by Starting Online Communities* (Hoboken, NJ: Wiley, 2007) and L. Weber, *Marketing to the Social Web: How Digital Customer Communities Build Your Business* (Hoboken, NJ: Wiley, 2007).

3. An excellent introduction to the changing world of networks can be found in A-L Barabasi, *Linked: How Everything Is Connected to Everything Else and What It Means* (New York: Plume Press, 2003).

4. See U.S. Department of Commerce, "Statistical Abstract of the United States," Bureau of the Census, Washington, D.C., 2008, for a wealth of data on small firms.

5. See William B. Gartner, Barbara J. Bird, and Jennifer A. Starr, "Acting As If: Differentiating Entrepreneurial from Organizational Behavior," *Entrepreneurship Theory and Practice* (Spring 1992): 13–27.

6. See Rita McGrath and Ian MacMillan, *The Entrepreneurial Mindset* (Boston: Harvard Business School Press, 2000), 2–3.

Chapter 3: The Art of Innovation—Developing Ideas and Business Opportunities

1. This profile was constructed from the company's Web site and articles about the founders. Learn more about how SmartPak started and grew at www.smartpakequine.com and the analogous human services at www.cardinal.com/pharmacies/hospital/index.asp.

2. For a number of interesting anecdotes and insights illustrating how global trends are impacting the world of business, refer to Thomas L. Friedman, *The World Is Flat* (New York: Farrar, Straus and Giroux, 2005).

3. See www.miniwatts.com.

4. See www.boutell.com. By the time this book reaches print and is read, any data reported here will surely be outdated. You can visit the referenced sites to get an idea about how rapidly the Internet is expanding.

5. Information on international trade can be found at the World Trade Organization's Web site, www.wto.org.

6. These data were taken from a *Wall Street Journal* article on currency flows, August 4, 2004.

7. See an article in *The Deal,* July 2004. Since then, a number of leading U.S.-based venture capital firms have launched initiatives for investments in India and China.

8. The observation was made in 1965 by Gordon Moore, cofounder of Intel, that the number of transistors per square inch on integrated circuits had doubled every year since the integrated circuit was invented. The pace has slowed down a bit, but data density is still doubling approximately every eighteen months. Most experts, including Moore himself, expect Moore's Law to hold for at least two more decades.

9. Hans-Günther Hohmann (general manager, HP Germany), private conversation with one of the authors, at the Conference Board/McKinsey meeting on Corporate Innovation in Munich, August, 2000.

10. From a survey reported in Industry Week, January 2004 as part of the IW/MPI Census of Manufacturers, and also in 2004.

11. "Innovation Models in the 21st Century," a project funded by the National Institute of Science and Technology, by G. Susman and A. C. Warren within the Smeal College of Business, Pennsylvania State University, published in 2005 and to be found at www.smeal.psu.edu/fcfe.

12. For more about how companies manage agility, see Pal and Panteleo (eds.), *The Agile Corporation* (New York: Springer Press, 2005).

13. See William J. Baumol, *The Free Market Innovation Machine* (Princeton, NJ: Princeton University Press, 2002). There is an excellent short white paper of Baumol's ideas entitled "Entrepreneurship, Innovation, and Growth: The David-Goliath Symbiosis," which can be found at www.econ.nyu.edu/user/baumolw/sfg.pdf.

14. See Alan Afuah, *Innovation Management: Strategies, Implementation and Profits* (New York: Oxford University Press, 1998).

15. The Blyth Candles Web site, www.blyth.com, is an interesting place to learn how the humble candle can be "innovated" into a major business.

16. Clayton Christensen has written extensively about "disruptive innovation" and the difficulties large companies have in dealing with these. See *The Innovator's Dilemma* (1997) and *The Innovator's Solution* (2003) (with Michael Raynor), both from Harvard Business School Press.

17. From the U.S. Small Business Administration Report, "The State of Small Business: A Report of the President" (Washington, D.C.: U.S. Government Printing Office, 1995), 114.

18. In 2000 Korea's LG Electronics, Inc., launched an Internet-enabled refrigerator, followed by an Internet-ready washing machine in what it expects will eventually be a family of Net-ready home appliances. The Internet LG Turbo Drum washing machine can connect to the Internet to download new programs to match new fabrics. In addition, according to Merloni, another appliance maker, "in the case of [our] washing machines, smart RFID tags on clothes will enable the appliances to select the washing program appropriate to the items in the load. If any incompatible fabrics end up in the drum, such as whites with colored items being washed for the first time, the display will tell the consumer which items to take out."

19. See Jack M. Kaplan, *Getting Started in Entrepreneurship,* 2nd ed. (New York: John Wiley & Sons, 2001), 20–23.

20. See R. McGrath and I. Macmillan, *The Entrepreneurial Mindset* (Boston: Harvard Business School Press, 2000), 17–18.

21. See James Jiambalvo, *Managerial Accounting* (New York: John Wiley & Sons, 2001), 9.

22. Ibid., 23.

23. See Jack M. Kaplan, *Smart Cards: The Global Information Passport* (Boston: International Thomson Computer Press, 1996), 15–17.

24. See W. B. Walstad, *Entrepreneurship and Small Business in the United States: A Gallup Survey Report* (Princeton, NJ: National Center for Research in Economic Education and the Gallup Organization, 1994).

25. See R. M. Kanter, "Supporting Innovation and Venture Development in Established Companies," *Journal of Business Venturing* 1 (1985): 47–60.

26. See H. A. Simon, "What We Know about the Creative Process," in R. L. Kuhn (ed.), *Frontiers in Creative and Innovative Management* (Cambridge, MA: Ballinger Publishing, 1999), 3–22.

27. See Jeffry A. Timmons and S. Spinelli, *New Venture Creation* (Boston: Irwin McGraw Hill, 2006), 119–121.

28. See H. Stevenson and D. Gumpert, "The Heart of Entrepreneurship," *Harvard Business Review* (March–April 1985).

Chapter 4: Analyzing the Market, Customers, and Competition

1. This profile was compiled from interviews with Rappaport in 2008. You can learn more about American List Counsel at www.alc.com.

2. For additional reading on marketing, see P. Kotler, *Marketing Management Analysis Planning Implementation and Control,* 8th ed. (Englewood Cliffs, NJ: Prentice Hall, 1994).

3. For more on this topic, see C. Christiansen, *The Innovator's Dilemma: When New Technologies Cause Great Firms to Fail* (Boston: Harvard Business School Press, 1997). His main thesis is that attending to the needs of good current customers can systematically inhibit a business from understanding the needs of new customers.

4. See R. C. Bidettberg and J. Deighton, "Interactive Marketing: Exploiting the Age of Addressability," *Sloan Management Review* 33(1) (1991): 5–14.

5. See L. Fuld, *Competitive Intelligence* (New York: John Wiley & Sons, 1993), 9–10.

6. J. Crew issues gift cards with purchases of specified amounts for specific promotions. Interview with Scott Rosenberg, J. Crew, New York, February 2002.

7. See Leo Jakobson, "Growing Pains," *Alleycat News* (May 2001): 76–78.

8. See B. Tedeschi, "Spy on Your Customers (They Want You To)," *Smart Business* (August 2001): 58–66.

9. See K. Coyne, "Sustainable Competitive Advantage: What It Is, What It Isn't," *Business Horizons* (January–February 2002): 27–34.

10. See P. Kottler, *Marketing Management*, 10th ed. (Upper Saddle River, NJ: Prentice Hall, 2000). Kottler indicates that the firm should consider six factors in setting policies: (1) selecting the pricing objective; (2) determining demand; (3) estimating costs; (4) analyzing competitor's cost, prices, and offers; (5) selecting a pricing method; and (6) selecting the final price.

11. See P. Courtney and R. Mac Davis, *The Entrepreneur's Fast Track II Handbook* (Denver: Entrepreneurial Education Foundation, 1997), 109–112.

12. For further examples on viral marketing techniques, see D. Silver, *Smart Start-Ups: How Entrepreneurs and Corporations Can Profit by Starting Online Communities* (Hoboken, NJ: Wiley, 2007), L. Weber, *Marketing to the Social Web: How Digital Customer Communities Build Your Business* (Hoboken, NJ: Wiley, 2007), and the section on viral marketing in A-L Barabasi, *Linked: How Everything Is Connected to Everything Else and What It Means* (New York: Plume Press, 2003).

13. Other examples of viral marketing campaigns can be found at www.gluelondon.com.

14. See Jack M. Kaplan, *Smart Cards: The Global Information Passport* (Boston: International Thomson Computer Press, 1996), 40–41.

Chapter 5: Writing the Winning Business Plan

1. This profile was prepared using interviews with Shkolnik and members of the MIT business plan team.

2. See Jack M. Kaplan, *Smart Cards: The Global Information Passport* (Boston: International Thomson Computer Press, 1996), 187–190.

3. See Eric Siegal, *The Ernst & Young Business Plan Guide* (New York: John Wiley & Sons, 1987), 59–60.

4. See William A. Sahlman, "How to Write a Great Business Plan," *Harvard Business Review* (July 1, 1997): 2–5.

5. See Jack M. Kaplan, *Getting Started in Entrepreneurship* (New York: John Wiley & Sons, 2001), 95.

6. Ibid., 97.

7. Michael Bucheit (partner, Advanced Infrastructure Ventures Interview) interview, New York, May 2002.

8. See William A. Sahlman, "Some Thoughts on Business Plans," Harvard Business School, November 1996, 3–5.

9. Eric Major (angel investor) interview, New York, June 2002.

10. Ibid.

Chapter 6: Setting Up the Company

1. See Amar V. Bhide, "The Questions Every Entrepreneur Must Answer," *Harvard Business School Review* (November 1, 1996): 8–9.

2. Ethan and Matt were engineering students at Penn State. This profile was developed using a number of interviews and class visits by Ethan Wendle. You can learn more about their company at www.diamondbackcovers.com.

3. Robert Katz, Esq. (Cooper & Dunham LLP) interview, New York, May 15, 2002.

4. Sole proprietorships are very common for single owners and home-based businesses. See interview with Ann Chamberlain of Richards and O'Neil LLC law firm, New York, March 10, 2001.

5. For most companies that require financing, David Cohen, CPA, at J. M. Levy suggests a C corporation.

6. "To increase business within a state, entrepreneurs should file for a certificate of incorporation in the state where they conduct business. The state of Delaware has attractive advantages for companies and should be investigated." Alan Brody, Esq. (Buchanan Ingersoll Inc.) interview, Princeton, NJ, February 2001.

7. See S. Zellcke and K. Pick, "Unbalanced Boards," *Harvard Business Review* (February 2001): 1–2.

8. See Gordon B. Baty, *Entrepreneurship for the Nineties* (Englewood Cliffs, NJ: Prentice Hall, 1990), 219.

9. David Cohen (CPA, J. M. Levy and Company) interview, New York, June 2002.

10. Robert Katz, Esq. (Cooper & Dunham LLP) interview, New York, May 15, 2005.

11. Kurt Hoffman (consultant, Financial Services) interview, Princeton, NJ, July 2004.

12. Ibid.

13. Ralph Subbiondo (partner, Ernst & Young LLP) interview, New York, May 2002.

Chapter 7: Bootstrapping and Financing the Closely Held Company

1. Materials for this section were obtained from www.dyson.com together with a number of articles on James Dyson appearing in the popular press.

2. For a full review of bootstrapping techniques, see Lynn Neeley, "Bootstrap Finance," www.aoef.org/papers/2003/neeley.pdf, 2003.

3. See http://www.nvca.org and www.thomsonreuters.com for a wide range of information on global private data and trends. In addition, the site's daily news and statistics offer a snapshot of the U.S., European, and Asian private equity markets.

4. See Ellen Paris, "David vs. Goliath," *Entrepreneur Magazine,* November 1999.

5. "Microsoft Loses Patent Suit," Associated Press Announcement, February 23, 1994.

6. "Patents, an Inventor Wins but isn't Happy", Edmund Andrews, *New York Times*, December, 14th 1991.

7. See Eric Rosenfeld, *Credit, Where Credit Is Due: Using Plastic to Finance,* www.entreworld.org (accessed August 1, 1999).

8. Rick Smith interview, April 2002. Smith is an entrepreneur who received funding from his family when he started Smith and Solomon Training School.

9. Mary Gelormino (Fleet Bank) interview, New York, June 2002.

10. Small Business Administration, "Results on Small Business Borrowing Loans Study," Washington, D.C., 2001. The Small Business Administration's mission is to aid, counsel, and protect the small-business community. There is a wealth of information at the agency's Web site, www.sba.gov.

11. See Rick Stephan Hayes and John Cotton Howell, *How to Finance Your Small Business with Government Money: SBA Loans* (New York: John Wiley & Sons, 1980), 37–38.

12. To locate your local SBA office, go to www.sba.gov/localresources/index.html.

13. For detailed information about the SBIR and STTR programs, visit www.sba.gov/sbir. You can also find a complete guide of all federal funding programs for small companies for all government agencies, including topics of interest, available funds, and direct contact names, in the Federal Technology Funding Guide published annually by the nonprofit Larta organization. The report can be downloaded from www.larta.org.

Chapter 8: Equity Financing for High Growth

1. This profile was developed using interviews with Brezina as well as presentations in class. See also www.ycombinator.com as well as another so-called microequity fund www.dreamitventures.com.

2. See www.khoslaventures.com, the latest partnership started by Vinod Khosla, a long-time and highly successful venture capitalist formally with the famed firm Kleiner Perkins. For Khosla's views on venture capital, together with other well-known investors, see U. Gupta (ed.), *Done Deals, Venture Capitalists Tell Their Stories* (Boston: Harvard Business Press, 2000).

3. For more about Matt Brezina's company, see www.xobni.com.

4. The Kauffman Foundation has studied angel investing and angel networks in detail. An excellent report on angel networks can found at www.kauffman.org/pdf/angel_guidebook.pdf.

5. See Carl Simmons, "Every Business Needs an Angel," *Inc. Magazine,* Summer 2002, 2.

6. *Inc. Magazine* publishes a list of angel investors annually.

7. There are two excellent sources of data for the venture capital sector: Venture Economics, found at www.thomsonreuters.com, and the National Venture Capital Association, www.nvca.org, which reports on the annual Money Tree Survey with PricewaterhouseCoopers.

8. See Stephen C. Blowers, *The Ernst and Young Guide to the IPO Value Journal* (New York: John Wiley & Sons, 1999), 97–99.

9. See Linda A. Cyr, "A Note on Pre-money and Post-money Valuation," *Harvard Business Review*

(April 17, 2001): 2–5. This article provides a brief introduction to calculations inherent in premoney and postmoney evaluations at multiple stages of financing.

10. See Tom Copeland, Tim Koller, and Jack Murrin, *Valuation: Measuring and Managing the Value of Companies* (New York: John Wiley & Sons, 2000), 64.

11. Ibid.

12. Ibid.

13. See Shannon P. Pratt, Robert F. Reilly, and Robert P. Schweihs, *Valuing a Business: The Analysis and Appraisal of Closely Held Companies,* 3rd ed. (Homewood, IL: Irwin Press, 1996), 45–47.

14. Parviz Tayebati interview, June 2005.

15. Foster-Miller is an example of an R & D contract development company that in the past has derived a major part of its revenues from SBIR funding. See www.foster-miller.com.

16. This list was derived from one used by Adams Capital Management, a VC firm based in Pittsburgh.

17. This generic term-sheet was derived from one used by Adams Capital Management.

Chapter 9: Managing the Money

1. See R. Breasley and S. Myers, *Principles of Corporate Finance* (New York: McGraw-Hill, 1996), 224–250.

2. See www.investopedia.com for details on terms.

3. Alvin Katz was introduced to the authors by his nephew, who was in one of our classes. The profile was developed during a class visit and subsequent interviews.

4. For an easier way to use financial analysis and a CD for exercises on ratios, see Clifford Schorer, "Grow," (unpublished work, New York, 2001), 20–21.

5. Ibid., 41.

6. For a more complete explanation, see Donald E. Vaughn, *Financial Planning for the Entrepreneur* (Upper Saddle River, NJ: Prentice Hall, 1997), 12–15.

7. See Stephen C. Blowers, Peter H. Griffith, and Thomas L. Milan, *The Ernst & Young Guide to the IPO Value Journey* (New York: John Wiley & Sons, 1999), 97–99.

8. See Robert C. Higgins, *Analysis for Financial Management,* 3rd ed. (Burr Ridge, IL: Irwin Press, 1992), 346.

9. The original source for the financial documents of U.S. public corporations is the Securities and Exchange Commission's electronic data gathering, analysis, and retrieval system, also known as EDGAR, located on the Web at edgar.sec.gov. Other sites that have licensed EDGAR data include FreeEDGAR (www.freeedgar.com), EDGAR Online (www.edgar-online.com), and 10-K Wizard (www.10kwizard.com).

10. For a more detailed analysis, see Stephen C. Blowers, Peter H. Griffith, and Thomas L. Milan, *The Ernst & Young Guide to the IPO Value Journey* (New York: John Wiley & Sons, 1999), 132–133.

11. David Cohen (CPA, J. M. Levy & Company) interview, New York, June 2001.

Chapter 10: Discovering the Value in Intellectual Property: The Competitive Edge

1. Tony Warren, one of the authors, was an adviser for this company for more than three years and helped negotiate several corporate partnerships. The profile is based on firsthand experience of the company.

2. Other forms or types of marks include logos (such as the distinctive blue letters used by IBM) and slogans (such as Nike's "Just Do It"). Examples and application filing for a trademark provided by Eric Hirsch, New York, June 2001.

3. See Stephen Elias and Kate McGrath, *Trademark: Legal Care for Your Business,* 4th ed. (Berkeley, CA: Nolo Press, 1999), 297.

4. The USPTO keeps two lists of all trademarks that are registered: the principal register and the supplemental register. The lists specify the owner of the mark, the date the mark was registered, and the type of mark.

5. To avoid conflict, search state and federal trademark registers and the Thomas Registry at www.thomasnet.com. Explanations of and examples for the copyright symbols were provided by Eric Hirsch.

6. All states maintain trademark registers, but they are considered unimportant to trademarks.

7. Litigation can get expensive, running into tens of thousands of dollars in legal fees.

8. In the United States, the first business to use a trademark owns it.

9. Copyright protects the expression of ideas rather than ideas or methods in and of themselves.

10. Copyright generally provides a weaker form of protection than patent law.

11. Copyright law has been interpreted to protect a range of software that includes applications, programs, and video games. See "Licensing Best Practices: Strategic, Territorial, and Technology Issues" Alan H. Gordon (Editor), and Robert Goldscheider (Editor), 2006; Wiley, Hoboken, N.J. Gordon is a principal at Fish & Richardson, P.C.

12. Ibid., 28.

13. Ibid.

14. Design patents must consist primarily of drawings, along with formal paperwork and a filing fee.

15. A sample nondisclosure agreement can be found in Chapter 12 of this book.

16. There is a misconception that one must use a patent attorney. The law contains no requirement that one must have a patent attorney to file a patent application.

17. See Jack M. Kaplan, *Getting Started in Entrepreneurship* (New York: John Wiley & Sons, 2001), 242–243.

18. You cannot patent any process that can be performed mentally. The rule also applies to abstract ideas.

19. Also, there is no need to disclose details of the invention to the public, as you do with a patent.

20. See the article on reverse engineering at www.wikipedia.org for more details, examples, and the legal implications of reverse engineering.

Chapter 11: Business Models and the Power of Information

1. This profile was developed from private interviews. Visit DBi's Web site, www.dbiservices.com, to see how the DeAngelo brothers have expanded their mowing services into a multitude of markets. You can also see Neal DeAngelo discussing his business philosophy on the book's Web site.

2. See Michael Dell and Catherine Fredman, *Direct from Dell* (Cork, Ireland: Collins Press, 2006) for this quote, a discussion of the Dell business model and more insights into how Michael Dell started and grew Dell Computer Corporation.

3. For an interesting discussion on business models, "Making sense of business models", Susan Lambert, 2004 to be found at www.flinders.edu.au

4. IBM uses this definition for conveying the concept of business model innovation to its executives.

5. See, for example, H. Chesbrough and R. S. Rosenbloom, "The Role of the Business Model in Capturing Value from Innovation," *Industrial and Corporate Culture Change* 11(3): 529–555.

6. Chris Anderson, *The Long Tail, Why the Future of Business Is Selling Less of More* (New York: Hyperion Press, 2008).

7. General Fasteners is part of the MNP group of companies. More can be learned by visiting www.mnp.com.

8. For a detailed licensing how-to, see Richard Stim, *License Your Invention* (Berkeley, CA: Nolo Press, 1998). This book comes with a useful disc of all the necessary documents and forms needed for licensing. Also, the Licensing Executive Society provides useful contacts and further information on licensing at www.usa-canada.les.org.

9. See www.intertrust.com for a detailed description of the company's business. This site also links directly to the U.S. Patent and Trademark Office to see the thirty-seven patents owned by Intertrust in the field of digital rights manage-ment.

10. See www.amberwave.com for more details and what actions the company is taking to protect its intellectual property.

11. See the International Franchise Association and Horwath International, *Franchising in the Economy of 1990* (Evans City, PA: IFA Publications, 1991), 22–23. Also visit www.franchise.org for information on franchising and to review more than one thousand franchise opportunities.

12. A number of useful articles on franchising have appeared in *Entrepreneur* magazine, including discussions on the UFOC.

13. Based on an interview with George Homan in June 2004. You can learn more about the services Chem-Station provides at www.chemstation.com.

14. Some of the ideas in this section were first seen in "Knowing When to Outsource," *Tyme Management,* 2000, www.businessknowhow.com/Startup/outsource.htm.

15. Marcia Robinson and Ravi Kalakota, *Offshore Outsourcing* (Alpharetta, GA: Mivar Press, 2004).

16. Visit www.schoolwires.com to see how an ASP operates.

17. The term *Web 2.0* is difficult to define precisely. Broadly speaking, it describes a range of applications that use dynamic, two-way interactions on the Internet rather than static, one-way information exchange. The field is changing rapidly. For a discussion on the topic by the original user of the term, see www.oreillynet.com/pub/a/oreilly/tim/news/2005/09/30/what-is-web-20.html.

18. Visit www.vocalpoint.com to learn more. An independent review can be found at www.viewpoints.com/Vocalpoint-review-9a920.

19. See N. Chaddha, "Established 80 Alliances," *Forbes*, May 21, 2001, 76.

20. For the rationale behind this investment see http://bookseller-association.blogspot.com/2007/01/news-news-corp-and-newstand.html.

21. See M. Roberts, "The Do's and Don't's of Strategic Alliances," *Journal of Business Strategy* (March–April 1992): 50–53.

party should know to make a valid decision." This is a legal requirement in many cases, such as when seeking investors or lenders. It is considered fraudulent if you do not disclose *all* relevant information prior to taking funds from investors or lending money from a bank. The concept also applies when analyzing conflict-of-interest issues and ethical dilemmas where all stakeholders should receive full disclosure of all the facts in order to seek a justified resolution.

6. Ralph Subbiondo (partner, Ernst & Young, LLP) interview, New York, May 2002.

7. Sample of nondisclosure agreement provided by the Richards and O'Neil law firm, New York, 2001.

8. Kurt Hoffman (consultant, Financial Services) interview, Princeton, NJ, Aug. 2004.

9. David Cohen (CPA, Jacques M. Levy and Co.) interview, New York, June 2003.

10. See J. L. Nesheim, *High Tech Start-Up* (New York: The Free Press, 2000), 59–60.

11. See Dwight B. Crane and Indra Reinberg, "Employee Stock Ownership Plans (ESOPs) and Phantom Stock Plans," *Harvard Business Review, Boston*, (November, 2000), pp. 5–6.

12. See Brian Hall, Carleen Madigan, and Norm Wassman, "Stock Options at Virtuanet.Com Case Study," *Harvard Business School Review, Boston*, November, 2000. This paper describes issues facing founders of a high-tech firm in negotiating equity and stock options.

Chapter 12: Managing the Team

1. This profile was developed from several interviews with Paul Silvis as well as from presentations that he made to classes at Penn State.

2. See N. Pal and D. Panteleo (eds.), "The Agile Enterprise" (Berlin, Germany: Springer Press, 2005), 118ff.

3. Taken from a presentation made by Paul Silvis on human resource management.

4. This case was developed together with the authors' students who were faced with difficult conflict decisions on these and related topics.

5. The term *full disclosure* is defined as "the ethic to tell the full truth about any matter that the other

Chapter 13: Communicating the Opportunity

1. For an instructional guide on how to put an investors' presentation together, visit the "Learning Center" at http://ideapitch.smeal.psu.edu. This guide is used successfully in many courses at different universities and is also the basis of a virtual business plan competition.

2. Craig Bandes interview, July 2008.

3. Stanley E. Pratt, *Pratt's Guide to Venture Capital Sources* (Wellesley, MA: Venture Economics, published annually). For a list of libraries where you can find this complete guide, see www.worldcat.org.

4. William A. Frezza (partner, Adams Capital Management) interview, May 2004. Frezza can also be seen

talking about a number of topics in entrepreneurial companies on the book's Web site.

5. The authors thank a team of MBA students at Penn State for this example developed in the Opportunity Development Course in 2003.

6. We thank Ankit Patel, a member of an MBA class at Penn State in 2004, for his permission to use this material from a business plan competition based on concepts from Resco, Inc., in Kingston, Ontario.

Chapter 14: Scaling and Exiting the Venture

1. This profile was garnered from publicly available articles and a personal interview in October 2000 with Treffler.

2. David Carrithers (consultant and author of articles on employee culture and performance) interview. He can be found at www.businesshive.com.

3. Ibid.

4. Laurence Charney (partner, Ernst & Young) interview, New York, May 2001.

5. Ibid.

6. Michael Bucheit (partner, Advanced Infrastructures Ventures) interview, New York, June 2002.

7. See S. C. Blowers, *The Ernst & Young Guide to the IPO Value Journey* (New York: John Wiley & Sons, 1999), 97–99.

8. See Jack M. Kaplan, *Getting Started in Entrepreneurship,* 2nd ed. (New York: John Wiley & Sons, 2001), 173.

9. Blowers, *The Ernst & Young Guide,* 32–35.

10. See Ira A. Greenstein, *Going Public Source Book* (New York: R. R. Donnelley Financial, 1999), 5–7.

11. Laurence Charney interview, May 2001.

12. See Dwight B. Crane and Indra Reinberg, "Employee Stock Ownership Plans (ESOPs) and Phantom Stock Plans," *Harvard Business Review, Boston,* (November, 2000), pp. 5–6.

ACCREDITED INVESTORS: Individual or institutional investors who meet the qualifying SEC criteria with respect to financial sophistication or financial assets.

ADVISORY BOARD: A group of individuals willing to serve in an advisory capacity in exchange for stock or other benefits.

ANGEL: A private investor who often has nonmonetary motives for investing as well as the usual financial ones.

BOARD OF DIRECTORS: Individuals elected by stockholders of a corporation who are responsible to that group for overseeing the overall direction and policy of the firm.

BOARD VISITATION RIGHTS: The right to be present at board meetings as an observer but with no voting rights.

BOOK VALUE: The difference between the *tangible* assets of a company and its liabilities. For an early-stage company, the book value is often negative. As the company grows and matures, the value may be many times the book value.

BOOTSTRAPPING: Accessing cash and noncash resources to build a company, avoiding the sale of stock.

BRAINSTORMING: A management technique used to foster ideas, solve problems, set goals, establish priorities, and determine who on the team will be responsible for following through with the various tasks needed to accomplish the goals and priorities established.

BREAKEVEN ANALYSIS: A means of determining the quantity that has to be sold at a given price so revenues will equal cost.

BRIDGE FINANCING: Financing obtained by a company expecting to secure permanent financing (such as through an initial public offering) within a short time, such as two years.

BURN RATE: The cash needed on a month-to-month basis to sustain a company's operations (see **Runway**).

BUY-SELL AGREEMENT: Contract among associates that sets the terms and conditions by which one or more of the associates can buy out one or more of the other associates.

BY-LAWS: Rules under which a corporation is governed. These rules can be amended as provided by state law and the by-laws. Rules and regulations under which a board of directors operates a corporation.

C-CORPORATION: The most common form of business ownership and the one preferred by investors. As a separate legal entity apart from its owners, it may engage in business, issue contracts, sue and be sued, and pay taxes directly.

CASH-OUT: (1) The time interval before a company no longer has any cash for operations, also known as **runway;** (2) investors are said to cash-out of a company at a **liquidity event.**

CHIEF FINANCIAL OFFICER (CFO): A member of a company's upper management who oversees all the financial aspects of the business.

CLOSING: (1) In accounting, when the books are summarized in financial statements for a specific time frame and no further entries are allowed for this period; (2) in real estate, when the buyer and seller (or their agents) meet to finalize the transaction. Sometimes called the settlement, this is the point at which the transfer of property and funds takes place. The term also applies generally to business transactions such as an investment, loan, or company sales event.

COMFORT LETTER: A letter provided by a company's independent auditors detailing procedures performed at the request of the underwriters. The letter supplements the underwriter's due diligence review.

COMMERCIAL BANK: State or nationally chartered bank that accepts demand deposits, grants business loans, and provides a variety of other financial services. Typically used by the entrepreneur as an asset lender.

COMMON AND PREFERRED STOCK: Shares that represent the ownership interest in a corporation. Both common and preferred stock have ownership rights, but preferred stock normally has prior claim on dividends and assets (in the event of liquidation). Both common and preferred stockholders' claims are junior to claims of bondholders or other creditors of the company. Common stockholders assume the greater risk but have the voting power. They generally exercise the greater control but may gain the greater reward in the form of dividends and capital appreciation. The terms *common stock* and *capital stock* are often used interchangeably when the company has no preferred stock. Preferred stock may usually be converted into common stock upon a liquidity event.

CONTINGENT LITIGATION: A process in which an attorney will receive a percentage, typically 50 percent, from the proceeds of a successful lawsuit in exchange for not charging a fee for work done. Small companies sometimes use this process for patent litigation against larger companies.

CONVERTIBLE DEBENTURES: A form of investment whereby the investor loans the company funds carrying a "coupon," or interest, which usually accrues. Within a defined period, the investor may convert the loan and the accrued interest into stock at an agreed-on price. This arrangement gives an investor greater flexibility in managing the investment.

COPYRIGHT: An exclusive right granted by the federal government to the processor to publish and sell literary, musical, or other artistic materials. A copyright is honored for fifty years after the death of the author.

COVENANTS: Restrictive terms in a loan or stock sale agreement that protect the lender or investor.

DEBT CAPITAL: Funds or assets acquired by borrowing.

DILUTION: The reduction of a stockholder's percentage of ownership in an enterprise, usually arising from selling more common stock to other parties, sometimes called "watering the stock." Investors may require "antidilution" protection so their ownership position is protected in preference to the founders should certain milestones not be attained.

DISBURSEMENT: The act of paying out funds to satisfy a financial obligation.

D&O INSURANCE: An insurance policy that protects directors and officers of a company from lawsuits, particularly from shareholders. The cost of such insurance has escalated since the recent number of corporate fraud cases.

DUE DILIGENCE: The responsibility of those preparing and signing the registration statement to conduct an investigation in order to provide a reasonable basis for their belief that statements made in the registration statement are true and do not omit any material facts. Proper due diligence can help protect these parties from liability in the event they are sued for a faulty offering. The company, on the other hand, has strict liability for errors or omissions in the regulation statement. Due diligence is also undertaken by private investors and banks before reaching a final agreement on terms and releasing funds.

EARNINGS REPORT: A statement issued by a company reflecting its financial situation over a given period of time. This report lists revenue, expenses, and the net result.

EBITDA: The company's earnings before interest, taxes, depreciation, and amortization of long-term assets. It therefore reflects the inherent quality of the day-to-day operations of the firm.

ELEVATOR PITCH: A slang term referring to the twenty to sixty seconds an entrepreneur has to interest a venture capitalist in his or her business idea.

ENTREPRENEUR: Derived from the French word *entreprende,* meaning to undertake. Someone who is willing and eager to create a new venture to present a concept to the marketplace.

EQUITY: (1) Total assets minus total liabilities equals equity, or net worth; (2) money invested in a company that is not intended to be repaid but represents an ownership interest.

ESCROW: Placing money in a special and separate account under the control of another party, usually a financial institution, to be held until the completion of conditions set forth in an agreement.

ESOP: Employees stock ownership plan by which the employees can acquire ownership of a company over time. This transfer of ownership carries certain tax advantages and is one way in which founders and investors can create an exit strategy for themselves. This route is not favored by venture capitalists as the time frames are extended and the valuations usually low.

EXIT STRATEGY: (1) The way an entrepreneur gets his or her money out of the venture; (2) the vehicle for selling the enterprise; (3) what venture capitalists look for when funding new ventures—their way to realize the dollar profits from the investment. See **Liquidity Event.**

FACTOR: Financial institution that buys accounts receivable from a firm and bills customers directly, as opposed to a bank that lends on only accounts receivable. Factors can move quickly to get funds to a business but are usually the most expensive way to finance accounts receivable.

FINANCIAL INSTITUTION: Any firm that deals with money and/or securities. Banks, savings and loans, insurance companies, hard-asset lenders, credit unions, stockbrokers, consumer financial companies, and investment bankers, as well as a host of other highly specialized organizations are examples of the institutions that operate in the huge and highly complex world of finance.

FINANCIAL RATIOS: Measurements used to establish common standard figures that can be compared from year to year, company to company, or company to industry.

FINANCIAL STATEMENT: Periodic accounting reports of a company's activities, which usually include a balance sheet, an income statement, and a cash flow statement.

FINDER'S FEE: Commission paid to a person for furnishing to the payer a buyer or a property or for arranging an introduction that leads to a deal.

FORMS 10-K AND 10-Q: The annual and quarterly report public companies file with the SEC. The reports are prepared by the independent accountants of the company.

FRANCHISE: A right conferred by a franchisor to a franchisee to operate a business using a defined brand, image, and stipulated business processes in exchange for a fee usually based on a percentage of sales.

FULL DISCLOSURE: The ethic to tell the full truth about any matter that the other party should know to make a valid decision. There is a legal requirement in many cases, such as when seeking investors or lenders. The concept also applies when analyzing conflict-of-interest issues and ethical dilemmas where all stakeholders should receive full disclosure of all the relevant facts.

GAZELLE: A company that is growing its revenues by at least 20 percent per annum for four years in succession.

GOING PUBLIC: The process by which a corporation offers its securities to the public.

GOODWILL: The difference between the market value of a firm and the market value of its net tangible assets.

HARVEST: Liquidating the accumulated assets and equity of a venture. Converting profitable investment into cash to realize a profit.

INCENTIVE STOCK OPTION PLAN: Provision of **stock options** to employees as a component of compensation. Plans may be qualified or nonqualified, depending on the tax treatment sought.

INCOME STATEMENT: A financial statement that shows the amount of income earned by a business over a specific accounting period. All costs (expenses) are subtracted from the gross revenues (sales) to determine net income, which outlines the profit-and-loss financial statement (P&L).

INCUBATOR: Accommodation for early-stage companies providing low rent and shared services.

INFORMATION RIGHTS: The rights of a lender or investor to receive certain defined information concerning the progress of the company on a periodic basis. This right is commonly sought by lenders who seek an early warning if the company is not meeting its projections.

INITIAL PUBLIC OFFERING: A privately held company that elects to sell a portion of its common shares of stock to the public. Also referred to as an IPO. Often used when a small company seeks outside equity financing for expansion.

INTRAPRENEUR: A term coined by Gifford Pinchot III to identify an entrepreneur working within the confines of a corporation while retaining some degree of independence. Often the term *corporate venturing* is used.

INVESTMENT BANK: A company regulated by the Securities and Exchange Commission that acts as an agent for a company to sell stock to the public, private investors, or to another company. In the first case, they are said to act as an underwriter.

JOINT VENTURE: Usually refers to a short-lived partnership with each partner sharing in costs and rewards of the project; common in research, investment banking, and the health-care industry.

KEY-MAN INSURANCE: An insurance policy that protects investors or lenders from the death or disability of key employees on which an early-stage company may depend.

LETTER OF INTENT: A preliminary, nonbinding agreement between the company and the venture capital firm and/or investors specifying the terms of raising capital and the financial equity investment that will be contained in a formal agreement.

LEVERAGED BUYOUT: A method by which a firm is purchased by a private investment company and a significant part of the financing is accomplished using debt. These transactions require that the company have a dependable and sufficient cash flow to service the debt. The LBO firm may install its own management team or retain the existing management structure.

LICENSE: A right conferred on a licensee by a licensor to use intellectual property owned by the licensor under defined conditions in return for a license fee, usually in the form of a recurring royalty payment.

LIFESTYLE ENTREPRENEUR: An entrepreneur that starts and manages a company to fit their individual lifestyle rather than as a way of creating value for investors.

LIMITED LIABILITY CORPORATION: Also known as an LLC, a separate legal entity that allows a corporation to have "members" rather than stockholders. It is not subject to corporate tax, and therefore, tax liabilities or credits "flow through" to the members as in an **S-corporation.**

LIMITED PARTNERSHIP: A form of partnership composed of both a general partner(s) and a limited partner(s). The limited partners have no control in the management of the company and are usually financially liable only to the extent of their investment in the partnership. The majority of VC firms are formed as a limited partnership.

LINE OF CREDIT: Short-term financing usually granted by a bank up to a predenominated limit; debtor borrows as needed up to the limit of credit without needing to renegotiate the loan.

LIQUIDATION: The requirement by order of a bankruptcy court, sometimes called compulsory liquidation, that a business dissolve operations and sell off or dispose of assets by converting assets into cash.

LIQUIDITY EVENT: An event that occurs when the stock of a private company has a market for sale usually either through an IPO or a sale to another company. The venture capitalists' objective is to reach a liquidity event when they can "cash out" their shares and receive a "return on investment."

M&A TRANSACTION: A merger or acquisition of one company with or by another. This term is commonly used to describe the liquidity event in which an entrepreneur's company is sold to another.

MARGIN: The amount the entrepreneur adds to a product's cost to obtain its selling price. This is also called markup.

MARKETING PLAN: A written formulation for achieving the marketing goals and strategies of the venture, usually on an annual basis. Business plans always contain a marketing plan section.

MANAGEMENT BUYOUT: The purchase of a company by the management, often financed by a private equity firm; also called an MBO.

MEZZANINE FINANCING: Transitional money that helps entrepreneurial companies build to a level of growth that permits a public stock offering or a sale to another company, providing an exit strategy for investors.

MICROEQUITY FUNDS: Small amounts of financing provided by a localized network of angels targeted at very early stage (preseed) rounds of investment. They are often coupled with a strong mentoring network for entrepreneurs. Examples include DreamIt Ventures and YCombinator.

MULTIPLE: A firm's price-to-earnings ratio that is used for quick valuations of a firm. (For example, a firm that earns $5 million a year in an industry that generally values stock at ten times earnings would be valued at $50,000,000.)

NET PRESENT VALUE: The current value of a future cash flow stream, discounted back at a defined discount or interest rate; also known as NPV.

NEW VENTURE: A new business providing products/services to a particular market.

NICHE MARKET: A market in which a limited and clearly defined range of products is sold to a specific group of customers, often not supplied by an existing major company and hence suitable for a smaller company to serve.

NONCOMPETE/NONDISCLOSURE AGREEMENT: Legal agreement(s) that stipulates that the signees must not disclose confidential information about the company and/or product. It also prevents the signee from joining or starting a similar venture.

OFFERING: The financial "package" presented by a new venture.

OPERATING BUDGET: A financial plan outlining how a company will use its resources over a specified period of time.

PARTNERSHIP: Business association of two or more people. There are two types of partnerships: general and limited.

PATENT: Federal governmental grant to an inventor giving exclusive rights to an invention or process for twenty years from date of filing. A U.S. patent does not always grant rights in foreign countries.

POSTMONEY VALUATION: The valuation accorded a company after investment by venture capitalists or angels.

PREMONEY VALUATION: The value accorded a company prior to investment from venture capitalists or angels.

PRIVATE EQUITY: An umbrella term for investments that include venture capital and buyout funds. Sometimes used (especially in Europe) as a synonym for venture capital.

PRIVATE PLACEMENTS: A transaction involving the sale of stocks or bonds to wealthy individuals, pension funds, insurance companies, or other investors. It is done without a public offering or any oversight from the SEC.

PROPRIETARY: That which is owned, such as a patent, formula, brand name, or trademark associated with the product/service.

PROVISIONAL PATENT: A low-cost patent application filed with the U.S. Patent and Trademark Office, which establishes the date of an invention. This application is not published or reviewed by patent examiners and may be abandoned later, or it may be used as the basis of a full patent application.

PUBLIC OFFERING: The sale of a company's shares of stock to the public by the company or its major stockholders.

QUIET PERIOD: The period starting when an issuer hires an underwriter and ending 25 days after the security begins trading, during which the issuer cannot comment publicly on the offering due to SEC rules.

REGISTERED STOCK: Stock that has been registered with the SEC and, thus, can be sold publicly.

REGISTRATION RIGHTS: The right that a shareholder has to register her stock along with the founders at the time of an IPO.

RESTRICTED STOCK: Issued stock that cannot be traded until the restriction deadline has passed. Founders' stock is usually restricted for up to one year after a company has gone public as the new investors do not want to see the insiders selling too early and, thereby, devaluing the share price.

RETURN ON EQUITY: Measures the return on the owner's investment in the company and is perhaps the most important measure of a business's financial viability; also known as ROE. The higher the ratio, the higher the rate of return on the owner's investment.

REVOLVERS: Another term for a bank line of credit, which enables companies to borrow and use funds as necessary, usually with a one- to two-year payback requirement.

RISK CAPITAL: Another term for equity investing, sometimes also referred to as investment capital or venture capital.

ROAD SHOW: The process during a public offering in which the management of an issuing company and the underwriters meet with groups of prospective investors.

ROUNDS OF INVESTMENT: Investments made at different stages of a company's growth. These are referred to as "preseed" when the idea is embryonic and "seed" when the company builds a prototype before it has any sales. Those are followed by a series of development rounds called "A," "B," "C," and so on.

RUNWAY: The time until a company no longer has any cash on hand to continue its operations; also referred to as **cash-out.**

SALES PER EMPLOYEE: An important measure of your firm's overall productivity, its ability to manage the overhead associated with its workforce, and its long-term financial health. The higher the sales per employee, the more productive your employees.

SARBANES-OXLEY ACT: An act passed by Congress in 2002 to protect investors from the possibility of fraudulent accounting activities by corporations; also called SOX.

SBA LOAN: A variety of loan programs that assist owners in obtaining financing (SBA does not provide direct loans to businesses). The most common source of SBA financing is the 7(a) loan guaranty, which is obtained through a lender and receives a guarantee of repayment from the SBA (the collateral holder).

S-CORPORATION (SUBCHAPTER S-CORPORATION): A firm that has elected to be taxed as a partnership under the subchapters provision of the Internal Revenue Code.

SCALE-FREE NETWORK: A network that grows not through contacts between local neighbors, but through nodes that provide immediate benefit to visitors. One example is the "hub and spoke" structure of most airlines. Such networks have become more prevalent through the Internet. (See **social network.**)

SERIAL ENTREPRENEUR: An entrepreneur who starts and exits several companies one after the other.

SOCIAL NETWORK: A network of individuals who have a common interest. Recently such networks have been created using the Internet as the meeting venue. Examples include Facebook, MySpace, LinkedIn, and others.

SOLE PROPRIETORSHIP: A business firm owned by only one person and operated for his or her profit.

SPIDERWEB MODEL: A visual representation of an early-stage company indicating its fragility and that it can be severely damaged suddenly by events coming unexpectedly from many directions.

STAKEHOLDER: A person or entity that has an interest, financial and/or otherwise, in the outcome of an action. In a start-up situation, the list includes owners, investors, lenders, employees, customers, suppliers, landlords, and others.

STANDSTILL AGREEMENT: An agreement between two parties that they will not enter into another agreement for a defined time. This allows parties to invest in due diligence processes without the concern that their efforts will be preempted.

START-UP CAPITAL: Money needed to launch a new venture before and during the initial period of operation.

START-UP STAGE: A stage of development a company may experience, characterized by a need for planning, people, and financial resources.

STATEMENT OF CASH FLOWS: A financial statement that reflects the increases and decreases in cash for a certain time period.

STOCK CERTIFICATE: A document issued to a stockholder by a corporation indicating the number of shares of stock owned by the stockholder.

STOCK DIVIDEND: A proportional distribution of securities to the company's stockholders.

STOCK OPTIONS: A right to buy a stated number of shares in a company at a defined price (the strike price) within a defined time period. Stock options are often used as part of the compensation for key persons in a company. The owner of the options can "exercise" them within the defined period, and if the stock price has appreciated, they will have a capital gain. If the share price has declined below the strike price, the options are "under water" and have little or no value.

STOCKHOLDER'S EQUITY: The portion of a business owned by the stockholders.

SYNDICATION: A means by which investors or bankers spread their risk by bringing in partners to share the transaction.

TEASER: A slang term for a one- or two-page document that provides just sufficient information to grab the attention of an investor or lender without disclosing too much. A written version of an elevator pitch and similar to an executive summary.

TERM LOAN: A loan that must be fully paid back by an agreed date. If a lender does not meet the terms of the covenants of the loan, the lender may have the right to "call the loan" by shortening the term.

TERM SHEET: A summary of the principal conditions for a proposed investment by a venture capital firm or lender.

TOTAL AVAILABLE MARKET: The total annual sales that a company would derive if it were able to capture 100 percent of its targeted market; also called TAM.

TRADEMARK: A brand or part of a brand that is given legal protection because it is capable of exclusive appropriation.

UNDERWRITER: An intermediary between an issuer of a security and the investing public, usually an investment bank.

VENTURE CAPITAL: Money from investment pools or firms that specialize in financing young companies' growth, usually in return for stock.

VENTURE CAPITAL VALUATION METHOD: A method used by venture capitalists to value a young company based on a discounted value of an anticipated exit using either an IPO or, more likely, a sale to a large company.

VENTURE CAPITALIST: An investor who provides early financing to new ventures—often technology based—with an innovative product and the prospect of rapid and profitable growth.

VESTING PERIOD: The time between the issuance of a benefit or right and the time it can be accessed. This often applies to stock options, which may not be exercised until the recipient has been with the company for a defined time.

VIRAL MARKETING: A means by which customers are acquired through recommendations from existing customers and users. The Internet often supports such marketing methods.

WARRANT: An option to buy for a stipulated price a certain amount of stock that is transferable and can be traded.

WORKING CAPITAL: The amount of funds available to pay short-term expenses, such as unexpected or out-of-the-ordinary, one-time-only expenses. Working capital is determined by subtracting current liabilities from current assets.

INDEX

A

Accountability, 296
Accountant selection, 146
Accounting fees, public offerings and, 383
Acquisitions/buyouts
  private equity firms and, 185
  venture capital process and, 197–198
Action plans, 97
Adjusted book value, 205
Administrative services, 173
Advances, licensing and franchising and, 303
Advertising, 67, 102
Afuah, Alan, 41
Aggregators, 87
Allen, Paul, 27
Alliances, exit strategies and, 368–369
Amazon, 43, 234, 300
Amberwave Inc., 303
American List Council, 66
Angel investors, 193–194, 348
Annual budget preparation, 246–248
Antidilution protection, 221
Antidilution rights, 192
Antioco, John, 46
Apple Computer, 72
Application service providers, 309–310
Articles of incorporation, 134–135
Aspiring entrepreneurs, 6
Asset valuation, 205–206
Assimilation, hiring process and, 322–323
Attorney selection, 145–146
Authority conflicts, partnerships and, 142
Automatic conversion, venture capital
  terms and, 221

B

Balance sheets
  book value and, 234–237
  burn rate and, 235–237
  current-liabilities-to-net-worth ratio
    and, 240
  current ratio and, 239
  debt-to-worth ratio and, 241
  fixed-assets-to-net-worth ratio and,
    240–241
  goodwill and, 237
  quick ratio and, 239–240
  sample, 234
  solvency ratios and, 240
  total-liabilities-to-net-worth ratio and,
    240
  typical cash flow statement, 236
Balch, John, 160–161
Bandes, Craig, 346
Bank loans, 162
Bartering for goods and services, 159
Baumol, William, 41
Bayh, Birch, 61
Bayh-Dole Act (1980), 61
Better Business Bureau, 281
Bezos, Jeff, 29
Blyth Candles, 42–43
Board of directors
  C-corporations and, 132
  equity financing and, 225
Bonforte, Jeff, 183
Book value, 205
Bootstrapping techniques, 158–161
  bartering for goods and services, 159
  contingent litigation, 160
  cooperative purchases, 160
  credit cards, 161
  expensive equipment access, 159
  no or low rent, 159
  outsourcing, 160
  renting or leasing equipment, 159
  suppliers' and customers' help,
    159–160
  trading intellectual property rights,
    159
  used equipment, 159
Breakeven analysis, 252–254
Breakeven formula, 253–254
Brezina, Matt, 183
Bridge financing, 190–191, 197
Bucheist, Michael, 134
Budget preparation, 246–248

Building to order, 296
Bureau of Indian Affairs, 170
Burn rate, 235–237
Business incubators, 172–174
  administrative services and, 173
  easy networking and, 174
  expert help and, 174
  flexible space and leases and, 173
  for-profit incubators, 173
  funding and, 174
  increased credibility and, 174
  management help and, 173–174
  publicly sponsored, 173
  specialization and, 174
  types of, 173
  university related, 173
Business mergers, 185, 375–376
Business models
  competitive strategy and, 298
  corporate partnering and, 311
  cost structure and, 298
  databases and, 299–300
  definition of, 297–298
  Dell example, 295–297
  licensing and franchising and,
    301–307
  locking in customers and, 300–301
  market segments and, 298
  outsourcing resources and, 307–310
  profit potential and, 298
  social networks and, 310–311
  supply chain value and, 298–299
  value chains and, 298
  value proposition and, 298
Business opportunity evaluation, 51
Business plans
  action plans and, 97
  advertising/public relations/promotion
    strategies and, 102
  attracting investors and, 94
  business concept and, 96
  characteristics of, 94
  development and, 54–55
  drafting of, 96
  executive summary and, 96–97

Business plans (*Contd.*)
  financial plans and, 103–104
  format and content of, 99–104
  full business plans, 97
  funds required and, 103–104
  goals and objectives and, 94–95
  likelihood of success and, 93
  management team and, 103
  marketing and sales and, 99–102
  objectives identification and, 95–96
  operations plans and, 102
  outlines and, 96
  performance benchmarks and, 95
  preparation time and, 98
  pricing strategy and, 101–102
  reviewing and updating and, 97
  roadmap guide for writing, 121–125
  securing capital and, 95
  targeting selected groups and, 97–98
  testing feasibility and, 93
  understanding failure of, 104–105
  value of, 93–94
  writing process and, 95–97
Business sales, 369–370. *See also* Exit
    strategies
  buyer search and, 371–372
  closing deal and, 375
  due diligence and, 374–375
  initial meetings and, 372–373
  Lehman formula fee schedule, 372
  letter of intent and, 373–374
  negotiating and, 373
  offer evaluation and, 372–373
  professional intermediaries and,
    371–372
  purchase agreements and, 375
  sale memorandum and, 370–371
Business start-up, 143–147. *See also*
    Ownership forms
  accountant selection and, 146
  attorney selection and, 145–146
  directors and officers insurance and,
    147
  domain name registration and, 147
  federal identification number and, 146
  first sixty days guide and, 145
  first thirty days guide and, 144–145
  first year end guide and, 145
  insurance issues and, 147
  name registration and, 146
  state registration and, 147
  Web site registration and, 147
Business-to-business (B2B) sales, 38
Business-to-consumer (B2C) sales, 38

Business valuation
  adjusted book value and, 205
  asset valuation and, 205–206
  book value and, 205
  cash flow estimates and, 202
  discounted cash flow valuation and,
    206–208
  early-stage investments and, 202–203
  earnings valuation and, 204–205
  exit valuation and, 203
  later-stage valuation and, 204
  liquidation value and, 206
  motivational issues and, 203–204
  strategic sales and, 202
  venture capital model and, 202–203
Bust-up fees, 374
Buyer searches, 371–372

C

C-corporations, 132–138
  advantages of, 136–137
  attracting capital and, 137
  board of directors and, 132
  Certificate of Incorporation and,
    134–135
  continuity and, 137
  corporate officers and, 132–133
  corporate stock and, 135
  disadvantages of, 137–138
  double taxation and, 137
  incorporation process and, 137
  limited liability of stockholders and,
    136
  registration and, 133–134
  shares authorized and issued, 136
  skills, expertise, knowledge and, 137
  stockholders and, 132
  taxes and, 135–136
  transferable ownership and, 137
Capital access
  C-corporations and, 137
  currency trading and, 39
  partnerships and, 140–141
  public offerings and, 377
  sole proprietorships and, 131
Capital accumulation, partnerships
    and, 141
Cardinal Health, 45
Cash flow forecasts, 249–252
  cash flow disbursements and, 250
  cash flow revenues and, 250
  cash flow statements and, 251

commercial loans and, 165
  reasons for, 249–250
  revenue and disbursement
    reconciliation and, 250–251
  starting, 250–251
  venture capital model and, 202
  worksheet design and, 251
Cash flow statements, 236, 243–244
Cash generated measurement, 245
Certificate of Incorporation, 134–135
Character, as factor in commercial
    loans, 165
Chasteen, Ron, 160–161
ChemStation franchise model, 306–307
Chin, Fanny, 139
Christensen, Clayton, 43
Chverchko, Matt, 128–129
Citibank, 184
Class A stock, 135
Class B stock, 135
Clean breaks, employee termination
    and, 324
Coca-Cola, 286
Collaborative filtering, 300
Collateral, commercial loans and,
    165–166
Combination segmentations, 72
Commercial bank loans, 162–167
  banker relationship and, 167
  cash flow and, 165
  character and, 165
  collateral and, 165–166
  contribution and, 165
  debt terms and, 166–167
  interest rates and, 166
  personal credit ratings and, 164
  preparing loan proposals and, 164–165
Commercializing New Technologies (V. K.
    Jolly), 9
Communication. *See* Opportunity
    communication
Community bank loans, 163
Compaq, 296
Competitive advantage, 58
Competitive analysis. *See also* Marketing
    analysis and plans
  attribute measurement and, 75
  product or service positioning and,
    75–76
  questions to consider and, 74–75
Competitive pricing, 101
Competitive strategy, constructing
    business models and, 298
Complaints, 70

Confidentiality
   employee termination and, 324
   equity financing and, 227–228
   investors' presentations and, 354–355
Confidentiality agreements, 278, 328–329
Conflict analysis, 327
Conflicts of interest, 325–327
Consulting agreements, 328, 333–337
Contingent litigation, 160
Continuity
   C-corporations and, 137
   partnerships and, 141
   sole proprietorships and, 131–132
Contribution, marketing plans and, 77
Contribution to venture, commercial loans
   and, 166
Control loss, public offerings and, 378
Control needs, entrepreneurship and, 7–9
Conversion, venture capital terms and, 221
Cooperative purchases, 160
Copyrights, 269–272
   obtaining, 270–271
   protection and enforcement of,
      271–272
   symbol, 270
Corporate culture, 319–320
Corporate investments, strategic
   partnerships and, 200–201
Corporate officers, 132–133
Corporate partnering, 311
Corporate stock, 135. *See also* Stock
   options
Cost of goods sold, 246
Cost-plus pricing, 101
Cost structure, business models and, 298
Creative Calendar, 139
Credit card funding, 161
Credit ratings, commercial loans and, 164
Cultural attributes, successful companies
   and, 320
Currency trading, 39
Current-liabilities-to-net-worth ratio,
   240
Current ratio, 239
Customers
   capturing data on, 300
   complaints and, 70
   customer satisfaction programs, 70
   identification of, 68–69
   Internet-related expectations and, 38
   just-in-time marketing and, 70
   lifetime value and, 70
   linking with transactions and, 70
   locking in of, 300–301

marketing analysis and, 69
one-to-one contact and, 295–296
points of pain and, 70

D

Daring Visionaries (Ray Smilor), 6
Data analysis, market research and,
   53–54
Databases, creating value using, 299–300
DBI Services, 294–295
DeAngelo, Neal, 294–295
Debt
   commercial loans and, 166–167
   debt financing, 161–162
   preparing financial projections and, 245
Debt-to-worth ratio, 241
Delaware, incorporation in, 133
Dell, Michael, 36, 295, 319
Dell Computer, 40, 43, 45, 295–297
Delphion, 276
Demand pricing, 101
Demand registration, equity financing
   and, 222–223
Demographic segmentation, 72
Denoble, Alex, 5
Design patents, 273
Digital rights management, 303
Direct salesforces, 78–79
Directors' insurance, public offerings
   and, 383
Disclosure document program, patent
   ideas and, 280
Discounted cash flow valuation, 206–208
Disruptive innovation, 43
Distressed companies, private equity
   and, 184
Dividends, equity financing and, 222
Dole, Robert, 61
Domain name registration, 147
Double taxation, 137
Due diligence
   business sales and, 374–375
   equity financing and, 189–190
Due diligence checklist (prospective
   investor), 214–219
   agreements, 216
   corporate documents, 214
   employee relations, 215
   financial/accounting, 218
   financings, 215
   governmental licenses and, 217
   insiders, 215–216

insurance and, 217
litigation and regulatory compliance,
   217
management/directors, 215
real property matters, 216
sales and marketing, 216
securities matters, 214–215
taxes, 218
technology matters, 216–217
trade/analyst reports, 216
Duress, 9
Dyson, James, 155–156
Dyson case, 155–156, 302

E

Early-stage financing
   securing of, 157
   venture capital model and, 197,
      202–203
Earnings valuation, 204–205
EBIT (earnings before interest and taxes),
   242, 247
EBITDA, 247
Edison, Thomas, 42
Ehrlich, Sanford, 48
Elevator pitch, 353–354
Elting, Liz, 367
Employee incentives, public offerings
   and, 377
Employee termination, 323–324
   clean breaks and, 324
   confidential information and, 324
   guidelines for, 324
   professionalism and, 324
   reasons for, 324
Employment agreements, 328, 331–332
Energy investments, 185
Entrepreneurial characteristics, 5–10
Entrepreneurship process, 21–30
   company setup and, 27
   conducting opportunity analysis, 26–27
   financial partners and sources of
      funding, 27–28
   finding early mentors and, 23–24
   five-stages of, 25–29
   growth period and, 29–30
   managing stress and, 24–25
   plan development and, 27
   plan implementation and, 28
   resource determination and, 28
   spiderweb model and, 22
   venture scaling and harvesting, 28–29

Equifax, 164
Equipment access, 159
Equity financing. *See also* Venture capital
    angel investors and, 193–194
    antidilution rights and, 192
    board membership and, 191
    bridge financing and, 190–191
    business value and, 202–208
    corporate investments and, 200–201
    due diligence and, 189–190
    due diligence checklist and, 214–219
    forced buyouts and, 192
    fundamentals of, 183–193
    later rounds and, 192
    management decisions and, 192
    microequity and, 194
    piggybacking and, 192
    pre- and postmoney valuation and, 189
    preferences and covenants, 191–193
    private equity and, 184–187
    private placements and, 199–200
    public stock and, 183–184
    registration rights and, 192
    selling to partner and, 367
    stock classes and, 187–188
    strategic partnerships and, 200–201
    warrants and, 188–189
Ernst & Young, 96
Ethical dilemmas
    conflict analysis and, 327
    conflicts of interest, 325–327
    full disclosure and, 327
    gut-feel test and, 327
    resolution of, 327
Ethnic segmentations, 72
Excitement creation, investments
    and, 359
Exclusivity, licensing and, 302
Executive summary, business plans
    and, 96–97
Exit strategies. *See also* Business sales
    creation of, 366–367
    identifying alliances and, 368–369
    mergers and, 375–376
    negotiation process and, 369
    nonconfidential introduction kits
        and, 368
    plan of action and, 368–369
    public offerings and, 376–383
    sample meeting agenda and, 368–369
    selling equity to partner and, 367
Exit valuation, 203
Expansion financing, venture capital
    and, 197

Expenses, public offerings and, 379,
    382–383
Experian, 164

F

Facebook, 23, 310
Factoring, 162
Fair and Accurate Credit Transitions Act
    (ACTA) (2003), 164
Family funding, 161
Feasibility studies. *See* Marketing analysis
    and plans
Federal government funding
    federal sources, 167–168
    minorities and women and, 170
    Small Business Administration
        programs and, 168–169
    Small Business Innovation Research
        program, 169
    Small Business Technology Transfer
        program, 170
    state and local financing initiatives,
        170
Federal identification number, 146
Feedback, employee, 324
Fees
    franchising and, 305
    licensing and, 302–303
Fiduciary responsibilities, public
    offerings and, 379
Filtering, collaborative, 300
Financial Accounting Standards Board
    (FASB), 256
Financial partners, finding, 27–28
Financial projections, 245–248
    cash generated and, 245–246
    profits and, 245
    sales volume and, 245
Financial statement footnotes, 244–245
    acquisitions and divestitures/
        discontinued operations, 245
    debt, 245
    general description of business,
        244–245
    intangible assets, 245
    legal proceedings, 245
    subsequent events, 245
Financing agreements, 360–361
Firing employees. *See* Employee
    termination
Fitzgerald, Gene, 303
Fixed-assets-to-net-worth ratio, 240–241
Fixed costs, pricing methods and, 77

Flexibility, partnerships and, 140–141
Flexible space, business incubators and,
    173
Focus groups, 88
Forced buyout terms, 192
Ford Motor Company, 161, 184, 301
Foreman, Richard, 28
Form S-3 registration, 223
Founders' buyback agreements, 225
Franchise agreements, 304–307
Frezza, Bill, 349
Friends, startup funding and, 161
Full disclosure, ethical dilemmas and,
    327
Funding. *See also* Bootstrapping
    techniques; Investor location
    bank loans and, 161–162
    business incubators and, 174
    factoring and, 161–162
    family and friends and, 161
    finding sources of, 27–28
    securing early funding, 157
    self-funding, 157–161

G

Garage start-up, 159
Gates, Bill, 27, 29, 183
General Fasteners, 301
General Motors (GM), 301
General partnerships, 140–142
Geographic segmentation, 72
Gisholt, Paal, 36, 45
Global knowledge sharing, 37
Go2Athlete.com, 310
Goodwill, accounting treatment of, 237
Google, 37
Government funding sources, 167–170.
    See also Federal government funding
Graef, Ted, 22
Greif Packaging, 38
Groegen, Robert, 42–43
Gross profit, 243, 246
Grove, Andy, 29
Growth capital, 184
Growth entrepreneurs, 7
Growth period, entrepreneurship process
    and, 29–30
Gut-feel test, ethical dilemmas and, 327

H

Harvesting, venture, 28–29
Hewlett-Packard (HP), 39, 159

Hills, Gerald E., 67
Hiring practices, 321–323
    interviewing and, 322–323
    legal documents and, 322
    mentoring and assimilation and,
        322–323
    searching and, 321
    stock options and, 322
Homan, George, 306

I

IBM, 296
Ideas. *See also* Innovation
    converting into opportunities, 49–50
    finding and assessing, 48–49
Incentive stock options (ISO), 329.
    See also Stock options
Income statements
    return on investment and, 242–243
    return on total assets and, 243
    using ratios for profitability and,
        242–243
    value of, 241–242
Income taxes, 246
Incorporation, state of, 133–134
Incremental innovation, 41–42
Information rights, equity financing
    and, 224–225
Information sources, market research
    and, 53
Infrastructure investments, 185
Initial public offerings (IPOs). *See* Public
    offerings
Innovation
    business management and, 56–57
    competitive advantage issues and, 58
    converting ideas into opportunities,
        49–50
    creating evaluation framework and,
        57–58
    definition of, 41
    disruptive, 41–42
    evaluation process and, 50
    existing business analysis and, 46–47
    finding and assessing ideas and,
        48–49
    five phases to success and, 50–59
    importance of, 40–41
    incremental, 41–42
    learning innovation skills, 43–44
    market issues and, 57
    market research and, 52–54
    opportunity costs and, 51

    patent protection and, 58–59
    plan development and, 54–55
    points of pain and, 46
    radical, 41–42
    resource need determination and,
        55–56
    seizing opportunity and, 51
    technology trend intersections and,
        45–46
    time horizon and, 51
    twentieth century, 44
    types of, 41–42
Insurance issues, 147
Intangible assets, 245
Intel, 43
Intellectual property *See also* Patents
    choosing representatives and, 279–280
    confidentiality agreements and, 278
    copyright value and, 269–272
    from idea to patent to enterprise, 285
    licensing and, 302
    nondisclosure agreements and, 278
    patent value and, 272–278
    protection of, 40, 278–280
    registered patent agents and, 278
    registered patent attorneys and, 279
    reverse engineering and, 287
    reviews of, 225
    trade secrets and, 286–287
    trademark value and, 266–269
    trading rights and, 159
Interest rates, commercial loans and,
    166
Intermediaries, business sales and,
    371–372
Internal rate of return (IRR), 255
Internet
    customer expectations and, 38
    finding mentors and, 23
    growth of, 37–38
    online surveys, 88
    Web site registration, 147
Intertrust, 303
Interview guide, 323
Intuitive Controls Inc., 22
Inventory costs, 241
Investment decision analysis, 254–256
    company statement evaluation and,
        255–256
    internal rate of return and, 255
    net present value method and, 254–255
Investor benefits, public offerings and,
    376–377
Investor evaluation process, 359–360

Investor location, 347–349. *See also*
    Funding
    initial conversations and, 348
    tips regarding, 348–349
Investors' communication
    confidentiality and, 354–355
    meeting preparation, 354–359
Investors' presentations
    after the presentation, 359–361
    presentation tips, 359
    template for, 356–358
Investors rights, venture capital terms and,
    221–225
Issued shares, C-corporations and, 136
iTunes, 300

J

JetBlue, 75
Jobs, Steve, 29
Johnson, Scott, 22
Johnson & Johnson (J&J), 184
Jolly, V. K., 9
Just-in-time marketing, 70

K

Katz, Alvin, 232–233
Kearns, Robert, 161
Khosla Ventures, 183
Kibblewhite, Ian, 264–265
Kodak, 43
Kohlberg Kravis Roberts & Co., (KKR),
    198

L

Later-stage business valuation, 204
LeafBusters Inc., 44, 350–353
Leases, 173
Leasing equipment, 159
Legal documents
    consulting agreement, 333–337
    employment agreement, 331–332
    sales and marketing agreement, 339–342
    separation agreement, 337–339
Legal fees, public offerings and, 383
Legal issues, 327–329
    confidentiality agreements, 328–329
    consulting agreements, 328
    employment agreements, 328
    sales and marketing agreements, 328
    separation agreements, 328

Legal restrictions, sole proprietorships and, 130

Lehman formula fee schedule, 372

Letter of intent, 373–374

Leveraged buyouts (LBO), 184, 197

Liability
C-corporations and, 136
partnerships and, 141

License agreements, 301–303

License fees, 302–303

Lifestyle entrepreneurs, 6–7

Limited liability company (LLC), 142–143

Limited partnerships, 140–142

LinkedIn, 23, 310

Liquid Piston, 92–93

Liquidation events, 222

Liquidation value, 206

Litigation, contingent, 160

Loan proposals, 162, 164–165

Local government funding sources, 170

Loyalty programs, 70–71

M

Management decisions, equity investors and, 192

Management help, business incubators and, 173–174

Management incentives, public offerings and, 377

Market identification, 68–69

Market penetration, 78–80

Market research
data analysis and, 54
data collection and, 53
designing and executing studies and, 54
informal focus groups and, 88
information sources and, 53
marketing plan writing and, 86–87
online surveys and, 88
preliminary questions and, 52–53
primary market research, 87–88
secondary market research, 88
techniques, 86–88

Market segmentation, 71–73
business models and, 298
combination segmentations, 72
demographic segmentations, 72
ethnic segmentations, 72
factors in, 73
geographic segmentations, 72

psychographic segmentations, 72
questions regarding, 73

Market stand-off, equity financing and, 223

Marketing analysis and planning. *See also* Competitive analysis; Market segmentation
advertising/public relations/promotion, 67
current and best customers and, 69
customer identification and, 68–69
future activities and, 68
loyalty program value, 70–71
market identification and, 68–69
niche or target markets and, 69
one-to-one marketing and, 69–70
outside factors and, 69
potential customers and, 69
pricing strategy and, 67
sales and distributions and, 67
setting objectives and, 67
site analysis and, 68

Markup pricing, 101

Massing, Daniel E., 61

MasterCard, 161

McDonald's, 304

McGrath, Rita, 51

McVicker, Wayne, 4

Mentoring, 23–24, 322–323

Mergers. *See* Business mergers

Merz, Ernest, 22

Mezzanine capital, 185

Mezzanine financing, 197

Microequity, 194

Microsoft, 43, 160–161, 302

Minard, Becky, 36, 45

Minimums, licensing and, 303

Mining the long-tail, 300

Minorities, government funding sources and, 170

Minority Business Development Agency, 170

Money management. *See also* Balance sheets
annual budget preparation and, 246–248
balance sheet and, 233–241
breakeven analysis preparation and, 252–254
cash flow forecast preparation and, 249–252
cash flow statements and, 243–244
financial projections preparation and, 245–248

income statement and, 241–242
investment decision analysis and, 254–256
sample budget projections, 247–249
stresses of, 257
taxes and filing, 256–257
understanding financial statement footnotes, 244–245
using ratios for profitability, 242–243

Moonlighting, self-funding and, 158

Moore's law, 39

Motivational issues, business valuation and, 203–204

Motorola, 39

MySpace, 23, 310

N

Name registration, business-startup and, 146

Napster, 303

NASDAQ, 184

Negotiating business sales, 373. *See also* Business sales

Neoforma, Inc., 4, 311, 321–322

Net income, 247

Net present value (NPV) method, 254–255

Net profit margin, 243

Netflix, 46, 300

Networking, 23–24, 55, 174

New York Stock Exchange, 184

NewsCorp, 311

NewsStand, 311

Niche markets, 69

Nokia, 39

Nonconfidential introduction kits, 368

Nondisclosure agreements (NDA), 225, 278

Nonqualified stock options (NQSO), 329

Nonunique products, 296

O

Office of Minority Enterprise Development (MED), 170

Office of Small and Disadvantaged Business Utilization, 170

Officers' insurance, public offerings and, 383

One-to-one customer contact, 295–296

One-to-one marketing, 69–70

Online surveys, 88

Operating expenses, 246
Operating profit/loss, 246
Operating profit margin, 243
Operations-oriented pricing, 77
Opportunity analysis, 26–27
Opportunity communication
    creating excitement and, 359
    dealing with rejection and, 360
    elevator pitch and, 353–354
    financing agreement and, 360–361
    investor evaluation process and,
        359–360
    investor location and, 347–349
    investors' presentation, 354–359
    post-presentation, 359–361
    teaser preparation, 349–353
Opportunity costs, 51
Other income and expenses, 246
Outsourcing
    application service providers and,
        309–310
    as bootstrapping technique, 160
    business plans and, 307–310
    checklist for, 308–309
Ownership forms
    C-corporations, 132–138
    choosing best form, 129
    limited liability companies, 142–143
    organizational structure comparison
        chart, 143
    partnerships, 140–142
    S-corporations, 138–140
    sole proprietorships, 129–132

P

Parachute payments, equity financing
    and, 225
Part-time consulting, self-funding and,
    158
Partnerships, 140–142
    advantages of, 140–141
    attracting limited partners and,
        140–141
    business models and, 311
    capital accumulation and, 141
    capital pool and, 140–141
    complementary skills and, 140
    continuity and, 141
    disadvantages of, 141–142
    division of profits and, 140
    ease of establishment and, 140
    flexibility and, 140–141
    general partnerships, 140

liability and, 141
limited partnerships, 140
personality and authority conflicts and,
    142
restrictions of elimination and, 141
taxation and, 140–141
Patel, Ankit, 353
Patents, 272–278
    application process and, 282
    classifications and, 273
    disclosure document program and, 280
    drafting claims and, 283
    evaluation screening for, 58–59
    financial considerations and, 284
    licensing and, 284–285
    long-term coverage and, 40
    new patent activity, 274
    nonobviousness and, 275–276
    nonprovisional applications and, 283
    patent pending, 284
    patent portfolios, 272–273
    potential invalidation and, 276–277
    prior art searches and, 280–282
    process of, 276
    provisional applications and, 282–283
    qualifications for, 274–275
    review process and, 284
    right questions and, 273–274
    sample acceptance letter, 277
    steps to enterprise, 285
    utility and novelty and, 275, 277–278
Patronage-oriented pricing, 77
Peak season pricing, 77
Pegasystems Inc., 366
Periodic reporting, public offerings
    and, 379
Personal contacts, 55
Personal liability, sole proprietorships
    and, 131
Personality conflicts, partnerships and,
    142
Piggybacking, equity investors and, 192,
    223
Plan implementation, entrepreneurship
    process and, 27–28
Plant patents, 273
Points of pain, 46, 70
Polaris Industries, 160–161
Pommerenke, Pamela, 52
Positioning, product or service, 75–76
Postmoney valuation, equity investments
    and, 189
Power investments, 185
"Pratt's Guide to Venture Capital," 349

Preferred stock, 135
Premoney valuation, equity investments
    and, 189
Presentations, public offerings and,
    381–382
Pretax income, 246
Price/earnings (P/E) multiples, 204–205
Price elasticity, 78
Pricing methods
    contribution and, 77
    fixed costs and, 77
    rationale and, 76–77
    sales strategy and, 76–77
    semivariable costs and, 77
    value and, 76
    variable costs and, 77
Pricing objectives, 77–78
    operations oriented, 77
    patronage oriented, 77–78
    revenue oriented, 77
Pricing strategy, marketing plans and, 67
Primary market research, 87–88
Prior art searches, 281–282
    agencies and organizations and, 281
    cautions regarding, 281–282
    government resources and, 281
    Internet searching, 281
Privacy loss, public offerings and, 379
Private equity, 184–187
    distressed or special situations and,
        184
    energy and power investments and, 185
    growth capital and, 184
    infrastructure investments and, 185
    initial public offerings and, 185
    leveraged buyouts and, 184
    mergers or acquisitions and, 185
    mezzanine capital and, 185
    recapitalization and, 185
    rounds of investment and, 186–187
    venture capital and, 184
Private placements, 199–200
Procter & Gamble (P&G), 310
Product information enhancement, 70
Product life cycle acceleration, 40
Production costs, 241
Professionalism, employee termination
    and, 324
Profits
    gross profit, 243, 246
    measurement of, 245
    net profit margin, 243
    operating profit margins, 243
    partnerships and, 140

Profits (*Contd.*)
  potential and business models, 298
  ratios and, 242–243
  sole proprietorships and, 130
Promotion strategies, 67, 102. *See also*
  Marketing analysis and planning
Proprietary rights agreements, 225
Prospectus, public offerings and, 380
Psychographic segmentation, 72
Public Company Accounting Oversight
  Board (PCAOB), 237
Public offerings, 376–383
  accounting and legal fees and, 383
  acquisition path and, 377–378
  benefits of, 376–378
  capital access and, 377
  control loss and, 378
  corporate reputation and, 377
  delivering value and, 383
  directors' and officers' insurance
    and, 383
  disadvantages of, 378–379
  expenses and, 382–383
  financial condition improvement
    and, 376
  future financing opportunities and,
    377
  initial and outgoing expenses and, 379
  management and employee incentives
    and, 377
  management freedom to act and, 379
  managing IPO event, 379
  meeting expectations and, 383
  new fiduciary responsibilities and,
    379
  periodic reporting and, 378
  privacy loss and, 379
  prospectus and, 380
  quiet periods and, 381
  registration filing and, 380–381
  registration process and, 379–380
  road show presentations and, 381–382
  shareholder/investor benefits and,
    376–377
  shareholder portfolio diversification
    and, 377
  underwriter selection and, 382
  underwriters' compensation and,
    382
Public stocks. *See also* Public offerings;
  Stock options
  classes of, 187–188
  equity investment and, 183–184
Purchase agreements, 375

Q

Questions, market research and, 52, 73
Quick ratio, 239–240
Quiet periods, public offerings and, 381

R

Radical innovation, 41–42
Rappaport, Donn, 66
Recapitalization, 185
Redemption, securities, 221
Registration expenses, equity financing
  and, 223
Registration process, public offerings
  and, 379–380
Registration rights, equity investors
  and, 192
Regulation D, 199–200
Rejection, finding investors and, 360
Rent, bootstrapping techniques and, 159
Renting equipment, 159
Research in Motion, 39
Resignations, 325
Resources
  cultivating advanced resources, 56–57
  determination of, 28, 55–56
  financing requirements and, 56
  personal contacts and networking, 55
  technical skill requirements and, 56
Restek, 318–319
Return on investment (ROI), 242–243
Return on total assets, 243
Revenue-oriented pricing, 77
Reverse engineering, 287
Right of first offer, equity financing
  and, 224
Right of first refusal, equity financing
  and, 223–224
RJR/Nabisco, 198
Road show presentations, 381–382
Royalties
  franchising and, 305
  licensing and, 302–303
Running royalties, 302–303

S

S-corporations, 138–140
  advantages of, 138–139
  choice of, 139–140
  disadvantages of, 139

S-curve, 41
Sale of business. *See* Business sales
Sales, annual budget preparation and, 246
Sales and marketing agreements, 328,
  339–342
Sales channels, 78–80
  direct salesforces, 78–79
  sales agents, 79
  trade shows, 79–80
  viral marketing, 80
Sales strategy
  marketing plans and, 67
  pricing methods and, 76–77
  pricing objectives and, 77–78
Sales volume measurement, 245
Sanders, James, 199
Sarbanes-Oxley Act of 2002, 237–239
  analyst conflicts of interest and, 238
  auditor independence and, 238
  commission resources and authority
    and, 238
  corporate and criminal fraud
    accountability and, 238
  corporate fraud accountability and,
    239
  corporate responsibility and, 238
  corporate tax returns and, 239
  enhanced financial disclosures and,
    238
  Public Company Accounting Oversight
    Board and, 237
  studies and reports and, 238
  white-collar crime penalty
    enhancement and, 238–239
Scale-free networks, 23–24
Scaling, venture, 28–29
Schoolwires Inc., 310
Schorer, Clifford, 97
SCORE (Service Corps of Retired
  Executives), 25, 168
Secondary market research, 88
Secured loans, 163
Segmentation. *See* Market segmentation
Self-esteem, employee termination
  and, 324
Self-funding, 157–161
  bootstrapping and, 158–161
  moonlighting and, 158
  part-time consulting and, 158
Selling equity, 367
Selling memorandums, 370–371
Semivariable costs, pricing methods
  and, 77
Separation agreements, 328, 337–339

Serial entrepreneurs, 6
Service mark, 266
Shareholder benefits, public offerings and, 376–377
Shares authorized and issued, 136
Shkolnik, Nikolay, 92–93
Silvis, Paul, 318–319, 324
Site analysis, marketing plans and, 68
Skaldic, R. J., 9
Sleeping assets, 159
Small Business Administration
    business size standards and, 168
    funding programs and, 168 169
    loan application and, 168
Small Business Innovation Research (SBIR) program, 169
Small Business Investment Company, 168
Small Business Technology Transfer (STTR) program, 170
SmartPak, 36, 45
Smilor, Ray, 6–7
Smith, Adam, 183
Social networks, business models and, 310–311
Sole proprietorships
    access to capital and, 131
    advantages of, 130–131
    characteristics of, 129
    continuity and, 131–132
    disadvantages of, 131–132
    discontinuing, 131
    legal restrictions and, 131
    owner skills and capabilities and, 131
    personal liability and, 131
    profit incentive and, 130
    simplicity and, 130
    start-up fees and, 130
    total decision-making authority and, 130
Spiderweb model, 22
Stac Electronics, 161
Staged investments, 183
Standstill, 228
Start-up costs
    franchising and, 305
    sole proprietorships and, 130
State government funding sources, 170
State registration, business start-up and, 147
Statement of cash flows (SCF), 243–244
Stock options, 225, 322, 329
Stock purchase agreements, 225

Stockholder liability, C-corporations and, 136
Stocks. See Public offerings; Public stocks; Stock options
Strategic partnerships, 200–201
Strategic sales, 202
Stress, 24–25, 257
Study design, market research and, 54
Sugginono, Ralph, 96
Supply chain, capturing value in, 298–299
Sweat equity, 158
Syndication, 188
Syndicom.com, 310

T

Targeting, business plans and, 97–98
Taxation
    C-corporations and, 135
    filing and, 256–257
    partnerships and, 141
Team management
    business ethics and, 325–327
    conflicts of interest and, 325–327
    corporate culture and, 319–320
    cultural attributes and, 319–320
    firing employees and, 323–324
    hiring practices and, 321–323
    legal issues and, 327–329
    resignations and, 325
    stock-option agreements and, 329
Teaser preparation, 349–353
Technical skill sources, 56
Technological obsolescence, 39–40
Technology transfer, 303
Term sheets, 360
Territories, licensing and, 302
The Entrepreneurial Mindset (Rita McGrath), 51
Threadless.com, 310
Time horizon, innovation and, 51
Toro, 299
Total-liabilities-to-net-worth ratio, 240
Trade barrier elimination, 38
Trade secrets, 286–287
    advantages and disadvantages of, 286–287
    protection of, 287
Trade shows, market penetration and, 79
Trademark Electronic Application System (TEAS), 268
Trademarks
    enforcement of, 268–269

keys to, 266
    registration benefits and, 268
    registration of, 266–268
    symbols, 269
Transfer of registration rights, equity financing and, 223
Transferable ownership, C-corporations and, 137
TransUnion, 164
Trefler, Alan, 366

U

Ultrafast Inc., 264 265
Underwriters, public offerings and, 382
Uniform Franchise Offering Circular (UFOC), 304
Uniform Trade Secrets Act (UTSA), 286
Up-front fees
    franchising and, 305
    licensing and, 302
UPS, 201
U.S. Copyright Office (USCO), 271
U.S. Patent and Trademark Office (USPTO), 267, 272
Used equipment, 159
Utility patents, 273

V

Value chains, 298
Value networks, 298
Value pricing, 101
Value proposition, business models and, 298
Variable costs, pricing methods and, 77
Venture capital
    acquisitions/buyouts financing and, 197–198
    basics of, 195–196
    characteristics of, 184
    corporate partners and, 201
    development stage and, 197
    early-stage financing and, 197
    expansion financing and, 197
    finding, 348–349
    fund stage and, 197
    funding decisions and, 196–198
    location and, 197
    model, 202–203
    recent statistics and, 198

Venture capital (*Contd.*)
   selection guide and, 198–199
   specialized industries and, 196
   term sheet, 219–221
Viral marketing, 79, 311
Virtual clusters, 37
Virtual knowledge networks, 37
Visa, 161
Visibility, marketing plans and, 67

Vision for company, 26–27
Vocalpoint, 310

W

Wal-Mart, 299
Warrants, 188–189
Web 2.0 technologies, 310
Web site registration, 147

Wendle, Ethan, 128–129
Whitman, Meg, 29
Women, government funding sources
   and, 170

Y

YCombinator, 183